EYEBALL TO EYEBALL

The Inside Story of the
Cuban Missile Crisis

EYEBALL TO EYEBALL

DINO A. BRUGIONI

Edited by Robert F. McCort

Random House New York

Library of Congress Cataloging-in-Publication Data

Brugioni, Dino A.
Eyeball to eyeball: the inside story of the Cuban missile crisis
/ by Dino A. Brugioni; edited by Robert F. McCort.—1st ed.
p.   cm.
Includes index.
ISBN 0-679-40523-2
1. Cuban Missile Crisis, Oct. 1962.   I. McCort, Robert F.
II. Title.
E841.B76   1991   973.922—dc20   91-52820

Manufactured in the United States of America

24689753

FIRST EDITION

Book design by Carole Lowenstein

This book is dedicated to
Arthur C. Lundahl.
His vision and leadership made
photo interpretation the guardian
of the national security.

For my grandchildren

Preface

The denouement of the Cuban missile crisis was an elegy to a vanishing era in world affairs. It marked the end of an epoch in national and international history when a grim rivalry between social orders climaxed in a confrontation that could have led to thermonuclear war. We had gone to the brink, as we had vowed we would, but when we arrived at that point, instead of unsheathing our swords and striking, we stepped back and pondered the stupidity that had gotten us into such a position. With a sigh of relief, we determined that in the new era, we would never again permit our international policy to be so simplistic and jingoistic; that our national leaders would think long and cautiously before making warlike policy statements. Safeguards had to be established to prevent future crisis situations from rapid deterioration into nuclear confrontations. We owed this much to ourselves, and to the world.

The Soviet Union had attempted, clandestinely, to move a massive nuclear strike force into Cuba, construct it rapidly, and seize a position of nuclear superiority that it could present as a fait accompli. The missile, military, and naval bases established in Cuba were an extension of Soviet nuclear power and not relevant merely to the defense of Cuba; the military and political benefits to the Soviets had international implications. It was a gamble—large, premeditated, reckless. It became a colossal Soviet blunder. The Soviets completely misjudged the character of the U.S. presidency, the mood of the country, and our ability to "find out" what they were doing. The U.S. public would not have tolerated acquiescence to an offensive missile base ninety miles from our shores, and any president would have been obliged to take strong action. The United States could not have tolerated such a base without undermining any claim to leadership in the West. Militarily, as General Maxwell Taylor would remark, the Soviets chose the wrong issue and the wrong battlefield. President Kennedy would meet this threat with a firmness moderated only by wisdom and diplomacy.

The discovery of the missiles in Cuba was an event so sudden and so unexpected, despite vague unsubstantiated information to the contrary, that mankind even today has not fully recovered its breath. Yet the Cuban missile crisis confirmed something of vital importance to every living and still-unborn inhabitant of this world—that two great nuclear powers could confront each other and back down.

It can be said that the United States, in resolving the crisis, scored an impressive victory—probably the greatest achievement of the Kennedy administration. It was a case where we, rather than the Soviets, set the terms for negotiation. The Cuban missile crisis has had many highly salutary consequences in international relations. Because of it—not in spite of it—there has been a perceptible lessening of tensions between the two superpowers. There are those who maintain that Cuba today continues to stare us insolently in the face. The subsequent flow of arms from Russia into Cuba allowed it to develop into the third most formidable military power in the hemisphere, exporting its revolution and sending military personnel to Nicaragua, Ethiopia, and Angola. Resolving the crisis eliminated only the immediate and obvious threat, but nothing more. The Soviets, we reasoned, had made a serious mistake. They had chosen to challenge the U.S. on its home ground, but the Soviets had miscalculated and we had a marvelous opportunity to inflict a severe wound, or exact a promise that the Soviets would never again interfere in the affairs of Latin America. Instead, we were the ones who made the promise. The president had made a completely gratuitous pledge not to invade Cuba—a pledge that had never been given before.

The starting point of the Cuban missile crisis of October 1962 is exceptionally difficult to fix. Some analysts assert that the crisis began with the visit of Soviet first deputy premier Anastas I. Mikoyan to Cuba in February 1960. Others feel it began with the Bay of Pigs fiasco of April 1960. President Kennedy's first meeting in Vienna with Khrushchev in June 1961 is believed by some analysts to be the starting point of the crisis. Khrushchev bullied the president, and may have judged Kennedy weak because of his handling of the Bay of Pigs affair, his inaction during the construction of the Berlin Wall, and his wavering in deciding on a firm policy in Laos.

I trace the crisis back to President Eisenhower's concern for good intelligence and his interest in aerial reconnaissance. Without the U-2, there may have been no crisis—only an accomplished fact. The U-2 and low-altitude-aircraft photographs of the Soviet missile sites in Cuba were not just the common variety of aerial photos but marvelous examples of what a combination of the science of optics, film production, processing, and specially designed aerial platforms could produce.

During a crisis, many meetings, actions, words, and thoughts go unrecorded. Many studies of the Cuban missile crisis concentrate almost exclusively on the behavior of White House principals and tend to ignore the impact of photo intelligence or the military moves that the U.S. was making and how the Soviets and Cubans reacted to those moves. I was privileged to be a part of a group of dedicated individuals at the National Photographic Interpretation Center who furnished the information derived from the analysis of aerial photography to the policymakers, information that played a major role in resolving the crisis. What follows is the story of those efforts.

DINO A. BRUGIONI
Hartwood, Virginia
1991

A Note to the Reader

I was one of the original cadre of twelve people who, under the direction of Arthur C. Lundahl, organized the National Photographic Interpretation Center (NPIC) in the mid to late 1950s. During the Cuban missile crisis, because of the current information the interpretation of reconnaissance photography was providing, the center became a focal point of many related and diverse activities. I was the chief of a unit responsible for providing all-source collateral information to the photo interpreters as well as managing collation and processing of intelligence data derived from the exploitation of photography acquired by various national-level aerial reconnaissance programs. Each morning during the crisis, Mr. Lundahl would review pertinent details of the all-source notes and briefing boards before conveying that information to the United States Intelligence Board (USIB), the Executive Committee (EXCOM) of the National Security Council, and the president. Returning from these briefings, he would inform his staff chiefs of the recipients' reactions and their continuing intelligence needs. Lundahl was an astute observer, and I made detailed notes of what he had seen and heard so the center might better respond to the concerns and needs of policymakers. John Hughes, special assistant to the director of the Defense Intelligence Agency (DIA), appeared each morning at the center to pick up a duplicate set of the briefing materials and notes and kept us posted of the reactions and needs of the secretary of defense, the Joint Chiefs of Staff, and other high-ranking Defense Department officials. Service chiefs of the Army, Navy, and Air Force photo-interpretation detachments at the Center also got copies of all the briefing materials and posted us on the reactions of the various Unified and Specified commands. Aerial photography from a variety of reconnaissance units was delivered to the

Center at all hours of the day and night during the crisis, usually by high-ranking military officers who knew intimately what was happening during the actual collecting of the information.

My unit also prepared all the notes for the materials carried by ranking CIA and diplomatic officials to de Gaulle, Diefenbaker, Macmillan, and Adenauer. I questioned the Agency personnel upon their return about what had happened during these meetings. Ray S. Cline, CIA deputy director for intelligence, and Colonel David S. Parker, deputy director of NPIC, provided details of the briefing of foreign delegates in Stevenson's office and the preparation of Stevenson's speech prior to his confrontation with Soviet delegate Valerian Zorin. Later, Huntington "Ting" Sheldon, a senior CIA official and intelligence expert, assigned as John J. McCloy's intelligence support officer during the critical discussions with the Russians relative to the removal of the missiles and Il-28 bombers from Cuba, gave additional "firsthand" information on McCloy and Stevenson's personal negotiations with Kuznetsov. He also revealed more fully how he created the PSALM control system. When the UN was considering sending observers to Cuba, senior CIA official William Tidwell told me what happened during his discussions with U Thant's military advisers. We were made aware of U.S. battle plans and targets, and we provided field units with information and photography for their assigned missions. I was a participant in several postmortems conducted on the crisis, and I conducted interviews with Agency principals involved in the crisis for an Agency historical project. I am indebted to Sherman Kent for providing details on the discussions in the United States Intelligence Board and to Sidney Graybeal for discussions in the Guided Missile Astronautic Intelligence Committee. I met with military participants in the crisis and reviewed a number of oral histories, and I want to thank General Maxwell Taylor for providing information relative to discussions in the EXCOM and to General Lyman Lemnitzer and Admiral Alfred Gustave "Corky" Ward for their time and patience reviewing details of the preparations for an invasion of Cuba as well as their reactions to the crisis. I am also indebted to the U.S. Naval, Marine Corps, and Air Force historical centers, which provided information or reports pertinent to the crisis. Over the intervening years, I frequently attended intelligence briefings given by Mr. Lundahl and was able to question officials who were involved in the crisis. I corresponded with a number of people who, although not directly involved in the crisis, met with the president during that crucial period and solicited from them opinions on the president's mood and reactions. As one of the

Agency officials who made the presentation of a photographic exhibit that I had prepared for CIA headquarters on the tenth anniversary of the crisis to the John F. Kennedy Library, I was allowed to review library documents pertinent to the crisis as well as a number of transcripts of "secret" recordings made during the period.

Contents

EYEBALL TO EYEBALL

Eisenhower and
Reconnaissance

"A unique opportunity for comprehensive
intelligence."

—DR. EDWIN H. LAND

AFTER WORLD WAR II, U.S. military leaders felt comfortable, almost complacent, with the technological advantage seemingly attained by the U.S. during the war. Production lines were tooled for the B-36 intercontinental bomber and plans were well under way for the design and production of B-47 medium and B-52 heavy jet bombers. Planning for series production of nuclear weapons had begun. Successive events in the immediate postwar period, however, provided ample indications that the Soviet Union, by its intransigence on many international issues, was destined to be the principal adversary of the United States in world affairs. The Berlin blockade was only one early indicator of suspect Soviet actions that confronted President Truman in 1948.

Despite wartime technological advances, the United States sorely lacked basic intelligence on the Soviet Union. Although some limited human intelligence (humint) and some Luftwaffe photography of the Soviet Union during World War II were available, they did not provide the substance or volume of information required for current strategic intelligence estimates. On August 29, 1949, the Soviets detonated a nuclear device at Semipalatinsk, in Central Asia. It came as a surprise to the fledgling U.S. intelligence community, which generally believed that the USSR was some five years behind the U.S. in nuclear development. The intelligence community had little knowledge of the details of that event, or where and how the weapon had been produced. Subsequent attempts to procure strategic intelligence on the Soviet Union resulted in repeated failures. Vast areas of the USSR had been curtained off from the outside world, and Soviet military preparations, production, and deployment activities were carried out in the utmost secrecy. All of their strategic capabilities—bomber forces, ballistic missiles, submarine forces, and nuclear weapons plants—were concealed from outside observation. The Soviet air defense system, a prime consideration in determining U.S. retaliatory policies, was also largely an unknown factor.

The resources for gathering such vital intelligence information were denied to U.S. collection efforts and alternative methods were either not available or had not been developed. The physical barriers established along the Soviet-Bloc borders curtailed the movement of human intelligence sources. Sources of communications intelligence (comint) were also being made more secure and, thereby, increasingly denied. The situation was regarded by President Eisenhower as intolerable—both from the viewpoint of adequate U.S. warning and U.S. military preparation to meet the menace and from the point of view of being able to take countermeasures in the event of a surprise attack.

There was a tendency at the time for U.S. resources to get locked into inflexible departmental attitudes. There was also considerable difficulty in making corrections once mistakes were identified. Most analysts believed that the Soviets were copying and following U.S. practices—that they were taking the same route we had taken to solve research-and-development and production problems. As we were to see later, this was an enormous fallacy.

The U.S. military services had adopted an attitude that they had proprietary responsibilities for military intelligence and that the Central Intelligence Agency was duplicating their efforts. This parochial attitude frequently hindered overall objectivity. Intelligence papers prepared by a second agency were often automatically rebutted rather than objectively considered and coordinated. Too frequently, the challenges were merely bureaucratic. More frequently than not, military estimates were an inventory of ignorance rather than the precise analysis of a situation. If a CIA intelligence estimate was contrary to the prevailing thinking of a particular military service, there was an immediate howl that the Agency, and perhaps the other services, was encroaching on that service's specific area of responsibility. There was a need, realized by General Walter Bedell Smith and, later, Allen Dulles, for an independent estimate, and the CIA was the logical agency to produce it—because, supposedly, it had "no ax to grind." Prior to 1953, the U.S. intelligence community had concluded that the Soviets had little capability for intercontinental attack. Their main bomber, the Tu-4 Bull, a copy of the U.S. B-29 bomber, had no in-flight refueling capability and, because of its limited range, could only reach the U.S. on a one-way mission. A large turboprop version of the Bull, the Barge, appeared in the July 1951 Soviet air show at Tushino airfield. The U.S. intelligence community concluded that there would be series production of the Barge. The Barge, however, never went into series production.

The U.S. monopoly on strategic nuclear weapons was not significantly challenged by the Soviet detonation of a nuclear device because the Soviets would have to progress from testing to production while the U.S. nuclear stockpile already was continuing to grow. We were unaware at the time that Soviet spy Klaus Fuchs, who had worked in the United States at Los Alamos during World War II, had passed details of the plutonium and uranium bombs to the Soviets, along with descriptions of their design and method of construction. It was the Defense Department's judgment at the time that future wars would be protracted wars of attrition. The U.S. therefore embarked on a program of establishing forward air bases in Europe, Africa, and Asia, perfecting in-flight refueling techniques, and reinforcing NATO. Reports were being received, however, that the Soviets were also building a strategic air force, and from German scientists repatriated from Russia, it was learned that the Soviets were also building a strategic ICBM force. It was therefore essential—indeed vital—that we learn more about the Soviets' strategic warfare capabilities.

It was known that more than fifteen hundred Soviet manufacturing plants had been dismantled and moved from the Moscow, Leningrad, Ukraine, and Western USSR areas as the German armies advanced into the Russian heartland during World War II. These plants had been shipped to the Urals, Siberia, and to Kazakhstan and Central Asia. Cities like Sverdlovsk, Irkutsk, Omsk, Novosibirsk, and Tashkent had grown phenomenally. Little was known, however, about the precise location or production operations at these reconstructed and expanded plants. Since most of them had been dedicated to defense production, it was essential to know how many aircraft, tanks, guns, and missiles they were producing at their new locations. It was known that a nuclear industry was being established in the Urals, but little detailed information was available.* We also knew that the Russians were dismantling many of the German missile, aircraft, armament plants, and research establishments and relocating them in newly constructed plants beyond the Urals. We not only had to have hard evidence for national intelligence estimates, but we needed it now. We needed the information to plan our defense establishment and to assure that we did not spend our defense dollars foolishly or excessively. We also needed the information for targeting the Soviet Union for our B-47 and B-52 strategic bombers.

The nucleus of the Central Intelligence Agency had been formed from a cadre of wartime Office of Strategic Services (OSS) agents. Many of these agents had been recruited from Ivy League and other prestigious Eastern universities, and a number of ranking officials were from prominent or wealthy Eastern families. Most were proficient in foreign languages and had traveled extensively or had lived abroad. These ex-OSS officers had continued to foster the nexus between espionage, the "Eastern establishment," and the academic community by recruiting individuals largely with backgrounds similar to theirs, in favor of the more traditional liberal-arts-based "substantive" intelligence. The ultimate result was a bias against scientific and technical intelligence. In the 1950s, however, it became increasingly clear that more precise information was required on the scientific and strategic production capabilities of the Soviet Union. Soviet science was generally recognized as being of high quality, but Soviet engineering efforts left a lot to be desired. It also became clear

---

* In an article, "The Kyshtym Connection," in the March 1990 issue of the *Bulletin of Atomic Scientists*, I describe how a map obtained by Herbert Hoover while he was a mining engineer in Russia in the 1900s enabled us to pinpoint Russia's principal plutonium plant and the source of the material for their first nuclear weapon.

that the required information was not being provided by human or electronic collection systems. The wide expanse of the Soviet Union and its overwhelming penchant for secrecy and security hindered both humint and comint collection efforts. What was needed was a system that could collect detailed information over a wide area and do it quickly, efficiently, and effectively. The only apparent system that could answer that requirement was aerial photography.

In June 1952, the Massachusetts Institute of Technology (MIT), under U.S. Air Force sponsorship, released the epochal Beacon Hill Report, entitled "Problems of Air Force Intelligence and Reconnaissance." Dr. Edwin Land, the eminent photo scientist, played a leadership role in formulating the report, which advocated radical approaches in the application of scientific methods to obtain the information needed for national intelligence estimates. Noting the successes of Allied aerial reconnaissance during World War II, the report also recommended that wartime methodologies be considered for further study.

Shortly after General Dwight D. Eisenhower assumed the presidency in 1953, he indicated rather forcefully that he was not pleased with the currency of U.S. intelligence collection and estimating activities. The president made frequent references to the postwar findings of the U.S. Strategic Bombing Surveys (USSBS), which showed that wartime analysis of aerial photography was amazingly accurate and that some 80–90 percent of U.S. military intelligence came from it.*

Eisenhower was convinced that reconnaissance was the answer

---

* The United States Strategic Bombing Survey was established by the secretary of war on November 3, 1944, pursuant to a directive from President Roosevelt. Its mission was "to conduct an impartial and expert study of the effects of aerial attacks on Germany, to be used in connection with air attacks on Japan, and to establish a basis for evaluating the importance and potentialities of air power as an instrument for military strategy for planning the future development of the United States armed forces; and for determining future economic policies with respect to the national defense." The conclusion of the USSBS in the Pacific was: "Although viewed with indifference and skepticism at the beginning of World War II, aerial photography ultimately became one of the most single important sources of intelligence in the Pacific War. They played an important part in more phases of military and naval operations than any other source." Among the officers involved in the Pacific study who would later achieve national prominence were Paul H. Nitze, John Kenneth Galbraith, and Fred Searls, Jr.

and revealed his thinking to General George Goddard, the ranking U.S. Air Force expert on reconnaissance. General Goddard met frequently with CIA intelligence analysts and loved to quote Eisenhower's concern about good intelligence: "Without it you would have only your fears on which to plan your own defense arrangements and your whole military establishment. Now, if you're going to use nothing but fear and that's all you have, you are going to make us an armed camp. So this kind of knowledge is vital to us."[1]

General Walter Bedell Smith, a close friend of Eisenhower, assumed his duties as director of the CIA on October 7, 1950. Smith soon realized that the traditional means of obtaining information did not apply to the Soviet Union. General Smith was well aware of the contributions that photo interpretation had made during World War II,[2] and on August 9, 1952, he authorized the establishment of a photo interpretation unit within the Agency's Office of Research and Reports. During World War II, over three thousand U.S. men and women had been trained in the art of photo interpretation. Most returned to civilian life. A number, however, remained in the military services or worked as civilians in military organizations.

The truce ending hostilities in the Korean conflict in July 1953 provoked a thorough reexamination of U.S. military and political strategy by the Eisenhower administration. From these deliberations came the policy of "massive retaliation." The threat of a prompt nuclear response by the U.S. to any Communist aggression was announced, and U.S. military planners began creating contingency plans for nuclear strikes on the Soviet Union.

The United States detonated its first thermonuclear device on November 1, 1952. Because of the U.S. atomic monopoly and the successful test of the hydrogen device, President Eisenhower proposed a $5 billion defense cut. Only a few Air Force generals and a small number of congressmen and senators protested. However, the Soviet test of a thermonuclear device on August 12, 1953, came as a complete surprise to the U.S. intelligence community.

Later that year, a U.S. attaché stationed in Moscow spotted a heavy jet bomber at the main Soviet aircraft test and development airfield at Ramenskoye, outside Moscow. It, too, was a surprise, since it was not a copy of a U.S. bomber but was of indigenous design. It appeared to be a counterpart of the B-52, which at the time was in about the same stage of development. It would be designated the Myasishchev-4 and given the NATO code name Bison. Later, the bomber was spotted at its production plant at Moscow/Fili.

A single Bison bomber was seen in the air on April 18, 1954, and several Bisons were seen in rehearsals for the annual May Day celebrations. The rehearsals lasted for several weeks—two bombers were flown one day, two the next, and three the following day. Consistently, they flew down the parade route and over the Kremlin. Across the street from the Kremlin, on the roof of the U.S. Embassy, attachés with long-focal-length cameras photographed the bombers each time they appeared. The exposed film was expedited to Washington for processing. Enlargements of the photos revealed two-digit bort numbers in the teens on the nose of the bombers, indicating series production of at least twenty of these bombers. A number of intelligence analysts raised the possibility that different numbers were being painted on a relatively small number of bombers, but the U.S. Air Force, which at the time had the prime responsibility for estimating Soviet bomber strength, would not agree with this evaluation. Democrats, led by former secretary of the air force Senator Stuart Symington of Missouri, charged the Eisenhower administration with permitting the Soviets to exceed the U.S. in bomber strength. They questioned why the Soviets would want to deceive the United States, and thus began the "bomber-gap" controversy in strategic intelligence.

Allen Dulles became the director of the CIA on February 26, 1953, and would later admit that the U.S. intelligence community had been "taken." In his book *The Craft of Intelligence*, Dulles commented on the rehearsals and the air show and the number of Bisons seen: "The number far exceeded what was thought to be available. The impression thus given that many more had lately come off the assembly line and that the Soviets were therefore committed to an increasing force of heavy bombers. Later, it was surmised that the same squadron had been flying around in circles, reappearing every few minutes. The purpose was to emphasize Soviet production. In fact, they were soon to shift the emphasis to missiles."[3] Be that as it may, the Soviets now had nuclear weapons and an intercontinental bomber to deliver those weapons over the U.S.

The U.S. Department of Defense, spurred by the U.S. Air Force, called for estimates on Soviet bomber production for the next five years. The Air Force saw the Bison as the main element in a large Soviet intercontinental bomber force. When completed, these estimates were rife with speculation and qualifying footnotes. The U.S. Air Force estimated there would be more than thirty Bisons in the Soviet inventory by the end of 1955 and about five hundred by mid-1959. When President Eisenhower received those estimates, he ordered Secretary of Defense Charles E. Wilson to speed up U.S. B-52 bomber production. In testimony before Congress in 1956, Neil H. McElroy, who replaced Wilson as secretary of defense, testified that the Soviets would have six to seven hundred Bison bombers in long-range operational units by 1969. (Actually, only about a hundred were ever produced.)

The years 1952 and 1953 proved to be especially fortuitous for the CIA. It hired two of its most brilliant innovators, who, literally, would become prime movers in projecting the Agency into the era of scientific and technical intelligence. Richard M. Bissell, a noted economist by training and experience, possessed innovative and organizational talents since unequaled in the intelligence community. Calm, deliberate, articulate, and a good listener, he had taught economics at Yale before World War II. Wartime service included stints with the Department of Commerce and the War Shipping Administration and, later, with the Economic Cooperation Administration. Bissell also served on a number of interdepartmental government committees concerned with wartime industrial production. After the war, he returned to teaching at MIT but resumed his governmental service in the administration of the Marshall Plan. Bissell, more than any other individual, was responsible for fostering the "technical" collection systems that became the mainstay of modern intelligence. In 1954, the Agency gave him the innocuous title of special assistant for planning and coordination. Realistically, he was the Agency contact with academic, scientific, industrial, and technological organizations, with the express purpose of ferreting out ideas applicable to intelligence collection. Bissell was aware that he would be asked to present bold ideas, and he didn't restrict himself to presenting the ideas of others. He was one of the few planners in the U.S. government capable of bringing projects from conception to reality, quickly, efficiently, and economically. He was the organizer, the innovator, the risk taker, the man who felt equally comfortable talking to columnist Joseph Alsop or to Dr. Edwin Land, who described Bissell as the best organizer in the U.S. government.

Bissell's program for development of a viable reconnaissance system created a need for specialists to interpret the photography acquired. To meet that need, the Agency lured the brilliant photo-interpretation expert and photo scientist Arthur C. Lundahl away from the U.S. Naval Photographic Intelligence Center (NAVPIC) at Anacostia, D.C. Lundahl, a graduate geologist of the University of Chicago in 1942, served as a photo interpreter at Adak, Alaska, during World War II, where intelligence information was derived from aerial photographic missions flown over the Aleutian Islands, Japan, and the Kuriles. Wartime photo intelligence successes convinced Lundahl that photo interpretation afforded virtually limitless peacetime, military, and civilian application opportunities. Intrigued by the wealth of information that could be derived from applying analytic and photogrammetric methods to aerial photography, Lundahl, more than any other individual in Washington, realized that aerial photography of sufficient quality—and supplied on a periodic basis—could answer a number of difficult intelligence questions posed by the Cold War. Lundahl had served as chief of the NAVPIC Photogrammetric Division and, subsequently, as assistant chief engineer between 1946 and 1953. He immersed himself in all aspects of NAVPIC activities and became a recognized authority on photogrammetric engineering and its photo interpretation applications.

Lundahl, an extremely articulate speaker, had a distinct talent for making highly technical material understandable to the layman. He had lectured frequently on photo interpretation at the Agency and had caught Bissell's eye. He joined the Agency in 1953, with a mandate to organize "a first-class photographic intelligence center." Lundahl recalls: "Bissell strongly supported my efforts in so many ways. He clearly understood that we had to push concurrent research and development efforts to develop a wide variety of optical mechanical devices for the exploitation of photography specifically tuned to new formats of imagery to be collected from a wide variety of collection platforms."

The U.S. continued to be frustrated in the early 1950s by its inability to penetrate the Iron Curtain to obtain information on the

Soviet nuclear-delivery capabilities that threatened Western Europe, Japan, and the U.S. The Strategic Air Command (SAC) expressed serious concern that it did not have the target intelligence required for its B-47 and B-52 bomber wings. General Curtis E. LeMay, commander of SAC, pressed for ways and means to strengthen U.S. air intelligence and reconnaissance capabilities and asked the Air Force to determine if a special reconnaissance plane could be built.

On March 27, 1953, a design study for such a plane was issued by the Air Force for a single-seat subsonic aircraft with an operational radius of 1,500 statute miles, flying at altitudes of 70,000 feet, and capable of carrying a variety of cameras. Three firms submitted designs: Fairchild submitted the M-195; Bell, the X-16; and Martin, a stretched-wing version of the Canberra bomber, later designated the RB-57D. The Air Force favored the RB-57D and ordered twenty of them. The U.S., meanwhile, attempted to acquire intelligence information on the Soviet Union using oblique cameras with focal lengths of 100, 240, and 500 inches on peripheral flights of denied areas by RB-47, RB-57, and RB-36 aircraft. But the Soviets reacted every time a U.S. reconnaissance aircraft attempted to procure information on Soviet installations along its coasts, and several U.S. planes were shot down.

The Pearl Harbor syndrome was still very relevant in the Eisenhower administration, and the president on numerous occasions expressed his fear of a surprise attack—"a fear which haunted Eisenhower throughout his Presidency."[4]

On March 27, 1954, President Eisenhower expressed his grave concern for better intelligence on the Soviet Union at a meeting of the Science Advisory Committee of the Office of Defense Mobilization. He said, "To anyone bearing the responsibility for the security of the United States, the situation was highly unsatisfactory." The vulnerability of the United States to surprise attack and the lack of current strategic intelligence on the Soviet Union were predominant topics at the meeting. Four months later, on July 26, the president asked Dr. James R. Killian, president of MIT, "to direct a study of the country's technological capabilities to meet some of its current problems." The problems listed were principally concerned with intelligence needs. Killian accepted the challenge on August 27, 1954, and established a special panel of experts. Dr. James Fisk, of the Bell Telephone Laboratories, was appointed Killian's deputy. Others on the panel were: Marshall A. Holloway, Los Alamos Scientific Laboratory; Leland J. Havorth, Brookhaven National Laboratory; Lee A. DuBridge, California Institute of Technology; James H. Doolittle, Shell Oil; James P. Baxter, Williams College; Robert C. Sprague, Sprague Electric Co.; and Dr. Edwin H. Land, the eminent photo scientist. Dr. Land was subsequently appointed to Project 3 of the Technological Capabilities Panel (TCP), the so-called Land Panel, concerned with the development of new reconnaissance programs. Jimmy Doolittle, familiar with the value of aerial reconnaissance in World War II, supported Land's view that "every known reconnaissance technique should be used."

A number of unique proprieties can be attributed to aerial photography: 1) it captures and freezes an instant in time; 2) it can be studied at length and in detail by persons from a wide variety of backgrounds and disciplines; 3) it constitutes a precise geometric record that can be measured, scaled, quantified; 4) it becomes a record of the earth's surface—a catalog of things, activities, and relationships; 5) it is duplicable and manipulable—can be enlarged, enhanced, and reproduced; and 6) it can provide near-synoptic coverage of large areas.

Dr. Edwin H. Land's panel was guided by his personal credo: "My motto is to select things that are manifestly important and nearly impossible."[5] He maintained that "discoveries are made by some individual who has freed himself from a way of thinking that is held by friends and associates who may be more intelligent, better educated, better disciplined, but who have not mastered the art of a fresh, clean look at the old, old knowledge."[6] He once remarked that all governmental research and development activity eventually follows a well-worn path toward bigness, turf protection, security, inertia, and incompetence. Under Dr. Land's leadership many learned men and women—leaders in academe, science, and industry—generously gave of their time and talents; research laboratories made their resources and facilities available; and industry displayed a willingness to cooperate in the manufacture of highly sophisticated hardware.

As happens rarely in scientific pursuits, five major breakthroughs applicable to gathering intelligence came together in the postwar period. Among the major developments in chemistry was a thin, tough plastic called estar. The thinness of estar, used as film bases by the Eastman Kodak Company, permitted enormous quantities of film to be spooled onto a single film roll or magazine. This technique in turn allowed reconnaissance to be conducted over larger territorial areas and for extended periods of time. This film was subsequently referred to as thin base film (TBF) and could be specially ordered only from Eastman Kodak. At Eastman, scientists Joe Boone, Ford Tuttle, Raife Tarkington, Al Soren, and Ed Green worked not only in the development of the film but also on designing machines to process it.

Rocket development during World War II had ushered in a new era of concern for atmospheric and space phenomena, both celestial and man-made. At Harvard University, the renowned astronomer and lens designer Dr. James Baker* had designed revolutionary lenses for the observation of celestial bodies. The unprecedented efficiency of these lenses suggested that they could be applied, conversely, for looking from space to earth. During World War II, the resolving power of the best aerial photographic lenses was about 25 lines per millimeter. Baker was given the responsibility by the CIA to design the lenses for the cameras that would be used in a viable reconnaissance system and he, in turn, chose Dr. Rod Scott of the Perkin Elmer Corporation to supervise their production. The original Baker lenses were capable of resolving about 75 lines per millimeter. Later versions of these lenses had a resolution capability of nearly 125 lines per millimeter. Baker was no novice to aerial reconnaissance. He had served with Colonel George W. Goddard during World War II, designing lenses for the aerial cameras of that period.

The fifties also saw the beginning of the electronic age. The introduction of computers to the production lines was opening new vistas in a number of highly technical areas. Until that time, the custom

---

* It has been said prior to the advent of computers, a lens designer would be fortunate to design about three lenses in a lifetime. Baker was the first to use the computer to aid in the design of aerial photographic lenses and he developed a series of lenses that were used by the CIA.

grinding of aerial camera lenses was a slow and laborious process. Experiments revealed that computers could also be applied to the precise work of driving the lens-grinding and -polishing machines. The resultant lenses were not only of superior quality but could be produced much more economically.

The aerial cameras used in World War II were large, heavy, and bulky. To achieve wide-area and stereo coverage, it was necessary to mount three cameras in reconnaissance aircraft—one pointing straight down and one pointing to each side. This camera system was called tri-metrigon. It was usually necessary to station an operator among the cameras to assure that they were operating properly. After the war, Dr. Land suggested the development of an automatic camera with a lens barrel capable of rotating from side to side and filming from horizon to horizon. It was called the panoramic camera, and a wide expanse of earth could be covered with each rotation.

In 1953, Dr. Baker had specified the focal length and formats of the cameras to be designed and the Hycon Corporation of East Pasadena, California, was selected to produce them. Under the leadership of William McFadden, Richard H. Perley, Wilton A. Stewart, and Leroy A. Lofftus three cameras, the A, B, and C, were designed and later produced. The design of the B panoramic camera, weighing about 450 pounds, incorporating the Baker lens, and utilizing the thin base film developed by Eastman Kodak, looked especially promising to Dr. Land.

With regard to intelligence applications, these breathtaking technological advances materialized against a background of limited progress in covert operations. The need for decoupling of traditional ways of acquiring intelligence was obvious to most policymakers.

The U.S. military services had continued the practice of converting bomber or fighter aircraft for reconnaissance purposes during World War II and in the postwar period. Flying these aircraft unescorted, in clear conditions suitable for obtaining photographs over denied areas, however, seriously diminished the chances for survival. In December 1953, Clarence L. "Kelly" Johnson, the chief aircraft designer at the Lockheed Aircraft Corporation, was asked by the U.S. Air Force to investigate the possibility of modifying the F-104 fighter he had designed and increasing its performance characteristics for reconnaissance purposes.*

It didn't take Johnson long to come to the conclusion that there were too many drawbacks in redesigning or modifying combat aircraft for reconnaissance purposes. The obvious solution was an aircraft that could fly both higher and faster than its potential interceptors. Johnson therefore felt that an entirely new design was required. His unique concept was to put a jet engine inside a glider—the huge glider wings would have to support the entire weight of the aircraft but still would have to be of very light construction. At the same time, Johnson's design would permit an extraordinary range at extended altitudes with the engine idling. In March 1954, he submitted his design, labeled the Lockheed CL-282 (later to be designated the U-2), to the U.S. Air Force, only to have it rejected. But word of Johnson's plane, along with the other designs, had reached the members of the Killian committee. They asked for a briefing from the Air Force of the various aircraft they were considering for reconnaissance purposes.

Dr. Land saw that Johnson's design, along with the scientific advances in film, lenses, and camera development, could constitute a viable reconnaissance system. Dr. Land had become disenchanted with the Air Force's system of assigning specific tasks to a variety of offices in managing the research, development, and testing phases of an individual aircraft. In this arrangement, hundreds of major and minor changes were often incorporated into an aircraft, thereby lengthening its test and development program. Although the Ridenour Committee in 1949 had recommended that: "Satisfactory progress in Air Force research and development can be made only when

---

* Kelly Johnson has been associated with Lockheed as chief engineer, vice-president for advanced development projects, senior vice-president for advanced development projects, senior vice-president, member of the board, and after his retirement as a senior consultant. His long list of aircraft credits reads like a who's who of renowned U.S. aircraft: the P-38 fighter, the Hudson bomber, the Constellation commercial transport, the F-80 and F-90 jet fighters, the U-2, and the SR-71. Johnson is the holder of more professional and government awards than any other free-world aerospace engineer. Among these awards are the Sylvanus A. Reed Award, Wright Brothers Medal, Collier Trophy, twice Aviation Man of the Year, General Hap Arnold Gold Medal Award, National Academy of Engineers Founders Medal, Thomas D. White Defense Award, and the CIA Distinguished Intelligence Medal.

a single agency, headed and staffed by technically qualified personnel, is charged with this single purpose and is given the entire job,"
the Air Force's research-and-development establishment had developed into a plethora of technological installations scattered about
the country, each with technological preserves of their own. All of
these organizations had grown phenomenally, staffed with effete
personalities who jealously guarded their specific turf. Because of all
of these ramifications, delivery of new or improved equipment was
seldom on schedule. Land found the situation most depressing. He
once remarked that organizations were more concerned with protecting traditional franchises than with exploring new areas of technical activity. This was also the period of interservice rivalry, when
the defense establishment was going through the throes of reorganization, consideration of roles and missions, and budget cuts. President Eisenhower, aware of the bickering, stipulated that the U-2
"should be handled in an unconventional way so that it would not
become entangled in the bureaucracy of the Defense Department or
troubled by rivalries among the services."[7]

Considering the feuding and biases between the Air Force and its
contractors, and an apparent lack of direction in the Department of
Defense regarding reconnaissance matters, Dr. Land, in a November
5, 1954, memorandum, entitled "A Unique Opportunity for Comprehensive Intelligence," suggested to Allen Dulles that the Agency
assume the leadership role in the application of technological intelligence collection techniques: "We told you that this seems to us the
kind of action and technique that is right for the contemporary version of CIA; a modern scientific way for the Agency that is always
supposed to be looking, to do its looking. Quite strongly, we feel
that you must assert your first right to pioneer in scientific techniques
for collecting intelligence—and choosing such partners to assist you
as may be needed. The present opportunity for aerial photography
seems to us a fine to start."[8]

There was some consternation within the Agency regarding the
future financial impact of the U-2 reconnaissance system. When
Colonel Lawrence "Red" White, the executive director of the
Agency, suggested that maybe the Agency should let the Defense
Department do the interpretation, Dulles put his glasses on his fore-
head, as he often did, and said, "Red, you don't think that after I've

taken all those photos, I am going to let someone else interpret them."

On November 1, 1954, Kelly Johnson was invited to Washington and questioned in detail by Bissell and Lawrence Houston, the Agency's general counsel, about producing the U-2. The Agency had a protected fund for which no special accounting was made. Dulles, however, had made it a practice to inform President Eisenhower about all such expenditures. Houston was told of these expenditures. Johnson was confident that the U-2 would fly at 70,000 feet for extended periods and be a stable camera platform. The discussion turned to the cost of producing twenty U-2's. Houston remembers: "Kelly said this would save us a good bit of money but he would use his best people on the production line and that this would cost us a bit. I said we had twenty-two million [in the reserve fund] and Kelly said he thought this would do. He took our draft letter to California and came back about 10 days later. He said Mr. [Robert] Gross [Lockheed's president] and their Comptroller thought twenty-two was too low and they wanted twenty-six outside."[9] Johnson said that Lockheed understood the fund limitations and could proceed using the $22 million and call for additional funds if needed.

On November 24, 1954, Dulles answered Land's memorandum of November 5 stating that the Agency would be willing to take on the responsibility of not only developing the U-2 but also of interpreting the photos taken by it. On December 4, 1954, the president approved the proposal for construction of the U-2's, and on December 9, 1954, the Agency and Lockheed signed the contract. And so a deal was struck that has since been described as the biggest intelligence bargain in history.

The development of the U-2 represented a radical departure, both in the system itself and in the program for clandestine overflight of foreign territories. Although a special antiradar paint would be applied to the U-2, the risks of being detected were great and the political repercussions, which would surely follow, would be both domestic and international. Eisenhower decided that the need to obtain up-to-date factual intelligence on the Soviet Union far outweighed the political considerations. In retrospect, we can realize that the often desperate and dangerous route Eisenhower took to seek the truth through aerial reconnaissance now seems very plausible and rational. Indeed, it has become the accepted avenue for better understanding between the U.S. and the Soviet Union and also a better method for resolving the problems of day-to-day diplomacy.

Kelly Johnson picked a small staff and a team of twenty-nine engineers and technicians and moved them into a Lockheed hangar at Burbank, California, in December 1954. This secret workshop became known as the Skunk Works, a reference to the popular L'il Abner comic strip wherein, as with Hairless Joe's "Kickapoo Joy Juice," few knew what Kelly Johnson was brewing at his design institute. The problems to be overcome in the development of the U-2 were enormous. Johnson's managerial style was to involve all of his engineers—each was personally responsible for the ultimate success of the project.

Development of the U-2 commenced with the realistic assumption that it would be a short-term, high-risk operation. Though the chances of success were at best uncertain, the need was so urgent that the risk of failure was acceptable to President Eisenhower. Although the program faced many challenging problems as development and testing proceeded, there was no flagging in the determination to make the system work—and in the shortest time possible. Johnson emphasized that development of the U-2 was like moving an aircraft directly from the design phase to combat. This phase of the development of the U-2 was best described by Tom Braden, an ex-CIA employee, when he once remarked, "Only arrogant men would insist on building the U-2 spy plane within a time frame which military experts said could not be done."

Johnson chose the Pratt and Whitney J-57 jet engine as the power source for the U-2. The Shell Oil Company developed a special fuel for the U-2 to operate at high altitudes. Because it burned so well, it was labeled lighter fuel, to distinguish it from other jet fuels. Johnson also began to drive his engineers to save weight, admonishing them that he would "trade his grandma" for several pounds' weight reduction. From that moment on, every pound saved was referred to as a grandma. "Simplicity, simplicity of design," Johnson would extoll at each morning meeting with his engineers.

The final wing design was so superb that it weighed only three pounds per square foot, one third that of a normal aircraft. The long wingspan, however, posed problems for the installation of landing gear and aircraft stability on landing and takeoff. The engineers proposed placing the main landing gear inside the fuselage and installing tiny landing gear, called pogos, near the wingtips. On takeoff, the pogos would be jettisoned; on landing, as the aircraft lost forward momentum, ground personnel would run alongside and reinsert them into the wings. Skids were also mounted on the wingtips as precautions on landing. Witnessing U-2 takeoffs and landings was somewhat akin to watching cop drills in a Keystone comedy. When Lundahl first saw the U-2, he described it as a black vulture on crutches.

This was a unique period in the development of a new and vital reconnaissance system. The twenty U-2's were produced for $22 million. Risks were taken, bottlenecks were broken, red tape minimized, new techniques developed, and feedback established.

There was another problem. President Eisenhower asked Allen Dulles at one point: "Who are you going to get to fly it?" Dulles replied that pilots were being recruited from U.S. Air Force units, thanks to the efforts of Lt. Gen. Emmett "Rosie" O'Donnell, Jr. "You won't have many volunteers to fly over Russia," the president responded. Dulles assured the president that General O'Donnell had a number of potential recruits. The president frowned. "Are they going to be soldiers of fortune?" Dulles replied that if it got narrowed down to recruiting soldiers of fortune, they would be Americans. The president frowned again. "It would seem that you could be able to recruit some Russians or pilots of other nationalities." Dulles said he would try. Four Greek pilots were eventually recruited, along with a Polish one. Two of the Greek pilots were subsequently brought to the United States and allowed to train in the U-2; however, their flight proficiency was so poor that they were dropped from the program. The Polish pilot was never allowed to fly the U-2.

Concomitant with Johnson's development of the U-2, Lundahl began to structure the intelligence organization within the CIA required to exploit the imagery acquired by the U-2. Lundahl was given a free hand in recruiting and selecting personnel. Early in 1955, Hans "Dutch" Scheufele, William F. Banfield, and I were told by

Dr. James M. Andrews, the director of the Office of Central Reference, and Dr. Joseph Becker, his executive officer, that we had new jobs and that we were not to discuss our new assignments with anyone.

I had been recruited by the CIA in March 1948 and was a member of a unit responsible for creating the Agency's industrial register of detailed information on foreign-production facilities worldwide. I had flown in sixty-six aerial bombardment missions and numerous reconnaissance missions during World War II and was familiar with the target dossiers that had been created for bombing purposes. I became an expert on Soviet industrial installations and, using knowledge gained from World War II experiences, had created all source dossiers on thousands of Russian installations. These dossiers included Luftwaffe reconnaissance photography taken of Russia during the war, along with blueprints of plants in Russia built by U.S. and foreign firms during the prewar and wartime period.* This, and other such targeting systems, was necessary to support U.S. capabilities to strike strategic enemy targets and ultimately evolved into the U.S. Air Force's "Bombing Encyclopedia."

Dutch Scheufele was fluent in German and had worked as a translator of World War II German documents on Soviet industries. William Banfield was a photo laboratory specialist. The three of us were told to report the following day to Lundahl's office, where we joined nine other men—Myron Krueger, Jack W. Gardner, Norman Beckett, Zigmund Lenchert, Clifton Mulinaux, Sidney Stallings, W. Reece Walker, John Wilson, Charles F. "Chick" Camp—to form the cadre of a photo-intelligence division in the Agency's Office of Research and Reports.

Lundahl, aware of the difficulties encountered by the photo interpreters during World War II, conceived of his organization as a wagon wheel. The photo interpreters would be the hub of that wheel

---

* For example, all of the Ford River Rouge Plant equipment used to manufacture the Model A Ford had been purchased by the Russians and installed in a newly built plant in Gorki during the early 1930s. A number of Ford workers, including Walter Reuther, were sent to Russia to help them start production of the Russian version of the Ford. Austin Engineering had designed the large steel combine at Stalinsk; General Electric equipment was used in the Dnieper Dam; and the Badger Company had been involved in building four Lend-Lease oil refineries. Searches were also made in the Library of Congress for information on plants built by other Western nations.

and the radiating spokes of specialists would make the wheel turn. Specialists would be hired in the following categories: collateral information support, editorial, photogrammetry, graphics, photo-processing laboratory, printing services, automatic data processing (later computers), three-dimensional model making, and mail and courier support. The loyalty, enthusiasm, devotion, and total commitment engendered among his original "twelve apostles" by Lundahl in Q Building and, later, Quarters I—an abandoned barracks that housed a WAVE contingent during World War II—convinced him that photo interpretation could resolve many current intelligence problems. Photo interpretation had traditionally been the private preserve of the military, especially the Air Force, which was extremely sensitive to the Agency's encroachment on its territory.

Three camera systems were being considered for use in the U-2: The A consisted of three 24-inch focal-length cameras, one vertical and two obliques; the B was a 36-inch focal-length panoramic camera that fired from seven positions to provide horizon-to-horizon coverage; and the C camera was a single 66-inch focal-length camera used for special purposes. During the winter of 1955 and the spring of 1956, specialists Louis Franceschini, Cliff Mulinaux, Myron Krueger, and I were much involved in evaluating imagery acquired by these systems on test missions. The A cameras functioned perfectly, but problems developed in both the B and C camera systems. The B camera, in hitting one of its seven stops, would frequently bounce and create a smeared image. The C camera had a variety of problems which seemed insurmountable. The operational people favored the A camera, but our specialist's "team," especially Lou Franceschini, insisted that the B was a far superior camera in both resolution and swath width and that the stops of the camera could be "dampened."

We were so impressed with the quality and quantity of the imagery obtained by the B system that we doubted whether the old methods of interpreting photography—i.e., using paper prints and four-power stereoscopes—were practicable any longer. If it continued to be done in this manner, we had no doubt that substantial data imaged on the film itself would be lost. We recommended that interpretation be done from duplicate film positives rather than with paper prints. It also was soon recognized that if photographic interpretation was to be performed properly, new equipment for processing, interpretation, and mensuration would have to be developed.

The unique and highly technological progress made in photographic acquisition systems made it urgently necessary to match user capability to the new collection systems. Lundahl therefore reorganized his forces to concentrate on developing a "family" of equipment designed specifically to extract all the information captured on the film. Robert Neasham, Duane W. "Doc" Linker, Chris Mares, and John Cain were hired for this developmental work. Lundahl also pressed industrial and government laboratories to the limits of their imagination in order to establish and maintain equality of capabilities. Linker and Neasham conducted a series of experiments with medical microscopes and X-ray light tables. The outgrowth of these experiments was an enhanced light source for exploiting the duplicate positives and a microstereoscope with rhomboids for stereoscopic viewing of the film. Mares and Cain were concerned with the development of new mensuration devices.

During this period, Lundahl and his executive officer, Chick Camp, were also involved in negotiating a permanent home for the center. The nondescript Steuart Motor Car Co. Building was selected in a crime-ridden area of the Washington ghetto at 5th and K Streets, NW. The four upper floors of the building would become the division's home, while the three lower floors would still be occupied by the motor car company, along with the Steuart Real Estate Office. The building was not air-conditioned, and there were heating problems in winter. Lundahl invited the U.S. military services to station interpreters at the center. While the Army promptly accepted, the Air Force remained aloof and the Navy decided to participate on only a limited basis.

Lundahl met with the Agency's deputy director for intelligence, Robert Amory, about reorganizing the organization to accommodate the service elements. Amory agreed and Lundahl chose the title Photographic Interpretation Center for his new organization.

Air Force Colonel Osmond "Ozzie" J. Ritland had been working with Bissell, and he and lower-ranking Air Force officers were doing everything possible to aid the CIA in its photo-collection and -interpretation efforts. Meanwhile, at the Pentagon, there was an angry undercurrent as to how the Air Force could allow a task properly assigned to them to slip away to the CIA. Air Force photo-interpretation units were directed not to cooperate with Agency personnel in their attempt to establish a photo-interpretation center. At Omaha, General Curtis LeMay regarded SAC as the free world's primary deterrent to the Soviet Union and assumed that it should have the dominant role in acquiring strategic intelligence. While General LeMay cooperated with the Agency in providing logistical support, he too, to paraphrase one of his senior officers, was "bent out of shape" because the Agency was becoming involved with photo interpretation. In one of his staff meetings, LeMay said about the U-2: "We'll let them develop it and then we'll take it away from them."

The Soviets staged an all-out spectacular air show over Moscow on Aviation Day in July 1955. A formation of fifty-four Tu-16 Badger medium jet bombers, along with Bison heavy jet bombers and MiG fighters, zoomed overhead. Then, the flyby of a large turboprop strategic bomber designed by the renowned designer A. A. Tupolev, later designated the Tu-95 Bear, would add additional fuel to the "bomber-gap" controversy.

Meanwhile, in the U.S., Kelly Johnson was progressing with developing the aircraft, and Bissell was investigating a dry lake bed in Nevada, within the atomic test area and adjacent to the Nellis Air Force Base gunnery range, as a site for flight testing the U-2. It was called Groom Lake, Watertown Strip, or Paradise Ranch and air crews and technicians began arriving for training in the summer of 1955. On August 1, 1955, just eight months from the day that Kelly Johnson had gotten the go-ahead from the Agency, the U-2 was ready for its first test flight. Pilot Tony LeVier took the plane up, with Johnson observing its performance, flying alongside in a T-33 chase plane. There were problems not only with the airplane and its J-57 engine, which would frequently flame out at high altitudes, but also with the space suits, the helmets, and face plates. Problems also surfaced with providing liquids and food to the pilot. It was finally decided that the pilot feed himself with food and water by inserting a plastic tube through the opening of the face plate of the helmet. "Liquids were stored in a plastic bottle and food (much like baby food) was stored in tooth-paste-like tubes and squeezed through the tube as desired. Commonly used foods were applesauce, peaches, beef and gravy. Liquids used were water and fruit juices. The food and liquid were normally carried in a pocket of the leg of the pilot's coverall which was worn over the partial pressure suit."[10] The U-2 pilots became so proficient with the U-2 that they could land and taxi the aircraft to a hardstand without the use of the pogos. The sleek U-2 was all flush riveted and had a wingspan of 80 feet and a fuselage length of 49 feet and 7 inches. Its range was approximately 5,000 nautical miles. With power loss at altitude, the U-2 could glide over 300 miles.

During this period, Eisenhower frequently talked about a possible disarmament agreement between the U.S. and the Soviet Union. The stumbling block for such negotiations was on-site inspection, a prerequisite that was rejected summarily by the Russians. The advances in photo technology and the development of long-range jet aircraft—and the possibility of their application to aerial reconnaissance—were intriguing to those of us in intelligence concerned with the problems inherent in arms control and disarmament.

Eisenhower was extremely receptive to the idea of using aerial reconnaissance as the vehicle for inspection and compliance with any proposed disarmament agreement. He asked that the issues inimical to such a system be studied. Three groups were involved in submitting ideas and proposals: 1) the "Quantico group," headed by Dr. Max Millikan, an MIT professor and former head of CIA's Office of Research and Reports; 2) an Air Force group comprising specialists from SAC, the Air Research and Developmental Command, and specialists from the Office of the Secretary of the Air Force; and 3) a CIA group.

The studies produced by these groups were lengthy, detailed, and full of qualifiers. The president preferred short, pithy memos—i.e., fact one, fact two, fact three, and conclusion. Eisenhower subsequently asked an old Army colleague and confidant, General Lucian K. Truscott, senior representative of the D.C.I. in West Germany, to return to Washington and apprise him of the pros and cons of a disarmament proposal using aerial reconnaissance. Truscott was made a deputy director to Allen Dulles.

My superior, James M. Andrews, asked that I meet with General Truscott and show him the types of information that we were holding on Russian plants. Truscott asked what I would want in addition to aerial photos of Russian plants. He was rather surprised when I showed him the many blueprints already collected and how they facilitated the interpretation of aerial photos. Truscott asked me to accompany him to the White House, where we met Nelson Rockefeller, a presidential aide on foreign affairs, who was most impressed with what could be done with a combination of blueprints and aerial photography. Rockefeller was the focal point in drafting a proposal for Eisenhower for a summit conference to be held in Geneva in July 1955. He presented a draft proposal on "Open Skies" to Secretary of State John Dulles, who had promptly rejected it. We were told later that there had been several heated discussions on the proposal between Rockefeller and Dulles in Eisenhower's office and that Dulles had won out.

President Eisenhower attended the Geneva summit meeting, but the meeting was not going well because of the intransigence of the two Soviet leaders, Bulganin and Khrushchev. Eisenhower raised the issue of the danger of surprise attack—that there should be concern "to find dependable ways to supervise and inspect military establishments so there can be no frightful surprises." There was no response from either Premier Bulganin or Khrushchev. Eisenhower asked Rockefeller to come to Geneva as fast as possible with the Open Skies draft proposal.

On Tuesday, July 21, 1955, President Eisenhower surprised Premier Bulganin with the proposal. Eisenhower admitted later that he spoke quickly and, in part, extemporaneously. It was, however, from his heart when he said, "I've been searching my heart and mind for something I could say here that would convince everyone of the great sincerity of the United States in approaching the problem of disarmament."

Eisenhower proposed that the following steps be taken immediately:

"To give each other a complete blueprint of our military establishments, from beginning to end, from one end of our countries to the other; lay out the establishments and provide blueprints to each other.

"Next, to provide within our countries facilities for aerial photography to the other country—we to provide you with the facilities within our country, ample facilities for aerial reconnaissance, where you can make all the pictures you choose and take them to your country to study, you to provide exactly the same facilities for us and we to make these examinations, and by this step to convince the world that we are providing as between ourselves against the possibility of great surprise attack, thus lessening danger and relaxing tension. Likewise, we will make more easily attainable a comprehensive and effective system of inspection and disarmament, because what I propose, I assure you, would be only a beginning."

Although Bulganin stated that Eisenhower's proposal would be studied, it was subsequently rejected by the Russians. Bulganin, in a speech to the Supreme Soviet on August 4, 1955, stated that "aerial photography cannot give the expected results, because both countries stretch over vast territories in which, if one desired, one could conceal anything." Khrushchev would later call the plan "a bold espionage plot." (According to Ambassador Dobrynin, in an address at Georgetown University in November 1989, Khrushchev initially favored accepting the Open Skies proposal but was voted down by the Politburo for fear it would legitimize spying against the Soviet Union. Dobrynin said Khrushchev thought accepting the plan would be a propaganda triumph for the Soviets, since he was certain the U.S. Congress, at the time, would not allow Soviet aircraft to fly over the U.S.)

Eisenhower still thought the plan had merit and asked the CIA and the Air Force to come up with a publication describing the plan and the whole photo-taking and -interpretation process. Lundahl and I worked with the Air Force to produce a magazine-size publication entitled "Mutual Inspection for Peace" (which the CIA published), which became a classic description of the aerial-reconnaissance, photo-interpretation, and inspection process.

Eisenhower Uses the U-2 to Provide Vital Strategic and Tactical Information

"During the four years of its operation, the U-2 produced intelligence of critical importance to the United States."

—President Dwight D. Eisenhower

WITH THE FAILURE of the Open Skies proposal at the Geneva summit, the U.S. government pursued the U-2 program full steam ahead. There was a shakedown of the processing machines at Eastman Kodak and the Photo Interpretation Center had conducted several drills for reporting the intelligence that would be obtained from the U-2 photography. There were problems in procuring a water-chilling machine for the Steuart Building so that film could be processed and developed. All of these and hundreds of other problems were being solved, since the time was soon approaching for the deployment of the U-2's to Wiesbaden airfield in West Germany under the spurious 1st Weather Reconnaissance Squadron, Provisional (WRSP-1). During this period, U-2 photographic development flights were being conducted in the U.S. and the results were spectacular. President Eisenhower was kept fully informed and was periodically shown photographs of the test flights by Bissell and Lundahl. Eisenhower would remark: "Proof of the plane's capacity to produce photography of excellent definition was striking. I was shown photography, taken from an altitude of 70,000 feet, of some of our important cities. On these we could easily count the automobiles on the street and even lines marking the parking areas for individual cars. There was no doubt about the quality of the information to be obtained."[1] Lundahl and James Q. Reber were sent to England and Germany with government-to-government agreements and "to make U.S. officials witting of the resource of the U-2 program and also to see if all of the pieces fit together." Later, Lundahl would again travel to Europe with the results of the missions.

Allen Dulles had given the important job of target selection for the U-2 missions over Russia to Reber, a highly respected CIA staff officer. He in turn formed the Ad Hoc Requirements Committee (ARC), with representatives from the various intelligence services. Representatives would argue vociferously for missions covering targets that were of particular concern to them. Reber would listen patiently to their arguments, reflect on them, and then decide which flight track would be the most beneficial in satisfying the intelligence needs relative to the national estimates.

A select number of participants would meet in Reber's office to draft a request for presidential approval of the mission. CIA staffer Sidney Graybeal would normally write a paragraph stating what information the particular mission could produce relative to missile estimates; Herb Bowers, the information relative to strategic bombers; and Henry Lowenhaupt, for nuclear weapons. A flight track would be drawn in straight lines among the prime targets. It was my job to show, by bending or by departing slightly from the straight flight lines, that we could pick up bonus targets such as industrial installations, military camps, fighter airfields, etc., along the way. We thus attempted to maximize the intelligence take from each mission. For every delineation I would recommend, James Cunningham, the flight planner, would carefully compute the fuel required for such delineations. When the flight plan was complete, Reber would compose a justification for the mission. One paragraph would cover the potential take for missile information, another for nuclear, the third for bombers, and the fourth on the numbers and types of bonus targets that could be accrued. This memo, not over a page and a half, would be skillfully crafted by Reber into a justification for approval by President Eisenhower. Often, U. Alexis Johnson would look at the memo and make appropriate comments representing the Department of State's view. The memo justifying a mission would be given to Allen Dulles, who would forward it to his brother, Secretary of State John Foster Dulles.

The secretary of state kept a relentless vigil over all senior officials, including his brother, on international affairs but especially anything having to do with the Soviet Union. Allen Dulles kept a low profile regarding aerial reconnaissance, content to confide his views and memos to his brother. The secretary of state would take the memo to the president. Eisenhower reviewed and personally approved every U-2 mission over Russia. The requesting memo would come back with the president's approval, which was good for ten days. Mission planners would then consult the weather charts and wait until the weather along the flight track was 80 percent cloud-free before the mission would be launched. Weather Central had indicated that the best weather for western Russia was between June 20 and July 10, 1956. There was a hitch, however, to all the planning for the first U-2 mission. General Nathan F. Twining, the Air Force chief of staff, had been invited to Russia during this period and he indicated that he would attend. It was decided, therefore, that two test missions would be flown over Eastern European countries. These missions were extremely successful and a number of briefing boards were created and shown to the president.

The first U-2 mission over the Soviet Union took place on July 4, 1956. It was flown with the A camera and covered a number of long-range bomber bases in western USSR, along with targets in the Leningrad area. The Russians attempted more than twenty interceptions of the U-2. MiG fighters were photographed desperately trying to reach the U-2, only to fall and tumble back to an altitude where they could restart their flamed-out engines.

Photo interpreters at the center looked at the photography with abject fascination. A number of briefing boards were produced on Soviet long-range bomber airfields; no Bison bombers were observed, but nuclear weapons' loading pits were evident at all the airfields. Briefing boards were also made of Russian cities, especially Leningrad, where shipyard production of submarines and naval combatants was clearly visible.

Lundahl showed the intelligence significance of each board as the president listened intently. Lundahl remembered that the president "asked questions about very specific targets that were of great national interest. He was impressed with the quality of the photography and asked questions about the resolution and the altitude the pictures were made from. He also asked questions about intercept attempts and questions about any Soviet reaction." Lundahl described the president as being "warm with satisfaction" after seeing the results from the first mission. A warm and friendly relationship developed, Eisenhower admiring Lundahl for his articulate presentations and Lundahl enjoying the president's support for the reconnaissance programs.

It was an exciting era—a new age of discovery, and, for the first time, we had the capability to derive precise, irrefutable data on the vast land mass and physical installations of our principal adversary —and the data was only a few days old. It was also a learning and collaborative experience between the policymakers, intelligence analysts, and photo interpreters. The analyst literally stood at the photo interpreter's shoulder and was made acutely aware of the exploitation process and of the photo interpreter's nuances and jargon. The policymakers began comparing the information derived from the U-2 with other sources of information. Often when presented with information from other sources, the president would ask, "How does this compare with the U-2 information?"

The second U-2 mission, on July 5, over Moscow and the southern Ukraine, was particularly daring since Moscow was defended by two concentric rings of SA-1 surface-to-air missile sites, totaling some 3,600 launchers. But the U-2 piloted by Carmine Vito slipped in without being detected. When Vito was asked recently what his reaction was when he saw that the flight line would take him through the SA-1 defenses not once but twice, coming and going, he said, "Hell, it was my job and I just flew the mission to the best of my abilities." Subsequent U-2 missions crisscrossed long-range bomber bases in the western areas of the Soviet Union.

These missions were generating accurate, current information in greater quantities than had ever been contemplated. Much to our surprise, the Russians had not employed any camouflage and concealment efforts. Time and again, we knew we were reporting information that was dispelling existing notions and intelligence estimates, and we took a certain vicarious pleasure in proving the value of aerial photography over other intelligence sources. Analysts began reevaluating assumptions regarding Soviet strategic capabilities. Within a few weeks, analysis of the U-2 photography had dispelled the bomber-gap myth.

On July 10, 1956, the Soviet Union protested to the State Department that "a twin-engined medium bomber of the United States Air Force"[2] had violated Soviet airspace on several recent occasions. The Soviets probably thought they were being overflown by the twin-engine stretched-wing RB-57D Canberra. While the Soviets cited a number of cities in western Russia that were overflown, no mention was made that the U-2 had flown over Moscow, Leningrad, and most of the principal cities of western USSR. The State Department waited until July 19 to reply to the Soviet note, and by that time, the most critical U-2 missions had been completed. The State Department reported carefully to the Soviets that: "A thorough inquiry has been conducted and it has been determined that no United States military planes based, or flying in or adjacent to the European area at the time of the alleged overflights could possibly have strayed, as alleged, so far from their known flight plans, which carefully exclude such overflights as the Soviet Note alleges. Therefore the statement of the Soviet Union is in error."[3]

Lundahl's combination of energy, memory, intelligence, knowledge, and articulateness was making quite a name for him and the art of photo interpretation. After the president was briefed on the takes from each mission, Lundahl would proceed to the secretary of state, the secretary of defense, the Joint Chiefs of Staff, congressional leaders, and the chiefs of the various intelligence directorates. Lundahl quickly became the most respected and honored intelligence officer in the intelligence community. He was a superb photo interpreter and photogrammetrist and could articulate the characteristics and technical specifications of the new collection system. This ability, combined with a warm enthusiasm and a strong empathy with his audiences, was daily proving the value of photo intelligence in the estimative process. After each mission, Kelly Johnson would come to the Center and we would brief him on the results of the mission. Such other distinguished visitors as General Jimmy Doolittle, Dr. Edwin Land, and Dr. George Kistiakowsky also came to our nondescript but vital facility in the Steuart Building.

The U-2 was designed and approved originally for gathering strategic intelligence on the Soviet Union, but President Eisenhower also considered using it to acquire current and detailed information in tactical situations. Political tensions between Britain, France, and Egypt over Egyptian nationalization of the Suez Canal were causing apprehension at the White House, particularly when it became apparent that the British, French, and possibly the Israelis were making preparations to attack Egypt. When Eisenhower warned the British not to attack, they began to mask all of their military preparations. Eisenhower convened a meeting of Senate and House leaders and told them of the British and French attitudes. He said, "I don't like to do this to my friends, but I will G-2 [use intelligence on] them if I have to." He directed U-2's be deployed to obtain information on the Middle East situation.

The first U-2 mission was flown over Egypt, Israel, Jordan, Lebanon, and Syria in late August 1956. We were surprised to find a number of French-supplied Dassault Mystère fighters and Sud Vautour fighter bombers at Israeli airfields. Eisenhower was shocked when shown the photos and felt that he had been betrayed by the Israelis. In a memorandum for the record dated October 15, 1956, Eisenhower added the following note: "Our high-flying reconnaissance planes have shown that Israel has obtained some 60 of the French Mystère pursuit planes, when there had been reported the transfer of only 24."[4] He ordered the U-2 surveillance stepped up, and it was during this period that U-2's were staged out of Adana, Turkey.

Surveillance of Anglo-French activities was maintained through periodic coverage of the staging bases at Valletta, Malta; Toulon, France; and Cyprus without the British, French, or Israelis knowing about it. The British had closed a number of areas and bases in Cyprus to foreign observation and began deploying their troops in large tented areas in remote locations. The Center developed the science of "tentology"—by counting the number of tents and the number of personnel assigned to each tent, we were able to report to the president the increasing number of troops the British were stationing in Cyprus. When French Nord Atlas transports were seen at Tymbou airfield and Hunter fighters and Canberra bombers arrived at Akrotiri airfield, Eisenhower was notified that an invasion was imminent. Heavy lightering activity was later seen at Limassol transferring troops to landing ships. The U-2 photographs were also carefully studied to ascertain ship movements, staging areas, activity at airfields, and possible amphibious and paradrop areas. U-2's were overhead filming the invading forces. In fact, a U-2 pilot was filming the Cairo area when he saw the British Canberra bombers coming in for a bombing run on Cairo/Almaza airfield. The pilot made a complete turn and filmed the results of their bombing. When the pre- and postmission photos were shown to Eisenhower by Lundahl, the president reflected for a moment and then remarked, "Twenty-minute reconnaissance. Now that's something to shoot for."

One of the most successful tactical U-2 operations involving U.S. armed forces was during the Middle East crisis of 1958. The growing influence of President Nasser and the UAR posed a threat to Lebanon, and President Camille Chamoun of Lebanon announced that the danger posed by the threat to Lebanon's sovereignty forced him to ask for assistance from Europe and the United States. In response to a formal request for U.S. intervention, Eisenhower decided to send U.S. forces to Lebanon. U-2 imagery was used in planning the invasion. On the evening of July 15 and the morning of July 16, over 3,500 U.S. Marines landed on the beaches south of Beirut and took control of the international airfield. Supplies for the troops and additional troops were landed and deployed to predetermined locations. Missions were flown over the area and a vigil was maintained on all of the positions where U.S. troops were deployed. Surveillance of Egypt and Syria for possible armed intervention was also maintained. When all the troops were subsequently withdrawn on October 25, 1958, and the final briefing boards of the troop withdrawal were shown to President Eisenhower, he remarked, "The troops will never know that they had a guardian angel watching over them."

The so-called missile-gap controversy began on August 27, 1957, when the U.S. detected the Soviets had carried out the first successful test firing of an ICBM. On January 25, April 19, May 21, and August 30 of that year, the U.S. attempted four highly publicized test flights of the intermediate-range Thor missile. All ended in failure. On June 11, a test flight of the Atlas ICBM had also ended in failure. The impact of the Soviet test, and subsequent firings, served to convince the intelligence community that the Soviets were readying a deployment program involving a substantial number of ICBMs. The

Soviets had also demonstrated the reliability of their boosters by a series of successful space launches. It was logically assumed that they would deploy the missile, which had been designated the SS-6.

Then on October 4, 1957, two weeks after the Soviet ICBM firing, the Soviets launched Sputnik, followed a month later by placing a live dog into orbit. To respond to the Soviet space accomplishments, an attempt was made to launch the Navy's Vanguard satellite in December. The Vanguard malfunctioned, rose a few feet above the ground, and exploded. The launch was viewed by millions on nationwide television and added to the feeling that the U.S. had fallen far behind the Soviets in missile technology. The American public was confused, angry, and in a near hysterical state concerning education, science, and scientists. The Department of Defense, especially the U.S. Air Force, seized upon the issue arising out of this potential threat and gained the support of sizable elements of the Congress, both Republican and Democrat. The claim that the Soviets were outpacing the U.S., both in production and deployment of ICBMs, was given added impetus by Khrushchev in both public and private statements. Without sufficient intelligence, the claim could neither be substantiated nor refuted. The pressure on the president reached its peak in the early months of 1958. Eisenhower would later write: "There was rarely a day when I failed to give earnest study to reports of our progress and to estimates of Soviet capabilities."[5]

In the 1957–1959 period, the targeting of U-2 missions over the USSR was shifted to seek out ICBM production and possible deployment areas in the Urals and Siberia as well as atomic-energy-production and development sites. A number of U-2 missions were flown over these areas, but no ICBM deployment areas were identified. The Soviets had only one launch pad (stand) at their main ICBM and space test center, at Tyura Tam. We measured the aperture of the launch pad (stand); it was an extremely large one and its size raised some doubts whether a missile that large could be successfully deployed for operational purposes. (It wasn't until the Paris Air Show in 1967 that the Soviets exhibited the SS-6 publicly. The four conical multichambered boosters strapped to a sustainer confirmed our earlier hypothesis that the missile's size made it difficult to deploy either in a soft or silo configuration.) The only place where the Soviets deployed the SS-6 was at the Plesetsk Missile and Space Center. U.S. national estimates continued to project Soviet ICBM capabilities for the year 1963 to range from the Army's estimate of two hundred deployed sites to the Air Force estimate of seven hundred sites. By the end of 1960, however, photo-interpretation and other efforts had failed to produce evidence of a single deployed Soviet ICBM site outside of Plesetsk.

During this period, U-2 missions were flown from a number of foreign bases. In England, Macmillan was being periodically briefed on the resultant photo intelligence. President Eisenhower decided that Chancellor Konrad Adenauer should also be briefed. Lundahl and Dutch Scheufele were selected, and when they arrived in Bonn, they were met at the chancellor's residence by David K. E. Bruce, the U.S. ambassador to West Germany, and John Bross, a senior Agency official. Ushered into the chancellor's office, they were greeted by the chancellor and Reinhard Gehlen, chief of West German Federal Intelligence Agency (FIA). According to Lundahl: "I showed the Chancellor one briefing board after another on the whole gamut of Soviet strategic weapons and targets. He looked at the photography carefully and couldn't believe what he was seeing. He seldom showed any emotion and usually listened with a stoic face. Several times, he asked that translators elaborate on the terms I was using. He was so impressed with the quality of one briefing board that he threw back his head, brought his fingers to his mouth, shook his head in disbelief and exclaimed: '*Fabelhaft! Fabelhaft!*' [Fabulous, fabulous.]" About this time, Adenauer's secretary entered and said Senator Estes Kefauver was waiting. The chancellor asked if the senator could join in the briefing. Bross said no, the senator wasn't cleared. The chancellor's stoic face broke into a smile.

Eisenhower was displeased with intelligence estimates on the Soviet Union. He wanted an impartial look at the information being gleaned from the U-2 photography. He asked his science adviser, Dr. George B. Kistiakowsky, to form a panel of experts to evaluate the Russian strategic capabilities versus those of the United States. Such experts as Dr. Kistiakowsky, Dr. William Pickering, Werner Von Braun, Clark Millikan, Simon Ramo, General John B. Medares, Herbert York, and the heads of laboratories from major U.S. weapons development laboratories took part in the exercise. Two future deputy directors of the Agency, Albert D. Wheelon, of the Ramo Wool-ridge Corp., and Carl E. Duckett, of the U.S. Army's Ballistic Missile Agency, were also among the group.

At the Center, we made hundreds of enlargements of U-2 photos, drawings, and stereograms of Soviet missile, nuclear, aircraft, and biological and chemical installations for use by the panel of experts in what Kistiakowsky called a "comparative evaluation."[6] Discussions between the experts and Center photo-interpretation experts went deep into the night. I was placed in charge of the logistics, message center, and physical comfort of the scientists while they were at the Center. Lundahl had given the scientists a free run of the Center to speak to anyone they desired. After nearly a month of effort, the panel issued its report: The U.S. was far ahead of the Soviet Union not only in weapons research but also in the deployment of strategic weapons. What emerged was that the Russians were not comparable to the U.S., as the U.S. military and industrial complexes had repeatedly emphasized in the yearly congressional budget battles. Perhaps Kistiakowsky phrased it best when he complimented our efforts, stating, "We went looking for a body but only found a skeleton." The report stimulated considerable reflection on the part of President Eisenhower, and he later expressed serious concern about the danger of an unbridled U.S. military-industrial complex.

British pilots had been trained to fly the U-2, and in 1958, President Eisenhower pressured Prime Minister Harold Macmillan to have his pilots fly missions over the Soviet Union. On August 24, 1958, Macmillan approved the use of British pilots and they began flying missions over targets concerned with Soviet strategic capabilities.

The success of the U-2 in providing current information during the Suez crisis also prompted Eisenhower to continue to use the U-2 in tactical situations. Probably one of the best examples of how U-2-derived intelligence was used by President Eisenhower occurred during the summer of 1958. Intensified Chinese Communist military activity in the Formosa Strait had provoked repeated engagements between Chinese National Air Forces, flying F-84 Sabre jets, and Chinese Communists, flying MiG-17's. Sporadic naval skirmishes also occurred near the offshore islands of mainland China. The Chinese Communists were shelling the Chinese Nationalist-held islands of Quemoy and Ma-tsu, and it was feared that the Chinese Communists would attempt to invade these islands. President Eisenhower authorized U-2 missions to be flown, not only over the islands but also over the mainland. We were able to report with a high degree of confidence that there was no imminent preparation for the invasion of the offshore islands or Formosa itself. Eisenhower looked at all the briefing boards, stroked his chin as when he pondered a decision, and said, "We'll see what we can do about it [the dogfights]." In September, he decided to provide the Chinese Nationalists with Sidewinder air-to-air missiles. Commencing in mid-September, the Chinese Nationalists shot down over 100 MiG fighters in aerial dogfights. The U.S. government also provided the Chinese Nationalists with information as to rendezvous areas of boats and junks that could be used for an invasion. The Chinese Nationalists began bombing and strafing these areas. The offshore Quemoy-Ma-tsu island crisis was resolved.

In March 1959, a Tibetan revolt against Communist Chinese rule was crushed and the Dalai Lama went into exile in India. Eisenhower authorized U-2 flights over the area to assess the situation. The aerial photography clearly showed that the Chinese Communists completely ruled the principal cities, that they had constructed a number of military installations and airfields and were in Tibet to stay. Eisenhower, based on the information derived from the aerial photos, decided not to support any effort by the Tibetans to regain control of their homeland.

Also in 1959, the North Vietnamese began to infiltrate troops into Laos in the Sam Neua and Phong Saly provinces of northern Laos. At the time, the United States maintained friendly relations with the existing Laotian government. At the end of July, Communist-led Pathet Lao guerrillas began attacking Laotian army posts. A state of emergency was proclaimed in Laos and the Laotian government called for help from the U.S. On August 25, the Laotian government asked for military aid from the U.S. and President Eisenhower reported that its request "was under study as a matter of urgency." The president authorized U-2 missions over North Vietnam and Laos. The Vietnamese order of battle in North Vietnam was derived from the U-2 photography, but we could not determine whether the trails leading from Vietnam into Laos were used by people in their normal course of daily life, by animals, or by the infiltrators. We also told the president the difficulty of seeing anything under the jungle canopy and pointed out that the numerous caves in the Sam Neua area could provide shelter for the invading guerrillas. Eisenhower reflected for a long while on the briefing boards, recalling his personal knowledge of guerrilla operations and making specific references to the difficulties the U.S. Army had encountered with the Moros in the Philippines and the operations of the Tito guerrillas in Yugoslavia during World War II. "In such terrain," he remarked, "the advantage clearly lies with the enemy." Considering Eisenhower's military background and his knowledge of the conditions under which a war would have to be fought in Vietnam, Mr. Lundahl and I have discussed a number of times that it is doubtful that Eisenhower would have committed large numbers of U.S. troops to fight in Vietnam.

Even as the U-2's were bringing back this invaluable information for use of policymakers, Dr. Land was challenging his colleagues to organize the research and development for an even more effective reconnaissance aircraft. In November 1958, the final report of the Land Panel suggested that "The successor reconnaissance aircraft would have to achieve a substantial increase in altitude and speed; be of reduced radar detectability; suffer no loss in range to that of the U-2; and be of minimum size and weight." President Eisenhower was briefed on July 20, 1959, on the successor aircraft to the U-2. It would fly at three times the speed of sound at an altitude of 85,000 feet. It was officially designated the A-11, later to be known as the SR-71. Eisenhower, however, would always refer to it as "the big one."

In a June 1959 interview with Averell Harriman, Nikita Khrushchev threatened Harriman regarding Berlin: "Your generals talk of maintaining your position in Berlin with force. That is bluff. If you send in tanks," Khrushchev said with angry emphasis, "they will burn, and make no mistake about it. If you want war, you can have it, but remember it will be your war. Our rockets will fly automatically."[7] His colleagues around the table chorused the word *automatically*. We were asked to attempt to verify Khrushchev's threat. The Soviets still had only one large missile-launch position at that time, at the Tyura Tam Missile Test Center, and several at Plesetsk. In the same interview with Harriman, Khrushchev claimed that the USSR had shipped numerous rockets to Communist China and that these had been planted in the hinterlands behind the coastline. "The rockets," Khrushchev boasted, "have adequate range to blast the Chinese stronghold of Formosa." He added arrogantly that "Communist strength is now more than adequate to immobilize and, if necessary, destroy the powerful U.S. Seventh Fleet patrolling the Formosa Strait."[8] At the very same time that Khrushchev was making these threats, U-2's were crisscrossing China at will, unchallenged by Chinese Communist defenses. Analysis of the photography proved that while the Chinese had a missile-test facility at Shuangcheng Tsu, there were no offensive missile sites in mainland China. Indeed, the Chinese Communists could hardly challenge a single U.S. destroyer, much less the powerful U.S. Seventh Fleet.

Analysis of aerial photography of Soviet forces in East Germany, however, left no doubt that the Soviets could resist any forced entry into West Berlin by the Allied powers. Whenever the East Germans deliberately slowed or stopped traffic at various checkpoints along the autobahn leading to Berlin, there would be an inevitable demand in the United States that the Allies force their way into West Berlin. On one such occasion, careful analysis of aerial photography of one checkpoint revealed a number of carefully concealed Soviet tanks positioned with barrels aimed directly at the checkpoint—at point-blank range.

President Eisenhower decided that there should be some method of informing the American people that much of what Khrushchev was saying about his missiles was pure bluff. Eisenhower was a personal friend of Henry R. Luce, who had supported him in all of his campaigns. When Luce was told that the administration would provide classified information for an article on Soviet strategic capabilities, he selected Charles J. V. Murphy, Washington bureau chief for *Fortune* magazine, who was also a colonel in the Air Force Reserve and a specialist in defense- and intelligence-related matters. We showed Murphy U-2 photos of Soviet missile installations and provided him with information on their locations, facilities, and capabilities. Murphy wrote a stinging exposé about Russian strategic limitations. When the article was previewed by Secretary of State Dulles, however, he thought it revealed too much about U.S. reconnaissance capabilities and refused to let Murphy print it. (Much later, after Eisenhower had left office and Kennedy had been assassinated, Murphy's article, entitled "Khrushchev's Paper Bear," was published in the December 1964 issue of *Fortune* magazine.)

Meanwhile, concern was shifted to Cuba. On January 8, 1959, after a week-long victory march from Santiago de Cuba, Fidel Castro triumphantly entered Havana, and was immediately faced with a faltering economy and a thoroughly disorganized society. Two months later, Castro nationalized the Cuba Telephone Company, marking the beginning of confiscation of U.S. properties in Cuba. Castro was invited to the United States by the American Society of Newspaper Editors and he visited Washington in April. Eisenhower was on a golfing vacation and left Vice-President Nixon to meet with Castro. Nixon and other U.S. officials warned Castro about the dangers of further confiscations. The nationalization, however, continued throughout 1959, despite warnings from the Eisenhower administration. Two weeks before President Kennedy's inauguration, Eisenhower broke diplomatic relations with Havana.

Not long after Castro's takeover, more than a year before the Russians began sending arms to Cuba, unevaluated intelligence reports began warning of offensive missile sites being constructed in Cuba. The most persistent rumor in Cuba and in Cuban refugee colonies in the U.S. was that the Russians were constructing a missile site in the Zapata swamp. Eisenhower authorized several flights over the swamp to be made by "off-course" U.S. Navy reconnaissance aircraft, ostensibly on their way to Guantánamo. Detailed examination of the photography failed to reveal any missile-related equipment or activity. While no great worry was expressed by the U.S. military about Castro's ragtag army, there was some concern about the Cuban Air Force, which previously had been in a state of almost complete disorganization. Most of its former officers had been imprisoned or dismissed and many of its former enlisted personnel had deserted. The Cuban Air Force was designated the Cuban Rebel Air Force (CRAF) by Castro but had no operational units per se. It had eighty-four aircraft, all propeller-driven with the exception of seven U.S.-provided T-33 jets. Castro had been negotiating with the British and others to acquire additional jets. It was estimated that he had less than sixty pilots, although sixteen were undergoing training in Mexico and several were being trained in Venezuela. In spite of this, the intelligence community was impressed when, on July 26, 1959, in celebration of the beginning of Castro's revolution, the CRAF, assisted by civilian pilots, managed to get twenty-nine aircraft into the air in a flypast over Havana. The aircraft consisted of eight Sea Furys, nine B-26's, four T-33's, two F-47's, four C-47's, one C-54, and one C-46. It would be the T-33's that would bomb the supply ships and cause the failure of the Bay of Pigs landing. Cuban air defenses had no intercept-type fighters, no early-warning radars, no ground-control radars, no airborne-intercept-radar equipment, and only a few anti-aircraft weapons left over from World War II. Cuba did not have any weapons sufficient to challenge U.S. reconnaissance capabilities.

There was considerable controversy regarding the political orientation the Cuban leader would adopt in charting his country's future. On February 13, 1960, a "commercial aid pact," in which the Soviets agreed to buy up to a million tons of sugar annually over a period of four years, in addition to granting Cuba a $100 million-dollar loan, was signed by Premier Castro and Anastas Mikoyan. Five months later, the U.S. Congress, in retaliation for Castro's anti-U.S. policies, voted to give the president discretion to cut quotas of Cuban sugar imports to the U.S. A series of incidents escalated tensions between the United States and Cuba. Then, on April 16, 1961, Castro for the first time referred to the Cuban revolution as "socialist," and during his 1961 May Day speech he announced that Cuba was entering into an "era of socialist construction." The speech that received the most publicity, however, came on December 2, 1961, when he proclaimed that he "believed absolutely in Marxism" and that "he had for some time."[9]

U-2 flights continued over the Soviet Union, and the information obtained continued to enhance national estimates that the United States had achieved a superior strategic position. Reports to Congress and statements by administration officials started to reflect that strategic strength. During this same period, Soviet military policy underwent far-reaching appraisals and innovations, culminating in a newly created Strategic Rocket Forces, an expanded Air Defense Force, and an expanded subsurface navy. On January 14, 1960, Khrushchev addressed the Supreme Soviet, and while he painted a rosy picture of the Soviets versus the United States in economic matters, he made note of the widening strategic gap between the U.S. and the Soviet Union: "Realization that the international situation has changed, that a basic shift has taken place in the balance of power between the socialist and capitalist states, is increasingly spreading in the Western countries. Numerous statements by government and business leaders are devoted to this subject."[10]

The expanded Soviet air defense was noted in the deployment of surface-to-air-missile sites. The first Soviet surface-to-air missile, the SA-1 (Guild), was deployed only around Moscow and in fixed installations. Because of the threat posed by B-47 and B-52 bombers and reconnaissance missions by the U-2, the Soviets subsequently developed a more sophisticated mobile surface-to-air system, designated the SA-2 (Guideline). Guideline missiles employed in the SA-2 system were first observed in the November 7, 1957, Moscow parade; operational deployment of the system began in 1958. Obviously, the state-of-art of the SA-2 system was such that it had the capability of downing a U-2. This deployment was disturbing to those of us who were involved in U-2 flight planning.

By 1959, SA-2 missile sites were not only being deployed around the principal Soviet cities but also at strategic industrial installations deep in the Urals and Siberia coincident with our intelligence interests and objectives. Flight tracks were adjusted so that the U-2 would come no closer than twenty-five miles to such a site.

On May 1, 1960, just fifteen days before a scheduled four-power summit conference was to convene in Paris, Gary Powers's U-2 airplane was brought down by an indirect hit from a near-miss SA-2 missile near Sverdlovsk, in the USSR. Powers would later relate that there was an explosion behind him, followed by a brilliant orange light, while he was flying at an altitude of about 70,000 feet. Almost immediately, the nose of the aircraft pitched into a steep dive and Powers began procedures to escape the doomed U-2. Powers's flight had begun at Peshawar, Pakistan, passed over Stalinabad, the Tyura Tam Missile Test Center, the nuclear plants in the Urals, and was to proceed to the ICBM missile base under construction at Yurya, the missile test center at Plesetsk, the submarine shipyard at Severodvinsk, the naval bases at Murmansk, and then on to Bodo, Norway.

(Khrushchev was on the reviewing stand for the May Day parade when Marshall Biryuzov, head of the Soviet defense forces, came up to the stand and whispered to Khrushchev that a U-2 had been downed in the Urals.) Four days later, Khrushchev, in a long speech before the Supreme Soviet, announced that an American plane flew into Soviet territory and was shot down. (In 1990, *Red Star*, the Soviet army newspaper, revealed there was confusion among ground-control and air-defense forces at the time. They believed the missile that exploded behind Powers's U-2 had missed its target and fired a second missile. That missile struck a MiG-19 tracking the U-2, killing its pilot.)

On the day of Khrushchev's announcement, a State Department spokesman told the press that the department had been informed by the National Aeronautics and Space Administration (NASA) that "An unarmed plane, a U-2 weather research plane based at Adana, Turkey, piloted by a civilian, had been missing since May 1. It is entirely possible that having a failure in oxygen equipment, which could result in the pilot losing consciousness, the plane continued on automatic pilot for a considerable distance and accidentally violated Soviet airspace." We at the Center had not been informed beforehand of the cover story, and when the State Department announcement was made, Lundahl shook his head. It could be embarrassing, since Powers's U-2 was well into the mission and about half of the 5,000 feet of film had been exposed. Since the film was wound tight and safety-based, it therefore would be extremely difficult to ignite. Lundahl notified CIA headquarters that even in a crash, he was sure the Soviets would have recovered some of the exposed film.

I was put in charge of a damage-control unit established at the Center to receive and evaluate all the press reports and photographs that the Russians were issuing. One such photo depicted Khrushchev holding an aerial photo purportedly from the downed U-2. Lou Franceschini and I examined the photo. It had the unique 9 × 18-inch format of the B camera used in the U-2, and when it was examined under the high-power optics, we could authenticate the clock imprint in one corner. Although the Russians had printed the photo backward, there was no doubt they now had positive proof that Powers was on a reconnaissance mission and was not merely flying a weather-research mission and off-course, as the State Department maintained. Lundahl again notified headquarters of our findings.

The Russians then did a foolish thing. They released a photograph purportedly of the crashed U-2. When I viewed the photograph, I knew immediately it wasn't the U-2 because the U-2 is flush-riveted and I could clearly see several rows of prominent rivets on the plane in question. Lundahl called that information to headquarters. The Soviet photo was forwarded to Kelly Johnson, who held a press conference describing in detail why the plane in the photo was not a U-2 but probably a Russian Il-28.

On May 6, a State Department spokesman again denied that any American plane had ever deliberately violated Soviet airspace and said it would be "monstrous" to claim that the U.S. was trying to fool the world about the real purpose of Powers's flight. But the U.S. had fallen into Khrushchev's carefully laid trap. On May 7, Khrushchev again spoke to the Supreme Soviet: "Comrades, I must tell you a secret. When I was making my report I deliberately did not say that the pilot was alive and in good health and that we have got parts of the plane. We did so deliberately because had we told everything at once, the Americans would have invented another version." Khrushchev demanded an immediate apology from President Eisenhower, which was not forthcoming. Eisenhower instead said that although activities such as the U-2 flight over Russia were distasteful, they were "a vital necessity in the world as it is today." The downing of the U-2 cast some doubt as to whether the scheduled four-power meeting in Paris between the United States, the Soviet Union, Great Britain, and France would be held.

In the United Kingdom, Prime Minister Macmillan was, according to John M. Clarke, a senior CIA official, "quite sensitive over how to treat the likely parliamentary question that might occur from the opposition as a consequence of the U-2 flight. The West was not entirely sure of what Powers may have told the Soviets, including perhaps divulging the British role in the 'American' program. When the inevitable question came, i.e., What is Her Majesty's position toward Powers and the shootdown of the U-2? the Prime Minister responded, 'But for the grace of God, it could have been one of our boys.' This response admitted nothing and as is tradition on official secrets, required no further elaboration."[11]

Throughout history, it has been the practice for governments never to admit intelligence activities, especially clandestine operations. The U-2, however, was no ordinary spy, and the big question was whether or not President Eisenhower should admit personal complicity in U-2 operations. Some advocated an attempt to salvage the summit conference by maintaining silence in Washington and leaving the matter to the usual exchange of angry diplomatic notes. A number of irate congressmen and national leaders recommended that Eisenhower punish, either by reprimand or dismissal, selected officials who had been intimately involved in the U-2 operations. Allen Dulles, in conversations with Eisenhower, had offered to resign. Eisenhower explained, "The thought that such action would provide at least an implication that the flight had taken place without my authorization or possibly even without my knowledge and that I had been the victim of overzealous subordinates."[12]

Other congressmen and senators called for the cancellation of the entire program. Adlai Stevenson, the unsuccessful Democratic candidate for president in 1952 and 1956, was extremely critical, charging that Eisenhower had given Khrushchev "the crowbar and sledgehammer to wreck the conference." Senator John F. Kennedy, a leading presidential hopeful, was asked by a student in Portland, Oregon, what he would have done in President Eisenhower's place in Paris. Kennedy said he had recalled that Khrushchev had set two conditions for continuing the summit conference—an end to the U-2 flights, which the president had in fact ordered, and an apology. Concerning the apology, Kennedy told his audience, "This might have been possible to do," and then continued that if Mr. Khrushchev had asked the president to express regret, "That would have been a more reasonable term."[13] A furious debate ensued in the Senate, with Senators Everett Dirksen and Hugh Scott charging Stevenson and Kennedy with "appeasement" and "irresponsibility." To quell the debate, Allen Dulles decided to brief the entire Senate on the benefits that were derived from the U-2 program.

Mr. Lundahl was told that he would be allowed precisely thirty minutes and that this should be the briefing of his lifetime. Lundahl gave us the task of organizing the effort, and I carefully reviewed all the contributions that the U-2 missions had made to the national estimative process, along with the many crises wherein the intelligence derived had been employed to resolve policy issues worldwide. A number of spectacular briefing boards were created, and Lundahl rehearsed himself intently on the substantive content of the boards, to assure that he could effectively deliver the information within the prescribed thirty minutes.

Lundahl remembers the chamber he and Dulles entered as being "filled with senators, many in angry or combative moods." Mr. Dulles, wearing one of his usual English tweed suits, introduced Lundahl. He then lit his curved tobacco pipe and settled back to enjoy Lundahl's startling presentation, which upon completion provoked a standing ovation from the senators present. Mr. Dulles was so surprised by the reaction that when he rose to his feet, his lit pipe tumbled into his lap, setting his tweed coat afire. Lundahl, taken aback, did not know whether to simply stand there and accept the senators' acclaim or to seek a glass of water to throw on his inflamed director.

In Paris, General Charles de Gaulle, after being reassured that the head of each of the participating states would attend, announced that the four-power conference would be held as scheduled. Eisenhower meanwhile asked to be briefed by the Agency on the status of the A-11 (SR-71) aircraft and the satellite-reconnaissance development program. He was told that the A-11 would not be ready for at least another year while the satellite program was on schedule.

Eisenhower arrived in Paris on May 15, 1960, and called on General de Gaulle that afternoon. De Gaulle told Eisenhower that Khrushchev had been to see him, was highly agitated about the U-2 overflights, and was still demanding an apology from President Eisenhower. De Gaulle said, "You obviously cannot apologize and I will do anything I can to help you." Eisenhower replied that as president, he had to ascertain the Soviet threat to the United States—and to world peace—and that there was no other way than using the U-2. De Gaulle agreed. Eisenhower decided that de Gaulle should see some of the photographic materials acquired by the U-2 over the Soviet Union. Washington was notified, and that afternoon Lundahl and Cunningham were on their way to Paris.

Lundahl, Cunningham, and a translator were driven to the Elysée

Palace and escorted to de Gaulle's office. De Gaulle was alone. Lundahl opened the package of briefing materials and moved toward de Gaulle in order to brief him at his desk. De Gaulle rose, walked toward Lundahl, and asked him to place the graphics on a large conference table, where he stood looking down at them. Knowledgeable of his poor eyesight, Lundahl handed him a large magnifying glass. De Gaulle asked a number of questions about the focal length of the cameras and the speed and altitude at which the photography was acquired. Frequently, as Lundahl unfolded details depicted on the briefing boards, de Gaulle would take a magnifying glass in hand and lift the board to carefully analyze the details that could be seen on the photography. His initial response to what he saw was expressed, cryptically, in French, *"Formidable! Formidable!"* When the briefing was completed, de Gaulle thanked Lundahl, paused, reflected for a moment, and then said, "This is one of the most important programs the West is currently involved in and it is something that must continue." De Gaulle assured them that he would so inform President Eisenhower.

The four-power conference was held in the Elysée Palace. De Gaulle purposefully waited to walk in with President Eisenhower. He whispered his thanks for the briefing and said, "Now I see why Khrushchev is so mad." De Gaulle explained that since Eisenhower was the only chief of delegation who was chief of state as well, he should be allowed to speak first. Khrushchev, very agitated, demanded to speak first. Eisenhower nodded assent to de Gaulle. Khrushchev launched a flamboyant attack against Eisenhower and again demanded that the U.S. president apologize for the U-2 overflights. Khrushchev returned again and again to his static theme that the Americans were surreptitiously sending spy planes over the Soviet Union and, indeed, over the world.

De Gaulle had listened patiently, but his patience had worn thin. He looked directly at Khrushchev and said, "You're making too big a fuss about this matter." Khrushchev drew back in surprise. De Gaulle continued, "There is probably a ton of Russian iron [referring to Russian satellites] coming through French space every day without my permission. I have no idea what is inside those satellites and you have not told me. But I am not making a big fuss."

Khrushchev replied, "My hands are clean. We do not do things like that."

"Then tell me how you took some of the pictures of the Soviet Union taken from a satellite that you are so proud of."

"In that satellite, we had cameras."

"Aha, in that one you had cameras," de Gaulle continued. "But you are not sure if all of them have cameras."

"I am only concerned with that which is over the Soviet Union with a man in it. That it doesn't have men in it doesn't bother me."

De Gaulle drew himself up to his full height and said, "I understand."

Eisenhower assumed his arched-brow grimace and, knowing that the U.S. photo satellite program was about to begin, doodled "Most interesting."

The conference collapsed because of Khrushchev's intransigence on the U-2 issue. Khrushchev undoubtedly knew of the SR-71 and the Soviet inability to stop it if it were used in reconnaissance missions over the Soviet Union.

Eisenhower responded to Khrushchev's ostentatious rage with temperate words, patience, and dignity. He calmly explained that reconnaissance was, and is, a necessity—that it was vital for the United States to know what went on behind the Iron Curtain. Eisenhower's public admission that he had authorized the U-2 flights, the first time any nation had publicly admitted that it was engaged in espionage, was characteristic of a man who always had the courage to act on his convictions. The incident also emphasized the vital importance that leaders of the twentieth century attached to aerial reconnaissance. Eisenhower explained, "Our deterrent must never be placed in jeopardy. The safety of the whole free world demands it. As the secretary of state pointed out in his recent statement, ever since the beginning of my administration, I have issued directives to gather, in every feasible way, the information that is required to protect the United States and the free nations against surprise attack and to enable them to make effective preparations for defense."

Upon his return from the aborted conference, Eisenhower decided to speak to the nation and to reassure the public that he knew what was going on in his government. Here was an unprecedented opportunity to show the American people and the world, with spectacular aerial photography, what the Soviets were concealing. A stick-it-in-their-teeth atmosphere prevailed at the White House. Robert Montgomery, the famous movie actor and producer—now the assistant to the president for TV presentations—was especially aware of a magnificent opportunity. Montgomery had envisioned a series of spectacular briefing boards that would be attached to the walls of the Oval Office, and as the president spoke, the television cameras would focus on them. Lundahl placed me in charge of preparing the required materials. On my own, I had the idea that maybe the president might like to show the comparison of U.S. and Soviet installations. So in addition to about forty other briefing boards, ten briefing boards were made comparing our long-range bomber airfields, shipyards, nuclear installations, and missile and aircraft plants with theirs. I had a briefing board made of the San Diego complex, to be compared with facilities in Leningrad.

James C. Hagerty, the president's press secretary, selected a number of the boards and left to show them to the president. He returned after a few minutes, saying that Eisenhower had rejected the idea of showing all the briefing boards. "The boss has decided against using these because it would probably make our relations with the Russians much worse than they are." Rather than releasing photography of Soviet installations for public display, the president had selected the single briefing board I had prepared of the San Diego Naval Air Station, showing the airfield, aircraft, hangars, and runway markers in great detail. The president said that the American people could understand and relate to such a picture. (When I went to the White House to pick up the remaining boards, I was surprised to find Hagerty was showing the entire package to Walter Winchell, the noted newspaper columnist and a staunch supporter of the Eisenhower administration.)

In his televised address, Eisenhower predictably emphasized the need for good intelligence: "Our safety, and that of the free world, demand, of course, effective systems for gathering information about the military capabilities of other powerful nations, especially those that make a fetish of secrecy."[14] He then added, "Aerial photography has been one of many methods we have used to keep ourselves and the free world abreast of major Soviet military developments. The usefulness of this work has been well established through four years of effort. The Soviets were well aware of it. Chairman Khrushchev has stated that he became aware of these flights several years ago. Only last week, in the Paris peace conference, he confirmed that he knew of these flights when he visited the United States last September."[15]

The Soviets had been quite successful in maintaining secrecy about their industrial and military establishment. The U-2 had effectively compromised much of that secrecy. As for critics of the program, Eisenhower later utilized another time-honored Midwestern practice of responding to a question with a question: "Would you be ready to give back all the information we secured from our U-2 flights over Russia if there had been no disaster to one of our planes in Russia? I have never received an affirmative response."[16]

Eisenhower informed officials that U-2 flights over the Soviet Union would be discontinued and gave two reasons: 1) the utility of the U-2 was limited because of the new Soviet SA-2 surface-to-air missiles; and 2) considerable progress was now being made in the developmental program of photographing the earth from space.

Eisenhower would later sum up his opinion of the U-2: "During the four years of its operations, the U-2 program produced intelligence of critical importance to the United States. Perhaps as important as the positive information—what the Soviets did have—was the negative information it produced—what the Soviets did not have. Intelligence gained from this source provided proof that the horrors of the alleged 'bomber gap' and later the 'missile gap' were nothing more than imaginative creations of irresponsibility. U-2 information deprived Khrushchev of the most powerful weapon of Communist conspiracy—international blackmail—usable only as long as the Soviets could exploit the ignorance and resulting fears of the free world."[17]

In addition to providing the president and the Congress with information essential to their decision making, the U-2 provided the Department of Defense and the respective services with reams of details on Soviet targets.* This knowledge alone saved billions of dollars in development of appropriate counterweapons. The U-2 photography also provided precise geodetic data for targeting our missiles and to produce accurate, up-to-date charts for the Strategic Air Command's B-47 and B-52 bombers.

There are a number of references in books on Powers's U-2 flight[18] and the Kennedy assassination to the effect that Lee Harvey Oswald provided the Russians with data on the U-2 that was subsequently used by the Soviets in downing Gary Powers's U-2. Most of these accounts focus on the fact that in 1957, Oswald, then a seventeen-year-old U.S. Marine Corps private, was assigned to the 1st Marine Aircraft Wing, based at Atsugi Naval Air Station, about twenty miles west of Tokyo, as a trained radar operator. During the period Oswald was assigned at Atsugi, U-2's used the naval air station as a staging base for missions over the Soviet Union. Oswald returned to the U.S., and on October 31, 1959, renounced his U.S. citizenship. At the U.S. embassy in Moscow, he indicated that he would tell the Russians everything he knew about U.S. radar operations and something else he termed "of special interest."[19] The knowledge derived from radar intercepts—i.e., course, altitude, and speed—is the same whether learned from U.S. or Russian radar operations. The Soviets certainly had begun to compile data on U-2 performance beginning with the first mission over the USSR on July 4, 1956. On subsequent missions, the data was refined so that in a relatively short period the Soviets had an accurate record of U-2 characteristics. The Russians had publicly confirmed the fact that they had been tracking and were knowledgeable about U-2 operations. (In addition to using MiG-17's, MiG-19's, and later MiG-21's in zoom-climb intercept techniques, the Russians recently admitted that they also tried to use an Su-9 Fishpot fighter stripped of its armor to climb and ram the U-2.) All of these

---

* Allen Dulles succinctly summed up the contribution of U-2 overflights during congressional testimony in August 1960: "It is extremely difficult for me to sum up in words the significance of this effort to our national security. I do not wish to exaggerate, nor do I wish to belittle other vital intelligence programs. The photographic coverage and the data derived from it are an inseparable part of the whole national intelligence effort. But in terms of reliability, of precision, of access to otherwise inaccessible installations, its contribution has been unique. And in the opinion of the military, of the scientists and of the other senior officials responsible for our national security it has been, to put it simply, invaluable."

intercept attempts were vectored by ground-control stations, so the Russians were well aware of the U-2's altitude, course, and speed.

Khrushchev continued his bluster on July 9, 1960, when he addressed the All-Russian Teacher's Conference. After making note of his displeasure at American missiles' being emplaced in Italy and aimed at Russia, and that Eisenhower had announced that the U.S. would no longer be buying sugar from Cuba, Khrushchev said, "We, for our part, will do everything to support Cuba and its courageous people in their struggle for freedom and national independence." Then Khrushchev warned: "It should not be forgotten that the United States is not so inaccessibly distant from the Soviet Union as it used to be. Figuratively speaking, in case of need Soviet artillerymen can support the Cuban people with their rocket fire if the aggressor forces in the Pentagon launch an intervention against Cuba. And let them not forget in the Pentagon that as the latest tests have shown, we have rockets capable of landing in a particular square at a distance of 13,000 kilometers. This is a warning to those who would like to settle international issues by force and not by reason."[20]

On August 18, at 12:57 P.M., the U.S. Discoverer XIV space satellite was launched from Vandenberg Air Force Base in California into an orbit, having an apogee of 500 miles and a perigee of 120 miles. The reentry vehicle was ejected over Alaska on its seventeenth pass. In the recovery area, which encompassed a 200-by-60-mile rectangle, six C-119's and one C-130 flew within the area called the ball park. Three other C-119's patrolled an "outfield" area, embracing an additional 400 miles. All aircraft flew an assigned search pattern. At 3:46 P.M. on August 19, one of the C-119 Flying Boxcars, piloted by Captain Harold E. Mitchell and his nine-man crew, searching in the "outfield" area, hooked the parachute and the 84-pound capsule in midair at an altitude of 8,500 feet and hauled them aboard.[21] A new era of reconnaissance had begun. On this first successful photographic satellite mission, carrying a twenty-pound roll of film, we gained more than 1 million square miles of coverage of the Soviet Union—more coverage in one capsule than the combined four years of U-2 coverage. (The capsule is now on display at the Smithsonian's National Air and Space Museum.)

The Soviets, especially Khrushchev, deliberately took every opportunity to create the impression internationally that the Soviets were far ahead of the United States in all aspects of military might. Khrushchev boasted endlessly about Soviet scientific discoveries and industrial accomplishments. Americans were told by Khrushchev that "we will bury you." It was a carefully planned and fostered fear of the unknown, and this would explain, at least in part, Khrushchev's rage about the U-2. Lundahl and I frequently discussed how frustrating it must have been for Soviet military leaders to know that for four years an aircraft was overhead photographing their territory and yet they could do nothing about it.

The front page of *The New York Times* on August 20, 1960, headlined the first successful midair recovery of the reentry capsule and on the opposite side of the front page announced the end of the U-2 trial and conviction and sentencing of Gary Powers. One photographic-collection period of the Soviet Union was ending while another was just beginning.

The missile-gap controversy had become an election issue during the 1960 campaign, with the Democratic candidate, John F. Kennedy, charging that the U.S. was lagging behind the Soviets. By this time, of course, with successive satellite missions, we had searched the Soviet Union and come to the conclusion there was no missile gap. Both Eisenhower and Vice-President Richard Nixon knew this fact. Nixon, running for president on the Republican ticket, knew that the charges Kennedy was making were not true. Eisenhower was adamant that no references to this new information was to be made, for security reasons. I've often wondered if Nixon would have challenged Kennedy on this important issue if the close 1960 presidential election had not gone in his favor. Eisenhower arranged for President Kennedy to be briefed on the fact that the missile gap did not exist shortly after his election. Though McGeorge Bundy said later in a *Foreign Affairs* article in April 1963 that "it was with honest surprise and relief that, in 1961, he [the President] found the situation much less dangerous than the best evidence to the Senate had indicated the year before," Kennedy would never recant his election-year speeches condemning the missile gap. He gave McNamara the task of informing the public that the missile gap did not exist.

In the meantime, relations with Cuba continued to deteriorate, and President Eisenhower authorized the first U-2 flight over Cuba on October 27, 1960. The mission did not reveal anything of significance. Its value lay in the importance of establishing a baseline of data on Cuba from which we could monitor succeeding events.

Eisenhower did not allude to Cuba in his State of the Union message to Congress on January 13, 1961. By the end of his administration, from information obtained from aerial reconnaissance, Eisenhower knew that the actual balance of strategic power was strongly in favor of the United States and was moving forward to an even greater U.S. advantage. Eisenhower implored, "We must not return to the crash-programs psychology of the past, when each new feint by the Communists was responded to in panic. The bomber gap of several years ago was always a fiction, and the missile gap shows every sign of being the same."

Just a few days before he was to leave office in January 1961, President Eisenhower signed National Security Council Intelligence Directive Number Eight, which established the National Photographic Interpretation Center under CIA administration, with multidepartmental staffing and Lundahl as director.

It is remarkable that in a period of only eight years, President Eisenhower had introduced four revolutionary reconnaissance systems into the U.S. inventory: the Genetrix aerial photographic balloons; the U-2; the SR-71; and the photographic satellite.

President Kennedy and "the Cuba Problem"

*"The enemy has no aerial photographic systems
like ours."*

—PRESIDENT DWIGHT D. EISENHOWER

MANY INDIVIDUALS play a role in the education of a president, and this was certainly true in the case of President John F. Kennedy. He chose his mentors well. He had the gift of judging his peers objectively, without the slightest taint of envy. Impressed by knowledge, he listened attentively and intently to new and unfamiliar ideas. He had great powers of concentration and an intellect capable of rapid assimilation. During his election campaign, he was briefed on intelligence but not on any of the reconnaissance systems.

A warm bond of genuine friendship developed between President Eisenhower and President Kennedy. Soon after Kennedy's election in November 1960, President Eisenhower had the president-elect briefed in depth by Bissell and Lundahl on all photographic-intelligence systems. President Eisenhower sat in on several of these meetings, informing Kennedy on the various arrangements made with foreign countries in the sharing of intelligence derived from the collection systems. Kennedy became intrigued with the whole process of photo collection and interpretation. President Eisenhower would often interrupt, emphasizing how valuable intelligence had been in his decision making. Eisenhower and Kennedy shared an insatiable craving for knowledge of their Soviet adversary, and photo interpretation became a prime source of satisfying that craving. When Eisenhower talked about reconnaissance, there was an enthusiasm in his voice quite different from that when he talked about political matters. Eisenhower told Kennedy triumphantly after one of the briefings, "The enemy has no aerial photographic systems like ours."

The task of educating President Kennedy on photo interpretation devolved upon Arthur Lundahl. Lundahl was a key official who established a close working relationship with both President Kennedy and the assistant to the president for national security affairs, McGeorge Bundy. Lundahl's articulate, erudite, and succinct explanations of what was seen on aerial photography were always welcome at the White House. The president wanted technical information presented in a straightforward manner, free of military jargon, so it would be comprehensible not only to him but also the average person. In one of his early briefings of the president, Lundahl explained that the U-2 camera could photograph a swath about 125 nautical miles wide and about 3,000 nautical miles long on over 10,000 feet of film. Lundahl drew the analogy that each foot of film was scanned under magnification in much the same manner that Sherlock Holmes would scan evidence or look for clues with a large magnifying glass. "Imagine," Lundahl would suggest, "a group of photo interpreters on their hands and knees scanning a roll of film that extended from the White House to the Capitol and back." Kennedy never forgot the analogy. When other high officials were briefed on the U-2 at the White House, the president would call on Lundahl to repeat the story.

Lundahl and President Kennedy hit it off famously. Periodically, Lundahl would update the president in private briefings on the latest finds from both U-2 and satellite photography. The president's discomfort from a chronic back ailment, the usual cluttered condition of the presidential desk, with its many mementos and reams of reading material, and the very nature of the large photographic briefing materials to be presented required that a certain special physical arrangement be made. Lundahl would enter the Oval Office and the president would leave his cluttered desk and be seated in the famous rocking chair that had been custom-designed to alleviate his back problem. The rocking chair was positioned in front of a round coffee table. Lundahl would be seated on the sofa to the right of the president, and the director of the CIA frequently would be seated on the president's left. Removing the silver cigar humidor and ashtray that were usually on the table, Lundahl would arrange his briefing materials and provide the president with a large magnifying glass. The president then drew up his rocking chair close to the table and, using the magnifying glass, began to study the latest photography as Lundahl briefed.

According to Lundahl, the president was a good listener. He liked good lead-in statements. Lundahl knew this and carefully selected and arranged his words so he could gauge the president's reaction as he spoke. Once he asked Lundahl to remain after a briefing. He was eager to know more about the photo-interpretation process. "Where do you get photo interpreters? How much do you pay them? How do you train them? Are they satisfied with their work?" He indicated that he would like to visit the center and observe the high technology of interpretation at work. Lundahl was afforded a unique opportunity because of his position. He admired the president's intellect and courage, and in turn, the president came to admire Lundahl for his intelligence and grace in making a difficult task look exceptionally easy. He came to know the president as a friend and was privy to share the laughter, heartaches, secrets, moods, defeats, and triumphs that occurred during the Kennedy years.

Intelligence, like knowledge, is power. Photographic intelligence, because of its currency, reliability, and relevancy, is an especially effective tool when it is applied to matters concerning strategic balances of power and knowledge of a crisis. Colonel—later General—Andrew Goodpaster became powerful during the Eisenhower administration performing this important national-security-affairs function. McGeorge Bundy—who had been appointed assistant to the president for national security affairs after the Bay of Pigs invasion and also had an instinct for power—assumed the intelligence-watchdog role in President Kennedy's administration. Intense, articulate, and intelligent, Bundy kept close track of the satellite, U-2, and other aircraft missions being flown—and their results. Any photography shown to the president had to be passed through Bundy's office in the White House basement. Extremely flexible, he would drop his regular duties to see the latest takes of photography and be briefed on them. Dean Rusk and Robert McNamara would frequently meet with the CIA director and Lundahl at the White House to see the photography and hear the briefings before meeting with the president. More often than not, Bundy would state the significance of the information and its U.S. foreign policy implications. While Bundy exhibited great intellect and insight, he was never pompous or overbearing. Because of Bundy's knowledge and prescience, however, many intelligence officers were uncomfortable if they were required to remain in his office for an extended period.

The Bay of Pigs affair had been treated the world over as a fiasco and a serious political setback for the president of the United States.[1] The Bay of Pigs also ended the intelligence careers of two distinguished men, Allen Dulles and Richard Bissell. Allen Dulles had set the course of the Agency so that his loss as a manager would not be irreparable, but the greater loss would be Richard Bissell, the progenitor of technical intelligence collection. Most intelligence professionals agreed that Dulles had stayed too long. Some even said that he would have stayed with the Agency until he was carried out. But the image "the old man" had created would not easily fade. Dulles was known affectionately to his people as the great white case officer. He, perhaps more than any other individual, had shaped the organization and operation of the CIA. He had the vision, endurance, and stamina to create the organization that would supply the intelligence answers for the 1950s and 1960s. His greatest accomplishment, however, was the recruiting and training of a group of intelligence professionals who could match any organization in the world. His concern in his later years was to build a new headquarters building at Langley, Virginia. Dulles had hoped that Lieutenant General Charles Pearre Cabell, the deputy director of the Agency, would remain and provide the continuity for the reconnaissance and other programs underway, but he too would soon be leaving, because of a most unfortunate incident.

The president, on April 22, 1961, appointed General Maxwell Taylor to head an investigation of the CIA's role in the Bay of Pigs disaster and the next day asked Attorney General Bobby Kennedy to assist Taylor in that investigation. Other members of the Taylor probe panel included CIA director Allen Dulles and Admiral Arleigh A. Burke, the chief of naval operations.[2] Information from their report was leaked to Charles J. V. Murphy, Washington bureau chief for *Fortune* magazine. Murphy wrote an account of the Bay of Pigs invasion highly critical of President Kennedy and thereby incurred the president's wrath.[3] The president was furious. Suspecting that General Cabell had leaked information, he asked for his resignation. Cabell tried to explain to the president that he was not the source of the leak, but to no avail. On January 31, 1962, he resigned as deputy director and retired from the Air Force. He was replaced by Major General Marshall "Pat" Carter. A number of years after President Kennedy's death, Murphy was doing another story related to intelligence and Lundahl and I were directed to cooperate with him. He revealed to us that Admiral Arleigh Burke had been the source of his Bay of Pigs information. The admiral felt that the president had "chickened out" in not calling for Navy fighter aircraft to cover the Bay of Pigs invasion. Murphy said that Burke had nothing but disdain for President Kennedy and his "bagman" at the Department of Defense, McNamara.[4]

After the Bay of Pigs, Cuba became a continuous thorn in the sides of the Kennedys. The president had made it clear, however, that he did not intend to abandon the Cubans to Castro and the Communists. To many Cubans, that indicated the threat of another invasion. Cuba had become a partner in the Communist adventure, and Russian "experts" began to move into offices of the various Cuban ministries. While this was welcomed by old-time Communists, the idealists in the Cuban revolution began to resent the way the Russians began to institutionalize the Cuban revolution, making Cuba become a surrogate in the export of Soviet Communism. Provided with the necessary financial and logistical support, Cuba began to push a more radical solution—the Guevara-style revolution. Bold, brazen, poorly planned, and often not very discreet, one Cuban covert operation after another in Latin America was unmasked or failed. Although the Russians had admonished the Cubans to go slowly, Castro and Che Guevara were not left much room to maneuver in international relations. Che and Castro's credentials as revolutionaries were being tarnished by the presence of the Russians and by their own operational failures.

After the Bay of Pigs, all the U.S. and Cuba had in common were a morbid mutual suspicion and the expectation of more years of hostility. Castro, after a series of severe diplomatic setbacks, believed more than ever that the very survival of Cuba was seriously threatened. He felt a sense of bitterness and isolation toward the U.S. and Latin America. The Bay of Pigs and subsequent Soviet arms shipments to Cuba served to fortify Castro's already arrogant attitude toward President Kennedy and the United States. Castro praised the Cuban revolutionary spirit and said that its influence beyond Cuba's borders "intimidated Americans." Castro had publicly proclaimed in many flamboyant speeches before the assembled multitudes in Havana Square the need for revolution throughout Latin America. He chided Kennedy for the Bay of Pigs disaster and boasted that at Playa Girón, "the imperialists had suffered their greatest defeat in Latin America." He referred to President Kennedy as "the chief of the pirates" and later boasted that he had exacted a $62 million ransom that would further finance the Cuban revolution. He said contemptuously, "Let them continue to send expeditions." He regarded Kennedy's assumption of responsibility for the Bay of Pigs, and his efforts to ransom the captives, as an unparalleled mark of weakness. He felt that with the increased influx of Soviet arms, the United States would be extremely reluctant to attack Cuba again.

The sharp increase in Soviet support for the Castro regime provided further evidence of Khrushchev's conception of the political weakness of President Kennedy. The Soviets clearly regarded Cuba as a much more valuable asset over the long run in trying to formulate revolution in Latin America, and Khrushchev proceeded on the assumption that this policy entailed few risks of confrontation with the United States. The Soviets seemed confident they would be able to capitalize on the opportunities created by Castro's urgent need for assistance. President Kennedy became concerned about Castro's and Khrushchev's statements.

In an address before the American Society of Newspaper Editors on April 20, 1961, Kennedy warned: "Let the record show that our restraint is not inexhaustible. Should it ever appear that the inter-American doctrine of noninterference merely conceals or excuses a policy of nonaction—if the nations of this hemisphere should fail to meet their commitments against outside Communist penetration—then I want it clearly understood that this Government will not hesitate in meeting its primary obligations, which are to the security of our Nation. Should the time ever come, we do not intend to be lectured on 'intervention' by those whose character was stamped for all time on the bloody streets of Budapest."[5]

Khrushchev's call for "a new revolution" had triggered alarm and uncertainty in the U.S., particularly among the military. Khrushchev's penchant for "free-wheeling" policymaking also generated controversy within both the Department of Defense and the Department of State, and between them as well.

After Kennedy's meeting with Khrushchev in Vienna in June 1961, the president asked for a copy of all of Khrushchev's speeches, which he studied carefully. He also called for interpretations of a number of them by experts at the CIA, State, and Defense. Khrushchev's proclamations were viewed as ominous warnings and challenges.

The Soviet military supply effort to its Communist allies in the Eastern European countries and China, as well as Egypt, Syria, and Indonesia, had followed a distinct pattern, and it was obvious to intelligence analysts that Moscow had a shopping list for exporting armaments. The initial shipments would include small arms, automatic weapons, trucks, and other logistical equipment to handle the heavier military pieces that would follow. Armor shipments would consist of T-34 and T-54 tanks, SU-85 and SU-100 assault guns, BTR-40 and BTR-50 armored personnel carriers, and PT-76 amphibious tanks. Antitank weapons would include the 57mm antitank gun and the Snapper antitank missile. Artillery would normally be 76, 85, 100, 122, 130, and 152mm howitzers and guns, along with truck-mounted rocket launchers, 82 and 120mm mortars, and FROG (Free Rocket Over Ground) missiles. Naval shipments would consist of the P-4 and P-6 patrol boats, Kronstadt submarine chasers, KOMAR guided-missile patrol boats, and often Gordy-class destroyers and Whiskey-class submarines. Aircraft included the MiG-15 (Fagot), MiG-17 (Fresco), MiG-19 (Farmer), and MiG-21 (Fishbed) fighters, An-2 (Colt) light transport aircraft; Il-14 (Crate) transport aircraft, Il-28 (Beagle) light bombers; and Mi-1 (Hare) and Mi-9 (Hound) helicopters. Anti-aircraft weapons included the 37mm, 57mm, and 85mm guns and SA-2 (Guideline) surface-to-air missiles. A variety of engineering equipment, staff vehicles, and special purpose vehicles would also be sent.

Initially, Khrushchev and the Soviets denied or attempted to evade the issue that they were sending arms to Cuba. But the U-2 was over Cuba at least once a month, and significant items of intelligence interest included the detection of Colt transport aircraft at Campo Libertad near Havana; Hound and Hare helicopters at Playa Baracoa airfield; a large concentration of Russian field artillery pieces in storage areas in Havana city and at Campo Libertad airfield on Havana's outskirts; some forty tanks and self-propelled guns at the Managua military camp; and new airfields under construction at Santa Clara, Cienfuegos, Siguanea, and Playa Girón.

Most analysts were lulled into believing that what had happened in Egypt, Syria, and Indonesia would appear to be happening in Cuba. The Soviets purportedly were providing military equipment to these countries to enable them to defend themselves against the "imperialists," but in reality, they were trying to influence the military and foreign policies of the host government.

The Bay of Pigs had damaged the Agency's image, and Allen Dulles resigned on November 29, 1961. The president appointed John Alexander McCone to become the director of the CIA. McCone, silver-haired, always impeccably groomed and fastidiously dressed, assumed the leadership of the Agency on November 29, 1961. His conduct of this office was to result in the most distinguished chapter of his public service to the nation.

Born into a working-class Irish Catholic family in San Francisco, McCone exhibited all the traits of the classic self-made man. Educated as an engineer at the University of California, he became a calculating and highly successful businessman, industrialist, and banker. His actions, always highly principled, were governed ultimately according to the dictates of his own conscience—completely independent of the personal desires, problems, or concerns of either his peers or his subordinates. He was a taciturn and demanding individual who dominated his colleagues and provoked the best performance possible from them. Cold and remote, he was characterized by one of his chief Agency aides as having "ice water, not blood, flowing through his veins." He was violently anti-Communist and looked on Khrushchev and Communism as he would look upon business adversaries. A staunch conservative, he was also a devout Roman

Catholic who frequently went to mass before going to his office and who had held many honorary and functional positions in Catholic institutions. He had been made a knight of Saint Gregory, the highest honor for a Catholic layman, by Pope Pius XII.

When McCone came to the Agency, most of the intelligence professionals were convinced that his principal objective was "to stabilize and refloat the vessel" after its near-disastrous foundering on the shoals of the Bay of Pigs. Few felt that he would remain for an extended period. His uneventful tenure as chairman of the U.S. Atomic Energy Commission did little to recommend him to Agency professionals as director. He had little historical or political knowledge of the Soviet Union, except for a passionate hate of monolithic Soviet Communism. It was his unequivocal conviction that the Soviets would risk anything in the pursuit of world revolution and that they would respect only brute military force in response.

McCone was a complex personality, difficult to know and evaluate. He was a poor boy who had become a multimillionaire; a tyrant at the office who could be tender with family and friends; a conservative in a liberal Democratic administration; a confidant who could also advise; a man who felt secure in insecure situations; and as intelligence officers were soon to learn, he possessed an uncanny ability to think clearly about complicated matters. He was a man who helped shape the course of events rather than merely be carried along by them. He let it be known that he would grant no interviews and would make no public speeches as director of the Agency.

McCone had a job to perform and he set about getting it done. The Dulles legacy was a cadre of devoted professionals—which McCone knew and appreciated; but no longer would there be the paternalistic attitude of Allen Dulles. The Dulles era, with its Ivy League syndrome and emphasis on clandestine methods, had ended and now would come the age of technical intelligence. Those who didn't perform to McCone's stringent standards were soon transferred or replaced. Shortly after he became director, McCone was invited to visit the Agency's computer center "for morale purposes." Allen Dulles frequently visited Agency components that were experiencing difficulties and often gave a pep talk "for morale purposes." McCone declined the invitation with the acid comment that he was the director of the Central Intelligence Agency, not a shop foreman. He said that if the computer center was dependent upon him for morale, there must be something wrong with its management. There were few subsequent requests for him to visit the working echelons of the Agency.

McCone selected his team: Richard Helms, deputy director, plans; Ray Cline, deputy director, intelligence; Robert Bannerman, deputy director, support; Lyman Kirkpatrick, Jr., executive director; Lawrence Houston, general counsel; Sherman Kent, Office of National Estimates; and John Bross to handle interagency coordination problems.

McCone started immediately to rebuild the bridge to the White House and to restore relations with the Congress and the departments of State and Defense, which had been strained to the breaking point by the abortive Bay of Pigs invasion. New men, with family names unfamiliar to the Eastern establishment, began to move into positions of prominence in the Agency. They were experts in such disciplines as optics, electronics, chemistry, physics, engineering, and photography. Many were World War II veterans educated under the provisions of the GI Bill. McCone was not addicted to the fashionable view that all that was happening in Cuba had happened before in Egypt, Syria, Iraq, and Indonesia. On one occasion, he complained that reading existing intelligence reports on Cuba was like grabbing a ball of fluff—there was some substance but little to hold on to. Having opted for technical rather than clandestine intelligence collection methods, McCone was particularly attracted to aerial photography as a source of both tactical and strategic intelligence.

McCone used his personal friendship with the Kennedys, especially Bobby, to reestablish close communications between the Agency and the White House. Unlike most cabinet members, McCone was afforded easy, frequent, and direct access to the president. At a typical meeting with the president and the National Security Council, McCone would introduce the subject of the meeting and then call on his experts to present the evidence and details. Carefully choosing his words, he would often summarize their presentations and then dismiss the experts. When questioned by the president or council members, he would sometimes take positions oblique to the intelligence presented. In so doing, he would always qualify his remarks by indicating that he was speaking as John

McCone, "private citizen." He enjoyed being at the center of power, the man whose opinion was being sought in the formulation of policy, the go-between. His genius was stating the facts in an un-equivocal fashion.

McCone had reached down in the Agency to appoint two bright young intelligence officers as his special assistants—Enno Henry "Hank" Knoche[6] and Walter Elder. Knoche would later comment that it was a joy to work for an individual who stretches your abilities to the utmost.

McCone had a high regard and admiration for the constitutional role of Congress in the formulation of national policy and was always straightforward with answers when questioned by senators or con-gressmen. Some say he never forgot that many in Congress opposed his nomination as director of the CIA and he was determined to prove his worth.

Congressman Jamie L. Whitten of Mississippi said of McCone, "He gave it [intelligence] to you straight and unadulterated. That's the way we liked it. Not like McNamara, who applied a lot of frills and attempted to turn the intelligence to his own benefit."[7] Senator Stuart Symington of Missouri said of McCone, "The old man's intelligence presentations were always welcomed on the Hill, and we looked forward to them."[8]

While McCone was becoming acquainted with the Agency, the covert war against Cuba was continuing under the leadership of William King Harvey, who headed up the important Task Force W in the Agency's Directorate of Plans. Harvey was a huge man with a massive head, with a frightened shock of hair encircling a near-bald pate. He had a gnarled brow, and cold protruding eyes set into a red face. When he moved about, he wheezed and grunted like an animal. He was also a man of extraordinary personal ambition. He had transferred to the CIA from the FBI and became one of the Agency's outstanding case officers. He was hard-drinking and pos-sessed of an enormous ego and a Jekyll/Hyde personality, but his brashness and flamboyance were counterbalanced by a certain tend-erness and propensity to help the underdog. (During his Berlin as-signment, he would work long hours carefully planning covert operations that would ruin the careers of KGB officers. In contrast, walking home from his office, he often encountered destitute children for whom he would compassionately provide food and clothing.) A gun fancier since his days as an FBI agent, he often carried two loaded pearl-handled pistols in his belt. Frequently, he would place them on his desk or point them at subordinates or visitors to emphasize a particular point. He reveled in the planning and execution of covert operations. He had the imagination and audacity to carry out bold covert plans but also was fully aware of the countermeasures his adversaries might employ.

Harvey had quickly established his reputation in the Agency. Early in his career, a flood of East European and Russian defectors to the West provided compelling information that the British intelligence services had been penetrated by the Soviets. It was Harvey, not James Angleton, who fingered Guy Burgess and Donald Maclean as British agents in Washington working for the Soviet Union. He also pointed to Kim Philby as ''the third man'' when Burgess and Maclean defected to the Soviet Union. But it was in Berlin that Harvey enhanced his reputation as a covert operator. Using a radar station as a cover, he masterminded the digging of an eighteen-hundred-foot tunnel from West Berlin into East Berlin. It was about twenty-five feet deep; all the dirt was removed in small wooden boxes. The tunnel provided access to the main Moscow-Berlin underground communication lines, and taps attached to those lines for nearly a year provided thousands of tapes, which kept translators busy for several years.

In 1960, Harvey was brought back to Washington to head Task Force W. He was given responsibility for intelligence gathering, propaganda, and sabotage raids against Cuba. He was also made chief of Project Mongoose, an elaborate plan to unseat Castro. The failure of the project was first disclosed publicly during a 1975 Senate investigation.[9]

Edward Lansdale had touted Harvey as the modern-day James Bond to the president and Bobby Kennedy. From their first meeting, there developed a hate relationship between Bobby and Harvey. Harvey looked suspiciously at Bobby's suggestions as those of an amateur and openly questioned Bobby's judgment. Harvey's propensity for drink and his tendency to speak his mind often generated hate and animosity toward him from his superiors.

Professionally, his plans were thorough and detailed; however, he would never reveal the whole plan, allowing for what he termed ''a freedom of action for the operators." He was not a friend or sympathetic to those of us in the Agency concerned with aerial photography. He looked upon us almost as adversaries, spying on his operations. As a matter of fact, we could often see that he was lying about the success of his operations. On one occasion, he asked us to bring in aerial photography of an operation and said he would prove us wrong about our conclusions. When we entered his office, in addition to the ubiquitous pistols, he had in his hand a foot-long stiletto. He cleaned his nails and then hurled the stiletto at a target hung on the wall of his office. We pointed out that the photography showed clearly that the operation was not a success. He berated us: "What in the hell does a bunch of quacks know about covert operations?" Once, while showing him that there was no visible damage to a building that was supposedly bombed, he remarked the damage was all inside. Another time, when we showed him pictures of an installation that supposedly had been burned but showed no outward damage, he picked up the phone and called Theodore Shackley, chief of the Agency's covert operations center, JMWave, in Miami, demanding to know in no uncertain terms whether his agents had actually gotten to the installation or had chickened out. When time and time again we continued to prove him wrong, Harvey demanded that we send photo interpreters to brief his Miami office.[10] After the abortive Bay of Pigs invasion in April 1961, President Kennedy placed the control of U.S. covert operations in the hands of the Washington Special Operations Group Augmented, headed by Bobby Kennedy.

Harvey and Bobby Kennedy continued to be at odds not only on operations but also on methods. Harvey would maintain to his superiors that Bobby was trying to conduct covert operations with little knowledge or experience, while Bobby would complain to the president that not enough covert action was being taken to unseat Castro. Bobby Kennedy had an office at the CIA headquarters building at Langley and would stop in that office several times a week on his way home to nearby Hickory Hill. Frequently, he would chat with Mr. McCone, but more often he would want to discuss the latest covert operations against Cuba with officers in the Directorate of Plans. Bobby had become so intrigued with covert operations that he was insistent on talking with Cuban exile leaders directly involved.

This brought him into violent disagreement with Harvey. Harvey argued unsuccessfully that someone of Bobby's stature and position should not be known to the covert operatives, much less be seen with them. After one of these meetings, Harvey came storming into his office stating that Bobby was carving a path in the operations so wide that a Mack truck could drive through. One participant in these discussions would later claim that Bobby could ''be charming one moment and could be a complete bastard the next.'' General Maxwell Taylor would remark, ''I don't think it occurred to Bobby in those days that his temperament, his casual remarks that the president would not like this or that, his difficulty in establishing tolerable relations with government officials, or his delight in causing offense was doing harm to his brother's administration.''

Ray Cline, the deputy director for intelligence, was convinced that it was Bobby's original objective after the Bay of Pigs fiasco to dismantle the covert part of the Agency. It soon became evident, however, that Bobby grew unalterably intrigued with the power inherent in intelligence operations and began to exercise it, much to the chagrin of those trying to run the operations. According to Cline: ''Both of the Kennedy brothers, and particularly Bobby, felt they had been booby-trapped at the Bay of Pigs, and it became a constant preoccupation, almost an obsession, to right the record somehow. And I remember what people have said about the Kennedys in other contexts, that they learned from their father, 'Don't get mad. Get even.' ''

Harvey had undertaken three types of operations against Cuba. The first was the infiltration of agents; second, the logistical or cache operations, i.e., delivering provisions and equipment for indigenous groups opposed to Castro; and third, sabotage operations. It was the last that were most encouraged by Bobby Kennedy, with the hope that, through the sabotage of certain key Cuban industries, Castro could be brought to his knees. Harvey had assured the Special Operations Group that such operations could and would be conducted. There were a number of industries singled out for sabotage: the Esso oil refinery in Havana, the Moa Bay nickel-mining operations, the oil refinery at Santiago de Cuba, a number of large railroad bridges, and a number of oil and gas storage installations. While the infiltration of agents was going well, along with the placement of caches, the most important sabotage operations were going awry, and of course, the failures of those operations could be seen on aerial photography. More often than not, secondary and tertiary targets were being hit. The oil refinery at Santiago de Cuba was to be sabotaged, for instance, but when it was discovered to be defended, a lumber mill was hit instead. Bobby Kennedy was furious. Our visits to Harvey's office were growing more frequent and, always, with more bad news. On one occasion, I accompanied photo interpreter Ray Gripman. He looked at me and said, "You know we are going to be about as popular as the proverbial fart in church." I said I knew, but perhaps a better analogy would be that of the messenger bringing the bad news to "King" Harvey.

Although operation after operation against Cuba was going sour, Harvey continued to blame Bobby. He began to refer to the Kennedys as fags, an implication that they were not physically up to the task demanded of them and that they remained in the closet instead of confronting Castro.*

Harvey was not the only one discontented with the Kennedy administration's foreign policy, especially toward Cuba. U.S. congressmen and senators began to criticize and make suggestions, much to the consternation of the Kennedys. Senator Fulbright delivered a long speech in the Senate on May 9, 1961, entitled "A New Approach to the Latin American Policy of the United States," which was regarded by the Kennedys as an appeasement to Castro.[11]

When Khrushchev assumed power in the Soviet Union, he also inherited a serious foreign policy dilemma. Soviet military doctrine under Stalin had been dominated by ground-forces marshalls and generals, who advocated a large and strong conventional army capable of not only defending the Soviet Union but also of sweeping through Europe, destroying opposing armies, and occupying their territories. Nuclear weapons were regarded as an extension of tube

* The relationship between Harvey and the Kennedys continued to deteriorate, and after the missile crisis, the president asked that Harvey be replaced. In January 1963, Harvey was removed and sent to Rome. He was replaced by Desmond FitzGerald. Harvey's problems with drink continued. On one occasion, he was driving home at night and at high speed when he was stopped by an Italian patrolman. Harvey got out of his car, drew his pistol, placed it at the patrolman's temple, and asked what was the problem. The patrolman, with eyes bulging, thought he had stopped a mafia chief and was going to die meekly. He said, "Nothing." Harvey said, "That's what I thought," and got in his car and drove away.

artillery, to be delivered by medium (Badger) and light (Beagle) bombers. The bombers had been produced in quantity for this role and were based opposite the NATO forces in European Russia. Later, bases were built in the Soviet Far East to oppose the U.S. forces in Japan, Okinawa, and South Korea. Although the "first strike" might be nuclear, the traditionalists reasoned that the decisive role would still be played by massed armies, which could destroy similar opposing forces and occupy enemy territory.

Khrushchev saw a serious flaw in the reasoning of his military advisers. He was concerned because the United States was developing a massive nuclear strike force consisting of B-47 and B-52 bombers, Polaris submarine-launched ballistic missiles, and intercontinental missiles. He stressed the preeminence of strategic nuclear forces to his marshalls and diminished the need for large conventional forces. A massive nuclear strike aimed at Russia during the first few hours of battle could be decisive. He determined that the most urgent of Soviet priorities should be the production of intercontinental ballistic missiles and the creation of a missile-firing submarine force.

In his report to the Supreme Soviet on January 14, 1960, Khrushchev stressed the continuing American hostility to the Soviet system and advocated a new military policy. He stressed the decisiveness of missiles armed with nuclear warheads, as opposed to conventional military forces. To achieve this posture, he advocated a drastic cut in the Soviet ground forces and an enhancement of Soviet rocket-forces capability. This stance generated widespread discontent and disagreement among ground-forces officers, the largest segment of the Soviet armed forces.

Medium- (MRBM) and intermediate-range (IRBM) ballistic missiles offered the USSR the quickest prospect for neutralizing the NATO threat, and Khrushchev ordered that priority be given to their production and deployment. To oversee this effort, the Strategic Rocket Forces (SRF) was formed from existing artillery and long-range bomber units. A group of men representing interlocking directorates formed the nucleus of the Strategic Rocket Forces. Marshall M. I. Nedelin, a tough-minded artillery commander, was made the first commander of the SRF and served until his death, in 1960. (Although the Soviets said he had died in a plane crash, we knew that not only he but a number of others had died when an ICBM exploded on its pad at the Tyura Tam Missile Test Center.) Khrushchev also relied on his son, Sergei, who was working in V. I. Chelomei Missile Design Bureau, for advice on missile matters.

By 1961, we had determined through the analysis of satellite photography that construction of more than six hundred MRBM and IRBM pads, most in a soft configuration, were underway in the USSR. This scale of deployment was not without a price for the Soviets. Funds were cut from the development of new Soviet ground-force weapons, and only a few pieces of military hardware moved from the design institutes to the factories. The Soviet ground forces, along with the tactical air forces, suffered a decline during the 1959–1963 period.

Senator J. W. Fulbright, owing to his position in the Senate and briefings from the CIA, was well aware that the military balance of power favored the U.S. In a speech entitled "Some Reflections upon Recent Events and Continuing Problems," on the floor of the Senate on June 29, 1961, he reflected on Cuba and said: "The possibility of Soviet missile bases and jet aircraft bases in Cuba is frequently noted. I suppose we would all be less comfortable if the Soviets did install missile bases in Cuba, but I am not sure that our national existence would be substantially in greater danger than is the case today. Nor do I think that such bases would substantially alter the balance of power in the world today. What would substantially alter the balance of power in the world would be precipitate action by the United States resulting in the alienation of Latin America, Asia, and Africa."[12] Some U.S. military observers would later hold that Khrushchev's thinking about a missile venture into Cuba had been encouraged by the senator's remarks.

As it became increasingly apparent that Soviet supplies and arms were flowing to Cuba, Soviet merchant shipping came under close scrutiny. All acquired photography of ships en route to Cuba by a variety of organizations was sent to the National Photographic Interpretation Center. Photographs were taken from various vantage points—from shore, from other ships, and from aircraft flying at low, intermediate, and high altitudes. Because of the variety of cameras and focal lengths, the film came to the center in many sizes and formats. Overhead photography taken by U.S. Navy, Marines, and Coast Guard aircraft usually included port, starboard, bow, stern, and overhead views of the ships. Vessels moving through the Bosporus and the Mediterranean were photographed by the U.S. 6th Fleet and by squadrons stationed in Sicily and Spain. Once the ships passed Gibraltar or left the Baltic, they were photographed by planes operating out of Kindley Naval Air Station, in Bermuda, and the naval air station, at Jacksonville, Florida. As the ships approached Cuba, they were picked up by the Marine photo squadron based at Guantánamo and by Coast Guard planes operating out of Miami. Ships were photographed if they were declared to be of "special interest" by the Office of Naval Intelligence.*

When the Soviets first began sending armaments abroad, it was frequently carried as deck cargo on merchant vessels. In an attempt to conceal and protect those shipments, the Soviets covered the weapons with packing crates or placed them in special shipping containers. Many of these ships were old U.S. Liberty ships or ships constructed in Western shipyards, and their dimensions, and often their blueprints, were available. Lundahl asked that the crates and containers be carefully analyzed and measured using photogrammetric means. He labeled the science of measuring, identifying, and cataloguing the crates and their contents *cratology*. By the time of the Cuban missile crisis, cratology was firmly established as an intelligence technique.

Most shipping crates containing Soviet aircraft were delivered to selected foreign airfields, and periodic photography of those fields, as well as airfields in the Soviet Union, made it possible to observe the crating or uncrating of various aircraft components. Not only were the crates measured, but protrusions on the crates for toolboxes, rotors, etc., along with the shipping hooks, were carefully analyzed and catalogued. The crates were then identified as specifically containing such things as fuselages, wings, engines, rotors, and so forth.

---

* To be of special interest, a ship had to meet one or more of the following criteria:
  a. It was a known arms carrier.
  b. It transited the Bosporus at night.
  c. It reported tonnage well below its capacity and rode high in the water—a normal indication of military cargoes.
  d. It made a false declaration of its port of destination.
  e. It carried suspicious cargo.
  f. It declared for Cuba.
  g. It was the subject of other pertinent information.

By August 1962, NPIC had identified seventy-five Soviet or Soviet-chartered ships that had reached Cuba or were en route carrying a variety of military cargo.

The Cuban fear of another invasion from the U.S. subsequent to the Bay of Pigs was very real. They expected that the next invasion would be accomplished with regular U.S. troops rather than with Cuban mercenaries. Tanks and self-propelled guns usually seen at Managua, the main armor depot, were seen deployed along the coast, particularly in the Playa Girón area. In June 1961, the first MiG 15/17 was identified at San Antonio de los Baños airfield. The number of these aircraft seen in Cuba continued to grow throughout the summer. By November 1961, there were twenty MiG 15/17's and ten MiG 19's at the San Antonio de los Baños airfield. Deployment of Soviet aircraft was also observed at other airfields. Eight MiG-15/17's were seen at Camagüey Airfield in November, and Soviet Il-14 transports were noted at José Martí airfield outside Havana. Construction at the Santa Clara airfield to accommodate high-performance fighters also was accelerated.

By the end of December 1961, military equipment seemed to mushroom throughout the island. Concentrations of tanks were seen not only at Managua and Havana but also at Camagüay and Santa Clara. Anti-aircraft positions sprouted around Cuba's principal cities and military installations. Soviet air-warning radars were being installed along Cuba's northern coast. One of the readout requirements levied on the Center by the Joint Chiefs of Staff was to pinpoint and report all Cuban gun positions around the Guantánamo naval base. Arcs were then scribed on the ranges of the guns. All new trenching was reported, especially those near the fences of the naval base.

Although President Kennedy was willing to accept the idea of a Cuba armed beyond its needs following the Bay of Pigs, the growing Soviet presence provoked increased concern because of the political effect it was having in Latin America. The beleaguered Cuban economy was riddled with fundamental weaknesses, but the Soviets had propped up other regimes and had often spoken of the Communists' ability to protect the smaller nations from the "imperialists" both militarily and economically. By the middle of 1961, the increasing flow of military supplies and the technicians to show the Cubans how to use them was strong evidence that the Soviets would not be reversing their policies but were, instead, determined to sustain the Castro regime.

The Twenty-second Communist Party Congress convened in Moscow in October 1961. Khrushchev discussed, among other things, the strategic problems facing the Soviets. He had been brooding about the inferior Soviet strategic position and consequently painted a dark picture to the delegates. Khrushchev reiterated that any war involving NATO and the Warsaw Pact would be nuclear from the start and would be largely decided by massive nuclear exchanges during the first several hours. He also knew that the U.S. Strategic Air Command had targeted specific Soviet cities for immediate destruction and that ''city busting'' was being advocated by General LeMay to bring Russia quickly to her knees. He also knew the adverse strategic imbalance would grow even larger in the future.

The survival of the Soviet Union became the paramount concern. The 20 million Soviet war dead of World War II and the destruction left by that war remained uppermost in Khrushchev's thoughts and, undoubtedly, in the consciousness of most of his countrymen.

During this period, the Soviets were putting forward peace and disarmament proposals. Some, in hindsight, were probably sincere. Unfortunately, these proposals alternated with Khrushchev's dire threats of Soviet missile and nuclear power. The U.S. military, State, and Agency officials regarded all the proposals as a wide-ranging propaganda effort. Some went so far as to state that these proposals were designed to stall for time so the Soviets could build up their forces. General Taylor would remark that ''you just couldn't hear the signal from all the noise.''

We had prepared an elaborate briefing on U.S. versus Soviet strategic-weapons capabilities in early fall 1961. It was presented by McCone and Lundahl to President Kennedy and subsequently shown to Rusk, McNamara, and other ranking U.S. officials. (It was prepared in a manner similar to the methods used in the more recent Department of Defense publication *Soviet Military Power*.) President Kennedy was so impressed with the briefing that he decided that Khrushchev should be warned that the U.S. was fully knowledgeable of the meager Soviet strategic capabilities. Roswell L. Gilpatric, deputy secretary of defense, had also seen the photographic materials and in the speech at Hot Springs on October 21, 1961, came to the point: "Our confidence in our ability to deter Communist action or resist Communist blackmail is based upon a sober appreciation of the relative military power of the two sides. We doubt that the Soviet leadership has, in fact, any less realistic views, although this may not be always apparent from their extravagant claims. While the Soviets use rigid security as a military weapon, their Iron Curtain is not so impenetrable as to force us to accept at face values the Kremlin's boasts. The fact is that this nation has a nuclear retaliatory force of such lethal power that an enemy move which brought it into play would be an act of self-destruction on his part. The U.S. has today hundreds of manned intercontinental bombers capable of reaching the Soviet Union, including six hundred heavy bombers and many more medium bombers capable of intercontinental operations because of our highly developed in-flight refueling techniques."[13] Then as if to add salt to the wound, Gilpatric added, "We have accelerated deliveries of Polaris submarines and hastened the development schedule for a greatly improved version of the missiles they carry. We have expanded the development of the Minuteman, our solid-fuel, land-launched missile, and enlarged its production capacity. We are proceeding simultaneously with the development of air-to-ground missiles, such as the Skybolt, in order to extend the useful life of the manned bomber further into the missile age."[14]

The next day, Secretary Rusk confirmed that "Mr. Gilpatric was making an official statement. It was a well-considered statement and it was based on the facts."

Two days later, Marshall Rodion Y. Malinovsky, the Soviet minister of defense, addressed the Twenty-second Communist Party Congress. Most newspapers seized on one of his statements and headlined it. Malinovsky said, "I must report in particular that the problems of destroying missiles in flight has been successfully solved." Authorities were searched out and quoted as to how far along the Soviets were in the antimissile field. Largely overlooked in this context was Malinovsky's endorsement and implementation of the Khrushchev January 1961 speech emphasizing the need for strategic force while cutting back on conventional forces. Malinovsky announced a new and accepted military doctrine when he said Khrushchev's 1961 report "made a profound analysis of the character of modern war, and this lies at the basis of Soviet military doctrine. One of the important theses of this doctrine is that a world war, if it should nevertheless be unleashed by the imperialist aggressors, will inescapably assume the character of a nuclear-rocket war, that is, a war in which the main striking force will be nuclear weapons, and the main means of delivering these weapons to their targets will be rockets.

"In this connection, war will both begin differently from before and will be waged in a different way. The use of atomic and thermonuclear weapons with unlimited possibilities of delivering them to any target in a matter of minutes by means of rockets make it possible in the shortest period to achieve decisive military results at any range and over immense territory. The targets of crushing nuclear strikes, together with the groupings of enemy armed forces, will be industrial and vital centers, communication junctions—everything that feeds war.

"A future war," Malinovsky noted, "if it is not averted, will have an unprecedented destructive character. It will lead to the deaths of hundreds of millions of people and whole countries will be turned into lifeless deserts covered with ashes."[15] Malinovsky also noted Gilpatric's speech, saying it was made with President Kennedy's approval and that Gilpatric was "brandishing the might of the United States, he threatened us with force."[16]

The Soviets and Defense Department officials continued the "war of words." On January 19, 1962, Secretary McNamara said the U.S. was capable of destroying "the Soviet target system." Reacting, Marshall Malinovsky, on January 24, in an interview with *Pravda* and *Izvestiya*, declared that the Soviets had the power "to wipe off the face of the earth with a single nuclear-rocket attack all the industrial and administrative centers of the United States and to destroy entire countries that might offer their territories for American military bases."

Khrushchev was being stung repeatedly by U.S. statements. He was desperately trying to maintain the Soviet image abroad and at the same time mitigate the criticism he was receiving from both the military and the party at home. But what really commanded the Soviet military and Khrushchev's attention and further frustrated their efforts was the U.S. breakthrough in solid-propellent technology. The first of over a thousand Minuteman missiles were being produced for emplacement in hardened silos in the fall of 1962. By comparison, the Soviets were still having problems with their liquid-fuel rocket program. Then, too, all of their deployed missiles were in a "soft" configuration rather than launch silos. Dissent in the Soviet ground forces persisted. It was still argued that war could occur without the use of nuclear weapons. These dissenters pointed to the postwar Greek, Korean, and Indochina experiences. Later, they argued that large armored forces were still required to exploit the gaps torn in the enemy lines by nuclear weapons. The destruction of the NATO armies and the occupation of Western Europe could only be accomplished by a well-equipped army. But Khrushchev's will and policy prevailed, and Malinovsky would later state: "Real reasons exist which from the government and the Communist party must strengthen the Soviet armed forces. We do not intend to be inferior in any way to our probable enemy."

Khrushchev had announced a halt in the reduction of the number of Soviet ground personnel in 1961 because, as he explained, of the growing crisis in Berlin, but more probably to placate ground-forces commanders. There seemed to be some concern among Politburo members as to the opinions of Marshall Sergei S. Biryuzov. Biryuzov, who headed the Soviet Defensive Forces (PVO), instrumental in downing Powers's U-2, had assumed command of the fledgling Soviet Rocket Forces, replacing Marshall K. S. Moskalenko. Biryuzov was closely allied with Khrushchev and Malinovsky. Biryuzov was Malinovsky's chief of staff in the 2nd Guards Army in the defense of Stalingrad during World War II. During the battle of Stalingrad, Khrushchev was the political commissar in the southern Ukraine and had established a close relationship with officers whose careers he helped advance in later years and who, in turn, would help him establish and consolidate his political power in the unstable years after Stalin's death.*

Khrushchev had shuffled the top echelons of the army and installed leaders he trusted and who believed in his policies and positions. This group of officers became the envy of their colleagues and at times were contemptuously referred to as the Stalingrad group. The

---

* Biryuzov, along with a Soviet delegation sent to celebrate the twentieth anniversary of the liberation of Belgrade, would die in 1964 in an airplane crash on Mount Avala, outside Belgrade.

most prominent included Malinovsky and Biryuzov, along with A. A. Grechko, K. S. Moskalenko, N. I. Krylov, V. I. Chuikov, I. Kh. Bagramyan, P. I. Batov, M. V. Zakharov, I. I. Yakobovsky, A. A. Yepishev, and V. A. Sudets. Some analysts maintain it was probably Marshall Biryuzov who advocated the deployment of missiles to Cuba, after listening many times to Khrushchev's frustrations and in an attempt to please his leader and ingratiate himself with Malinovsky.

In Washington, diplomatic relations also were not going well, and the Soviets decided to replace Ambassador Mikhail "Mike" Menshikov—who was wooden, uncompromising, and unimaginative—with forty-three-year-old Anatoly Fedorovich Dobrynin. Dobrynin was considered by the Soviets to be one of their outstanding specialists in the field of American relations. Although he had served as a civilian engineer in an aircraft plant during the early war years, in 1952 he became counselor, and later minister counselor, to the Soviet embassy in Washington. He remained in the United States until 1955, when he returned to Moscow. From 1957 to 1960, he served the Soviet delegation to the UN as undersecretary for political and security council affairs. From 1960 until his appointment as ambassador in 1962, Dobrynin headed the American department of the USSR Ministry of Foreign Affairs.

Dobrynin was at Vienna with Khrushchev during the first Kennedy-Khrushchev meeting, where he impressed Kennedy with his knowledge of the United States. When asked about Dobrynin's appointment as ambassador, Kennedy remarked, "At last they've sent a son of a bitch to Washington that can speak and understand English." The personable Dobrynin wasted no time establishing close and cordial relations with Secretary of State Rusk, Press Secretary Pierre Salinger, and Bobby Kennedy.

Beginning in January 1962, and continuing throughout the summer, Soviet personnel began arriving in Cuba in large numbers. A portion of the boys' reformatory at Torrens was being used as a Soviet processing and command center. From there they were dispatched in groups to a number of remote areas throughout Cuba. These personnel undoubtedly were involved in the planning and site preparation for the missile sites and military equipment to follow. Whenever personnel lists were intercepted by the U.S., a number of names like Petrov and Ivanov appeared—names in Russia equivalent to Smith and Jones. It was obvious that the Soviets were concealing the real names of experts visiting Cuba. One such delegation was headed by Marshall Biryuzov. He was carried as "the engineer Petrov." By mid-February, reports began to flow into the U.S. of Soviets being seen in large numbers throughout the island. The task of site selection was made easy for the Russians. (The Cubans provided them with excellent geological and geographical data, along with large-scale topographic maps, which had been produced in the late 1950s by a U.S. contractor under the auspices of the U.S. Army Corps of Engineers and the U.S. Army Map Service. Ironically, it was these same maps that U.S. photo interpreters and intelligence analysts used to plot all new Soviet construction in the island.) China had strongly supported the Cuban revolution, and reports were also being received in the U.S. of Chinese Communist, or "mongol," troops in Cuba. Reports of troops arriving from Africa were frequent, too, but were never substantiated.

CIA director McCone was disturbed by the Cuban developments and the monthly U-2 overflights were increased from one to two. Flown on clear days, and in the early morning hours before rain clouds appeared, nearly all of Cuba could be photographed on each mission. By January 1962, there were over two hundred humint reports of missile activity in Cuba. None, however, were confirmed by photography.

The Kennedy administration had decided it was time to isolate Cuba. On January 22, 1962, Latin American foreign ministers met at Punta del Este, Uruguay, and U.S. secretary of state Dean Rusk denounced Cuba as a Communist bridgehead in the Americas. Three days later, they proposed the expulsion of Cuba from all organizations of the Organization of American States, the termination of all trade with Cuba, and the setting up of a Special Security Committee to protect against Sino-Soviet intervention in the Western Hemisphere. The final resolution of the conference on January 31 achieved the U.S. aim insofar as it proclaimed the isolation of Cuba. Fourteen nations voted to exclude Cuba from participation in the inter-American system; six important nations, however, abstained from the voting—Argentina, Mexico, Chile, Brazil, Bolivia, and Ecuador. On February 7, 1962, the U.S. decreed a total embargo on trade with

Cuba, except for medicines and similar supplies. The State Department also requested that NATO nations impose sanctions on their trade with Cuba, but only Turkey, West Germany, and Belgium gave token support to the request.

In the March 31, 1962, issue of *The Saturday Evening Post*, Khrushchev saw in print what he had always suspected. In an interview with Stewart Alsop, President Kennedy announced that a change had occurred in America's military policy. The president stated that the U.S. must be prepared to use nuclear weapons at the start—come what may—of a clear attack on Western Europe, for example. In an obvious warning to Khrushchev, the president added, ''in some circumstances we might have to take the initiative.''[17] Kennedy had hoped that with this warning, Khrushchev might avoid situations like Berlin that could lead to ''global thermonuclear war.''

Khrushchev later denounced the president for adopting a policy based on ''a nuclear initiative.'' *Pravda* reported that President Kennedy had concluded that the U.S. was ''entitled to strike the first atomic blow, to become the initiator of a war of aggression.'' Malinovsky had no doubts about the meaning of President Kennedy's statement and would later write: ''These declarations correspond to the conception of preventive war using nuclear and other weapons of mass destruction, contained in the military doctrine of the United States, and clearly show the aggressive trend in American military plans.''[18] President Kennedy, somewhat embarrassed by Soviet and other foreign reaction, asked that the State Department brief newspaper, radio, and TV reporters on the conditions under which he would order the use of nuclear weapons against an enemy. The State Department, rather befuddled by being tossed a hot potato, issued a statement attributed to the president that there had been no change in U.S. strategic policy. The statement sought to clarify but only further muddled the military circumstances in which the U.S. would resort to nuclear war. Try as he might to mitigate the Soviet reaction to his original statement, the president had provoked Khrushchev and the Soviet military into an undesirable reaction.

Secretary McNamara, in his Ann Arbor address of June 16, 1962, advocated that both countries should concentrate only on striking military targets and not cities in the event of war: ''The United States has come to the conclusion that, to the extent feasible, basic military strategy in a possible general nuclear war should be approached in much the same way that more conventional military operations have been regarded in the past. That is to say, principal military objectives, in the event of a nuclear war stemming from a major attack on the alliance, should be the destruction of the enemy's military forces, not of his civilian population."[19] The worrisome aspect of McNamara's position was that a policy of counterforce and retaliation did not add up to the Soviets. They said that with this counterforce strategy the United States had accepted a first-strike policy. In 1962, neither country had a strategy for flexible nuclear options.

While the Soviets did not have a viable intercontinental ballistic missile (ICBM) force, they did have both medium-range ballistic missiles (MRBM) and intermediate-range ballistic missiles (IRBM). But they had never before placed these missiles outside their borders, although there had been past crises when it might have been advantageous for them to have done so.

The introduction of offensive missiles in Cuba would certainly legitimize an American invasion, and obviously, there must have been some old-line Politburo members who would have been wary of risking an adventure of this magnitude. Little is known about the scope of the opposition to placing missiles in Cuba, but it is known that the Khrushchev adventure was supported by A. N. Kosygin, F. R. Kozlov, L. I. Brezhnev, and A. I. Mikoyan. The Soviet military leaders, except the Stalingrad group, it appears, had been generally reluctant to become involved in Cuba, partly out of fear of being associated with a military misadventure and, secondly, because they realized the difficulty of maintaining supply lines for Soviet forces so far removed from Russia in the event of a confrontation with the United States. The most outspoken were Marshalls K. S. Moskalenko, P. I. Golikov, and V. I. Chuikov, who represented the conservative element of the military against Khrushchev.

On April 3, 1962, Ramiro Valdés, Cuban minister of the interior, and, on April 29, Osmani Cienfuegos, minister of public works, and Joaquin Ordoqui Mesa, army chief of supply, arrived in Moscow. At the time, it was thought they were in Moscow seeking aid to improve sanitation and public works in Cuba. In hindsight, they were probably being told by the Soviets of the logistical needs of the

Soviet missile forces that were to arrive in July, August, and September.

In May 1962, General A. A. Yepishev, an MGB officer closely linked to Khrushchev, was selected to replace Marshall P. I. Golikov, a career military officer, as head of the Main Political Administration of the Army and Navy. Yepishev undoubtedly was responsible for the tight control and security of the movement of Soviet missiles to Cuba, and acting under Khrushchev's direct authority, he could investigate, remove, or break the resistance of any attempt to counter Khrushchev's Cuban policy either within the ground forces or the Ministry of Defense. With Khrushchev and Yepishev now firmly in charge, acquiescence in the military became politically prudent.

There is no clear evidence when the Soviets decided to place offensive missiles in Cuba, although it has been the subject of much speculation. The most accurate guess is that the decision was made sometime between the fall of 1961, when it became clear to the Soviets that their efforts in Berlin had failed, and January–February 1962, when Soviet military personnel began surveying specific areas in Cuba.

Certainly, the magnitude of the logistic effort, the extensive planning required, and the coordination necessary among the various ministries and among the military forces involved a high degree of security. The difficulties inherent in an effort of this magnitude would have been daunting even in normal times; but successfully transporting offensive missiles to Cuba during a time of tension and close observation was a formidable undertaking.

The initiation of such a mammoth supply effort, arriving in stages as it did, indicates that the Soviets employed a contingency plan developed long before its implementation. U.S. logistical experts have, in reviewing the movement of men and matériel to Cuba, concluded that this was an effort of the first magnitude and would have taken the U.S. at least six months of extensive planning and coordination. Castro has since claimed that the decision to put missiles in Cuba was taken ''at the beginning of 1962.''[20]

The Soviet supply effort can be categorized into five distinct phases: 1) the initial supply of conventional weapons, i.e., the MiG–15–17–19, tanks, artillery, and electronic equipment; 2) defensive equipment, i.e., the SAMs, coastal-defense missiles, and KOMAR patrol boats; 3) the Soviet protective force for the missiles; 4) the advanced aircraft, i.e., the MiG-21 and Il-28; 5) the MRBM missiles; and 6) the final phase that never materialized but was en route at the climax of the missile crisis, the emplacement of IRBMs.

Khrushchev has stated the idea of installing missiles in Cuba occurred during a visit to Bulgaria in May 1962. In a radio and TV address to the Soviet people when he returned, he said, "It should be said that on all these questions our Western partners are displaying intractability, an unwillingness to settle acute problems by peaceful means. They do not understand the changes in the balance of forces that have taken place in the international arena in recent years, and they are still trying to follow a 'position of strength' in relations with us.

"The founder of this mad doctrine is dead, as we know, but his doctrine is still alive, and the present leaders of the Western powers do not at all want to renounce it. But the 'positions of strength' policy, which did not bring laurels to its author, will not bring success to those who try to continue it in our times either. It is doomed to failure. Now, when the might of the Soviet Union and of the entire socialist camp has grown immeasurably, to indulge in threats is hardly serious, to say the least." More likely this was the time when Khrushchev gave the go-ahead to an already prepared plan for sending missiles to Cuba.

The former Soviet ambassador to Cuba, Aleksandr Ivanovich Alekseyev, has written that the decision to send the missiles to Cuba was made in a meeting held by Khrushchev in Moscow and attended by Kozlov, Mikoyan, Malinovsky, Gromyko, Biryuzov, and Sh. R. Rashidov and that in mid-May, Biryuzov and Rashidov visited Cuba and presented the idea to Castro. In later years, Sergei Mikoyan said that only his father opposed the emplacement of missiles in Cuba. Alekseyev states that in a meeting with Fidel Castro, Raul Castro, Ernesto Che Guevara, Osvaldo Dorticos, and Ramiro Valdés in Havana, the Cubans agreed to the installation of the missiles.

Meanwhile, at the CIA, Major General Marshall "Pat" Carter became the deputy director on April 13, 1962. The antithesis of

McCone, Carter was a bald, pudgy, jaunty man. Born on an army post, he was the son of an army general. He had served a considerable part of his career in the Washington area and had earned his spurs as a staff officer to General George C. Marshall during and after World War II.

General Carter was an incorrigible prankster whose impudence, roguery, and charm compensated for some of McCone's coldness and aloofness. Carter poked gentle fun at McCone's serious attitude, but never in McCone's presence. The director's office of the new CIA headquarters building at Langley was designed to include a connecting door with that of the deputy director so the latter could enter the director's office anytime he wished. When McCone first visited his office and was made aware of this arrangement, he demanded that the door be sealed off immediately. CIA Executive Director Col. Lawrence "Red" White prevailed upon the General Services Administration to accomplish the task that evening. Although the doorway was removed and the area sealed with paneling, a fine crack remained. General Carter thereupon wedged a fake rubber hand into the crack on his side of the wall so that it appeared that McCone was attempting to escape from his office. Another time, following a lengthy staff meeting, McCone remarked to the executive director that he would like a certain brand of cosmetics and a special brand of toilet tissue to be placed in the private bathroom of his office for the convenience of his fiancée when she visited. Several members of McCone's senior staff were rather surprised by such a request; McCone reiterated that one must be prepared for all occasions. Subsequently, General Carter decided that to emulate McCone he likewise had to be prepared to accommodate guests. Many of Carter's relatives were from rural farming areas, so he facetiously placed a special container in his office bathroom to hold a bag of corn cobs, a Sears Roebuck catalogue, and some Sunkist orange wrappers.

On one occasion, while Lundahl was briefing Carter, he noticed that the general was slouching down in his chair. Lundahl was seated in front of Carter's desk and thought something had gone wrong with the briefing. Moments later Lundahl felt something strike his legs. He looked down and saw a pair of large bare feet against his. Hesitant and surprised, Lundahl realized that the feet were fake and were being manipulated by Carter. Carter pulled the same trick on many who visited his office. The general also equipped himself with a telescoping briefing pointer, which he called his goosing stick, to use if he thought a speaker took too long to get his points across.

At the Agency, concern was being expressed on the stream of refugees from Cuba. As the numbers increased, so did the reports dealing with military activity in Cuba. About seventeen hundred Cuban refugees were arriving in Miami each week, but the facilities to handle these potential sources of information were woefully lacking. There was a bureaucratic nightmare of representatives from thirteen federal agencies competing with the CIA to interrogate the refugees. These included State, Commerce, Joint Chiefs of Staff, Army Counterintelligence, the Office of Naval Intelligence, the Air Force Office of Special Investigation, Health, Education, and Welfare, Immigration, Voice of America, the Border Patrol, the Coast Guard, and Public Health. In addition, local authorities and intelligence units from the Miami and Dade County police departments wanted to question certain émigrés. It is easy for a researcher or historian today to point to several agent reports, which are known from hindsight to be correct, and question why they were not acted upon. Many refugees, of course, gave valuable information; others gave unreliable reports or misinformation—some unintentionally, some with the hope of inducing the United States to strike or invade Cuba. Some agent reports were the result of fertile imagination and some information was undoubtedly planted by Cuban and Soviet agents. Separating the factual from the false was not as easy as it often appears to be in retrospect. Probably the most difficult task was checking out the "missile" sightings. Details of "missile" sizes and shapes were often lacking. Many of these missile reports upon being checked out proved to be telephone poles, torpedos, fuel-storage tanks, industrial piping, and maritime marker buoys.

The intelligence community proposed the establishment of a joint interrogation center at a former marine air base at Opa-Locka, a few miles from Miami, to process the Cuban émigrés and speed the flow of intelligence to Washington. The center was to be administered by the CIA and was to be known as the Caribbean Admission Center. It was approved by the president and went into operation on March 15, 1962. Those who had information of interest were to be fully interrogated. The information obtained could be placed into the following categories: missile sightings, rumors of missile or rocket launching pads or bases; loading and unloading activities; property seizures; evacuation of families; presence of tents; movements of military convoys; digging of trenches, emplacements, and tunnels; new road construction; closing or sealing off of roads or railroads; munitions storage; use of concrete in constructing military projects; activities at caves; construction of military camps, airfields, and radar stations; military training activity; all activity at unidentified installations; submarine or naval sightings; camouflage efforts; gun emplacements; military equipment sighted in farming or wooded areas; and Soviet, Czech, or ''mongol'' troop sightings. All these categories were checked against U-2 photography.

In addition, all reports of fires and sabotage, and reported closings of U.S. and other foreign-owned plants, were checked. Closings of sugar mills and other industrial installations due to shortages of spare parts or equipment breakdowns were investigated. Reports of newly constructed resorts and hotels were scrutinized, as was all information about Soviet-constructed plants or foreign-aid projects. Because there were so many refugees whose bona fides could not be established, the Agency placed qualifying comments on individual reports emanating from the interrogation center. As long as these comments were amplifications or informative, a definitive purpose was served. These comments, however, became increasingly evaluative, to the extent that they ultimately demeaned the substantive worth of the reporting system. Information was also coming from the military intelligence services, the FBI, press and broadcast accounts, friendly foreign sources, and businessmen. Many well-intentioned people wrote letters giving information to the president, the secretary of state, the director of central intelligence, congressmen, and others in government. All of these reports had to be evaluated. McCone directed Lundahl that he wanted all information checked against U-2 photography and the findings disseminated to the intelligence community. Beginning in May 1962, and continuing throughout the crisis, the Center published a ''Photographic Evaluation of Information on Cuba,'' which confirmed or denied humint information.

The CIA database on Cuba was an all-encompassing one. In addition to U-2 photography and reports from agents and refugees, there were an extensive ground photo file, blueprints of U.S. and foreign-owned firms in Cuba, and extensive studies in hydrographic, geological, speleological, forestry, agricultural, transportation, sugar production, ports, weather, and communication subjects.

Richard Helms would later point out some of the difficulties encountered in checking out these reports: "It was a mammoth undertaking, but where possible we checked every weapon report against U-2 photography of Cuba, and against other intelligence sources.

"One report, for example, claimed there were underground submarine pens at Matanzas. Our analysts had the facts to disprove this, given the geological structure of the shore line and the crucial inshore depths in the bay.

"Another report alleged that light bombers were being stored in a particular cave. We had comprehensive speleological surveys of Cuba, which showed that this particular cave curved sharply a few yards inside its entrance—too sharply to admit a vehicle, let alone an aircraft. We also had the photography to show that there had been no work to alter the shape of the cave.

"A merchant seaman gave us a detailed description of what he thought might be a rounded concreted dome covering missiles— complete with range and bearing from the pier where his ship was docked. A map of Havana and a recent city directory established that it was a relatively new movie theater."[21]

McCone also would later testify before Congress on the difficulties of verifying such information: "In the spring of 1962, there were other reports of heavy construction in Cuba. There were reports of underground hangars, heavily reinforced, that could house large numbers of aircraft. When these reports reached me, I ordered four complete mosaics of all of Cuba, and four overflights were flown in the month of June 1962. These flights disapproved the statements."

It was obvious that the Soviets were aware that refugees were being interrogated and that U-2 flights were continuing, so once the Soviets had decided to install the missiles in Cuba, they had to place an elaborate deception scheme into effect. In wartime, Winston Churchill said, truth was so precious that it should be attended by a bodyguard of lies. Throughout World War II, Churchill, in the vernacular of the intelligence officer, had "mousetrapped his security"—i.e., he planned deception on an international scale to shield his real motives and actions. His government had devised a sophisticated and extensive disinformation system designed to confuse a situation and distract the intelligence analysts of the adversary.

The Soviet doctrine related to concealment, camouflage, deception, and misinformation in support of military operations is called *maskirovka*. The central tenet of *maskirovka* is to prevent the adversary from discovering Soviet intention—i.e., to deceive the adversary about the nature, scope, and timing of a Soviet operation. Khrushchev had to be confident that the outcome of his adventure in Cuba would represent a major political success and a damaging defeat for President Kennedy, which gave the Soviets a powerful incentive to make *maskirovka* work. Lying is always an integral part of any *maskirovka* scheme, and deception has to play on, or reinforce, what the adversary believes and expects not to happen. Each lie has to be elusive and its confirmation should be difficult, if not impossible. While military activity cannot be concealed for long periods and is relatively easy to discern, Soviet political intentions were often extremely difficult to judge.

While Khrushchev would be the master of the *maskirovka* scheme, *maskirovka* in the Soviet armed forces is under the overall control of the Defense Counsel, the Ministry of Defense, or a specific branch of the service. The *dizinformatsiya*, or dissemination of false or misleading information, is an integral part of the *maskirovka* scheme. It was obvious that the political, economic, and military elements of the Soviet Union were all involved in the scheme of protecting the deployment of missiles in Cuba. The deception plan called for continuous and repeated assertions by high-ranking Soviet officials that no weapons that could threaten the United States would be put in Cuba. *Maskirovka* considers the enemy's intelligence capabilities and is designed to force the enemy to make an erroneous decision. It is based on careful and painstaking preparations, realism, secrecy, and allowance of time for enemy intelligence to reach a false conclusion. A successful *maskirovka* scheme also supports the existing or believed prejudices of the enemy. Legitimate overt activities often serve as a façade to mask the covert deployment. The Soviets were also probably aware that U.S. intelligence and military officials believed that the covert transfer of offensive missiles would be virtually impossible.

Khrushchev would also have to consider the threat of premature disclosure and its attendant political consequences. The Soviets also had to factor in U.S. monitoring capabilities in such a deception scheme. The Soviets were aware that the USSR's prestige and credibility were being placed on the line and that they probably had not fully considered the consequences of the miscalculations and unexpected developments if the project failed.

Khrushchev, in meetings with foreign heads of state and distinguished visitors, took every opportunity to create the impression that the Soviets were far ahead of the United States in military technology. He extolled the superiority of Soviet offensive and defensive missiles and would spontaneously interrupt himself and offer to show the visitors a classified film documenting his point. The visitors would be ushered into Khrushchev's private cinema, where they were shown a "secret" documentary film entitled *Rockets Defend the Peace*. The film had spectacular scenes of Soviet ICBM, ABM, submarine, aircraft, and SAM-missile programs. The impact of the film upon visitors who might be unfamiliar with advanced military technology had the desired propaganda effect. They in turn would report the "secrets" to which they had been made privy—just as Khrushchev had hoped they would.

The CIA had obtained a copy of the film and we had carefully evaluated it. Instead of being in an operational state, most of the missiles shown, we found, were still in the developmental and testing stages at various Soviet missile test ranges.

Yet even as the plan for sending missiles to Cuba was well under way, Khrushchev, speaking to the World Congress for General Disarmament and Peace on July 10, told of the Soviet desire for peace and disarmament. He stated: "Nuclear weapons are being located in an increasing number of countries. More and more military units are getting them. This continually heightens the danger of adventurist groups' starting a new world war."[22] He tried to refute the balance of power favoring the U.S. "At present the United States leadership has set out to impress upon their own people and the people in the Allied countries that the balance of strength has tipped in favor of the United States. Lately, the militarists talk more and more about nuclear war. Take Defense Secretary McNamara's speech of June 16.

He says in it that an understanding may be reached to use nuclear weapons solely for striking at the armed forces, and not at big cities. The U.S. press says that McNamara's statement had the approval of the White House, and interprets it as a sort of proposal to the Soviet Union on 'rules' of conducting nuclear war."[23] Showing his concern about the U.S. initiating a war, Khrushchev continued, "Some responsible U.S. statesmen go to the length of saying publicly that they are prepared to take the 'initiative' in a nuclear conflict with the Soviet Union."[24] Commenting on U.S. policy, Khrushchev asked, "I wonder how the American leaders came to adduce that the relation of strength has changed in their favor. They have nothing to back up this claim." Then, in typical Khrushchev braggadocio fashion, he threatened, "In order to insure its security, the Soviet Union was forced to develop in the last few years nuclear weapons of fifty, one hundred, and more megatons, intercontinental rockets, the global rocket, which is practically impervious to defense, and an antimissile rocket."[25]

In speaking to U.S. newspaper editors on July 16, 1962, Khrushchev bragged that his missiles could hit a fly in space, and he later told Mr. Felix McKnight, editor of the *Dallas Times-Herald*, that he had offered to show the documentary film on Soviet missiles to the World Congress on General Disarmament and Peace but said he had been turned down by the organization leaders because showing the film might be taken as a warlike gesture.

Meanwhile, there was an increase in Soviet shipping activity to Cuba, and during the month of June 1962, the Cubans exhibited increasing anxiety and sensitivity to U.S. violations of their airspace and territorial waters. The buzzing of Soviet and Cuban merchant ships at sea by the U.S. to obtain photos of their cargoes was also irritating. The Cuban press began to refer to these overflights as "spy flights" and "piratical actions" designed to gain information for aggression and sabotage against Cuba. On July 1, the Ministry of the Revolutionary Armed Forces (MINFAR) announced that henceforth it would publish a daily list of provocations against Cuba. The information provided in these announcements would normally give the date, hour, type of plane, altitude, area where the violation occurred, and the direction of the approach and exit of the flight. It was obvious that most of this data came from ground observations rather than radar illumination, since the U-2 missions were never mentioned.

In June and July, the Soviets began a policy of chartering Western vessels to carry general cargo from the Soviet Union to Cuba, reserving their own bottoms for carrying military cargo. On July 2, 1962, Major Raul Castro, Cuban minister of the armed forces and deputy premier, arrived in Moscow at the invitation of the Defense Ministry. He was received at Vnukovo airfield by Soviet defense minister Malinovsky, ranking Soviet military leaders, and the new Cuban ambassador to the Soviet Union, Carlos Oliveres Sanchez. (According to the Soviet ambassador to Cuba, Alekseyev, Major Castro met with Malinovsky and Biryuzov to work out an agreement for sending the missiles to Cuba.) On July 5, Raul Castro addressed the Soviet people on nationwide television. He boasted about the accomplishments of the USSR and Cuba, stating that the socialist camp was now stronger than that of the capitalists. He thanked the Soviet people, the Soviet government, and Nikita Khrushchev for their selfless "assistance and support of Cuba's cause for independence."

On July 8, the Central Committee of the Communist party and the Soviet Council of Ministers hosted a dinner in honor of Major Castro. In attendance were Kirilenko, Mikoyan, Suslov, Grishin, Demishev, Ponomarev, Malinovsky, and Khrushchev. Castro was toasted repeatedly by Khrushchev, and the Russian press reported that there was "an atmosphere of great cordiality and fraternal friendship."

While Castro emphasized the solidarity of the Cuba-Soviet friendship during his entire stay, the most revealing statements came from the Cuban ambassador, Sanchez, on July 3 in answer to questions as to his plans and thoughts on his new post. With regard to the agreements reached, Sanchez said, "They are being carried out very well to the benefit of both sides. It is necessary to emphasize especially that these agreements gave great advantages to Cuba." He concluded: "This aid from the Soviet Union to my country is one of the most important factors promoting the final victory of our revolution."[26]

Imagery intelligence obtained over the Soviet Union throughout the spring and summer allowed the intelligence community to formally quantify Soviet strategic forces and capabilities for National Intelligence Estimate 11-8-62, "Soviet Capabilities for Long-Range Attack." Its conclusion was that the United States strategic forces were clearly superior to those of the Soviets and that superiority would continue to grow. Sherman Kent, director of the Office of National Estimates, when seeing the tabulations in the estimate, said, "Hell, this isn't an estimate, it's a fact book." It was issued on July 6, 1962, and discussed at an NSC meeting on July 10, 1962. The president, appreciative of the information in the estimate, expressed concern as to how this new information should be used in the formulation of U.S. foreign and defense policies. He asked that a special study be made, and the "Report on Implications for U.S. Foreign and Defense Policy of Recent Intelligence Estimates" was submitted to the president in August 1962.

On July 16, 1962, a Tu-114 Cleat transport aircraft flew from Moscow to Havana. On July 17, Havana announced that Cuba and the Soviet Union had signed an agreement establishing a regular Moscow-Havana civil air route. Most intelligence analysts thought that the Tu-114 flights most probably were bringing ranking Soviet military officers—and, probably, sensitive electronic and signal-monitoring equipment—to Cuba.

U.S. ambassador to the Soviet Union Llewellyn E. Thompson made a farewell call on Premier Khrushchev in the Kremlin on July 25, 1962. Also in attendance was Arkady A. Sobolev, former Soviet representative to the UN and, later, a deputy foreign minister. A two-hour discussion over a wide range of topics ensued. Cuba, however, occupied only a small portion of that time. According to Thompson, there was no mention of Soviet arms shipments to Cuba, only a brief discussion of Soviet intentions to conclude a modest fishing agreement with Cuba. In our debriefing of Thompson, he said that Khrushchev brought up the previous U-2 flights over the Soviet Union several times, referring to the U-2 as "that beast" over which he had lost a number of sleepless nights. He emphasized, "And you're still flying it." Thompson felt that Khrushchev may have been probing for information on U-2 flights over Cuba. Khrushchev certainly must have been aware, from the coverage acquired by the Soviets from the Powers flight, of the excellent capabilities of the U-2 to discover missile sites.*

In a rare happening in the Soviet Union, Khrushchev and his wife gave a farewell party later for Ambassador and Mrs. Thompson at their dacha on the outskirts of Moscow. It reflected, in some manner, the extraordinary personal relationship and mutual trust that existed between Khrushchev and Thompson. Khrushchev summarized his relationship with Thompson: "We had a very free and easygoing relationship. He scolds me and I scold him."[27]

In Cuba, the Soviet military were frequently clumsy and overbearing in relations with their Cuban counterparts. Much of the Soviet activity at Cuban installations was serving Soviet rather than Cuban interests. They were exercising increasing control over the installations and turning them into exclusive Soviet enclaves. To some extent, friction and suspicions were an inevitable, even normal, feature of the Soviet-Cuban "friendship." The arms shipments gave Moscow a greater role in the formulation and execution of Cuban foreign policy. Castro had seen himself a modern-day Bolívar, destined to lead Latin America in its "war of independence" from the United States. In most of his speeches, he made an explicit call for violence and the necessity for revolutionary confrontation. But Castro also became suspicious of Soviet intentions regarding Cuban domestic affairs. The "Old Communists"—those in ranking positions in his regime who had belonged to the prerevolutionary Cuban Communist party—were capitalizing on increased Soviet influence to institutionalize their, and the Soviet, position.

Anibal Escalante, the leader of the old Communists, had begun to place his Bolshevik colleagues and cronies into key positions to dominate party policy. When Escalante took over the political organization, he removed a number of military officers from command. The reason stated was their apparent or stated lack of conviction for

---

* Thompson was no stranger to NPIC or to reconnaissance. He frequently visited the Center on home leave to be brought up-to-date on the latest photographic intelligence on the Soviet Union. He never wanted any fuss to be made over him. He always listened intently to the briefer, chain-smoking one Camel after another. He asked many questions and always expressed his gratitude when the briefing was completed.

the Communist party line. A number of these officers had fought with Castro in the Sierra Maestra and still had access to him. In mid-March 1962, they met with Castro on the Communist issue. Castro reassured the officers and, on March 26, cracked down on the old Communists with a vengeance. He charged Escalante and his colleagues with "sectarianism" and initiated a purge of the party. Escalante was forced to leave Havana for exile in Prague. The political apparatus Escalante had been building was quickly dismantled.

Castro's attack on Escalante had an immediate cooling effect on the Soviets. But their stake in Cuba was now too high, and they worked overtime to deny Castro's implied charges of Soviet complicity in the affair. It was unlikely that Castro believed that the activities of the old Communists constituted a serious threat to him. But he was warning the Russians to refrain from meddling in Cuban internal affairs. Soviet press commentary in April endorsed the removal of Escalante but called for an end to bickering among the Cuban revolutionaries. Castro and his closest advisers attempted to remain aloof and independent of the feeling that Moscow Communists would resort to any means to gain control of Cuba.

Soviet hard-sell tactics had now placed a number of chips on the table that allowed Castro a large degree of latitude and that Castro had hoped to cash in at a later date. The Soviet ambassador to Cuba, Sergei Kundriatsev, was suddenly recalled to Moscow on June 4, 1962. It was obvious that his performance as ambassador had not pleased either Castro or Khrushchev.[28] Kundriatsev was replaced by his deputy, Aleksandr Ivanovich Alekseyev. Khrushchev, in his memoirs, states that Kundriatsev was "unsuited for the service in a country just emerging from revolution," and that Kundriatsev "demanded" among other things "that the Cubans give him an official bodyguard." The real reason for Kundriatsev's removal was that he and Escalante had failed to put the hard-core Cuban Communists in control of Cuba and had incurred the displeasure of both Castro and Khrushchev.[29] Although Khrushchev described Alekseyev as a journalist friend of Fidel Castro, Alekseyev was known to Western intelligence agencies as a high-ranking agent of the KGB. In hindsight, the assignment of Alekseyev as ambassador provided additional security for the movement of the Soviet missiles to Cuba.

In Washington, the increased shipment of Soviet military equipment to Cuba disturbed McCone. He first expressed his fears that the Russians might introduce offensive missiles into Cuba on August 10, 1962, in a meeting with Dean Rusk, General Maxwell Taylor, McGeorge Bundy, and Bobby Kennedy. General Taylor would later relate to me that no one in the group was shocked at the idea and that it had certainly gone through his mind and had probably occurred to most of the policymakers. It certainly had been discussed in the intelligence community and by military contingency-planning staffs. McCone's action had brought the idea out in the open, but Taylor hastened to add, "McCone had no proof." He said, "There was nothing immediate the president could do about McCone's feelings, except to acknowledge the issue and possibly raise it in future discussions." McCone was bothered that there was no apparent reaction by the administration to his suggestion, and for nearly a week he brooded about possible Russian actions. He did express his fears to both his special assistants, Walt Elder and Hank Knoche. He did not, however, call for an estimate or express or discuss his fears with the United States Intelligence Board as was his prerogative or, as some would say later, his duty.

On August 21, at a meeting with McNamara, U. Alexis Johnson, and Generals Taylor and Lemnitzer, McCone assumed charge. It was obvious that in a week of brooding, McCone had carefully considered a number of Soviet alternatives. He discussed these, and then, according to General Taylor, McCone said, "I had to put myself in Khrushchev's shoes. And adopting Khrushchev's mental attitudes, I would have to believe what my intelligence officers were telling me and what the leaders in the United States were saying about our relative military strengths was true. Khrushchev is no fool. He's a conniving but a very pragmatic man. Men who are born poor are always like that." He was, in McCone's terms, "in the red and knew it."

McCone paused for a moment and then said, "If I were Khrushchev, I would put MRBMs in Cuba and I would aim several at Washington and New York and then I would say, 'Mr. President, how would you like looking down the barrels of a shotgun for a while. Now, let's talk about Berlin. Later, we'll bargain about your overseas bases.' " Then McCone warned, "That's the kind of situation that we can be faced with in the future, and we had better do some planning for it.''

There was general agreement that it could happen, but secretaries Rusk and McNamara still held that the buildup in Cuba was strictly defensive. They felt it would be out of character for the Soviets to place offensive missiles outside their own territory.[30] According to Taylor, the meeting ended before any formal action could be planned or taken. Taylor went back to his office and ordered that the intelligence ''be sifted again,'' but nothing was found that would support McCone's thesis. Taylor, however, did have the JCS review contingency plans for both striking and invading Cuba. At a planning group meeting on August 21, Ray Cline, deputy director for intelligence, also raised the issue that the Russians' buildup in Cuba could be more ominous than perceived.

McCone met alone with President Kennedy on August 22 and again presented the views as he had given the others. The president listened patiently and the next day at a National Security Council meeting asked that the following actions be taken: ''Analysis should be prepared of the probable military, political and psychological impact of the establishment in Cuba of either surface-to-air missiles or surface-to-surface missiles which could reach the United States.''[31]

That evening, McCone, a widower, left Washington for Seattle to prepare for his wedding to Theiline McGee Pigott, a widow. McCone and his bride would spend their honeymoon at Cap Ferrat, on the French Riviera. Before leaving, McCone instructed Ray Cline to publish a special report each day on the intelligence findings on Cuba and to forward a copy by cable to him in France. McCone responded to these cables with a number of questions. The cables were facetiously referred to by Cline as the honeymoon cables. One wag in the cable section, after receiving one of McCone's long cables, remarked: ''I have some doubts that the old man knows what to do on a honeymoon.''

The president and Bobby Kennedy had been experiencing growing disenchantment with Dean Rusk and the State Department. The time-consuming staff work and multiple meetings required to solve any problems had earned the State Department its nickname as the fudge factory. The department, being an old-line organization, bore the scars of frequent internecine wars between the foreign-service and headquarters personnel. Few new ideas were generated from within, and coordination and cooperation with other governmental departments was minimal. Any new thinking had to be thoroughly analyzed and painstakingly coordinated within the department through a long and laborious process. Bobby Kennedy was disturbed that State was not assuming its proper foreign-policy leadership role. This was especially true overseas. It was not an infrequent occurrence that when an ambassador wanted to see a foreign head of state, he would ask the CIA chief of station or the military attaché to make the necessary arrangements. Bobby Kennedy asked the State Department to establish an inter-agency departmental seminar, in an effort to initiate a more cooperative attitude. Bobby once remarked, "How in the hell can you expect U.S. personnel to coordinate in the field when their bosses are not speaking to each other in Washington?"

To those engaged in intelligence, State was known as the home of "the gray ladies"—elderly, well-read career women who were regarded as the mainstay of headquarters intelligence, and the "Jewish lawyers"—scholarly experts in the fields of international law, politics, protocol, and languages. They were there when they were needed, but in between times they were preoccupied attending international conferences or writing exhaustive research papers and books on their specialties.

State was considered by most in Washington to be a reactionary organization rather than a viable, responsive, forward-looking department. Solutions to problems were sought by looking backward rather than forward. It was no surprise, therefore, that few new programs originated with State. The Kennedys began to bring new, bright young people to the White House to formulate new ideas and approaches to foreign-policy problems.

A strong argument can also be made that the research and analysis elements of the intelligence community were not structured to handle events of the magnitude of the Cuban missile crisis. There were three groups of analysts at work within the intelligence community on separate but related problems. One group, concerned with Latin American affairs, was essentially focusing on the Cuban problem, the shipment of military equipment to Cuba, and its political repercussions in Latin America. The second group concentrated on the Soviet-Berlin problem, the Soviet threat to conclude a treaty with East Germany and to drive the Allied occupation forces from West Berlin. The third group dealt solely with Soviet strategic capabilities and created an estimate each year that dwelt solely on this subject. The preoccupation of each analysis group with its own problem, and the lack of coordination and interface between the groups, went largely unrecognized. There was a failure to realize that the problems were interrelated—that the solution of the Berlin problem might be related to developments in Cuba or that the Soviets might attempt to place missiles in Cuba to realign the balance of power.

Much of the analysis connecting the three areas was not accomplished until after the Cuban missile crisis had begun. It should also be mentioned that the two most influential committees of the United States Intelligence Board—the Joint Atomic Energy Intelligence Committee (JAEIC) and the Guided Missiles Astronautics Intelligence Committee (GMAIC)—were not directly involved with the Cuban problem prior to the discovery of the missiles in Cuba. The Defensive Missile Working Group of GMAIC would be called in only when the SA-2 surface-to-air missile sites were found in Cuba.

In mid-August 1962, agents and refugees began reporting the sighting of missiles in Cuba with sizes and shapes resembling the SA-2. Reports of property seizures along the coast, and the evacuation of civilian personnel from those properties, began to increase. Convoys of surface-to-air-like missiles were being seen with frequency throughout the island. Reports of Russian military personnel in these areas also began to increase. Rechecks of photography in several of the reported areas did reveal Soviet-style tents and construction equipment but no SA-2 associated equipment or sites. The consensus of intelligence analysts was that the U.S. should anticipate SA-2 defensive-missile deployment. This pattern fit with what had been seen previously in Egypt, Syria, and Indonesia.

On August 22, 1962, CIA leaders decided that the president should be warned of the possible deployment of an SA-2 surface-to-air missile system in Cuba. "The speed and magnitude of this influx of Soviet personnel and equipment into a non-bloc country is unprecedented in Soviet military aid activities; clearly something new and different is taking place. As yet limited evidence suggests that present activities may include the augmentations of Cuba's air defense system, possibly including the establishment of surface-to-air missile sites or the setting up of facilities for electronic and communications intelligence."[32]

Soviet shipping to Cuba was under close scrutiny, and on August 18, the Soviet merchant ship *Sovetskaya Gavan* was photographed with four large crates on its deck. Center photogrammetrists subjected the photographs to careful analysis and provided detailed dimensions of the crates. The configuration of the crates and the dimensions led to the conclusion that the *Sovetskaya Gavan* was carrying four KOMAR guided missile patrol boats to Cuba. Subsequent analysis of the Soviet freighters *Divinoles* and the *Severoles* revealed that they were each carrying two KOMARs. There was little apparent reaction in the intelligence community because KOMARs previously had also been sent as part of military-aid packages to other nations.

When campaigning began in July for the fall congressional elections, only one fundamental issue seemed of vital concern to both parties—the U.S. economy. But by August, the issue had become Cuba, and the Kennedys were growing increasingly sensitive about Republican charges that the Kennedy administration was weak on Cuba.

The intelligence community watched with interest on August 27, 1962, when the Cuban minister for industry, Ernesto Che Guevara, arrived in Moscow for a six-day visit. He headed a delegation that included Emilio Aragones Navarro, head of the Cuban militia. They met with Premier Khrushchev, visited a number of military installations, and, according to Alekseyev, brought the corrected and final missile agreement to Moscow. On September 2, the Soviet news agency Tass published a joint Soviet-Cuban communiqué acknowledging that the USSR had agreed to send military aid to Cuba. The communiqué was brief and devoid of details: "During the stay in the USSR of Ernesto Guevara Serna and Emilio Aragones Navarro, views were exchanged in connection with the threats of aggressive imperialist quarters with regard to Cuba. In view of these threats, the government of the Cuban Republic addressed the Soviet government with a request for help by delivering armaments and sending technical specialists for training Cuban servicemen. The Soviet government attentively considered this request of the government of

Cuba and agreement was reached on this question. As long as the above-mentioned quarters continue to threaten Cuba, the Cuban Republic has every justification for taking necessary measures to insure its security and safeguard its sovereignty and independence, while all Cuba's true friends have every right to respond to this legitimate request."

The Soviet passenger ship *Gruziya* arrived in Havana on August 27, 1962. A barrage of publicity was unleashed by the reception given the Russian "technicians" transported to Cuba aboard the ship. Some of the photography of the reception reached the Center on August 29 and 30. I showed it to Lundahl and he asked us to study it for "anything suspicious." The photographs were carefully analyzed both by photo interpreters and photogrammetrists. The "technicians" were young, a large percentage of them carried 35mm cameras, and several appeared to be Orientals. This might account for the reporting of "mongol" and Chinese troops in Cuba. None wore military uniforms or carried weapons. Five more such ships would arrive in the next ten days. Tass announced that they were transporting Soviet agricultural technicians as well as Cuban students who had studied in the Soviet Union. Estimates of the number of personnel on each ship varied from 350 to 1,000. The intelligence community thought the "number of arrivals as not less than 1,500." McCone would later testify: "We knew that the true figure [of Soviet personnel] could be considerably higher, but there was no way at that time to estimate the upper limit of the arrivals." By September 19, there were thought to be at least 4,000 Soviet personnel in Cuba. Most of the ships had unloaded at Mariel. Later, it was determined that some 8,000 to 9,000 Soviet troops had been unloaded during this period. Reports received from friendly nations and from newspaper correspondents indicated that hundreds of Russian troops in fatigues had been seen in Havana and also in seemingly endless convoys along Cuba's main highways. Many of the convoys appeared to be going to Torrens. Hundreds of young Russian men also had been observed in Havana, sightseeing, in cotton checked shirts and cheap trousers. Still, the intelligence community continued to carry a low estimate of the number of Soviet troops in Cuba.

At a press conference on August 29, President Kennedy was questioned about Senator Capehart's claim that Soviet troops were in

Cuba. The president replied that the United States had no evidence of Soviet troops in Cuba, but he cautiously added, "We are continuing to watch what happens in Cuba with the closest attention and will respond to—will be glad to announce any new information, if it should come, immediately."[33] Another reporter contradicted the president. He said, "Some of us were told at the State Department the other day that there were military personnel in Cuba, that these are military technicians and are the people who are probably going to operate missiles, similar to the Nike missiles. Is this in accord—"[34] The president, obviously annoyed, cut off the reporter, answering, "I don't know who told you that at the State Department, that they're going to operate missiles, because that information we do not have at this time. There certainly are technicians there. They may be military technicians. We do not have complete information about what's going on in Cuba, but in the sense that troops—the word *troops* is generally used—they've had a military advisory commission there for a long period of time, so there may be additional advisory personnel there or technicians. But on the question of troops, as it's generally understood, we do not have evidence that there are Russian troops there. There is an expanded advisory and technical mission."[35] When asked whether any anti-aircraft missiles had been shipped to Cuba, the president cautiously answered, "We have no information as yet. That doesn't mean that there haven't been, but all I am saying is that we have no such information as yet."[36]

In forming opinions, people seldom see the whole character of a president. The picture that emerged about President Kennedy was that he enjoyed meeting and jousting with the press. But the president was extremely sensitive to what was said and printed. This was especially true with respect to Cuba. There was a certain doubt, a pessimism that might be attributed to Yankee skepticism. But it could also be characterized as a tinge of irresponsibility and a restrained animosity if the press made him look bad. After the August 29 press conference, the president, who was extremely irritated by his poor responses to the reporters' questions regarding SAMs, asked Secretary Rusk and deputy CIA director Carter if either of them was withholding information from him. Carter, somewhat concerned and embarrassed, ordered Lundahl to review all previous aerial photography of Cuba. The review failed to reveal any SA-2 sites under construction. When informed of the result of the search, President Kennedy directed both Rusk and Carter that "in the future, any son of a bitch with any 'gut evidence' is to be kept within the intelligence community and away from the press and any hard evidence be reported to me immediately. Is that understood?"

The heavy influx of Russians into Cuba, of course, was distressing to the Kennedy administration. The Russians and Cubans stoutly maintained that only Soviet "technicians" were being sent to Cuba. They supposedly were experts in soil cultivation, irrigation, sugarcane growing, rice harvesting, and animal husbandry. They also, supposedly, were technicians training Cubans in the maintenance of the trucks, tractors, farm machinery, and industrial equipment that the Soviets had sent to Cuba. There was also the higher level of technicians—the economists, bureaucrats, political theorists, and teachers required to change the Cuban economy from one oriented toward capitalism to one oriented to communism. But the reporting, especially from Mexico, was indicating strongly that the Russians coming to Cuba were military troops. Luis Botifoll, a prominent Cuban exile, gave the following information to the American embassy: "The Soviet military presence in Cuba was a fact, and that among the thousands of Soviet technicians who recently arrived on the island, many appeared to be between eighteen and twenty years of age, too young to have had time to acquire any technical experience to impart to the Cubans." According to Botifoll, "these young Russians dress in sports clothes but give the appearance of having only recently completed their military training."[37] Another Cuban exile, Carlos Marquez, reported that at least twelve thousand Soviet soldiers had landed in the Cuban ports of Havana, Nipe, and Mariel.

Although not specifically acknowledged by the Cubans, Russian diplomats were justifying the presence of Russian technicians in Cuba by pointing to the migration of Cuba's professionals to the United States. The Soviets also accused those who had defected to the U.S. of absconding with funds and with gross mismanagement in Cuba. The fact that many of Cuba's former trading partners were now boycotting trade with Cuba was also cited as a reason why an augmented level of Russian help was needed. The Russians pointed with pride, for example, to the Esso oil refinery in Havana, which had originally been built to refine Venezuelan crude oil and now had been redesigned to handle the heavier Soviet crudes.

On August 29, 1962, a U-2 was dispatched to photograph the entire island of Cuba. The mission would be a milestone in the Cuban missile crisis. Although the flight covered the entire island, clouds obscured most of the eastern portion. But observations in the clear areas triggered alert mechanisms throughout the intelligence community. As one analyst stated after viewing the results of the mission, "The sirens were on and the red lights were flashing."

Within minutes after the film was placed on a light table, a Center photo interpreter assigned to the mission scan team shouted, "I've got a SAM site." Excitement spread, and other photo interpreters gathered around him to look at his find. There were subsequent shouts, and before the day was over, eight SAM sites in various stages of construction were found in western Cuba.

The SAM sites were located along Cuba's northern coast, at Bahía Honda, Havana, La Coloma, Mariel, Matanzas, San Julián, Cienfuegos, Santa Lucía, and Santa Cruz del Norte. A SAM assembly area was discovered near Santiago de las Vegas. The geographic placement of these sites was designed to provide a strategic area defense of the entire island rather than for the protection of specific key military installations.

Much would be written later that the sites had been placed in a trapezoidal manner to prevent detection of the emplacement of MRBM and IRBM sites. This simply was not true, as evidenced by the placement of the sites. Later, there were seven SAM support facilities located among the sites, designed to provide the logistical and repair support for the entire SAM network. The SAM sites were configured in the usual six launch positions encircling a central guidance area that we had become so familiar with, not only in Russia but in other areas of the world. In most cases, the sites were joined by an interconnecting road network, creating the familiar "Star of David" pattern. Photo interpretation and mensuration analysis, along with electronic radiation signals intercepted later, indicated that the latest guidance radar, the Fruit Set (model C), was being deployed at the sites.

A complete recheck of defector, refugee, and agent reports on the areas of SAM deployment confirmed humint reporting of tents, construction activity, military vehicles, and land expropriation. Many of these reports also had revealed the presence of Soviets at the sites. This accurate reporting prompted a close check of all other such suspect locations and the marking of maps for subsequent photo-reconnaissance missions.

All of us at the Center were convinced that something extraordinary was happening, involving an exceptionally large amount of Soviet military hardware and manpower, and that additional SA-2 sites would probably be found on subsequent missions. We also searched the photography for evidence of the KOMAR guided-missile patrol boats in the port of Mariel, since the U.S. Navy had spotted one at sea near the port on August 29. We found thirteen PT boats moored at piers north and south of Mariel airfield. Seven of the thirteen boats were KOMAR-class guided-missile boats and another was possibly being converted—the missile tubes were being installed.*

When Mr. McCone was briefed on the finds of the mission, he admonished contemptuously, "They're not putting them [the SA-2 sites] in to protect the cane cutters. They're putting them in to blind our reconnaissance eye."

Although the SAM missile launchers and radars were revetted, McCone quickly noted on the map we had provided that all the SAM sites were located near the coast, vulnerable to a knockout attack by low-flying bomber or fighter aircraft. He would subsequently seek evaluations from the Defense Department on the difficulty of striking the sites. The DOD report verified that the radar and the missiles were extremely vulnerable to both rocket and bombing attack.

When Cline was briefed on the mission finds, he asked that Bill Harvey, chief of Task Force W, also be informed so that covert personnel would be aware of and could concentrate on collecting information on the newly found sites. Harvey was briefed by Lundahl and William Tidwell, an assistant to Cline. He responded quickly that McGeorge Bundy and the president should also be briefed as

* On September 7, a presidential memo to the secretary of the Navy directed: "I would like to get a report on the ability of our destroyers to deal effectively with the new motor torpedo boats of the KOMAR class that the Cubans now possess."

soon as possible. Cline had already called Bundy to remind him of the president's expressed wish a few days before that he be promptly told of any SAM sites that were found.

Bundy said that the president would not be available that afternoon because he was preparing to fly to the Quonset Naval Air Station to meet his wife and children, who had returned from a month-long vacation in Italy. Recuperating from the death of their newborn son, Patrick, Jackie had visited her sister, Lee, and Lee's husband, Stanislas Radziwill, at Villa Episcopio in Ravello.

Bundy told Cline that Attorney General Bobby Kennedy was available, however, and might like to hear the briefing, since he would be seeing the president later that evening in Rhode Island.

On August 31, at 4 P.M., Lundahl, Tidwell, and Harvey waited outside the attorney general's office. After the group was ushered into Kennedy's office, Harvey made a brief introductory statement and turned the briefing over to Lundahl. Lundahl laid out the photographs and maps on Kennedy's desk and summarized the developments in Cuba. He pointed to the deployment patterns of the SA-2 sites and indicated that we would probably be seeing more. He then showed Kennedy the photo of the port of Mariel with seven KOMAR guided-missile patrol boats, explaining their function and mission in a sketch included on the briefing board.

Photography was an ideal medium for conveying information to someone with Bobby's forceful views and convictions. He was extremely interested, asked many questions, said he wanted to be kept up-to-date, and promised that the intelligence would be conveyed to the president that evening. Kennedy had attempted to take notes on the finds, but Lundahl provided him with a résumé of the information that I had prepared. Kennedy reiterated again that he and/or the president would want to see any further evidence of the military buildup. The briefing lasted about an hour, and Lundahl noticed that there was a chill between Kennedy and Harvey—that Kennedy avoided speaking to Harvey directly and that Harvey avoided eye contact with Kennedy.

This was Lundahl's first briefing of the attorney general, and he remembered him as being "a very sharp fellow, very perceptive, full of good questions. He didn't like long, involved answers. He cut through any wandering conversations and got right up to the things he wanted to know. In other words, when he heard the things he wanted to hear, he soaked it up like a blotter. But when you wandered off, he would jerk you back quickly to the subject in which he was interested."

Kennedy gave the summary of information that Lundahl had left to Nicholas deB. Katzenbach, a deputy attorney general, to draft a warning statement to be issued later by the White House.

According to Arthur Schlesinger, when the attorney general saw the draft, he recommended "stiffening it with an explicit statement that we would not tolerate the import of offensive weapons." The draft was revised and, in final, read, "while we had no evidence of significant offensive capability either in Cuban hands or under Soviet direction, should it be otherwise, the gravest issues would arise."[38] Bobby confronted Dobrynin about the SAMs, only to be assured that "the military buildup in Cuba was not of any significance."

The finding of the SAM sites brought the United States Intelligence Board into play, and Norman Smith, a defensive-missile specialist in the Agency's Office of Scientific Intelligence, came to the Center daily and began writing reports for the Board and the Office of National Estimates. Norm and other CIA analysts concluded that construction of the SAM sites was proceeding on a crash basis and some of them could be operational within two weeks. The report also stated that the Soviet shipment of military supplies showed no sign of letting up.[39]

At 2 P.M. on August 30, a U.S. Navy S2F Grumman antisubmarine search-and-attack bomber manned by three reservists on a training mission was fired on by two Cuban patrol craft of the GC-107 class. The aircraft, based at Florida's Boca Chica Naval Air Station, was over international waters, some fifteen nautical miles off the Cuban port of Cárdenas, when attacked. The reservists were from naval air units assigned to Andrews Air Force Base, outside Washington.

When the Defense Department flashed the report to the White House and thence to the president at Newport, the president was skeptical that the flight was a reserve-training mission. Knowing that an all-out electronic intelligence (elint) effort against the SAMs was being pressed and that the crew was from Washington, the president asked for verification of the flight plan. When told it was indeed a training flight, the president blasted, "What in the hell are reservists doing training so close to Cuba?" It was the last straw in a seemingly unending round of frustrations for the dispirited Kennedy. He then added sarcastically, "Have we run out of training space in the United States?"

Because of Republican attacks on the administration's Cuba policy and the demand of ranking Democrats in the Senate calling for a response, the president asked that before news of the incident was released to the press, a protest be drafted and presented to the Cubans. The protest sent to the American embassy in Bern was delivered to the Cuban government through the Swiss embassy in Havana on September 1. It was sharply phrased: "In any such incident in the future where United States aircraft or naval vessels are fired upon in or over international waters while in peaceful performance of their duties, the United States Armed Forces will employ all means necessary for their own protection and will assure their free use of such waters."[40] When questioned by reporters about the statement, Press Secretary Pierre Salinger said it meant that the Cubans had better not fire on any unit of the United States Armed Forces in the future or it would face the consequences. Fidel Castro answered the U.S. note with one of his own. He said, "We categorically affirm that this report by the United States Government is totally untrue. The incident in question is pure fabrication—a method in which Yankee policy is very experienced." He added: "In no case has Cuba answered provocation with provocation. Our rights have been violated hundreds of times and always, without exception, our reply has been a public protest and a denunciation before international bodies and world opinion."[41]

On August 30, 1962, a U-2 on an air-sampling mission intruded into Soviet airspace over the southern end of Sakhalin Island, just north of Japan. The pilot had been navigating on a wrong star. The Soviets waited until September 4 to protest. In a strongly worded note, they asserted that the U-2 had entered the airspace of the Soviet Union in the Far East, at a point sixty-five kilometers east of the town of Yuzhno-Sakhalinsk, overflying Soviet territory and territorial waters for nine minutes. The time given was 7:21 P.M. Moscow time (2:21 A.M. Washington time). This intrusion, the note stated, was a

"gross violation" of the Soviet frontier that was "obviously provocative in nature." The note repeated previous threats of retaliatory
action, including the destruction of bases of other nations used by
the United States to stage flights over the Soviet Union. Britain, West
Germany, Turkey, and Japan were named as countries where the
U-2 had again appeared since the 1960 Powers U-2 incident.

The Soviet note was carefully timed on the eve of a meeting of
the United Nations General Assembly. The vehemence of the protest,
together with the timing, was apparently an attempt to distract attention from the Soviets' growing involvement in Cuba. Another
obvious intent of the protest was to create uneasiness in countries
that permitted the United States to station U-2's on their territories.

In contrast to the initial reaction to the downing of the Powers
U-2, the United States replied to the Soviet protest by admitting that
"an unintentional violation may in fact have taken place." The note
went on to state that the pilot had "encountered severe winds during
his nighttime flight. If the pilot of the aircraft in question did in fact
violate Soviet territory, this act was entirely unintentional and due
solely to a navigational error under extremely difficult flying conditions." The note reiterated that there had been no change in the
ban of U-2 flights over the Soviet Union, a policy that had been
reaffirmed by President Kennedy on January 25, 1961.

The Russians vigorously rejected the explanation offered in the
U.S. note. They called the explanation that the U-2 may have been
blown off course by high winds a clumsy subterfuge "unworthy of
responsible politicians." In the propaganda effort that followed, the
Russians attempted to link the incursion with Powers's U-2 flight,
and they indicated that they were determined to apply additional
pressure to get a more apologetic statement from the United States
than that which had been submitted by the State Department.

President Kennedy was acutely aware of the off-year congressional
elections just two months away. It is an axiom that many of the
biggest problems a president must resolve are, themselves, the products of earlier decisions or solutions that he, and other presidents,
thought had been resolved. Cuba was such a problem. After the Bay
of Pigs fiasco and the subsequent Russian arms buildup in Cuba,
Kennedy had little room to criticize the Eisenhower administration
or the Republicans for their handling of the "Cuban problem," as

he had during the 1960 election. The raw material of politics and policies is reality. To the adversary belongs the right to criticize and/or philosophize on things as they would like them to be or think they should be. There was no need for the opposition to have an explanation or solution. This right to criticize is expounded during an election year and the year 1962 would prove to be no exception. The Republicans felt that Kennedy was vulnerable on Cuba and that Kennedy knew it.

A certain public disenchantment regarding Kennedy's handling of the "Cuban problem" was also evident. Charges that Kennedy was "soft on Communism and Castro" and that he was pursuing a "do-nothing" policy with regard to the Russians had been heard in the halls of Congress and was now being heard on the campaign trail and written about in the press. Some of the leaders in the Democratic party were even beginning to question Kennedy's courage. While the more influential Democratic senators were not ready to speak out publicly, their attitude on Kennedy's handling of the "Cuban problem" was increasingly unsympathetic. In an intelligence briefing of Senator Richard Russell on Cuba, Russell asked McCone, "When is the president going to get off his ass and do something?"

The president was pressed by powerful senatorial critics to enforce the Monroe Doctrine in the Cuban situation. It was generally felt by the administration that the presence of Soviet arms and technicians did not constitute a violation of the Doctrine, but at his news conference on September 2, the president stated that as far as he was concerned, the Monroe Doctrine still applied to Cuba. Still, he said that the U.S. government had no plans to invade Cuba.

Preconceptions and intuitive gut feelings were rampant throughout the government, but warning intelligence must be based on fact or indications. To the opposition, it appeared that the president had accepted the status quo in Cuba and there were only feeble efforts to alter the accomplished fact of Castro's Communist Cuba. Statements from the administration seemed to imply that it did not wish to intervene in Cuba again and that Kennedy would not challenge the Soviets' arms aid.

The Republicans knew that Kennedy was a shrewd politician and that in this election year he would seek to obviate the Republican charges on Cuba. Barbed Republican criticism of Kennedy, however, and his inadequate measures to deal with the "Cuban problem" were, as Senator Barry Goldwater termed it, beginning to draw blood. In a conversation later, Goldwater stated that he had warned a number of his fellow Republicans to be careful lest Kennedy do something before the election to pull the rug out from under them. Goldwater reiterated that he didn't trust either of the Kennedys and that a stunt of that type was characteristic of them, since they would do almost anything to win an election.

Running for reelection in 1962, Senator Homer Capehart spoke to a GOP meeting in Rockville, Indiana, on August 27 and said that the three to five thousand Soviet personnel in Cuba were not technicians but combat troops and that the president knew this. He chided the president that the Russians were pouring men and equipment into Cuba and the president was doing nothing about it. "How long will the president examine the situation? . . . Until the hundreds of Russian troops will grow into hundreds of thousands? . . . Until the little Cuban military force grows into a big Russian force? Whatever happened to the Monroe Doctrine? What the Russians are doing now and have been doing for many months has been in violation of that same Monroe Doctrine adopted in 1823. Never before have we allowed it to be violated."[42] Senator Capehart proposed that the United States invade Cuba. It was the boldest move yet advanced by the Republican opposition.

The Kennedy administration came to look upon Senator Capehart with loathing, a loathing he assiduously returned. Bobby would contemptuously refer to Senator Capehart as "the clod," and fomented a campaign to discredit him in favor of his young Democratic opponent, Birch Bayh.

Determined to make inroads into the Democratic congressional majority, the Republican leadership met on August 31 and set the theme for the upcoming campaign. The Republicans would assail the administration's foreign policy as being one of making concession to and retreat from that of the Russians. Senator Everett Dirksen, the GOP leader and principal spokesman, stated that by every standard, the administration's record in foreign affairs "has shown lack of understanding and initiative, the absence of an overall policy, and a tendency toward concession rather than standing on principal."[43] The Berlin Wall, the Russian shipment of military equipment to Cuba and Vietnam, and the situation in Laos were cited as failures of the Kennedy administration.

Then, on August 31, 1962, the day Bobby Kennedy was briefed on the SA-2 sites in Cuba, Senator Kenneth Keating of New York made the following startling announcement from the floor of the Senate: "I am reliably informed that between August 3 and August 15 at the Cuban port of Mariel, ten to twelve large Soviet vessels anchored at the former Marante docks. The dock area previously had been surrounded by construction of a high cinder-block wall. The Soviet ships unloaded 1,200 troops. I call these men troops, not technicians. They were wearing Soviet fatigue uniforms.

"Through August 13, five torpedo boats have been unloaded and now are moored at nearby La Base. There is every indication that the naval complement to handle these disembarked at the same time. Again let me emphasize that these men could not reasonably be called technicians. What are the Soviets planning to do with their new island fortress? What are they going to build with all this equipment?"[44]

We were tasked to scan available aerial photography and validate, if possible, Senator Keating's statement. We concurred that the Russians had indeed unloaded their vessels at the former Marante docks and that the immediate dock area had been surrounded by a high cinder-block wall. The torpedo boats referred to were identified as the KOMAR guided-missile boats (there were actually seven) moored at the former U.S. naval air station. The twelve hundred troops referred to was consistent with the number of Soviet-type tents recently seen in Cuba on aerial photography.

Senator Keating elaborated further on the Soviet "technicians." "Again let me emphasize that these could not reasonably be called technicians. On August 13, 1,000 non-Cuban personnel in fatigue uniforms were seen working in the area near Finca la Guatana, in all probability on or near a missile base located in that area.

"On August 3, a large convoy of military vehicles manned by Soviet personnel was observed on the highway in Las Villas Province. The convoy moved in military order and contained the first amphibious vehicles observed in Cuba; also jeeps, 6×6 trucks, and tracked trucks.

"On August 5, there was a movement seen of 64-vehicle convoy heading west on Carretera Central. The convoy was moving in military order. It included tanks, cannon-like trailers, and flatbed trailers.

"On August 8, there was observed a night movement of convoy on Carretera Central. Flatbed trucks were observed transporting concave metal structures supported by tubing. The convoy included a number of closed vans. The convoy appeared to be moving toward an installation 4 to 5 kilometers from Canimar in a closely restricted area believed to contain a rocket installation. There have been other observations of activities here, which have been confirmed."[45]

The convoys, the numbers and types of vehicles—closed vans (probably electronic and shop vans), cannonlike trailers (probably SA-2 transporters), metal structures supported by tubing (probably SA-2 launchers)—the direction of transit along Cuba's main highways, and the number of personnel involved were consistent with the known equipment and mode of transport and deployment of the SA-2. In some of the areas cited by Keating, SA-2 sites were found later.

Pravda noted on September 3 that "threats of the aggressive imperialist circles" had forced the Cubans to appeal to the Soviet government for armaments and the technical specialists necessary to train Cuban servicemen. A picture accompanying the article showed four hundred Cubans in military dress arriving in Odessa for training. It was assumed that these were the men who would be trained to operate the SA-2's.

The first Democrat to openly break ranks with the president was his longtime friend Senator George A. Smathers of Florida, who, on September 2, proposed that Cuba be invaded by a U.S.-sponsored military organization made up of Western Hemisphere nations. The president was furious. He phoned Smathers but Smathers held his ground, telling Kennedy that he had to take some positive action during this election year.

In his weekly letter to his constituents, also on September 2, Senator Strom Thurmond of South Carolina called for a U.S. invasion of Cuba. The longer it is postponed, the more difficult it will become, he maintained.

On September 3, Senator Keating resumed his attack on President Kennedy, asking that an inter-American mission be sent to Cuba to determine whether missile bases were being constructed. He wanted the whole question of Soviet arms deliveries to Cuba to be debated in the Organization of American States.

Senator Alexander Wiley of Wisconsin proposed that Cuba be blockaded by an inter-American "peace fleet" to keep Cuba from receiving military supplies.

Senator John Tower of Texas characterized U.S. policy with respect to Cuba and the USSR as one of "massive appeasement."

House Republican whip Leslie Arends of Illinois advocated enforcing the Monroe Doctrine and demanding that the Russians leave Cuba. He was careful, however, not to offer any proposals as to how this could be accomplished.

"Trigger-happy senators and congressmen have been whipping up anti-Cuban hysteria," Moscow lashed out. "The Neanderthal wing of the Republican party and others of this ilk are screaming that the people of Cuba, seven million strong, have aggressive plans against the United States. These arguments are ridiculous as they are cynical."[46]

Finally, on September 4, Pierre Salinger grimly read to White House correspondents the definitive statement by President Kennedy on Cuba. Salinger refused to answer any questions:

"All Americans, as well as all of our friends in this Hemisphere, have been concerned over the recent moves of the Soviet Union to bolster the military power of the Castro regime in Cuba. Information has reached this Government in the last four days from a variety of sources which established without a doubt that the Soviets have provided the Cuban Government with a number of anti-aircraft defense missiles with a slant range of twenty-five miles which are similar to early models of our Nike. Along with these missiles, the Soviets are apparently providing the extensive radar and other electronic equipment which is required for their operation. We can also confirm the presence of several Soviet-made motor torpedo boats carrying ship-to-ship guided missiles having a range of 15 miles. The number of Soviet military technicians now known to be in Cuba or en route—approximately 3,500—is consistent with assistance in setting up and learning to use this equipment. As I stated last week, we shall continue to make information available as fast as it is obtained and properly verified.

"There is no evidence of any organized combat force in Cuba from any Soviet Bloc country; of military bases provided in Russia; of a violation of the 1934 treaty relating to Guantánamo; or the presence of offensive ground-to-ground missiles; or of other significant offensive capability either in Cuban hands or under Soviet direction and guidance. Were it to be otherwise the gravest issues would arise.

"The Cuban question must be considered as part of the world-wide challenge posed by Communist threats to the peace. It must be dealt with as a part of that larger issue as well as in the context of the special relationships which have long characterized the inter-American system.

"It continues to be the policy of the United States that the Castro regime will not be allowed to export its aggressive purposes by force or the threat of force. It will be prevented by whatever means may be necessary from taking action against any part of the Western Hemisphere. The United States in conjunction with other Hemisphere countries, will make sure that while increased Cuban armaments will be a heavy burden to the unhappy people of Cuba themselves, they will be nothing more."[47]

The president had drawn a sharp distinction between offensive and defensive missiles, but the warning came too late. The Soviet ships *Omsk* and *Poltava*, carrying the first MRBM missiles, were on their way from Russia. On September 4, the Soviets would resort to the next step in their *maskirovka* scheme—the outright lie. That morning, Soviet ambassador Dobrynin sought out Robert Kennedy and perpetrated two outright lies. Dobrynin said he had received instructions from Khrushchev to assure President Kennedy that there would be no ground-to-ground missiles or offensive weapons placed in Cuba. Dobrynin also added that Bobby could assure the president that the military buildup was not of any significance. This despite the fact that U.S. estimates indicated the Soviets had shipped over $1 billion worth of military equipment to Cuba. Kennedy warned Dobrynin that the buildup was being carefully watched and it would be of the gravest consequence should the Russians place offensive missiles in Cuba. Kennedy was again assured by Dobrynin that it would never happen.[48]

Although Kennedy reported his conversation with Dobrynin to the president, Secretary of State Rusk, and Secretary of Defense McNamara, it never reached down to the intelligence community.

Those of us involved in U-2 mission planning were well aware of the danger of sending U-2's over defended territory. The vulnerability of the U-2 to the SA-2's had been dramatically substantiated by the loss of Powers's aircraft over the Soviet Union. The planners were also aware that in the event of a U-2 shootdown, the administration would have to justify the mission in terms of national security and the highest priority intelligence needs. There would be no phony excuse this time. James Q. Reber, the COMOR chairman, prepared a memo to that effect, which was forwarded to McCone and the president.

Although the Air Defense Working Group of GMAIC had been brought into the picture, they provided little intelligence or focus on the SA-2 problem. The Soviet SAM sites found on the August 29 U-2 mission over Cuba presented a second problem for flight planners. It was important to learn whether the Soviets had engaged in a limited deployment of SA-2 missile sites or whether an island-wide defense was being initiated, as we had presumed. There was also discussion at the higher echelons of the government about the possible transfer of U-2 flights from the CIA to the Strategic Air Command.

A U-2 mission was proposed for September 5. At the Center, we drew a map showing the cloud-covered portions of the August 29 mission. The September 5 mission would be designed to cover those areas hidden before—the central and eastern portions of the island. The U-2 made landfall about 100 nautical miles east of Havana, avoiding all of the SAMs found under construction on August 29. The flight plan would send the U-2 directly over the airfield at Santa Clara and then crisscross the easternmost part of the island several times, photographing Guantánamo, Santiago de Cuba, the Sierra Maestra Mountains, and the coastline. The missions were being flown out of Edwards Air Force Base in California, and by the time the U-2 reached Cuba, heavy clouds obscured most of the island. In the clear areas of the mission along Cuba's northeast coast, we found three new SAM sites—spaced in an almost equidistant pattern. These SAMs, along with the eight discovered previously, confirmed the fact that an island-wide defense network was being deployed.

At the Santa Clara (Camilio Cienfuegos) airfield, a MiG-21 Fishbed fighter aircraft and four Fishbed fuselage shipping crates were identified. The Fishbed could reach altitudes of 60,000 feet and speeds of over 1,100 knots. On a zoom climb, the MiG-21 could reach over 70,000 feet and therefore was an additional threat to the U-2. (In the U-2 missions over the Soviet Union, Soviet flyers had tried such maneuvers many times but were always wide of the mark.) These delta-wing fighters were being assembled at a rapid rate, and by the time the Soviet MRBM missiles were discovered on October 14, forty MiG-21's had been assembled. The MiG-21 came equipped with the AA-2 Atoll air-to-air missile, which was similar to the U.S. Sidewinder.

When Cuban pilots first began their flight training in the Fishbeds, the type of maneuvers they were practicing indicated that they were still in preliminary stages but progressing in their ability to handle modern fighters. They were, however, far from attaining combat proficiency. The U.S. Navy, responding to directives from Gilpatric, transferred Squadron VF-41, consisting of twelve F-4B Phantom 2 fighters from Oceana, Virginia, to Key West, Florida. The Phantom, at the time, was the fastest and most versatile fighter aircraft in the world, and VF-41 Squadron comprised some of the best fighter pilots in the Navy.

The Republicans relentlessly kept up their attack on President Kennedy. On September 5, 1962, at a news conference prior to a GOP fund-raising luncheon in Takoma, Washington, Senator Barry Goldwater proposed that the U.S. resume U-2 flights over the Soviet Union. "I think a few U-2 flights would be rather revealing."[49] (Had there been U-2 flights over the Baltic and Black Sea ports, it would indeed have been revealing in tracking MRBMs destined for Cuba being loaded into the holds of Russian ships.)

Meanwhile, Khrushchev was attempting to create an atmosphere of normality in Moscow. The Soviet press began giving considerable space and attention to problems related to Soviet agriculture. Khrushchev, it was reported, had taken personal command of Soviet policy designed to increase agricultural production. To emphasize this point, on September 4, Khrushchev sent a lengthy memorandum to the presidium of the Communist party of the Soviet Union entitled "Urgent Questions for the Further Development of Agricultural Production." On September 10, Khrushchev followed with a note to the presidium entitled "On Reorganization of Party Leadership of Industry and Agriculture."[50]

Although Soviet farm production for 1962 was normal, it had been disappointing the previous three years. Khrushchev had toured the farm belts, alternating between threatening rampages and playing the fatherly expert dispensing advice and criticism. Senator Allen Ellender, for many years the chairman of the Senate Agricultural Committee, who had toured Russia extensively, directly questioned Khrushchev's knowledge of agriculture. When Khrushchev responded that the Soviets knew more about farming than the capitalists, Ellender countered, "Then why in the hell do you leave all your equipment out in the open to rust? You will never see an American farmer leaving his most precious equipment out in the weather."

In early September 1962, Khrushchev had gone for a rest at Gagri, his home on the shore of the Black Sea. A delegation of American power engineers, headed by Stewart L. Udall, secretary of the interior, had visited a number of Soviet hydroelectric power plants, viewed high-voltage transmission lines, and talked to power-engineering scientists in late August and early September. Khrushchev invited Mr. Udall to visit him at Gagri on September 6. Although Udall would report that Khrushchev appeared a bit tired, he had lost none of his bravado—bragging to Udall that the Soviet Union was ahead of the United States in the construction of hydroelectric power plants. There was considerable talk about Udall's visit to the Soviet Union but no references to international affairs. The talks, according to the Soviet press, "were held in a friendly atmosphere." Udall brought back little information of intelligence value.

In Washington, the discovery of the additional SA-2 sites dominated the Special Group meeting on September 6. Colonel Ralph Steakley gave a briefing on aircraft-reconnaissance flights about Cuba in an effort to monitor the Cuban electronics buildup. Specially equipped B-47's and F3D aircraft were thrown into the gap, along with specially equipped Navy Constellations and SAC U-2's configured to collect electronic data. All of these aircraft contained automatic scanning devices to acquire SA-2-related signals.

In the meantime, Soviet ambassador Dobrynin returned to the

theme that the Soviets would do nothing to disrupt the U.S. fall campaign. In conversations with Theodore Sorensen, Dobrynin said that he had informed Moscow of his talk with Sorensen on August 23 and of Sorensen's concern about the Cuban buildup. Dobrynin said that at the end of August, Khrushchev had directed Dobrynin to seek out and tell Sorensen that "nothing will be undertaken before the American Congressional elections that could complicate the international situation or aggravate the tension in the relations between our two countries."[51] Sorensen countered that Khrushchev's message was both hollow and tardy. Dobrynin, however, stuck by the premise that the Soviets "had done nothing new or extraordinary in Cuba"[52] and that the buildup was "defensive in nature and did not represent any threat to the security of the United States."[53]

4

The Soviet Buildup
in Cuba

"The president was pissed."
—Major General Marshall "Pat" Carter

THE SA-2 SITES and the KOMAR guided-missile patrol boats were not the only significant discoveries on the August 29 U-2 mission. But the president would not learn of another startling discovery in Cuba until September 7. The reason for the delay was that a new missile site discovered near Banes did not resemble the familiar "signature" of Soviet SAM installations. After two days of detailed photo analysis, the Center identified the site as a "Possible Tactical SSM (surface-to-surface missile) Launch Site U/C" (under construction).

There were only two launch positions at the Banes site versus the usual six found at SA-2 sites. The launch positions were also different in configuration and arrangement. The SA-2 revetment is a drive-through one; those at Banes were not. To place a missile on the launcher at Banes, the transporter would have to be backed up to the launcher. The length of the missile transporters at Banes was about the same as that for the SA-2, but otherwise the transporters were entirely different. The Banes transporter was a "low-boy" type, with a unique humpback canvas cover rather than the sleek horizontal box of the SA-2. The Banes launcher was also different from that of the SA-2. It was slightly longer—38 feet instead of 28. The support or rectangular box effect seen under the SA-2 was not present at the Banes site. The flame deflector was trapezoidal, not rectangular as in the case of the SA-2. The Banes launcher consisted of two launching rails set 2.4 feet apart and it had side outriggers to stabilize the launcher. The base was supported by two axles (four wheels). In addition to the transporters and launchers, two Whiff-type radars were found, along with two generator vans. When the photo was shown to Lundahl, he was especially concerned about the launch rails. "Does it have a ski site appearance?" he asked. Lundahl was remembering the V-1 launch sites the Germans constructed during World War II. They had been referred to as ski-type launch sites. I pulled together all the information we had on the V-1 launch sites, but the photo interpreters, after reviewing the material, said that there was no correlation between the Banes site and the V-1 sites. Then Lundahl asked if we had seen any sites in the USSR resembling those in Cuba. Again, a review of all missile sites at the ranges and deployed sites in the USSR was made. Still, no direct correlation.* Lundahl asked if the site was directed toward the U.S. The answer was no.

The location of the site suggested a coastal-defense role, but the kind of a missile that would be fired from such a site and what its range would be was not determined. Since no missile had been found, the Banes site would become a high-priority target for continuing coverage. Roger Hilsman erroneously reported in his book that there was a "robot airplane with stubby wings" at the Banes site on the August 29 coverage.[1] Lundahl was under considerable pressure from the Defense Department to disseminate the information on the Banes site, but he deferred to his superior, Ray Cline. Because the president and his brother had shown such interest in new developments in Cuba, Cline asked that the information not be disseminated until the president had seen it and pressed Lundahl to complete his analysis as soon as possible. While a number of us favored the coastal-defense role, an equal number said they simply didn't know; therefore, Lundahl stuck with the title "Possible Tactical SSM Launch Site U/C." The missile for the

---

* There was a coastal missile installation at Balaklava but the launchers were protected by a massive concrete bunker.

Banes site would not be seen in Cuba until the coverage on September 29.

A meeting with the president was set for September 7. At 3:50 P.M., Secretary of State Rusk, Secretary of Defense McNamara, General Carter, Cline, Lundahl, and John McLauchlin, representing the Defense Intelligence Agency, were ushered into the Oval Office. The secretary of defense had asked John Hughes, a special assistant to the director of DIA, to attend, but Hughes was unavailable. John McLauchlin, Hughes's deputy, laughs when he recalls how a GS-12 represented the DOD at such a critical White House meeting. He felt ill at ease when he saw the nation's leaders' inquiring glances directed at him. He is sure they were wondering, Who in the hell is he? But no one asked.

The president was seated in his famous rocking chair, with McGeorge Bundy standing immediately to his left. General Carter told the president that detailed analysis of the August 29 U-2 photography over Cuba—in addition to providing data on the SA-2 sites and the KOMAR guided-missile patrol boats—had revealed a surface-to-surface missile site. He said that Cline and Lundahl would provide the details. Cline read a short prepared statement. He said that we knew little about the system, but analysts felt it was a defensive missile system that could be employed to repel an amphibious landing. He then asked Lundahl to describe the site. Lundahl removed the briefing board from a leather carrying case and handed it to the president. Lundahl looked over the top of the briefing board while explaining it to the president.

Lundahl said the site was near the town of Banes, in eastern Cuba, along its northern coast. It was three nautical miles inland but could cover seaward approaches to many of the beaches that were suitable for large-scale amphibious landings. Describing the site in detail, he said it contained revetted, inclined launchers with associated possible control revetments; canvas-covered missile transporters; Whiff-type radars; numerous vehicles and pieces of equipment; a tent area; and an open storage area. Lundahl said that we would probably see refinements at the site in the future. The president asked, "What, for example?" Lundahl replied, "Revetting of the major pieces of equipment and the missile itself." Lundahl hastened to add that the site might now be operational, with all the equipment present and properly emplaced, inasmuch as more than a week had elapsed since the August 29 coverage.

The president obviously was concerned primarily with whether the newly identified site was defensive or offensive in nature. Only three days earlier, he had informed the Russians that "the gravest issues would arise" if offensive weapons were introduced into Cuba. His anxiety was revealed when he pressed Lundahl on this possibility.

"How far will this thing shoot?" the president asked. Cline replied, "We think from twenty to forty nautical miles." The president seemed perturbed at such a wide divergence in range. Cline explained that based on an assessment of the radar's capability, a maximum range of forty miles was estimated. He said that the range was a function of the altitude of the site and the height of the surface target and the missile's radar.

The president was not satisfied with technical explanations. Lundahl explained that a key feature of such a system was the target illumination radar, which was not yet identified. Subsequent missions could refine the estimate, he explained.

The president, now more displeased, tried another tack. "Can it hit our ships at sea?"

Cline replied that it could if our ships came within range.

The president snapped, "That would make it an offensive weapon, wouldn't it?" Cline again explained that the site seemed designed to defend possible landing beaches. The president, growing impatient, said, "You've explained that before."

In an attempt to relate the weapon system to something within the president's frame of reference, Cline said that the missile could be compared to an unmanned guided kamikaze—that it had been evaluated to be a very effective weapon against naval vessels. Cline said, "It depends on how the missile is used; if it is fired at one of our sigint ships in international waters it is damned offensive. The weapon seemed to be capable of a dual purpose."

The president paused for a moment and reflected, obviously thinking of trying to explain the system to others. He asked, "Do we have something like that?"

McNamara replied, "No, we don't."

The president snapped, "Why in the hell don't we? How long have we known about this weapon?"

McNamara was flustered and did not respond. Cline, guessing, said, "For several years."

The president's face froze. He began to drum his fingers nervously and impatiently on the arms of the rocker. Lundahl knew that the quick, annoyed tapping betrayed his impatience and anxiety. "Damnit," the president said. "If that damn thing is in Cuba, we should know something about it."

General Carter, sensing that the president's questions and concern about the missile system would not be satisfied that day, stated that he hoped the president understood that he was only following the president's orders to report any new developments in Cuba to him personally and that the Banes site was such a development.

The president stood up and glared fiercely at General Carter and then muttered, almost to himself, "I do, but I don't want half-assed information." The president, obviously concerned about how he could act on such unevaluated information, said, "Go back and do your homework."

Carter was stung by the president's attitude and remark, and Cline stepped in, fearing that Carter might become argumentative. Cline said he understood the president's concern and that the CIA Office of Scientific Intelligence was conducting a search for information on the missile system and was also seeking advice from contract technical experts employed by the Agency and the Department of Defense. "We'll get our people together with those at Lundahl's Center," he promised.

The president listened impatiently. His brows were furrowed at a sharp angle; his face reddened; he was becoming visibly angry. His voice began to rise, "How sure are you that this is not an offensive weapon designed to strike targets in Florida?"

Lundahl explained that the site was located in the eastern part of Cuba with the launchers oriented eastward, away from the continental United States.

The president countered, "What do you know about this weapon?"

Somewhat embarrassed, Cline again said that we knew little about the system but felt that we had to report its deployment in Cuba.

The president snapped back, "I want no further reporting until the missile site has been completely evaluated and you can report back to me."

Secretary McNamara agreed and said that he would convey that message to DOD officials.

The president asked how widely the information would be disseminated. Lundahl replied that the Center's cables and reports were disseminated to a rather large number of intelligence organizations and military commands. Cline also indicated that multiple copies of the film and selected prints are normally made and routinely sent to military commands.

Still obviously angry, the president handed the briefing board back to Lundahl. Speaking to Carter and Cline, the president said, "We have to be very careful about any evidence of offensive weapons in Cuba. If such evidence is found, it must be kept very restricted and I want to be the first to know about it."

The president began a chopping motion with his right arm, emphasizing the need for security, and then his index finger shot out. Touching Cline's chest several times, his eyes glared fiercely, and he said scornfully, "If this information is in *The Washington Post* tomorrow, I'll fire both of you."

Still agitated, the president began to herd the group toward the door. Carter tarried and said, "Mr. President, we clearly understand your wishes in this matter. But just to make sure that we're all on the same wave length, may I say you do want us to know exactly what these things are so that we can report to you accurately?"

The president, considerably toned down, said, "By all means."

Carter continued, "Then in order to arrive at these conclusions, it certainly wouldn't be contrary to your wishes, or your order, that we, the analysts, talk back and forth with each other to compare our knowledge and winnow out our conclusions and to reject that which is inconsistent."

The president replied, "Most certainly not; that's exactly what I want to happen."

"I thought that's what you wanted," Carter said, "but others might have felt that each of us was to stay in isolation and try independently to arrive at a collectively agreed upon conclusion, which would have been hard to do."

The president then said, "No. Those people who need to know—those specialists, those experts who can talk to the photo interpreters, and with whom those photo interpreters can talk—can collectively arrive at a decision. That's what I want to happen."

General Carter paused at the door leading out of the Oval Office and looked back at the president. Cline grabbed his arm. Everyone had gotten the president's message.

Carter, Cline, and Lundahl left the White House about 5 P.M. Driving back to Langley, Carter rather ruefully said that it seemed every time McCone went out of town, some flap caught him on the bridge. Lundahl recalls: "Each person in the group was rather grimly convinced that we were dealing with a very serious situation and that it was going to take our very best efforts not only to satisfy the president but to satisfy the rest of the leadership in terms of what was really there."

Bundy later reported: "The president told General Carter that this information should not be included in intelligence publications pending more exact determination; he directed that no reports on weapons which might be offensive should be published without his approval."[2]

It was obvious that a special security system had to be invoked to ensure against any intelligence leaks or premature disclosures of offensive weapons in Cuba. The president had stated that it had to be "an ironclad system." Only those who must know should have access to such intelligence. Bundy remembered, "The president thought it important that no avoidable publicity should be given to reports which might turn out to be wrong, as has happened very often, before and after the Cuban crisis, in connection with Cuba. Given the obvious importance of the question and the intense interest surrounding it, the president was convinced that community-wide publication based on raw and unconfirmed reports on offensive weapons would greatly increase the danger of leaks which would add to the confusion surrounding the subject in the country."[3]

Lundahl and I have talked several times about the president's attitude. The president had come to rely heavily on aerial reconnaissance in making decisions, and in the past, the information had been presented in a succinct manner, not as an unknown as it had been in the case of Banes.

A great paradox existed in Washington. While there was no hard intelligence confirming the introduction of offensive missiles—and intelligence officers were confident that the Soviets would not be that irrational—most analysts were now sensitive to that possibility. All agreed that extraordinary precautions were to be taken should such information be confirmed.

When Carter returned to his Langley office, he was asked by an aide how the presidential briefing had gone. He answered, "The president was pissed!"

Carter called Huntington Sheldon, the CIA assistant deputy director for intelligence, into his office. Carter told him that as a result of a presidential directive, a security system had to be established that would absolutely safeguard the dissemination of highly sensitive information derived from the Cuban overflights should offensive missiles be found. Carter left it to Sheldon to determine how this should be accomplished. With that very broad and general directive, Sheldon proceeded to formulate the kind of system he thought would meet Carter's specifications. He could see immediately that an additional code word was needed to override all other code words to effectively implement what Sheldon called "monolithical" dissemination. Sheldon summoned security specialist Henry Thomas to his office and asked him to bring with him a list of available code names so that he might select one appropriate to the new control system. Working with Thomas, Sheldon chose the code word PSALM.

The sensitivity of information regarding offensive missiles in Cuba required that the special security system have extremely tight parameters. It didn't take Sheldon long to devise the system. The most sensitive decision that had to be made was who would have access to these materials and who would be responsible for clearing individuals to receive PSALM information. Sheldon prepared the implementation memorandum and took it to Carter. It was agreed that the plan would be discussed further with the United States Intelligence Board and approved by its members.

As usual, when a rigid security system such as this is adopted, there are always numerous complaints from individuals who feel their organization is being denied vital information. But because the system was established under USIB authority, and because the president's determination to keep such information tightly compartmented was known, the system was readily accepted by the intelligence community.

At the Center, Lundahl appointed Jack Gardner and me to work with Office of Scientific Intelligence offensive missile specialist Sidney Graybeal and defensive missile specialist Norman Smith on the Banes site.

The Banes site was situated on a hill with a commanding view of beaches and ports, suitable for large-scale amphibious operations. From existing maps and charts, the hilltop location was estimated to be 250 to 330 feet above sea level. This estimate was not sufficient for Lundahl, and he asked his photogrammetrists to compute the straight line of sight of the Banes site for elevations of 250, 300, and 330 feet above sea level. The photogrammetrists found that for a 250-foot elevation, the line-of-sight range would be 20.87 miles; for 300 feet, the range would be 22.86 miles; and for 330 feet, the range would be 23.98 miles.

Analysts at Langley also began to look at various possibilities for the Banes site: First, there was the SS-1—a destroyer-launched cruise antiship homing missile, using 30-foot-long launch rails; the SS-N-2—a KOMAR-class patrol-craft missile with inclined rails 25 to 30 feet long; and the SS-C-1—the "missile-in-a-bottle" first shown in the November 7, 1961, Moscow parade. The latter missile would be launched from an inclined ramp within a tube mounted on a large four-axle truck. None of these Soviet systems seemed to fit the Banes site.

Other intelligence analysts concentrated on the Whiff-type radar at the Banes site, which had not been seen deployed with any of the known Soviet surface-to-surface missile systems. Obviously, the radar was being used for target acquisition, and analysts looking at the radar concluded that the Banes missile would employ a radar beam-riding guidance with the terminal phase of the flight conducted by semiactive homing radar. Other analysts, however, expressed concern that if the missile had an inertial guidance system and a means of target acquisition, the range of the missile at the Banes site could be extended as far as 130 nautical miles. The beam-riding analysts prevailed.

Meanwhile, Gardner asked his photo interpreters to review again all of the Soviet missile test ranges and deployed sites. While this search was going on, Joe Seng, a photo interpreter specializing in nuclear sites, remembered a peculiar installation he had seen on U-2 photography of China. He pulled the film on the Lien-shan missile site and compared it with the Banes site. Although the Lien-shan site was a permanent installation, the spacings of the launchers and the radar at the two sites were remarkably similar. The Lien-shan site was also near the coast. A cruise missile that resembled a small MiG-15 fighter had been seen at the China site and this sent us scurrying for background files. We had previously noted the similarity of the MiG-15 to the Kennel AS-1 air-to-surface missile on photography. There were differences, however. The Kennel had a radome housing the receiving antenna atop the vertical stabilizer and a radome on the nose. The Kennel, of course, being a cruise missile, had no canopy. The Kennel was smaller, with an overall length of 27 feet, as compared to 33.4 feet for the MiG-15. The Kennel's wingspan was only 15.5 feet, as compared to 33.2 feet for the MiG. The leading edge wing sweepback for the Kennel was about 60 degrees, compared to the MiG's 36 degrees. The stall fence arrangement—two fences on each side—was seemingly the same for both.

The development of the Kennel was initially reported by German scientific returnees who had worked on a Soviet beam-rider guidance system called Komet. The missile was a product of the Mikoyan-Gurevich (MiG) design bureau and was developed originally to be used on the Bull bomber; it was later adapted for the Badger bomber. The Kennel was first shown to the Western world at the Leningrad Travel Air Show in July 1961. Launched from the Badger, it had ranges of 35 to about 55 nautical miles. Although the Kennel had not been seen before in a coastal-defense role, U.S. experts had now concluded that the Banes site was a cruise-missile site using a ground-launched Kennel-type missile with a range of about twenty-five miles. Both Cline and Carter were notified of the findings, and they made arrangements to see the president. (It was not until the January 3, 1963, parade in Havana that intelligence analysts saw close up the surface-to-surface version of the Kennel. In the meantime it had been given the designation SS-C-2 [Surface to Surface Coastal-2] and given the NATO code name "Samlet.")

On September 8, two Cuban MiG-17's made simulated firing runs over international waters at two U.S. Key West-based S2F Grumman antisubmarine search and naval attack bombers. The pilot of the bomber called for help, and two F4D Phantom fighters scrambled from Key West. Before they reached the S2F's, the MiG's had departed. When the president was informed of the incident, he said it was obvious that the defenses at Key West needed shoring up. When Vice-President Johnson was told of the incident, he said, "The next time they appear, shoot their asses out of the sky."

In Congress, Senator Everett Dirksen and Congressman Charles A. Halleck, the Republican minority Leaders, issued separate statements urging stronger U.S. policy toward Cuba. President Kennedy, on the afternoon of September 7, requested and received congressional authority to call up 150,000 reservists. Khrushchev and the Russians were surprised by the announcement. That evening in New York, Soviet ambassador Dobrynin sought out and assured U.S. ambassador to the UN Adlai Stevenson that only defensive weapons were being supplied to Cuba and that all this hysteria on the part of the U.S. government was unnecessary.

In the Soviet Union, the press turned its wrath on the president and the Congress and condemned what was called the growing military hysteria among U.S. politicians. The Russian press also belittled the U.S. reserve call-up, stating that modern weaponry negated the military significance of 150,000 reservists. Signed commentaries appeared in *Pravda* and *Izvestiya* pillorying President Kennedy and expressing support for the Cubans, charging that the call-up of reserves signaled that an "aggressive act was imminent." Other articles condemned the "anti-Cuban hysteria" in the U.S. but concluded that "all this ominous strength is without force behind the all-triumphant ideas which are being strengthened in Cuba." In the September 21 issue of *Red Star*, an article entitled "The Pentagon Rattles Sabers" heaped abuse on President Kennedy and denounced the Congress for granting the president the authority for mobilization of the reserve forces and for retaining personnel already on active duty. Lieutenant Colonel Gorin, the author of the article, belittled the U.S. for using the Cuban situation to initiate such drastic moves.

The Soviet press was also rampant with articles that encouraged the belief that the Soviet offensive and defensive forces were being brought to a high state of readiness. The Strategic Rocket Forces, the ground troops, the anti-aircraft defensive forces, and the navy, especially the submarine fleet—all were admonished to "be equal to their tasks" and to be ready to respond instantly to any aggression. "Duty, vigilance, and country" was repeated over and over. Many of the articles recalled the "glorious history" of the Soviet armed forces and stressed the need for precise execution of orders and instructions and "faultless discipline in all military personnel."

The drumfire of propaganda emphasized that the Soviets were in possession of awesome nuclear weapons of adequate quality and quantity, and prepared "to deliver crushing retaliatory blows against any aggressor that dared to unleash nuclear war." These same articles warned that it would be impossible for the U.S. to attack Cuba without punishment. "The foul schemes of the warmongers" must be brought down and the Soviets stood ready to render a "crushing blow to such imperialists."

Understandably, the U.S. intelligence community maintained a close watch on Soviet forces, using all available intelligence systems. Local troop exercising was observed, but there was little photographic evidence that unusual measures were being taken to bring Soviet forces to combat-readiness status.

Soviet propaganda grew more intensive and evolved into a full-fledged assault not only on the president and Congress but on the United States itself. U.S. foreign policy was characterized as having created a situation in which some kind of incident could develop into a catastrophe of world thermonuclear war. U.S. forces were portrayed as reckless and dangerous. U.S. troops in Guantánamo were reported firing on innocent Cuban civilians, and U.S. aircraft were said to be dangerously buzzing Soviet and Cuban ships. The Russians expended considerable effort to portray the U.S., and in particular the Pentagon, as having "aggressive designs in Cuba." Americans were admonished for failing to heed "the sensible voice of reason." The Pentagon was excoriated for increasing international tension and preparing to unleash a rocket-nuclear war against the socialist countries. In late September, the Soviet press admonished the U.S. government to "avoid action which could lead to war." Excerpts of articles from U.S. newspapers critical of the U.S. policy regarding Cuba were published in the Soviet press, along with stated opposition to U.S. policy by American officials, writers, and spokesmen. The Soviets were quick to reiterate any statement made any-where in the world that had an anti-American or pro-Castro tinge. There were articles expressing the readiness of the Soviet armed forces to render any necessary aid to Cuba. All these articles had a central theme: The Soviets were strong and the United States was weak.

During the September-October cocktail circuit, Soviet diplomats were buttonholing Western diplomats to pressure the United States to refrain from its warlike attitude. They were especially critical of the "Pentagon clique."

On Sunday, September 9, while a number of senior Agency officers concentrated on the Banes briefing and the president's testy reaction to it, other officers in the Agency's command center were following a Chinese Nationalist U-2 mission flying in clear weather deep over western China.* All appeared to be going well until the U-2 was approaching an important nuclear target. Suddenly, tracking of the U-2 ceased. Apprehension began to develop into fear both in Wash-ington and Taipei. Taipei later reported that the U-2 had failed to respond at an appointed time.

General Carter was notified that the U-2 was overdue and pre-sumed lost. Carter posted the White House and advised that Roger Hilsman, director of the State Department's Bureau of Intelligence and Research, be notified. Reached at home by telephone, Hilsman said that he was leaving immediately for his office and would like to be briefed as soon as possible.

CIA officers familiar with Chinese U-2 operations were dispatched to Hilsman's office. Obviously agitated, Hilsman asked a number of questions of the CIA officials. Had the U-2 been sold to the Chinese Nationalists? It had, by Lockheed. Who was the pilot? A Chinese Nationalist. How was it downed? Probably by a surface-to-air missile. Were there U.S. markings on the aircraft? No, it had Chinese Na-tionalist markings. Were there U.S. markings on the equipment? There were. Would the Chinese Nationalists assume responsibility for the mission? They would.

* Ray Cline, as CIA station chief in Taipei, had convinced President Kennedy to allow the Chinese Nationalists to fly the U-2 over Communist China. Although Allen Dulles expressed some reservations, he allowed Cline "to do the sales job" on the president.

Hilsman was certain that the Chinese Communists would protest vociferously that the U.S. was directly involved in these overflights. They undoubtedly would be supported by the Russians and by other Bloc nations. Hilsman's overwhelming concern was that the Chinese Communists would make the flight a cause célèbre, comparable to the Powers incident, to the profound embarrassment of the Kennedy administration.

Agency officials knew that the incident would generate renewed concern for the safety of the U-2's flying over Cuba and a call for a reassessment of the entire U-2 program. Plans for an all-out elint effort against Cuba and the jamming of the SA-2 Guideline radars were reviewed. The provision of armed fighter escorts would also have to be considered. Upon being notified of the loss of the Chinese Nationalist U-2, Bobby Kennedy's initial reaction was much the same as Hilsman's—an overwhelming concern for the effect on the president's image and the administration. He asked that not only the Chinese U-2 program but also the U.S. Cuban U-2 overflights be reviewed at the scheduled meeting of the Special Action Group on Monday, September 10. But late Sunday evening, a Peking radio broadcast reported the incident—not with a propaganda barrage but with a terse "A U.S.-made U-2 high-altitude reconnaissance plane of the Chiang Kai-shek gang was shot down this morning by an Air Force unit of the Chinese People's Liberation Army when it intruded over east China."

General Carter called Lundahl early on September 10 and said that the president would like a current briefing on aerial photographic systems for himself and General Eisenhower. General Eisenhower had recently returned from a six-week trip to Western Europe and had been invited to lunch by President Kennedy to discuss his trip and to be shown, in turn, the latest advances in photography and recent aerial photography of Cuba. Carter said he would meet Lundahl at the White House at 10 A.M., but the precise time of the presidential briefing was not set. President Kennedy had several items on the agenda for General Eisenhower, including a short tour of the White House to show him Mrs. Kennedy's remodeling project and the latest acquisitions of furniture and art.

The president was in an expansive mood. He enjoyed playing host to General Eisenhower. It was a father-son—or, as Lundahl would relate, a teacher-student—relationship. The president admired the general's role in World War II and all that he had done for his country as president. And now, as master of the grand mansion, Kennedy had the opportunity to play host to its previous occupant. President Kennedy had a warm smile and was making sweeping motions with his arms as he walked about the White House talking to General Eisenhower.

Carter was informed that the president would be lunching with General Eisenhower and that Carter, Lundahl, and his deputy, Col. David S. Parker, should have lunch at the White House dining room. Afterward, Lundahl set up his briefing materials on an easel in the Oval Office. Just before 2 P.M., President Kennedy and General Eisenhower came in. The president said to General Eisenhower, "You must certainly know these gentlemen?" General Eisenhower said that he did, shook hands with the briefers, and sat down at the president's right.

Carter made a few introductory remarks and then turned to Lundahl, who presented fifteen briefing boards on Soviet strategic industries and test centers. Lundahl had briefed President Kennedy numerous times and knew he liked opening remarks that gave him an immediate option on the presentation. The president reached into the humidor and took out a big black cigar and lit it. Senator Smathers had given him several boxes of Havanas and the president promptly had the bands removed and the cigars placed in the handsome silver humidor. Although he appeared to enjoy a good cigar, the president was not an adept smoker, often toying with and chewing on the cigar. He tried, however, not to be photographed with a cigar.

Part of Lundahl's presentation showed the improvements that had been made in the various photographic systems. General Eisenhower listened intently and asked questions about the systems in the research and development stages. He especially wanted to hear about the "big one, the very, very high-speed and high-flying aircraft [the SR-71]." General Carter gave Eisenhower the latest information on the progress of the program. The aircraft had made its maiden flight on April 26, 1962.[4]

President Kennedy, too, asked numerous questions. During the briefing, Lundahl was pleased to see the president smiling, delighted

with the general's questions and the answers given by the participants. The briefing lasted approximately forty minutes and all agreed
that the briefing was a success. General Carter, especially, felt relieved
and jokingly remarked, "At last, I can report some good news from
the White House to Mr. McCone." But Carter's elation would not
last long.

A Special Group meeting had been scheduled for September 10
in Bundy's office regarding aerial reconnaissance over Cuba. Carter
knew that Agency experts in U-2 reconnaissance were prepared to
fight for their existence, because both Rusk and Bundy were expected
to question, in depth, the further need for U-2 reconnaissance of
both China and Cuba. The meeting opened with an Agency review
of the reaction to the downing of the Chinese Nationalist U-2 the
day before. While the Chinese Communists condemned the "Chiang
Kai-shek clique" for the mission and linked the United States with
the overall reconnaissance efforts, they did not pursue an aggressive
propaganda campaign against the United States. We were later to
learn from Chinese Nationalist Air Force officials that had the Chinese
Communists attempted to make a cause célèbre of the incident, they
were prepared to release a number of aerial photos of Chinese nuclear
and missile installations to prove they had been flying over the mainland for years. Word of this plan was purposely leaked to known
Chinese Communist agents. The execution of this plan would have
been a distinct embarrassment to the Chinese Communists throughout the Far East, where the saving of face is of critical importance.
There was some surprise when the Russians reported the incident
in their press without comment. The severity of the ideological split
between Russia and Communist China was not fully appreciated at
the time. The U.S. policymakers were also pleasantly surprised that
the incident generated only token reaction from non-Communist
countries.

When the discussion turned to reconnaissance of Cuba, Carter
showed a map of the island depicting those areas that had not been
covered on the August 29 and September 5 missions and stated that
McCone would like to see those areas covered as soon as possible.
On McCone's orders, Carter asked the secretary of defense to consider
using tactical low-level reconnaissance against the highest-priority
target—the Banes missile site—and other targets along the coast that

would be suitable for such missions. The secretary of defense said he would consider the request. (Later, however, McNamara demurred, stating that he preferred the continued use of the U-2 against Cuba.)

Rusk and Bundy, however, immediately began to question the need to overfly Cuba with the U-2's. Were the intelligence objectives worth the inherent risks? Couldn't these objectives be met if the reconnaissance activities were carried out by peripheral flights utilizing oblique photography? Rusk's principal concern was that in the event a U-2 was downed by an SA-2 over Cuba, it would be the May 1960 Powers flight all over again and impact adversely on the presidency. Reconnaissance experts advised that the SA-2 missiles along the Cuban coast had a slant range of twenty-five miles, and it would be difficult to conduct reconnaissance of Cuba from that far out. Rusk felt a U-2 downed at sea was an entirely different question, but when the experts tried to point out the poor results that would be obtained from reconnaissance conducted twenty-five miles at sea, Rusk remarked, "Well, let's just give it a try." The same expert would later remark, "After all this time and the many photographs that had been shown to Secretary Rusk, I was surprised to see how stupid he was on reconnaissance."

There was obviously a great divergence of views among the Special Group members. Some held that the information derived from the U-2 flights was necessary to the national security and, therefore, the risk was justified. Others felt that if there were a U-2 shoot-down, U.S. public opinion would turn against the flights, with charges that such flights were illegal and immoral. All agreed, however, that should a U-2 be downed, the Soviets would exploit the propaganda value to the utmost.

Rusk was also determined not to entrust the handling of any downing of a U-2 to the CIA. Rusk had asked State to draft a contingency message that could be used in a future incident involving the U-2. He said that the explanation had to be convincing. When Bobby saw the draft, he was furious because it was almost a complete contradiction of what the president had been saying, that the weapons being sent to Cuba did not represent a threat to the United States. Rusk's draft, in effect, supported the views of the Republican opposition, that something sinister was going on in Cuba and hence the need for the U-2 reconnaissance effort. Bobby said there would be no further drafts. A statement would be prepared by the president if or when a U-2 was lost.[5]

The Special Group discussion continued about the number and the probable locations of SA-2 sites in Cuba. Postulations were made based on the locations and spacings of the SAMs we had already seen.

Bobby listened with impatience. Not surprisingly, Bobby had a healthy suspicion of the Agency, which was no doubt sharpened by his own investigation of the Bay of Pigs. While he was intolerant of those engaged in covert operations, he did seem to understand aerial photography and was a strong advocate of its use. But if Bobby was cool to the Agency, he was getting impatient with Rusk.

Rusk pressed on, supported by Bundy. The Kennedy administration faced a number of problems relative to the continued use of the U-2. The United Nations had convened in September and congressional elections were upcoming in early November. The downing of a U-2 could have dramatic repercussions in both situations. Rusk appeared obsessively concerned about the overflights of Cuba, even believing the flights could increase tensions to the point of war.

McCone, of course, had instructed Agency representatives to press for continued aerial surveillance of Cuba—that it was a vital necessity to cover the highest priority targets. Flight-track planning, however, was to be weighed against locations of known SAM sites and probable locations of others, especially where elint cuts indicated that SAMs were operational.

James Reber, the chairman of COMOR (Committee on Overhead Reconnaissance), unfolded a large map of Cuba on the conference table with various flight plans on it. Bobby strongly advocated the overflights and stuck to the postulation that even if a U-2 was damaged by an SA-2, it would glide, as Powers's U-2 had, for a considerable distance out of Cuban airspace. One participant said that Bobby was in a bad mood and had chided Rusk throughout the meeting. Rusk raised the question about the violation of Cuban airspace several times. Abrasive and flippant, Bobby said, "Let's sustain the overflights and the hell with the international issues." The same participant said the meeting became "hushed like a forest glen in the mountains when two big-horn rams prepared to square off. All the other animals stop what they are doing and watch and that's what we did."

A break in the meeting was called. When it resumed, the CIA proposal, with McCone's strong backing, called for a single high-level U-2 flight specifically designed to photograph the Banes cruise missile area as well as areas not covered on the August 29 or September 5 missions. The long flight plan was strongly supported by Robert Kennedy, but Secretary Rusk still expressed grave concern about so much time over Cuban territory. Should the U-2 be downed over Cuban territory, he repeated, the United States would be put in a poor position trying to rely on its rights to overfly international waters near the Cuban coasts. Bobby insisted on the long mission, and Rusk continued to maintain that the mission was too exposed.

As the impasse between them became more and more pronounced, the other participants disengaged completely from the debate. Reber, with puckish humor, would later relate, "When men of such rank involve themselves in planning mission tracks, good intelligence officers just listen." Finally, with Rusk still adamant, Bobby turned sarcastic. He looked Rusk squarely in the eye and said, "What's the matter, Dean, you chicken?" Rusk slumped abruptly in his chair and pondered for a long moment. Then he resumed an alert position and began clearly and forcefully to reiterate his views. He remained adamantly opposed to making long, "provocative" flights over Cuba. A compromise was reached. The flight plan would be changed. Four short flights would be substituted for one long one: one over the Isle of Pines, one over the area roughly east of longitude 77 west, and two legs along the coast—one north and one south. The president's approval would be required and that could mean several days before the mission could be launched.

Later that afternoon, Rusk again brought up, with McGeorge Bundy, the danger of continued U-2 reconnaissance. He pleaded with Bundy to use his influence with the president to curtail or halt the flights. Bundy then called General Carter and asked that the following questions be answered in thirty minutes:

1) How important was it to our intelligence objectives that we really overfly Cuban soil?

2) How much would we suffer if we limited our reconnaissance to peripheral reconnaissance?

3) Was there anyone in the operations or planning sections who might provoke such an incident?

Carter quickly gave the task of answering these questions to Dr. Herbert "Pete" Scoville, deputy director of research, and to James Reber. Scoville responded that he knew of no other intelligence source that could provide the timely information McCone was demanding and that we would suffer substantially if reconnaissance was limited to peripheral tracks. Scoville replied that he did not like the tenor of the last question but stated emphatically that all CIA U-2 operations were predicated on the safe return of the pilot and aircraft.

Late that afternoon, General Carter was called by Bundy and told that the approval given previously for one of the four overflights had been rescinded. Furthermore, Bundy said all future requests for a mission had to be sent through him to the president.

The next day, Rusk remained preoccupied with the fear of a U-2 loss. Grasping for straws, he asked Abram Chayes, the State Department's legal officer, to investigate the legal possibilities of having the U-2 flights conducted under the auspices of the OAS to legitimize them, reducing the political consequences should a U-2 be downed.[6] Rusk made a similar request to the Department of Defense.

At the Agency, Rusk's actions were seen as a stalling or stone-walling tactic. Forwarding proposals for comments and policy, along with asking for the formation of a committee to study something, were long-established State Department stalling ploys. General Carter did not inform McCone (in France) of the dispute. An Agency official would remark later that Carter "was standing in quicksand which was hardening into concrete, but Carter was too dumb to realize it." Still, the embittered officials at the Agency assembled a group to study Rusk's proposal. I sat in on several of the meetings. Even if all the appropriate legal papers were properly executed, it would be months before any action could be approved by the molasseslike OAS. In the meantime, word would certainly leak out to the Russians and Cubans, and the U.S. would be subject to a barrage of adverse propaganda. U-2 reconnaissance experts, however, punched a number of holes in Rusk's proposal. Prospective OAS pilots would have to have at least a thousand hours in single-engine jet aircraft and at least six months of training in the U-2 to properly execute the complex flying and navigation problems required on reconnaissance missions. There were few nations in Latin America that had such trained pilots. If a U-2 program for pilots other than Americans had to be created, it was doubtful if the Cuban overflights would ever be resumed. When that conclusion was reached, someone remarked, "Can't you see that's what that son of a bitch Rusk wants?" It all boiled down that even if the flights were to be conducted by the OAS, the pilots would have to be Americans. The Agency received some support when the General Counsel's Office of the Department of Defense quickly responded, on September 12, to Rusk's inquiry that the transfer of U-2 flights would not be legally permissible either under the UN or OAS charter.

On September 11, the Soviet government released through Tass a statement justifying its policy of sending military aid to Cuba, saying the arms and military equipment being sent to Cuba were strictly for defensive purposes. Then it went on to say: "The explosive power of our nuclear weapons is so great and the Soviet Union has such powerful missiles for delivering these nuclear warheads that there is no need to seek sites for them somewhere beyond the borders of the Soviet Union."[7] A series of short articles from Moscow, Leningrad, and a number of Soviet provincial capitals ran in *Pravda*, commenting favorably on the Tass release. Interviews with "indignant civilians" and military officers at "Hands off Cuba" rallies were published. Two days later, a full page of articles from Havana, Paris, Warsaw, Sofia, New Delhi, and Berlin voiced support for the Tass statement. Privately, Soviet diplomats around the world maintained that the Cuban affair was being blown out of proportion by the United States, and they argued for a cautious, restrained U.S. policy toward Cuba. The Soviets undoubtedly hoped that with this reassurance the United States would refrain from U-2 surveillance of Cuba long enough for deployment of the MRBM missiles already en route. The Russians were maintaining that Soviet ships were only carrying "necessary foods and foodstuffs to the Cuban people." But the Russians remained sensitive about their shipping to Cuba. "We can say to these people that these are our merchant vessels and what we ship in them is none of your business; it is the internal affair of the countries conducting this commercial transaction. We can say in the words of the popular expression, Don't stick your nose where it does not belong."

The reaction to the Tass statement was predictable. The Cuban press, of course, quickly claimed that Cuba had every reason to ensure its security, that it had a right to appeal to her friends, and that the friends had every legal reason to respond to that appeal. It warned the Cuban people to be ready for another Playa Girón and to remember the righteousness of Marxism and the Cuban revolution. The U.S., as usual, was portrayed as the bully of the hemisphere.

The increase in rhetoric between the U.S. and Russia regarding Cuba prompted Rusk to ask embassies for Latin American reaction to the president's September 4 statement, along with the Tass statement of September 11. Almost without exception, most newspapers were critical of U.S. inaction and saw the Cuba buildup as a matter of great concern. One Chilean newspaper claimed that "the Russian military buildup of Cuba is a crucial test for the Kennedy Administration, and U.S. reaction would prove whether Rio Treaty is worth the paper it is written on."[8] Others criticized U.S. policy on Cuba as "weak and inconsistent, implying U.S. should take decisive action to clean out Castro regime." Still others stated that the United States should take strong and direct action to alleviate the Cuban problem and eliminate Communist intervention. Rusk was surprised with this reaction, but apparently the cables were not forwarded to the White House.

In Washington, detailed analysis of the Banes site involved experts from all major organizations in the intelligence community. Cline emphasized to all participants that they had to work until there was unanimous agreement on the function and range of the missile site. The analysis was helped by further searching of the August 29 and September 5 photography, which revealed additional Banes-like sites under construction at Santa Cruz del Norte and Campo Florida. Both sites overlooked beaches perfect for amphibious landings. On the morning of September 13, the president was told by Cline that the Banes missile site had been evaluated by the intelligence community and found to be a short-range cruise-missile system with a range of twenty-five to thirty nautical miles for coastal defense against naval targets. The president seemed pleased that Banes posed no threat to the United States mainland or to the Panama Canal.

That afternoon at his press conference, the president read a statement seeking to clarify the issues. He took note of the recent increase in the movement of Soviet men and matériel to Cuba and restated the warning that the activity in Cuba was being closely watched: "Ever since Communism moved to Cuba in 1958, Soviet technical and military personnel have moved steadily onto the island in increasing numbers at the invitation of the Cuban government. Now that movement has been increased. It is under our most careful surveillance. But I will repeat the conclusion that I reported last week, that these new shipments do not constitute a serious threat to any part of this hemisphere."[9]

(It is puzzling why the Russians—if they believed that the president was not fully aware of what was happening in Cuba but had issued the explicit warning that Cuba was under "careful surveillance," which could only mean the U-2 missions—would not have activated the SAM system to discourage that surveillance.)

Finally, the president reiterated the principal American position: "But let me make this clear once again. If at any time the Communist buildup in Cuba were to endanger or interfere with our security in any way, including our base at Guantánamo, our passage to the Panama Canal, our missile and space activities in Cape Canaveral, or the lives of American citizens in this country, or if Cuba should ever attempt to export its aggressive purposes by force or the threat of force against any nation in this hemisphere or become an offensive military base of significant capacity for the Soviet Union, then this country will do whatever must be done to protect its own security and that of its allies."[10]

The warning to Moscow was no longer faint, but firm and hard. The only weaknesses in the president's warning, if there was weakness, lay with the president not stating what he would do if such activities were discovered.

Although the president's warning was explicit enough, it appeared that Khrushchev chose not to read the president correctly. Certainly, the U.S. seemed unaware of the magnitude of the Soviet venture. Khrushchev had made the decision to place the missiles in Cuba and it would now be difficult to reverse it. He could not reopen the issue without using the very argument used by the conservative marshalls who had opposed the venture in the first place. Those who supported the venture would attack him for not following through. The Soviets may have read into Kennedy's message that although he did not like the missiles there, he would have to accede because the U.S. had placed missiles in England, Italy, and Turkey.

The immediate Soviet response to the president's statement was a renewed, intensive propaganda campaign charging the United States with aggressive designs on Cuba. The Soviets again charged that U.S. aircraft were dangerously buzzing Soviet ships bound for Cuba. An editorial in the September 13 *Red Star* acknowledged that "a certain quantity" of arms had been sent to Cuba but that they were "exclusively for defensive purposes." Again, it reiterated that the Soviets had no need to install atomic missiles outside their borders.

The president was confronted with a nagging dilemma—caught between Soviet and Cuban charges that the U.S. was planning to invade the island and mounting congressional demands from both the Republicans and Democrats that he had to do precisely that. Adlai Stevenson was caught in a similar dilemma at the UN as to whether the United States might take offensive action against Cuba. On September 21, he made the following statement: "We are not taking and will not take offensive action in this hemisphere. For, as the president of the United States made clear last week, we and other countries in the Americas will not be deterred from taking whatever action is needed by threats from any quarter. But while we will not commit aggression, we will take whatever steps are necessary to prevent the government of Cuba from seeking to subvert any part of this hemisphere."[11]

President Kennedy was showing himself to be extremely sensitive about appearing to be the aggressor against Cuba. Statements from administration officials, however, seemed to imply that the U.S. did not wish to intervene in Cuba again and would not challenge the Soviets as to their arms aid. To the Republican opposition, however, it appeared that the president had accepted the situation in Cuba and was making only feeble efforts to alter the accomplished fact of Castro's Cuba with Russian forces at the back door of the U.S. Senator Goldwater charged that the president's September 13 statement "virtually promised the Communist world that the United States will take no action to remove the threat of Soviet armed might in the Western Hemisphere."

It was no secret to Kennedy that the Kremlin was inclined to brutal action whenever the U.S. looked weak or paralyzed, as it had in Hungary, but the president could not act without proof that there were offensive missiles in Cuba. At one point, he thought he could have issued stronger warnings than those of September 4 and 13. But after studying the statements again, he was convinced that they were as strong as he could make them without provoking a confrontation with the Soviets. He certainly could not impose a quarantine on Soviet ship movements, as his critics were demanding, or make a convincing case to the U.S. public, the United Nations, or for that matter to the world. Puzzled, he called for a National Intelligence Estimate on Cuba. But because of Bundy's and Rusk's stalling actions, there had been no U-2 photography of Cuba for over two weeks.

There was confusion at the Agency about "what and where" U-2 missions could or should be flown. When Bundy was called by the CIA, he appeared confused and said he interpreted the president's intention as approval for the four short missions outlined at the September 10 Special Action Group meeting. Planning for each of these missions began in earnest.

The most difficult task for the intelligence analyst is to determine the intent or will of the opposition. Sherman Kent, director of the Office of National Estimates, was well aware of this fact in the preparation of national estimates.[12] Kent called for all the humint, comint (communications intelligence), and photint (photo intelligence) information on the Soviet buildup in Cuba.

History is replete with examples of inaccurate conclusions drawn in advance of the facts. Once an advance conclusion is accepted, there is a tendency to reject information that conflicts with it. Kent, well aware of this fact, kept asking that we sift and resift all the information we possessed. At one meeting, I reported that we had no photographic evidence of offensive missiles in Cuba, but I hastened to add that we had not had any coverage of Cuba's interior since the August 29 and September 5 missions. I was immediately cut off by Kent, who stated, "That's another ball game that we are not to get involved in." Several Agency analysts pointed out that the flow of arms to Cuba was following an establishment of Soviet aid to other countries. They pointed out that the Soviets had sent I1-28 Beagle bombers and FROG missiles to other nations as part of their weapons package and these would also probably be sent to Cuba.

All participating Agency analysts and military representatives concurred in the draft estimate without exception.[13] Still, Kent was well aware of McCone's attitude and the controversy at the White House and that he would be asking General Carter, as acting director of the Agency, to sign the estimate. He carefully reviewed the Special National Intelligence Estimate draft several times. Still not satisfied with the draft in what it purveyed, he asked to see all the raw intelligence that reported offensive missiles in Cuba. There were about a thousand such reports, five of which contained some substance of truth and, in hindsight, indicated that the Soviets might place offensive missiles in Cuba. The rest had been proven invalid through the analysis of U-2 photography. Sidney Graybeal, the offensive-missile expert for the Agency, reviewed the five reports containing some valid data and, upon careful examination and verification analysis, concluded there were obvious errors—the same type of errors prevalent in refugee reporting on missiles. Kent read all the reports. When Graybeal affirmed that all of the reported information and sites had been checked against aerial photography, Kent was satisfied and reviewed the estimate for a final time.

Kent said it appeared impossible for anyone to sift "signals from noise" or to perceive a precise pattern. The estimate, Special National Intelligence Estimate (SNIE) No. 85-3-62, titled "The Military Buildup in Cuba," was approved by the United States Intelligence Board without objections and issued on September 19. The estimate indicated that: "We believe that the military buildup which began in July does not reflect a radically new Soviet policy towards Cuba, either in terms of military commitments or of the role of Cuba in overall Soviet strategy. Without changing the essentially defensive character of the military buildup in Cuba and without making an open pledge to protect Cuba under all circumstances, the Soviets have enhanced Cuban military capabilities, repeated in stronger terms their warnings to the U.S., and tied the Cuban situation to the general question of East-West confrontation."[14] Kent told me later that the consensus was the Soviets would realize that the deployment of an offensive capability in the Western Hemisphere would provoke U.S. military intervention. The estimate, therefore, covered four essential points:

1. That the USSR valued Cuba as a political base, and that the purpose of the buildup was to strengthen the Castro regime against an attack or attempts to overthrow the Castro regime. Cuba would be used by the Soviets as a springboard for subversion for Latin America.

2. That the military significance of the Soviet equipment sent to Cuba was defensive, both for air and coastal purposes. These shipments therefore did not conflict with the president's warnings. The Cuban concern over the prospects of an invasion were real and may have been intensified by the president's warnings of September 4 and 13.

3. That before the buildup was completed, the Cubans might receive light bombers or short-range missiles.

4. That the sending of MRBMs or IRBMs was weighed against the idea that the Russians might try to establish a submarine base in Cuba or provide the Cubans with Russian-made submarines; the establishment of a submarine base was rated most likely. The MRBM and IRBM postulation was carefully weighed and rejected.

McCone, winding up his honeymoon trip, was kept informed of the work being done on the estimate in Washington. He cabled his doubts about the conclusions reached in the estimate to General Carter after it had been prepared. McCone held to his position that the estimate failed to take into account the strong possibility that the deployment of the SA-2's was to hinder the U-2's from detecting the arrival of surface-to-surface missiles. McCone would later explain: "The majority opinion in the intelligence community, as well as State and Defense, was that this would be so out of character with the Soviets that they would not do so. They had never placed an offensive missile in any satellite area. I pointed out that Cuba was the only piece of real estate that they had indirect control of where a missile could reach Washington or New York and not reach Moscow. So the situation was somewhat different."[15] But McCone's telephone calls did not prevent the estimate's being signed by General Carter, issued on September 19, and sent to the president.

Although no one was present when the president read the report, word was relayed back that the president "felt better after reading it."

Much would be written later about the September 19 estimate and the whole estimative process. Subsequent to the crisis, numerous postmortems and investigations were conducted. The crisis would also be the subject of a number of analytical methods, typing and modeling experiments both within and outside the government.[16]

The accuracy of missile reporting was still open to question and the Washington atmosphere was skeptical of generalizations. The president's statements of September 4 and September 13 had raised the requirement of the quality of proof for any judgment that offensive missiles had been introduced into Cuba. On September 20, McCone cabled Carter again, asking that the Office of National Estimates reassess its findings. Kent and the office reviewed the estimate again and found no reason to change their conclusions. In later discussions with Kent, he told me his belief in the conclusion of the report was swayed by the fact that the Russian embassy was staffed with some of the best intelligence officers in the Soviet system and that these officers were constantly plumbing both White House and congressional feelings and he felt that certainly this information was being transmitted to Moscow. "Dobrynin," Kent said, "was no dummy to the West and he certainly must have been warning Khrushchev on the dangers of a U.S. riposte if the Soviets placed offensive missiles in Cuba." Kent would relate that the Soviet intelligence officers had fallen prey to a bad intelligence system, telling the top leaders only what they wanted to hear.

After the crisis, Sherman Kent would tell me and others that considering the evidence at the time, and if he had the estimate to do over again, he would have to come down hard again on the "no" position of the Soviets introducing offensive missiles in Cuba. He was supported by Thomas Hughes, deputy chief of INR, Department of State. Hughes would also later maintain that the State Department had fully weighed all indicators and there were no relevant ones that would support the introduction of offensive missiles into Cuba. Cline would also support Kent, stating that anyone could go back and pick needles out of haystacks, but based on the evidence at the time, it was the only call that could be made. Kent would later write that "They [the policymakers] seem to have gone out of their way to praise intelligence in its fact-finding role, but to be anything but grateful for intelligence utterances in the estimate category."[17]

For months after the crisis, Bobby Kennedy complained that not only had the estimate been wrong but that no one had informed the president that offensive missiles might be put into Cuba. That, General Maxwell Taylor would later remark, was simply not true. Bobby sat in on several meetings when McCone expressed his thoughts that indeed missiles might be introduced into Cuba.

Soviet diplomats later expressed their misinterpretation of the president's feelings and warnings, claiming they were meant for the Republicans and the American electorate during this election period rather than for the Russians. Although highly speculative, the purported Soviet reaction could be explained in that most Soviet diplomats the world over were not privy to information regarding what was happening in Cuba.

In early September, the Cuban Ministry of Foreign Affairs began to exert control over the movements of all foreigners in Cuba. News reporters and foreign embassy personnel were forbidden to travel outside the city limits of Havana. Within the city, all foreigners were shadowed by Cuban agents on foot and in cars. British embassy personnel, who had been providing substantial information to the United States, were especially harassed. To be caught near any military installation without authorization was to risk arrest and expulsion.

The roads leading to the Torrens Reformatory, headquarters of the Soviet forces in Cuba, were closed to normal traffic, but U.S. agents stationed along the road were reporting an ever increasing number of convoys to the reformatory. And in Havana, an unusually high number of Russian "tourists" were sightseeing in the streets or visiting the restaurants and nightclubs in the evenings. These "tourists," it was noted, were young and wore the same type clothes—cheaply made sport shirts and bell-bottom trousers.

About this time, several Soviet Baltic and Black Sea ports were suddenly closed to foreigners. It was normal for Soviet ports to be closed when munitions were being loaded. What, of course, was happening was that MRBM missiles were being put aboard ships under the strictest of security conditions and under the cover of darkness. The missiles were stowed deep in the holds, which gave no external evidence that the ships were carrying them.

Soviet ships made false declarations as to their destinations when they exited the Black Sea and the Bosporus. Little or no information was available on the unloading plans or types of cargo carried. Cargo records were falsified and the tonnage declared was well below what was being carried. Although the ships would declare from Odessa, from a variety of intelligence sources it was known that they had loaded at ports elsewhere. Often, ships going to Cuba declared for Conakry, Guinea. When the volume of traffic to Cuba increased, a number of ships would not give their destinations but would simply state they were carrying "general cargo" and "awaiting orders."

On September 15, the Soviet merchant ship *Poltava* was photographed en route to Mariel. The *Poltava* rode exceptionally high in the water, an indication that the cargo was of low weight but large in volume. So much military equipment, including missiles, falls into this category that no conclusion regarding the nature of the cargo could be made. One intelligence-collection organization even decided that the Soviets were sending these ships to remove from Cuba all the unnecessary excess military equipment they had provided. McCone was furious and after the crisis ordered that intelligence-collection organizations never analyze intelligence they had collected.[18] The deck of the *Poltava* contained seventeen cargo trucks, none associated with missiles.[19]

A significant feature of the *Poltava* was that it was a large-hatch cargo, and it was one of nine different series of large-hatch cargo ships being built at Soviet and world shipyards for the Soviet merchant fleet.[20] Free-world merchant fleets were also introducing units with large hatches into their fleets during this period. The main difference between the Soviet and free-world ships, however, was that the majority of the free-world units lacked the heavy lift equipment possessed by the Soviet ships to handle the heaviest pieces of commercial cargo. Each Soviet large-hatch ship was equipped with a sixty-ton boom adjacent to the large hatch. This factor contributed significantly not only to its utility as a commercial carrier but also to its capability to support military operations. Large-hatch ships of the *Poltava* type, as well as ships of the *Omsk* class, were used for the clandestine delivery of offensive missiles to Cuba in September 1962. The *Poltava* probably carried eight MRBMs in its hold.

Postmortems of intelligence operations leading up to the Cuban crisis gave rise to considerable controversy as to why these ships had not been identified as missile carriers and called to the attention of higher officials. The simple fact is that there were no external indicators that the ships were carrying missiles. Analysts, understandably, thought that the ships had been pressed into service to help deliver large quantities of military equipment that the Soviets were openly announcing was strictly defensive in nature.

Roger Hilsman, in commenting on intelligence operations during the Cuban crisis, stated that the ships that apparently brought the missiles to Cuba had been designed as lumber carriers.[21] The fact is that the *Poltava* and the *Omsk* were not lumber ships. While the large-hatch ships were certainly capable of carrying lumber, they had not been designed for that role and specific purpose.[22]

The *Poltava*, along with another large-hatch ship, the *Omsk*, were unloaded at the Mariel naval port, which had been used by the U.S. Navy during World War II as an antisubmarine warfare base. The Castro regime had put the base at the disposal of the Soviets, who had constructed a large cinder-block wall around the unloading area at the port so that none of the activity at the port could be observed by land-based agents.

The Soviet vessel *Kimovsk*, also carrying missile equipment, was unloaded at the port of Casilda. On October 2, the Soviet merchant ships *Krasnograd* and *Orenburg* would unload additional missiles at Mariel. The canvas-covered MRBM missiles were moved from the port in night convoys, under tight security, to remote sites in the interior, where they were concealed among the karst hills. The launch sites, however, constructed on areas expropriated from Cuban landowners, had no special security measures such as fences or walls and, more important, were completely exposed to aerial observation.

There were some eyewitness reports that missiles were unloaded on three nights following September 17. One report cited at least eight MRBMs observed on the highway leading from Mariel. These accounts were being evaluated at a higher level of credibility than before, but analysts remained skeptical about trailer and missile lengths since many had been seen at night or under difficult or fleeting circumstances. Then, too, a mass of such previous reporting had proven false. Sightings in the Mariel-Havana area looked particularly promising, but no aerial-reconnaissance missions had covered those areas for over a month. McCone would later testify to the House Appropriations Committee: "On September 21, we received our first agent report that there was the possibility and that report and other information led us to the conclusion of the fact that the missiles, the first missiles, probably arrived around September 8."

Furthermore there was considerable confusion as to what type of U-2 missions had really been authorized by the president. The Agency was told that there were no constraints on peripheral missions, and indeed, on September 17, a U-2 peripheral mission was authorized by the president. By the time the flight reached Cuba's coast from Edwards Air Force Base, the weather had closed in and the mission was aborted. There was no usable photography.

New rules for peripheral flights for the U-2 and other reconnaissance aircraft had been formulated. All reconnaissance aircraft were to fly no closer than twenty-five miles from Cuba's shore—the slant range of the SA-2 missiles. Confident and cocky, General LeMay sent several SAC RB-47 photographic planes along Cuba's coast. The results were very disappointing, the shoreline of Cuba barely visible on the oblique photos from that distance. LeMay then sent several B-52 bombers, configured for reconnaissance, aloft. The results were equally disappointing.

F8U Crusader and F3D Skynight peripheral missions were also conducted by the Navy. The Center looked at the photography, but we couldn't even distinguish the shore. Desperation in reconnaissance often results in jerry rigging. The Air Force borrowed an Army 100-inch-focal-length still camera. These cameras, mounted on huge tripods, had been used previously to photograph Soviet border defenses from extended ranges. The camera was placed in a Constellation transport aircraft, its long barrel protruding from an escape hatch. Another failure: The effect of the aircraft's vibration on the long barrel of the camera resulted in pictures that were blurred. LeMay then asked that a longer-focal-length camera, the "Boston," be employed. There were only two such cameras produced. One of the cameras installed in an RB-57 stretched-wing Canberra was designed to photograph deep into East Germany and Czechoslovakia while flying along the West German borders. The 240-inch camera was large and bulky and required manual adjustment and operation. It weighed over two thousand pounds. It was difficult to aim—an operator located the target with a monoscope with mechanical linkage to the camera. The camera port was six feet by three feet. A C-97 transport aircraft equipped with the "Boston" camera was flown to the United States from Rhein Main airfield in West Germany. The camera was extremely difficult to maintain, and the photography, more often than not, was disappointing. The peripheral missions along Cuba's shores would prove to be typical. The camera malfunctioned and the limited photography obtained was of little intelligence value.

The Soviet press during this period changed its tone and admitted that military aid was being sent to Cuba "in view of the threat of U.S. intervention." Where in the past the Soviets would only admit that "a certain quantity of armaments had been sent to Cuba," now it referred to the equipment being sent as being "exclusively for defensive purposes" or as being "the necessary arms for its [Cuba's] struggle against the imperialist Americans." There were also articles denying emphatically any Soviet need to install atomic missiles outside the Soviet Union.

Much to the consternation of the intelligence community, the administration policy was essentially one of watchful waiting, grasping at small straws that Castro was losing prestige, ardently hoping that his economy would collapse—that the Russians would eventually tire of paying the more than $1-million-a-day bill to sustain the Castro regime. The only positive step taken was to ask friendly foreign governments to restrict their shipping trade with Cuba. While a few smaller countries complied, larger nations such as the United Kingdom and Canada continued their trade with Cuba. U.S. congressional reaction was predictable—condemning and threatening the British with sanctions and denying intelligence, including satellite, to them. On September 18, former vice-president Nixon called for a "quarantine" of Cuba to halt the flow of Soviet arms. He urged President Kennedy to take "stronger action" against the Soviets and Cuba. On September 20, two Senate groups, the Foreign Relations and the Armed Forces committees, at a joint meeting approved a resolution sanctioning the use of force, if necessary, to defend the Western Hemisphere against Cuban aggression or subversion. The leader of this effort was Senator Richard B. Russell, who regarded President Kennedy as weak and ineffectual in dealing with Cuba and the Russians. Senate leaders also had consulted with leaders of the House Foreign Affairs Committee, along with leaders of both parties, in Russell's words, "to get the President off of his dead ass." Paragraph B of the resolution stated in unequivocal terms that the United States would work "to prevent in Cuba the creation or use of an externally supported military capability endangering the security of the United States."[23]

The president was angered not only by Republican criticism but also by ranking Democrats who were openly criticizing his handling of the Cuban problem. Kennedy, during this period, frequently quoted the following poem:

> Bullfight critics, row on row
> Crowd the vast arena full
> But only one man is there who knows
> And he is the man who fights the bull.
> —*Anonymous*

Reports of missiles being sighted in Cuba continued; the evidence that there were or were not missiles in Cuba had to be totally acceptable and convincing. Aerial-reconnaissance photography was the only way to make sure. It all devolved upon the president. A meeting of the Special Group was set for September 20, and Carter raised the possibility of using Ryan Firebee drones to acquire the necessary aerial coverage. The Firebee could fly at 40,000 feet, at a speed of about 600 miles an hour. The Air Force had also proposed that the Firebees could also be elint-configured to gather data on the operational status of the SAM sites. According to General Taylor, none of the participants were interested in approving their use. Meanwhile, Carter, prodded by McCone's insistent phone calls, then pressed for the resumption of U-2 overflights. Three types of U-2 missions were again proposed: one, a long overflight mission; four short "in-and-out" missions; or the continued peripheral missions. Rusk asked that the three proposals be combined into a single study and that the findings be presented at a Special Group meeting scheduled for a week later. Carter concurred with Rusk's proposal.

On September 21, Gromyko delivered a wide-ranging speech before the United Nations General Assembly. The Soviets, he insisted, desired peace, but he warned "that preparations for a rocket-nuclear war in the world are being developed day-by-day and that, consequently, the danger of its being unleashed is growing." Gromyko singled out Cuba as a problem of particular urgency. He charged the president was stepping up the training of U.S. forces and would attack Cuba should it pose a threat to the United States, the Panama Canal, or against any state in the Western Hemisphere. Gromyko commented acidly, "It is well known to every person of sound mind that Cuba is pursuing neither the first nor the second nor the third of the goals. This is also well known by the state leaders of the United States. They know very well that the help rendered by the Soviet Union to Cuba in the matter of strengthening its independence does not pursue any of these goals, since they are alien to our policy."[24]

He turned to the American desire to restrict shipping to Cuba: "The most free and easygoing officials in the United States, who are obviously losing control of their thoughts, are announcing that, if you please, it is necessary to control the movement of Soviet ships bringing goods to Cuba and from Cuba to the Soviet Union and the specialists who help Cuba to organize their industry and agriculture." He belittled the United States for "brink-of-war hysteria" and warned that the "Soviet Union has all it needs to meet any aggressor fully armed, and destroy him."[25]

Adlai Stevenson, the U.S. ambassador to the UN, responded to Gromyko's charges by saying that the U.S. and other countries in the Americas would take necessary steps against threats in the hemisphere. "We shall work closely with our inter-American partners. This intention does not, of course, derogate from our right, a right anchored in the United Nations charter, to protect our national security."[26]

The finding of additional SA-2 sites and the tracking of the U-2 and other peripheral flights by Cuban radars became particularly bothersome to Roswell Gilpatric in early to mid-September. A debate ensued between the CIA and the DOD as to whether, as a national policy, the covert overhead reconnaissance of Cuba be performed by the Department of Defense or, because of plausible denial, by the CIA with DOD support. Within the Agency, those in charge of U-2 operations believed that since the president had not acknowledged overhead reconnaissance of Cuba and since the operations were still being conducted as a covert undertaking, they deserved professional execution by a staff most experienced in conducting such operations—with the smallest circle of knowledgeable people possible. Agency leaders advocated to Carter that the U-2 operations remain under the command and guidance of the Agency, with any additional support required from the USAF and SAC to carry out the mission in military guise. Gilpatric, mindful of Bobby Kennedy's anger earlier in the month about U-2 reconnaissance of Cuba, was determined not to allow another Powers-like incident to blemish the Kennedy presidency. In mid-September, Gilpatric had met with General Carter and recommended that the Cuban U-2 flights be turned over to the Strategic Air Command. His reasons were: 1) the overflight requirements were becoming tactical rather than strategic; 2) there was a danger of possible armed conflict; 3) there could be possible embarrassment to the administration if an Agency U-2 was downed by Cuban SAMs; and 4) in the event the Cuban situation became further aggravated, the Agency's operational assets would be insufficient to keep up with reconnaissance demands. Gilpatric then told Carter that the president and Secretary McNamara also felt strongly that the overflights should be turned over to the Strategic Air Command. General Carter, ever responsive to his military background, agreed. He apparently did not consult McCone.

The Russians, meanwhile, must have become aware of the change in reconnaissance-flight patterns from overflights to peripheral missions. They probably felt that the danger of the missiles being detected had been lessened and that Kennedy may have retreated from a position of confrontation. The Russians, too, probably hoped that the observation of the SA-2 sites by previous U-2 flights might have induced the United States to halt reconnaissance of Cuba altogether. But they couldn't be sure.

In the midst of all this on September 25, 1962, Premier Fidel Castro announced that a Soviet-Cuban agreement had been concluded for the construction of a large fishing port in Cuba. The port would be under lease to the Soviets and would eventually become a headquarters for the Soviet Atlantic Fishing Fleet. Under terms of the agreement, the Soviets would finance the port and the Cubans would provide all the necessary labor and materials. Premier Castro did not give a date when construction would begin or where the port would be located. There were some indications that Castro made the announcement prematurely and caught the Russians completely off guard.

There was an immediate howl of protest from Congress, and U.S. newspapers began using the word *base* to describe the port. No one in the intelligence community believed that the port would be used solely for fishing. Some feared it would become a vast intelligence base for Soviet intelligence trawlers, which prowled the U.S. coast equipped with sophisticated electronic detection equipment. Others saw a more sinister connotation: The port would become a Soviet submarine base. The intelligence community feared a pattern might be emerging in Cuba that had been seen elsewhere. The Russians would first offer to make port improvements and would later grant naval aid in the form of PT boats, patrol craft, submarines, and destroyers. In the late 1950s, the Soviets had provided the Egyptians with eight W-class submarines and a number of combatants. In July 1962, the Soviets gave the Indonesians six W-class submarines and a number of combatants. At both Surabaja, Indonesia, and Alexandria, Egypt, Soviet personnel in host-country uniforms had been spotted.

At the White House this development was but another in a series of aggravations, and the irritation showed. The September 19 SNIE postulated that the construction of a submarine base would be more likely than the deployment of missiles. The president wanted to know if there was any indication as to where the "base" would be located. We thoroughly reviewed all of the U-2 photography along Cuba's coasts and rivers, but there was no evidence that any such construction was under way.

When Soviet foreign minister Gromyko left Secretary Rusk after a three-hour meeting on September 25, he was questioned by newsmen not only about the meeting and the port. He showed particular irritation toward newsmen using the word *base*. Turning to one of the newsmen, he said in English, "I would not use such terms as *base.*" On September 26, Congress completed action on a joint resolution expressing the determination to oppose with force if necessary any Communist aggression or subversion in Cuba. The Kennedys noted that the resolution passed the Senate on September 20 by a vote of 86 to 1 and passed the House of Representatives on September 26 by a vote of 384 to 7. The Congress was sending the president a strong message to get tough.[27]

The resolution, plus speculation about the "port," inspired lengthy articles in the Soviet press charging the U.S. with a wave of anti-Cuban hysteria and other "fabrications." The Russians ridiculed suggestions that the port would be used for military purposes. *Izvestiya* published an interview with V. M. Kamentsev, deputy chairman of the Soviet State Committee for Fisheries, who said that the port would be solely for Soviet fishing trawlers. He denied reports in the U.S. press that the port would be constructed near Banes; instead, it would be near the port of Havana.

Meanwhile, in Havana, the Cuban ministry informed correspondents that in the future, they would not be permitted to travel beyond Havana without a special permit. There was no explanation for the restriction.

The failure of reconnaissance efforts using the "Boston" camera, the RB-47's, and B-52's—along with the Navy's inconclusive reconnaissance efforts—brought demands by McCone that the U-2's be employed again. Permission was granted to use the U-2 cameras in an oblique mode flying closer offshore than before in "short-revelation overflights." Two peripheral missions were approved.

Even as some of the MRBM missiles were being moved to their sites in Cuba, Khrushchev, with considerable publicity, left Moscow on September 27 for a barnstorming tour of agricultural enterprises in the Turkmen and Uzbek republics. For four days he toured cotton-growing farms, irrigation projects, sheep farms, and petroleum industries, concluding his tour at Ashkhabad, the capital city of Turkmen SSR. On October 3 and 4, he resumed his tour, visiting irrigation projects, scientific-research institutes, cotton-equipment plants, and virgin land areas in Uzbekistan. The culmination of his trip would be an address on October 5, at Tashkent, to agricultural workers from Uzbekistan, Kazakhstan, Tadzhikistan, Kirgizia, Turkmenistan, Azerbaijan, and Armenia. In none of the speeches on this trip, which fill a volume, were there any signs of aggression or threats to the United States.[28]

The first successful U-2 peripheral mission was flown on the day Khrushchev began his tour, and its targets were the Banes cruise missile site, and the Guantánamo and Santiago de Cuba areas. These areas had been targeted before, but they had been selected this day because of clear weather conditions.

At the Banes site, a twenty-six-foot-long cruise missile with a wingspan of fifteen feet was clearly seen on one of the launchers. The tie with the Kennel-type missile was now complete. A total of four cruise missile sites had now been identified. In addition, about a hundred cruise missile crates were seen at storage areas at Mayarí Ariba, Guerra, and Santiago de Cuba, enough to establish at least fifteen more coastal-defense sites. Three new SA-2 sites were also found—Chapara, Los Angeles, and Jiguaní—and a SAM support facility was identified at Santiago de Cuba.

The cruise missiles, along with the additional surface-to-air missile sites, considerably strengthened the Cuban capacity to fend off another invasion, and bolstered the Kennedy administration theory that the buildup was for defensive purposes. As a result, the administration decided to counter Republican party charges against its Cuba policy in this election year. Democratic leaders were encouraged by President Kennedy to make themselves available to the Congress and the public media in an effort to explain administration policies.

Information on the Soviet buildup in Cuba, other than offensive missiles, was to be made public as soon as it developed. Roger Hilsman, director of Intelligence and Research at State, and Robert McNamara at Defense held backgrounders for the press. Secretary Rusk granted an interview to John Scali, the American Broadcasting Company's State Department correspondent, which was presented on TV on September 30. When Scali asked about the type of weapons in Cuba, Rusk (probably remembering President Kennedy's first reaction to the Banes site) said, "Now, I don't think that we ought to play with words on this question of defensive and offensive weapons. Any weapon is offensive if you are on the wrong end of it. But the configuration of the military forces in Cuba is a configuration of defensive capability."[29] Rusk then sought to clarify the administration policy. "What we are concerned about is the development of any significant offensive capability against Cuba's neighbors in the Caribbean, or against this country, and we are keeping a very close watch indeed on just that point."[30] Reemphasizing President Kennedy's warning on September 13th, he said, "We have great power in that area, and the President has made it very clear that whatever arms are in Cuba will stay in Cuba and that there will be no effort by Castro to move these arms into other countries."[31]

The second successful peripheral U-2 mission was flown on September 29 and covered the Isle of Pines and the Bay of Pigs area. A new SA-2 site, along with a cruise missile site similar to the Banes site, was discovered at Siguanea. The cruise missile site was on the top of a bulldozed hill, the launchers oriented westward toward the Yucatan Peninsula, away from the United States. The site overlooked beaches, obviously a defense against an amphibious operation.

Lundahl was concerned about the lack of information derived from reconnaissance since the August 29 and September 5 U-2 missions and asked us to come up with a map depicting that coverage. We plotted the coverage and found that outside of coastal areas, very little information about Cuba's interior had been obtained. We also pointed out that because of the oblique coverage, karst hills could be shielding missile installations. Lundahl took the map with him and briefed James Reber and, later, McCone. According to Lundahl, "McCone nearly came out of his chair when he saw the map. I pointed out to him the problem of the oblique cameras—that installations could be hidden behind hills." McCone grabbed the map and said, "I'll take this."

McCone called for a meeting of the Special Group for October 3. At that meeting, he took both Secretary Rusk and Secretary McNamara to task. He said that he was disturbed by the unequivocal statements that were being made by both State and Defense spokesmen to the effect that there were no offensive missiles in Cuba. McCone said there had been no aerial reconnaissance coverage of central or western Cuba for over a month—all flights since September 5 had been of limited penetration, or conducted peripherally. McCone concluded that as spokesman for the intelligence community, he could not make a definitive statement that there were no offensive missiles in Cuba. He told the Special Group that he would so inform the president.

Those around the table were getting used to McCone's persistence. Secretary Rusk's reaction to McCone's warning was to restate to his old fear that should a U-2 be shot down over Cuba, it would be difficult for the Kennedy administration to explain. SA-2 sites were capable of tracking and shooting down a U-2; the Chinese Communists had done it on September 10. "Plausible denial," Rusk maintained, was now a hollow phrase because it would be impossible to deny that aerial reconnaissance was being conducted if a U.S.-operated U-2 was downed. McCone then shifted his ground and advocated short U-2 overflights of Cuba flying south to north rather than the conventional west-to-east missions. McCone reasoned that the operational SA-2's were on the northern coast of the island and if a U-2 was flying a south-to-north mission and fired upon, it would be downed over international waters or at sea. The U.S. would then be in a better position to protest.

Bundy still insisted that the U.S. should try to achieve its reconnaissance objectives by flying peripheral missions. McCone, as usual, was well prepared and with maps and photography clearly showed that the peripheral missions could not confirm or deny the presence of offensive missiles.

McNamara sat passively as Rusk retorted that the greater the number of missions flown, the greater would be the chance for the loss of a reconnaissance aircraft. He wanted to know what the U.S. response to such a loss would be.

McCone finally said he would ask that a number of short-flight plans be drawn up for coverage of the entire island based on targets with intelligence priorities. These plans would be presented at the Special Group meeting scheduled for October 9. McCone candidly added that the degree of readiness of the SAM sites in Cuba had been evaluated. The majority of the SAM sites along Cuba's northern coast should be considered operational and they constituted a threat to flying conventional U-2 missions.

Direct military intervention against Cuba, of course, had to be considered. On October 1, McNamara had met with the Joint Chiefs of Staff. The purpose of the meeting was to discuss circumstances in which military action against Cuba might be necessary and toward which planning should be actively pursued. It was a lengthy meeting. Existing plans reviewed were: strikes against selected targets; airborne and amphibious assaults; the removal of the threat of Soviet weapons; and the necessary actions to stop the possible further export of Soviet arms and equipment to Latin America by Castro. There were three operations plans: 312, 314, and 316.

After the meeting, the Joint Chiefs ordered CINCLANT (commander in chief, Atlantic forces), located in Norfolk, Virginia, to review and update existing plans for a blockade, a strike, and an invasion of Cuba. On October 3, CINCLANT promulgated an operations order for the blockade of Cuba. The plans for the blockade were to include a task force of ships consisting of a blockading group, a covering group, a logistics group, and an antisubmarine group. Plans for joint military, naval, and air task force operations were to be reviewed and updated. These plans were to be coordinated with the Army's 18th Airborne Corps and the Air Force's Tactical Air Command.

Ever since the Bay of Pigs, CINCLANT, the JCS, and the unified and specified commands had prepared detailed contingency plans for Cuba. There were a number of options in each plan and each had a stated degree of urgency. Army planning extended down to the company level. Jump zones in Cuba had been selected for the airborne troops; beach fortifications and obstacles had been carefully charted; and target folders for the bombing or bombardment of military installations had been created. The mining of all Cuban harbors had been carefully planned. Admiral Alfred G. Ward of CINCLANT would later characterize these planning sessions: "We worked with the Army planners on many occasions and the lieutenant general in command of Ft. Bragg would come to our headquarters with his staff and we would plan on where the Marines would land, plan what cruisers would be needed in order to provide gunfire support, and what would be necessary to protect these landings. We made a regular invasion plan which would be available in event of need."[32] The blockade plan, according to Admiral Ward, required considerable modification and legal clarification.

On the same day, the Joint Chiefs of Staff ordered the Strategic Air Command to submit a plan for a Department of Defense reconnaissance program over Cuba. The SAC plan contained no provision for the use of CIA pilots but did require the use of the Agency U-2's. Two experienced SAC U-2 pilots from the 4080th Strategic Wing, at Laughlin Air Force Base, Del Rio, Texas—Major Rudolf Anderson, Jr., and Major Richard Heyser—were sent to Edwards Air Force Base to be checked out in flying the Agency's more advanced U-2's.

While the JCS was planning for the possible invasion of Cuba, Undersecretary of State George Ball, on October 3, was called before the House Select Committee on Export Control to testify on "Trading Relations between the Free World and Cuba." There had been considerable irritation and frustration among the congressmen and senators regarding NATO allies either trading or providing ships to carry supplies to Cuba. There was special sensitivity about British trade with Cuba.

After testifying on trade, Ball reviewed in great detail the Soviet arms shipments to Cuba. On missiles, he said that fifteen SAM sites had been established on the island and that the total might eventually reach twenty-five. Then he said, "In addition, three and possibly four missile sites of a different type have been identified. These sites are similar to known Soviet coastal-defense sites with a range of 20–25 miles. Quite likely several more sites will be installed."[33] When asked by Representative A. Paul Kitchin, chairman of the committee, if Cuba was becoming an offensive base, Ball confidently replied that our intelligence was complete, good, and very hard. "All the indications are that this equipment is basically of a defensive capability and that it does not offer any offensive capabilities to Cuba against the United States or the other nations of the hemisphere."[34]

In the meantime, mission planners were particularly harassed because it was the hurricane season. The 1962 season was marked by eight hurricanes: Alma, Becky, Carla, Celia, Daisy, Ella, Ester, and Hattie. On October 3, tropical storm Daisy began building up to hurricane strength in the Caribbean, dumping heavy rains on Cuba. Daisy headed up the U.S. coast to New England before battering Nova Scotia on October 8. Every available means for checking weather was employed on a daily basis.

The intelligence community maintained steadfastly after the crisis that it was the weather that had hindered reconnaissance over Cuba and not the interference of Rusk and Bundy. McCone was called to testify before the House Appropriations Committee after the crisis, and he insisted that weather had hampered reconnaissance. This brought a strong rejoinder from Congressman Jamie Whitten: "Are you sure it was weather for the whole period and not a decision to postpone the flights?" He added, "It makes you wonder if perhaps our intelligence agencies might not be finding and releasing that which supports governmental policy rather than keeping us aware of the danger to our nation."

McCone was not entirely truthful when he said, "I have the responsibility for coordination and guidance of the entire intelligence community—and when I returned [from his honeymoon, on September 23] and found that there had been some restriction, I immediately investigated to see whether that restriction was such that it had deprived the intelligence analysts and the policymakers of any vestige of information, and I found this was not the case." Congressman Whitten didn't buy the argument. He asked McCone acidly: "So you pulled all your planes in and rested on your oars from September 5 to October 14, relying on the fact that the government said these are defensive weapons." Congressman Whitten later told me he wanted it on the record that had reconnaissance been conducted, we would have known nearly a month before that there were missiles in Cuba.

When General Carroll and McNamara testified before Congress on the lack of U-2 flights during the month of September and October, they also blamed the lack of reconnaissance on bad weather, as did Taylor, who was confronted by Congressman William Minshall: "I am not a meteorologist but I do have these weather forecasts and for a period of 8 days it was clear. There were many days when there was only one quarter cloud cover. There were many days when the visibility was 7 miles or more."[35] Congressman Minshall in later hearings would be even more forceful: "The record has been gone over many times, but from the 5th of September, for a period of 39 days until the 14th of October, we went from an open field, wooded area, to a completed missile site. That is all we have got. Nothing in between. That is why I say someone was derelict between the 5th of September and the 14th of October in not conducting a more intensive aerial reconnaissance, whether high, low, or whatever."[36]

It wasn't the weather but rather the dereliction, bumbling, and intransigence of Rusk and Bundy that kept the U-2's from flying over Cuba and learning about the missiles far earlier than October 14. The stormy weather conditions would find a strong parallel in the political climate that pervaded the president's advisers.

In hearings after the crisis, Senator Stennis would remark that "the reconnaissance of Cuba was not pursued with adequate vigor during the arms buildup to provide coverage of all parts of the island with sufficient frequency—and that procedures for obtaining approval for flight plans based on COMOR targets was not conducive to permitting quick changes in a fast-moving situation."[37]

Between September 20 and October 2, agent and refugee reports dovetailed sufficiently to generate the hypothesis that something of unusual importance was going on in Cuba, possibly in the western portion of the island. Che Guevara, according to one agent's account, was promoting the thesis that the NATO nations constituted a belt of bases surrounding the Soviet Union. He reportedly had stated that in September Cuba was going to become the buckle in that belt. According to another agent, Castro's personal pilot claimed that mobile ramps for launching intermediate-range rockets were being built in Cuba. In late September, a former Havana Hilton hotel employee claimed that he had seen a large missile estimated to be 65 to 70 feet long. When shown photographs of Soviet missiles, he quickly pointed to the SS-4 MRBM. Another source, in the same time frame, claimed to have seen a 30-meter-long missile; still another claimed that the Soviets were constructing rocket sites that could strike the Panama Canal.

A report, from a CIA agent in Cuba, stands in hindsight but was never adequately credited for helping find the missiles. On September 15, this agent conveyed the information in secret writing in a letter mailed from Cuba via international mail to a drop in a foreign city. When the letter arrived at CIA headquarters, it was processed and the information made available throughout the intelligence community. The report defined a large trapezoidal area heavily guarded by the Soviets in Pinar del Río province—within a perimeter bounded by the cities of San Cristóbal, San Diego de los Baños, Consolacíon del Norte, and Los Pozos. He reported that all Cubans in the area had been moved out and that security was being enforced to prevent access to the area where very secret and important work, believed to be concerned with missiles, was in progress.[38] The report was carefully analyzed by the U.S. Cuban Task Force.*

Repeated reports of large missiles being sighted and deployed in Cuba could no longer be discounted, and U.S. intelligence analysts were seeking alternative methods to confirm the authenticity of the reports.

On October 4, COMOR tasked the reconnaissance planners to come up with a complete plan for reconnaissance of the island, and on October 5, McCone asked that the USIB again review the priority recommendations for a series of short overflights.

On October 5, a peripheral offshore U-2 mission was flown covering the area from Trinidad, Cuba, to the eastern tip of the island. The only intelligence information obtained was the finding of an SA-2 site under construction at Manzanillo.

Another peripheral U-2 mission was flown on October 7, this time from the eastern tip of Cuba westward to the Bahía de Buena Vista. Four additional completed SAM sites—Chamsas, Senado, Manatí, and Esmeralda—were found along Cuba's northern shore.

Osvaldo Dorticos, president of the Republic of Cuba, had asked to address the UN General Assembly in New York. On October 8, beginning at 10:30 A.M., he spoke for several hours, and at the time, his speech was regarded as boilerplate Cuban propaganda. In retrospect, however, it is interesting to note that Dorticos gave a strong hint that the deployment of missiles in Cuba was a fact and that they may have been imposed on Cuba. He said, "We are, I repeat, well equipped to defend ourselves, for . . . we can, of course, rely on our unavoidable weapons—weapons we wish we did not need and that

* Elie Abel, in his book *The Missile Crisis*, properly credits Colonel John Wright of the Defense Intelligence Agency for recommending the mission over San Cristóbal, but for the wrong reasons. Colonel Wright, fully aware of the covert report and the fact that the area had not been photographed since August 29, recommended an aerial-reconnaissance mission over the area. There were no SAMs deployed in a trapezoidal pattern near San Cristóbal, but neither were SAMs deployed in Cuba in the same manner as they were in the Soviet Union—i.e., a point rather than an area defense pattern. When MRBMs were found in the San Cristóbal area, the sites were not defended, as Abel claims, with a SAM at each corner of the sites. The trapezoidal SAM defense concept was also discounted by the Department of Defense hearings before the Congress for fiscal year 1964.

we do not want to use."[39] Dorticos made repeated utterances that Cuba was not and did not pose a problem for the U.S. or the Western Hemisphere. He expressed fear that the U.S. might attack Cuba and sounded the warning: "If this error is committed, we are giving warning that the aggressor against Cuba, despite ourselves and against our will could, as has been pointed out here, become the starting point of a new World War."[40] Dorticos also revealed Khrushchev's final fallback position when he was confronted with the missile pullout of Cuba. "If the United States could give assurances, by word and by deed, that it would not commit acts of aggression against our Country, we solemnly declare that there would be no need for our weapons and our armies."[41] In Havana, Raul Castro also boasted about Cuba's ability to fend off an invasion: "We are not prophets, and we cannot foretell the decisions of the feverish minds of our enemies, but we can, calmly and sincerely, say here that Cuba, its revolution, and its people are invincible. We will repel, crush, and annihilate any attempt to set foot on our country."[42]

The Cuban press also gave considerable play to Vice-President Johnson's statements. In answer to critics advocating a blockade of Cuba, Johnson warned, "A blockade will lead to a third world war."[43] In response to proposals being made by some opponents of the Kennedy administration that the U.S. forcibly stop ships from other countries from sending materials to Cuba, Johnson added, "The detention of a Soviet ship is an act of war."[44] He also declared that an American invasion of Cuba was a stupid idea.

On October 9, the COMOR committee met and again discussed all the possibilities for reconnaissance of Cuba. Agreement was reached that the best results, following McCone's recommendation, could be obtained from a U-2 overflight from south to north. The highest priority was accorded the western portion of the island, especially over the trapezoidal area, and the mission was to be afforded full elint and tracking support.

That afternoon the Special Group met in McGeorge Bundy's office and considered proposals for both high- and low-level coverage of Cuba, including the use of tactical reconnaissance aircraft and drones. The group agreed with COMOR's recommendation for four U-2 south-to-north overflights that would cover most of Cuba. Depending on the results of the first mission, others would be approved.

The mission would have to be approved by the president. The group also discussed the possible transfer of Cuban reconnaissance responsibilities to the Strategic Air Command. A final assessment of the capabilities of the Cuban SA-2 sites had been completed and it had been determined that any further U-2 missions over Cuba should be considered hazardous. At this meeting it was also decided that the CIA cover story that a Lockheed pilot was delivering a U-2 from the United States to Puerto Rico and had inadvertently overflown Cuba was unsatisfactory and no longer credible.

Dr. Joseph V. Charyk, undersecretary of the Air Force, had notified Gilpatric that the Strategic Air Command was now prepared to assume U-2 flights over Cuba. Carter, remembering the chewing out he had gotten previously from McCone, protested and said that he would have to consult McCone, who told Carter that he understood that the decision to transfer the operation had already been made by McNamara. Much to Carter's surprise, McCone said further that he had mentioned the proposed transfer to the president previously—that the U-2 missions were getting progressively hazardous and he might want to consider a transfer of the responsibilities to the military. There are indications that Gilpatric informed the president previous to the Special Group meeting that the transfer should be effected as soon as possible and that preparations already were well under way to affirm the transfer. The president expressed concern whether the SAC U-2 pilots were as proficient as those of the Agency. He was reassured that they were.

Meanwhile, at Edwards Air Force Base, Agency personnel were supervising the requalification of the SAC pilots to fly the Agency's U-2's. The weather was reviewed daily and it was unfavorable for flying on October 10, 11, 12, and 13.

In his October 9 column, entitled "On War over Cuba," Walter Lippmann supported the administration's contention that the arms being shipped to Cuba were for defensive purposes. Quoting a number of Ball's statements before the congressional committee, Lippman reported that it was on the basis of such sound intelligence information that the administration was basing its policy. "This intelligence estimate is based on an elaborate system of surveillance by sea, by air and by land and there is every reason to think that this accuracy is very high . . . little of military interest can happen without our knowing it. We do not have to guess about what is being landed at the Cuban ports or about what is being constructed on Cuban territory. We know and anyone who chooses to question the basis of our present policy must begin by proving that the intelligence estimates are wrong."[45]

Meanwhile Senator Kenneth Keating of New York, who on September 3 proposed an inter-American mission to determine whether offensive missiles were in Cuba, was not convinced of what either Ball or Lippmann were saying. On October 10, on the floor of the Senate, the senator made the most serious charge to date. Construction had begun, he said, on at least a half-dozen launch sites for "intermediate-range tactical missiles." He said that these sites would be operational within six months. He emphasized that his sources had substantiated the report completely and called on the administration to confirm or deny his allegation. Keating then attacked President Kennedy and Undersecretary Ball for not telling the whole truth. He referred especially to Ball's testimony to the House committee and seized on the phrase "quite likely several more sites would be installed." Ball, of course, was referring to the cruise missile sites and not to intermediate-range ballistic missiles. Keating defined his term *intermediate-range tactical missile sites* as being capable "of hurling rockets into the American heartland and as far as the Panama Canal Zone."

Keating quoted from the Lippmann article that the U.S. knew what was happening in Cuba. He then questioned whether the administration was revealing all the information it had in its possession. He criticized the administration for withholding vital information from the American people and said, "Our government is very well aware of the fact that within a matter of months, Cuba may have the capability of launching intermediate-range missiles, but the American people are being kept in the dark. The Soviets know the fact. The Cubans know this fact. But in the view of the administration our people are not entitled to know it." Then he appealed, "Mr. President, let us have all the facts, and have them now."

Keating's speech hit like a bombshell at the White House. Keating's implication that the U.S. government possessed information on offensive missiles in Cuba and was doing nothing about it infuriated President Kennedy. Kennedy initially suspected that information had been withheld from him and angrily called McCone, demanding to know if such information existed. McCone responded in the negative but then called Lundahl to see if anything had been discovered on the aerial photos. Lundahl said he had no such information, but if the occasion should develop when he did, he had explicit orders to make that information known to him post haste. McCone received the same answer from other Agency components.

When news of Keating's statement was flashed on the various wire services, a scramble ensued in the lower echelons of the intelligence community, with analysts calling one another to see if any information existed confirming Keating's statement. At higher levels, Thomas Hughes, the deputy chief of intelligence and research at State, also called the chiefs of the various Washington intelligence agencies or their deputies to see if they possessed any of the information Keating had released. The responses that Hughes received were also negative.

The substantive content and the manner of reporting the information released by Keating suggested that it had been from human sources; a strong feeling existed among intelligence analysts that Keating's sources were refugee reports. It was further assessed that the senator was accepting the reports with little reserve or suspicion. In intelligence jargon, the senator was taking the worst-case approach in intelligence analysis. Nonetheless, all previous reporting from refugee sources was checked. Again, the response was negative. There was some fear that Keating might even be receiving refugee reports from the interrogation centers before they were being received in Washington. Calls hurriedly placed to interrogation centers revealed that no such information had been received or processed. The established procedure was for staffs at the interrogation sites to flash such information to Washington.

Senator Keating did not reveal the locations of the "intermediate" missiles, but the implication was that construction was already under way. If construction was sufficiently advanced, the sites would certainly be seen on photography. It would be counter to Soviet practices to place all of the sites in one location. Lundahl asked us to search the island again and to look especially hard and carefully analyze any area with recent construction activity. Again, no offensive missiles sites were found.

It was considered possible that Keating's information had been a deliberate attempt by a dissident refugee source to embarrass and discredit the Kennedy administration before the November elections or to push the United States into taking action against the Castro government. In the past, the Agency had received a number of such outright false reports, and all of them had been discredited.

Could Keating have misinterpreted Ball's statement regarding tactical missiles to mean intermediate missiles without realizing the difference? But Keating had stated that his information was fully substantiated. The nagging question within the intelligence community was, who had substantiated it? Keating, it was known, did not have a trained intelligence officer on his staff or the background files to evaluate or substantiate such a report. The implication that Keating was promoting was that his information had been corroborated by government sources. Senator Keating had provided amazing, accurate information to the government in the past. Because the senator was from New York, careful consideration was given to the possibility that he was being provided information by a member of the Cuban delegation to the United Nations. The fact that Keating would never reveal his sources lent considerable credence to this theory.

McCone did not like the criticism that President Kennedy was receiving from Congress. He was a Republican and a contributor to the Republican party, and he felt he was the logical man to approach Senator Keating. No one knows what arrangements were made between McCone and Keating, but McCone was well prepared. He directed Lundahl to have a complete set of briefing boards on Cuba sent over to his office. Lundahl asked if he should accompany them in case there were questions. McCone said it wasn't necessary. When the boards were delivered to McCone by NPIC couriers, he carefully reviewed them, keeping some, discarding others. He then arranged them in the order he thought would be appropriate to brief Keating and asked NPIC couriers to wait outside his office.

But Keating did not appear at the appointed time. The NPIC couriers exchanged banter with McCone's secretaries. Several times, McCone came out of his office and asked if the senator had arrived. Then he asked that the senator's office be called. The reply was that the senator had not been in his office that morning but was campaigning in upper New York State, that he would go directly to McCone's office when he arrived in town. About an hour later the senator arrived at CIA headquarters. He was recognized immediately by McCone's secretary. She asked if he would like to take off his coat and hat while she informed McCone that he had arrived. The senator was left waiting for a good ten minutes and during that time he chatted with the couriers. Then the senator was ushered into McCone's office. Presumably, McCone showed the senator all of the briefing materials and then probably asked Keating for the source of his information. Keating would not reveal it.[46]

The couriers reported that voices began to rise. McCone said that he had laid his cards on the table and had been honest but that the senator was doing his country incalculable damage. The senator shot back that he would not change his announcement that offensive missiles existed in Cuba. McCone retorted, "Tell me where they are and I'll prove to you that they are not there." McCone offered to have a mission flown over any spot in Cuba that the senator indicated. The senator refused. McCone then took the tack that the senator was not patriotic. Senator Keating shouted that he didn't care what McCone thought and stalked out of his office. According to the couriers, Keating appeared highly disturbed, his face flushed as he grabbed his hat and coat and stormed out of the office.

McCone did not give up. On another occasion, he asked Lundahl to report to the Senate Office Building and wait for him. The purpose, he said, was to brief Senator Keating on the latest intelligence findings regarding Cuba. When Lundahl arrived at the Senate Office Building, he couldn't find McCone. He called McCone's office and was told by McCone's secretary that she had received a call from Senator Keating's secretary that he was busy and did not have time for McCone.

When the missiles were found, Senator Keating was criticized for not sharing the information with the intelligence community. Roger Hilsman would later write: "The charge that Keating was more interested in personal publicity than in his country's welfare may be extreme. But until the Senator comes forward with a better explanation than he has so far supplied, one of two possible conclusions is inescapable: Either Senator Keating was peddling someone's rumors for some purpose of his own, despite the highly dangerous international situation; or, alternatively, he had information the United States Government did not have that could have guided a U-2 to the missile sites before October 14, and at less risk to the pilot."[47]

Although a concerted effort was undertaken by the Kennedy administration to determine Senator Keating's source of information, all their efforts failed. Time-Life publications were suspect because their reporting on Cuba had been very accurate. A check with Time-Life reporters friendly to the administration also failed to reveal Keating's sources. In later years, Clare Booth Luce would state that some of her sources had furnished information on missiles being in Cuba and that the information had found its way to Senator Keating.[48] In Havana, Castro welcomed President Dorticos on his return from the UN General Assembly. In a long, rambling speech, Castro announced, "We have many weapons. Yes, many weapons, many and powerful weapons!"[49] Castro stated, "The security of the fatherland has been increased; for the fatherland will not be helpless; for the fact is that the fatherland will be strong; for the fact is that the fatherland with the help and support of its socialist brothers can reply to the imperialist attack."[50]

U.S. reconnaissance aircraft were still photographing Russian ships on their way to Cuba. On September 28, 1962, a new large-hatch Soviet ship, *Kasimov*, was photographed in the Atlantic with a deck cargo of ten 60-foot-long shipping crates amidships. The type of crates was not identified by the U.S. naval unit that took the photographs, and unfortunately, these important photos were delayed in transmittal to Washington and were not distributed to the intelligence community until October 9. Bill Crimmins, the NPIC expert on Soviet aircraft, immediately identified the deck cargo as being ten fuselage crates for the Il-28 Beagle bomber. Lundahl called Cline, who asked to see the photos. Thaxter Godell, the Office of Research and Reports analyst and also a cratology expert, confirmed that the crates were those for the Beagle bomber. After seeing the photos and hearing the evaluation, Cline called McCone. Upon arriving at McCone's office, Cline pointed out the delay in the pictures' reaching Washington. McCone gave Cline a pained look and caustically remarked, "How in the hell did the Navy get them to Washington, by rowboat?"

McCone listened attentively and then questioned Cline if by any chance anything else could be shipped in the crates. Cline said he didn't think so, pointing out the unique configuration and length of the crates. Cline had also been shown photographs of similar Il-28 crates photographed at close range in the Alexandria, Egypt, harbor and at Egyptian airfields. The U-2's had also photographed Il-28 fuselages being removed from their shipping crates in Indonesia.

McCone reflected momentarily, accepted the photographs and the analytical report, and asked his special assistant, Walt Elder, to inform Bundy that he wanted an appointment with him and the president as soon as possible. Before dismissing Cline, McCone asked when the *Kasimov* had reached Cuba. When told that it had arrived on October 4, McCone shook his head and said that the information wasn't intelligence, it was history.

The Il-28 Beagle is a twin-jet light bomber with a cruise radius of 750 nautical miles, capable of carrying a 6,500-pound payload of nuclear or conventional bombs. It originated at Sergei Vladimirovich Ilyushin's design bureau shortly after World War II and had been initially test-flown in 1948. Series production had begun in 1950. During the next decade, before production ceased, the Il-28 had been used extensively by the Soviets. As it began to be replaced by later models, the Il-28 began to appear in Eastern European Communist countries, Communist China, the United Arab Republic, North Korea, Iraq, and Indonesia.

CIA analysts had long considered it was only a matter of time until the Il-28 would be made available to Cuba, and we began to watch Cuban airfields for indications of preparations for handling the aircraft. We had watched Holguín airfield for more than two years. During the Batista regime, it had been a minor airfield. Shortly after the Soviets began sending aid to the Cubans, we noted that grading and new construction activity began at the field, and it appeared that the airfield was being constructed in a manner similar to those we had seen in the Soviet Union where the Il-28 had been operational. By 1962, the Holguín airfield had a 10,000-foot blacktop runway capable of accepting light jet bombers or high-performance jet fighters. Additional signs that the airfield was nearing operational military status were the anti-aircraft defenses being deployed around the perimeter of the field. Several Il-28 crates had arrived at Holguín.

San Julián airfield, in western Cuba, was another field kept under surveillance. This airfield had been constructed as an operational U.S. air base during World War II, and the U.S. Navy and the U.S. Army Air Corps had used it as a base for antisubmarine air patrols protecting convoys moving from the United States to Africa and Europe. When World War II ended, the Cuban Air Force took over the field for use as a training base, but it soon fell into disrepair. Although it was marginally operational in 1962, many repairs on the hangars and runways were needed. Renewed signs of activity were noted on the photography in the late summer of 1962, but San Julián was not photographed for a period of more than six weeks in the fall because of bad weather. By the time it was photographed again on October 14, 1962, twenty-one fuselage and component crates were seen. On photography of October 23, Il-28 bombers were seen being assembled.

McCone reviewed the *Kasimov* photographs and the substantive analytical information with the president. He told the president that the Il-28 was an obsolete bomber by current standards. The president asked if these bombers could be considered offensive weapons. McCone replied in the affirmative, but soon qualified his remarks by saying that it wasn't the type of offensive weapons that the president had defined. "What are you going to do with the information?" the president asked. McCone said it was being prepared for publication in the CIA Intelligence Bulletin. The president asked if the intelligence community was in agreement with the information. McCone said that he was sure of the photographic analysis and that he planned to pass the information to McNamara as soon as he left the president's office. President Kennedy then asked if the information should be placed in the "special category." McCone looked rather surprised but said that "he didn't think so."

Upon returning to CIA headquarters, McCone mentioned that he was puzzled that the president had alluded several times to information being placed in a "special category." One of McCone's aides flinched, realizing that General Carter had failed to brief McCone on the PSALM category and the president's concern for restricting dissemination of sensitive information.

McGeorge Bundy obliquely announced on Sunday, October 14, on the ABC television program *Issues and Answers*, that the United

States would accept the presence of Il-28 bombers in Cuba when he said, "It's true that MiG fighters have been put in Cuba for more than a year now, and any possible addition in the form of aircraft might have a certain marginal capability for moving against the United States." Later in the program, in answer to a reporter's question, Bundy stated, "So far, everything that has been delivered in Cuba falls within the categories of aid which the Soviet Union has provided, for example, to neutral states like Egypt or Indonesia, and I shall not be surprised to see additional military assistance of that sort." The Soviets, listening to that broadcast, would undoubtedly have been encouraged; they had played another trump card and the United States had passed.

COMOR objectives and mission recommendation and track for the north-to-south U-2 mission were reviewed by the USIB and the JCS. Word was later received that the mission had been approved by the president.

On October 12, General Thomas S. Power, commander of the Strategic Air Command, was called to Washington. Ushered into the office of the secretary of the Air Force, he was asked if the Strategic Air Command was prepared to take over all the duties of flying U-2 reconnaissance of Cuba. The secretary was especially concerned whether the SAC pilots were sufficiently proficient to fly the Agency's U-2's. General Power replied in the affirmative.

If Prime Minister Castro showed any concerns about the missiles being in Cuba, it was not apparent. On the evening of October 12, Castro visited the University of Havana. For almost two hours he spoke to the students. It was a rambling discourse. He suggested to the law students and professors that they make a thorough survey of the reforms of the judicial power and the social defense code. He promised that he would teach a class on law "within the next few days."[51] He also announced a new tourist plan would be inaugurated on December 15. He rambled on about the good results of the coffee harvest and a change in the price of guest houses at Varadero Beach.

While a number of contacts with Russian officials were made by members of the Kennedy administration and while they conveyed anger at what was happening in Cuba, none of these officials demanded that the Soviets define precisely what was happening there. The failure to ask pertinent questions could have been misconstrued by Khrushchev as an acquiescence. Ambassador-at-large Chester Bowles, the president's special adviser on African, Asian, and Latin American affairs, met with Soviet ambassador Dobrynin on October 13. The appointment had been of long standing, and prior to their meeting, Rusk had shown Bowles the photos of the Il-28's aboard the *Kasimov* and asked that Bowles re-raise with Dobrynin the issue of Soviet offensive weapons being sent to Cuba. Bowles would be leaving on October 14 for a four-week visit to Africa, but the luncheon conversation with Dobrynin was dominated by Cuban affairs. Bowles made a strong statement that the sending of Il-28's to Cuba would exacerbate U.S.-Russian relations. He then restated the administration's position of the seriousness of offensive missiles being placed in Cuba. When Bowles said that reports were being received that the Soviets were shipping offensive missiles to Cuba, Dobrynin was surprised and insisted that the reports were untrue. Bowles warned that he hoped Dobrynin was right, "but that if he was wrong, he would not be the first nor the last ambassador in modern history to be deceived or ignored by his government in such a situation."[52]

Stung by Bowles's attitude, Dobrynin contended that the Soviet presence in Cuba was no more provocative than the American Jupiter missiles in Turkey. The fact that Dobrynin mentioned intermediate-range missiles would suggest that he had prior knowledge of the Soviet missiles being sent to Cuba. When Bowles pressed Dobrynin about the president's distinction between offensive and defensive capabilities, Dobrynin immediately went into the Soviet fallback position. He stated categorically that the Soviet Union was not sending offensive weapons to Cuba and that he was fully aware of the dangers and consequences of doing so. Bowles summarized his conversation with Dobrynin in a memorandum to Secretary Rusk and the president.

The next Soviet attempt to mislead was a message from Khrushchev to Kennedy, delivered through Georgi Bolshakov. Bolshakov's cover was that of being a Tass correspondent and the editor of the English-language slick Russian propaganda magazine *USSR*, published and distributed in the United States. He was also the escort of distinguished Soviets visiting the U.S. and the expeditor of requests for prominent Americans to visit the Soviet Union. To the CIA, Bolshakov was known as a KGB agent, probably a colonel, an expert translator and an important confidential courier. He had been in Washington for nearly ten years and had a number of friends in the Washington press corps. An opportunist, he sought out prominent Americans for opinions, which he transmitted to Moscow. More importantly for the Soviets, however, he had attained a working relationship early in the Kennedy administration with a number of its members, including Ted Sorensen, Robert Kennedy, and Pierre Salinger.[53]

The exchange of confidential notes and messages between Khrushchev and President Kennedy began after their Vienna meeting, much to the consternation and chagrin of the State Department. These exchanges were bypassing established State Department channels. Bolshakov became the confidential courier for Soviet officials, and Pierre Salinger was his usual contact in the White House. Bolshakov visited Moscow frequently and was in Moscow on October 1 when he was summoned to the Kremlin for a meeting with Khrushchev and Mikoyan. Bolshakov carefully recorded the conversation in a blue notebook. Returning to the United States, he pressed for an appointment with Robert Kennedy rather than his usual contact, Salinger. In a conversation with Robert Kennedy in early October, Bolshakov stated that he would like an interview with President Kennedy since he had a personal message from Premier Khrushchev. It was obvious that Bolshakov wanted to see how the president was reacting insofar as the missiles were being emplaced in Cuba. Bobby refused the interview request outright but said he would carry the message to the president. With some reluctance, Bolshakov opened his notebook and said that he had met with Khrushchev and Mikoyan and that Khrushchev asked that Bolshakov assure the president that the weapons being sent to Cuba were strictly for defensive purposes. Mikoyan added that the missiles were for anti-aircraft purposes and could not reach the United States. Bolshakov was encouraged by Bobby Kennedy to put the notes in writing for the president. Information from this meeting was circulated throughout the intelligence community. In Robert Kennedy's book, after discussing the Tass statement of September 11, he writes, "During this same period of time, an important official in the Soviet Embassy, returning from Moscow, brought me a personal message from Khrushchev to President Kennedy, stating that he wanted the President to be assured that under no circumstances would surface-to-surface missiles be sent to Cuba."[54] There is little doubt that Bobby Kennedy was speaking of Bolshakov but he had misdated his talk as being in September while records show it to have been in October.[55]

But Bolshakov did not stop there. He also sought out columnists Stewart Alsop and Charles Bartlett and told them there were no offensive missiles in Cuba. In their column of October 20, Bolshakov was quoted by name as the authority. By the time Bolshakov had gotten around to putting his notes on paper and getting them to the White House, the missiles had been found. After reading Bolshakov's message and the Alsop-Bartlett column, Bobby Kennedy, realizing that he had been fully taken, sarcastically said, "That son of a bitch has got to go." Shortly after the crisis, Bolshakov, his usefulness having come to an end, was recalled to Moscow.

By the middle of October, the attitude of most Americans had changed significantly. The public generally was uncomfortable with Kennedy's handling of the "Cuban problem." Roscoe Drummond, after a reporting trip across the United States, would state, "The feeling is that the Administration policy is unclear, uncertain and more timid than the American people relish."

There was widespread feeling that the time had arrived for Americans to stand firm against the Soviets. Recommended actions ranged from repeal of the neutrality laws of 1939 to forming Cuban brigades to the outright invasion of Cuba by U.S. forces. Such recommendations harried the president, but he remained resolute in his resolve not to be rushed into brash action. To Senator Russell and other Senate leaders, Kennedy was perceived as being weak and indecisive.

President Kennedy felt that he had to speak out and he decided to go after his arch-critic, Senator Homer Capehart, in his own territory. The Kennedys held nothing but contempt for the senator. Bobby was now referring to Senator Capehart as the Indiana Clodhopper. President Kennedy had backed young Birch Bayh for the Senate seat held by the senator. On October 13, at the Indianapolis airport, the president spoke out. After outlining in detail the military strengths of the United States, he said, "This is no time for confused and intemperate remarks on the part of those who have neither the facts nor the ultimate responsibility."[56]

Again, endorsing Bayh, the president pointedly attacked his Republican adversaries as "Those self-appointed generals and admirals who want to send someone else's son to war and who consistently vote against the instruments of peace ought to be kept at home by the voters and replaced in Washington by someone who understands what the 20th Century is all about."[57]

The motto of the 55th Strategic Reconnaissance Wing of the Strategic Air Command was *Videmus Omnia*—"We see all." Although the wing did not have a precisely defined wartime activation role, as did the SAC strategic bombardment wings, the 55th was a special activity wing, performing dangerous and highly sensitive photographic and elint collection missions. The wing was based at Forbes Air Force Base, outside Topeka, Kansas, but had detachments of elint collection aircraft stationed at Yakota, Japan; Incirlik, Turkey; Ellison Air Force Base, near Fairbanks, Alaska; Brize Norton, England; and occasionally at Wake Island. It was an RB-47H elint aircraft from the 343rd Squadron of this wing, flying a peripheral mission in the Barents Sea, that was shot down by the Russians during Eisenhower's administration. Early in the Kennedy administration, the president had asked for a show of goodwill from Khrushchev, who responded by releasing two survivors of that mission.

Five RB-47 photo-configured aircraft from the 55th were deployed to Macdill Air Force Base, outside Tampa, Florida. In addition to its elint mission, the 55th was to photograph all ships coming to Cuba. The elint-configured RB-47H consisted of a crew of six—a pilot, copilot, a navigator, and three elint operators. Elint missions were flown usually three times a day around Cuba, recording all signals being emitted by Cuban surveillance radars and radars at surface-to-air missile sites. These same aircraft were also used to support the U-2 photographic missions. The pilots of these missions were required to note the weather over Cuba and to report it to the headquarters of the Strategic Air Command, which in turn passed the information along to U-2 mission planners.

By late September these flights were being illuminated by radars that appeared to be operating in a tracking mode. There were, however, no reactions to the missions—no fighter aircraft were scrambled and no anti-aircraft or SAM warning shots were fired. Because of the duration of the illuminations, and since the radars employed had height-finding capabilities, the Soviets and Cubans were well aware of all these flights. It was also obvious that the tracking data that the Soviets and Cubans were acquiring would give them the capability to shoot down a U-2.

October 14 – The U-2
Reconnaissance Mission

"A piece of cake—a milk run."

—U-2 PILOT MAJOR RICHARD S. HEYSER

T HE OPERATIONAL CONTROL of the Cuban overflights was officially transferred from the CIA to the Joint Chiefs of Staff/Strategic Air Command on October 12, 1962. On October 13, the CIA U-2 detachment at Edwards Air Force Base was transferred to McCoy Air Force Base, Orlando, Florida, which would become the U-2 operating base. McCoy AFB was much closer to Cuba and U-2 flights could be revised more readily to accommodate changes in weather. In mission planning of Cuba, a weather forecast of at least 75 percent of the primary area to be cloud-free was considered requisite for a successful reconnaissance mission. The general weather forecasts provided to the public by the U.S. Weather Bureau were inadequate for operational reconnaissance planning. Weather for U-2 mission planning was obtained from Global Weather Central, located at Offutt Air Force Base, near Omaha, Nebraska. The U-2 mission planners were concerned with the type and extent of cloud cover from ground level to the U-2 operational altitude of 70,000 feet rather than with forecasts that were limited to the visibility and ceiling readings associated with routine airfield operations in controlling aircraft take-offs and landings. While some parts of Cuba experienced good weather every day, mission planners had to be virtually certain that the principal targets would be clear—not only at the time of the forecast but from 12-to-24 hours in advance of the mission, so that the reconnaissance aircraft and photographic systems could be readied.

The weather cleared and Major Richard S. Heyser was given the nod to fly the first SAC U-2 mission over Cuba. Major Heyser and Major Rudolf Anderson were the first SAC pilots checked out by the CIA to fly the U-2F model; Major Heyser was considered the more proficient of the two. There would be only one mission flown on October 14 and Major Heyser was to be the pilot, with Major Anderson designated the backup pilot. Four hours before the flight, a backup U-2 was also made ready in case the primary aircraft was unable to fly.*

Major Heyser was billeted in the BOQ of the officers' club at Edwards Air Force Base in the California desert. After a high-protein, low-bulk meal at 11 A.M. on October 13, Heyser took the customary sleeping pill and shortly afterward fell asleep. He was awakened at precisely 8 P.M. EST. His takeoff was set for 11:30 P.M. on October 13. He would now follow a regimen that would put him over Cuba at 7:30 A.M. on October 14. He had ten minutes to shower and shave, ten minutes for a bowel movement, and ten minutes to get dressed. After dressing, he would be driven to the flight line, where the flight crew was busy preparing a CIA U-2F for takeoff. It was a newer model than the U-2A's and U-2C's assigned to SAC. The U-2F contained the powerful J-75 engine, a larger, more sophisticated power plant that developed 15,800 pounds of thrust compared with the 13,500 pounds of the J-57. This allowed the Agency U-2F's to fly about 5,000 feet higher than the SAC U-2's. Several of the Agency's U-2's were also configured for in-flight refueling and contained a myriad of black boxes for detecting ground radar tracking and hostile SAM firings.

The flight surgeon was waiting at the preflight facility. He gave Heyser an abbreviated physical examination, making careful notes

---

* James Daniel and John G. Hubbell's *Strike in the West*, published in 1963, reported that two missions were flown concurrently, one by Heyser and the other by Anderson. General Maxwell Taylor, in *Swords and Plowshares*, also erroneously identified Major Anderson as the pilot who flew the mission that discovered the MRBM missiles.

as he asked numerous questions of Heyser as to how he felt that day. After taking Heyser's blood pressure, temperature, and pulse, the flight surgeon checked to see if Heyser had any coordination problems. He asked Heyser to stand on the nearby scales to be weighed. Heyser would lose about five pounds during this mission. After executing all the necessary forms, the flight surgeon gave his permission for Heyser to fly the mission.

Heyser then moved to the dining table, where a sergeant served a low-residue breakfast, consisting of a lean steak, two eggs, toast, jam, and coffee. It was a leisurely breakfast lasting about forty-five minutes. U-2 pilots normally had several cups of coffee, which, they claimed, counteracted the effects of the sleeping pill taken the night before. Heyser paid 40 cents, the usual club price, for his breakfast. It was ironic that a man who was willing to give his life, if necessary, for his country would have to pay for his breakfast. After breakfast, Heyser started dressing for the mission. He donned long-john-type underwear, then put on his flight helmet and started the prebreathing process—breathing pure oxygen for about two hours. His helmet was periodically checked for condensation. During this period, Heyser was briefed on the weather, the flight track, turn points, checkpoints, defenses, call signs, emergency procedures, recall, and rescue. He was also told the altitude at which to expect condensation trails from the aircraft.

After these briefings, he was allowed to go to the bathroom one last time prior to being fitted into his pressure suit. There are provisions for urinating in flight but no provisions for defecating once strapped into the cockpit. In the early phases of U-2 flight training, pilots were offered diapers, but all felt that this was demeaning and chose the high-protein, low-bulk meals as an alternative. Two enlisted technicians helped Heyser dress. First, they helped him into his pressure suit and then into his heavy but comfortable flight boots. They carefully laced his boots and connected all the pressure hoses and electrical connectors to his suit. Before he donned his coveralls, a pressure check was made of his pressurized suit and helmet. His communication gear was also checked out.

Heyser was then disconnected from the in-house oxygen supply and hooked onto his "walk-around oxygen bottle." He walked to a waiting ambulance and was driven to his U-2. Heyser was assisted into the U-2 cockpit some thirty minutes before takeoff. Once he was strapped into his seat, his oxygen supply was transferred from the bottle to that of the plane. It seemed an interminable period, but all of these checks and counterchecks were necessary to assure a safe flight. Should there be an emergency, Heyser would switch back to the oxygen bottle, pull a yellow lever between his legs, and be ejected, seat and all, from the aircraft. Upon completing all the cockpit preflight procedures, the enlisted men departed and a second U-2 pilot who had preflighted the plane, and who also served as control officer, went over with Heyser the countdown of the preflight checklist.

The cockpit hatch cover was then closed and Heyser began the aircraft start-up procedure. The compression in the starter unit was activated while a fire engine was positioned nearby. With the U-2's engine started and warmed, Heyser taxied to the end of the runway. There, he ran still another checklist on his equipment. The safety pins on the pogos were removed by a ground crew. Everything had checked out and Heyser waited for tower clearance. When it came, Heyser shoved the throttle forward and the U-2 responded and began to move down the runway. As it gained speed and began to lift, Heyser dropped the pogos and then gently pulled back on his control stick. The U-2 lifted off the runway and began a mission that would have historic repercussions. Heyser recorded his takeoff time as the U-2 augured skyward. At altitude, Heyser went through still another checklist. All systems were go, and he pointed the nose of the U-2 toward Cuba.

At altitude, Heyser checked all his life-support systems; at this height, oxygen must be supplied under pressure or it would not enter the bloodstream. He sat uncomfortably in the cockpit in his skin-tight pressure suit. Later, the danger would possibly be from SA-2 missiles or MiG-21 fighters, but throughout the flight there was a more dangerous enemy—sudden decompression. He looked around and saw that his aircraft was leaving no contrails.

This mission, like all photographic-reconnaissance missions, was among the most carefully guarded of all military tasks. The mission number was G-3101 and the code name was Victor. Heyser set his course and settled back for about a five-hour flight. Mission G-3101 employed the B camera system, a high-resolution 36-inch-focal-length, large-format general-coverage reconnaissance camera designed to provide detailed information over an extremely large area. The camera was loaded with two rolls of film, each 9 inches wide and over 5,000 feet long. The rolls of film were placed parallel to the focal plane of the camera so that both rolls were exposed during each action of the shutter. The combined film size was 18 × 18 inches. The cameras would take an array of pictures from horizon to horizon. Coverage was in a seven-position mode (73.5 degrees left, 49.0 degrees left, 24.5 degrees left, 0 degrees or vertical, 24.5 degrees right, 49.0 degrees right, and 73.5 degrees right). The camera stops in each position and moves forward ever so slightly. This compensates for the speed of the U-2 as it passes over a stationary point on the ground and is called image-motion compensation. The seven positions cover an area about 100 nautical miles wide from horizon to horizon. The supply of film in the cameras made it possible to acquire about 4,000 paired aerial photos—i.e., to photograph a route of about 3,500 kilometers or from Washington, D.C., to Phoenix, Arizona. The high-sensitivity film in the U-2 camera ensured excellent aerial photography throughout the daylight hours. It was designed for photographic reconnaissance of military, industrial, and topographic objects and for aerial surveys from high altitudes. The definition of the film was remarkable for that day. It recorded photography with a resolution of 2.5 feet at nadir (objects 2.5 foot square on the ground could be seen) from altitudes of 65,000 to 70,000 feet. The resolution of the U-2 cameras was often exaggerated, probably through confusion with the low-altitude camera systems later deployed over Cuba. Roger Hilsman, the director of intelligence and research at State, for example, in his book stated: "At heights well over seventy thousand feet—almost fourteen miles—pictures were taken with a resolution of only two inches on a side, which means that the painted lines of a parking lot could be distinguished, for example, or the muzzle of a new kind of cannon peeking out of the wing of an airplane. In the hands of skilled photographic interpreters, these pictures could produce an unbelievable amount of extremely accurate information."[1]

Approaching the Isle of Pines from the south, Heyser checked to see if his aircraft was leaving any contrails and made the following notation on his chart: "On course 351." He turned the camera switch on and checked the voltage needle. It registered the desired 24 volts.

He could hear the whine of the camera's motor and the thump each time the long barrel of the panoramic lens locked into one of its seven positions. He noted the time as he flew northward over Cap Frances on the Isle of Pines as being 1231Z (7:31 A.M EST). He also recorded the altitude as being 72,500 feet. The course line of 351 degrees across Cuba took him over Davaniguas, Los Palacios, San Cristóbal, San Diego de los Baños, and Los Pozos. The names Los Palacios and San Diego de los Baños would have fleeting moments of notoriety. At 1243Z (7:43 A.M. EST), he left the island of Cuba and made a new course correction of 17 degrees.

When Heyser's U-2 touched down at McCoy Air Force Base at Orlando, Florida, the two large rolls of film were removed, placed in special shipping containers, and rushed to a waiting aircraft that took the film to the Naval Photographic Intelligence Center (NAVPIC), at Suitland, Maryland. While the film was being flown to Maryland, Heyser was debriefed. He regarded it as a routine mission. During his debriefing, he said the mission was "A piece of cake—a milk run," Air Force jargon for a mission in which there were no enemy fighters seen over Cuba and no anti-aircraft or SA-2 reaction.

6

October 15—Discovery of Offensive Missiles in Cuba

"The photographs one brings back are submitted
to stereoscopic analysis as organisms are
examined under a microscope; the interpreters
of these photographs work exactly like the
bacteriologists."

—ANTOINE DE SAINT-EXUPÉRY

O CTOBER 15 would be a routine day for the heads of state of two
of the most powerful nations in the world. President Kennedy
had been campaigning in upstate New York and had appeared
in the Pulaski Day parade in Buffalo on October 14. He stopped off
in New York City and had a late dinner and an extended conversation
with Adlai E. Stevenson, U.S. ambassador to the United Nations.
Leaving LaGuardia airfield at 11:50 P.M., the president arrived at the
White House at 1:40 A.M. on the fifteenth. He slept late that morning
and went to his office at 11:00 A.M., just in time to prepare to greet
Ahmed Ben Bella, the prime minister of Algeria.

In July 1957, the then junior senator John F. Kennedy had called
upon the Eisenhower administration to stop supporting France in
its war against the Algerian separatists led by Ahmed Ben Bella and,
instead, to back independence and self-rule for the Algerians. Kennedy's
demand had caused considerable controversy and had been
greeted coolly by Secretary of State John Foster Dulles. Dulles had
stated that if Kennedy wanted to tilt against colonialism, he should
concentrate on the Russians rather than the French. The hard-pressed
Algerians, however, had regarded the Kennedy statement as a generous
gesture and the initial break in the pro-French U.S. attitude.

When Ahmed Ben Bella became premier of Algeria, he expressed a desire to visit President Kennedy, and arrangements were made for his visit on October 15. At 11:15 that morning, Ben Bella was given an especially warm welcome on the South Lawn of the White House as cannons boomed out a twenty-one-gun salute. Although Ben Bella had publicly emphasized that he was not taking sides in the U.S.-Cuba dispute, he told President Kennedy that he would not mind functioning as an intermediary. The president apparently advised Ben Bella that the Russian buildup in Cuba was extremely disturbing to the United States and Castro should be warned that if he did anything to endanger the security of the United States, the president would take whatever steps necessary.

Two days later, Ben Bella arrived in Havana for a twenty-four-hour state visit. He was greeted warmly by Castro. The Algerian premier found Castro extremely belligerent and adamant against any concessions to the United States. Later that day, Castro made a vitriolic attack against the U.S. A communiqué issued after Ben Bella had departed claimed that Ben Bella had joined with Castro in demanding that the U.S. give up its naval base at Guantánamo.

The Castro announcement caused considerable concern in Washington. Senator Russell commented that the president had selected a poor friend in Ben Bella and the naiveté of the president had given the Republicans another issue in the upcoming elections. Officials at the State Department said that while they were unhappy about the statement, they were not surprised by Ben Bella's support of Castro inasmuch as Algeria had just gained its independence from France. When Senator Russell was made aware of the State Department response, he remarked, "Well, what would you expect from those apologetic bastards at State. Not one of them have ever run for office."

On October 17, when Ben Bella arrived in New York, he was met by the Czech ambassador to the U.S., Dr. Miloslov Ruzek, and Dr. Mario Garcia-Inchaustegui, head of the Cuban UN delegation. Later, Ben Bella also saw U Thant. Ben Bella was surprised that he had not been contacted by any U.S. representative to the UN to pass along information he had gained in his conversation with Castro. What Ben Bella didn't know was that the Soviet offensive missiles had been discovered while he was in Havana.

At 4:30 P.M. on October 15, the president met with Mohammed

Ali, minister of external affairs of Pakistan, at the White House for over an hour. Among other things discussed was the deteriorating situation between India and Communist China. That evening, the president had a quiet dinner with his father. Exhausted from the previous day's campaigning, and with his back giving him considerable pain, the president retired early. According to one source, he was "hurting"—White House jargon that the president was in more pain than usual.

In Moscow, Khrushchev met with Finnish president Uhro Kekkonen in his Kremlin office on the same day. After their meeting, Khrushchev, Kekkonen, and Kekkonen's wife, Sylvi, a well-known author, strolled casually about the Kremlin grounds. Early that morning, the Soviets had announced they would conduct extended-range rocket firings—i.e., ICBMs—launched from Tyura Tam missile test range downrange to the Pacific during the period from October 16 to November 30. The possibility that the firing of long-range missiles in the Pacific was meant to impress and intimidate President Kennedy cannot be discounted.

That same day, Khrushchev's findings on his trip to Central Asia, entitled "Several Questions of Planning Economic Development in Central Asia," were presented to the presidium of the CPSU Central Committee. That evening, Khrushchev and his wife attended a ballet performance at the Bolshoi Theater. There had been no apparent pressing problems throughout the day; all appeared peaceful and tranquil in Moscow. If Khrushchev was in any way aware of the U-2 flight over the Cuba missile sites and possible discovery of missiles, he gave no outward sign of it.

At the new CIA headquarters building in Langley, Virginia, the day also began with meetings for some of the principals who would later be involved in the crisis. At 9:10 A.M., Ray Cline opened the Second Conference on Intelligence Methods. Participants were foreign-intelligence chiefs, along with senior officers from the CIA, DOD, and State.

Paul J. Pigott, Mrs. McCone's son, who had been injured in an auto race at the Riverside Raceway in California on October 14, had died at the March Air Force Base hospital. McCone had left Washington to accompany the body to Seattle and to make the necessary funeral arrangements. McCone had planned to open the conference, and Cline conveyed the director's regrets. The first speaker was McGeorge Bundy and his topic, "Intelligence in an Age of Acceleration," would be particularly applicable the next day. He was followed by Roger Hilsman. As the week's program continued, the Commonwealth intelligence chiefs were to become more and more suspicious that a crisis was brewing as their U.S. hosts mysteriously excused themselves from the business and social functions of the conference.

Monday, October 15, began as a beautiful fall day in Washington. Because of the poor parking facilities around the Steuart Building at 5th and K streets in northwest Washington, car pools were encouraged. From the suburbs of Virginia and Maryland and from the city, car pools made their way to the National Photographic Interpretation Center. Leaves on the trees had just begun to turn. The beauty of the trees along Skyline Drive in Virginia and the strengths and weaknesses of the Washington Redskins football team were current topics of conversation. Most of the parking spaces near the building were in alleyways or in spaces rented in the backyards of nearby homes and businesses. Broken bottles, abandoned autos, and trash littered the area. Frequently, a car-pool member would get out and remove the broken bottles and glass before a car could park.

The Steuart Building was a nondescript seven-story structure built during World War II. The Center occupied a total of fifty thousand square feet on the fourth through seventh floors. There were no restaurants or cafeteria facilities in the building and food service was a particular problem, especially for persons working at night. When there was time, sandwiches and coffee could be bought at a nearby all-night diner. Most employees brought bag lunches and dinners from home. Before entering the Steuart Building each morning, others stopped at the Center City Market. The market was a conglomeration of small shops selling everything from the cheapest cuts of meats to imported delicacies, from patent medicines to freshly cut flowers. But every morning, freshly baked breakfast rolls and freshly brewed coffee and tea were available. Properly fortified, employees passed through the security turnstiles of the Steuart Building en route to their offices. They were always greeted cordially by guard George

Bailey, who knew everyone by first name. Eunice Stallings, the elevator operator, a cigar-smoking woman who did *The New York Times* crossword puzzle in record time, took the employees to their appointed floors.

A mere physical description of the squalid building amid its squalid surroundings in Washington's 2nd Police Precinct reveals little as to what NPIC was all about. It was a unique multidepartmental national-level organization. The formal structure was controlled, staffed, and funded by the CIA, but the informal organizational structure also comprised special detachments from the Army, Air Force, and Navy. They were under the administrative control of "service chiefs," who contributed personnel for photo-interpretation projects of national interest such as the exploitation of photography acquired over Cuba.

The National Photographic Interpretation Center, however, was synonymous with its director, Arthur C. Lundahl. Lundahl was responsible for the conception and evolution of photographic interpretation as it was performed at the Center. His ingenuity was reflected not only in Center activity, but also at all the military-intelligence agencies involved in photo-interpretation activities. From the inception of NPIC and its predecessor organizations, beginning in 1955, Lundahl's visionary approach and methods of deriving intelligence from photography and collateral sources were dismissed by many as too revolutionary to last. Basically, he aimed at fusing ideas and experiences that previously had been considered unrelated or incompatible. Drawing on World War II experiences, he juxtaposed and fused the skills of seven different disciplines: photo interpretation, collateral information and data processing, photogrammetry, graphics and publication support, technical analysis, and distribution and courier support. The result was a team of experienced personnel that inspired great confidence from other intelligence and government officials. The Center's organization and skill represented the first modern technological approach to intelligence collection, processing, and dissemination. NPIC supervisory personnel recognized their unique opportunity and worked hard at making the Center a model of organization and production.

Lundahl's leadership was reinforced by an unusual level of talent throughout the organization. Allen Dulles, the director of the CIA, and his deputy, Lieutenant General Charles P. Cabell, extended Lundahl a free hand in selecting personnel to staff the Center. Although the Steuart Building left much to be desired in physical amenities, Lundahl would frequently remark: "Where a choice be necessary, give me good men in poor ships rather than the converse." A particularly distinguishing feature of Lundahl's managerial genius was his ability to find gifted people and to establish an atmosphere of creativity in which they could work. Many new organizations are burdened with a percentage of castoffs. But Lundahl's most unique and significant contribution was his ability to lead and inspire others. He was unparalleled in winning the complete respect, admiration, and devotion of all those with whom he came in contact—presidents, the Congress, the military services, the intelligence community, the scientists, contractors and, of course, the personnel of the Center. The imagination and dedication of the people selected by Lundahl for managerial responsibilities can never be overestimated. These managers, in turn, supervised young, talented, and dedicated personnel. Although Lundahl set high standards for his employees, he permitted his staff an extraordinary degree of independence. He laid down few guidelines or specific rules. He believed that his staff would function better if given wide latitude. In return, he received an exceptional sense of commitment from his employees and a great response of new ideas. The employees at the Center had in Arthur Lundahl an ardent believer in, and a prophet of, photographic interpretation. He could articulate with great feeling the meaning of the photo-interpretation methods and the value of information obtained from the photography. Lundahl, in his words, didn't believe in a droning presentation but rather in an exploding one. Aerial photography was his ammunition.

Even the security system at the Center reflected the singularity and uniqueness of the organization. The security accorded the U-2 program and the photo intelligence derived from it was never breached. Great effort had been expended to place the program in a separate security system and give it a set of special code words. Some maintain this system gave Lundahl extraordinary freedom to move information directly from the Center to the president. Others maintained that the novelty of aerial photography made it a new toy for the intelligence-service chiefs and other government leaders.

It was also the knot that tied together the many bits and pieces of information gathered from other collection sources. Analysts now had the means to confirm or deny their suspicions or hypotheses. NPIC was uniquely qualified, staffed, and ready on October 15.

At the Naval Photographic Intelligence Center, the film from mission 3101 was processed under stringent quality and security controls. The film was carefully edited and titled, and the duplicate positives from the processors were spooled and packaged in film cans.

NPIC's operations officer, Hans F. Scheufele, maintained constant contact with the collection and processing sites so that scheduling information would be available to Center components and the exploitation teams could be apprised of the delivery time of the film. He kept this information posted on a large blackboard on his office wall. He also issued daily bulletins on "Proposed Staffing and Time Completion Estimates," which listed specific personnel assigned to exploit a given mission and the arrival time of the film.

This particular day had all the appearances of being routine. Lundahl had scheduled a 9:30 A.M. meeting with his division chiefs to discuss training. There were many problems associated with training photo interpreters in the technicalities of identifying modern weaponry on photography. Lundahl encouraged Center personnel to make on-site familiarization visits to U.S. missile, nuclear, electronics, and related industrial facilities. On such trips, Center personnel could become thoroughly familiar with U.S. weapons and the photographic "signatures" of each system. This familiarity would aid them in recognizing similar systems in denied foreign areas. There were always problems—clearances, transportation, money—in arranging such trips. As he prepared for the meeting, Lundahl glanced out his office window overlooking 5th Street. With some annoyance, he noted that a U.S. Navy truck parked in front of the building entrance was blocking traffic. Two armed Marines had dismounted and taken positions immediately behind the truck. An armed Navy officer and an enlisted man entered the truck from the rear, lifted a box off the truck, and carried it into the Steuart Building.

Lundahl smiled, shook his head, and noted how good intentions often become counterproductive. Every effort had been made to keep the Steuart Building looking as innocuous as possible. Yet the regulations for transporting U-2 film by the military services specified that movement of the film be made under armed guard. The U.S. Navy was following the rules to the letter. But in doing so, it was revealing that personnel in the Steuart Building were undoubtedly engaged in some extremely classified and sensitive work.

Robert Kithcart of the NPIC registry, a businesslike reserve paratroop captain who was in charge of all the film and files retained in the Steuart Building, received the box. Eight cans of film—numbering 464 frames for each camera—were in the box. Kithcart duly recorded the receipt time in the log—0955—and affixed film library control numbers 11476 through 11483 to the cans of film. He then placed the film in a wire basket to be delivered to Earl Shoemaker, the exploitation coordinator for this mission.

After being notified that mission 3101 had been successfully flown over Cuba, personnel at the Steuart Building prepared to exploit the photography and, when the exploitation was completed, to report their findings in a SITSUM (situation summary) for the mission. The usual procedure was to cable the SITSUM immediately to watch offices throughout the intelligence community. Some days later, it would be disseminated by courier in hard-copy form to a broader distribution of intelligence analysts in the Washington area and throughout the JCS unified and specified commands.

Marvin Michell, the collateral-support information specialist for the mission, had performed preparatory tasks for many of the U-2 missions over Cuba. He had plotted the mission flight track on a World Aeronautical Chart and noted all the targets that should be covered by the photography and the reporting requirements for each target. He had requested computer listings and histories of the targets of concern. The photo interpreters would also be provided with a worksheet for each target with all its identifiers (installation name, location, geographical coordinates, target numbers, sorting codes), along with the target brief, which contained a printout of previous photographic coverages, readouts of the target, as well as a summary of the requirements and related collateral intelligence. There was a packet of collateral materials for each target, containing a map, photo chips, and various intelligence documents. Knowing what support materials would be required, Michell selected reference materials on what might be seen: missiles, aircraft, airfields, ports, and industries.

He carefully assembled the paper printouts from the computers, along with the target dossiers, and sorted them according to the assigned teams of photo interpreters. When word came that the film had arrived in the building, Marvin wheeled a library cart full of the target packets and reference materials to the area where the photo interpreters were waiting.

Earl Shoemaker had his photo-interpretation teams ready. He had checked the flight track; this would be a short mission in terms of film footage to be exploited. The cans of film had arrived and were distributed among the various teams. The interpreters began cranking the reels of duplicate positives onto the light tables.

Normally, six photo-interpretation stations were employed in scanning Cuban photography. But since mission 3101 was of short duration, with just eight cans of film, only three stations were used. The three stations were manned by six photo interpreters—three teams of two interpreters each—representing the CIA, Army, Air Force, and Navy. Backup, or special, teams of photo interpreters would be provided as needed. Various types of photographic-viewing equipment were used, including hand-held tube magnifiers with magnification from 7 to 13 power; fixed stereoscopes with magnifications of 2.4 or 7 power; zoom stereoscopes with magnifications ranging from 10 to 60 power; and roll-film viewing tables with a built-in light source over which the film passed. Most of the equipment had been designed and built for the Center specifically to exploit U-2 photography. (The light tables, along with the stereoscopes used on this mission, have since been given to the Smithsonian Air and Space Museum.)

The photo interpreters who scanned these missions found Cuba intriguing: the hot morning sun; the afternoon rain clouds; the strange vegetation of the palm, coniferous, and deciduous trees; the tall marsh grass; the sugarcane fields in the plains; the small towns where people gathered; the large estates overlooking beautiful beaches; the thatched roofs of the peasant huts; the plush resort towns; the rich expanses of *fincas*, or ranches; the ubiquitous baseball diamonds; the cosmopolitan look of Havana and the sleepy and forgotten appearance of Santiago; the Sierra Maestras rising abruptly behind the coast; the small railroads leading from the sugar-processing centrals to the cane fields; the loneliness of the large prison on the Isle of Pines; the salt flats; the many boats and fishing yards; and the roads that cross and crisscross the island.*

As they examined the film, the interpreters wrote their observations on the worksheets provided and passed them to their team leaders for review. An editor then checked the sheets for style and completeness and handed the edited sheets to the mission coordinator for approval. From him, the worksheets flowed to a keypunch operator. One IBM card was punched for each line of text. The cards were then fed into a computer processor, which printed out a proof run in subject order (missiles, airfields, etc.) for final edit and review. Each evening, a corrected proof would be run, and the final version of the SITSUM would be ready for transmittal by cable and hard copy to the intelligence community. The SITSUM for mission 3101, however, would not leave the Steuart Building for several days.

The two cans of the film covering the San Cristóbal and the trapezoidal area of concern were given to the scan team of Gene Lydon, a CIA photo interpreter, and Jim Holmes, an Air Force interpreter, for exploitation. Scanning the countryside, they spotted military vehicles and tents. The equipment and tents observed along fence rows suggested preparatory work for an SA-2 site. The two interpreters searched for the Fruit Set guidance radar and the missile launchers to identify another SA-2 site. None were found. Because cruise mis-

---

* Photo interpreters develop signatures—indicators that act as a mechanism by which natural, cultural, or man-made objects can be identified on aerial photography. Distinguishing elements of an image scene that lead to a photo-interpretation signature include:

1. Shape—relates to the general configuration of an object (distinguishing a factory from a school)

2. Size—relates to the dimensions, surface, and volume of an object (bombers vs. fighters)

3. Tone—refers to the brilliance with which light is reflected by an object

4. Texture—is the frequence of a tone change within the image (in crop analysis, the differences between a field of corn vs. that of wheat)

5. Pattern—refers to the spatial arrangement of the objects (especially true for deployed weapons)

6. Shadow—describes the condition wherein an intervening object prevents the direct sun rays from striking certain areas shown on the imagery (important for three-dimensional study and mensuration)

7. Site—is the location of an object in relation to its environment (geographical location, i.e., on hills, valleys, etc.)

8. Scale—is the ratio of image size to object size, may be varied by optical instruments

9. Association—is the interrelationships of objects observed

sile sites had been identified along Cuba's coasts, their attention shifted to searching for cruise missile launchers and attendant guidance radars. Again, none were found.

Then they spotted six long canvas-covered objects. Lydon and Holmes made rough estimates of the measurements of the objects several times. Each time, their measurements showed the objects to be more than sixty feet long. It was then about noon, and both men paused for lunch. After lunch, they resumed their efforts but still could not positively identify the canvas-covered objects. The equipment appeared to be missile-associated, so the film was labeled "possible missile-associated installation" and handed to Shoemaker. Shoemaker assigned the film to the missile backup team, which consisted of four interpreters representing the Air Force, Army, Navy, and CIA. Jim Holmes, a civilian Air Force employee, was a soft-spoken, yet tough-minded and intense, photo interpreter. A native of Pittsburgh, Pennsylvania, he was only twenty-nine but a veteran of twelve years of government service. He began his government career at seventeen as a GS-2 cartographic technician at the Army Map Service, where his aunt was a training officer. She made sure his training was especially thorough. This thoroughness and his meticulous eye for detail were to pay off that day. His training in map compilation work also made him aware of unnatural features on aerial photography. An Army veteran, he was also a night student at American University.

Twenty-two-year-old Second Lieutenant Richard Reninger was the Army member of the team. Born in Laramie, Wyoming, he had a B.A. in history from the University of Wyoming. He had graduated from the U.S. Army Photo Interpretation School at Fort Holabird in June 1961 and was assigned to the missile backup team at the Center the following May. Reninger was a tall, erect, and slender young man with a stern face. He was affable but generally quiet. He had a no-nonsense approach to problems and was painstaking in detail. The subtle differences in models of military equipment had been stressed heavily at Fort Holabird. Dick was an expert on military hardware and knew most of the equipment basic to Soviet line divisions.

A native of Maine, Joe Sullivan, a civilian Navy employee, was a puckish, attractive Irishman. At fifty, he was the senior member of the team, with nineteen years' experience with the stereoscope. He was reserved, thoughtful, and extremely courteous. He was especially appreciated by colleagues for his sense of humor. Joe had served in World War II as an aerial phototopographer both in photo-reconnaissance squadrons and in engineering topographic companies in the Army Air Corps. This background, combined with subsequent experience at the Army Map Service and with the Navy, made him extremely familiar with topography and mapping.

Vince DiRenzo was the CIA representative on the team. From Shenandoah, Pennsylvania, he was thirty-two and a former Marine. He joined the Agency in 1956 fresh from the graduate school of geography at Clark University. His abilities were as bright as the Marine sheen he constantly maintained on his shoes. He was affable and possessed a good sense of humor. Joe Sullivan made constant fun of the "Crooks" and "Marsh Wheeling" cigars that Vince smoked. Vince, too, was very meticulous. He and his branch chief, Bob Boyd, had performed detailed support studies for covert operations. Vince had also reviewed all of the aerial photography taken in the Berlin corridor and carefully categorized and prepared an excellent file of stereo pairs of all SA-2 support equipment and other military hardware observed in Soviet army units in East Germany.

The "possibly missile-associated installation" was given to DiRenzo, the missile backup team leader. After scanning the photography, DiRenzo determined that several tasks had to be completed before the function of the sites could be determined. The location had to be established, the canvas-covered objects measured precisely, the support equipment counted and categorized, and a "negation date" established to determine the most recent photography on which the equipment had not been present.

The team began a systematic analysis of the photography. Reninger measured the canvas-covered objects, DiRenzo and Holmes began to identify the support equipment, and Sullivan determined the location of the site. It was situated in the Sierra del Rosario Mountains, about fifty nautical miles west-southwest of Havana, and Los Palacios was the nearest town. After surveying previous coverage of the area, he confirmed that this was an area of new activity; nothing had been seen or reported there before. The measurements, computed manually by all members of the team, of the canvas-covered objects kept falling in the sixty-five-to-seventy-foot range. DiRenzo scanned the target area and identified eleven trucks and fifteen tents in the immediate vicinity of the canvas-covered objects and twenty-eight other trucks scattered throughout the area. A convoy of ten trucks—two trucks with trailers and eight unidentified vehicles—was approaching the area.

DiRenzo returned to the canvas-covered objects and reexamined the equipment. None appeared to be related to SA-2 missiles. U-2 photography over the Soviet Union in 1959 and 1960 had revealed patterns of SA-2 deployment. DiRenzo consulted the stereograms of the missile and missile-support equipment. The equipment at this site appeared to be much larger than that seen at the Soviet SA-2 sites. Questions reeled in his mind. Its position and size did not correspond to anything seen in Cuba before. Was it real or dummy equipment? The support equipment gave few clues. DiRenzo concluded that the canvas-covered objects were missile transporters for an undetermined system.

It would have been easy to have been lulled into accepting the premise that these were defensive and not offensive missiles. The group checked its work again, searching for something that might have been missed, some clue that might better explain this find.

DiRenzo called me and said he needed some support regarding the missiles. I called on Jay Quantrill, who worked for me and who was the Center's collateral specialist on missiles, to accompany me to Vince's work station. Jay had read all that had been published on SAMs and MRBMs and had distilled all pertinent information into loose-leaf volumes, called black books. In addition to information provided by the Soviet Penkovsky, the MRBM books contained hundreds of photographs taken at various Moscow parades. First, we slowly flipped through the SS-3 book and then began to flip through the SS-4 book. When we flipped to a photo of a full-side view of the SS-4 missile, Vince said, "That sure looks like it." The black-book photograph became a key element in identifying the site as a possible MRBM site, along with the missile's dimensions. The team considered numerous possibilities and tried different approaches but kept returning to a surface-to-surface missile, about sixty-five to seventy feet long.

DiRenzo was assured and straightforward when he contacted his chief, Bob Boyd, and announced, "We've got MRBMs in Cuba." Boyd asked that the analysis be rechecked. It would have been easy at this point to report the findings as unidentified missiles, but DiRenzo returned to his microstereoscope and reanalyzed the missiles, along with other members of the team. Their conclusion remained the same. At 4 P.M., DiRenzo asked that I accompany him, along with the collateral support book, and approached Shoemaker and said, "We've got big missiles in Cuba." Shoemaker's immediate question was "How big?" So many previous reports of missiles had turned out to be SA-2's that Shoemaker had memorized the standard length of the SA-2 as being thirty-five feet. When DiRenzo said, "About seventy feet," Shoemaker asked, "What does that make them?" DiRenzo replied, "The SS-3 or the SS-4," at which point I opened the book to the Moscow parade picture of the SS-4.

After reviewing the evidence on the size and shapes of the missile transporters with Reninger at about 4 P.M., Shoemaker said, "We've got to let Mr. Lundahl know before he goes home." Shoemaker and Boyd went to their division chief, Jack Gardner, and his intelligence production officer, Gordon Duvall. They, too, reviewed all the information and, after looking at the imagery, concluded that these were indeed canvas-covered surface-to-surface missile transporters.

By five o'clock car pools were waiting. But obviously, it was necessary to continue work on this mission's "find." At that point, it was also decided that each member of the team should notify his "service chief." Holmes was unable to contact Air Force lieutenant colonel Robert Saxon, so he sought out Ted Tate, Saxon's civilian deputy. Tate asked Holmes to continue working and said that he would take his car pool home. Tate returned to the Steuart Building later that evening. Reninger informed Army colonel George C. Eckert, his commanding officer. Joe Sullivan, however, had problems. His chief, Lieutenant Commander Pete Brunette, was also in his car pool. Brunette had a dinner engagement that evening and had left his work area promptly at 5 P.M. He had called several times from the guard's desk on the first floor asking Joe to hurry. Joe said he was working on a project and that Lundahl was about to be briefed. A few minutes later, Brunette called again. Joe answered, saying that they had just found some additional information. Brunette answered rather angrily, "Goddamnit, Joe, if you keep finding new things, I am going to go off and leave you." Sullivan called Brunette's deputy, Clay Dalrymple, and explained what he was working on. Dalrymple went downstairs and posted Brunette on the details. Brunette immediately canceled his dinner plans and came to the area where the missile team was working.

Lundahl was called by Gardner, and Duvall escorted him into the room where the backup team was working. Lundahl had a distinctive list to his walk as a result of an old football injury. He was immediately recognized by us in the semidarkened enclosed room. "I understand you fellows have found a beauty," he said as he approached.

We nodded agreement almost in unison. DiRenzo escorted the director to the light table he had set up with the missile photos. DiRenzo pointed out the missile transporters on the frame. Lundahl swung the microstereoscope over the stereo pairs and carefully adjusted it. "There are six of them," he said, and began to examine the area. "It looks like a field expedient," he added.

DiRenzo agreed and pointed out the convoy. He said the picture was taken at the right time since the equipment was just arriving at the time of the exposure.

Lundahl turned from the table and looked at us and then said, "I think I know what you guys think they are, and if I think they are the same thing and we both are right, we are sitting on the biggest story of our time."

Lundahl rose from the light table and sat on a drafting stool. He was grave as he listened to Reninger, who said that preliminary mensuration indicated that the missile transporters were approximately sixty-five to seventy feet long. I then stepped forward and put the collateral-support book in Lundahl's lap. Reninger explained that the SS-3 (Shyster) missile was fifty-four feet long and that the SS-4 (Sandal) was seventy-four feet long. Then, showing Lundahl the Moscow parade photos of the SS-4 along with detailed drawings, Reninger said, "I believe they are the SS-4." DiRenzo agreed.

After the discussion, Lundahl rose and walked a short distance.

His hands were clasped behind his back. We remained silent. The strange stillness suggested the extreme seriousness of the moment. Lundahl looked at us and said, "If there was ever a time I want to be right in my life, this is it."

He asked if anything had been committed to paper. He was shown a few notes that related to the site location and the size and number of the missile transporters. Again, seated on the drafting stool, Lundahl pointed to each of us by name and asked if we agreed the missiles in question were MRBMs. Each reply was affirmative. He then asked if there were any other possibilities. DiRenzo mentioned what is always considered at such a time—the possibility that these missiles were dummies. All signs, however, pointed to their being real. Then, too, it was doubtful that all the support equipment around the transporters could be fake. The Center had been accused of tending to exaggerate rather than underrate a photographic find. But Lundahl knew the implications of this find all too well. He did not doubt or delay reacting to the situation. The ruddy-complexioned, silver-haired director looked at each of us again. "Gentlemen, I am convinced. Because of the grave responsibility of this find, I want personally to sign the cable."

All of those present knew these images represented a grave moment in history. All knew that the future turn of events would surely involve the president personally. Lundahl asked who knew about the find. Jack Gardner said that the "service chiefs" had been informed but had been told not to divulge the information to their superiors until the analysis had been completed. Lundahl asked Gardner to invoke the code word PSALM on all the information. I was the custodian of the closely held directive for the Center and said that I would furnish it to Gardner.

Lundahl asked if any photographic enlargements had been produced. Sullivan said no. He added that they only had the duplicate positive; the original negative was still at NAVPIC, where they were producing additional duplicate positives. It would take several hours to make photographic prints. Besides, the duplicate positive was required for further analysis of the site. Lundahl said he understood.

Lundahl asked that all those present remain and work through the night if necessary to glean all the information possible from the images. He said, "Make any excuses you want to your car-pool members, your wives, and any others you may have obligated your-selves to this evening." Lundahl left, saying he was going to call Cline.

I ran downstairs and told my superiors, Hans Scheufele and Bill Banfield, that photographic-laboratory support would be needed that night and that they should keep essential personnel at work.

It was always difficult to get through to CIA headquarters on the secure phone line at that time of evening. On his way downstairs to his fifth-floor office, Lundahl was thinking how he could clearly and unmistakably get his message across to Cline if he had to use open phone lines. There was a good working relationship between Cline and Lundahl. Cline was one of the founding fathers of the Agency, held a doctorate from Harvard in history and international relations, was a Phi Beta Kappa, and had earned his Agency reputation as a China expert. He had replaced Robert Amory in March 1962 as the deputy director of intelligence. Cline had full confidence in Lundahl and the abilities of his people.

At Langley, the first of the formal series of meetings of the intel-ligence methods conference had ended at 5:30 P.M. and Ray Cline had returned to his office. He had only been there a few minutes when the secure phone rang. Lundahl identified himself and said, "Ray, our worst fears are coming to pass in Cuba, because it looks like something more than defensive missilery is being deployed. In fact, we are convinced and ready to publish at your command an indication of the insertion of what seems to be medium-range ballistic missiles into Cuba. We don't know the full extent of their distri-bution, but we have found six missile transporters in a place called Los Palacios, about fifty nautical miles west-southwest of Havana. I have a team working the rest of the night, and by tomorrow we'll have a better fix on the situation. As you know, we have never seen this particular missile system deployed outside the Soviet Union. Therefore, we have to go very cautiously because it is new ground that we are breaking. But the dimensions, at least as they are coming out so far, the supporting equipment, as far as we can detect it, and the associations on the ground all seem to be clearly vectoring in on the conclusion that there are Soviet MRBM missiles in Cuba."

Cline was incredulous. He paused and asked, "Are you fellows sure?"

Lundahl replied, "Yes, I am sorry to have to maintain it, but we are sure."

Lundahl added that Center personnel had been working on the material since noon, and within the last half hour they had reached a point where they felt sufficiently sure to tell him. Lundahl indicated that precise mensuration, full interpretation of the sites, and photo-lab enlargements would not be complete until much later that night.

"Are they ready to fire?" Cline asked.

Lundahl answered that he didn't think so, since the equipment was dispersed and no pads or erectors were evident and that it appeared that some of the equipment was just arriving.

"How many missiles have you got?" Cline asked.

Lundahl said that we could clearly count six large missile transporters.

Cline said, "Well, we've got to get on this one right away. I'll get hold of Carter." Cline then added, "Art, I'll rely on you, of course, to keep me posted. But in the absence of any other contacts, I want you to plan to be in my office with the evidence by seven-thirty tomorrow morning."

Lundahl agreed. The call had been made. Lundahl recollected his thoughts. A lot of questions would certainly be asked tomorrow and he should have answers or explanations for as many as possible.

One of my duties was to prepare all of the briefing notes for Lundahl, and he called me down to his office and explained that the notes on all of the materials that were to be produced that night should be as complete as possible. I said I would cover every item of possible interest.

Thoughts swirled in Lundahl's mind. Why would the Soviets leave the missiles and all the support equipment exposed in an open field in such a manner that they would certainly draw a photo interpreter's attention? The Soviets certainly had ample evidence of the advanced quality of U.S. reconnaissance and interpretation abilities—enough, certainly, so they should have known that such sites would not escape detection. A number of U.S. Genetrix balloon cameras had fallen into Soviet hands in 1956 and the Soviets had thoroughly studied their optical and film qualities.[1] Lundahl then concentrated on the events of the Powers U-2 flight. He remembered Khrushchev saying in a speech on May 7, 1960, that "a competent expert commission" had been established to examine the plane and its equipment. He remembered Khrushchev had grudgingly admitted that "The camera used is not bad; the photographs are very clear."[2] Professor Gleb A. Istomin's description of the U-2's camera and its film at the Powers trial was so detailed and so accurate that it was almost like reading pages from the contractor's technical manual.[3] Istomin also noted that compared with the film used in the "spy balloons," the film in the U-2 had been improved "for a number of specifications essential for high-altitude aerial reconnaissance of military, industrial, and topographic objects."[4] Amron Katz of the Rand Corporation, while participating in the December 1960 Pugwash meeting in Moscow, was asked by a prominent Soviet scientist about the kind of film used in the U-2. When Katz asked the reason for the question, the Soviet scientist responded, "They were damn good pictures."[5]

Lundahl thought of President Eisenhower's speech following the Powers U-2 incident and the photo of the San Diego Naval Air Station the president had shown on a nationwide telecast. The Russians were surely aware that if we could observe parking-lot stripes about six inches wide, we certainly could see seventy-foot missiles in Cuba. During the American Society of Photogrammetry annual meeting, the Soviets could be seen picking up all the free literature on U.S. cameras and exploitation equipment from the research and development organizations, the armed forces, and commercial firms. Lundahl also had had a number of the articles translated from Russian journals dealing with reconnaissance, photo interpretation, and photogrammetry. These articles indicated that the Russians were well aware of Western advances in optical and film technology.

Lundahl then tried a different tack. Why had the Soviets employed extensive security in transporting the missiles from the USSR to Cuba yet, once in the field, there were no security procedures to avoid overhead observation?

Why would the Soviets deploy their missiles to Cuba at this time of year? Lundahl recalled questioning me about the weather in Cuba during October. The October weather was characterized by strong winds, torrential rains, thunderstorms and, often, hurricanes. Maybe, Lundahl rationalized, the Soviets had planned to move the missiles in and set them up under this weather umbrella. But this would be risky since there would be days of clear weather when there could be reconnaissance flights. It was clear to Lundahl that the Soviets had blundered seriously. It seemed that Russian military authorities failed to consider their operation was being closely watched. (In 1989, the Soviets would admit that "Moscow operated in the spirit of the traditional old thinking. One could hardly expect the secret to go undetected by American intelligence, which kept a close eye on Cuba and was disturbed by the nature of its growing ties with the Soviet Union. But that is precisely the special power of old thinking, made strong by tradition: It can not always be explained rationally, and it manifests itself in a vacuum from which public pressure has been 'pumped out' and in which authoritarianism engenders voluntarism.")[6]

Lundahl checked his calendar for any appointments that would conflict with the next day's briefings. He wrote *crash* and *MRBM* on the page for October 15. He looked back at the page for October 14, on which he had jotted *mission 3101*. Printed on the right of the calendar's date was DWIGHT D. EISENHOWER BORN 1890. Lundahl thought how ironic it was that on the former president's birthday, the reconnaissance vehicle that Eisenhower had sponsored and that was to give him so much good intelligence on which to base his decisions—and also the heartbreak of the Powers flight—was to deliver the critical evidence that the Russians had deployed offensive missiles in Cuba.

The evening of October 15 was a night of parties, not atypical for Washington during the month of October. The secretary of state was hosting a dinner party for Foreign Minister Gerhard Schroeder of West Germany at the State Department dining room. The secretary of defense was attending a Hickory Hill seminar at Bobby Kennedy's home in McLean, Virginia. General and Mrs. Maxwell Taylor were giving a formal dinner party at their Fort McNair residence in southwest Washington. The guests of honor were to have been Mr. McCone and his wife, to celebrate their recent marriage. Before departing to make funeral arrangements for Mrs. McCone's son, McCone called General Taylor and asked that the party be held as scheduled since so many arrangements had been made. Also, as McCone would later relate, those invited included Deputy Secretary of Defense Roswell Gilpatric, Deputy Undersecretary of State U. Alexis

Johnson, Lieutenant General Joseph Carroll, the director of the Defense Intelligence Agency, and Major General Marshall Carter, the deputy director of the CIA, who had been working hard on the Cuba problem and needed the relaxation that such a party would provide.

At CIA headquarters, General Carter had planned an informal reception for the Commonwealth conferees of the intelligence methodology conference in the Agency's executive dining room. Although Cline was the conference host, he delayed his arrival until 6:15 P.M. to ponder the impact of the new intelligence find. Cline walked into the executive dining room, called Carter aside, and gave him the startling report. Cline indicated that it would take NPIC several hours to wrap up a definitive report with a fully considered analysis along with the aerial photos of the site. They discussed the task of alerting the White House and the intelligence community. Carter said he would be going to the dinner hosted by General Taylor and that he would inform Bundy, General Taylor, and General Carroll there.

Cline checked with Taylor and was told that Bundy was not on the guest list. Checking further, Cline found that Bundy was hosting a dinner party for Charles E. "Chip" Bohlen, the newly appointed ambassador to France. Cline decided to verify whether General Carter had notified Bundy. When he learned from General Carter that Bundy had not been notified, Cline told Carter that he would assume the responsibility of notifying him.

At about 9 P.M., Cline called Bundy at his home and said: "Those things we've been worrying about in Cuba are there." Bundy's reaction was, "You're sure?" Cline said that he had received a call from NPIC that they had found medium-range ballistic missiles in Cuba. Cline explained that his analysts had studied the photos with the NPIC interpreters and were convinced they were offensive missiles. Cline reemphasized that the Center was still working on the imagery and that substantive intelligence officers would be assessing the find. Mr. Bundy indicated he wanted to see the photography as soon as practicable and that he would draw up a schedule of what should be done. Cline promised to have the evidence and the assessment for Bundy the first thing in the morning.

Much has been said about the fact that McGeorge Bundy did not immediately inform the president. Several influential senators would later be extremely critical of Bundy, claiming he had no authority to withhold such vital information from the president. One senator, finding that Bundy was hosting a dinner, would caustically remark that the call interrupted the dessert, something that is not done in the Washington cocktail and dinner circuit.

When a Washington newspaper later questioned Bundy's inaction, the president also facetiously asked why Bundy had not called him. Bundy responded with a memorandum, FOR YOUR MEMOIRS. The memorandum, in part, said: "Its validity would need to be demonstrated clearly to you and others before action could be taken. The [photographic] blowups and other elements of such a presentation would not be ready before morning . . . [To] remain a secret . . . everything should go on as nearly normal as possible. In particular, there should be no hastily summoned meeting Monday night. This was not something that could be dealt with on the phone . . . What help would it be to you to give you this piece of news and then tell you nothing could be done about it till morning? . . . You were tired [from] a strenuous campaign weekend, returning . . . at 1:40 Monday morning. So I decided that a quiet evening and a night of sleep were the best preparation you could have."[7]

Cline next called Roger Hilsman at his home. He had difficulty indicating over the insecure phone that he meant MRBMs ("mediums") rather than aircraft ("medium bombers"). Cline would later tell me that he also thought Hilsman had had too much to drink that evening, making his call even more difficult. Finally, after several repetitions, Hilsman got the message. Hilsman, who always tried to ingratiate himself with the White House, said he would get in touch with Bundy and the president. Cline told him that that was already done. Hilsman then said he would alert Rusk and Martin.

Meanwhile, Norman Smith, the SAM specialist, had been at the Center to study SA-2 deployment when the MRBM site was found. At 6:30 P.M., he called Sidney Graybeal, his division chief. Smith said that the Center had found something hot and that Graybeal should come to the Center as soon as possible. Graybeal arrived approximately one hour later. He was shown the imagery under the stereoscope and given a description of the find. He agreed that these had to be offensive missiles.

Graybeal told the missile backup team that he did not wish to disturb them in their work but would like to remain, listen to their conversations, and jot down all pertinent details. At 8:30 P.M., Graybeal called Cline and stated that the information was hard and there was no doubt in his mind that these were offensive missiles. Cline asked Graybeal to be in his office the next morning to help write an appraisal of the find.

Col. David Parker, the deputy director of NPIC, called John Hughes, a special assistant to the director of the Defense Intelligence Agency, and asked him to come to the Center as soon as possible because of an important discovery. Hughes and John McLauchlin, a photo interpreter specialist who had worked at the Center, arrived at the Steuart Building at 7 P.M.

Hughes reviewed the duplicate positives, talked to the photo interpreters and to Sidney Graybeal, and carefully jotted salient facts on a small pad. Convinced that these were offensive missiles, he and McLauchlin proceeded to General Carroll's Bolling Air Force Base home. General Carroll was dressing for the dinner he would attend at General Maxwell Taylor's residence. Hughes and McLauchlin were admitted to General Carroll's quarters and the general listened as Hughes briefed from his notes. Agreeing that the evidence was hard, General Carroll called Roswell Gilpatric, and said that Hughes and McLauchlin were coming over to fill him in on some new and very important intelligence on Cuba.

Hughes and McLauchlin got in Hughes's old yellow DeSoto. The DeSoto was experiencing transmission problems and painfully growled each time Hughes pressed on the accelerator or made a turn. McLauchlin kidded Hughes, "We have the secret of the century. I hope we can get it to the proper people." Hughes retorted, "If this thing breaks down, you'll run the rest of the way on foot." They arrived at Gilpatric's apartment, at 4201 Cathedral Avenue in northwest Washington, just as Gilpatric had finished dressing for the Taylor dinner. Hughes presented the facts from the notes and then said that the photographic prints and laboratory work would not be ready until morning. Gilpatric asked Hughes to be prepared to brief Secretary McNamara first thing the next morning. Since McNamara was at Bobby Kennedy's home attending a Hickory Hill "seminar," a private self-improvement program, Gilpatric waited until McNamara got home and posted the secretary of defense at about midnight.

Hughes returned to the Center and began to prepare his notes for the next morning's briefing.*

Lundahl asked me to provide him with a map showing Cuba and the United States. He asked me to swing a 1,100-mile arc on the map, the range of the MRBM from the area where the missile site was found. Within the arc in the United States were an ICBM base, eighteen SAC bomber and tanker bases, three major naval bases, and such populated areas as Washington, Dallas, Atlanta, and New Orleans. Outside the continental United States, the Panama Canal and U.S. bases in Puerto Rico could be reached by the MRBMs. Lundahl asked that I include the map in his briefing case for the morning meeting with Cline.

Cline, meanwhile, continued to make and receive telephone calls throughout the evening. He asked his teenage daughter not to use the telephone and should she receive any calls to make them as brief as possible. While Cline was on the phone, his daughter was in a nearby room doing her homework. She overheard her father make what he thought were very guarded telephone calls. Upon completing several calls, Cline walked into the room where his daughter was studying. She looked up and without hesitation said, "Are there missiles in China or Cuba?"

Cline would later tell me that his principal concern that evening was what would be said at the White House the next morning and he trusted Graybeal's and Lundahl's judgments in responding. Graybeal went over the sizes of the SS-3 and SS-4 and agreed with the photo interpreters that the missiles had to be the SS-4. The main question for Graybeal now was why the Soviets would send over the advanced SS-4 rather than the older SS-3. Both systems were road-mobile and could be deployed with no heavy construction necessary for launch pads or support buildings. Both the SS-3 and SS-4 were single-stage liquid fueled guided missiles that could carry a 3,000-pound warhead to a maximum range of 700 nm and

---

* The world would get to know Hughes's abilities when, four months later, on February 6, 1963, Hughes and Secretary McNamara appeared on national television and gave a detailed photographic review of the introduction of Soviet military personnel and equipment into Cuba, emphasizing, of course, the introduction and removal of the offensive missiles.

1,100 nm, respectively, with a CEP (circular error probability) estimated in the 1-to-1.5-nm range. The SS-3 required liquid oxygen as an oxidizer, while the SS-4 employed storable propellent combinations—red fuming nitric acid as the oxidizer and kerosene as fuel. The SS-4 could carry a nuclear warhead up to 3 megatons (the Soviets later said it carried a 1-megaton warhead). From logistical and operational standpoints, the deployment of the SS-4 would certainly be more advantageous.

Graybeal asked me if the missiles had been sighted on any of the ships coming into Cuba. I said I did not think so, and a quick review of maritime shipping photography with Bill Culkin and Darrell Herman, the Center's shipping specialists, gave no hard evidence of Soviet offensive missile shipments nor did other information indicate Soviet ships were carrying offensive missiles to Cuba.

Examination of the aerial photography indicated that the missiles and missile equipment had been shipped from the Soviet Union as an integrated road-mobile unit suitable for field deployment. The time required to reach operational readiness, therefore, would be quite short. Assuming that the necessary fueling and handling equipment were available, that communications equipment was being installed, that warheads were in Cuba or en route, an operational capability could exist within weeks. No facilities to store nuclear warheads at the missile sites could be found. Graybeal assumed that there would be direct communications from Moscow to the sites and he said he would investigate that possibility the next day.

When the question of range came up, I showed Graybeal the map that had been prepared for Lundahl showing the range of the SS-4. He asked that I also plot the 700 nm range of the SS-3 on another map. The SS-3 could reach such targets as Savannah and New Orleans, seven SAC bomber and tanker bases, and one important naval base. Graybeal looked at the maps and reflected for a moment and then said, "After seeing that map, there's no doubt I would deploy the SS-4."

NPIC photo-laboratory personnel had waited since 5 P.M. that evening for the photo interpreters to relinquish the duplicate positives so they might make the necessary prints, enlargements, and additional duplicate positives for study. Jimmy Allen, a photo-laboratory section chief, had much experience waiting for imagery from the photo interpreters. He contentedly puffed on a large cigar. Jack Davis, the new chief of the photo laboratory, waited nervously.

At 8:30 P.M., Earl Shoemaker brought a duplicate positive frame to the laboratory. Within a few minutes, the number of enlargements and contact prints to be printed changed several times. Normally, a control code word was given to priority or special laboratory-processing work. When Allen asked what code word should he apply to the Cuban material, Davis replied, "This is all so confused, a good term might be mass confusion." All the photo-laboratory work done that night and throughout the missile crisis received priority treatment if it bore the title "Mass Confusion."

At 8:30, Gardner initiated a requirement that the missile trans- porters be precisely measured by the Center's photogrammetrists using comparators. Leon Coggin was listed as the off-duty photo- grammetrist. He had just moved into a new apartment and the tele- phone had not yet been installed. On departing that evening, Coggin told Dick Reninger jokingly, "If you need me, you are going to come after me." Coggin, however, had left word that if he had to be reached, his nearest coworker, Eugene Ricci, should be called. Gard- ner reached Ricci, who drove five miles to Coggin's apartment only to knock on the door and see that Coggin had guests. Ricci was brief: "I am sorry, but you've got to go in to work right now."

An around-the-clock atmosphere soon pertained at NPIC—one of sleeplessness and anxiety, as the interpretation of each subsequent mission unfolded further significant events. But it was now 8:45 P.M. and past time-out for dinner. Most stepped out of the Steuart Building onto 5th Street. It was a warm fall night and most crossed over New York Avenue and 6th Street to Havran's Restaurant, a favorite after- hours eating place for Steuart Building people and policeman from the 2nd Precinct. Hamburgers, french fries, pies, and coffee were popular menu selections—in fact, the only food available.

Joe Sullivan had not eaten his bag lunch from home. He remained in the Steuart Building and reviewed what had to be done. The precise location in degrees, minutes, and seconds of the MRBM missile site had not been done and Sullivan concentrated on this task. The landscape—particularly around the loaflike karst hills north of the site—resembled those seen on picture postcards. And the fields in the area all looked alike. He selected the best maps of the area at a scale of 1:50,000. Ironically, the maps bore in bold red letters the caveat FOR OFFICIAL USE OF GOVERNMENTS OF CUBA AND UNITED STATES ONLY. The agreement to produce these charts had been made under the Batista regime. Sullivan used the pertinent frames of photography. He tried to locate prominent landmarks in the vicinity of Los Palacios. As he scanned the photography, large objects at a second military encampment caught his attention.

He called out, "I've got something new."

Gardner, seated nearby, came to Sullivan's station. "What do you have?"

Sullivan said, "I don't know."

Gardner then asked, "What does it look like?"

Far from vividly describing the objects, Sullivan said, "They look like boats."

"Boats?"

"Yes, boats." Sullivan was very emphatic.

"That's a funny place for boats—in the middle of an island," Gardner, a reserve naval officer, added.

Recollecting, Gardner thought they could be pontoon boats or other boats used by army engineering units. He then asked, "What kind of boat?"

"Like a big whale boat," Sullivan replied.

The other team members returned from dinner. Reninger then took his turn at the scope to confirm Sullivan's observations. He confirmed Sullivan's two "boats" and, searching the area, reported laconically, "Here's another one just like the other two. And here's a fourth."

Holmes took his turn at the scope, and Sullivan asked him to check out the linear objects leading from each boat. Holmes said, "I think those are cables."

Then it was DiRenzo's turn. He followed the cables. The pattern was complete, and the picture emerged with sudden clarity. The boatlike objects were the launcher erectors. It was another field-deployed MRBM site. Near woods were seven missile transporters, and an eighth was found in the woods. They, too, were roughly measured and again the length kept coming out in the sixty-five to seventy-foot range. Nearby were two large tents measuring about a hundred feet long. There were several other areas of interest, one consisting of a number of personnel tents, and along a treeline a variety of equipment associated with the SS-4 missile system was observed. The site was pinpointed at 22 degrees and 40 minutes north and 83 degrees and 17 minutes west and was given the place name of the nearest town—San Diego de los Baños. This site was further along than the Los Palacios site, and although it appeared that no missiles were on the launcher erectors, it was felt that this site would soon be operational.

The impact of finding a second MRBM launch site just two nautical miles from the first was sudden and overwhelming. The evidence that the objects were missiles and that the site was for the SS-4 was now incontrovertible. The course of events changed dramatically with the finding of the second site and the fact that the sites were not there on the last previous known coverage of the areas, on August 29. NPIC personnel were acutely aware that the coverage afforded this mission was extremely limited, and the gnawing question was how many sites could be in other areas of Cuba not seen since August 29.

The search continued, and a third area, 4.2 nautical miles west of the large town of San Cristóbal, came under close scrutiny. It was labeled as an "unidentified installation." It also was new to the area, about ten miles from the Los Palacios and San Diego de los Baños sites. It lay in a valley but, again, near the sugarloaf karst hills that rise in the area. It had many of the same characteristics of the other sites but contained no missiles or erector launchers. However, it was suspect enough and I encouraged the making of still another briefing board. One of my responsibilities was to title the briefing boards, and I was loath to title the new find "unidentified installation" because I was convinced that "unidentified installation" would raise questions among the intelligence analysts and policymakers. After a long discussion with DiRenzo, I suggested that it should be titled "Military Encampment." It was agreed to have Lundahl state that the site needed additional attention and coverage. In the notes I prepared for Lundahl, I stated it was a "Military encampment located in a wooded area and it contained seven new buildings, fourteen large tents, fifteen smaller tents. Extensive open storage of canvas-covered equipment. Area appears under development and bears attention." The next time the installation was seen, it would be identified as a full-fledged MRBM site, and because San Cristóbal was a larger town than either Los Palacios or San Diego de los Baños, the intelligence community ultimately designated the three sites in this area the San Cristóbal MRBM sites 1, 2, and 3, respectively.

Additional details of the three MRBM missile sites were derived from mission 3101 and subsequently reported. At the San Diego de los Baños site there were seven large tents, each 100 feet long by 15 feet wide. Continuing analysis led NPIC to postulate that these tents could probably be used to prepare and check out the missiles, mate the missile to the nuclear warhead, or just to protect the missiles from the elements; as there was insufficient time to clearly identify their function, it was decided not to annotate them on the early photography. A variety of terms would later be used to identify their function: missile shelter tent; missile checkout tent; and missile ready tent. The latter term was ultimately chosen for purposes of consistency and clarity of reporting. A number of "unidentified" vehicles were also seen at both the San Diego de los Baños and Los Palacios sites. Again, there was insufficient time to have them measured or fully analyzed and they were labeled in early reporting as "equipment" at the San Diego de los Baños site and "convoy" at the Los Palacios site. Analysis of subsequent photography of the sites enabled identification of the equipment as oxydizer trailers and fuel transporters.

At approximately 10:30 P.M. on October 15, Leon Coggin placed the mission 3101 film on the Mann comparator at NPIC and began measuring the missiles. The measuring mark or crosshair was placed on the extremities of the object being measured. The comparator then automatically recorded on paper tape the X and Y coordinates of each position. Each measurement was made several times in order to obtain an average value. Reninger assisted Coggin in identifying the objects and equipment to be measured. The procedure took about an hour. At 11:30 P.M., Coggin entered the coordinates and appropriate computer programs into NPIC's ALWAC computer. The ALWAC was an early vacuum-tube computer and tests had been designed to check the accuracy and computer's performance. After Coggin ran the first test, line-voltage problems developed, causing the computer to drop bits (digits) during the test routine. Few people knew computers like John Wyman, the senior NPIC computer operator, and Coggin called him at home. Wyman asked for the voltage reading at the power supply cabinet that supplied the various computer components. Wyman told Coggin to vary some of the voltages and then try the test routines again. Coggin followed Wyman's instructions, got the desired results, and started the computations. The computer malfunctioned three times, and each time Coggin called Wyman. Finally, the tests were clear and Coggin began to process the tapes from the Mann comparator. The length of the missile transporters consistently came out at least 67 feet in length and 9 feet in width. The 67-foot measurement of the transporters with missiles was almost identical with that of the SS-4 observed in the Moscow parades, less their nose cones. The SS-3, also measured at a parade outside Moscow, measured only 54 feet, less the nose cone. The SS-3 was therefore incompatible with the missiles observed in Cuba.

At 1:45 A.M. on October 16, Gardner wanted the missile transporters at the second MRBM site measured. The computer was operating well now, and Coggin turned out a string of measurements. All of the measurements were the same as those of the first site. At 3 A.M., Coggin asked Shoemaker if any other measurements would be needed. Shoemaker replied in the negative and Coggin turned off the computer and comparator. He wrote a note asking Wyman to check his calculations the next morning. Wyman verified Coggin's work and noted that the computer had functioned admirably.

Dean Frazier's phone rang at 3 A.M. Gardner was on the line asking Dean, the Center's graphics duty officer, to round up a graphics crew and come to work immediately. Gardner indicated that several briefing boards had to be prepared for Lundahl before 6 A.M. Dean's crew—graphic analysis officer Dan McDevitt, illustrator Glenn Farmer, and headliner (typesetting) operator Loretta Huggins—arrived at the Steuart Building at about 4:30 A.M. and found the annotated photographic prints ready for layup. Frazier and McDevitt began preparing the briefing boards and Farmer the vu-graphs. Miss Huggins prepared the type for both. Frazier and McDevitt finished first. They logged the titles of the briefing boards and their control numbers.

Briefing boards were the established medium for presenting intelligence during this period. They mirrored the missions, visually reporting situations at the moment the photographs were taken. Free of ephemeral data, the boards showed graphically and precisely what the target looked like at a specific second, day, month, and year.

Three briefing boards and three vu-graphs were prepared from mission 3101:

1. MRBM Launch Site, San Diego de los Baños
2. Military Encampment (Missile), Los Palacios
3. Military Encampment, San Cristóbal

Later, the Center began designating and numbering MRBM and IRBM sites as they were found. The first three sites at San Cristóbal were numbered MR-1, MR-2, MR-3, and the Sagua la Grande sites MR-4 and MR-5. The Guanajay IRBM sites were numbered IR-1 and IR-2 and the Remedios site IR-3. As the crisis progressed, this system was dropped.

October 16–The President
Is Informed

"Are you sure?"
—PRESIDENT JOHN F. KENNEDY

LUNDAHL ARRIVED at the Steuart Building at 6 A.M. on October 16 and carefully reviewed the briefing boards and notes that Shoemaker and I had assembled. They seemed to impart an extraordinary, almost surrealistic, feeling. In stark stillness, they depicted a moment in time that had been frozen as visual history. It was as if the world was holding its breath for a moment. And the effect was total, devastating loneliness. Shoemaker went over the details seen on the photography. Lundahl then examined several of the Moscow parade photographs of the SS-4 that I had placed in his briefing packet. He went over again the performance and range of the SS-4.* He took the 3-by-5-inch cards and feverishly jotted down additional notes on the information I had covered. He said he would study the notes further on his way to Langley.

Frank Beck, the courier, was waiting. Lundahl closed the large

---

* The initial version was first seen in the November 7, 1957, Moscow parade and the latest version was seen in the November 1961 parade. The missiles were deployed in battalions of four launch positions each; the missiles could be launched singly or in salvo. After a launch, the battalions could move to a resupply point, reload with new missiles, and then deploy to a new launch position.

black briefing board case and said, "Let's go." He paused and asked Shoemaker and me to thank all the people who had worked through the night and to send them home to get some sleep. It was 7 A.M.

About the same time, Walt Elder, a special assistant to the DCI, called McCone in Seattle and cryptically reported, "That which you always expected has occurred." McCone, silent for a moment, replied, "Does the president want me back?" Elder replied, "I am sure that the president will need all the help he can get." McCone said, "I can fly back to Washington as soon as possible." Elder replied, "I knew you would. An Agency plane is on its way to pick you up."

Lundahl and Beck arrived at Ray Cline's office at 7:30 A.M. Personnel from the substantive intelligence analysis offices jammed the room. Since Cline had not seen the photos, Lundahl placed the briefing boards on Cline's desk and everyone in the room listened, almost in awe, as Lundahl pointed out each salient feature. Lundahl noticed that Sherman Kent, director of the Office of National Estimates, was shaking his head from side to side, in total disbelief that the Soviets would do something so earthshaking. After Lundahl finished briefing Cline, he stepped back so that those gathered could review the photography for themselves.

Ed Proctor, a division chief concerned with military and economic matters, was contemplative as he looked at the photographs. He tapped his pipe against his teeth. Soon he would spend many sleepless hours in the Steuart Building reviewing and writing evaluations of the intelligence derived from subsequent high-and-low-altitude reconnaissance missions. But that day at 11 A.M., he was scheduled to address the intelligence methods conference on "Problems in Determining the Cost of Soviet Weapons Systems."

Cline, Lundahl, and the courier, Beck, left the CIA headquarters for the White House shortly before 8 A.M. As they were crossing the lobby, they overheard a new receptionist speculating with an older colleague as to why so many "Methodists" were visiting the Agency, thinking that all these visitors had some religious affiliation. Conference delegates entering the building as Lundahl and Cline emerged tried to engage them in conversations and, being intelligence officers, wondered why they were obviously in such a hurry with the courier and large bag of briefing boards. Later, Walter Pforzheimer, longtime Agency legislative counsel, would write a frequently quoted poem about the departing members of the intelligence methods conference.[1]

At the White House, Cline, Lundahl, and Beck went directly to McGeorge Bundy's office in the basement. They waited only a few minutes in his outer office before Bundy came out. Cline summarized the photo-intelligence findings and asked Lundahl to explain what had been found as he had in Cline's office. Cline answered several questions about the type and range of the missiles.

Bundy told the men to wait in his outer office while he went back inside. He made a telephone call and then took the elevator to the president's private quarters. The president, sitting on his bed and still in his pajamas, was looking at the morning newspapers. An article on page one of *The New York Times* entitled "Eisenhower Calls President Weak on Foreign Policy" caught his attention. Eisenhower, campaigning in Boston the previous day for Republican candidates in the off-year elections, had for the first time assailed President Kennedy's handling of foreign affairs. He called the Kennedy record for the past twenty-one months "dreary" and "too sad to talk about." Three weeks before, at Harrisburg, Pennsylvania, Kennedy had criticized Eisenhower's foreign policy. Now at Boston, Eisenhower defended his administration and challenged Kennedy. "In those eight years, we lost no inch of ground to tyranny. We witnessed no abdication of international responsibility. We accepted no compromise or pledge word or withdrawal from principle. No walls were built. No threatening forces were established. One war was ended and incipient wars were blocked."[2] These were obvious references to the Berlin Wall and Russian military shipments to Cuba, Laos, and North Vietnam. Kennedy understood politics, and Eisenhower, as the titular head of the Republican party, was trying to get some of his fellow Republicans elected. These charges and countercharges did not diminish the respect these two men had for one another, as we shall later see.

Bundy told the president about the missiles being in Cuba and together they reviewed the president's appointments for that morning. The only free time was at 11:45. The president asked that a meeting of all principals be scheduled for that time.

. . .

While the momentous decisions regarding Cuba were about to be made at the White House, military activity was occurring in other parts of the United States that would eventually have a direct bearing on the Cuban missile crisis. A number of military exercises were under way that would later provide a measure of cover when the time came to alert U.S. forces for movement toward the southeastern United States.

PHIBRIGLEX-62 (Amphibious Brigade Landing Exercise), an annual routine training exercise in the Caribbean, was scheduled for the period October 15–20. It would be one of the largest ever staged. Amphibious Squadron 8 of the Atlantic Amphibious Force, at Little Creek, Virginia, had just taken aboard the 2nd Battalion of the 2nd Marines. Thousands of Marines would eventually be loaded onto fifteen assault ships. The task force would also include four aircraft carriers and twenty destroyers. The Marines were to assault Vieques Island, ten miles east of Puerto Rico. Although these naval exercises had been conducted annually "to train and exercise naval forces to conduct amphibious assault," this year's exercise would be more realistic than in years past and would test the Navy's ability in four important areas: naval air bombardment, live ship fire against armor and targets on shore, the landing of Marines, and combat support ashore. The Navy considered Vieques Island an ideal locale because it permitted the use of live ordnance, had excellent beaches, and allowed the Navy to practice landings in a near-combat atmosphere.

The Cubans were convinced this exercise was a prelude to an imminent attack on their island and began alerting their forces.

The amphibious force flagship for the exercise, USS *Mount McKinley*, was to take on reporters at Roosevelt Roads in Puerto Rico and allow them to view the naval bombardment and the landing of Marines. But because of the high seas after hurricane Ella and the subsequent cancellation of the exercise, the reporters never got aboard. On October 20, the ships of this task force would receive urgent messages alerting them to expect new sailing orders.

The U.S. Army and U.S. Air Force were engaged in exercises "Three Pairs" and "Rapid Roads" concentrated in central Texas.

Units of the 82nd Airborne Division, the attacking force, were waiting at Connally Air Force Base, at Waco, Texas, when orders came through ordering them to return to Ft. Bragg on October 20. The Tactical Air Command fighters that were to support the 82nd Airborne troopers received orders to proceed to airfields in Florida. The First Armored Division, which was to be the aggressor force, was told to load its tanks and head back to its home base at Ft. Hood.

And in the South Atlantic, UNITAS, the third annual antisubmarine training exercise with South American navies, was nearing completion.

On the morning of October 16, Khrushchev was at work early, probably to catch up on tasks that had accumulated while he was vacationing at Gagri on the Black Sea. He sent a lengthy report to the president of the CPSU Central Committee on "The Kara Kum Canal and Its Economic Significance." The canal was but another of Khrushchev's agricultural schemes that was in trouble. The capital expenditures had risen enormously and the construction of the canal was behind schedule. Production at agricultural enterprises in the areas served by water from the canal also was lagging seriously. He maligned the ministry of agriculture because the assimilation of the land during canal construction lagged seriously behind the construction of the irrigation schemes. Cotton was not being planted to coincide with the receipt of water and the state was losing money. Khrushchev threatened that these shortcomings had to be eliminated. He justified the priorities and expenditures that he had authorized for the canal and stated that the significance of the canal would be realized once the work was properly coordinated.

Khrushchev would probably read the daily military newspaper, *Red Star*, for it was one of his favorites. There was an article in it that day that Khrushchev would certainly endorse. It was by V. Kudryavtsev, who stated that the American leaders had embarked on an aggressive policy as the result of their overestimation of their superiority in missile-nuclear weapons. Kudryavtsev asked, "Where does this outburst of American self-assurance come from?" and then tried to bolster the Soviet military with the statement "Only a few months ago the same President of the United States admitted that the relative capabilities of the United States and the Soviet Union are at best equal." Kudryavtsev, in the best Khrushchev tradition, threatened, "It has been known for a long time that people who rely on force usually respect and understand most of all those people who are able to respond with force."

Later that day, Khrushchev sent for U.S. Ambassador to the Soviet Union Foy Kohler. Khrushchev stated emphatically that the Soviet Union would take no action on Berlin until after the U.S. elections and that the message should be sent to President Kennedy. Khrushchev also told Kohler that he understood that Fidel Castro's announcement that the Soviets would be constructing a fishing port in Cuba had caused the president some political trouble with the Republicans. He said that the announcement would not have been made had he been in Moscow at the time and implied that Castro had gone off half-cocked. He then reemphasized that military equipment sent to Cuba was strictly of a defensive nature. He added that he would probably visit the UN in late November or early December.

It was obvious that the president had called Bobby Kennedy concerning the missiles in Cuba because at about 9 A.M. on the morning of October 16, he came storming into Bundy's office asking to see the photography. Cline repeated his assessment and Lundahl took Kennedy over the three briefing boards, pointing out the fourteen missiles. Kennedy looked at the photos and moaned, "Oh shit! Shit! Shit! Those sons a bitches Russians." Lundahl described Bobby's movements as being like those of a prizefighter. He walked several times about the room, snorting like a prizefighter, smacking the palm of one hand with his fist. Kennedy might have been thinking about his recent conversation with Georgi Bolshakov, who said that he carried a personal message from Khrushchev to President Kennedy and that Khrushchev wanted the president to be assured that under no circumstances would offensive missiles be placed in Cuba. And Kennedy may have recalled, as he expressed in his book, that "On September 11, Moscow publicly disclaimed any intention of taking such action and stated that there was no need for nuclear missiles to be transferred to any country outside the Soviet Union, including Cuba."[3]

Bobby was extremely bitter, seeing now the evidence that he and the president had been deceived by the Russians and at the highest of levels. In fact, the missiles were on their way to Cuba at the same time those assurances were being forwarded by Chairman Khrushchev.

Bobby Kennedy came back to Lundahl and Cline. The seriousness of the moment was broken when Kennedy pointed to the map NPIC had prepared showing the range of the SS-4. He pointed to the map and asked, "Will those goddamn things reach Oxford, Mississippi?" Before Lundahl could stop himself, he replied, "Sir, well beyond Oxford." He then looked up to catch a slight gleam in Kennedy's eyes and a wry smile on his face. Oxford, Mississippi, of course, was where the Kennedys were having trouble attempting to register James Meredith into the University of Mississippi. Bobby thanked Lundahl and Cline and said he was going up to talk to the president. When Lundahl returned to the Steuart Building and told about Bobby's Oxford remarks, it was decided all subsequent maps showing the ranges of missiles deployed in Cuba would also show as reference points such principal cities of the United States as St. Louis, New York, Atlanta, and, in the same bold type, Oxford, Mississippi.

Bundy announced that the president would be keeping his scheduled appointments that morning but that a special meeting was scheduled for 11:45 and that Lundahl and Cline were to remain for the meeting.

At 9:30 A.M., the president welcomed the astronaut Walter Shirra, Mrs. Shirra, son Walter, Jr., and daughter Suzanna to the Oval Office. Earlier that month on the third, Commander Shirra, the fifth American in space, had completed nearly six orbits aboard Sigma 7 before landing in the Pacific, 275 miles northeast of Midway. As was customary in those days, he was invited to the White House.

The president exchanged pleasantries and then began joking with Suzanna. He asked if she would like to see Caroline's pony, Macaroni. She replied, "Yes," delightedly. While the president was showing the Shirras the White House grounds, more high-ranking officials began arriving. C. Douglas Dillon, the secretary of the treasury, came to Bundy's office and asked to see the photographs. An urbane, scholarly New York Republican, Dillon was a popular figure in the Kennedy cabinet. Tall, bald, outgoing, studious, and unpretentious, he was listened to when he spoke. Suave and courteous, he was one of Kennedy's favorite cabinet members. Possessed of a quick grasp for complex detail, his penetrating intellect enabled him to contribute precise logic to resolving problems not only in the Treasury Department but in other departments as well.

Lundahl repeated his briefing. Dillon listened intently and didn't question the analysis. "How sure are we that there are not other sites on the island?" he asked. Lundahl explained that we did not have recent coverage of the island but that we were reviewing all past coverages. Dillon said, "I gather then our greatest need is to have the island completely photographed." Lundahl agreed. Dillon thanked Lundahl and Cline, but not before remarking, "This evidence poses many problems for this administration. We'll be depending on you fellows for some of the answers." Dillon excused himself stating that he, Henry Fowler, and Myer Feldman had an appointment with the president. According to Dillon: "The meeting with the president for a few minutes on October 16 was obviously business unconnected with the Cuban missile crisis."[4]

At 9:30 A.M., General Carter arrived at Bundy's office. Cline felt that Carter, as the acting DCI, should handle the scheduled 11:45 meeting. Carter agreed, and Cline advised him that Lundahl would perform the briefing but that he would be sending over Sidney Graybeal, the Agency's offensive missile specialist, to provide analytical backup to Lundahl if needed. Cline said he would get back to his office and assure that the DCI, then on the West Coast, learned what was happening at the White House. He said he would also continue the research and analysis, and prepare an assessment of the find. General Carter concurred with his plan.

Earlier that morning, at about 6:30, John Hughes arrived at NPIC to procure a duplicate set of the briefing boards that had been produced during the night for the Department of Defense. After Shoemaker and I had finished briefing Lundahl, we met with Hughes. Shoemaker discussed the two additional sites that had been found during the night. I gave Hughes a duplicate set of the notes I had made for Lundahl. Hughes asked a lot of questions, made copious notes, and said that he had to leave to brief General Joseph Carroll at the Pentagon. The general was waiting, and after listening to John's review of the information developed during the night, they discussed the questions that would probably be raised by McNamara and Gilpatric.

At approximately 8 A.M., General Carroll received a call that McNamara had arrived in his office and was eager to see "the new information." McNamara would later indicate that he recalled having seen the pictures at either 10 P.M. or midnight on Monday, October 15. The fact is that McNamara did not see the pictures until 8 A.M., Tuesday, October 16. When General Carroll and Hughes arrived in McNamara's office, Gilpatric and General Taylor were with him. According to Hughes, McNamara was very animated, moving around the briefing boards on the desk as Hughes explained the items. McNamara would also later report seeing the four-slash ground pattern that bore an ominous resemblance to the configuration of Soviet missile sites.[5] There were no slash marks evident on mission 3101 photography. The four characteristic slash marks were not seen until later, when the IRBM sites were found on subsequent photography. Hughes said that McNamara began "asking unanswerable questions"—i.e., for information not verified on the boards. Gilpatric was concerned about obtaining additional photography of the sites, while General Taylor was "very pensive and pragmatic." Taylor, and later McCone, would relate that while the Soviets could not precisely anticipate when the U.S. would discover the missiles, it was foolish for the Soviets to deploy the missiles without first bringing their SAM defenses to a maximum state of readiness. In retrospect, if the Soviets had downed a U-2, it would have placed President Kennedy in a most awkward position.

Within minutes, according to Hughes, there was a call from the White House setting up the 11:45 meeting "in the strictest of secrecy." General Taylor stated he would like to convene an emergency meeting of the Joint Chiefs of Staff at 10 or 10:30 A.M. that morning. General Taylor returned to his office and asked that calls be placed immediately to the individual members of the JCS or their deputies. Admiral Anderson, chief of naval operations, was lecturing that morning to the Industrial War College, at Fort McNair in southeast Washington, while General Curtis LeMay, Air Force chief of staff, was in Europe. General Taylor asked that LeMay be recalled immediately. Both General Earle G. Wheeler, chief of staff of the Army, and General David Shoup, commandant of the Marine Corps, were in their offices.

General Taylor had asked that JCS members be briefed on the Cuban photography as soon as possible. A team of Army briefers at the Steuart Building was assembled to brief the Army chief of staff. Colonel George Eckert, Major Frank Kinkle, and Lieutenant Richard Reninger took duplicate photographic copies of the briefing boards and hurried across the city to the Pentagon to the office of General Wheeler.

A methodical planner of his work, General Wheeler had, as an indispensable member of his staff, an aide who carefully maintained his appointment schedules. The general's morning was usually filled with briefings on the many problems that arise in managing a modern army. These briefings were normally given by general officers or colonels of the general staff.

Colonel Eckert approached the appointments officer, insisting that he must see General Wheeler immediately. The appointments officer checked his list and noted that Colonel Eckert was not scheduled. He then asked Colonel Eckert what he wished to discuss with the chief of staff. Colonel Eckert said he was sorry but he could not reveal the subject. The appointments officer surveyed the group—a colonel, a major, and a lieutenant. To his practiced eye, this was an obviously unimportant delegation. He was not going to risk censure by interrupting the briefings in progress or scheduled at the insistence of a mere colonel who would not state his mission. Colonel Eckert was asked to wait until the scheduled briefings were completed. An interminable period of nearly an hour passed without a summons. Colonel Eckert again approached the appointments officer, emphasizing that the subject he had to discuss was of the utmost importance. By this time, the scheduled briefings had ended and the three officers were finally ushered into General Wheeler's office.

When the office door closed, Colonel Eckert abruptly stated his mission, "Sir, last evening the National Photographic Interpretation Center discovered two MRBM sites on photography flown over Cuba on October 14." General Wheeler reeled back in his chair, breathing heavily. "Oh no!" According to Colonel Eckert, the general appeared stunned, as if he had been hit by a baseball bat. Several seconds passed before the general regained his composure. He listened intently while Lieutenant Reninger displayed the photographs and briefed the general in detail on the findings. General Wheeler then asked how sure was the Center that these indeed were MRBMs. Colonel Eckert replied, "Very sure." General Wheeler promptly used his telephone, setting up an immediate briefing of the same information for several of the generals on his staff, along with Major General Alva R. Fitch, assistant chief of staff for intelligence. General Wheeler then thanked the three officers and, accompanying them to the door, said loud enough for the waiting appointments officer to hear, "If any further information is developed, I want to be informed immediately." Colonel Eckert smiled as he passed the appointments officer. The three officers waited in the ACSI briefing room, and as the generals arrived, their clearances were checked. One of the generals who had been briefing General Wheeler that morning did not have the necessary clearances and was asked to leave. Lieutenant Reninger smiled: a small bit of sweet revenge for the enforced wait.

The Center also prepared additional copies of the briefing boards and notes for the Navy and Air Force. Lieutenant Colonel Robert Saxon took the briefing boards from the Steuart Building to General LeMay's office and Lieutenant Commander Pete Brunette took copies to Admiral Anderson's office. Brunette raised the issue of briefing General Shoup. An aide to Admiral Anderson reminded Brunette that the Marines got their information, as far as intelligence was concerned, from the Navy and you never brief the commandant of the Marine Corps before you brief the chief of naval operations. When Brunette questioned that judgment, the aide said, "You just let us worry about that."

That same morning, Secretary Rusk had a discussion in his office in the State Department with U. Alexis Johnson, Edwin Martin, and Roger Hilsman on the missile find. He then went to National Airport to greet His Royal Highness Hasan al-Rida al-Sanusi, the crown prince of Libya, and arrived at the White House shortly after McNamara. McNamara told Rusk that he, Roswell Gilpatric, and General Taylor had been briefed that morning by General Carroll and John Hughes. Lundahl went over the photography with Rusk, and McNamara listened intently to see if there had been any additional information or change in the intelligence since he had been briefed earlier that morning.

At 10:30 A.M., the president met with the White House Panel on Mental Retardation. He participated actively in the discussions for forty-five minutes, giving no indication of the news on Cuba that he had received just a few hours earlier.

From 11:15 to 11:45 (White House log for Tuesday, October 16, 1962, John F. Kennedy Library), Chip Bohlen paid his official farewell call on the president prior to leaving to assume the post of U.S. ambassador to France. In his book *Witness to History*, Bohlen misdated the visit as being on the seventeenth.[6] Bohlen said that the president was so preoccupied with the Cuban missile sites that he did not mention France once. Ambassador Bohlen is again in error when he stated that the president showed him the aerial photos. According to Bohlen: "The pictures, the president told me, showed sets of twenty-four medium and sixteen intermediate range missile sites."[7] The president, however, would not see the pictures himself until the meeting at 11:45 A.M., at which time only two medium-range missile sites (that would eventually have four pads each) had been identified on the aerial photos. The IRBM sites were not found until later photo-reconnaissance missions had been flown and interpreted. Bohlen said he agreed with the president, that the existence of the missile bases could not be tolerated and that they had to be removed.

A large group had gathered in Bundy's office by this time, when a call came that the president had finished with his meeting with Ambassador Bohlen and was proceeding to the Cabinet Room. After all the participants were seated in the Cabinet Room, General Carter read a prepared statement that MRBM missiles had been discovered on U-2 photography of October 14 at two locations and that Lundahl would brief the group using enlargements of that photography. The president was seated, as usual, at the center of the long conference table in the Cabinet Room, with his back to the windows. Lundahl had placed the briefing boards on an easel at the far end of the room near the fireplace. He gave a brief description of the MRBM sites and then asked permission of the president to come to the table and show him the evidence at close range. The president replied, "By all means." Lundahl approached the conference table and stood between the president and Secretary Rusk. Handing the president a large magnifying glass, as he had on numerous previous occasions, he placed the briefing boards on the table in front of the president and proceeded to point out details of the three sites.

Lundahl was acutely aware that photo interpreters can recognize and point out things that the unsophisticated and untrained eye would easily miss. He therefore dwelt on the enlargements of the missiles. The photography itself seemed unrevealing, a panorama of farmland with strange objects parked in the fields. But these objects, Lundahl pointed out, were alien to the environment. The photo interpreters could quickly identify the pastures, croplands, orchards, tobacco and cane fields, and the karst hills. They could also quickly recognize the sugar centrals, the tobacco-drying barns, the cattle sheds, etc. The alien objects, difficult for the untrained eye to discern or evaluate, were immediately apparent to the photo interpreter. Lundahl pointed out the missile transporters, the tents, the launcher erectors, and other objects. Everyone was quiet as the president took the magnifying glass and studied the photography. After asking a few questions, he turned to his right and, looking Lundahl straight in the eye and carefully spacing out his words, asked, "Are you sure?" Lundahl was anxious to be measured in his response but at the same time leave no doubt in the president's mind that the evidence was conclusive. Lundahl replied, "Mr. President, I am as sure of this as a photo interpreter can be sure of anything. And I think, sir, you might agree that we have not misled you on anything we have reported to you. Yes, I am convinced they are missiles."

Although Robert Kennedy agreed at the time that there were indeed missiles on the photography, missiles that posed a threat to the United States, he would later write: "Photographs were shown to us. Experts arrived with their charts and pointers and told us if we looked carefully we could see there was a missile base being constructed in a field near San Cristóbal, Cuba. I, for one, had to take their word for it. I examined the pictures carefully and what I saw appeared to be no more than the clearing of a field for a farm or the basement of a home. I was relieved to hear later that this was the reaction of virtually everyone at the meeting, including President Kennedy. Even a few days later, when more work had taken place at the site, he remarked that it looked like a football field."[8]

There was no scraping visible on the photography, no clearing of a field, and nothing that resembled the construction of a basement. Either the untrained eyes of those present were seeing things that were not on the photography or Bobby had forgotten those things that had been pointed out by Lundahl to him and the president. Ironically, the photography on which the missiles were discovered appears as the frontispiece in Bobby's published account of the crisis.

The president's eyes rose again from the photos. He looked at Lundahl again and asked, "How long will it be before they can fire those missiles?" Lundahl stated that Sidney Graybeal, the Agency's expert on offensive missiles, would comment on that question. Graybeal moved into position next to Lundahl. He discussed the SS-4 missile system, its range, and what was known about its operational-readiness status. He deferred on the president's question because the system had been transported overseas by ship and there undoubtedly would be some time delay in bringing the missiles back to operational status. He added that there was no way of knowing exactly how long it would be before the missiles were operational, but it was more likely to be a matter of days rather than hours.

McNamara asked where the nuclear warheads for these missiles were located. Graybeal expressed no doubt that they were stored somewhere in Cuba or would soon be sent to the missile sites. He said it was normal Soviet practice to transport the warheads with the missiles but that there was no evidence, as yet, whether the warheads were or were not there. McNamara told the president that it was very important to learn the location of the nuclear warheads. Lundahl added that a thorough search was being made by the Center of all the airfields, military installations, and storage depots. Questions continued about the missiles—what was known about them, what payloads they would carry, how far could they fire, and so on. Lundahl and Graybeal tried very carefully to differentiate what was known and what was unknown. Lundahl intimated that more missiles probably would be found and that additional photographic coverage was needed. The question-and-answer period lasted for over ten minutes.

The briefing left a peculiarly somber mood in the room. The worst fears had come to pass and the worst of conjectures were on many minds. Dramatic reaction was uppermost in many minds—war, with all its new, devastating connotations—a nuclear confrontation. Lundahl would relate: "In an age which demanded immediate response and rebuttal, the president listened to all remarks and weighed all positions without surprise. He had the curiosity, sensitivity, and intellect to assimilate any proposition. With that grace and charm, he stimulated the best in all those with whom he came in contact and that day was no exception."

According to Lundahl, "The president never panicked, never shuddered, his hands never shook. He was crisp and businesslike and speedy in his remarks and he issued them with clarity and dispatch, as though he were dispatching a train or a set of instructions to an office group." General Taylor would confirm the president's attitude: "Kennedy gave no evidence of shock or trepidation resulting from the threat to the nation implicit in the discovery of the missile sites but rather a deep but controlled anger at the duplicity of the Soviet officials who had tried to deceive him."[9]

Lundahl removed the boards from the table. The president turned to the group and said he wanted the whole island covered—he didn't care how many missions it took. "I want the photography interpreted and the findings from the readouts as soon as possible." The discussion then turned to how many U-2 missions could be flown and the possibility of using low-altitude aircraft. McNamara cut that discussion short, saying that he and General Carter would meet with their reconnaissance experts that afternoon and report back to the president.

At the conclusion of the meeting, the president turned to General Carter and Lundahl and said he wanted to express the nation's gratitude to the men who had collected these remarkable photographs and to the photo interpreters for finding and analyzing the missile sites. Carter graciously accepted the compliment and motioned to Lundahl and Graybeal to remove the briefing boards and prepare to leave the room.

The Cuban missile crisis was on!

When Lundahl returned from the meeting at the White House, he held a meeting in his office and warned us that "all hell was going to break loose" and for us to be prepared to receive a lot of photography in the coming days. He outlined specific duties and responsibilities in getting ready for the influx of photography. He then told of McNamara's concern as to where the nuclear warheads could be stored and asked Gardner to meet with his people and come up with a list of possible storage areas.

The search for additional prospective MRBM missile sites assumed near frantic proportions. A request was received from the Defense Department to tabulate all buildings large enough to accommodate an MRBM missile. Military installations, warehouses in port cities, and factory buildings throughout the country were quickly surveyed and their identification affirmed. A search of the heartland of Cuba revealed that only the *centrales*, or sugar-processing centers, had buildings large enough to house the missiles. These facilities comprised the very essence of the Cuban sugar industry. There were about 150 of these mills, most containing the large crushing and processing buildings along with the warehouses, equipment storage buildings, and repair yards. At no time during the crisis was any MRBM or IRBM equipment seen at these facilities, yet because of their size for possible storage of missiles, they were targeted for destruction in the event of war. Lundahl asked specifically that existing ammunition storage areas be checked for any recent changes such as additional security fences or special security measures.

When asked if all the missile sites had been negated, Gardner replied in the affirmative. He suggested that two comparison briefing boards be created on each site: on the left side, showing the area as it was when last seen on August 29, and on the right side, showing the site on the October 14 coverage. Lundahl agreed and the completed boards showed graphically that the missile sites were not present on August 29 and did much to diffuse the concept that the sites had initially somehow been overlooked or missed. Lundahl would later relate that he did not have to do much in the way of convincing of the Center's interpretation ability when these boards were shown.

The president was scheduled to have lunch with Sampson Field, chairman of the board of directors of the Printing Company of America, on October 16. The appointment had been made several weeks before so that the president could discuss the Medicare program and how to get public support for it in the Congress. At noon, Kenneth O'Donnell met Mr. Field in the Fish Room and took him to lunch, stating that the president was preoccupied and would see him at a later hour. Finally, at 4 P.M., Field was ushered into the Oval Office and was surprised to see that the president was terribly upset, belying his earlier calm. Field would later describe the president as looking as though "he was coming out of a hell of a binge."[10] The president, impatient, did not sit down but stormed about the room, with Field following, seemingly unaware that Mr. Field was in the room. Field saw immediately that his thoughts on Medicare would have no effect on the disturbed president. After a few minutes, Field excused himself and left the Oval Office. Mr. Field would later describe to his wife the president as being "punch-drunk" when she asked how his meeting with the president had gone.

At 1 P.M. on October 16, a meeting was held in McNamara's office to formulate plans for the stepped-up U-2 reconnaissance missions the president had directed. In addition to McNamara and General Carter, CIA officials concerned with the U-2 program and ranking Air Force officers were present. McNamara stated that the question of presidential approval for U-2 missions no longer applied and he wanted the greatest number of missions flown in the shortest period of time. Emphasizing that it was his responsibility to give the president a firm idea of what the threat was to the United States, he asked about the logistics, aircraft, and pilot problems. Because U-2 operations had been shifted to McCoy Air Force Base, in Orlando, Florida, McNamara was told that the maximum number of U-2 missions that could be flown daily with existing assets would be six, flying from early morning to late in the evening. The big question, however, was the weather. Mission planners said that since they did not have to have each mission track approved, they could get weather reports from Weather Central and also have airborne weather observers flying around Cuba reporting the weather. U-2 missions could then be launched to fly over the areas that were clear. McNamara emphasized the need to get the whole island covered as soon as possible and gave the mission planners wide latitude in making reconnaissance decisions.

Questions arose about the number of Air Force pilots qualified to fly the Agency U-2's. A decision was reached to use both SAC and CIA U-2 pilots to cover all of Cuba. The CIA pilots were to be used only in "extreme circumstances" and they would be recommissioned into the Air Force and given Air Force credentials. Two CIA pilots reported immediately to Orlando.

The feasibility of low-altitude reconnaissance missions also was discussed. Questions arose as to which organization should fly them and what numbers of low-altitude missions would be required. Lundahl was consulted by Carter and recommended that the U.S. Navy had the best low-altitude capabilities. The Center maintained close liaison with the various service reconnaissance-technical squadrons and was well versed in the capabilities of the various aircraft, camera systems, and photo-intelligence officers.

The Navy had devoted considerable time and effort to develop an effective low-altitude jet reconnaissance capability. Commander (later Captain) Willard D. Dietz had perceived and pushed for the development of small-format aerial cameras (70mm and 5 inches) to replace the Navy's bulky $(9 \times 9 \times 18$ inch) K-17 and K-38 cameras used in World War II and Korea. His purpose was to reduce the external size of the camera systems so that ongoing fighter aircraft designs could accommodate a viable camera suite without major airframe alterations. His foresight would pay off during the crisis. Dietz worked with the best research-and-development personnel of the Navy, and these men collaborated closely not only with the camera manufacturers and research laboratories but also with the reconnaissance units and the fleet. Their efforts had resulted in the development of the Chicago Aerial Industries, Inc.'s KA-45 and the KA-46, six-inch-focal-length framing cameras with a film width of five inches and a capacity of 250 feet of film. The cameras could be used in the forward, vertical, and oblique positions. The system had been installed in the F-8U-1P Crusader and fully tested and proven.[11] Pilot training in low-level navigation and photographic reconnaissance had been implemented in naval fleet squadrons since 1953. This training, coupled with the proper camera system, onboard computers, and optimized low-level performance of the aircraft, provided a capacity of more than a hundred miles of photographic coverage, traveling at 100 to 500 feet above the ground within a 250 nm radius from the operating base. It was no secret in Washington that the Navy had the best totally integrated low-altitude reconnaissance capabilities in support of the intelligence community.

Lundahl recommended that the Navy's Light Photographic Squadron No. 62 (VFP-62) be selected if low-altitude reconnaissance was instituted over Cuba. Since its activation in January 1949, VFP-62 had stressed the acquisition of aerial photography, along with low-altitude navigation and instrument training. "Whether flying alone, or with an escort, the photo pilot had to navigate to the maximum of his radius or action, find a small target such as a bridge or railroad intersection, and then get home. Getting home is important to the photo pilot because his mission is not accomplished until the finished prints are delivered."[12]

Members of the squadron had seen duty around the globe and had operated from the flight deck of twenty-two different carriers. Photographing some of the Cuban missile sites hidden in the karst hills and among the pine trees would be difficult, but we felt this squadron could accomplish the mission. The squadron was based at the U.S. Naval Air Station, Cecil Field, just outside Jacksonville, Florida. It could easily stage out of the Key West Naval Air Station and return its film to the naval air station at Jacksonville for processing.

As a result of the meeting in McNamara's office, Lundahl received a call from Admiral Anderson's office that a member of his staff would visit the Center and help in drafting a cable alerting Light Photographic Squadron Sixty-two. The finished cable read: "Recent U-2 photography of Cuba has revealed the existence of certain installations which may require further evaluation through the use of large-scale high-resolution photography by LANT F-8U-1P aircraft. A high level decision whether or not to conduct the required overflights is expected shortly. Once authority is granted for these operations, rapid accomplishment becomes essential. Therefore operations should be conducted from the closest base to the area of interest consistent with operational factors. Guantánamo, however, will not be used except for emergency. Recommend Key West. Your comments/concurrence is desired.

"It is accordingly requested that VFP-62 be alerted for the mission of conducting low-altitude photography missions over Cuba, 1,000 feet or below. For the present, earmark eight (8) suitably equipped F-8U-1P aircraft for this mission and place four of these in a four-hour alert status commencing 171400Z. Obtain equipment and make plans to expand this number to a maximum of sixteen. Every feasible action will be taken to expedite arrival of processed film in Washington. Augmentation of photo processing personnel if necessary, use of jet couriers, and other time conserving steps are directed. Process film at Jacksonville. Deliver original negative plus one dupe positive to the National Photographic Interpretation Center, Washington, D.C. Direct liaison with NPIC authorized.

"A list of targets is provided below. The list will also be provided to the VFP-62 representative arriving at JCS response to reference. You will be advised of additional targets as they are developed.

PRIORITY 1—Canvas covered trailer vans, tents, 4 buildings under construction 4.0 nm ENE San Diego de los Baños at 22-40-05N-83-17-55W.
PRIORITY 2—Canvas covered trailers, vehicles and tents, 5.8 nm North of Los Palacios at 22-40-50N-83-15-00W.
PRIORITY 3—Vehicles, tents, buildings 4.12 nm NW of San Cristóbal at 22-42-40N 83-08-15W.
PRIORITY 4—Installation under construction, including earth covered revetments. 23-03N/82-06W.
PRIORITY 5—Installation under construction, including drive-thru buildings and earth covered structures. 13 nm South of Havana at 22-56N/82-24W.

UNCLASSIFIED nickname for this project will be BLUE MOON."

Later, the additional instructions were cabled to VFP-62.[13]

Joe Sullivan, the Navy photo interpreter on the NPIC "discovery" team, had gone home about 4:30 A.M on October 16, having been told by his supervisors to take the day off but to be available. After sleeping about six hours and having received no calls, Sullivan decided to get a much-needed haircut. He called home from the barber shop to see if he had received any messages. His wife answered and said his supervisors were desperate to get in touch with him. When Joe reached his supervisor, Clay Dalrymple, he was told in no uncertain terms to "get his tail over to the Pentagon as fast as possible" because there was going to be a special meeting of the GMAIC (Guided Missile Astronautics Intelligence Committee). Sullivan had a difficult time finding a parking space at the Pentagon but arrived just in time to present the photographic evidence of the missile deployment.

Dr. Albert "Bud" Wheelon, CIA chairman of the committee, listened to all the arguments and rationales for other possible missile deployment areas in Cuba; after an hour of discussion, he suggested that rather than single out one suspect deployment area, the whole island should be covered photographically as soon as possible. Wheelon realized that there had to be both organization and specific methodology to distill the vast volume of information that would be derived from all the aerial photography flown over Cuba and interpreted by the National Photographic Interpretation Center. He realized, too, that this photographic lode had to be incorporated with other sources and succinct and definitive reports created for the policymakers. Wheelon, in addition to being chairman of GMAIC, was also the director of the Agency's Office of Scientific Intelligence. Wheelon, thirty-three at the time, was an MIT physicist who had come to the Agency from the Ramo-Woolridge Corporation. He got along well with McCone and on the evening of October 16 met with McCone and sketched out procedures for handling and reporting information concerning the crisis. He recommended that selected representatives of all of the standing United States Intelligence Board's scientific committees transfer their activities on an ad hoc basis to NPIC in order to expedite their considerations of the findings from the photography. McCone approved, and the next day, representatives of the GMAIC, the Joint Atomic Energy Intelligence Committee (JAEIC), and members of the Agency's Guided Missile Task Force began moving certain of their files to NPIC.

Robert F. Kennedy was something of a rarity in government. By the age of thirty-five, he had acquired a reputation for a vigorous and unorthodox style. He possessed a crusading spirit and was aggressively frank, not to say brash, in his dealings with both peers and subordinates. Impatient and combative by nature, he was extremely conscious of his ability to influence the ideas, opinions, and decisions of his brother. The president enjoyed telling stories at his expense while Bobby, disdainful of failure and ridicule, masked his sensitivity with assertiveness, abruptness, and restlessness. Bobby yearned to establish his own identity. He also attempted in every situation to enhance his own ability. In September 1962, he would leave his personal imprint on the civil rights movement by placing James Meredith in the University of Mississippi at Oxford, Mississippi, and a month later in international relations during the Cuban missile crisis.

Bobby was most receptive to praise and flattery, especially coming from his peers. When he was abrasive and, at times, obnoxious and self-centered, he was usually greeted with stony silence by those dealing with him, who knew that in reality, they were dealing with the president. All of the cabinet members were extremely aware that Bobby was the point man, the lightning rod of the Kennedy administration. When Bobby's actions reflected careful thinking, there would be flashes of admiration from the president. When it was shoddy, the pain of compassion would flash across the president's face. When it exasperated the president, he would dress down Bobby as all older brothers do their siblings, completely oblivious as to who was present. But Bobby had a sly sense of humor, using it often to cover his habitual indiscretion. He was extremely sensitive to adverse criticism of the Kennedy administration; he was a total political animal standing guard over his brother's image. He could be mean-spirited and vengeful to any reporter he thought was "out to get the president." It became obvious to all in the administration that Bobby was the follow-up man on administration policy, the prod for action. He made up his own mind and then hastily announced his decision, regardless of consequences. His judgments on people and policies were generally sound and well-balanced. The Kennedy administration had engaged in a search for new approaches and ideas, and Bobby was the channel for the review of new and better approaches to old problems.[14]

The president formulated a group of special advisers to advise and assist him in decisions affecting the missile crisis. It became known as the Executive Committee (EXCOM) of the National Security Council and would be formally established by National Security Action Memorandum 196, signed by the president on October 22, 1962.[15] It comprised 1) the president's most trusted advisers within the administration; 2) experts on Soviet and Latin American affairs; and 3) two elder statesmen. The initial advisers were Dean Rusk, Robert S. McNamara, Robert F. Kennedy, C. Douglas Dillon, John McCone, General Maxwell Taylor, McGeorge Bundy, and Theodore

Sorensen. Others who participated either as experts or when their superiors were not present were Undersecretary of State George Ball, Latin America Assistant Secretary Edwin M. Martin, Deputy Undersecretary U. Alexis Johnson, and former U.S. Ambassador to the Soviet Union Llewellyn Thompson; Deputy Secretary of Defense Roswell Gilpatric and Assistant Secretary of Defense for International Security Affairs Paul H. Nitze; Deputy Director of the CIA General Marshall Carter, and Vice-President Lyndon Johnson, Kenneth O'Donnell, Adlai Stevenson, and U.S. Information Agency Deputy Director Donald Wilson.

The first meeting of the EXCOM opened with a briefing on the photographs by Lundahl and intelligence estimates of the magnitude of the Soviet effort in Cuba, including the earliest date that operational readiness of the missile sites could be achieved. It was agreed that Cuba should be placed under virtually constant aerial surveillance. The president had asked that several "old hands" be included in the EXCOM deliberations. He specifically asked that Robert Lovett be included. Dean Rusk recommended that his longtime friend and colleague Dean Acheson also become a member because of his quick grasp of complex issues. The president approved.

Acheson was an imposing figure because of his forceful personality, shrewdness, and precise vocabulary. He also could be ruthless and domineering in attempting to have his will prevail. Acheson had been the principal architect of the postwar policy that advocated containment of the Soviet Union, and he had also been the principal originator of the diplomatic tactics and strategy of that era. Acheson saw the Soviet Union as an implacable and permanently hostile enemy, a threat to the free world. He had always advised President Truman to take a tough and threatening stand toward the Soviet Union—strength being the only thing the Communists understood. An advocate of stern action, he saw few advantages in negotiating with the Russians on Cuba. He emphasized several times that Soviet authorities were not moved by negotiations, only by strength. But Acheson was also a critic of strategic military thinking. On this, he was to note that military recommendations are usually premised upon the meticulous statement of assumptions that, often as not, are quite contrary to the facts and yet more often than not control the conclusion.

Upon entering his first EXCOM meeting, Acheson sat back and listened for nearly an hour. He was not impressed with its functioning. The strict protocol method he had instituted in the National Security Council meetings during the Truman administration was not being followed by the EXCOM. Policy was being decided through an argumentative process rather than the presentation of clear, concise papers. Although the meeting was supposedly chaired by the secretary of state, Robert Kennedy dominated the discussions.

Tall and erect, his face saturnine, marked by heavy upslanting brows and his carefully clipped mustache, which he constantly stroked with impatience during the meeting, Acheson expressed his views forcefully and lucidly on the international implications of an insufficient response to the Russian move in Cuba. General Taylor supported Acheson's position, commenting that one does not plan a military operation of the magnitude of the Russian operation in Cuba with the expectation that it would fail. Khrushchev, Acheson said, undoubtedly thought that the United States would acquiesce —that it would not go the military route. Acheson said a demonstration of American military superiority was a prerequisite for a successful solution. General Taylor saw the secret, unprecedented Soviet move into Cuba with nuclear missiles as a major effort to change the strategic balance of power and advocated a preemptive air strike, an airborne assault, and an invasion to wipe out the missile bases. This position represented the strong views held by the Joint Chiefs of Staff, especially by General LeMay. Taylor warned that unless the U.S. met this challenge, it would invite the Soviets to make similar moves elsewhere and to demand concessions in other parts of the world. Acheson emphasized this was not the time to condescend. If the missiles were left in Cuba, it would inflict enormous damage on Western power, influence, and prestige and be tangible proof to the world of overwhelming Soviet military power and of U.S. impotence; Communist and extremist elements in Latin America would be strengthened, while U.S. prestige in those countries would be substantially weakened. It could be further rationalized that if the United States was incapable of defending its own shores, it certainly would not prove capable of defending the hemisphere. Acheson insisted that if the Khrushchev challenge was not met, if there was any vacillation, uncertainty, faint-heartedness, if it was not met boldly—head-on—the Soviet assertion of political and moral superiority could be established in the eyes of the world. The Soviet gains, Acheson maintained, would be practically limitless across the board—politically, morally, economically, and militarily. Taylor would later relate to me, "I let Dean Acheson speak for my position. His views were my views exactly. In fact, he might have been even a little to my right."

Robert Kennedy disagreed. "The United States," he said, "would be damned in the eyes of the world forever should such a military operation be undertaken." He also expressed strong opinions on how history would record his brother's role, and he argued vehemently against a surprise U.S. attack. Several times during the discussions, he reminded the group of Pearl Harbor, maintaining that a surprise attack would irreparably hurt the image of the United States through-out the world just as it had Japan. He capped his argument by saying that he did not want his brother to go down in history as the American Tojo.

Dean Acheson listened with a touch of arrogance. He would later accuse Bobby of "high school thought, clichés, and cheap shots" to persuade. And Acheson was appalled that the principal advice to the president would come from a "leaderless, uninhibited group." Bobby would later be characterized by Acheson as one who felt "all the world was beholden to him." And, at another time, that Bobby in the EXCOM deliberations was "like Captain Bligh on the foredeck." Acheson said the crisis could not be reduced into simplistic terms of good or bad as Bobby was desperately trying to do. Acheson held that any diplomat worth his salt would consider the advantages and disadvantages of any proposed decision.

The scene had a certain irony. Bobby, who had previously taunted Rusk, McNamara, and others on the need for a more aggressive policy toward Cuba, was now telling the assembled group that the United States should pursue a more cautious policy—that the president had to weigh more carefully the true interests of the United States. Acheson, who had no qualms about confronting Bobby Kennedy, shot back, "The true interest of the United States is to bloody well get those missiles out of Cuba." A participant said that Rusk, who was responsible for asking for Acheson to attend these deliberations, throughout the discussions sat "like a constipated owl." Although he held definite views, he dared not express them in front of Acheson.

When Bobby pressed General Taylor for reassurances that the missile sites could be destroyed by bombing, Taylor replied that planners "prudently would have to allow for the likelihood that some retaliatory forces could survive a disarming attack. It was reasonable to conclude that there would be a retaliatory strike, however minimal, against the United States."

To the intelligence community, the Cuba venture had the Khrushchev stamp—bold, imaginative, costly, wishful thinking, and not thoroughly thought through. Khrushchev's unshakable belief in Soviet Communism guided almost all of his actions. His emotional and uncompromising outlook, his impetuousness and disregard for political risks were serious vulnerabilities. He was showing signs of becoming more extreme in both his foreign and domestic policies. The pursuit of his highly personalized crusade frequently took insufficient account of political obstacles or risks. He was uncompromising in his attitude toward, and contemptuous of, others whom he suspected of negotiating or aiding the Chinese. Similarly, he was convinced that the Soviet "Virgin Lands" program should work and plowed up half of the Siberian plain to prove it. Russian problems and setbacks in the waning years of Khrushchev's regime, in considerable part, grew out of his activism and the allure of his personal ability to convince the world of the wonders of Communism.

The Soviet plan, as best can be determined, was to conceal the missiles from the Cubans and American public but not the Kennedy administration. The areas chosen for deployment were on remote ranches, in hill country shielded by karst knolls. The missiles had been unloaded in secrecy by the Soviets and moved to the Cuban countryside at night. Concealing the missiles from the Cubans kept precise information from filtering through refugee sources to the U.S. news media. The Russians apparently never expected a demand for quick withdrawal of the missiles. If there was U.S. acquiescence, and it appears that the Russians expected it, then the U.S.-Soviet nuclear balance of power would achieve some measure of parity. If the president did not acquiesce, lengthy negotiations would ensue in which the Soviets would try to exact large concessions. First and foremost would be Berlin. It was clear from later events that one of the last Soviet fallback positions would be a Cuba-for-Turkey missiles proposal. There was reason to believe that Khrushchev had promised Castro the Soviets would intervene if the U.S. attacked. Castro believed that the USSR had made the decision to defend Cuba at all costs and that the Soviet people were ready to fight for the Cubans.

The EXCOM meeting rambled on with no decisions. In later years, Acheson characterized this meeting as "a floating crap game for decisions." There would be a meeting with the president at 6:30 P.M.

Sorensen summarized the first day of EXCOM deliberations for the president: "The Soviet purpose in making this move is not understood—whether it is for the purposes of diversion, harassment, provocation or bargaining. Nevertheless, it is generally agreed that the United States cannot tolerate the known presence of offensive weapons in a country 90 miles from our shore, if our courage and commitments are ever to be believed by either allies or adversaries. Retorts from either our European allies or the Soviets that we can become as accustomed as they to accepting the nearby presence of MRBM's have some logic but little weight in this situation."[16]

Taylor remained with the president after the meeting. He could not assure the president that aerial bombardment alone was sufficient to render the Cuban missile sites ineffective. He argued that the mobility of the MRBMs was a factor that had to be considered. The MRBM equipment seen on the photography was positioned in open fields, and Taylor could not be certain whether additional equipment might be under cover. He said if he were a Russian and planning the operation, he would certainly hold a number of missiles in reserve. He also concluded that inasmuch as the photography was all daylight coverage, he could not be certain that the Russians would not take advantage of the cover of darkness. General Taylor was convinced that once the missile sites were brought under fire, the Russians would certainly employ evasive tactics. He cited the old artillery adage, "When brought under fire, shoot and scoot." General Taylor added, "If one of them gets away, it will be the one whose warhead will fall on Washington." He expressed his strong conviction that any bombing had to be accompanied by a full-scale invasion. He chided Bobby privately for his continued analogy of the Cuban situation with Pearl Harbor. He emphasized that surprise was an essential element in military planning and operations and told him that any other course of action would be, in the general's word, "stupid." General Taylor couldn't seem to make that point with either Bobby or the president, and he would later remark that "the president put the JCS cynicism in his pocket and looked for rainbows." Others looked upon Bobby as relentless in insisting that all avenues be explored before accepting an all-out war as the only recourse. His central theme and motive was to reject despair bombing.

The question was again asked why the Soviets would place the missiles in Cuba. It had been stated by a number of U.S. military men, including General LeMay, and even by McCone, that the reason the Soviets deployed the MRBM, and later the IRBM, missiles in Cuba rather than in the European satellite countries was that the missiles in Cuba did not have the range, in the event they fell into unfriendly hands, to be turned on Russia. They maintained that the Russians did not trust having missiles deployed in Bloc countries— that the East German rebellion, the Polish demonstrations, and the Hungarian revolt in the 1950s were still too fresh in the Soviets' minds. The simple truth was that the Russians didn't have to deploy offensive missiles to the satellite countries. From within their own borders they could launch the 1,100-mile MRBM or the 2,200-mile IRBM and strike any major Allied base in England, Western Europe, North Africa, or the Middle East. To prove the point, I had Steve McCloskey, chief of the NPIC map unit, scribe arcs from the various Soviet IRBM and MRBM missile sites to the respective maximum distances. I showed the map to Lundahl, who in turn showed it to McCone, and the argument as to why the Soviets had not placed MRBMs or IRBMs in the Eastern European countries faded. Yet McCone in later testimony before Congress would persist with this argument.

The Soviets had lived under the shadow of U.S. strategic bases since the end of World War II. They had learned to live grudgingly with them, but they were always uneasy when force comparisons were made. First, they had seen the Soviet Union ringed with strategic bomber bases. Later, they watched as bases for sixty Thor medium-range missiles were built in Britain. Still later, they saw the construction of bases for thirty Jupiter missiles in Italy and fifteen in Turkey, and the deployment of Matador and Mace tactical cruise missiles in Germany. The Soviets in turn had deployed medium- and intermediate-range missile systems targeted to nullify these threats.

Despite all of the Soviet actions, nuclear superiority was strongly in favor of the United States, and Khrushchev believed that a base in Cuba would reduce the strategic imbalance. Khrushchev probably also felt that Americans would understand the Soviet move into Cuba the same way he did—that is, the placing of nuclear weapons on an opponent's periphery by any of the great powers was an accepted fact of life in the Cold War era. It can only be assumed that the Soviets did not regard the move as a provocation for war.

The president was the guest of honor at a party given by columnist Joseph Alsop at his Georgetown home for Chip and Avis Bohlen during the evening of October 16. Kennedy, according to Alsop, was an uncharacteristically poor guest on that occasion. He sat preoccupied, morose, and did not mingle with the other guests. What was to have been a festive going-away party for the Bohlens was being adversely affected by the uncommunicative president. Alsop also realized that something was wrong, probably having to do with U.S. relations with Russia, when the president took Bohlen by the hand and led him into the garden. A long, animated conversation ensued. The president solicited Bohlen's feelings and attitudes regarding the crisis. He also warned Bohlen that he might have to cancel his departure for Paris and alerted him to think of some reason for not going. Bohlen said that the only thing scheduled was a speech he was to give in New York before going to France.

The accelerated increase in U-2 missions, along with the movement of U.S. military forces, must have alerted the Soviets, yet they made no effort to prevent or delay U.S. reconnaissance efforts over Cuba, indicating that they assumed the American reaction to their missile ploy would be nominal. This was evident in that the Soviets proceeded to deploy the missiles even subsequent to President Kennedy's pointed public statements of September 4 and 13, which clearly indicated that he possessed photographic evidence of the Soviet military buildup in Cuba and warned of "grave consequences" should offensive weapons be introduced into Cuba. One must conclude that the Soviet leaders did not regard the possibility of U.S. detection, either by photography or other sources, as critical to the success or failure of the venture.

The Soviets had grossly miscalculated on a number of counts.

There was a misconception in the Soviet Union that U.S. presidents were not prone to make unpopular decisions during an election year, especially in the months preceding that election. The Soviet observation was that the president would either not make a decision, not reveal it to the public, and thus embarrass the administration, or acquiesce to foreign demands in order to keep from losing votes. Sherman Kent, on reviewing the actions of the Soviet embassy in Washington during the crisis, said, "There were a lot of people there that had their heads up their asses to believe that the president and the nation would accept the missiles in Cuba without doing something about it."

One reason often given for the Cuban venture was that the Soviets were beginning to take their own propaganda of "national wars of liberation" and their economic and military aid programs to underdeveloped third-world nations too seriously. While it is true that Khrushchev had involved Russia in a number of projects in areas heretofore reserved to Western nations, it was hard to imagine that missiles in Cuba could be placed in the same class with conventional military aid to other nations. The Soviets were deeply involved in the Middle East and North Africa, providing military aid to Syria and Algeria and substantial economic and military aid to Egypt. In Africa, Khrushchev had meddled in the Congo and had established close ties with Ghana, Guinea, and Mali. In the Pacific, the Soviets had supplied over $1 billion in military aid to Sukharno. The Soviets had combined diplomacy from a position of strength with economic programs, military aid programs, virulent propaganda, and open threats in order to either bring down French, Dutch, English, and Portuguese colonialism or to make those nations assume a low profile in their former colonies. It is interesting to note that a number of the economic programs in these same areas had been considered by Western nations and rejected. Whatever the rationale employed, the objective appeared to be clear—confront the president after the midterm election with a fait accompli in Cuba. Khrushchev would then have a vantage point from which he could bargain for a definitive settlement on Berlin and German questions and later the removal of U.S. bases abroad.

Some in the intelligence community maintained that Khrushchev's decision to deploy the missiles testified to his determination to deter any U.S. intervention to weaken or overthrow the Castro regime, which he was firmly committed to support. A September Tass statement warned the U.S. that an attack on Cuba could lead to a nuclear conflict. The Soviets believed that the presence of the missiles, when it became known to the U.S., would act as a deterrent to any U.S. action against Castro. They also believed that the missiles would act as a deterrent to any U.S. action in Berlin. This was also implicit in the September 11 Tass statement. Moscow sought to pirate Berlin as a hostage for Cuba.

The success of Sputnik in 1957 and the later Soviet manned space launchings put Khrushchev at the pinnacle of his political power. It was a gratifying personal triumph. He was now the unchallenged leader of the Communist party. Since the overthrow of Bulganin, he had wielded near dictatorial control. Malenkov, Molotov, and other political opponents were forced into exile, far removed from Moscow. With his power consolidated at both national and regional levels, Khrushchev was ready for new ventures.

But by 1962, public support for Khrushchev had fallen sharply, due primarily to his ineffective leadership. An Agency expert characterized his style as being "bombast and Band-Aids" in addressing the problems facing him. He was suddenly besieged by new sets of problems arising from the misuse of his power. The quarrel with China was out of control and far more serious than was realized in the West; the "Virgin Lands" program was collapsing; and the economy was being grossly mismanaged. In general, however, the Politburo, the Soviet military, and the vast majority still backed Khrushchev's international adventurism—some enthusiastically, others blindly. Khrushchev's split with the Chinese, however, was widely resented by the Communist parties outside Russia, especially those in Western Europe.

There was a decided need for an expert on Kremlin politics to be an EXCOM member. Although Chip Bohlen, former U.S. ambassador to Moscow, was highly regarded in Washington as a qualified candidate, he was about to leave for France. Bohlen, a personal friend of the president, was a Politburo theoretician, well informed on Communist party dogma and history. He did sit in on some of the EXCOM deliberations and he was alarmed by the strong recommendations for military action. He argued for private discussions with Khrushchev. Bohlen was chided by McCone that Khrushchev would regard such discussions as a weakness in U.S. resolve and cost the United States the bargaining initiative. "The objective," McCone, a hard-liner, would reiterate again and again, "was to get the missile out of Cuba." Personal discussions with Khrushchev, he maintained, would not encourage the Soviets to remove the missiles. McCone was strongly supported by Rusk, Acheson, and General Taylor.

Bohlen then proposed that the president send Khrushchev a strongly worded message, and based on the response, the U.S. could plan its course of action—blockading, striking, or invading Cuba. Bohlen would later write that no one could guarantee that withdrawal could "be achieved by diplomatic action but it seems essential that this channel be tested before military action is employed."[17]

Averell Harriman, another possible EXCOM candidate, had been tucked away as a State Department functionary, consulted only infrequently as a historian of a bygone era—the Stalinist period. Although he occasionally wrote Kennedy memos on current Russian affairs, the president seldom consulted him with respect to the current ruling Communist leaders.

Llewellyn "Tommy" Thompson, having only recently returned from Moscow, was, without a doubt, the best-informed man as to what was currently happening in the Kremlin. Knowing Thompson's clinical approach to the Soviets, the president actively sought his advice. A thoroughly experienced, humane, and sensitive diplomat, Thompson was extremely knowledgeable as to what Khrushchev's moves and moods might be. In diplomacy, one does not necessarily equate flamboyance and drama with effectiveness and objective results. Tommy Thompson was low-key all the way. In his baggy brown tweeds, standing motionless, chain-smoking Camel cigarettes, he would listen attentively, his pensive face looking troubled. When he did speak, he chose the most opportune moment and the most appropriate language to make his point. He was obviously the man best trained and prepared for the role he would assume in the crisis.

Thompson was a "nuts-and-bolts" man. He freely admitted his knowledge, which was substantial, on what he knew of Khrushchev, but he just as readily admitted his shortcomings. During one EXCOM discussion, Bobby, looking at Thompson, asked rather insolently,

"Well, what does the Russian expert think?" Thompson reacted with, "I am afraid I am not much of an expert. If you would have asked me several weeks ago, I would have told you that the Russians would not send the missiles to Cuba."

Thompson loved to tell the story that Khrushchev looked disdainfully on so-called Kremlinologists. According to Thompson, Khrushchev said: "They don't understand the Politburo. They are from a highly educated nation and they look upon us as being equally highly educated. They don't know that we are dominated by an unimaginative and unattractive bunch of scoundrels."

October 17—Options and Courses of Action

The objective of all dedicated employees should
be to thoroughly analyze all situations, anticipate all problems prior to their occurrence,
have answers for these problems and move
swiftly to solve these problems when called
upon. However, when you are up to your ass
in alligators, it is difficult to remind yourself
that your initial objective was to drain
the swamp.

—SIGN ON NPIC WALL

AMIDST ALL THE BUILDUP of U.S. military forces in Florida, the weather bureau kept a close watch on hurricane Ella as it moved toward Florida on October 16. It packed winds of about ninety miles an hour. Scientists at Cape Canaveral postponed the Ranger 5 moon shot because of the hurricane. The weather bureau had forecast that the area between Palm Beach and Daytona Beach would be the most endangered. The hurricane, however, suddenly veered northward out over the Atlantic. As happens so often after a hurricane, there is a cleansing-and-clearing effect of clouds, and on October 17, the skies over Cuba were clear.

Early that morning, two U-2's began flying reconnaissance missions covering the length and breadth of Cuba. Before the day ended, a total of six U-2 missions would be flown, along with a massive elint collection effort on the part of the military services and the NSA. McCone and Bundy met with the president from 9:35 to 9:55 A.M. and reviewed the intelligence-collection activities that would be accomplished that day. McCone could not rationalize the failure of the

Soviets to activate the SA-2 tracking radars to monitor the U-2, elint, and other military flights.

The fact that the SAM sites were not activated, and the failure of the Soviets to immediately work around the clock to complete construction of the MRBM sites, proved to be a fatal error on their part. It has been postulated that the failure to activate the SAM sites might have been a blunder on the part of the Soviet military and the KGB. The movement of the missiles to Russian ports, the shipping of the missiles and support equipment to Cuba, and the unloading in Cuban ports were controlled by the military and the KGB. Once the SA-2 missile equipment had arrived at the designated sites in Cuba, however, the PVO, or air defense forces, took over; once the MRBM equipment arrived at its designated site, Strategic Rocket Forces personnel would take over. There had been hints in the past of the lack of cooperation between the PVO and Strategic Rocket Forces personnel and it is entirely possible that neither force knew what the other was doing in Cuba. The SA-2 sites, for example, had been heavily reveted, while the MRBM sites had been constructed in open fields and in a soft configuration.

The United States Intelligence Board met that morning at 8:30 and authorized a Special National Intelligence Estimate to be drafted on the situation. They also advised the administration not to adopt a position of acceptance of the Soviet buildup in Cuba and also advised against giving the Soviets any advanced indications of possible U.S. actions.

The visit of Dr. Gerhard Schroeder, foreign minister of the Federal Republic of Germany, to Washington had been arranged some time prior to October 17. At 10 A.M., Dr. Schroeder, K. Heinrich Knappstein, the West German ambassador to the U.S., Dean Rusk, Walter C. Dowling, U.S. ambassador to West Germany, along with a number of American and German aides, met with the president for over an hour and a half. Schroeder's discussion with the president, according to Martin J. Hillenbrand, director of the Special Berlin Task Force, assumed the nature of a tour d'horizon in which a number of topics were discussed, including such items as U.S.-German relations, the NATO alliance, and the security of the West.[1] The president, as usual, in these meetings was an active listener as well as a participant,[2] but he couldn't put the Cuban missiles from his mind. After lunch, the president departed the White House and motored several blocks to St. Matthews Cathedral to attend services in commemoration of the National Day of Prayer. There, too, according to Dave Powers, his mind was preoccupied with Cuba.

Lundahl held a prolonged staff meeting at the Center on the morning of October 17 to structure operational changes for the duration of the Crisis. Center personnel were equally divided into two twelve-hour shifts, with the shift change at 8 A.M each morning. Robert Boyd was put in charge of one shift of the photo interpreters and Gordon Duvall the other. Photo interpreters would brief Lundahl on photo intelligence derived the previous day at a morning meeting that would take place at 6:30 to 7 A.M. Duvall and Boyd and I would be at that meeting. My staff would have prepared notes for Lundahl on each photographic briefing board, along with other pertinent collateral information. Notes on operational matters, such as the number of missions to be flown, the weather, etc., would have been prepared by Dutch Scheufele.

Various film-processing sites also worked around the clock during the crisis. Navy and Air Force jet transports shuttled exposed film from the U-2 missions to the airfields nearest to the processing sites, and the processed film was expedited, similarly, to Washington and the Center for exploitation. Eastman Kodak also went into shift operations to meet the increased demand for aerial photographic film. Camera manufacturers were alerted, and their best technicians, along with truckfuls of spare parts, were sent to Orlando, MacDill, and Boca Chica to make sure that cameras were maintained and functioned properly. Additional Lockheed U-2 technicians and maintenance personnel were dispatched to Orlando to keep the U-2's flying.

The EXCOM met several times in George Ball's State Department conference room on October 17. The missile sites were reviewed, and Lundahl's feeling that more would be found was reflected in the EXCOM minutes: "It must be assumed that this is the beginning of a larger buildup."[3] Strong arguments were presented by General Taylor that the Soviet move was a major effort to alter the balance of power, yet the memo sent to the president that night stated: "It is generally agreed that these missiles do not significantly alter the balance of power—i.e., they do not significantly increase the potential megatonnage capable of being unleashed on American soil, even after a surprise American nuclear strike."⁴ But Taylor's strong feeling about the presence of the missiles was reflected in another paragraph: "Nevertheless it is generally agreed that the United States cannot tolerate the known presence of offensive nuclear weapons in a country 90 miles from our shore, if our courage and our commitments are ever to be believed by either allies or adversaries. Retorts from either our European allies or the Soviets that we can become as accustomed as they to accepting the nearby presence of MRBM's have some logic but little weight in this situation."⁵

The question of notifying allies was also discussed: "It is also agreed that certain of our NATO allies would be notified but not consulted immediately prior to any action by the United States; that certain Latin nations would at least be notified; and that, if there is to be military action, the President would withhold announcing the existence of the missiles and the justification of our action until after that action had been completed."⁶ The prospect of military action occupied a large portion of the meeting. A comparison of the strategic forces of the United States and the Soviet Union in October 1962 was made, and the overwhelming power advantage of the U.S. forces was awesome. It was estimated that the U.S. nuclear-strategic lead advantage was at least 7 to 1. (Soviet officials, in meetings with Americans in Moscow in January 1989, stated that the ratio was more than 15 to 1 in favor of the U.S.)

The U.S. inventory included more than 600 B-52 bombers, about 400 of which were equipped with the standoff Hound Dog air-to-surface missiles; there were about 700 B-47's and 900 tankers to refuel them on their way to Russia if necessary. The Russian bomber fleet consisted of about 100 Bison heavy jet bombers and 80 Bear turboprop heavy bombers. U.S. tactical forces included 2,500 fighters and 500 transport aircraft, augmented by 15 reserve troop carrier wings, 11 Air National Guard reconnaissance squadrons, and 5 communication squadrons. In addition to Air Force strategic units, there were 16 U.S. Navy attack carriers, with more than 400 attack bombers stationed in the Atlantic, Pacific, the Mediterranean, and the Caribbean.

The Soviets had a few short-range missile-firing submarines, which, in an all-out effort, were capable of launching some 100 short-range missiles. None of these submarines, however, had ever been deployed close enough to strike the U.S. and none were in the Atlantic or Pacific at the time. There was nothing in the Soviet arsenal to compare with the nine U.S. Polaris submarines—*George Washington, Patrick Henry, Theodore Roosevelt, Robert E. Lee, Abraham Lincoln, Ethan Allen, Sam Houston, Thomas A. Edison,* and *John Marshall*—on station and capable of launching 144 nuclear-tipped long-range missiles and destroying the principal cities in the Soviet Union.

These and other statistics of strategic power were reviewed again and again, but the results were always the same. In a conflict with the Soviet Union, there was overwhelming evidence of U.S. superiority. The gnawing question that remained was that, knowing the preponderance of U.S. strength, why would the Soviets try such a desperate move? The U.S. had seldom been known to back down from a position of strength. The United States not only enjoyed total supremacy in conventional arms in the Caribbean crisis area but also possessed 229 ICBMs at the time—mainly Titans deployed in silos —and the Atlas missile, deployed in semihardened "coffin" configurations. The Russians, at the time, had only about forty-four ICBM sites, all in soft configurations. (General Dmitri Volkogonov, in meetings with Americans in Moscow in January 1989, stated that only twenty of the Soviet ICBM sites were operational at the time.) But the capability comparison did not stop there. Further, the Russian bombers would have had to penetrate the sophisticated NORAD air warning system, pass through U.S. and Canadian fighter-interceptor defenses, which had proven time and again an ability to intercept and shoot down Russian bombers in simulated raids. Even if the Russian bombers did penetrate the warning systems and get past the interceptors, the U.S. also had the proven and formidable Nike and Bomarc surface-to-air-missile systems defending America's principal cities and military and industrial targets.

Although there were no bombing experts present during the EXCOM meeting, there was general agreement that a "50-sortie, 1-swoop" strike was sufficient to destroy a single MRBM complex. However, before an air strike on the missile sites could be seriously considered, the Cuban air defenses would have to be neutralized. It was agreed that a "200-sortie raid" would be sufficient to destroy Cuba's MiG air defense fighters, the SA-2 sites, and Cuba's "retaliatory capacity."

There was disagreement, however, as to what was required and what would constitute a "surgical strike." The number of strike aircraft required to destroy Cuba's total war-making capability was also questioned. While it was true that the MRBM missile sites were located in isolated areas in the hinterland, a number of the airfields, military camps, and supporting installations were situated in populated areas in the larger Cuban cities. As the discussion of the estimate of the number of aircraft required for an all-out attack against Cuba increased, there was some doubt as to whether the Tactical Air Command, along with U.S. Navy aircraft, had the capacity to conduct the necessary bombing operations in the shortest period of time.

During the afternoon of October 17, EXCOM discussions again turned to the U.S. bombing of the missile sites, and Bobby Kennedy, while not objecting to General Taylor's remarks about not being sure of the total destruction of all missiles sites, called General Walter Sweeney, the commander of the U.S. Air Force Tactical Air Command, and received the same answer that he had gotten from General Taylor—i.e., Sweeney could not guarantee total destruction of all the missile sites in a one-strike operation. Later, General Sweeney would brief the EXCOM that it would take four strike aircraft for each MRBM launcher—in other words, sixteen aircraft for each MRBM site, eight aircraft for each SAM site, and twelve aircraft for each of three airfields that contained either fighter or bomber aircraft. The initial strike on Cuba would involve some 250 sorties. At the height of the crisis, there were 850 strike aircraft in Florida and on carriers at sea, along with 62 fighters for defense of Florida.

General LeMay had returned from Europe and knew that the question of bombing the sites was being discussed by the EXCOM. He was incensed that he, as Air Force chief of staff, had not been consulted. When he found out that General Sweeney had been approached by Bobby, his pique was intensified. But Bobby did consult General LeMay later by phone, since he hadn't gotten the response he had hoped for from General Sweeney. Bobby carefully phrased his questions to LeMay, "How many of the SAC bombers were designed to carry nuclear weapons?"

LeMay replied curtly, "All of them."

Bobby then asked, "How many of them could carry conventional bombs?"

LeMay responded without hesitation, "None of them. They weren't built to carry iron bombs."

Bobby then posed another question: "How many of the SAC bombers maintained on alert were loaded with nuclear weapons?"

Again, LeMay replied, "All of them."

(All of the SAC bombers assigned an international bombing role were configured to carry only nuclear and chemical munitions. It wasn't until the Vietnam conflict that SAC B-52 bombers would be reconfigured and crews trained to drop conventional "iron bombs.")

Bobby was flabbergasted and speechless. LeMay, meanwhile, was hoping that he would be invited to the White House to give expert advice on the bombing of Cuba.

There was a pause, and Bobby mumbled his thanks and hung up. LeMay looked at an aide and sarcastically said, "What a dumb shit!"

Bobby would later inform the president to be extremely careful in authorizing LeMay to initiate any bombing missions without very specific instructions as to the type of ordnance to be used.

The president admired LeMay as a good soldier. His feelings about soldiers, as described later by Arthur Schlesinger, were: "It's good to have men like Curt LeMay and Arleigh Burke commanding troops when you decide to go in," he told Hugh Sidey. "But these men aren't the only ones you should listen to when you decide whether to go in or not. I like having LeMay head of the Air Force. Everybody knows how he feels."[7]

Some EXCOM participants expressed concern about Guantánamo in the event of an attack on Cuba. There was agreement that dependents would have to be evacuated prior to such an attack. McNamara said that he would have such a move studied. Discussions evolved about other plans for destroying the missiles. General Taylor disagreed strongly with a plan for a "commando raid, under air cover, by helicopter or otherwise, to take out missiles with bullets, destroy launchers and leave." There were questions, "whether Moscow would be either able or willing to prevent Soviet missile commanders from firing on United States when attacked, or Castro and/or his Air Force or any part of it attacking U.S. mainland. This includes the further question of whether, if a military strike is to take place, it must take place before these missiles become operational in the next 2 weeks or so."[8] Whether Senate and congressional leaders should be briefed on the crisis was discussed. It was decided not to brief any of them, for fear of disclosure. The question was raised whether the president should cancel the remainder of his prescheduled campaign speeches. Until specific courses of action and decisions were made, it was agreed that the president should continue with his scheduled campaign speeches.

Specific courses of action were discussed and the attendant military and diplomatic actions weighed. The following alternative recommendations were made to the president for consideration:

> "TRACK A—Political action, pressure and warning, followed by a military strike if satisfaction is not received.
> "TRACK B—A military strike without prior warning, pressure or action, accompanied by messages making clear the limited nature of this action.
> "TRACK C—Political action, pressure and warning, followed by a total naval blockade, under the authority of the Rio Pact and either a Congressional Declaration of War on Cuba or the Cuban Resolution of the 87th Congress."[9]

Among the various tracks, the political actions, pressures, and warnings included the following: Letters to Khrushchev that the missile bases would be struck if they weren't dismantled, summoning him to a summit, and offering to withdraw the missiles from Turkey. Other suggestions were letters to Castro, bringing the threat of peace before the UN, taking the threat to the hemisphere to the OAS and obtaining authorization for action. Acheson would press for a declaration of war against Cuba stating that the Soviets would find "their bayonets had struck steel instead of mush." Another suggestion was to confront Gromyko when he visited the president on October 18.

As the talk of a blockade became more a possibility as a proposed course of action, two naval officers from the Joint Chiefs of Staff visited the Center. Their concern was to define the "interception area" where ships could be stopped. They said they wanted to make the interception beyond the range of air cover from Cuba. They, of course, knew the range of the MiG-21's, and they asked if they could see the location of all of the surface-to-surface missile sites, the SAM sites, and the airfields where the MiG-21's were deployed. We had all these installations plotted on a large map. They decided that intercepts could be made safely within five hundred miles of an arc, with its center at Cape Maysí, located on the eastern tip of Cuba. When they saw that a lot of the military activity was also located in the Havana area, they swung a second arc five hundred miles from Havana.

The Joint Chiefs
of Staff

"A quartet playing different tunes."
—Pentagon Scuttlebutt

Following the Bay of Pigs debacle, President Kennedy adopted a decidedly skeptical approach to decisions on military matters. Although he sought unanimous opinions from the JCS, he was dubious of their collective wisdom. When he asked for separate opinions from each member, he didn't have the military expertise to meld them into a course of action. After the Bay of Pigs, he would never again accept the parochial military judgments of the JCS without question. Although he had personally taken the blame for the Bay of Pigs, the president had a cynical appraisal of what had gotten him into the predicament. He regarded the Joint Chiefs' call for military action against Cuba as deplorably unrealistic.

The JCS, for their part, had a divided opinion of the president's leadership qualities. Some regarded him as decidedly weak in relations with the Soviets and Cuba. They especially questioned the president's knowledge of military matters, and after the Bay of Pigs wanted to make sure, in General Taylor's words, "they wouldn't be caught on the gang-plank alone."

President Kennedy brought General Maxwell Taylor to the White House as military consultant to the president after the Bay of Pigs. Taylor enjoyed the confidence of both the president and Bobby and advised the president on a broad range of national-security matters. It was in Taylor's office, room 303 in the Executive Office Building, that the powerful 303 Committee met and reviewed all covert CIA operations. On the 303 Committee were McNamara, Rusk, Taylor, and McCone. When the president subsequently designated Taylor as Chairman of the Joint Chiefs of Staff, a JCS liaison office was created in the White House, ostensibly to work with McGeorge Bundy, the president's assistant for national security affairs. In reality, the liaison office was to keep Taylor personally informed on all military matters of particular concern to the president.

Keeping peace among the Joint Chiefs of Staff required all the tact and patience that General Taylor could muster. The general felt that since the president was woefully lacking in knowledge on the U.S. military, it would become his duty to make the president fully aware of the military approach to problems. He constantly reminded the president of the realities and complexities of mobilizing and moving modern armies. Some would argue that the Joint Chiefs of Staff played a far less prominent role in the Cuba missile crisis than was generally accepted—that the military was controlled by General Taylor and that Taylor, in turn, was controlled by the president. There was also distrust between the JCS and McNamara. McNamara had come to the Pentagon with little or no knowledge of things military, and immediately brought in Alain Enthoven, Charles Hitch, and a coterie of "whiz kids" and began immediately to question all of the building blocks the military had established since World War II.

General Taylor was haughty, urbane, intelligent, and eloquent. Athletic since his academy days, he was one of the better tennis players in the Washington area for his age. He would smile when asked if it was true that one of the prime considerations in selecting his aides was their tennis-playing abilities. His friends called him "the book general" because he possessed all of the principal qualities stressed in West Point textbooks—vision, judgment, a broad spectrum of knowledge on tactics, and patience. A strikingly handsome man, he was articulate despite a slight lisp in his speech. Among the postwar generals, he is ranked by Army historians second only to General Matthew Ridgway as a writer whose words needed little ghosting or editing. Devoted to his old comrades of the 101st Airborne Division, he proudly wore a tie clasp bearing the screaming eagle insignia. He attributed his appointment as superintendent of West Point after the war to the loyalty and endorsements of Division comrades.

Always the dedicated army man, Taylor would smile when questioned about having made his stars so fast. He reminded his questioner that it had taken him thirteen years to make captain. Disillusioned at the slow rate of promotions, he recalled that at times, he had lost favor even in his own family. His grandfather was a Confederate soldier and his grandmother an unreconstructed southern sympathizer. On seeing Taylor in his West Point uniform for the first time, said she that she never thought she would ever see the day when a blue Yankee uniform would be allowed in her house. When Taylor's promotions were slow in coming, she insisted that the North was still punishing the South. Taylor told her that was not true and she took a different tack—that Taylor must be doing something wrong and for him to "get with it."

Meetings of the Joint Chiefs of Staff were alluded to by some as a three-ring circus. General Curtis E. LeMay, Air Force chief of staff, was characterized by one observer as always injecting himself into situations "like a rogue elephant barging out of a forest." There are many stories of LeMay's crudeness in dealing with his colleagues on the Joint Chiefs of Staff. He found the meetings dull, tiring, and unproductive. Petulant and often childish when he didn't get his way, LeMay would light a cigar and blow smoke in the direction of anyone challenging his position. To show utter disgust, he would walk into the private Joint Chiefs of Staff toilet, leave the door open, urinate or break wind loudly, and flush the commode a number of aggravating times. He would then saunter calmly back into the meeting pretending that nothing had happened. When angry with individual staff members, he would resort to sarcasm; if that failed, he would direct his wrath to the entire staff.

General Taylor, on the other hand, always considered the consequences of any action. "What will be our position if we fail?" was one of his most persistent questions. Often he would ask his subordinates, "What are we doing that may provoke a response?" He would often deliberate a problem by showing how differently a politician and a military man would approach the problem. General David M. Shoup, commandant of the U.S. Marine Corps, always

looked backward to World War II for analogies and his recommendations were, for the most part, wide of the mark. General Earle G.
Wheeler, chief of staff of the U.S. Army, has been referred to as a
mechanic, concerned only with the response after a decision was
made—but made by someone else.

But the Joint Chiefs of Staff were unanimous during the crisis in
calling for immediate military action, believing that a blockade of
Cuba would be ineffective. A military attack was essential. The strike
plan they advocated was a massive attack on all missile sites, all
airfields, and all military camps, and invading the island. With the
specter of Soviet nuclear weapons in Cuba a probability, prudence
called for strikes to eliminate all sources of retaliation.

General LeMay was the leading advocate of the manned bomber.
His beetle brows, jutting jaw, sagging jowls, shock of slicked-down
black hair, and the ubiquitous brown cigar gave him the visage of a
bulldog. Profane, demanding, restless for power, he was the undis-
puted builder of the greatest fleet of destruction ever assembled. He
had helped pioneer air transport in the pre-World War II days, led
wartime combat forces in Europe and the Pacific, served as SAC
commander for seven years and for two years as the vice-chief of
staff before becoming chief of staff of the U.S. Air Force in 1961. He
had personally selected "Peace Is Our Profession" as the motto for
the Strategic Air Command, and in one of his "prepared" lectures
for visiting dignitaries at SAC headquarters in Omaha, he would
speak boldly of his indomitable belief that peace could be achieved
only through strength. Conveniently omitting historical fact, he
would reiterate how Roman strength had achieved Pax Romana;
how the British, through their naval and military strength, had
achieved Pax Britannica; and, with unabashed gall, how his bombers
were achieving Pax Atomica (once during a lecture, he resorted to
the term Pax Americana). LeMay loved to compare SAC to a porcupine. The porcupine, he would say, was never provocative. "His
desire is to live at peace. But the mere fact that he is armed is the
essence of deterrence." At SAC, LeMay practiced what he thought
was a simple philosophy—uncompromising safety, patriotism, and
an instantaneous readiness for combat.

It was for his past accomplishments that LeMay was admired in
Washington, and he was well aware of this. For all of his power at

Omaha, he had few intimates among his associates in Washington. While he insisted on standard operating procedures in all operations of his command, he was not personally averse to abrogating channels in achieving his objectives. He still had the support of many powerful senators and congressmen. LeMay, however, was uneasy in Washington. He saw himself as an outsider, yet continually prided himself as the only authority on warfare available to the JCS. Most of all, he felt that the Joint Chiefs of Staff dallied over vital decisions and were not responsive. LeMay had come to Washington expecting the worst, and he was not disappointed. While he had ridden roughshod over the acquiescent officers to build SAC, he could not find such acquiescence in the Pentagon. LeMay received the many distinguished visitors to the Strategic Air Command like a king receiving his subjects. Many of the visitors, indeed, were defense contractors, who were likely to exaggerate their praise of LeMay and SAC. LeMay loved to bait these visitors and his briefers. One of his former aides said that "nothing pleased the old man more than shooting a briefer down in flames." This, it appears, added to an already egocentric attitude.

LeMay had a deep-seated antagonism toward what he termed "so-called thinkers," by which he meant those whose views were opposed to his. In later years, for example, he would forbid anyone from the Rand Corporation to see him or any of his official papers. On occasion, Herman Kahn, the mathematician, futurist senior physicist and military analyst, and later the director of the Hudson Research Institute, met LeMay at SAC. As Kahn moved through the headquarters building, he noted that many desks bore signs reading "Peace Is Our Profession." The portly Kahn slipped one of the signs under his tentlike coat. When he walked into LeMay's office, he plopped the sign down on the general's desk and said, "I am here to prove that war is your profession, not peace." A stormy session followed in which the two argued their views forcibly. Kahn maintaining that the policy of deterrence, known officially as "mutually assured destruction," was unworkable and that techniques of survival must take a large place in policy planning. Later, LeMay was to remark that he liked "that lard-ass son of a bitch." Actually, Kahn's position corresponded to the views that LeMay never expressed in public.

LeMay's bible was the Single Integrated Operational Plan (SIOP), the master nuclear-war plan created by the Joint Chiefs of Staff and approved each year by the administration in power. The SIOP had five options, the fifth being a first-strike plan. LeMay monitored all the conditions of each plan during the crisis and was prepared to launch a first strike if the president authorized it.[1] LeMay regarded the missiles in Cuba as an intolerable situation. He felt the Soviets had put them in Cuba to attack SAC bases. There could be little doubt that the greatest fear that the Soviets had were of General LeMay and the bombers of the Strategic Air Command. The loss of warning time posed by the missiles in Cuba would also degrade SAC's ground-alert bomber force. LeMay knew the threat of nuclear attack was not only against the SAC bases but also against the principal cities of the nation.

There are many anecdotes about LeMay. One of the more quotable was: "Moses came down from the mountain followed by General LeMay with the 'Big Pig' [Basic Intelligence Planning Guide] and a SAC supplement." In one address to SAC crews, LeMay was quoted as saying: "There are only two things in this world, SAC bases and SAC targets." LeMay loved to bait the Navy. He felt strongly that the Navy's Polaris submarines should be under the control of the Strategic Air Command. As one entered the corridor leading to LeMay's SAC office, there was a model of the Polaris submarine with the SAC insignia emblazoned on it. LeMay had asked the JCS for control of the Polaris submarines. Admiral Arleigh A. Burke, as chief of naval operations, fought the Air Force every way he knew, in the Navy, among the JCS, in Congress, and in the press. The Navy lost partial control of the Polaris fleet when the Joint Strategic Target Planning Staff was created, with the commander of SAC as director and a vice-admiral as deputy director. In an encounter with Navy officers, LeMay said that the best antisubmarine system was "to boil the ocean with nukes."

Arrogant, zealous, and narrow-minded, LeMay contemptuously referred to Cuba as a "sideshow" and said that the main enemy was Russia. When he was asked what he would do with Cuba, he contemptuously replied, "Fry it."

Despite his pungent dialogue and impressive quotations, General LeMay continued to maintain an attitude of fully confident optimism.

In later years, he explained during an interview why he had been able to remain confident. If a war had started, he said, he would have failed in his mission as chief of staff. To fulfill his mission, he had built the Strategic Air Command into an effective deterrent and an ominous counterforce. The SAC counterforce strategy, he maintained, was designed to confront the enemy with certain destruction of his military force in case he attacked the free world. When the Cuban crisis occurred, LeMay stated his efforts in producing a massive strategic deterrent had produced a major dividend.

General Taylor, responding to my inquiry as to his personal view of General LeMay, said that as a bomber commander there was none finer. LeMay had built the Strategic Air Command into a fine fighting machine, exacting both devotion and discipline from his men. Everyone in authority knew that SAC was ready if called upon. "But a good bomber commander," Taylor hastened to add, "doesn't automatically make a good chief of staff, and appointing LeMay as chief of staff of the Air Force was a big mistake." Soon after being appointed chief of staff, LeMay began the infighting that SAC thrived on and interservice squabbles began to surface. Few in the Pentagon wanted to revert back to the feuds of the 1950s, and several ranking officers admonished LeMay to "control his tongue."

LeMay continued this modus operandi when Taylor became Chairman of the Joint Chiefs of Staff. Taylor stated that LeMay "would jam that damn cigar in his mouth and place a chip on his shoulder and parade through the halls of the Pentagon looking for a fight." Taylor felt LeMay was the most politically naive military man he had ever met and that LeMay's running for vice-president with George Wallace, along with other events, bore him out. LeMay's presentations to Congress and his off-the-cuff remarks to congressmen and senators often took weeks of effort for the JCS to clarify. Taylor was aware that LeMay wasn't a "team man" and, after admonishing him on two particular occasions, called him in and "read the riot act." Taylor was in a position to do this for two reasons: He was Kennedy's man in the Pentagon and he understood the total military needs of the country, not just those of the Air Force. LeMay subsequently perpetrated a rumor throughout the Air Force that

Taylor was out to get the Air Force and its appropriations. He began meeting privately with powerful House and Senate leaders, skirting both the secretary of defense and the Chairman of the Joint Chiefs of Staff. LeMay's arrogance was apparent in a later remark that what General Taylor did really made little difference—that when he (LeMay) left SAC, it would slowly die. The friction between LeMay and Taylor was well known in the Pentagon. When LeMay's reappointment as chief of staff of the Air Force was pending, Taylor recommended that he "be put out to pasture." LeMay, however, was reappointed.

JCS members after the crisis remained extremely sensitive about their reputations for recommending an all-out assault on Cuba. General Lyman L. Lemnitzer, former chief of staff of the Army, would defend the JCS actions: "I believe the Joint Chiefs of Staff played their normal and appropriate role during the Crisis. They provided sound military advice to the President, Secretary of Defense and other officials during the Crisis and had important influence on the final decision. There have been efforts to portray the Joint Chiefs of Staff during the Crisis as war-mongers or hawks during the Crisis pressing for invasion and air strikes, which is not true. It was, however, their duty to make contingency plans for the various developments as they occurred, to include an invasion plan if that was decided on by the President. In other words, the normal relationship took place between the military and the civilian branches of the government; the military made recommendations and the civilian political leaders decided."[2]

General Shoup would also react when Bobby Kennedy criticized the Joint Chiefs of Staff's actions during the crisis in a *McCall's* magazine article. "It is not fair to say that the Joint Chiefs of Staff recommended to the exclusion of any other course that we go right in and blast the missile sites off the face of the earth. I'm pretty sure that nobody recommended in my presence unequivocally that we immediately wipe out the missile sites with bombs without any other consideration of the implications."[3] Bobby would later relate the Kennedys' concern regarding LeMay: "General Curtis LeMay, Air Force Chief of Staff, argued strongly with the President that a military attack was essential. When the President questioned what the response of the Russians might be, General LeMay assured him there would be no reaction. President Kennedy was skeptical. They no more than we, can let these things go by without doing something. They can't, after all their statements, permit us to take out their missiles, kill a lot of Russians, and then do nothing. If they don't take action in Cuba, they certainly will in Berlin. The President went on to say that he recognized the validity of the arguments made by the Joint Chiefs, the danger that more and more missiles would be placed in Cuba, and the likelihood, if we did nothing, that the Russians would move on Berlin and in other areas of the world, feeling that the U.S. was completely impotent. Then it would be too late to do anything in Cuba, for by that time all their missiles would be operational."[4]

The performance of General David M. Shoup was less than distinguished during the crisis. Seemingly uninformed on a number of details of the war plans and seriously lacking knowledge of Cuba, he had difficulty making contributions to the discussions. As one observer remarked, "Shoup never seemed to engage the problem." Sitting passively in meetings, he would support one side of a position and then the other. Often in response to a very specific question, he would switch to irrelevant matters such as his experiences in Marine landings in the Pacific during World War II. As a colonel in 1943, he was the senior officer ashore and won the Medal of Honor during the landings at Tarawa in the Gilbert Islands. In three days of fighting, the Marines lost 948 dead and 2,072 wounded.

The only lasting impression Shoup made on President Kennedy on Cuba concerned Tarawa. During a meeting of the president with the Joint Chiefs of Staff, Shoup asked if he could show the president some information that might be pertinent to the invasion of Cuba. The president graciously accepted and General Shoup reached into a zippered case and removed a briefing board. The president was a little dumbfounded seeing a large map of the United States. General Shoup then reached behind the board and superimposed an acetate overlay of the outline of Cuba. The president was surprised to see that Cuba was over seven hundred miles long and nearly a hundred miles wide at its widest point. Shoup then made an analogy with Tarawa during World War II, citing the casualties taking an island that was barely two miles long. Marine casualties at Tarawa and other Pacific landings in World War II had a lasting impact on General

Shoup's thinking, as would the Cuban missile crisis. In his State of the Corps message on January 3, 1963, he would say, "Only by the grace of God and an aerial photo is it possible to make these remarks to many of you in person rather than to your spirits. For this I am truly thankful." He spoke in simple, staccato phrases, like a drill instructor addressing recruits. One of his battle reports was frequently quoted in Marine publications as an example of succinct battle reporting: "Casualties many; percentage dead not known; combat efficiency: we are winning." He stressed the human consequences of the invasion, especially if the Cubans fought as hard as he thought they would.

Shoup's constant reverting to World War II experiences irritated most of his colleagues, but especially General LeMay. The firepower, conditions, tactics, and the enemy had changed. One just couldn't apply World War II conditions to the Cuban missile crisis. On one occasion during a discussion with the president, Shoup looked at the president and rather flippantly remarked, "Mr. President, you have a problem." President Kennedy corrected him, "General, we have a problem."

General Earle G. "Buzz" Wheeler became the Army chief of staff on October 1, 1962. In March of that year, Wheeler had been promoted to full general and appointed deputy commander in chief of the United States European Command, headed by General Lauris Norstad. Norstad was also the supreme commander of the North Atlantic Treaty Organization forces. At that time, Wheeler was regarded as a possible successor to General Norstad. Wheeler was a protégé of General Maxwell Taylor. When Taylor became Chairman of the Joint Chiefs of Staff and General George H. Decker retired as chief of staff of the Army, Wheeler was Taylor's, as well as the president's, choice to succeed Decker. During the presidential campaign of 1960, General Wheeler, as director of the joint staff of the JCS, had been called upon to brief candidate Kennedy on military developments and military situations worldwide. Kennedy was impressed with Wheeler's succinct and orderly presentations.

General Wheeler began his army career as an enlisted man in the National Guard at the age of sixteen. He had served in the Guard for four years, rising to the rank of sergeant before receiving an appointment to the United States Military Academy in 1928. An excellent student, he was ranked 62 in a class of 292 at graduation. During the 1930s, he served in China for three years and attended the Fort Benning Infantry School, finishing first in his class. When Pearl Harbor plunged the United States into World War II, Wheeler had attained the rank of captain. He was sent, in 1942, to intensive advanced training at the Command and Staff School at Fort Leavenworth, Kansas. Again, he finished first in his class. While others on the Joint Chiefs of Staff had seen extensive combat duty in World War II, General Wheeler had only five months of duty in Europe as a division chief of staff in the final months of the war.

Wheeler had achieved prominence as an administrator and expert on supplies, training, and logistics. He had also earned a reputation as the general most capable of effectively presenting the U.S. Army's conventional-arms position, as opposed to the U.S. Navy and U.S. Air Force positions advocating the preeminence of long-range strategic weapons systems. It was while he was director of plans in the Office of the Deputy Chief of Staff for Military Operations that Wheeler first caught the eye of General Taylor. General Taylor had subsequently entrusted a number of important staff duties to Wheeler. Since it was well known that Wheeler was a protégé of General Taylor, LeMay was immediately suspicious of him. Taylor and Wheeler were very much alike in mannerism, speech, and in action. LeMay referred to Wheeler as Polly Parrot. LeMay had also facetiously said that one of Wheeler's ribbons was for "fighting the Battle of Fort Benning during World War II," an obvious reference to Wheeler's lack of combat experience.

Wheeler nevertheless was a "by-the-numbers" general and would later be criticized for a lack of imagination and single-minded doggedness when he became the Chairman of the JCS. As early as 1962, General Wheeler was advocating strong military action in Vietnam and, later, as Chairman of the JCS, helped conceal the fact that bombing raids had been conducted in Cambodia. His support to the Johnson and Nixon administrations regarding Southeast Asia was unquestioning. Wheeler was a total military man, completely devoted to the Army and the United States. He also had a heart problem and suffered from high blood pressure. During the Cuban missile crisis, one of his staff officers said he was eating high-blood-pressure pills like they were candy. He also chain-smoked king-size cigarettes in a long brown holder.

Admiral George W. Anderson, fifty-five, the chief of naval operations, was known throughout the Navy as a sailor's sailor. Tall (six feet, two inches), handsome, personable, and a superb strategist, he had been picked by Kennedy's first Navy secretary, John Connally, to replace the flamboyant and often self-determined Arleigh Burke. It was reported that when Kennedy saw Anderson's service file, he told Connally he would feel comfortable with Anderson at the helm. Beloved by Navy men wherever he served, Anderson had made his name as commander of the Sixth Fleet in the Mediterranean. A devout Catholic, he saturated his men with what became known popularly as the 3M's (memorandums, maxims, and man grams) on clean living. He was a man whose looks and actions garnered nicknames. Because of his good looks, he was affectionately known as Gorgeous George. Because of his sermonizing on the evils of prostitution, he earned the nickname Straight Arrow. Because of his penchant for detailing medics to dispense penicillin to prostitutes ashore and to men returning from liberty, he was known as the V.D.M.D. He abhorred foul language, and some of his messages on cursing were considered classics by petty officers who made them part of the Blue Jacket's Manual. For this trait, he was dubbed Snow White.

Anderson had a sincere compassion for the sailor's personal and family problems. Those closest to him felt that this compassion resulted from his first wife's death from cancer. A captain who served with Admiral Anderson in the Mediterranean recalled that not showing compassion to a sailor in distress could bring a dressing down from Anderson that one would not soon forget or want to experience again. Anderson was probably the best informed JCS member on Soviet military policy. He frequently described Soviet strategy in this manner: "To pose to the opposition courses of action characterized only by disadvantages, risks, expense, and controversy, while retaining the initiative to revert if necessary to a position no worse than the status quo ante."

. . .

President Kennedy, claiming that he "owed one to Abe," left Washington at 3 P.M. in the afternoon of October 17 for a five-hour campaign tour of Connecticut to aid the reelection campaigns of Abraham A. Ribicoff for the Senate and John N. Dempsey for governor. Under Ribicoff's leadership, Connecticut was the first state to support Kennedy's bid for president. Ribicoff had also labored hard for Kennedy at the 1952 and 1956 Democratic conventions. When Kennedy was elected president, he asked Abraham Ribicoff to become head of the new Department of Health, Education and Welfare. Although Ribicoff took the job, he didn't like it or the pressure, became restless, and chose to run for the Senate. The president spoke on Ribicoff's behalf at the Bridgeport airport, at Waterbury, and at New Haven. He addressed domestic issues and the need for more Democrats in Congress. He carefully avoided any international issue, which then prompted *Time* reporters to write: "Through it all, the President avoided anything more than passing references to the international problems of the U.S. Cuba might as well have been on another planet."[5]

When he returned to the White House that evening, Sorensen was waiting and handed him the memo outlining EXCOM discussions that day. The president supposedly said, "We cannot live with such a threat. One way or another, the missiles must go."

That same Wednesday, Vice-Admiral Alfred Ward, commander of the Amphibious Forces U.S. Atlantic Fleet, received a call from a CINCLANT staff captain, who told him that he would be relieved of his command the next day. Ward quickly asked, "What have I done wrong?"

The reply, "I don't know."

"Who will replace me?"

Again, the curt reply, "I don't know."

Frustrated, Ward asked to speak to Admiral Robert L. Dennison, commander in chief of Atlantic Forces. He was told, "He's too busy. He can't talk to you."

Ward then called his friend Vice-Admiral Wallace M. Beakley, Admiral Dennison's chief of staff. Beakley told Ward that he would be replaced either on Thursday or Friday by Vice-Admiral Horacio Rivero.

Admiral Dennison was making these changes in command with

the approval of Admiral George Anderson, chief of naval operations. Both Anderson and Dennison had agreed that since war seemed likely, it would be best that the commander of the Second Fleet, the working fleet in the Atlantic, be assured of a long tenure of command. Ward was later called and told that the change-of-command ceremony would be on Saturday, October 20, at Norfolk and that he would be in command on the Second Fleet. On Thursday, Friday, and Saturday, ships of Ward's future command were being ordered by Admiral Dennison to sea. Fleet oilers, ammunition, and other supply ships were also putting to sea, prepared to refuel and replenish the destroyers that would later be on the blockade stations. In addition, two TACAN-equipped navigational ships were positioned in the Florida Straits to support CINCLANT operations. Ward called Beakley again. "Beake," Ward asked, "what are you doing to my fleet? I want to see Admiral Dennison." Beakley replied, "You will see him tomorrow. Admiral Dennison is scheduled to be the principal speaker at the change-of-command ceremony."[6]

On Saturday, October 20, Admiral Ward reported to the heavy cruiser *Newport News*, the flagship of the Second Fleet. The brief change-of-command ceremony was conducted on the fantail of the cruiser berthed at Norfolk, Virginia. Admiral Dennison was not present. He had sent word to Ward that he would meet him at the Norfolk Naval Air Station at the conclusion of the ceremony and fill him in on the details. Ward quickly shook hands with the guests at the ceremony and then hurried to the naval air station, where he boarded Admiral Dennison's plane for a flight to Washington. Ward would tell me later that never in the history of the Navy had he seen anything so mysterious. En route, Dennison told Ward about the Cuban missiles and showed him the updated plans for a blockade of Cuba. Ward was told that he would be in charge of implementing the blockade if the president authorized it. Dennison asked Ward to study the plan in depth because it would be discussed with Admiral Anderson and then presented to the Joint Chiefs of Staff. The plan had been basically approved by the JCS with just the stipulation that qualified Russian language officers would be aboard all ships on the blockade line. Naval officers who were Russian linguists, and who were on duty in or near East Coast ports, were issued orders to be in Norfolk and aboard designated ships by Sunday, October 21.

Ward would write later, "Each ship on the quarantine line had on board a Russian language interpreter. This was quite a feat. Fortunately, plans had been made for such a contingency. Of interest, as a Cruiser Division Commander in the Pacific, I had a fine officer as my Flag Lieutenant and aide, then a lieutenant named William (Bill) Martin, a brilliant young officer who was a great help in working with the Japanese, Chinese, Filipinos, and Southeast Asian nationals. When it became desirable to have an interpreter on board ship of the Cuban quarantine, orders went out. Fortunately the 'computer' was prepared. To my amazement on Sunday morning, Bill Martin showed up. I asked him, 'Why?' and he replied, 'I am your Russian language interpreter.' I had no knowledge of that capability but it was a great benefit."[7]

At the JCS meeting on the morning of October 18 the special JCS-CINCLANT operational plan on Cuba went into effect. The Joint Chiefs of Staff were responsible for the overall plans, and CINCLANT (Commander in Chief, Atlantic), located in Norfolk, was responsible for the preparation and implementation of plans for joint military, naval, and air task force operations. The JCS designated the commanding general of the U.S. Continental Army, General Herbert B. Powell, and the commander of the Tactical Air Command, General Walter B. Sweeney, as Army and Air Force commanders in chief of the Unified Atlantic Command of Admiral Dennison. This was done to facilitate quick and orderly implementation of the plans already approved. Admiral George W. Anderson was designated to act for the JCS in all matters relating to the blockade and General LeMay was to handle all reconnaissance affairs.

MacDill, Homestead, and McCoy air force bases, as well as the Key West Naval Air Station, had been placed on a full-alert status on the afternoon of October 17. The SAC U-2 detachment commander at Orlando notified the Strategic Air Command and the CIA that he intended to use one of the CIA U-2 pilots on a reconnaissance mission scheduled for October 18. That decision was reversed that evening by Joseph Charyk, the undersecretary of the Air Force. The Air Force was not about to lose control of what it considered to be its mission. Majors Heyser and Anderson were still the only Air Force pilots checked out in the Agency U-2's that had J-75 engines. On October 18, General Geary of SAC was still concerned and inquired if he was to use Heyser and Anderson again or the two Agency pilots assigned to the detachment. McNamara insisted that he wanted only the Agency's U-2's used, so this meant that Anderson and Heyser would have to fly them. This, all agreed, was extremely dangerous, since fatigue and inattentiveness went hand in hand. Still, Charyk refused to allow the Agency pilots to fly the missions. One of the Agency's U-2's was in standdown status on October 19, as were Heyser and Anderson. On October 20, it was decided to alternate Heyser and Anderson in the Agency U-2's.

10

October 18–
More Surprises

<blockquote>
"Just listen to him."

—AMBASSADOR LLEWELLYN E. THOMPSON
</blockquote>

THE FILM FROM U-2 MISSIONS flown on October 17 was being processed, and the first of it reached the Center late in the evening of the seventeenth and the morning of the eighteenth. Photo interpreters immediately began to scan the film. Searching the area of Guanajay, just west of Havana, the photo interpreters spotted new military activity. Four slash marks—excavations for missile launch pads—caught their eyes. The spacing of the launch pads was radically different than for the launchers seen at San Cristóbal. The pads also appeared to be more permanent in nature. It was also immediately apparent that, when completed, this installation would be more sophisticated than those at San Cristóbal. There were two concrete batch plants at Guanajay, and the construction activity was much heavier than that seen at San Cristóbal. Excavations for fuel tanks and cables were being dug and concrete was being poured at some of the launch pads. The launch pads were paired and conduits for cables led from the center of each launch pad to a control bunker. Pad separation at these sites was 700 to 800 feet, rather than the 500 to 600 feet for the San Cristóbal MRBM sites. A missile servicing building had been roofed over and was nearing completion. Revetments for launch support vehicles were also under construction.

No missiles or missile-associated equipment were seen, however.

Searching nearby, the photo interpreters found a prefabricated concrete nuclear warhead storage bunker under construction. Joe Seng, Chris Dole, and Wilbur Dodd, the expert interpreters on nuclear matters, immediately indicated that the bunker was similar to those seen in the Soviet Union. David Doyle and Geoffrey Langsam were the Center's photo-interpretation experts for Soviet IRBM sites. When Doyle was shown the photos of the sites in Cuba, he opened one of his books and there was a photograph of an identical site in Russia. There was no doubt among the interpreters that the Soviets were also constructing SS-5 IRBM sites in Cuba.

Mr. Lundahl was hastily summoned. He listened intently as the interpreters revealed details about the site. He wanted to know the details of any differences between the sites at Guanajay and those at San Cristóbal. He was shown photos of the SS-4 MRBMs and sketches of the SS-5 IRBM. Lundahl was told that the SS-5, NATO code-named SKEAN, was a single-stage intermediate-range ballistic missile. It had been flight-tested in June 1960 and had been seen deployed in both soft and silo configurations in the Soviet Union. Unlike the SS-4, it had no aerodynamic fins. There were no ground photos available of the SS-5. (It would not be shown until the November 1964 Moscow parade.) The SS-5 was 82 feet long and had a diameter of 8 feet. Its range was 2,200 miles and it had been deployed initially in the Soviet Union in the summer of 1960. The SS-5 was rated as carrying a 5-megaton warhead. Lundahl asked numerous questions about the nuclear warhead bunker. He told the interpreters to keep searching, and then he looked at me, paused for a moment, and asked, "What will these IRBM sites reach in the United States?" I said I would go to our map library and bring the information to him in his office. There, Steve McCloskey and I swung a 2,200-mile arc from the Guanajay area; the only portion of the United States that was not covered was the Pacific Northwest—i.e., Seattle, Spokane, and points in Oregon and northern California. Most strategic targets on the North American continent could be reached, along with key locations in Central America and the northwestern portion of South America.

Lundahl called Cline and posted him on the latest find. Cline's response was a slow, "Good God!" Lundahl warned Cline that this might not be the end of the missile sightings—that more photo-reconnaissance missions would be arriving at the Center from the processing sites. Cline thanked Lundahl and said he would inform McCone immediately. Cline asked that the photo interpreters keep working, and Lundahl replied that the Center was operating around the clock.

The atmosphere at the Center was tense. The search of the photography continued. There were more calls like, "I've got another one," and then the measuring, checking, and analysis would continue. In a search of the Guanajay area, a second IRBM site was found. Again, the four slash marks were identified in a ranch area. Trees had been removed and two control bunkers were being dug. Extensive track activity was present leading from a farm road to the site. Site no. 1 was further along than site no. 2. It had been begun on or about September 30, while site no. 2 had been started in the October 1–5 period. Both sites had not been present on the coverage of August 29.

In the Remedios area, about 185 miles east of Havana, still another IRBM site was found. The initial construction of the site was evident, and Soviet crews had completed major sections of the footings for the pads and control bunkers. Scarring for cable conduits could be seen leading from the control bunkers to their respective launch pad areas. A concrete batch plant was located nearby and a tent camp for the troops was located in a forest. A check of past photography also revealed that this site was not present on the September 5 U-2 mission.

In a search of the Sagua la Grande area, some 150 miles east of Havana, two MRBM sites were found nestled in the karst hills. The missile-ready tents were deployed, the fuel and oxidizer transporters positioned, erectors were on the launch pads, and MRBM transporters were nearby. A large tent camp was also present. The sites were not present on the September 5 photography. In the San Cristóbal area, a fourth MRBM site was found. The "military encampment" had evolved into the third MRBM site there.

By the time all of the U-2 missions were scanned, the count stood at four MRBM sites at San Cristóbal and two MRBM sites at Sagua la Grande. Each of the sites contained four launch positions, some with eight missiles. The presence of the eight missiles indicated a refire capability at each launcher. There were no missiles or missile support equipment at the IRBM sites. Later, when Lundahl called Cline to report the total number of missile sites, Cline made a slow whistling response and said there could be no doubt that Cuba had been developed into a Soviet strategic base with a significant strike capability against almost all targets in the U.S. This, Cline said, was not the token show of military equipment that the Soviets had given to other non-Soviet countries.

The USIB met that morning and formulated its operational plan, which continued throughout the crisis. The USIB would be briefed each morning by Lundahl, would consider the joint evaluation report prepared by intelligence officers at the Center, and then estimate the possible consequences of U.S. actions as various proposals evolved. The intelligence board would also task the Office of National Estimates for special national intelligence estimates (SNIE) when necessary.

At nine o'clock that morning, the EXCOM met again in George Ball's office at the State Department and approved the blockade of Cuba. Before considering the public speech on the blockade prepared for the president by Sorensen, Secretary McNamara telephoned Admiral Anderson at the Pentagon and asked that the CINCLANT blockade position and policy papers that were promulgated on October 3 be worked out as soon as possible. The plan, he said, should also contain a scenario and implementing instructions for the blockade. The CINCLANT plan was modified to include these provisions, and by 1:30 P.M. on October 18, the plan was completed. The blockade would be directed against offensive weapons, within the charter provisions of the Organization of the American States and the Rio Treaty. At 1:45 P.M., the plan was sent to General Taylor for approval.

On October 20, Admiral Dennison, Admiral Ward, and General Taylor went to the White House. While Admiral Ward waited outside the Situation Room, Admiral Dennison and General Taylor presented the completed plan to the full EXCOM.

According to Admiral Dennison, Bobby Kennedy took a major part in the discussions. Bobby made it clear that the president had chosen the word *quarantine* rather than the more provocative word *blockade*, which in international law connotes an act of war. Neither, he explained, would sit well with the Soviets. Khrushchev would later state that even *quarantine* was indeed "a hard lump to swallow."[1] At 9 P.M. that evening, the Joint Chiefs would meet again, this time with ranking officers from all the services to review the execution of Operations Plan 312 concurrently with the implementation of the blockade. According to Ward, General Taylor dominated the meeting "and was superb," and "there were no major differences between any of the services and all decisions were unanimous."

At the Center, on the evening of October 18, intelligence analysts meeting to review the information uncovered by NPIC photo interpreters had a spirited discussion. State and Defense analysts contended that since no missile transporters, erectors, or support equipment were seen at the Guanajay and Remedios sites, they might be the permanent launch sites for the MRBMs seen at San Cristóbal. The CIA and Army analysts held that the missile equipment probably had not arrived or might be stored nearby. David Doyle, the NPIC IRBM photo interpreter expert, was summoned. He went through a long list of similarities of the Guanajay sites with those in the USSR. The construction and deployment patterns of the Cuban sites were identical with IRBM sites seen in the Soviet Union. It was a most convincing presentation, but the initial report on Guanajay and Remedios went out describing them as fixed field sites. Later that evening, it was resolved that the Guanajay and Remedios sites were for the IRBMs. That evening, too, ordnance experts arrived at the Center. They examined the aerial photographs to determine the types of ordnance that would be required to destroy the sites. Both the SS-4 and SS-5 sites were in a soft configuration and were extremely vulnerable. The experts estimated that overpressures of less than 10 pounds per square inch would be sufficient to "kill" either the SS-4 or SS-5 missile sites. Any bomb in the U.S. inventory would do the job.

We had anticipated that questions would be asked by the president, the EXCOM, and ranking congressional leaders as to why these sites weren't found sooner and why there had been a lack of coverage in the past month. Lundahl and I agreed that briefing boards depicting past coverages of the sites, along with the appropriate maps and charts showing their location on the island, should be prepared. Three hinged panels were prepared showing the information derived from the photo coverage of August 29 or September 5, when there was nothing present at the sites, the coverage of October 14, and the coverage of October 17 or 18. The president felt that these materials strongly supported his position regarding the sequence of events leading to his awareness of the Soviet missile activity in Cuba. When this photography would later be released to the press, the president specified that these materials be given the widest possible distribution.

Lundahl was certain that questions would be asked whether Cuba had been completely covered by the U-2 missions flown on October 17 and 18. The coverage of each mission was plotted, and when the work was complete, about 97 percent of Cuba had been photographed. The 3 percent not covered was in the Sierra Maestra Mountains. A check of previous coverages showed that there were few roads there and the team felt with a high degree of confidence that we had found all of the missile sites in Cuba. Lundahl took the map with him to show mission planners and McCone.

Data from a variety of intelligence sources was essential to evaluate the scope of the Cuban missile threat. Information from news services, foreign publications, radio monitoring, domestic collection, diplomatic traffic, attachés, communications intercepts, and clandestine collection would ultimately be brought to bear on the problem. The full "all-source" intelligence approach was applied to the Cuban missile crisis. Of special value was prior information provided by Colonel Oleg Penkovsky during his service within the Soviet GRU, the Soviet military intelligence organization.

Born at the time of the Russian civil war in 1918, Penkovsky had been educated in the Soviet system. He had joined the Communist party in 1940 and distinguished himself in World War II as an artillery officer. Later trained as an intelligence officer, he rose through the military ranks and became socially prominent in the Soviet elite. There the story might have ended, but on his own initiative, Colonel Penkovsky decided to reveal important Soviet military secrets to the United States and Great Britain. He was not recruited or coerced into his new cause. In the winter of 1960, two unsigned letters were received from Penkovsky, offering to make contact with Western intelligence representatives and supply information. The importance of Oleg Penkovsky's information made this one of the most productive intelligence operations in history. He was a trained intelligence expert who knew the value of specific information and who had access to an almost unbelievable number of secret documents. He had decided that in the interest of world peace, he must counter Soviet plans for nuclear war. During the sixteen months before he was discovered, the CIA received and processed more than 5,000 frames of microfilmed information. From these secretly photographed documents we had accurate information on the latest Soviet weapons and missile strategy.

Photo interpreters can recognize, identify, and accurately describe in detail natural and cultural features on photography not apparent to unsophisticated or untrained eyes. Their writing style, however, is often cryptic, terse, and military-oriented. Of necessity, this type of reporting has to be reworked and collated for presentation to policymakers. Dr. Edward Proctor of the Agency's missile task force devised the reporting format used in the crisis and honed it into a crisp, informative, narrative style to accommodate both the data obtained from aerial photos and other sources of information. The resulting reporting was further refined by the USIB so that the information presented to the EXCOM and the president was not merely a compendium of facts and undigested reporting but rather up-to-the-minute situation reports that represented the consensus view of the intelligence community.

And so a pattern developed. Photography acquired by U-2 missions flown in the morning would be processed in the afternoon, then analyzed in the late afternoon and nightly at the National Photographic Interpretation Center. Teams of photo interpreters working with missile and nuclear experts from other components of the intelligence community produced situation summaries that were disseminated the following morning. To keep track of information other than the photography, a special situation room was established in the Agency's Office of Current Intelligence, at Langley, Virginia. John Hicks, who had recently returned from a tour of duty in Australia, was placed in charge and had the responsibility for issuing the CIA daily bulletin. After being briefed each morning at the Center on the information generated the previous evening, Lundahl would depart for a briefing of the United States Intelligence Board, which met each morning at 8 A.M. in the East Building of the Agency, located in the Foggy Bottom section of Washington.

The USIB was the highest level of all national intelligence committees, acting as a board of review for all strategic estimates and current intelligence assessments. The Board was also cognizant of all clandestine collection efforts. Until January 1962, the director of the Central Intelligence Agency presided as chairman of the USIB and also acted as the CIA member. McCone decided that the chair could be more impartial if he served as chairman of USIB with the CIA deputy director representing the Agency. Other members of the board in October 1962 were: Roger Hilsman, director of intelligence and research, State Department; Lieutenant General Joseph F. Carroll, director of the Defense Intelligence Agency, Department of Defense; Major General Alva R. Fitch, assistant chief of staff for intelligence, Department of the Army; Rear Admiral Vernon L. Lowrance, assistant chief of naval operations (intelligence), Department of the Navy; Major General Robert A. Breitweiser, assistant chief of staff, intelligence, United States Air Force; Lieutenant General Gordon A. Blake, director, National Security Agency; Major General Richard Collins, Joint Staff; Mr. Henry S. Traynor, assistant general manager for administration, Atomic Energy Commission; and Mr. Alan H. Belmont, assistant to the director, Federal Bureau of Investigation.

During the Cuban missile crisis, McCone further felt that he could not serve as chairman of the USIB while simultaneously functioning as an EXCOM member charged with reviewing USIB recommendations. He asked General Carter, deputy director of the Agency, to chair the USIB, with either Ray Cline or Sherman Kent to represent the Agency. During the crisis, the USIB reviewed all intelligence on Cuba prepared the night before; reviewed all estimates prepared by the Office of National Estimates; approved recommendations for photo collection; and reviewed all papers prepared in response to questions raised by the president or EXCOM. Items for consideration by the EXCOM were also screened by the USIB.

After Lundahl's daily briefing of the USIB, he would proceed to brief the EXCOM. The EXCOM met several times daily, usually at 10 A.M. and 2 P.M., in the Cabinet Room of the White House during the early days of the crisis and thereafter usually in George Ball's Conference Room at the State Department. Thus the latest intelligence derived from U-2 photography was described and expedited to the White House through this special channel. Whenever McCone thought the president should be informed about items of special significance or whenever the president expressed an interest, Lundahl, usually accompanied by McCone, would proceed to the White House. The president was briefed at least once a day with the aerial photos. At one meeting with the president, McCone raised the question of how and when the photographic evidence should be shown to congressional leaders. The president asked that the full PSALM security directive be sustained. When McCone proposed that congressional leaders be briefed immediately, the president hesitated and stated he needed additional time to consider the evidence and to explore various options for action. When it was proposed that the Congress not be told at all, the president responded, "Good God! No. We'll be portrayed as having resorted to subterfuge and outright misrepresentation, since the facts will become known." Reflecting on the magnitude of what had already transpired and conscious of his role in history, the president, ever the political animal, said rather solemnly, "I'll be the Neville Chamberlain and Senators Capehart and Keating will be the Winston Churchill of this affair."

The visit of Eisaku Sato, former Japanese minister of finance and now minister of international trade and industry, had been arranged several months in advance and was part of a regular series of meetings between Japanese and American cabinet members set up the previous year by C. Douglas Dillon, secretary of the Treasury.

On the morning of October 18, Michael V. Forrestal, along with Averell Harriman, escorted Sato to the White House and Forrestal was informed by McGeorge Bundy of the presence of Russian missiles in Cuba. Forrestal was also told that while it was important to maintain all of the president's scheduled appointments, they were to be shortened as much as possible within the limits of avoiding a crisis atmosphere. At 1 P.M., the Japanese minister was ushered into the Oval Office. The president, according to Forrestal, was more of a listener than a talker at such meetings, unless he had a particular point to make. The president and Sato agreed that relations between the U.S. and Japan were extremely good at the time and were being handled well at the ministerial level.[2]

The president was convinced that the Soviets would apply pressure to seek a solution to the Berlin problem. Experience had made everyone in the intelligence community chary of prophesying what Khrushchev might do next. A meeting of Soviet foreign minister Andrei Gromyko with the president had been scheduled for October 18 for some time, and Kennedy debated whether he should confront Gromyko with the evidence or whether he should cancel the appointment. Gromyko was in Washington en route to Moscow, returning from a speech he had delivered at the UN. Having decided to meet Gromyko, the president was determined to be prepared. The president's schedule was left open that afternoon both for conversation with Gromyko and for action if necessary. Responses had been prepared in case Gromyko presented a fait accompli or merely engaged in diplomatic conversation. The president gave considerable thought to this meeting and the possibility of a vitriolic confrontation with Gromyko. Lundahl had met with the president, and the president had asked that he be provided with a selection of briefing boards that could be used if he confronted Gromyko with the evidence. Lundahl asked that I go along with him to be a liaison between the White House and the Center should additional materials be needed. I, along with other intelligence officers, waited in the White House Situation Room in case our knowledge and expertise became necessary.

The president had also asked Sorensen to draft a message from him to Khrushchev to be presented to Gromyko, stating that military action would be employed to solve the crisis.[3]

Ambassador Thompson advised the president to be cautious in handling Gromyko since the Executive Committee was not completely set in its course of action. "Just listen to him," was Thompson's recommendation. As Thompson was to tell Chalmers M. Roberts and a number of others, "It is rather like a man finding his wife unfaithful. She may know that he knows. But when he tells her, things are different then. He had better be prepared, for things will begin to happen."[4]

When Gromyko and Anatoly Dobrynin, the Soviet ambassador,

arrived at the White House, they walked somberly past reporters with heads lowered, refusing to answer any questions. They were ushered into the Oval Office. Waiting were the president, Secretary of State Rusk, and Ambassador Thompson.

Although Berlin dominated the first portion of the conversation, Gromyko then introduced the subject of Cuba and condemned the anti-Cuba hysteria being whipped up by the U.S. press and said that Washington was overreacting to the Cuban situation. Gromyko assured the president that the Soviet assistance to Cuba was "pursued solely for the purpose of contributing to the defense capabilities of Cuba," and that "training by Soviet specialists of Cuban nationals in handling defensive armaments was by no ways offensive," and that "if it were otherwise, the Soviet government would never become involved in rendering such assistance."

The expressionless countenance and unflinching stare with which the president confronted Gromyko, as shown in a series of photos taken by the White House photographer during the meeting, must have indicated to Gromyko that the president knew that he was lying.

Gromyko denounced and belittled the Kennedy administration's call-up of 150,000 reservists. He reminded the president that this was the twentieth and not the nineteenth century. New and modern weapons had obviated the necessity for call-ups. When Gromyko saw the president flinch, he said that he was speaking frankly since he knew the president appreciated frankness. He added that it appeared to the Soviets that the United States was again preparing to invade Cuba.

The president snapped that we had no intention of invading Cuba but that the Soviets had set out on a course that was extremely distressing and of considerable concern to the United States. The U.S. reaction could no longer be constrained. There was a change in attitude in the United States. Turning to Dobrynin, he said the Soviet ambassador had certainly noticed this and could vouch for it.

The president warned that the Soviet activities were serious and that he had not received a satisfactory explanation of them from the Soviets. The president then looked at Gromyko with eyes that were hard and emotionless. "Do you understand our concern?"

"Perfectly," Gromyko responded in a toneless voice.

The president, still eyeing Gromyko, then said, "So there is no misunderstanding," and took copies of his September 4 and September 13 statements and read portions of them aloud, including "the gravest issues" portion. He then warned that the personal assurances he had received from Khrushchev were keeping him from taking action, but that the situation was becoming increasingly dangerous.

The president grimaced at Gromyko's unprecedented indulgence in secrecy and deception. (Gromyko would later explain that since President Kennedy had not asked him directly about the missiles being in Cuba, there had been no need for a direct answer to the president's question.)

Paraphrasing Khrushchev, Gromyko advised against any blockade, stating that all problems were resolvable by negotiations. It was the final invitation to acquiesce. The president refused.

As Gromyko left the president's office, Kennedy whispered to Rusk and Thompson, "That lying bastard." There was a touch of vindictiveness and a feeling of betrayal in his voice. He had been deceived by the Russians—at the highest of levels—and the deception had been deliberate. From that moment on, he professed a hate for Gromyko and often referred to him as "that lying bastard."

The question has often been raised whether Dobrynin knew about the missile deployment at that time. Normally, one would expect that the ambassador to the United States would be informed on such matters. Dobrynin has steadfastly maintained that he did not know about the missiles in Cuba.[5]

When Gromyko and Dobrynin left the White House, Gromyko was jovial with reporters. The meeting, he said, was, "Useful, very useful."

After the Gromyko meeting, the president went back to his desk to work on campaign speeches scheduled later that week. Lundahl and I had gone into the Oval Office to retrieve the briefing materials that NPIC had prepared for the meeting but which the president had chosen not to reveal to Gromyko. The president was working with Sorensen when it was announced that Robert Lovett was waiting to see him. Robert A. Lovett, a man for whom the president had profound respect, had been invited by the president to be a member of the EXCOM. Mr. Lovett had arrived while the president was preoccupied with Gromyko and had been waiting in McGeorge Bundy's office. He had been briefed by Bundy on the missiles and then brought upstairs to the president's outer office. The president, as a gesture of respect, asked Sorensen to personally escort Mr. Lovett into the Oval Office. Then, remembering a point he wanted incorporated into the speech, the president recalled Sorensen and asked Bobby to do the honors. Bobby stuck his head out of the office door and called out to the waiting guest, "Hey, you!" The president, preoccupied, seemingly paid no attention. Lovett, calm, dignified, and reserved, did not respond. "Hey, you," Bobby called out a second time, and Lovett quizzically pointed to himself.

"Yes, you!" Bobby said with some irritation. "Come here!" The president slammed his pen to the desk, ran his hand across his brow and, thoroughly disgusted, screamed out, "Goddamn, Bobby!"

To us, it wasn't evidence of a brotherly feud or family infighting, it was simply the president dressing down a younger sibling who just happened to be the attorney general of the United States. We hastily packed our briefing materials and left.

11

Military Preparations

"Bring the task force units to the proper state
of operational readiness with reference to the
T.O.E. and supplies."

—GENERAL HAMILTON HOWSE

O N THE AFTERNOON OF OCTOBER 18, Lieutenant General Hamilton
Howse, commanding general of STRAC and the XVIII Airborne
Corps, summoned the commanders of the following units to
report immediately to his headquarters at Fort Bragg, North Carolina:
Major General Charles W. G. Rich of the 101st Airborne Division,
Fort Campbell, Kentucky; Major General John F. Ruggles of the 1st
Infantry Division, Fort Riley, Kansas; Brigadier General Charles Bil-
lingslea of the 2nd Infantry Division, Fort Benning, Georgia; Major
General Ralph E. Haines, Jr., of the 1st Armored Division, Fort Hood,
Texas; and Major General John J. Throckmorton of the 82nd Airborne Division, Fort Bragg, North Carolina. The respective commanders were briefed with aerial photos provided by NPIC on the
strategic threat posed by the presence of Soviet offensive missiles in
Cuba. General Howse then gave specific instructions—including the
sensitive security measures to be employed—in bringing their commands to full-alert status. They returned to their respective headquarters on October 20 to find a simple and terse message waiting
from General Howse: "Bring the task force units to a proper state
of operational readiness with reference to T.O.E. [table of equipment]
and supplies."

There were sixteen army divisions at the time—eight overseas and eight in the continental United States. The 82nd and 101st Airborne divisions were alerted for immediate movement. The 1st Division, at Ft. Riley; the 2nd Division, at Ft. Benning; and the 4th Division, at Ft. Lewis, were also alerted for possible immediate movement. The 2nd Division would be moved to New Orleans for embarkation. The 1st Armored Division, at Ft. Hood, was also ordered to prepare to move to Ft. Stewart, Georgia. The various commanders assembled their staffs and gave detailed instructions for the movement of men and matériel from their commands to Georgia or Florida. The largest U.S. mobilization of men and equipment since World War II was under way.

The first priority was to establish an impenetrable air-defense umbrella over the gathering forces in Florida. Just ninety miles and five minutes' jet flying time from Havana, Key West would become one of the principal bases of the crisis. When told of the impending crisis, Rear Admiral Rhomad Y. McElroy, the base commander, cleared Key West International airfield and the nearby Key West Naval Air Station at Boca Chica of all utility and support aircraft in order to accommodate the strike, reconnaissance, and defense aircraft that had already begun arriving. All leaves were cancelled at the base. A large new control tower was constructed overnight at the international airfield. From Cherry Point, North Carolina, aircraft from Marine Air Group 14, under the command of Colonel John E. Conger, began to arrive at the naval air station. Navy Squadron VF-41, having been transferred to Key West from Oceana, Virginia, on October 6, was patrolling along the Florida keys and the north shore of Cuba. The planes and personnel of VFP-62 had also arrived and a photographic laboratory was being set up in one of the hangars.

On October 19, an attack squadron from the Marine Air Corps Station, Beaufort, South Carolina, was transferred to the Roosevelt Roads Air Station in Puerto Rico to bolster defenses there. The KC-135 tankers, normally stationed at Homestead Air Force Base, south of Miami, were transferred to Bergstrom Air Force Base, outside Austin, Texas. Twenty-six F-102 Delta Dagger fighters were deployed to Homestead, and twenty-four F-106 Delta Dart fighters were deployed to Patrick Air Force Base, near Cape Canaveral. F-100's also began to arrive at Homestead and F-101B's were lined up wingtip to wingtip at Tyndall Air Force Base. Six Lockheed RC-121 high-altitude radar picket aircraft were deployed to McCoy Air Force Base, outside Orlando, Florida. The RC-121 were converted Super Constellations that mounted large electronic bulges and contained about half a ton of sophisticated electronic listening equipment. Included was an airborne computer that automatically transmitted information to air-defense warning centers.

MacDill Air Force Base, outside Tampa, would become the main Air Force fighter defense base during the crisis. MacDill would also host the Tactical Air Force's 363rd Tactical Reconnaissance Wing from Shaw Air Force Base. The wing consisted of two squadrons of RF-101 reconnaissance aircraft and one squadron of RB-66 and EC-66 elint aircraft. Navy Patrol Squadron No. 56, from Norfolk, was transferred to Guantánamo to locate and track all Cuba-bound shipping. The twenty-six B-47's of the 306th Bombardment Wing of the Strategic Air Command, normally stationed at MacDill, were flown in a combat manner to Hunter Air Force Base, outside Savannah, Georgia. Fighters from the 12th and 15th Tactical Fighter wings of the Tactical Air Command also began to arrive at Florida airfields. The United Strike Command had been activated and headquartered at MacDill in September 1961. The reason given for headquartering at MacDill at that time was that it gave an additional mission to the base. In reality, it was to have a command headquarters for any military action against Cuba.

At the naval air station at Boca Chica, there were seventy-six fighters, fifty-seven attack aircraft, and ten patrol aircraft. At the airfield of the U.S. naval base at Guantánamo, there were seven fighters, twelve attack, and five patrol aircraft. At Key West International airfield there were twenty-six fighters and five antisubmarine aircraft.

The highest priority for rail, air, and truck movement were afforded to the Army air defense battalions, equipped with Hawk and Nike Hercules surface-to-air missiles. From Fort Meade, Maryland, Fort Bliss, Texas, and as far away as Fort Lewis, Washington, equipment moved southward to defend Opa-Locka, Homestead, and MacDill airfields.

The Hawk surface-to-air missile battalion at Fort Meade, Maryland, was ordered on a moment's notice to proceed post haste by road to Key West, Florida. The loading was quickly accomplished, but it was quite evident that there had been little regard for weight loading or orderliness in the packing of the equipment. U.S. Highway No. 1 was selected by the unit as the route to Florida. Moving through Virginia, an alert state highway patrolman noticed that a number of the trucks appeared to be overloaded and had the convoy follow him to a weighing station. There, his suspicions were confirmed. The military officers protested vehemently that they had an important defense mission to perform in Florida and that precious time was being wasted. Undaunted, the patrolman said that it was his experience that military convoys were always in a hurry. Furthermore, the Army would be granted no exemption from the highway-patrol mission of protecting the state highways from damage. To the consternation of the convoy officers, the patrolman calmly proceeded to write out a warning notice to the U.S. Army to be more careful in future loading of convoys.

Ammunition and supplies were moving by rail from all parts of the country. Food rations came from such inland storage depots as Bonner Springs, Kansas, where emergency supplies were kept in underground caves.

The Air Defense Command had directed the large ballistic-detection radar at Morristown, New Jersey, and the space-tracking radars at Laredo, Texas, and Thomasville, Georgia, be aligned for missile warning from Cuba. Navy picket ships put to sea and formed several warning barriers along the Atlantic Ocean and Gulf of Mexico.

The 82nd Airborne, at Fort Bragg, North Carolina, and the 101st Airborne, at Fort Campbell, Kentucky, were the first Army units alerted for deployment. A number of contingency plans had been developed for partial- or full-division deployment. The plan chosen required the full combat deployment of both divisions in Cuba. The problems of marshalling and outloading two airborne divisions were monumental. Much had to be done, and all knew that they were racing the clock. Large numbers of transport aircraft would have to be diverted to support such an operation. More than eight hundred Lockheed Hercules flights would be required for initial notification to execute the plan. The plans for deployment of the airborne divisions had been rehearsed and tested many times, but they would be rehearsed and tested again. Emphasis would be placed on the immediate combat aspect affecting personnel and administration. The assumption was that there would be heavy fighting in Cuba and the Cubans would be using all the modern weapons at their disposal. The estimated total U.S. casualties for the first few days of the operation would be about a thousand a day.

The packing of all cargo and extractive parachutes had already begun. Engineer units were practicing repairing bomb craters on runways. Bridging, assault, boat, and river crossing crews practiced more intently than ever because it was the rainy season in Cuba.

The plan stipulated that the 82nd would be loaded at Pope Air Force Base, near Fort Bragg, and at Seymour Johnson Air Force Base, near Goldsboro, North Carolina, and would be intermediate-staged at Eglin Air Force Base and Sanford Naval Air Station, in Florida. The 101st would be loaded at nearby Campbell Air Force Base and Stewart Air Force Base, near Nashville, Tennessee, with intermediate staging at Tyndall, McCoy, and Patrick air force bases, in Florida. The drops would be made at altitudes from 700 to 900 feet. Airborne commanders knew there would be a number of problems conducting military operations in Cuba in October. It was the rainy and hurricane season, with the attendant clouds, high winds, and rains—certainly not the best jump weather. There was an additional problem. The drop zones would be in valleys that contained sugarcane fields and cattle ranches. By the end of October, the sugarcane fields would have reached their maximum heights of seven to ten feet. In addition to the cane stalks posing a hazard for the landing parachutists, they also presented a rally and maneuver problem. The cane fields also gave the opposition excellent areas from which to conduct guerrilla operations and to harass the airborne troops.

Cane fields must be replanted periodically, and by October the old cane fields would have been plowed and replanted for the succeeding year's harvest. The plowed fields would be rain-sodden, making maneuver by wheeled vehicles extremely difficult. Concern was also expressed that the Cubans might employ chemical-warfare agents against invading airborne troops. Chemical exercises had been conducted, with talc and smoke simulating actual attacks.

The airborne troops were issued a number of instructions for the care and treatment of prisoners of war. They were specifically warned that any "Sino-Soviet-Bloc personnel" observed or encountered would be carefully handled and taken into protective custody.

Three tons of maps, charts, and aerial photos containing up-to-the-minute intelligence were delivered to each airborne division headquarters for distribution down to regimental levels. To assure proper interrogations of prisoners of war, Spanish-speaking military-intelligence personnel were assigned to both division and regimental headquarters.

Liaison with the Department of State revealed that the department had no specific plan for accepting responsibility for the handling and feeding of captured Cuban prisoners of war and refugees. Although there were generalized plans for the occupation and military government, there were no detailed plans for the types and numbers of indigenous Cuban administrators required. There were also no specific plans for the prevention of starvation, disease, or civil unrest. The Army Intelligence Center, at Fort Holabird, Maryland, was tasked to provide linguists and specialists in field operations for intelligence and counterintelligence.

The 82nd Airborne would be dropped further inland than the 101st. The 82nd's objective was to seize the San Antonio de los Baños military airfield and the José Martí International airfield just outside Havana. The 101st would take the military airfields at Mariel and Baracoa, along with the port of Mariel. There would be air drops of dummy personnel to confuse the enemy. These, however, would not be ordinary dummies. They would be armed with recorded tapes to create firefight noise. The enemy would have difficulty distinguishing the real from the phony when these dummies were dropped early in the morning of D-Day. The Marines would come ashore at a number of famous beaches on Cuba's northern shore between Havana and Mátanzas* and link up with the airborne divisions. Once the beaches and the port of Mariel were secure, the 1st Armored Division would be put ashore. They would head down the highways to isolate Havana and then head for the missile sites. Some units of the 1st Armored would strike southward to cut the island in half. Tactical air support would be provided by the Marines, the U.S. Navy,

---

* The Soviets and the Cubans also expected the invasion to come ashore on the beaches and had deployed cruise coastal missile sites at Santa Cruz del Norte and at Campo Florida.

and the Air Force Tactical Air Command. Carriers would stand off-shore with Bell UH-1 Iroquois and Boeing CH-47 Chinook helicopters ready to ferry fuel, ammunition, and supplies ashore.

After reviewing the jump plans, airborne regimental and company commanders who had jumped in Normandy and remembered that a number of their buddies had been lost when they mistakenly dropped in swamps, rivers, or lakes asked that those jumping near bodies of water be issued life vests. The U.S. Air Force and Navy complied and thousands of inflatable life vests were sent to the airborne divisions.

The packing of all cargo and extraction chutes had been accomplished by October 17. The ammunition and food required had been palletized by October 19. In addition to the Lockheed C-130 Hercules squadrons required to carry the divisions to Cuba, twenty-one Fairchild C-119 Packet reserve troop-carrier squadrons were alerted.

General Maxwell Taylor had more than a passing interest in the status of the airborne divisions, especially the 101st, his old outfit. He was pleased when he received the following message from the commander of the 101st: "The troops understand the seriousness of the national crisis and are prepared to meet whatever demands placed on them."

The First Division, the "Big Red One," at Fort Riley, Kansas, also had been placed on alert. The mission of the 82nd and 101st Airborne divisions would be to secure the airfields in Cuba that would permit the First to land. A master sergeant stationed at Fort Riley at the time said that the division was "fully cocked" for movement—men waited in their barracks, duffel bags packed, weapons cleaned and cleared. Trucks required to move units of the division to the nearby SAC airfield were aligned in the barracks area. For several days the transport companies would rehearse their journey to the airfield.

A relatively new and large air-conditioned classroom at Homestead Air Force Base was selected to be the command center for the forces mobilizing in Florida. Carpenters quickly installed sliding map panels along two walls, and communications experts began stringing cables to connect elaborate communication consoles. Mobile communications and auxiliary vans were neatly lined up along one side of the classroom building.

At the U.S. Army Pictorial Center, in New York City, Major Robert

Vaughn received an order from the headquarters of the U.S. Continental Army Command, at Fort Monroe, Virginia, to install a closed-circuit television system at the Florida command site. Vaughn knew such a system was at Fort Gordon, Georgia, but unfortunately it had been dismantled and placed in a convoy and was on its way to the Brooke Army Medical Center, in San Antonio, Texas, for demonstration purposes. Georgia and Alabama highway patrolmen were alerted to stop the convoy and reroute it to Homestead, where it would be met by Major Vaughn. Vaughn arrived at Homestead, surveyed the classroom, and informed General Herbert B. Powell, the commanding general of the U.S. Continental Army Command, that emissions from the TV gear could be detected some five hundred feet from the command post. Powell, impatient because of all of the small details being thrust upon him, yelled at a staff officer, "Goddamnit, string barbed wire around this place and place MPs around the wire." Concertina wire was strung some seven hundred feet around the command posts and MPs took up stations around the wire.

Maps and charts were hung on the wall panels and the latest information on the Cuban situation was posted. The panels were used to conduct briefings several times daily. The closed-circuit television system permitted this data to be transmitted simultaneously to the offices and conference rooms of admirals and generals newly assigned to the task group coordinating the response to the Cuban missile threat.

By October 22, a vast armada of aircraft would gather at Homestead, along with thousands of flyers, technicians, defense specialists, and staff officers. The BOQ and enlisted men's quarters were operated on the "hot bunk" principle—three men would be assigned to each bunk—someone would sleep in the bunk at all hours and the mess halls would remain open around the clock.

Air Force transport aircraft arriving at the Key West International airfield from the First Missile Brigade of Fort Sill, Oklahoma, were given priority treatment. The C-123's taxied to one end of the field and began disgorging their cargo of Pershing missiles. A battery of four missiles and their support vans were dispatched to an unobtrusive spot about a quarter-mile from the naval air station. Nuclear warheads were mated to the missiles and the missiles erected for launching. The atmosphere within the control van was particularly eerie, according to a sergeant. Periodically, the computers would automatically check all systems for launch, the panel lights seemingly bouncing about in endless confusion before they stopped, informing the control officer that the four missiles were prepared, upon proper verification, to be launched at a moment's notice to obliterate their target—Havana.

The 15th Field Hospital departed Fort Bragg by rail for Opa-Locka, Florida. One of the freight cars developed wheel trouble and the train did not arrive in Florida until October 27. Air Ambulance detachments were ordered to bring their units up to strength. Some were ordered to Fort Benning. It was emphasized that each medical unit was to be stocked with fifteen days of supplies.

Several signal companies, including the 202nd Signal Company, departed for Homestead AFB.

A concern was emphasized about replacements if an invasion was begun. The 90th Replacement Battalion at Fort Lewis was ordered to move to Fort Benning and to establish a replacement station there.

In order to provide the logistics required, the 2nd Logistical Command was directed to move from Fort Lee, Virginia, to Opa-Locka Air Force Base, Florida.

Roswell Gilpatric was concerned that anti-American feeling would be intensified in Latin America. It was feared that thousands would gather and march on American embassies or presidential palaces demanding that the Americans negotiate with the Soviets. On October 18, at 9 P.M., Gilpatric authorized the shipment of riot-control equipment from U.S. stocks to Latin American countries.

The afternoon of October 18, the Department of Defense issued a news release that was largely overlooked by news reporters—that the military services and defense agencies had been ordered to prepare fallout-shelter utilization plans for the military installations under their jurisdiction. Existing public fallout shelters would also be allocated to the military. "The public shelter spaces made available will be allocated to troops other than those required to sustain operations, and to civilian employees and dependents. An excess or deficit in space is to be reported to local civil defense authorities."[1]

The president was still convinced that the Soviets would continue to apply pressure to seek a solution to the Berlin problem. He remembered that in his meeting in Vienna, Khrushchev made a number of seemingly friendly overtures to him in other areas of the world but was adamant and intractable over Berlin. On July 12, 1962, the Soviets had issued a significant statement on Berlin indicating that the Western powers were not displaying the proper attitude or understanding of the need for a German peace treaty and vowing that the Soviet Union, along with other peace-loving states, "will solve the question of signing a German peace treaty without the participation of Western powers." On August 22, 1962, the Soviets announced the abolition of the Office of the Soviet Berlin Commandant, and the following day the East Germans announced the appointment of an East German commandant. Simultaneous with this announcement came a large military exercise by the East German Army. Security measures were tightened around Berlin, and East German Army units were seen conducting drills adjacent to Allied accesses to Berlin. East German leaders Ulbrecht and Stoph spent the entire month of August in the Soviet Union discussing Berlin and other major problems.

Soviet diplomats had indicated privately for months that Moscow favored a quick solution to the Berlin problem and had made repeated references that the Soviets were going to conclude a peace agreement with the East Germans "in the not too distant future." The Soviets had also taken a number of steps to signal their annoyance with the Kennedy administration policy of doing nothing about Berlin. Khrushchev was finding less and less room in those days to exercise his penchant for political maneuver. He had likened Berlin to a bad tooth that had to be extracted to ease the pain. But he also realized that the Soviet initiative for solution of this problem was slipping away. American self-assurance and the new momentum that Kennedy had applied to missile development and deployment would further enhance the strategic advantage in favor of the United States.

12

October 19– Return to Washington

"Slight upper respiratory (infection) 1 degree
fever. Weather raw and rainy. Recommend
return to Washington."

—PRESIDENT KENNEDY'S NOTE
TO PIERRE SALINGER

THERE WERE POLITICAL DEBTS to be paid and political promises to
be kept. The congressional election was only three weeks off,
and the president was fully aware that he could later be criticized
for campaigning instead of staying in Washington, once the secret
of the missiles became known. Yet he had promised political leaders
in Illinois, Ohio, Wisconsin, and the state of Washington that he
would assist them in the campaign, and if he didn't appear, there
would be a number of questions that would be difficult to answer
without revealing that a national crisis was imminent.

It was an established phenomenon that in off-year elections, the
party in power stood to lose an average of forty-five House seats and
five Senate seats.[1] It was recognized that the 1962 campaign was
not going well for the Democrats. The president also knew that Ted
Kennedy's senatorial candidacy in Massachusetts would revive
charges of dynasty and nepotism that had been made when the
president had appointed Bobby attorney general.

The president arrived at his office at 9:44 A.M. on October 19.
Waiting were General Taylor, Rusk, McNamara, Bobby, and Admiral
Anderson. Anderson, acting for the Joint Chiefs of Staff, outlined
the finished plan for the blockade of Cuba. The president listened

intently and asked a number of questions about implementing such a blockade. Rusk answered that a State and Defense task force was looking into all the legal aspects of the blockade, while Anderson said that he and his staff would check and recheck all the military details. From the president's questions and his reactions, it was obvious that he had decided on the blockade as the initial move by the administration against the Russians. The president again said, however, that he didn't like the word *blockade*. Anderson assured him that from now on all references would be changed to *quarantine*.

The president also wanted to be assured that there should be no leaks whatsoever on the missiles being in Cuba while he was away from Washington. He had criticized the Eisenhower and Nixon administrations on Cuba during the 1960 presidential campaign. Now, his administration was faced not only with a military but also a political problem.

Remembering that the United States had broken the Berlin blockade with an airlift, General Taylor remarked that he had asked Pentagon experts to determine Soviet transport aircraft capabilities for a similar effort in Cuba. The distance between Cuba and the nearest Communist-held territory was approximately 5,100 miles. Taylor reported the only Soviet aircraft with that range was the Tu-114 Cleat, with a maximum range of 6,200 miles. The Cleat could accommodate 170 to 220 passengers, but there were only about fifteen Tu-114's in the Soviet inventory. Then, too, there were probably few Soviet pilots or navigators experienced enough to fly such distances. An airlift, while possible, was highly unlikely. Nonetheless, Taylor asked that the U.S. Air Force be alert to such an effort.

All of the crisis planning and management was conducted in an eerie atmosphere of almost total security. The arrival and departure of big black limousines at the White House would certainly be noted by newsmen and was to be avoided at all costs. The critical EXCOM meetings, as the crisis progressed, continued to be held in Undersecretary of State George Ball's Conference Room at the State Department. Often, the EXCOM members would arrive in one or several cars. One evening, McCone recalled that the majority of the EXCOM members crowded into a single car to avoid newsmen. McCone said,

"We were pushed into the car like the clowns at the circus." When McCone made the comparison to the EXCOM members, he said, "We were all having a good laugh when it suddenly dawned on me, What a wonderful target for an assassin—all of the government leaders in one car." After that experience, members began coming and going at State in their own or unmarked cars and using hidden or unmarked accesses to the building.

Intelligence officers, as a group, have an inane aversion to reporters. By training and inclination, the intelligence officer is secretive and withdrawn. The good reporter is an extrovert who wants everything in the open and is aggressive in his zeal for getting the story. The intelligence officer and the reporter, however, also enjoy a mutual respect. Respect for reporters, especially for the corps of newsmen in Washington, makes intelligence officers wary of being seen at the White House. Their mere presence there is interpreted by reporters as an indication of the existence of an undisclosed story.

Intelligence officers were also wary of being in the office of the presidential press secretary, Pierre Salinger, whose attitudes and actions inspired uneasiness on their part. Salinger never appeared to understand the curious, compartmentalized world of the intelligence services. President Kennedy had once warned McCone, "If you have a secret, do me a favor—don't tell Salinger." Salinger seemed to have difficulty distinguishing between unclassified and classified information. His gregarious nature often led him to try to please reporters and to maintain good relations with the press by giving them, perhaps inadvertently, the missing pieces of the puzzle they were trying to solve. Salinger had not been told of the missiles being in Cuba by the president.

But the alarm bells were beginning to ring. The secrecy of the proposed Kennedy moves regarding Cuba was holding—but just barely. Reporters at the White House were smelling a story and kept probing and asking embarrassing questions.

At 10:35 A.M. on October 19, the president walked onto the South Lawn to a waiting helicopter and was flown to Andrews Air Force Base, from where *Air Force One* would whisk him to Cleveland, Ohio. When *Air Force One* landed at Hopkins Airport, the president was

greeted by a rousing welcome from the sixty-eight-member Saint
Edward High School Band of Lakewood, Ohio, and his good friends
Governor Michael V. DiSalle, Senator Frank J. Lausche, and Congressman Michael J. Kirwan. DiSalle found the president somber
and more preoccupied than usual. He expressed concern and asked
if the president felt well. Kennedy responded that he had a cold
coming on, and if it did not improve before he reached Chicago, he
would return to Washington. He also said that there was another
matter pending that he would discuss with him at a later date.[2] When
the motorcade reached downtown Cleveland and the president saw
the large crowds, his mood changed. Governor Lausche said the Ohio
reception was an especially friendly one and the president momentarily forgot the problems in Washington. At Public Square, his address was, according to Lausche, excellent. "He had a very responsive
and enthusiastic audience."[3]

On his return to the airport, the president stopped at Saint Edward
High School and Brother Charles Krupp, the school principal, presented the president with a spiritual bouquet from the faculty and
student body. The president deeply appreciated the gesture and the
impact of the spiritual blessing for his personal and presidential well-
being."[4]

The president was off to Springfield, Illinois, arriving at Capitol
airfield at 2:15 P.M. He was greeted by Governor Otto Kerner and
Congressman Sidney Yates, who was seeking Senator Everett Dirksen's Senate seat. The president was motored to Lincoln's tomb, after
which he proceeded to the Illinois Fairground Coliseum, where he
spoke on matters of interest to Illinoisans—agricultural prices, housing, and employment. Then the president was off for Chicago.

The president arrived at O'Hare airfield at 4:30 P.M. and was met
by Mayor Richard Daley. At the Sheraton-Blackstone Hotel a by-
stander flashed a placard regarding Cuba: "Less profile—More courage." The trip to Chicago was ostensibly to endorse Congressman
Yates as a political favor to Mayor Daley. According to Yates, "The
president was in a serious mood. At the evening meeting, however,
he joked occasionally." Yates went on to say that the president "was
not interrupted by calls from Washington during the time I was with
him."[5] It was known that the president, in fact, favored the reelection

of Senator Dirksen. Dirksen, the Republican whip, had often supported administration programs in Senate voting and was preferred by Kennedy and Vice-President Johnson rather than having Senator Thomas H. Kuchel, whom the vice-president detested, succeed Dirksen as the Republican whip in the Senate. That evening, the president, along with Mayor Daley and Congressman Yates, attended a reception and dinner of the Cook County Democratic party. Later in the evening, the president addressed precinct captains at the Aerie Crown Theater. At both functions, the president warmly endorsed Congressman Yates while Mayor Daley beamed his approval, but at no time during his Illinois stay did the president attack or criticize the incumbent Dirksen.

A new phase of analysis of the U-2 imagery began on October 19 at the Center to determine whether (or when) the MRBM missile sites in Cuba would become operational. Criteria were developed by the GMAIC, and the Center applied that criteria in the analysis of all the imagery being received. To be considered operational, all four of the missile erectors had to be in place, with cables leading to the launch control building. The missiles, missile ready tents, generators, fueling vehicles, etc., also had to be present. On October 19, we reported to Lundahl that two of the Cuba MRBM sites met the criteria and were therefore considered operational.[6]

That same day the EXCOM meetings continued, but in a more hectic atmosphere. Lundahl briefed the group that morning, revealing still more details of the magnitude of the Soviet threat. He briefed on the latest details of the IRBM sites, and when he said that the Center considered two of the MRBM sites to be operational, the group, according to Lundahl, "became nervous and jittery. It was obvious that the president's hand was needed. Robert Kennedy made a few grim remarks and left the meeting. He tried to contact the president in the Midwest but was unsuccessful."

Dean Acheson was visibly disturbed about the illogical manner in which the EXCOM discussions were being conducted. He looked at a number of White House staffers "trooping in and out" of the EXCOM meetings and found their experience and basic intelligence

in high-level policymaking seriously lacking. He was especially critical of Theodore Sorensen and Kenneth O'Donnell. He would later
remark, "I just couldn't see what a ward politician would know
about war and peace." To Acheson, this was the time for action.
Disgusted, he stopped attending the meetings and retreated to his
farm at Sandy Springs, Maryland, but not before telling friends and
associates that he was totally disenchanted with the EXCOM and
the president. He referred to the president as "a cow with seven
stomachs, constantly ruminating and incapable of culminating in a
digested decision." He added that McNamara was "pin-pricking the
situation with erudite nonsense," and that he was also "slicing the
salami so thin that it was losing both its form and substance." Nor
did Bobby Kennedy escape the Acheson rapier. "Bobby," he said,
"had so many hands on his backside he looked like a tarantula."

Robert Kennedy left the October 19 afternoon EXCOM meeting
after hearing more bad news from Lundahl and stepped into a telephone booth in a little alcove. Lundahl recalls that Bobby was very
agitated, and determined to get in touch with the president. This
time, he was quickly connected with the president in Chicago and
began to tell his brother of the serious situation that had developed.
He closed the phone-booth door as someone approached. The gist
of his conversation was that the situation had developed far more
rapidly than had been expected. He advised the president to cut his
trip short, using any excuse he felt appropriate.

Robert Kennedy was probably the most misjudged person during
the crisis. It was, and still is, a period when critics tended to fasten
on a word or phrase to pass judgment on an individual. In Bobby's
case, this resulted in an injustice, since many of his spontaneous
words and phrases were strong and biting. He was the driven one—
the eyes and ears of the president: brilliant, insecure, clever, manip-
ulating, but possessing an outstanding ability to assess a situation,
be it domestic politics or international crisis. The president relied
heavily on his younger brother's advice. At about eight o'clock the
next morning, October 20, the president handed Pierre Salinger a
note: "Slight upper respiratory (infection) 1 degree fever. Weather
raw and rainy. Recommend return to Washington." He then told
Salinger about the missiles being in Cuba. Newspapers that afternoon
showed pictures of the president, his throat wrapped in a scarf,

wearing a hat; the announcement was made that he was returning to Washington.

The relatively small scale of the U-2 photography presented problems to the policy planners. Even when objects were enlarged from the U-2 photography, it was evident that the president, Bobby, and others were still having difficulty fully understanding the detailed information that was being derived from the photography. Lundahl asked NPIC support staffers to make photographic stereo pairs of enlargements of some of the sites. Lundahl would instruct EXCOM members and others in viewing the stereo enlargements in illuminated viewers, which helped but was slow and laborious. To help clarify discussions concerning the possible striking of SA-2 sites and destruction of the nuclear storage bunkers in Cuba, Lundahl had the NPIC model shop construct models of a typical SA-2 site with its six launchers and a separate model of a single SA-2 launcher with a human figure to scale, in order to give the president an idea of the size of the launcher. The nuclear warhead storage bunker model was constructed so that the president could see how it looked both with earth covering and a portion of the bunker exposed to show interior construction details. It also had human figures for scale comparison. The president was most appreciative of this effort, and the models remained in the White House Situation Room until the crisis was over.[7]

On the evening of October 19, McNamara had asked the Joint Chiefs of Staff, along with the service secretaries and office heads, to stay in Washington for the next six weeks. He explained that this was necessary for "consultations on defense budget planning."

The alert actions and movements of U.S. forces did not escape the Soviets. Radio Moscow characterized U.S. naval maneuvers in the Caribbean as preparations to carry out an invasion of Cuba and called such maneuvers "ridiculous" and "outdated." The Soviet Union now had rockets with hydrogen warheads that could strike any designated target around the world. The official Red Army newspaper, *Red Star*, in the article "Washington in the Fog of War Psychosis," stated, "Washington is acting as though it is in a state of war against Cuba." The article compared U.S. imperialism with a "ferocious and powerful shark" and then threatened that "the times are gone when imperialistic sharks may go unpunished after seizing and swallowing other countries."

The Office of National Estimates issued a "crash" estimate on October 19, "Soviet Reactions in Certain US Courses of Action on Cuba," concluding that the Soviets would not risk nuclear war over Cuba. A second "crash" estimate on October 20, "Major Consequences of Certain US Courses of Action on Cuba,"[8] stated: "We believe that the Soviets would be somewhat less likely to retaliate with military force in areas outside Cuba in response to speedy, effective invasion than in response to more limited forms of military action against Cuba."[9]

The October 19 estimate finally recognized the rationale of the Soviet venture in Cuba: "A major Soviet objective in their military build-up in Cuba is to demonstrate that the world balance of forces had shifted so far in their favor that the US can no longer prevent the advance of Soviet offensive power even into its own hemisphere."[10] The estimate also heightened the EXCOM awareness about the military implications of the Soviet missile deployment in Cuba. The danger of the Cuban-based missiles lay in their first-strike capabilities. The estimate continued: "For a pre-emptive or first strike, Cuban-based missiles would possess an advantage over Soviet-based ICBMs in that they would approach the U.S. with a shorter time-of-flight, and from a direction not now covered by U.S. BMEWS [Ballistic Missile Early Warning] capabilities."[11]

There would be yet another surprise in Cuba that week: Three Soviet armored combat groups were found on the U-2 photography of October 17 and 18. A fourth group was found on later photography.

In July and August, the Soviet and Cuban press had carried glowing accounts that the Soviets had sent skilled mechanics and agricultural experts to Cuba and promised they would change Cuba's traditional sugar-oriented economy into a modern industrial one. Soviet ships unloading at Mariel and other ports were seen on U-2 photography, but there was little or no evidence that skilled mechanics or agricultural experts and agricultural equipment were present.

The tents in the four armored groups were unique in that they were pyramidal and of Soviet design rather than the U.S. squad-type tents given to the Batista government and subsequently used by Castro's militia. Reported by photo interpreters, these camps were evaluated by the intelligence community as being training camps for Cubans, since there had been a substantial increase in the numbers of Cubans being inducted into the armed forces. NPIC kept insisting that these facilities were probably Soviet, since the military equipment observed on photography was parked in unit formations rather than the haphazard formations seen at indigenous Cuban installations.

The intelligence analysts maintained that the acquisition of large quantities of sophisticated military equipment and the rapid expansion of the Cuban armed forces had left Cuba with a serious shortage of skilled manpower. The shortage of qualified personnel extended especially to the officer and noncommissioned officer corps. Although Castro had announced that Cuban military personnel had been trained both in the USSR and in Cuba to man the sophisticated Soviet equipment, most U.S. military intelligence experts regarded this as obvious propaganda, because the proper training of MiG-21 pilots and SAM and KOMAR crews would require from one to three years. Analysts believed that the buildup was making Castro more dependent than ever on technical and advisory assistance from the Soviets and these were the camps where the Cubans were being trained to handle Soviet arms. When a variety of pieces of military equipment were reported at the tent camps, it was thought that these facilities might be temporary equipment transfer points—i.e., places where the Soviets turned over military hardware after it had been unpacked or made combat ready after the long journey from the Soviet Union. As one U.S. general, downgrading the Russian threat, stressed in his briefings, it was the place "where the cosmoline was removed."

There were continuing reports that the Cubans were having difficulty integrating the new equipment into their inventory despite extensive Soviet assistance. It was estimated that the Cuban armed forces consisted of about 75,000 regulars, 100,000 militia, and 100,000 homeguard. By the first of September, the U.S. intelligence community had upped its estimate to 5,000 Soviet personnel being in Cuba, but adhered to the view that these were military instructors, advisers, and trainers and not organized in combat units. Most of the interior regions of Cuba had not been photographed during Sep-tember. None of the four combat groups were present on August 29 photography. In addition to the tents, buildings similar to the U.S. World War II tar-paper barracks were being constructed. Military equipment seen at these installations indicated that highly mobile armored combat groups were present. The most modern Soviet ground combat equipment was present—T-54 tanks, assault guns, tactical rocket launchers, antitank weapons, and personnel carriers. With some variations, the Soviet military equipment seen was the equivalent of a medium tank battalion, an infantry battalion, a FROG artillery battalion (two launchers), and a Snapper antitank company. Scattered among the groups were a 120mm mortar company, an antiaircraft unit of 37 and 57mm guns, and an engineer bridging company.

The camps were strategically located. The Artemisa installation was designed to protect and provide coverage of the western section where the MRBMs were located; the Remedios garrison provided coverage for the central area where the IRBMs were located; the Holguín camp guarded the eastern section of the island. The Havana area and the Soviet headquarters at Torrens were guarded by the Santiago de las Vegas camp. The photo interpreters kept hammering away that these sites, since they showed an abnormal degree of organization not only in the construction of the military facilities but also in how the military equipment was organized. The equipment was parked in precise unit formations within motor pool areas. The Center tried on numerous occasions to show comparisons of the four installations with those in the Soviet Union. But intelligence analysts reviewing the raw information the photo interpreters were providing continued to maintain that the facilities were manned by Cubans.

NPIC was also maintaining through its analysis of the photography that there were more Russians in Cuba than previously estimated. On October 22, analysts revised their estimate that there were 8,000 to 10,000 Soviets in Cuba. It wasn't until October 24 that the in-telligence community agreed with photo interpreters that each of these four installations probably housed 1,500 Soviet personnel. The number of Soviet personnel in Cuba was revised upward to 22,000. (The Russians later maintained that there were almost 40,000 Soviets in Cuba at the height of the crisis.) The Russians did nothing to shield the identity of these special forces. This was particularly evident at the Santiago de Las Vegas installation. When it was overflown by U.S. low-altitude aircraft on October 25, Soviet ground-force-unit symbols and insignia were seen implanted in flagstone and flowers in front of garrison areas. The symbols for Soviet motorized rifle, infantry, and airborne units were clearly visible. One unit proudly displayed the Elite Guards Badge, the Russian equivalent of the U.S. Presidential Unit Citation. These four combat groups were quickly targeted, and ordnance, including nuclear, was selected for their destruction in the event of a U.S. invasion.

In May 1963, the Senate Preparedness Investigation Committee would take the intelligence community to task for not recognizing these forces earlier as being Soviet: "Notwithstanding some reports that many of the Soviets arriving in Cuba after mid-July were military units, and notwithstanding the evidence of a drastically increased buildup in modern and sophisticated ground weapons, the intelligence community did not identify the presence of Russian organized ground combat forces in Cuba until October 25 when new pictures obtained by low-level photography, coupled with a reanalysis of previous photography, led to the conclusion that there were, in fact, four organized, mobile and powerful armored units in Cuba." The report continued: "The failure to identify the presence of organized Russian combat units in Cuba and the underestimation of Soviet personnel present merits special comment. At that time, that is, on October 22, our plans for a possible landing of forces in Cuba, which were already substantially complete, were necessarily based on the information that our invading forces would be opposed only by indigenous Cuban troops. The fact of the matter is that the native Cuban forces would have been reinforced by a highly trained, powerful and mobile Soviet armored unit possessed of tremendous striking power. . . . The true order of battle of the enemy had not been ascertained at the time of the completion of plans for possible landings of our forces in Cuba. This omission could have resulted in our paying a much higher price in casualties in the occupation of Cuba than had been anticipated."

These Soviet combat groups were no match for the airborne and the tank division being alerted in the U.S. The question was asked: Why were such units sent to Cuba? The most plausible answer was that the Soviets felt that President Kennedy, after being told of the discovery of the missiles, would not order a U.S. force to invade the island but would instead send "Free Cuban" brigades such as those sent in the Bay of Pigs invasion. Against these and other such counterrevolutionary groups, the four Soviet combat groups were more than a match.

The Soviets also must have realized that in placing their SS-4 and SS-5 missiles in Cuba, they were giving the United States an opportunity to observe their more recent advances in missile technology. They also realized that the missiles would be deployed in remote, exposed areas, with little or no protection. The U.S. had always displayed a high interest in Soviet military technology, and CIA and the U.S. Army had specially trained units whose mission was to intervene and physically extract such equipment from difficult-to-penetrate areas. The Soviets had decided that their rocket forces would have to be protected by Soviet armed forces. They did nothing, however, to shield the identity of these combat forces from observation and discovery.

13

October 20—Setting the Course of Action

"We have to get someone better at the UN or
put some starch in the son of a bitch's
[Stevenson's] back."

—Robert Kennedy

At about one o'clock on that Saturday afternoon, October 20, word was received at the Center that Robert Kennedy and Robert McNamara would pay a visit. Some fifteen minutes later, a black limousine rolled up to the entrance of the Center, and Kennedy, McNamara, Gilpatric, and McCone stepped out. They were quickly ushered to the seventh floor of the Center, where photo interpreters were exploiting the latest U-2 photography.

The first concern of the four important visitors appeared to be the certainty of our identification of the newly discovered IRBM sites, especially the Guanajay site, which was the nearest to completion. The photo interpreters took turns showing the differences in size and configuration between the MRBM and IRBM sites, pointing out features upon which the identifications were based. Bobby frequently interrupted with questions, his face serious as he listened to details. Dave Doyle, the IRBM expert interpreter, showed satellite photography taken over the Soviet Union of the IRBM sites, calling attention to four prominent slash marks indicative of the initial construction of the pads. McCone listened patiently, obviously quite proud of the professionalism of the explanations provided by the interpreters. All of the visitors were convinced that the Soviets were indeed installing IRBMs, in addition to the MRBM sites in Cuba.

Kennedy asked if he could see photographs showing the progress being made on the construction of the MRBM sites. A series of photographs was spread out on a large table which graphically portrayed the feverish pace of construction at the sites. Bobby then asked if the photo interpreters would prefer to see the missile sites on larger-scale photography acquired by low-altitude photographic-reconnaissance missions. The reply was a unanimous yes. The interpreters asked that the launch positions be given priority consideration in targeting.

Lundahl invited the visitors to view the missile sites at light tables fitted with stereoscopic viewers. The four visitors took turns at the light tables, while photo interpreters pointed out details of what they were seeing. Photography of similar missiles in the Moscow parades was also shown to the visitors.

At this point, Air Force brigadier general Robert N. Smith arrived at the Center. General Smith, director of intelligence of the Strategic Air Command, was an old friend of Lundahl. He brought with him the latest U-2 photography that had been processed by the Strategic Air Command's 544th Reconnaissance Technical Wing at Omaha. It was not unusual for high-ranking officers to accompany such film shipments inasmuch as the photography was extremely sensitive from a security standpoint. Escorting mission film to the Center also afforded field-command officers an opportunity to view the latest photography firsthand, with immediate access to the most recent intelligence derived in Washington.

General Smith asked to see Lundahl and was directed to the seventh floor. When he walked into the interpretation area, he immediately recognized McNamara and Kennedy, who were viewing photography at the light tables. The dumbfounded general stopped in his tracks, stunned by the unexpected sight, then started backing to the door. He was stopped by Lundahl, who had moved across the room to greet him. The shaken Smith whispered to Lundahl, "Since when do you hire such talent to do your interpretation? I knew you were good, but not that good!" Lundahl smiled and then introduced General Smith to the visitors.

Now the visitors continued to other light tables, where photos of airfields, coastal-defense positions, and surface-to-air missiles sites in Cuba were displayed, but McNamara took Kennedy back to the photos of the MRBM missile sites. Kennedy turned to McNamara and said that it did not appear to him that the sites would be difficult to strike. McNamara agreed. Finally, McCone asked Bobby and McNamara if they were satisfied with what they had seen. Both replied in the affirmative. Bobby then asked the interpreters if they were getting enough sleep. Lundahl interrupted, stating that the Center was working on a two-shift basis and would continue to operate that way. Bobby then moved about the room shaking the hands and encouraging everyone to keep up the good work.

The unannounced purpose of the visit to the Center was to confirm details of the findings to help draft a televised address to the nation by the president and for an important meeting to be held at the White House. The president arrived back at the White House at 1:30 P.M. October 20. Because he was supposedly suffering from a cold, and in order to avoid further arousing the suspicions of news reporters, the National Security Council would not meet in the Cabinet Room; the president, instead, selected the Yellow Oval Room of the mansion. The room had been completely redecorated recently as a result of Mrs. Kennedy's restoration program and contained priceless furniture, which had been acquired from private donors. Lundahl remarked that the room looked like something out of *Better Homes and Gardens.*

Lundahl, Cline, and McCone arrived at the White House shortly before 2 P.M. They were taken to a foyer on the second floor, where they waited. The time for decision as to what actions the U.S. would take regarding Cuba had arrived. At 2:30 P.M., over thirty participants, including all of the members of the EXCOM and other invitees such as Robert Lovett and Adlai Stevenson, had gathered in the Yellow Oval Room. A problem of logistics developed because there were not enough seats to accommodate the group. The couches and chairs were soon filled and finally folding chairs were brought in. McCone and Lundahl surveyed the room to determine the best placement of the easel that would hold the briefings boards. The area next to the windows and in front of a marbletop table was selected. Lundahl opened the ubiquitous black bag containing the briefing boards with the latest photographic information and placed them on the easel. Still, the arrangement of the room was not conducive to a briefing. Most were reluctant to rearrange the priceless furniture and merely turned or twisted in their seats to see better. The president walked into the room and said with a wry smile, "Gentlemen, today we're going to earn our pay." He then waved to McCone to begin the meeting. McCone gave Cline the task of summarizing the totality of the missile threat as it had been reassessed overnight. Cline reviewed the types and numbers of weapons present in Cuba and the current status of shipping to the island.

When Lundahl took over, he first made sure the president, in particular, had a clear view of the easel. Because some of the participants could not see the briefing boards, he concentrated on describing each one while pointing out details. He focused on the stage of construction at each missile site: Several MRBM sites were operational and a number of others would be operational within hours. Lundahl reported that the operational MRBM sites could fire missiles within six to eight hours of a decision to launch. With regard to the IRBM sites, he said it was estimated that these would not be operational for at least five to six weeks. Lundahl then displayed briefing boards showing fuselage crates of twenty-two IL-28 jet light bombers, one of which was being assembled. He also showed photos of thirty-nine MiG-21 jet fighters, of which thirty-five were assembled; twenty-four SA-2 sites, of which sixteen were considered operational; four cruise missile sites, of which two were operational; and twelve KOMAR cruise-missile patrol boats, all considered operational.

When Lundahl finished he turned to the president and said, "Mr. President, gentlemen, this summarizes the totality of the missile and other threats as we've been able to determine it from aerial photography. During the past week we were able to achieve coverage of over 95 percent of the island and we are convinced that because of the terrain in the remaining 5 percent, no additional threat will be found there."

The president was on his feet the moment Lundahl finished. He crossed the room directly toward Lundahl and said: "I want you to extend to your organization my gratitude for a job very well done." Lundahl, rather embarrassed, hesitantly thanked the president. The president then extended his hand and smiled. Lundahl was again surprised.

The president told the assembled group that he felt the threat was clearly evident and that his course of action must likewise be very clear. The discussion then turned to the course of action that would later be described as the "blockade route." The president decided to initiate the "quarantine" but to delay it long enough to permit consultation with U.S. allies.

It was soon obvious to those present that Adlai Stevenson did not approve the stated course of action. Stevenson had been humiliated by two crushing presidential electoral defeats that had been traumatic experiences for him. Yet a towering ego remained. He had desperately wanted to be Kennedy's secretary of state but, of course, had been passed over. Kennedy instead had selected Dean Rusk, a man he had never met and who had not contributed to his campaign figuratively or substantively. It was known around the White House that Kennedy had chosen Rusk primarily on Robert Lovett's recommendation. When Rusk became secretary of state, Stevenson was encouraged not only by the president but also by his loyal followers to accept the UN post. Stevenson took the UN appointment after he had been reassured by both Rusk and Kennedy that he would have a strong voice in shaping U.S. foreign policy.

But Stevenson's tenure at the UN was only a few months old when, as he later expressed, he was "dropped on his head by the Washington establishment." During the Bay of Pigs, he had stoutly maintained at the UN that a photo he had shown of a B-26 bomber that had landed in Florida was that of a defecting Cuban. He learned later that the pilot and bomber were both CIA-managed. He never forgave Rusk or the CIA for not apprising him of the true facts of the Bay of Pigs invasion. He was a man of eloquence and charm but extremely sensitive to criticism. At the same time, he was often insensitive of the feelings of others. He knew that the Kennedys didn't want or need him in foreign policymaking. But at the UN, he had become an all-American hero overnight who tried to give credence to the U.S. position, however ill-defined it might be. Stevenson had quickly established a rapport with his UN colleagues, including the Russians. In a speech he had stated, "I believe many of our ster-

eotypes about the Russians are mistaken. We regard them as un-
dilutedly ideological and constantly plotting world revolution. I don't
think they are." The UN ideally suited Stevenson's talents. He had
quickly established an honesty and integrity with fellow delegates,
one of them going so far as to state that Stevenson was "incapable
of betrayal or opportunism." He had a prodigious capacity to serve,
and his frequent cables to Rusk reflected a deep and abiding concern
for world peace. Although Stevenson kept Rusk fully informed on
matters at the UN, there was a persistent complaint that Washington
was making Cuba policy decisions on which the U.S. UN representatives were not being informed or consulted. Stevenson had established an enviable reputation with the press and media, and his
performance as ambassador enjoyed wide approval in American public opinion, a fact that did not go unnoticed by the president and
Bobby.

But as a political practitioner rather than a Cold War dogmatist,
Stevenson was regarded in Washington as a compromiser, not a man
of strong convictions. This reputation was probably not wholly deserved. A willingness to listen to all sides, a skill in parliamentary
maneuvering, a mastery of subtle witticisms, and a deftness in per-
suasion marked him as an ideal man for the UN post. In light of
events that followed, he may have been ahead of his time. By October
1962, differences in opinion, approach, and policy were beginning
to appear between Kennedy, Rusk, and Stevenson. Stevenson was
frank and open on these differences, and news reporters were beginning to print them. Stevenson had brought his old friend Eleanor
Roosevelt to the UN, where she, too, would have a decided impact
and probably make the greatest contribution of her life to humani-
tarian issues. But in Washington, the Stevenson-Roosevelt-Harri-
man-Lehman liberal faction of the Democratic party were regarded
as mavericks—not to be trusted—capable of bolting from the Kennedys. In addition, Stevenson was openly critical about Ted Kennedy's running for the Senate in Massachusetts, and had criticized
the Kennedy family for being oblivious to the fact that this was
hurting the Democratic party. He characterized the Kennedy family
as "always being at the trough." His obvious dislike for both Ted
and Bobby, and to a lesser extent the president, was being quoted
around the Georgetown cocktail circuit.

Stevenson was adamantly opposed to either an air strike or an invasion of Cuba and expressed himself forcefully on these points. He proposed instead that the full peacekeeping machinery of the OAS and the UN Security Council be brought to bear. Stevenson stated rather emphatically that the president was only considering a military proposal (the quarantine) and there was no expressly stated political program. Stevenson also expressed the fear that events in such a charged atmosphere could easily lead to a military escalation. While McCone and others wanted to force the Soviets to the wall militarily, Stevenson continued to advocate political and diplomatic actions. Throughout all the briefings, and when the quarantine was being promulgated as policy, Stevenson remained passive. However, now when it came to the overall policy on resolving the crisis, Stevenson spoke out strongly for compromise. He questioned why the U.S. could not remove the Jupiter missiles from Turkey and Italy in exchange for the removal of Russian missiles in Cuba. He thought the U.S. should be ready to negotiate the elimination of all foreign missile bases "in the context of pending disarmament treaties," which, unfortunately, at the time were not well defined.

Stevenson's attitude brought him into a sharp collision with his colleagues in Washington. Bobby maintained an air of disgust. The president was taken aback by Stevenson's view, although of course he tried not to show it. Dillon, Taylor, and McCone criticized Stevenson openly. Stevenson, for his part, attempted to qualify his position. If the Cuban issue were to be resolved at the UN, Stevenson maintained, judging by past performance, the so-called nonaligned nations would support the U.S. cause if it were properly justified. Stevenson, who had a flair for the dramatic, warned that the alternative to negotiations was to "dig the Russians out of Cuba with bayonets." The only course, he insisted, was the "neutralization" of Cuba, both politically and militarily, into an entity similar to Austria. He spoke of the "demilitarization" of Cuba, that all Russian arms were to be removed and UN observer teams would be sent to ensure that the arms were not reintroduced. In return, the U.S. would have to guarantee the territorial integrity and "political independence" of Cuba.

Stevenson was the cynosure of all eyes. One participant would state that "Stevenson was 180 degrees from all the thinking that had gone on the previous week." General Taylor asked: "In the demilitarization of Cuba, would the United States be asked to 'demilitarize' Guantánamo?" Stevenson replied in the affirmative. Taylor shot back that if Guantánamo was "demilitarized," it would leave the U.S. with nothing. Stevenson responded by dismissing the military importance or utility of Guantánamo. McCone shook his head in disgust and later said, "The man was advocating another Munich." After the crisis, Stevenson wrote his friend Arthur M. Schlesinger that he was misunderstood.[1] Stevenson amplified his "demilitarization" of Guantánamo: "A United States demand for total Soviet evacuation of Cuba would inevitably produce counter demands, and the achievement of such a major political change in Cuba would justify similar "demilitarization by us of Guantánamo, the military utility of which was limited anyway."[2]

Stevenson also incurred McCone's wrath when he implied that the missiles themselves might not be in Cuba and that the photographic evidence was not conclusive. McCone, a devout Catholic, later facetiously referred to Stevenson as the St. Thomas of our generation. Stevenson also expressed his concern about the draft of the president's proposed October 22 speech, which was read to the group. He again repeated his doubts about the photographic evidence. Later, he would write: "We felt it was not entirely clear that the missiles themselves were actually present in Cuba and that we were demanding their withdrawal and withdrawal of other offensive weapons, as well as dismantling of the sites."[3] The president refused to consider any of Stevenson's political program in his initial actions.

Although President Kennedy feared that he might provoke another melee, at the close of the October 20 meeting he polled each participant on his final position and recommendation. The arguments Stevenson had advanced found no proponents. As Stevenson later related to his UN staff, "I was alone." Outraged and seething, Bobby turned to the president and said loud enough for others to hear, "We have to get someone better at the UN or put some starch in the son of a bitch's back."

Bobby felt strongly that Stevenson would not pursue the U.S. initiatives at the UN with adequate vigor, and said as much to Rusk, McCone, and the president. McCone had previously recommended that a tough negotiator be appointed to "help Adlai." When the president asked for a specific recommendation, McCone suggested John J. McCloy. The president approved McCone's recommendation without question. McCloy, former high commissioner to Germany, was summoned by the president from a business trip in Frankfurt, West Germany. Because the regular commercial plane from Frankfurt to New York had just left, Kennedy sent one of the presidential planes to pick up McCloy.

Ostensibly to provide the U.S. delegation with a bipartisan flavor, McCloy's real charge was to pressure Stevenson into action. He nominally would serve as a special adviser to Ambassador Stevenson. McCloy had established a reputation with the Russians as a tough negotiator and they would take particular note of his assignment to the UN. There was considerable agreement in some U.S. government circles with the statement in a Russian broadcast: "They evidently no longer rely on the abilities of Mr. Stevenson. It has been reported that President Kennedy has appointed a special assistant for Cuban affairs in the United Nations, John McCloy, the well-known banker."[4] McCloy would later write: "I was asked to go to the United Nations in New York, generally, I suppose, the objective was to strengthen Ambassador Stevenson's hand there. I had heard that some feared Mr. Stevenson might not take a strong enough attitude with the Russians. Perhaps because of my confrontations in Berlin, I had a reputation for firmness but I really do not know why I was asked to assist. I did not, however, find Stevenson at all weak in dealing with the Soviets. On the contrary, after he realized the Soviets had badly dissembled with him he was both firm and tough with them."[5]

Acheson had stated forcefully in the EXCOM meetings that a strike and invasion were the only answers. General Taylor, who also supported the military position for an invasion, listened in stony silence as plans for the implementation of the quarantine were discussed. He was confronted with a paradox. He was Kennedy's military man, obliged to support the president, but he also knew that doubt was being openly expressed in the JCS and the Pentagon as to whether he was sufficiently pressing the military point of view.

In the international political arena, it was McCone, not Rusk, who was the prime mover in encouraging the U.S. to seek support from its allies both in the Western Hemisphere and Europe. At the appropriate moment, McCone felt they should be brought into the discussions and shown the aerial photos of the Cuban threat. McCone rationalized that the Soviet actions threatened not only the security of the Western Hemisphere but that of Berlin. McCone further argued that the U.S. would receive support since the prospect of Communism in the U.S. backyard was untenable. The question of who to notify had been discussed at some length at the Saturday meeting. The president felt that Macmillan, de Gaulle, Adenauer, and Diefenbaker should be made personally aware of the crisis details in advance of his address to the nation. Questions were also raised about briefing the leaders of Turkey and Italy because of the U.S. Jupiter missiles deployed there. It was decided that the Italians and Turks would be notified in advance, but not by a personal presidential emissary.

The president suggested that each national leader receive a personal letter from him, be briefed on the details of the Cuban situation, and be allowed to read an advance copy of the president's proposed address. McCone suggested that copies of the aerial photographs also be shown. It would be convincing and reassuring to these leaders, McCone reasoned. When some doubt was expressed whether our ambassadors could convey the adequate impact of the photographic evidence, McCone proposed sending a senior CIA officer along to brief the photography and answer any questions.

The president was particularly uncomfortable because Dean Acheson had declined to continue to serve on the EXCOM and was sulking at his Maryland farm. He felt that it would take someone of Acheson's stature to dissuade de Gaulle from his resentful attitude toward the United States and convince him of the justification of the U.S. position. Since U.S. ambassador-designate to France, Bohlen, was already on the high seas en route to his post in Paris, President Kennedy suggested that Acheson be approached and asked to deal with de Gaulle. Acheson was working on a lecture to be given at the University of California the following Wednesday but responded with delight to a personal call from the president, and accepted the assignment.

Sherman Kent, of the CIA, was selected to accompany Acheson to Paris. Kent, an ex-professor of history at Yale, had served as a division chief in the Office of Strategic Services during World War

II. He returned to Yale in 1947 and remained there until 1950. In November 1950, he was invited to the Agency for a thirty-day consultancy. He remained there for the next seventeen years—sixteen of them as the director and chairman of the Board of National Estimates. An expert on French history, possessed of a keen sense of humor, and well informed on the situation in Cuba, he was the ideal choice to accompany Acheson.

Walter "Red" Dowling, U.S. ambassador to West Germany, was on home leave visiting his ailing mother in Georgia. When called by Rusk, he terminated his leave and flew immediately back to Washington. R. Jack Smith, deputy chief of the Office of Current Intelligence of the Agency, was selected to accompany Ambassador Dowling to brief Adenauer in Bonn. Smith, with a doctorate in history, was an articulate spokesman on the USSR and Cuba.

After consulting with Secretary Rusk, President Kennedy selected Livingston T. Merchant to brief Prime Minister Diefenbaker of Canada, where the U.S. had no ambassador on post at the time. W. Walton Butterworth, the ambassador-designate, was not scheduled to assume his duties until December 7. Merchant was at a Princeton-Colgate football game when notified that he had been selected to be the president's special emissary to the Canadian government. He hurried to Washington to receive his instructions. Merchant had been U.S. ambassador to Canada from 1956 to 1958 and had established cordial relations with Prime Minister Diefenbaker and ranking members of the Canadian Parliament. Because of his outstanding performance in Canada, Merchant had returned to Washington to serve as undersecretary of state for political affairs from 1958 to 1961. In 1961, he was again appointed ambassador to Canada, serving until April 9, 1962, when he resigned from the foreign service. McCone selected William Tidwell, special assistant to the deputy director for intelligence, Ray Cline, to make the photo presentation in Ottawa. Suave, learned, and articulate, Tidwell had gained a reputation for handling special assignments for the Agency. He also knew the photo-interpretation process well and had served previously as a senior analyst in Soviet matters.

Since Ambassador David K. E. Bruce was on station in London, it was decided that Chester Cooper, a senior Agency representative in London, along with Ambassador Bruce, would be briefed by Acheson and Kent, and then Cooper and Bruce would in turn brief Macmillan.

While Washington was preparing to brief the Allies, Admiral Ward—to assure the success of possible amphibious landings in Cuba—decided that exercises be conducted in Florida in as near realistic manner as possible. A number of projected landing areas in Cuba were at or near beach-resort areas. Hollywood Beach, near Fort Lauderdale, Florida, was selected for the exercise to simulate the beaches east of Havana. The sea off Fort Lauderdale was rough in the predawn chill, and it was late morning before the Marines and Army infantrymen climbed down nets from the landing ships offshore into the bobbing personnel landing craft. LSTs were preparing to move toward the shore to disgorge tanks and armored personnel carriers. The littoral behind the landing zone, situated along the central portion of Hollywood Beach, was dense with hotels, motels, restaurants, and bars. The landing was delayed several hours, and by the time the men and equipment hit the beach, the sunbathers had already gathered under their umbrellas. The tanks, armored personnel carriers, and infantrymen soon added to the crowded conditions on the narrow beach.

It was a case of mutual attraction. Instead of obeying the instructions of a forward observer located in a jai-alai court, some of the Marines began immediately fraternizing with the attractive girls on the beach; others busied themselves posing for photographs in their combat gear for the tourists, while an even greater number of soldiers headed for the bars. One officer in the landing party remembered: "We had one helluva time rounding up that group for reembarkation." Admiral Ward later characterized the exercise as about the closest thing to the Keystone Kops that he had ever seen. He never reported the Hollywood Beach fiasco to his superiors but, instead, emphasized that the landing exercises at Huchinson Island, Fort Pierce, and near Port Everglades went as planned.

The president on several occasions during the crisis expressed deep concern about the number of civilian casualties that could result from a nuclear conflict. From the very outset of his administration, the president had expressed displeasure with the status of the federal civil defense program and its lack of organization and preparedness. He felt strongly that the federal government was not doing enough to inform and protect the civilian population. On July 25, 1961, he had endorsed the construction of civilian shelters for protection from radioactive fallout: "In the event of attack, the lives of those families which are not hit in the nuclear blast and fire can still be saved if they can be warned to take shelter and if that shelter was available. We owe that kind of insurance to our families and our country."[6] Following the Berlin crisis of 1961, the president and the Congress took a new look at the U.S. civil defense program and placed a relatively high priority on the designation and stocking of civil defense shelters. Funds had been provided by the Congress to accelerate the program.

On October 20, 1962, the president asked for a status report on the U.S. civil defense program; he didn't like what he learned. Although some 60 million fallout-shelter spaces had been found in more than 112,000 structures throughout the country, the actual designation and marking of these structures by the Army Corps of Engineers and the Navy Bureau of Yards and Docks was far behind schedule. The owners and managers of many of the large buildings, especially in the larger cities, were reluctant to allow their buildings to be designated as civil-defense shelters. The principal objection was the responsibility imposed to provide emergency storage areas for food, water, and medical supplies and, in effect, relinquish effective control of those areas. The 1962 status report also showed that more than $80 million worth of emergency supplies—including water containers, food rations, medical supplies, sanitation equipment, and radiation detectors—were being produced by eighty-five prime contractors but that little of this production was available in federal warehouses only two weeks prior to the Cuban missile crisis. Kennedy ordered that distribution of the available supplies to the shelters begin immediately. Training centers in shelter management and radiological-defense techniques had been established in Battle Creek, Michigan, Brooklyn, New York, and Alameda, California; but in April 1962, only 2,900 personnel throughout the country had been trained.

There were, however, some positive aspects to the 1962 status report. Air raid warning systems had been installed and tested in all major cities and in most small towns. There were over 31,000 federal, state, and local radiological monitoring stations, whose function was to provide accurate, timely information on the extent, intensity, and duration of radiological hazards from a nuclear detonation.

Soon after the transfer of the civil defense program to the Defense Department, the president prodded Secretary McNamara to provide more nuclear-related information to the public. The result was the issuance of the civil defense handbook *Fallout Protection: What to Know and Do About Nuclear Attack*. By the time of the missile crisis, more than 31 million copies of the booklet had been distributed.

Military targeteers had been moved into the Center, physically, to update and maintain their target lists. My staff, charged with photo-derived databases, worked closely with them. Among the military targets were all POL (petroleum, oil, lubricant) storage areas in Cuba. (These were considered vital targets because all of Cuba's crude oil came from Russia, and if the storage areas, especially gasoline, were struck, it would have an immediate impact on Soviet and Cuban war-making capabilities.) There was concern that inexperienced photo interpreters were targeting all storage tanks as POL tanks. I issued a memo cautioning them: "Do not identify any and all storage tanks you may see as POL storage. Please check your collateral sources, blips, port studies, etc., because many of these storage tanks contain molasses, alcohol, or rum. The same applies to pipelines. Many of the pipelines in the port areas are molasses pipelines."

14

October 21–
Notifying the Allies

"Are they warm?"
—Konrad Adenauer

O N SUNDAY OCTOBER 21, following Lundahl's appearance before the United States Intelligence Board to inform them what had been learned from aerial photography during the previous twenty-four hours, McCone took him aside and said: "I want you to go right away and brief General Eisenhower, and get there promptly." McCone then turned to other business.

Lundahl and his courier, Frank Beck, hastily bundled up the photographic briefing boards and headed for the door. Lundahl stopped and turned toward McCone with a puzzled expression on his face.

"What's the matter?" asked McCone.

Lundahl said, "Sir, may I ask one question?"

"Yes," was McCone's curt answer.

"Where is General Eisenhower?"

Mr. McCone laughed and said, "I should have told you. He'll be at my house, of course."

Lundahl hustled through morning traffic to the McCone residence on Whitehaven Street, in the Foxhall section of northwest Washington. Briefing there, Lundahl had found, was always uncomfortable because the house was filled with priceless artifacts. Setting up easels in a room where the furnishings were precisely arranged meant that a false move could smash an art object worth a fortune. Nevertheless, the briefing materials were quickly made ready with the help of Walter Elder, McCone's aide. General Eisenhower had not yet arrived and Lundahl was in doubt as to how to proceed once he made his appearance. These doubts were quickly resolved at about 9:30 A.M. with the arrival of McCone, who gave precise directions as to what was to be covered and what points were to be emphasized. He also personally placed the easel and told Lundahl where to stand. He had never done this before, and even finished his instructions with, "I want you to speak clearly as you always do." Lundahl, who had a reputation as one of the most articulate briefers in the intelligence community, was taken aback. McCone's cryptic request was clarified when Lundahl went to move a table slightly and found that wires were running to it. The table had been strategically placed between Lundahl and the general. The room was bugged, and Eisenhower's reactions and remarks would be recorded and, presumably, sent to the White House.

General and Mrs. Eisenhower arrived in a limousine and were greeted in front of the house by the McCones. Mrs. McCone adroitly maneuvered Mrs. Eisenhower to the garden behind the house, leaving the general free for the briefing. Eisenhower entered the room where Lundahl was waiting and greeted him warmly with a firm handshake. Eisenhower was directed to the predesignated chair and Lundahl began the briefing. As Lundahl indicated, little preamble was needed since the general was intimately familiar with NPIC products. Lundahl showed a plethora of briefing boards detailing the buildup. He placed particular emphasis on the MRBM and IRBM sites. Eisenhower wanted to know about the operational status of the missile sites, concerned more with the IRBM sites since most of the U.S. strategic striking force was within their range from Cuba. Eisenhower was also shown a briefing board of the SA-2 sites. Eisenhower, of course, remembering the downing of Gary Powers by an SA-2, asked a number of questions about the Cuban SA-2 sites and if they had yet tracked and fired at the U-2. McCone then told Eisenhower that the EXCOM had considered three courses of action: 1) destruction of the sites by conventional bombing; 2) bombing in conjunction with an invasion of the island; and 3) blockade of the island together with further steps in sequence to assure the removal of the missiles. McCone told Eisenhower that the president had already come to the conclusion that the first plan would not be useful and actually detrimental to U.S. interests. Eisenhower told McCone he was not in a position to make judgment on options 2 or 3 because of insufficient background data. He did say that whatever the administration decided, it had his full support. He also advised that the Joint Chiefs of Staff be consulted before any military action was taken. The briefing lasted about forty-five minutes.

The president and Mrs. Kennedy attended the ten o'clock mass at St. Stephen's Church on Pennsylvania Avenue and returned to the White House shortly after 11 A.M. The president reviewed the draft of his proposed speech to the nation for about an hour, and around noon, Dean Acheson arrived to receive final instructions on carrying the president's message and letters to Europe. *Air Force One* was readied at Andrews Air Force Base, prepared for the journey to England, France, and West Germany. Edward Enck, the NPIC courier, arrived early with three large satchels containing the materials to be used to brief the European leaders on the Cuban threat. Wearing a sidearm, Enck checked his weapon before placing the briefing materials in a special security compartment aboard the aircraft.

I had coordinated the production of the four packets of materials, one each for the teams going to London, Paris, Ottawa, and Bonn. Dutch Scheufele prepared the manifests.*

Sir Kenneth Strong and several members of the British delegation to the methodology conference in Washington had been briefed by Ray Cline on October 19 on the totality of the Soviet threat in Cuba.

---

* Each package contained the following:
   1. A locater map of Cuba
   2. Soviet Ships Carrying Jet Light Bomber Crates to Cuba (Kasimov)
   3. Surface-to-Air Missile Base in Cuba (Bahía Honda)
   4. Surface-to-Air Missile Assembly Depot (Santiago de las Vegas)
   5. Guided Missile PT Boats Along Cuban Coast (Mariel)
   6. Surface-to-Surface Cruise Missile Base (Banes)
   7. Soviet High Performance MiG Jet Fighters in Cuba (Santa Clara airfield)
   8. Soviet Light Jet Bombers (Beagle) Being Uncrated and Assembled in Cuba (San Julián airfield)
   9. Medium-Range Ballistic Missile Base in Cuba (San Diego de los Baños)—later designated San Cristóbal No. 1
  10. Soviet Ballistic Missiles on Trailers Next to Launchers in Cuba (Calabazar de Sagua)—later designated Sagua la Grande No. 2
  11. Intermediate-Range Ballistic Missile Base in Cuba (Guanajay)

The hope was that these experienced intelligence officers would properly inform their governments of the missile threat and the possible responses by the Kennedy administration. It was also hoped that Prime Minister Macmillan, after being so informed, would support the president in the blockade and other foreign policy moves. Macmillan had been dubbed Unflappable Mac by his British proponents. According to a British observer, however, when the prime minister was informed of the missiles in Cuba, Macmillan was "very much in a flap." He expressed doubt about the information, stating that there must have been some misinterpretation of the photos. When told that the missiles were discovered by the National Photographic Interpretation Center, he still maintained that he wanted to see "hard evidence."

Air Force One, carrying the president's emissaries, made its first stop late Sunday at the Strategic Air Command's air base at Greenham Common, some forty-five miles west-southwest of London. David K. E. Bruce, U.S. ambassador to the Court of St. James, greeted Acheson and the others warmly. Bruce had been told to be armed when he greeted the plane since Acheson and Kent would be carrying highly classified data. When Bruce saw the armed NPIC courier standing nearby, he told Acheson to reach into his overcoat pocket. Acheson did and found a service revolver. Bruce said, "See, I came prepared." Driven to Admiralty House, Acheson and Kent briefed Ambassador Bruce and Chester Cooper, both of whom were impressed with the amount of data contained in the briefing package.

On Monday, October 22, about noon, Chester Cooper accompanied Ambassador Bruce to 10 Downing Street. The only other person present was the prime minister's private secretary. It soon became obvious to Bruce and Cooper that Macmillan was well aware of the Cuban situation, having undoubtedly received advance word from Sir Kenneth Strong and also from the British ambassador in Washington, David Ormsby-Gore. Macmillan, in a perturbed mood, immediately began to downgrade the Cuban missile threat. Sarcastically, he observed that the British had learned to live under the shadow of Russian missiles and that the Americans might have to make a similar adjustment. Macmillan, seemingly blissfully ignorant of the president's feelings, was not at all sympathetic to the American position as stated by Ambassador Bruce. Lord Alec Douglas-Home,

Britain's foreign secretary, joined the group and, hearing the discussion, realized that the American visitors would be transmitting their impressions of the prime minister's reaction to the president and feared his oblique demeanor undoubtedly would be misunderstood. He tried to mitigate Macmillan's adamant position.

As Cooper moved in to show the photos, Macmillan looked at several of them and then waved Cooper away. He began to comment on Kennedy's handling of the crisis, critical that the president had acted without consulting him personally. The Americans were surprised, knowing that the prime minister had previously been made aware of Kennedy's feelings. Macmillan said that Kennedy should confront Khrushchev privately rather than "going on the telly." He expressed doubts that the United States could muster enough support at the UN for its position and also doubted the blockade could be enforced.

The prime minister gave a clear warning to Ambassador Bruce of the damage that could be done to his government if he were not allowed to show the aerial photos to the British public. It was absolutely essential that the photos be shown. Just as President Kennedy was under increasing pressure from the American Congress to take stronger action on Cuba, so also was the prime minister receiving pressure to disassociate himself from Kennedy. Clearly, Macmillan's warning to Bruce was that, although he was reluctant to do so, without the hard evidence to show the public, he would have to moderate his support of the president. Macmillan would give no firm indication of his actions or support for the U.S. position to Ambassador Bruce.

Macmillan asked that the opposition be briefed. The leaders of the Labor shadow government, Hugh Gaitskell and George Brown, later met with the prime minister and were then briefed by Sherman Kent on the missile threat. Gaitskell had assumed that the missiles were of the surface-to-air variety and was shocked when told they were surface-to-surface long-range variety. He previously had made public statements of the "so-called missiles" in Cuba. Now, when he saw the threat, he began to ask questions as to why the Russians would send such missiles to Cuba. The usually ebullient George Brown had no comment that was remembered by Kent.

Gaitskell drew an analogy between Turkey and Cuba, strongly

suggesting that there was a way to negotiate the issue—i.e., the U.S. should withdraw its missiles from Turkey in exchange for the Soviet withdrawal of missiles from Cuba. When the Americans clearly showed displeasure with this suggested solution, Gaitskell expressed annoyance at not being previously informed on the course of U.S. actions. To fortify his position, he said confidently that the prime minister also felt that way.

Upon their arrival at Evreux Air Force Base, outside Paris, at about 1:30 A.M. local time, on October 22, Dean Acheson and Sherman Kent sped in two small French staff cars with curtains drawn to the home of Cecil Lyon, U.S. chargé d'affaires in Paris. The French did not want Dean Acheson recognized by even the casual Paris by-stander, much less by foreign-service personnel at the Elysée, who would have recognized him on sight. Precautions were taken at all stations. Dignitaries from the American embassy, the American mission to the North Atlantic Council, along with the U.S. military attaché, were briefed by Kent, who also outlined the course of action that the president would be taking. At about 4:30 P.M. Paris time (11:30 A.M. in Washington), two small French staff cars took Acheson, Lyon, and Kent to the Elysée. Although they entered the Elysée through the regular entrance on rue du Faubourg St. Honoré, once inside the courtyard the cars stopped at the nondescript basement entrance. The three Americans were escorted into the basement and led through a series of steel doors, which were opened only when the French escort gave a password. The atmosphere of intrigue was reminiscent of a seventeenth-century novel. Kent, an authority on the French who also possessed a great sense of humor, was inspired to ask Acheson, "D'Artagnan, is that saber loose in the scabbard?"

"Aye, Porthos," Acheson roared.

"Be on the alert. The cardinal's men may be waiting," added Kent.

After climbing several small stairways, they emerged into the ante-room of the president's office. Acheson and Lyon were ushered into de Gaulle's office first. De Gaulle asked Acheson: "Are you here to consult with me or to inform me?" Acheson frankly told the French leader that he was there to inform him. He then gave de Gaulle a verbal summary of the situation in Cuba and presented him a letter from President Kennedy. He told de Gaulle that the president would be addressing the nation that evening (U.S. time) on the threat and took out a copy of the president's speech. Acheson was well known as a raconteur, and the briefing of de Gaulle became one of his favorite topics. At Washington seminars and at cocktail parties, he told the story, which was then retold by others.*

Sherman Kent waited with the package of photos to show de Gaulle. When Acheson offered to show the photos to de Gaulle, he made a waving motion. "A great nation such as yours would not take such a serious step if there was any doubt. I need no such evidence. For our purposes, the missiles are there." Then Acheson diplomatically rephrased the offer: "Would the general as a military man care to look at the photographs to see the advancement that has been made in aerial reconnaissance?" To this, de Gaulle consented, and Acheson asked Sherman Kent to step forward. Kent recalled: "I was glad Mr. Acheson prevailed. One of the great moments of my life was being able to take the photographs and put them on the general's desk, with the feeling that of all the people I had ever seen, here was a man whose eyesight was least able to cope with the niceties of these photographs." Kent noticed that de Gaulle's eyes were hidden behind glasses with lenses that appeared to be almost a half-inch thick. He also knew that cataracts had been removed from both of the general's eyes. Kent politely asked if the general would care to look at a Cuban airfield, hoping that he could at least see the runway. Mr. Kent showed the photo of the Santa Clara airfield. He recalled that de Gaulle "picked up a magnifying glass and proceeded to identify MiG-21's on the runways with more aptitude than myself." The general also made note of several items that Kent had overlooked in his briefing.

When Kent showed the photographs of the MRBM and IRBM sites, de Gaulle asked whether the missiles contained nuclear warheads. Kent replied that although we could not identify any, the U.S. was sure they were in Cuba and would eventually be held

* There are two published versions of the story, one in *Life* magazine and the other reported by C. L. Sulzberger.[1]

in the special storage buildings such as the one seen at Guanajay.

De Gaulle continued to hold the magnifying glass as Kent showed other briefing boards. When Kent produced the KOMAR guided-missile patrol boats at Mariel, the interpreter could not translate the term *cruise missile* to de Gaulle's satisfaction. Fortunately, there was a diagram of the winged cruise missile on the graphic. De Gaulle looked at the sketch and said, "Ah, yes."

Kent breathed a sigh of relief when he finished his briefing, and the general removed his glasses. He realized that as an instructor briefing the general on U-2 photographic interpretation, he had met a most apt pupil.

The general asked at what altitude the pictures had been taken. When told fourteen miles, he said, "*C'est formidable! C'est formidable!*"

The general asked if President Kennedy had considered the possibility that the Russians might move in Berlin. Acheson responded that it had been considered, but should the Russians move, it would mean war. De Gaulle assured Acheson it would not come to war.

When de Gaulle asked Acheson why Khrushchev had placed the missiles in Cuba, Acheson replied it was a big Khrushchevian gamble. De Gaulle agreed. De Gaulle told Acheson that he could reassure the president that France would support him in the crisis. "It's exactly what I would have done," he assured Acheson. He also asked that his thanks be conveyed to President Kennedy for sending a man of Acheson's stature to brief him.

Air Force One flew on to West Germany with Ambassador Dowling, R. Jack Smith of the CIA, and the NPIC courier, Enck. Adenauer had been electioneering in Hanover when notified that special emissaries from President Kennedy were being sent to West Germany to brief him on a matter of utmost concern, and he returned hurriedly to Bonn. Adenauer received Dowling and Smith at the chancellor's official residence. Ambassador Dowling introduced Smith. (Smith later frequently told the humorous story that Adenauer was aware that many U.S. intelligence officers had pseudonyms like Smith or Jones. Adenauer had met Smith on a previous occasion, and when Smith was introduced, Adenauer with a sly smile said, "Still?") Dowling gave the chancellor a copy of the president's address and then asked Smith to show the photos. Adenauer was no stranger to U-2 photography, having been appraised previously on its fine points by Lundahl on U-2 flights over Russia in 1957. As Smith* unfolded the Cuban evidence, Adenauer was as usual an attentive listener. He was familiar with what could be seen at such altitudes but had a number of questions regarding the missiles. At one point he asked in German, "Are they warm?" When Smith said that some were considered operational, Adenauer asked if they were "ready to light."

After the briefing was concluded, the chancellor told Ambassador Dowling to inform the president that he could expect the chancellor's total and unqualified support. He also said he was not surprised that the Russians would try such a maneuver.

Although Livingston T. Merchant and William A. Tidwell had arrived in Ottawa on Sunday evening, October 21, they did not meet with Canadian prime minister Diefenbaker and his secretary of state for external affairs, Harold C. Green, and the minister of national defense, Douglas S. Harkness, until about 5 P.M. the next day. Merchant introduced the prime minister and others to Tidwell, who presented the photographic evidence of the Soviet military buildup in Cuba. According to Tidwell, the three Canadians sat with abject fascination on the quality of the photography and the analysis. Like the other world leaders, the prime minister remarked that the "evidence was overwhelming" and seemed confident that Kennedy would gain the support he needed throughout the Western world. He thanked and complimented Tidwell for the quality and scope of the briefing.

After Tidwell had finished, Merchant handed the prime minister a copy of President Kennedy's proposed nationwide speech, which he read slowly. Pausing momentarily, he said he could understand the president's bitterness about being deceived by Soviet foreign minister Gromyko. He was sure that Gromyko must have known that the missiles were being installed in Cuba while at his meeting with the president on October 18. However, Diefenbaker felt that the manner in which President Kennedy was stating his bitterness toward Gromyko in the address could be misinterpreted as an attack on the Soviet government. But he agreed that the reference to

* In 1971 Smith was one of ten persons selected to receive the National Civil Service League Career Service award for "his formidable contributions to our nation's security in numberless situations of grave national concern."

Gromyko should remain in the address, since the visit had been carried by the media. He felt, however, that the wording of the attack should be strictly limited to Gromyko. He questioned the use of the word *dishonest* and suggested the softer *dishonorable* with regard to Gromyko; Khrushchev might take *dishonest* as a personal affront and might be provoked to break diplomatic relations with the United States or at least recall Soviet representation to the UN. The best diplomatic efforts would be required to resolve the crisis. Merchant told Diefenbaker he would inform the White House of his comments immediately.

The prime minister added that it appeared to him that the real problem at the UN "would be to get people to believe the charge without benefit of the intelligence briefing. He said that he thought the best tactic would be for members of the UN to actually go and see the sites for themselves."[2] He told Merchant further to transmit to the president Canada's readiness and willingness to do whatever possible to bring peace to Cuba. He said he would meet with his cabinet and discuss the threat posed by the missiles and that although he didn't know how the crisis ultimately would be resolved, he would offer Canadian troops as part of a UN truce inspection team. He asked Green to ensure that Canadian airspace and Canadian air transport facilities were denied to the Soviets.*

Tidwell remembered another event on his return trip to Washington. "We had a 707 from the VIP squadron at Andrews assigned to us, and the three of us—Merchant, the security man, and myself—rattled around in that huge space. We flew down past New York and down Chesapeake Bay, turning northwest to approach Andrews from the southeast. That approach put us where we could see Washington in the background. We were all uncertain as to the possible Soviet reaction, and concerned that it might be an irrational

---

* Tidwell remembers that after the briefings were completed and the Canadians had left, "I turned the briefing boards over to the security officer and proceeded to inspect the room for notes or other classified information. I picked up Diefenbacker's notes and preserved them." Tidwell also recounts that "we heard that the prime minister had made a speech in Parliament saying that the UN should send a team to Cuba to verify the facts of the situation. The Kennedy brothers appear to have taken offense at this, feeling that Diefenbaker was questioning the integrity of the U.S. It was clear to me that they had mis-read him, and I tried to correct the impression, but I was too junior to make such an impression."[3]

reaction. Just as we neared Andrews, I saw a bright light in the sky shooting directly toward Washington. I thought 'My God, is this what a missile looks like? Or is it a meteor?' For a moment my heart stood still—then it burned out—it was a meteor!'"[4]

That afternoon commencing at 2:30, the president met with the EXCOM at the White House. The opening discussion centered around the third draft of the president's speech for October 22. The president listened intently to the recommendations of the committee about proposed changes. Then Admiral Anderson was asked to go over the details of the quarantine. The admiral, using maps and charts, explained how destroyers making an intercept would use the international code K (You are to stop at once) or ON (You are to heave to at once). The complete spectrum of signaling devices was to be used; international code signals, flag hoists, blinking lights, radio, and loudspeakers. Should there be a need for Russian linguists, the Navy had assigned one to each destroyer on the picket line. If an intercepted ship did not respond, a shot would be fired across its bow. If the ship still didn't stop, "minimum force" would be applied to damage a nonvital part of the ship. When President Kennedy inquired about what constituted a nonvital part, Admiral Anderson responded that a shot would be fired at the rudder. When the president asked for reassurance that the Navy's gunnery would be that accurate, Admiral Anderson replied that at close range it would be. The president directed that in all instances all possible restraint was to be used to avoid personal injury or loss of life. Any ship that failed to adhere to instructions would be disabled but not sunk. Tows would be attached and the ship taken to the nearest of the following ports: Charleston, South Carolina; Fort Lauderdale, Florida; or Roosevelt Roads and San Juan in Puerto Rico.

Throughout the presentation, Admiral Anderson exuded an air of confidence. He was convinced that the professional competence and level of experience of U.S. Navy officers, both afloat and ashore, were unequaled by those of any other fleet. Anderson said that although the Soviets had maintained a large fleet of surface ships and submarines for a number of years, they had rarely ventured far from Soviet shores. They were prepared primarily for a defense against

Western carrier task forces. The Russians, Anderson maintained, had little ability to deploy to distant forward areas and to supply those forces. This was a critical weakness of the Soviet naval forces, and Admiral Anderson sought to exploit it.

Admiral Anderson summed up for the president, as was his manner, in a crisp, succinct fashion. There were three tasks the Soviet Navy had to perform in the event of an all-out war: counter U.S. fleets deployed all over the world with matching force; guard the Soviet lanes of communication; and assist the Cubans in repelling an invasion. The admiral radiated confidence in the U.S. Navy. "The Russians," he declared, "could do none of the above effectively."

When the meeting ended at about 5 P.M. and Admiral Anderson was placing his charts in his folders, the president approached and said, "Well, Admiral, it looks as though this is up to the Navy." Anderson replied, "Mr. President, the Navy will not let you down."[5]

Vice-President Lyndon B. Johnson has stated in his memoirs that President Kennedy kept him well informed on all international crises while he was vice-president. The Cuban crisis was no exception. The vice-president returned to Washington on the evening of October 21 from a campaign trip to Hawaii. The president, meanwhile, asked McCone to be sure to brief the vice-president thoroughly on all aspects of the Cuban situation as soon as he returned. McCone alerted Lundahl to be ready. At 8:30 P.M., Lundahl arrived at the vice-president's Foxhall Road home, in northwest Washington. He was accompanied by his courier, Frank Beck. A knock on the vice-president's door brought a clatter of heels from within the house, as though several people were rushing to the entrance. The door opened slowly, revealing Mrs. Johnson and her daughters, Lynda and Luci. The women, obviously expecting someone else, dropped back when they saw two unfamiliar faces. Lundahl quickly explained his mission, and Mrs. Johnson graciously asked them to enter, ushering them into a small study at the rear of the house. She explained that her husband was just having his dinner, following a late arrival of his airplane, and would be with them shortly.

The vice-president came into the study about fifteen minutes later. His attire was a bit disheveled—no coat, tie knot askew, his hair slightly tousled—and he was obviously tired from his trip. He greeted the two intelligence officers warmly, remembering Lundahl from previous briefings. The amenities over, he said, "Well, what have we got here?" Lundahl replied, "Mr. Vice-President, this is the briefing to which Mr. McCone referred. Would you prefer for us to proceed immediately or wait until Mr. McCone arrives?" The vice-president said, "Why don't we go ahead." The vice-president assumed a casual position in a large chair, one leg over the arm, and listened intently. Lundahl was about halfway through the briefing when Mrs. Johnson brought McCone into the study. When told by Lundahl that the vice-president had asked that he proceed with the briefing, Mr. McCone said, "I am glad you did that." At this point, the vice-president rose to turn off a radio that had been playing softly in the background, but McCone suggested that the volume be increased to forestall any possibility that the room might be "bugged." The vice-president nodded agreement and said, "Oh, I hadn't thought of that."

The briefing continued, and the vice-president interrupted at only one point, about the question of visibility—could it have been possible to detect the missiles before October 14? Lundahl explained that the atmosphere must be perfectly clear for high-altitude aerial cameras to obtain usable photography. The weather before October 14 had provided some good days for sunshine and recreational purposes, but there had been haze and high cloud layers that could have prevented successful U-2 reconnaissance. The vice-president pondered the explanation a moment and then said, "Now, go over that one again for me." Lundahl complied, providing additional details. Satisfied, the vice-president said, "Now I understand. There is a difference between clear weather for sports and so forth and clear weather for taking pictures."

The vice-president then asked questions about the rate of construction of the missile sites. When informed that the Russians were constructing the sites at an unprecedented rate, he asked, "Suppose they don't stop constructing them after the president issues the warning tomorrow night?"

"Then blood will flow," McCone said just above a whisper.

The vice-president shook his head. His lanky frame was half slumped and half stretched out in the leather chair. He thanked

McCone and Lundahl for the briefing, saying that he was now up-to-date for the next day. It was about 10:15 P.M.

On the same evening, a Soviet Tu-114 Cleat transport with 140 passengers was closely followed by U.S. fighter aircraft before landing in Havana. It was later assumed by the intelligence community that the transport carried ranking missile officers sent to Cuba to assure that there would be no accidental launchings with respect to missiles that might be targeted against the U.S.

The U.S. Navy had a long-standing plan for the emergency evacuation of dependents from "Gitmo," the U.S. naval base at Guantánamo, Cuba. When the U.S. severed diplomatic relations with Cuba in January 1961, it was made clear to the Castro regime that the U.S. would continue to operate the base under rights granted in the 1934 treaty and would retaliate against any Cuban attempt to interfere with base operations. When Castro later shut off the base's water supply, the U.S. immediately began to construct a desalinization plant and, meanwhile, tankered in water from the United States. Guantánamo remained a year-round training base for ships and aircraft of the Atlantic fleet. The base also was used for sea trials, defense of the Panama Canal, and served as a base for antisubmarine-warfare fleet elements.

One of the first issues President Kennedy raised during the crisis was whether U.S. dependents at Guantánamo should be evacuated. At the time, there were over 900 families, comprising about 2,800 women and children, living on the base. The Navy had strong feelings that the removal of the dependents might be regarded by the Soviets and the Cubans as a sign of weakness and would also send a signal that the U.S. was aware of the missiles being in Cuba. The Russians and Cubans would then undoubtedly upgrade their military and naval defenses. Secretary of Defense McNamara had insisted that the Navy dependents be removed. It had not yet been established that McNamara was reflecting the president's views. In an attempt to convince McNamara of the value of keeping the dependents in Guantánamo, the assistant secretary of defense for international security affairs, Paul Nitze, and Admiral Ward met with him. Nitze pointed out various reasons why it would be inadvisable to pull out the

American civilians. McNamara listened patiently, but it was obvious that his mind was made up. McNamara stood up and said, "Mr. Secretary, you have your instructions to get the dependents out of Guantánamo Bay. Please carry out those instructions."[6] Mr. Nitze then suggested that in order to forestall any political criticism of the president by the Republicans and misinterpretations by the Russians and Cubans, the women and children should be replaced by Marine combat troops. McNamara liked the recommendation, particularly for political reasons. McNamara said that he would pass on the Nitze/Ward recommendation to the president.

Preparations were made to airlift and sealift Marine combat units to Guantánamo. The Marine force on the island would be under the command of tough Marine brigadier general William R. Collins. The president asked that all dependents be out of Cuba before his address to the nation on the evening of October 22. On Friday and Saturday, October 19 and October 20, four ships: a transport, *Upshur* (T-AP 198); a seaplane tender, *Duxbury Bay* (AVP 38); a refrigerator ship, *Hyades* (AF-28); and a landing ship, *Desoto County* (LST 1171) dropped anchor in Guantánamo Bay.

Monday, October 22, began as a routine day at the base. Sailors and Marines had had their breakfasts and were at duty stations, civil servants were at their offices, and children had gone to school. Most of the women were doing their laundry or household chores. Shortly before 11 A.M., the morning routine was interrupted by phone calls and messengers. Each family was told to pack one bag per person and prepare to evacuate the base within fifteen minutes. While the majority complied, some women felt it was just another drill until informed that it was real. The children were brought home from school at 11 A.M. and the mothers, after packing, prepared their quarters for a long absence. At about noon, ambulances and trucks began to move all hospital patients to the airfield. A short while later, about three hundred dependents arrived at the airfield in trucks. Five C-130 Lockheed Hercules transports were waiting to be loaded.

At about the same time, school and military buses began stopping at each house and, when loaded, moved either to the transports or to the piers and waiting ships. On the ships, the long wait for processing and form filling was having a disturbing effect on the apprehensive mothers and impatient children. Admiral Edward J.

O'Donnell, commander of the naval base, ordered that all processing cease, that the dependents be taken aboard as quickly as possible, and that further processing be done at sea. Loading was completed shortly before 4 P.M. The *Upshur* was loaded to capacity, with 1,730 passengers; the *Duxbury Bay* took on 351; the *Hyades*, 286; and the *Desoto County*, 92.[7]

Before the ships departed Guantánamo, Admiral O'Donnell read the following messages over the ship's loudspeakers:

> "To you who have had to leave your homes at Guantánamo, I send my deep regrets. I know you do so with sadness, for some of you also leave behind your husband, others, your father—your jobs as well as your homes. It is my most earnest hope that circumstances will permit your return. I send my warmest greetings and best wishes to you and those you leave behind.[8]
>
> (Signed) John F. Kennedy"

O'Donnell then read another message:

> "The calm and serene manner with which you have accepted the threat of possible personal danger while living at Guantánamo has been viewed with admiration and respect. Now our judgment dictates that you should leave the scene of an increasing danger to your safety. I am sure you will accept this action with the same fine spirit that has been so obvious throughout your stay at Guantánamo. Rest assured that we will do all possible to provide for your welfare in the days ahead.
>
> (Signed) George Anderson"[9]

In Norfolk, Rear Admiral James C. Dempsey, commander of the Amphibious Training Command of the U.S. Atlantic fleet, was preparing to receive the dependents. It was decided that the Little Creek Amphibious Base, on the outskirts of Norfolk, would be the reception and processing area and that some of the four ships would dock there and the others at pier 12 at Norfolk. The chief of naval personnel, Vice-Admiral W. R. Smedberg III, was dispatched by Admiral Anderson to Norfolk to assure that activities in the Norfolk area regarding the dependents were being coordinated.

The C-130 transports bearing the patients and others were to land at the Norfolk naval air station. Flight plans for one of the C-130's, however, had to be changed. It made an emergency landing at the Cherry Point, North Carolina, Marine Corps air station. Mrs. Louise K. Kittleson had to be rushed to the hospital, where later that evening she gave birth to a daughter.

Many of the women aboard the ships did not have time to say goodbye to the husbands and fathers who were at their duty stations at Guantánamo. But it had not seemed to adversely affect their conduct aboard the *Upshur*. Mothers took turns mixing formula, caring for children, sleeping, housekeeping, and aiding in the paper processing. Teenage boys worked in the galley aiding the Navy mess cooks, and teenage girls aided in serving the meals.

But if their performance aboard ship was outstanding, the performance of the Navy wives waiting to receive the Gitmo dependents at Norfolk was equally admirable. Captain Nelson P. Watkins, commander of the Little Creek base, had asked his wife to coordinate the efforts of Navy wives and the Navy League auxiliaries in the Norfolk area.

Dependents airlifted out of Cuba, where temperatures were in the nineties, arrived in Norfolk at 4:05 P.M., where the temperature was a cool fifty-one degrees. Navy men and Navy wives quickly wrapped the children in blankets and warm clothing and transported them to the Little Creek base for processing. Transportation personnel made the necessary air, bus, and rail reservations, while personnel from the Navy Exchange had set up a booth to cash checks. Navy stewards mixed baby formula late into the night. Red Cross Gray Ladies worked in shifts in a makeshift nursery. Local hospitals and Navy wives had donated more than three hundred cribs.

The Navy transport ships headed for Norfolk were scheduled to arrive Thursday, October 25. For three days, volunteers had visited Norfolk merchants to solicit clothing and money. Civic clubs, religious organizations, and veterans' groups had collected used clothing and shoes. Volunteers at Little Creek sorted the clothing and shoes and arranged them on racks and tables by sizes. At 2 P.M. Thursday, the *Upshur* docked at pier 12 of the Norfolk naval base as a Navy band played and over five hundred Navy, Marine, and civilian volunteers waited. As the children boarded buses, they were given apples, bananas, and comic books. Sailors and Marines loaded their baggage. The *Hyades* followed the *Upshur* at pier 12, while the *Desoto County* and the *Duxbury Bay* were docked at a Little Creek quay. By noon Saturday most of the Guantánamo dependents had processed through Little Creek and departed for reunions with family and friends throughout the U.S.*

The Navy had made careful record of all of the movement of the dependents and that information was sent to Guantánamo to reassure anxious husbands and fathers.

If the Cubans thought the Americans were showing signs of weakness by evacuating service families from Guantánamo, they were soon to see an impressive display of strength as cargo aircraft began landing at the airfield. By the evening of October 22, 3,600 Marines and 3,200 tons of equipment had been airlifted by the Military Air Transport Service (MATS). It was a dramatic signal to the Russians and Cubans that the U.S. intended to defend Guantánamo. The Russian intelligence estimate was that "the garrison had been increased from 8,000 to 18,000 personnel from the 2nd Marine Division, and reinforced with 150 tanks, 24 anti-aircraft missile systems, and 70 recoilless guns. The number of airplanes had been increased to 120."[10] The actual defense force deployed at Guantánamo during the crisis consisted of 5,750 Marines, a Hawk missile battery, 155 tanks, 105mm artillery pieces, three gunfire support ships, two Marine air attack squadrons, and a patrol squadron. Two aircraft carriers were in the area to render support, if necessary. While the U.S. had regarded this as a strictly defensive operation, the Soviets and Cubans viewing the U.S. Navy "conducting uninterrupted intensive reconnaissance along the Cuban shores and approaches" came to the

---

* Rear Admiral O'Donnell, commenting later on the evacuation, was to write: "I think that the great theme in any story about the evacuation should be the enormous steadiness and self-reliance of our Navy wives. I had never thought much about it in the past, but close association here has made it clear to me that the wives of our Navymen absorb the quality of self-discipline and are strengthened by the same process that goes into the formation of a first-class sailor. The wives showed a toughness of spirit and a no-panic attitude which must be a source of pride to the services and the country."

After seeing the courage of the women at Norfolk, Vice-Admiral Smedberg would later write: "One of the greatest strengths of all the services is the wife who accepts the many sacrifices she is called upon to make because of her understanding of her husband's part in insuring the security of our nation."

conclusion that Guantánamo was "actively being prepared as a bridgehead for military operation."

The Cubans reacted sharply to the landing of the Marines. That night, Cuban military forces were placed on an increased state of readiness. Soviet intelligence collection also reflected increased concern and sense of immediacy. Soviet intelligence ships were deployed off the coast of Florida to monitor the buildup of U.S. forces there.

The movement of troops from all areas of the United States to Florida, the lights burning deep into the night at the State Department, the Defense Department, the CIA, and the White House made a number of reporters suspicious of the White House story that another Berlin crisis was brewing. *The New York Times* team of Max Frankel and his boss, James "Scotty" Reston, had pieced together the story that the crisis actually involved offensive missiles being emplaced in Cuba. They called Pierre Salinger with their story, and within minutes the president was on the line asking them not to print it. The *Times* agreed to withhold the story.

15

October 22— Address to the Nation

"Both our will and our patience
will be tested."
—PRESIDENT KENNEDY

L EADERSHIP is rarely clearly understood or appreciated at the time
it is being exercised. Yet, considered in the proper historical
perspective, we are often amazed when we realize how we
would have fared without it. The Cuban missile crisis demanded
inspired leadership, and the president was up early the morning of
October 22 making a number of telephone calls. It would be a day
of conferences, consultation with congressional leaders, informing
Allied governments, and most important, giving an explanation to
the American people. The president went to his office at 9:15 A.M.
to review his speech to the nation. He had to express himself with
simplicity, clarity, and forthrightness. He had to use words that conveyed strength without provoking fear. He had to evoke spontaneous
support from all segments of society for an action of which they were
not yet aware, had not pondered or contemplated. The truth, simply
stated, had to be a central theme. The president reviewed his speech
alone, making only several minor corrections.

An hour earlier, aboard the cruiser *Newport News*, Admiral Ward
assembled the commanding officers and unit commanders of the
cruisers, destroyers, and escort ships based at Norfolk. Vice-Admiral
John W. Ailes III held a similar conference with the destroyer com-

manders based at the Charleston naval base. All were briefed on the crisis and on the forthcoming presidential address to the nation concerning the quarantine. They were told to round up their crews as quickly and as unobtrusively as possible and put to sea that afternoon for an indefinite period. All instructions for movements of ships prescribed "minimize public attention." Some of the ships had recently returned from duty with the Sixth Fleet in the Mediterranean and had many men on leave. Not one of the commanders expressed any dismay at being ordered to put to sea on such short notice and, in some instances, without a full complement of men.

The Second Fleet units assigned to the Caribbean were Task Forces 135 and 136. Task Force 135, consisting of two powerful attack carrier groups built around the nuclear-powered USS *Enterprise* and the USS *Independence* along with an underway replenishment group and fifteen screening destroyers, was proceeding to positions off the southern coast of Cuba. Task Force 136, the blockading force, consisted of the aircraft carrier *Essex*, cruisers *Newport News* and *Canberra*, along with an underway replenishment group and nineteen destroyers. The quarantine line as prescribed in the operations order consisted of twelve destroyer stations, sixty miles apart, on an arc 500 miles from Cape Maisí on the eastern end of Cuba with the cruiser *Canberra* with two escorting destroyers backing up the northern end of the line and the cruiser *Newport News* and two destroyers backing up the southern end of the line. The *Essex* and five destroyers were assigned the western end of the line.

At the same time, Admiral "Whitey" Taylor's Antisubmarine Warfare Force had the additional task of intercepting and tracking Soviet merchantmen. Navy patrol aircraft, along with SAC bombers, maintained surveillance over the broad ocean areas between Europe and Cuba, reporting movements of Soviet and Bloc shipping.

The amphibious force at Little Creek loaded the U.S. Marines of the Fleet Marine Force of the Atlantic fleet. This landing force was augmented by a brigade from the Fleet Marine Force based in Southern California. A total of ten battalions of Marines were afloat in the vicinity of Cuba.

President Kennedy that morning called former presidents Hoover, Truman, and Eisenhower. The calls to Hoover and Truman were more courtesy than substance, advising them of the upcoming crisis and his impending address to the nation. With President Eisenhower, Kennedy re-reviewed in some detail the proposals to bomb the missile sites, to bomb the missile sites as well as conduct amphibious and airborne landings on the island, or to blockade the island and take the necessary steps to assure the removal of the missiles from the island. The president said he had decided to put the third plan into effect. Eisenhower agreed that the first plan "would not be useful and would be detrimental to our cause." Eisenhower still maintained that he was not in a position to make a choice between the second and third plans since he "was not in possession of all the background files and communications and international conversations" that would give him a basis for making that decision. When Kennedy appeared uncertain as to what Khrushchev's reaction would be, Eisenhower offered the president a bit of advice. If the Russians resorted to any military action, he emphasized that the president should follow the course of action recommended by the Joint Chiefs of Staff. Eisenhower assured the president, however, that whatever he decided to do, he would have his wholehearted support.

At 10 A.M., the president met with the EXCOM. There were no indications Soviet naval forces were going on a higher alert, but McCone did report that early that morning a Soviet F-class (Foxtrot) submarine had been spotted on the surface in the mid-Atlantic recharging its batteries, and several hundred miles to the north, a Soviet long-range Z-class (Zulu) submarine was photographed near the Soviet auxiliary Terek.

Lundahl, in his briefing to EXCOM, had decided, with McCone's concurrence, to present the photographic evidence of the readiness posture of the offensive and defensive missile systems in Cuba. An offensive missile site, Lundahl said, could be considered fully operational when it was capable of salvoing its first missiles within six to eight hours and had a capability to refire within an additional four to six hours. Lundahl pointed out the various photographic indicators that would reflect such a capability: the erector/launchers in place and the cabling between the launchers, the control areas, and power generators installed. The missile checkout tent, along with the necessary checkout equipment, would be present. The oxidizer and fuel trucks would be evident in proximity to the launch site. Facilities for the launch crews would also be evident.

Lundahl shocked the group with the Center's opinion, shared by the intelligence community, that four of the MRBM sites had already became fully operational and that the remaining two sites would probably reach that status later that week. Photography indicated that the Soviets were working on the missile sites at an extremely rapid rate. Lundahl also revealed that it appeared that "the Soviet objective in Cuba is to attain full operational capability at all sites as soon as possible, rather than to prepare a single site for an emergency launch capability as soon as the missiles and equipment arrive in the area." The earliest estimate for the full operational capability for an IRBM site was December 1, with a more likely date being December 15. Lundahl emphasized that as yet, neither the IRBM missiles themselves nor support equipment for them had been discovered.

Lundahl then showed photos of the Il-28 Beagle bombers being assembled at San Julián airfield. Careful analysis of the shipping crates seen at the field estimated that at least thirty-five bombers were present.

Twenty-two of the twenty-four SA-2 sites in Cuba were considered fully operational, and an additional SAM assembly area had been discovered that morning, bringing the total of assembly areas to seven. There were at least thirty-nine MiG-21 fighters in Cuba, all of them deployed at Santa Clara airfield. There were twelve KOMAR guided-missile boats in Cuban ports, eight at Mariel, and four at Banes. There was no evidence that they were being made ready to put to sea.

Construction was continuing on the nuclear storage bunkers, but Lundahl acknowledged that the Center had not as yet identified any nuclear warheads. The presumption had to be that they were in close proximity to the missile sites.

After Lundahl was dismissed, the president asked that draft copies of his television speech be reviewed by EXCOM members. A few minor changes were made. The president then gave his approval to precautionary measures to put the military forces of the United States in a posture to respond to any contingency.

One place of concern was Berlin. When the president returned to Washington from Vienna in June 1961 after his meeting with Khrushchev, he recommended the formation of a special task force to handle the Berlin problem. In his address to the nation on June 6, 1961, he reported: "I will tell you now that it was a very sober two days. . . . We have wholly different views on right and wrong, of what is an internal affair and what is aggression. And above all, we have wholly different concepts of where the world is and where it is going."

Privately, the president had lamented his unpreparedness at Vienna in dealing with Khrushchev on the Berlin issues. Kennedy let it be known to the intelligence community: "I had a pocketful of sand while Khrushchev had concrete." He added, "In the future, I don't want to allow Khrushchev to ball an issue into a take-it-or-leave-it proposition. I also want to provide him with some powerful alternatives for his unilateral actions."

The Khrushchev attitude on Berlin had continued to bother Kennedy, and on July 25, 1961, he would report to the nation: "Seven weeks ago tonight, I returned from Europe to report on my meeting with Premier Khrushchev and the others. In Berlin, as you recall, he intends to bring to an end—through a stroke of the pen—first, our legal rights to be in West Berlin and secondly, our ability to make good on our commitments to two million people of that city. That we cannot permit." Then as a warning to Khrushchev, the president added: "I hear it said that West Berlin is militarily untenable; and so was Bastogne; and so, in fact, was Stalingrad. Any dangerous spot is tenable if men—brave men—will make it so. We cannot and will not permit the Communists to drive us out of Berlin, either gradually or by force." The president ordered that draft calls be doubled and tripled in the coming months, along with the call-up of a number of reserve units. Khrushchev decided to play hardball with Kennedy and less than three weeks later the Berlin Wall went up, literally cementing the division of Berlin.

Following Vienna, the perturbed president made known his dissatisfaction with State Department officials concerned with Berlin. He characterized them as being dull and unimaginative and said that the Berlin problem could not be handled through the maze of regular channels. He ordered the secretaries of State and Defense to personally prepare contingency planning recommendations on Berlin. The president stressed the need to have someone in charge of the Berlin problem on a full-time basis, supported by an interagency staff. He stated emphatically that he was not going to "get diddled out of Berlin."

The acrimony between the Soviets and the U.S. continued into the fall of 1961, when Gromyko met with the president on October 6 with the aim of easing the Berlin crisis. At one point during his two-hour talk with the Soviet foreign minister, the president responded to a Gromyko proposal: "You have offered to trade us an apple for an orchard. We do not do that in this country." When the president was asked about the progress made in his meeting with Gromyko, he replied, "Zero."

Although Secretaries McNamara and Rusk also had been aware of possible trouble in Berlin, both claimed that the pressure of other duties did not allow them to devote full time to the Berlin issues. Diplomatic overtures on Berlin were needed, but all the president was receiving from State was evidence of tensions and bickerings among the various desks, especially the German, Russian, and West European.

After some internal scrimmaging among the State officers, European assistant secretary Foy Kohler emerged as the quarterback of the State team. McNamara had asked Paul Nitze to represent him on military contingency planning, and the Joint Chiefs of Staff had named Major General David Gray as their representative on the presidential planning committee on Berlin. Operating under a loose arrangement called the Interdepartmental Coordinating Committee, Kohler and Nitze worked closely to produce two studies requested by Kennedy. The president still did not like the informal arrangement and again asked that a task team on Berlin be established. The German desk at State adopted a sandbagging and disruptive attitude, fearing they "would lose control of the Berlin problem" to the Pentagon. When Bobby became aware of the full scope of the bickerings, he reported the fact to his brother, but not before telling Rusk and McNamara that the president "was prepared to kick some asses around" if they did not subscribe to his wish for a Berlin task force. It was formally activated on August 13, 1961. Strong management by Kohler and Nitze smoothed out many of the differences, and before long the task force began to function effectively. When key decisions were required, they would request a joint meeting with the president, along with Rusk, McNamara, Bundy, Taylor, and Martin Hillenbrand, director of the German desk at State.

The Berlin task force was entrusted with coordinating all activities relating to Berlin, including daily problems of the air corridors, road and rail accesses, harassment, passports, visas, etc. Formulation of the long-range crisis and contingency planning policies also were undertaken. Their efforts were coordinated not only among the White House, State, and Defense, but also with the Washington ambassadorial group, which included the British, French, and German ambassadors to the United States. Coordination was also effected with the NATO allies, the various NATO agencies, and the U.S. ambassadors to Russia, the UK, France, and West Germany to preserve the Allied presence in Berlin.

By the time of the Cuban missile crisis, Kohler had become U.S. ambassador to Moscow and Hillenbrand, a brilliant careerist and Kohler's former deputy, had been selected to head the interagency Berlin task force. Hillenbrand wrote to me in 1978: "Although Robert Creel had become Director of the Office of German Affairs, the exclusive line responsibility for handling Berlin problems rested with me and other officers assigned to the Berlin Task Force."[1] Hillenbrand had seen that the basic contingency planning regarding Berlin was complete and ready for implementation.

On October 22, 1962, at 11 A.M., the president met with Rusk, Ball, Bundy, Hillenbrand, Thompson, Nitze, and Michael Forrestal on the Berlin problem. Any U.S. action toward Cuba could bring a reciprocal action against Berlin, and the president listened intently as Hillenbrand outlined the projected course of action in response to possible Soviet moves. The president expected, at a minimum, that the Soviets and East Germans would hinder the movement of food and supplies to Berlin. Looking at Thompson, the president said, "Suppose Khrushchev says to me, 'Well now, you've blockaded Cuba and I've blockaded Berlin. How do you like that?' " Thompson responded, "It will be 1948 all over again."

At 11:47 A.M., Paul Nitze, in his capacity as the assistant secretary of defense for international security affairs, along with a Pentagon expert, briefed the president on U.S. troop dispositions in Berlin and West Germany. (At the Pentagon, when the Joint Chiefs of Staff discussed the Soviets threatening to send troops to encircle Berlin, General LeMay had said the solution was a simple one: We threaten to send the bombers to Moscow.)

The president then asked for assurances from Rusk that all U.S. diplomatic and consular posts abroad would be fully informed on what the president would be doing: "I don't want any screw-ups on this one," he said.

Rusk replied that a copy of the president's speech would be sent to all posts that afternoon, followed by a circular detailing the various diplomatic actions that would be taken. Rusk handed the president a copy of the six-page State circular, which had been previously reviewed by Michael Forrestal and Bundy.[2]

The president then reviewed with the group the "State scenario" —the briefings, meetings, and notes the State Department would be responsible for accomplishing that evening. Rusk reviewed again with the president what he would be telling Dobrynin of the president's action at his meeting with him scheduled for 6 P.M.

The White House meeting ended at twelve-thirty, and the president and Dave Powers went for a swim. After the swim, he and Powers ate lunch in the Family Dining Room.

Shortly after noon on October 22, White House press secretary Pierre Salinger called Robert Fleming of the American Broadcasting Company, the pool coordinator that month for the three networks. Salinger asked for thirty minutes of network time for the president, commencing at seven o'clock that evening, on a "matter of highest national urgency." The press and media had been hounding Salinger on Sunday for information on the military movements from the Southern states to Florida and Georgia and were firmly convinced now that something big was brewing concerning Cuba. Salinger assembled his staff to make sure that all the necessary actions regarding the president's speech to the nation were being taken. A note made by the president reflected his concern that the press also be informed: "Is there a plan to brief and brainwash key press within 12 hours or so—New York Times—Lippmann—Childs—Alsop— key bureau chiefs?"[3]

At 3 P.M. that day, the president met with the National Security Council in the Cabinet Room; the Joint Chiefs of Staff were also invited. Final measures to put the U.S. military "in a posture to respond to any contingency'' were approved. Approval was also given to the Joint Chiefs of Staff to conduct low-level aerial photographic-reconnaissance missions over Cuba commencing on October 23. General Taylor and Admiral Anderson reported that ships of the U.S. Navy had moved to positions to enforce the quarantine. The Council formally established the Executive Committee of the National Security Council when it approved Action Memorandum 196. The president was designated chairman of the EXCOM and asked that the EXCOM meet with him daily at 10 A.M. for the remainder of the crisis. Actually, the EXCOM met with him only sporadically during the crisis.

There had been a general feeling among the Joint Chiefs that their views were not being properly elucidated by General Taylor and that Taylor was withholding information from them. The Joint Chiefs had asked to meet with the president to explain their points of view. At this meeting, Taylor gave them their opportunity. When all of the agenda items had been covered, the president said that he wanted to review the military actions he was proposing. At that moment, General Taylor, with the foreknowledge of the president, excused himself and indicated that each member of the JCS was free to speak for his particular service. Taylor knew that the members of the JCS favored military action, but when the president finished his discussion, he asked for any rebuttals. There was some discussion but no rebuttals. Taylor would later remark that ''the JCS tigers turned out to be pussycats.'' His actual remark to his staff was that ''all their tiger blood had turned to piss.'' LeMay later claimed that Taylor ''had boxed the situation,'' waiting until all the plans had been formulated before giving the JCS ''a crack at the president.'' LeMay added, ''I wasn't born yesterday. I can spot a setup when I see one.'' Taylor admitted later that in retrospect, it would have been difficult for members of the JCS to speak up at that late hour and in the presence of the secretaries of Defense and State. At meetings with the JCS later that week, when objections were again raised, Taylor told them, ''Well, you had your chance and didn't say a thing.''

At 3:45 P.M., while the National Security Council was still in session, G. Mennen Williams, assistant secretary of state for African affairs, arrived at the White House with A. Milton Obote, the prime minister of Uganda. The prime minister had brought along James

Simpson, his minister of economics; Grace Ibingira, the Ugandan minister of justice; John Kakonge, the secretary-general of Uganda's People Congress; and Apolo Kironde, Uganda's representative-designate to the United Nations. Since economic aid to Uganda was to be a topic of the meeting, Secretary Williams had brought along A. G. Matthews and Edmund Hutchinson, from the U.S. Agency for International Development. After the completion of the National Security Council meeting, they were ushered into the Oval Office, along with Secretary Rusk. Prime Minister Obote and his economic minister began immediately to enunciate the economic problems of emerging Africa. Kennedy listened intently as the discussion then roamed over a broad range of topics. Several times, Rusk attempted to speed up the discussion and expedite the departure of the group. The president, obviously enjoying the discussion, held up the flat of his hand several times as a signal to Rusk that he was aware of his time limitation. Mennen Williams would write later: "The President was very good about seeing African visitors and I can remember the impact on Africa of his breaking up cabinet meetings to see Africans, because I heard the President of Malawi tell his own political leaders of such an incident with great pride and effect."[4]

At 4 P.M., the president was scheduled to meet with his cabinet. When McCone asked if the president would like to have the cabinet briefed by him and Lundahl, the president said no. Mr. McCone also wondered if the president would like to show the cabinet members some of the aerial photos of Cuba. The president replied, "No, it just might confuse the issues." The cabinet was assembled, and the president promptly announced that offensive missiles had been discovered in Cuba and that he would address the nation at 7 P.M. on radio and TV. According to one participant, the president was like a professor counseling his class before an exam, allowing no questions or discussion. Orville Freeman, the secretary of agriculture, remained behind and asked the president if any consideration had been given to prospective food problems if the crisis continued for an extended period. The president replied that it had not been considered. Freeman said his department would be on top of the situation "with detailed plans to move it [food] where needed."[5]

The president remarked later that the cabinet had sat dumbfounded and had not participated. In retrospect, there were many specific questions that should have been raised by the respective cabinet members. But the Kennedy cabinet was not accustomed to being integral to the administration's decision-making process. Although careful consideration had been given to military planning, the administration had given little or no consideration to the impact of an extended crisis on the civilian sector. Walter W. Heller, chairman of the Council of Economic Advisers, had listened attentively to the president at the meeting and subsequently returned to his office and called a meeting of his aides. "I knew that we would have to do some high-pressure work at the Council of Economic Advisers," he said later, "to spell out the economic impacts and policy measures that would have to be taken if the missile crisis were not resolved peacefully. Questions about tax measures, possible shortages and rationing, possible price and wage restraints or controls, and the like had to be explored quickly."[6] As a starting point, he asked his staff to review the planning done in the Berlin crisis of 1961.

There was another event during the crisis that reflected how pertinent thoughts may be sidetracked, how priorities may be perverted, and how great men can get involved in tangential minutiae. A protracted discussion had ensued in the EXCOM as to what the Latin American reaction to the president's forthcoming speech would be. Most of the EXCOM members decided that anti-American feeling would be high, would intensify, and that radical elements in several Latin American countries were of such numbers that serious problems could result. There was fear that pro-Castro and pro-Communist groups would cause extensive disorder if the United States attacked Cuba. These groups, it was believed, had plans for organizing strikes, marches, sabotage, and anti-U.S. demonstrations. It was also feared that demonstrations would erupt at U.S. embassies and that sabotage against U.S. property throughout Latin America would ensue. Concern also was expressed about the safety of U.S. nationals in certain Latin American countries where the intensity of these actions could topple governments.

Roswell Gilpatric knew the military and police forces of a number of Latin American nations would be alerted immediately after the president's speech. There were questions as to whether these forces could handle the anticipated anti-U.S. demonstrations, and Gilpatric reported that the Department of Defense was engaged in an all-out effort to supply these forces with antiriot equipment. The U.S. Army had been tasked to survey U.S. stocks of riot-control equipment. Permission was also granted to the Army to contact any police department of the larger U.S. cities to borrow equipment from them if necessary.

As events unfolded, there were some small demonstrations and some bombings, but the EXCOM fears were largely unfounded. Communist parties and other pro-Castro groups in Latin America were apparently caught unaware and unprepared to respond to the president's action. Moscow, of course, could not give the Communist parties sufficient instructions as to what to do. None of the Latin American governments, it also seemed, had thought out in advance what to do if such a critical situation developed. The populace was more concerned about receiving news of the situation than demonstrating.

The president had summoned congressional leaders to Washington from various parts of the country to apprise them of the Cuban situation. With November elections barely two weeks away, most were out campaigning in their home states. Air Force, Navy, and National Guard planes were dispatched to bring them back to Washington. Senator Thomas H. Kuchel, the minority whip, campaigning at San Diego, California, donned a pressurized flying suit and was rushed to Washington in a jet fighter. He made sure, however, that he was photographed in the suit. Senator Everett Dirksen, the minority leader, along with Republican Leslie C. Arends, the House Republican whip, were flown in from Chicago. House Speaker John W. McCormick, along with Senator Leverett Saltonstall, an assistant leader, and ranking minority members of the Armed Forces Committee were picked up in Boston. Representative Charles Halleck, the House minority leader, who was pheasant hunting in South Dakota, was met in Sioux City, Iowa, along with Senator Bourke R. Hickenlooper, chairman of the Senate Republican Policy Committee; and the same plane stopped in Minneapolis for Senator Hubert Humphrey, the Senate deputy majority leader. Congressman Carl Albert, the House majority leader, who was campaigning in Indiana, was picked up in Indianapolis. Congressman Thomas B. Morgan, chairman of the House Foreign Affairs Committee, was flown in from Pittsburgh. Still other planes brought in Senator J. W. Fulbright, chairman of the Senate Foreign Relations Committee; Senator Alexander Wiley, ranking Republican member of the Foreign Relations Committee; and Congressman Robert Chiperfield, the ranking minority member of the House Foreign Affairs Committee.

Vice-President Johnson and Senator Richard B. Russell, chairman of the Senate Armed Forces Committee, along with Congressman Carl Vinson, chairman of the House Armed Forces Committee, and Senator George A. Smathers, were already in Washington.

Hale Boggs, the Democratic whip, was deep-sea fishing in the Gulf of Mexico. An Air Force plane, after making several warning passes over the boat, dropped a plastic message bottle. The message: "Call Washington—urgent message from president." His boat headed immediately for a nearby oil rig, and Boggs was helicoptered to an airfield, where a two-seat jet trainer was waiting. He struggled into the pressure suit and parachute. He was flown to Andrews Air Force Base, near Washington, and was helicoptered from there to the White House lawn "still smelling of fish," he was later to comment.

The president expected accusations and doubts from the Republicans. He had based his presidential campaign on the theme that the Eisenhower administration had been negligent, that Castro had come to power during that administration. The Kennedy administration's position that Castro had been contained and would soon fall now had little meaning, and Kennedy had to take special precautions that the meeting with the congressmen and senators would not degenerate into political rhetoric. Bobby was to stay away from the White House and from news reporters, since any remark he made could make him a ready target for the Republicans.

At 5 P.M. that Monday afternoon, President Kennedy waited for the congressional leaders in the Cabinet Room. Flanking him at the table were Secretary of State Rusk and Secretary of Defense McNamara. At the far end of the table sat McCone, Cline, and Lundahl. The president was obviously tense, and fumbled nervously with his tie. He was smoking a cigar, unusual for him at these meetings, and he drummed nervously on the table, waiting for everyone to enter. The room was soon packed. All chairs were occupied and people were standing several deep along the walls. The doors were closed.

The president apologized for the inconvenience he had caused the legislators by interrupting their campaigns. He said, however, that the nation was facing an international emergency—offensive missiles capable of striking the United States and Latin America had been discovered in Cuba. Mr. McCone and his briefer would provide the details. He announced that he had ordered Vice-President Johnson and all his cabinet members to cease political activities immediately, and he added that he too would take no further part in the campaign. He then turned the meeting over to McCone.

Mr. McCone made a short statement summarizing the findings that had been presented to the National Security Council earlier in the afternoon and asked Lundahl to show the telltale photographs.

As Lundahl began to unfold the pictures of the MRBM and IRBM launch sites and their ranges, an incredible hush settled over the room. When he remarked that a number of these MRBMs were operational, he heard a number of deep breaths, and everyone looked at the president. The president's eyes were evasive. Lundahl then told of the disposition of Il-28 bombers, the location of the MiG-21 fighter airfields, the cruise missile sites, the SA-2 missile defenses, and the KOMAR guided-missile patrol boats.

When Lundahl had finished his presentation, he felt as if everyone was looking at him "as though I were holding a cobra rather than a pointer in my right hand." The enormity of the threat was being seen and heard for the first time by the congressmen and senators, and they were obviously surprised and angered. Attention then shifted to the president. A great buzzing arose among the group.[7]

The buzzing died down as the president, backed by Rusk and McNamara, explained the plan for the quarantine as the first step in response to the Soviet challenge. The silence was broken by Senator Smathers. He saw an immediate threat to the state of Florida. His antagonistic tone surprised the president. "How long has this been known?" he demanded, implying that the president had withheld information from the Congress and that Senator Keating had been right all along.

Lundahl patiently showed that the buildup had occurred during the period of bad weather in late September and early October and that the first photographic evidence of the offensive missiles being in Cuba had been acquired only a week before. Smathers insisted that the weather in Florida had been nice during this period and implied that it must have also been like that in Cuba. Lundahl explained, as he had to Vice-President Johnson, that many weather factors affect aerial reconnaissance. Visibility factors from an altitude of seventy-thousand feet were far different than one might imagine on the ground. The skies had to be relatively clear of cloud cover, haze, or fog and remain clear for several hours over a relatively large area. Lundahl scanned his audience to see if he had been clear. As he came to the vice-president, the vice-president leaned forward and gave him an unambiguous wink as if to say, We went through that last night, didn't we?

Senator Russell, the powerful chairman of the Senate Armed Services Committee, anger tightening his voice, spoke out against the administration plan and proposed instead an immediate invasion of Cuba. The president gave the senator an agonized glance. What he feared most had started to happen. The president responded that military action had been considered, but that he was against such action because it would mean a confrontation before the Russians had a chance to react to the U.S. challenge. Russell shot back that this was no time for halfway measures. He reminded the president that he had warned Khrushchev on September 4 and again on September 13, and that there had been a joint congressional resolution that the United States would not tolerate an offensive base in Cuba. All the warnings, Russell maintained, had gone unheeded. The Soviets had pressed the U.S. to the wall and it was now time to fight back. The president asked the group to remember that Khrushchev was impulsive. Russell countered that the Russians had actually struck the first blow and that immediate action on the part of the United States would result in fewer casualties in the long run. "I hope for few or no casualties," the president added quickly as he saw Senator Russell's fervor, his cavernous face and hawklike nose prominent under the glaring lights.

As chairman of the Foreign Relations Committee since 1959, Senator William Fulbright regarded himself as an authority on what constituted America's national interest. He joined Senator Russell and also criticized the blockade as a weak step. The president disagreed that stopping Soviet ships was more risky than outright bombing. Fulbright was adamant. "The blockade will not work. It's the worst choice possible. It will bring a confrontation with the Soviets rather than the Cubans. Put the pressure on the Cubans," he insisted. The president had respect for his former colleagues in Congress and he listened intently.

Almost frantically, others joined in the discussion and voiced a number of apprehensions and fears. They had seen the evidence but were puzzled and befuddled by the president's reaction. The cold-blooded threat of these missiles must be met with an equal strength.

The earlier arguments during the week were being repeated. The president sat silent, studying each speaker, then he slumped in his chair, his hands shielding his eyes. Choosing his words carefully, he spoke, his voice devoid of emotion. He had chosen his course of action and he was sticking by it.

Several lawmakers were struck by his humility, a quality that had not been impressed upon them in the past. But this was election year, and Congressman Charles Halleck, a Republican leader in Congress, naturally had to consider the impact of the president's address on the upcoming election. He again asked how long the president had known this information. The president replied that it had been brought to his attention the previous Tuesday morning but, he explained, the full extent of the deployment was not fully known until Friday. Halleck felt that it would have been better if the members of Congress had been informed earlier. The president replied that he had hoped to assemble the lawmakers on Sunday, but because they were out campaigning, it was physically impossible. Halleck said that although he would certainly support the president, he would like to have the record show that he had been informed, not consulted. Speaker McCormick, however, felt that "under the circumstances, I think the legislative leaders were brought in at the right time."[8]

Senator Russell asked, "What are the JCS recommendations?"

Kennedy evaded the question.

"I'll bet they didn't recommend the quarantine."

Kennedy spread his palms wide and upward and lifted his shoulders in a hopeless gesture of resignation and said, "We went through all that last week."

Representative Morgan expressed his full support for the president, that the president should call the bluff of the Russians and stand firm.

Kennedy told them all that if we attacked Cuba, the Russians would probably invade Berlin and that would bring on nuclear war, with each country salvoing missiles. There would be millions of Americans killed. He stated rather forcefully that he would rather exercise his options as planned.

The president explained that the "quarantine" against ships carrying offensive missiles was the best route for two reasons: 1) it would give Khrushchev food for thought; and 2) it would give the U.S. flexibility in implementing alternative measures. The president, however, did not rule out bombing or invasion in consultation with Congress. American military forces had been alerted and were prepared to move should he give the order.

Senator Russell tried another tack: "You're going to have to invade Cuba sooner or later. Do it now and you'll have fewer complications." Whoever advised the president to opt for the blockade, he said, was dead wrong. The senator was sure it had not come from the military.

Kennedy slouched in his chair, in stony silence. All the "cool" that had characterized his handling of the Congress and the press in the past had vanished. His temper and impatience began to rise. Russell could see the president was getting angry, but he pressed on. With his chin thrust forward, he looked squarely at the president and almost disdainfully asked, "You have told us everything, haven't you?"

Congressman Thomas Morgan spoke up. His impression of the missile sites was that they constituted "clear evidence of an intent to establish the capability for an easy nuclear attack on the United States. The photos were very good quality, and made the sites plain to see."[9] He stated his "concern for the nation when these sites are completed for they would constitute an imminent danger to the security of the United States."[10]*

Senator George A. Smathers's immediate impression was that the

---

* Although there was some consternation among the legislative leaders, who were disgruntled at having been brought into the crisis at such a late date, in later years most agreed that it would have been difficult to keep the missile sites secret had the Congress been briefed previously. Senator Leverett Saltonstall would later write to me, "My immediate impression was that the President and our nation had to show that such threats could not be tolerated. I believe that the President took the right steps in connection with the whole Cuban crisis."[11]

situation was dangerous and could become a disaster. War could bring devastation to Florida, yet he supported the president's feeling that the executive has to be in charge of such situations.[12]

Senator Mike Mansfield asked many questions—bold, searching questions designed to assure himself that the president had considered all alternatives. Later that evening, he issued the following statement: "The leadership expressed full support for the president and recognizes that he and he alone had to make the decisions in light of all the information available."

Senator Russell, still perturbed with the speed of the Soviet buildup, asked Lundahl if it could have been possible to detect the buildup on photography before October 14. Lundahl replied that he was sure we would have detected the missiles had we had coverage of Cuba's interior.

Senator Dirksen said the president could count on his support. Later that evening, the Republican leaders who had attended the meeting issued the following statement: "We Republican leaders met today at the White House at the urgent request of the president. We listened to a report of the Central Intelligence Agency, the secretary of State and Defense; we were told of the unanimous report of the National Security Council and the Joint Chiefs of Staff; were informed by the president of his already determined course of action, which he later stated in his broadcast for all the world to hear. Americans will support the president on the decision or decisions he makes for the security of our country. The president has asked the leadership to stay in Washington for further consultation, and we will do so."

Lundahl noted that Senator Wiley, at the advanced age of seventy-eight, was having great difficulty understanding the intelligence evidence and the policy being enunciated. Finally getting the president's attention, he said, almost naively, "Now, I think we ought to tell the Russians that they should not do a thing like that." The president paused momentarily and looked patiently at this fine old gentleman who had served his country so well. Instead of being brusque, he answered in a slow, understanding fashion: "We've told them all these things, but they ignored us. And now we must do something else." It was an admirable trait of the president to be brittle, crisp, and full of spontaneous humor in one instance but equally gentle and considerate to age and infirmity in another. Patting Senator Wiley on the hand, President Kennedy announced that he had to leave to get ready for his speech to the nation. He stood up and said he was going to the family quarters to change.

Senator Russell took a last vindictive shot at the departing Kennedy. "When there is a cancer," he said, "the only solution is to surgically remove it. It won't go away." The president gave a shudder, half deliberate, half involuntary. Senator Russell continued, "You've gotten some good advice here tonight, you had better consider it." The president shrugged his shoulders again and lifted his hands questioningly; everyone noticed the pained look on his face. The president's voice was nearly brusque when he said he positively had to leave and began to move toward the door.

Senator Hubert Humphrey looked at Kennedy's tormented face and rose. Humphrey knew Kennedy, knew the president was angry and that he must find some pretext to talk to him before his speech and calm and reassure him. He moved quickly toward the president and, placing his hand on Kennedy's shoulder, expressed his support. The president said that if he had known the presidency would be so rough, he would have let Humphrey beat him in West Virginia. Humphrey replied, "I let you beat me because I knew it was tough." They both smiled.

The president had made no compromises and hoped he had generated no irretrievable animosities, but he was hurt and disappointed by the adverse congressional reaction to his plan. Sorensen was waiting impatiently at the door. As the president reached him, he said contemptuously, "If they think this office is a prize, they can have it."

The president had left McCone and Lundahl with the congressmen and senators. It was now 6:33 P.M. Groups of congressmen and senators were still talking, their voices loud and angry because Kennedy had left them uneasy. Others made their way out the doors to waiting limousines. Still others approached Lundahl, seeking more details from the aerial photos.

Returning from the White House briefing, Congressman Charles A. Halleck said to an aide, "You remember my prediction a month ago? I said he'll pull the rug from under the Republicans on the Cuba issue. Well, that's what he's done."[13]

Soviet ambassador Dobrynin had been asked to meet with Rusk at the State Department at 6 P.M. that evening. Arriving a few minutes early, Dobrynin evaded reporters' questions and hurried to Rusk's office. Rusk handed Dobrynin a copy of the president's speech, which was also being transmitted to U.S. Ambassador Foy Kohler in Moscow, for presentation to the Soviet Foreign Ministry. As Dobrynin read the speech, perspiration appeared on his forehead. Dobrynin obviously realized that his superiors in Moscow had completely misread the mood of the U.S. president and the American government and the speed with which Americans can be brought together in unified support of national interests. Dobrynin peered at Rusk, stating that he had not been made aware of the events in question and paused as though hoping for further information from Rusk. The secretary of state said that the president planned to outline his course of action on national television within the hour. Dobrynin peremptorily left Rusk's office, charged past waiting reporters, and returned to the Soviet embassy.

At 6:30 P.M. on October 22, Admiral Anderson formally requested Canadian and British navies to assist in reporting the positions of Soviet merchant ships and submarines. There had always been excellent cooperation among the Canadian, British, and U.S. naval intelligence reporting systems. Anderson also solicited the cooperation of Latin American navies. Messages were sent to the chiefs of naval operations of Chile, Brazil, Colombia, Ecuador, Argentina, Uruguay, and Peru. Later in the crisis, Argentina dispatched two destroyers, as did Venezuela and the Dominican Republic; these six destroyers plus the U.S. destroyer *Mullinnix* comprised Task Force 137, commanded by Admiral John A. Tyree. Brazil replied that it, too, would participate with destroyer patrols off its own coast.

Just before the president went on the air at 7 P.M., twenty-two U.S. jet fighters scrambled into the evening sky from bases in Florida. This action was termed an airborne alert by the Joint Chiefs of Staff—a precautionary measure "in the event of a rash action by the Cubans."

Promptly at 7 P.M., the president personally took charge of the crisis and initiated steps to force a Soviet retreat from Cuba and the Western Hemisphere. Addressing the nation from the Oval Office, he stated that the recent acquisition of "unmistakable evidence" revealed that a series of offensive missile sites were being prepared in Cuba; that "several" were for MRBMs and that others were apparently for IRBMs. This "urgent transformation of Cuba into an important strategic base," the president said, was an explicit threat to the peace and security of the Americas. This capability had been created in spite of "repeated assurances" by responsible Soviet spokesmen that the buildup in Cuba had been of a "defensive character." Moreover, these offensive weapons were introduced in spite of his warnings of September 4 and September 13. He quoted from the Soviet government's statement of September 11, which declared that the weapons were "designed exclusively for defensive purposes" and that there was "no need" to send offensive weapons to Cuba.

The president specifically directed his anger toward Soviet foreign minister Gromyko—that Gromyko on October 18 in the president's own office had stated that the weapons being sent to Cuba were "solely for the purpose of contributing to the defense capability of Cuba." He quoted Gromyko's assurance with regard to offensive weapons that the Soviet Union "would never become involved in rendering such assistance." The president characterized all these statements as false and described the missile buildup as a "deliberately provocative and unjustified change in the status quo which cannot be accepted by this country." He was determined to secure the "withdrawal or elimination" of the missiles and announced his immediate course of action. A "strict quarantine" was being imposed on all offensive military equipment under shipment to Cuba. He warned the Soviets that in the event of "continued offensive military preparations," further action would be justified. The Soviets were further warned that "any nuclear missile launched from Cuba" against any nation in the Western Hemisphere would be regarded as a Soviet attack on the United States and would provoke a "full retaliatory" response against the USSR. The president realized he had set a "difficult and dangerous" course and alluded that "many months of sacrifice and self-discipline lie ahead," in which "both our will and our patience will be tested."

The president could only have been pleased with U.S. public reaction to his speech—that the public was behind him in his endeavor to achieve an agreed-upon long-term solution to the Cuba problem, by war if necessary. His arguments gave the entire Western world direction, cohesion, and purpose.

When the president was speaking, A. Milton Obote, the prime minister of Uganda, watched him on television at the Blair House. He said with great feeling that he was impressed that the president of the United States had taken forty-five minutes out of a busy schedule earlier that day to talk with the leader of a small and internationally insignificant African country; to discuss that country's problems when the president was faced with the gravest of decisions on matters vitally affecting the security of the United States. He went on to say that he took the president's concern as evidence of the depth and sincerity Mr. Kennedy had for the problems of Africa and other underdeveloped countries.[14]

Khrushchev predictably regarded the president's speech as an ultimatum. It was not explicit at the time it was delivered, but it would become so on October 27. The president had not set a time limit for compliance; he had spoken of "months of patience." He also had not threatened any specific punishment for noncompliance—but it was implied.

The president went back to his quarters after the address but returned to the Oval Office at 7:44 P.M. McGeorge Bundy had left the following note: "Mr. President: The one thing I left out of the message to the Prime Minister [Macmillan] is that if the Soviet nuclear build-up in Cuba continues, it would be a threat to the whole strategic balance of power, because really large numbers of missiles from this launch could create a first-strike temptation. Any such shift in the balance would be just as damaging to our allies as to us. The missiles that are there now do not create this hazard but a further build-up would. This is probably the most important single justification of our action from the point of view of the future of the west as a whole."[15]

At NPIC, there was continued processing of U-2 missions that day, and a series of briefing boards were made to be used that night to inform a number of U.S. and foreign dignitaries. At the State Department at 7:30 P.M., Edwin M. Martin, assistant secretary for Latin American affairs, and U. Alexis Johnson, deputy undersecretary of state, briefed the ambassadors from the Organization of American States. At the Pentagon, Major General Robert A. Breitweiser, assistant chief of staff for intelligence in the Department of the Air Force, briefed the army, navy, and air attachés of the Organization of American States, along with the attachés from the NATO nations. At 8 P.M., Dean Rusk and Roger Hilsman briefed the ambassadors from neutral and nonaligned nations.

Secretary McNamara and Abram Chayes informed the press at the Pentagon that night on the legal aspects of the quarantine, emphasizing the distinction between a quarantine and a blockade. Chayes said that while a quarantine may have some elements of a blockade, blockade usually connotes an act of war; a quarantine was not an act of war. The quarantine, in this case, was applied as a purely defensive, not offensive, measure. After all of the questions pertaining to the quarantine were answered, the press demanded to see the evidence of the MRBM missiles in Cuba. A number of briefing boards were brought out, and the press was shown (off the record) for the first time the details seen on the aerial photography.

While pointing out the slash marks characteristic of IRBM sites, McNamara pointed out details: "As you can imagine, photo interpreters working on literally thousands of feet of film trying to pick this kind of a situation out—here are some more scars over here, and you try to examine the landscape of Cuba and separate this type of scar from this type of scar—it is a tremendous task. And they have been working twenty-four hours a day since that time on this tremendous mass of material to try to sort out the probable from the improbable. And it is based on that very, very thorough analysis by literally hundreds during this week that we arrived at these conclusions. And I might say we have satisfied ourselves personally that the conclusions that you were informed of tonight were correct."[16] While the press was convinced of the data derived from the aerial photos, they were told not to photograph the briefing boards. When asked when and if they might be released, McNamara said that might be possible at a later date.

At 7 P.M. Washington time on October 22, the Pentagon placed the entire U.S. military establishment on Defcon 3 (defense condition), an increased state of alert. The greatest mobilization since World War II was under way. SAC B-47 bombers were dispersed, according to plan, to over thirty predesignated civilian airfields in the United States. At two SAC bases in Spain, three in Morocco, and three in England, B-47's were loaded with nuclear weapons and given preflight inspections by their crews.

Simultaneously, a massive airborne alert was begun by U.S.-based B-52 bombers and KC-135 tankers. The bombers were loaded with nuclear weapons. Most communications from headquarters to the bombers were in the clear, as were those from the bombers to headquarters. The Soviets would learn—if they did not already know—that in a crisis, the Strategic Air Command carried a powerful, resounding signal from the United States. The alert lasted for thirty days of continuous flight operations—2,088 sorties in 48,532 continuous hours of flying time, in which 20,022,000 miles were flown without a fatality. Over 70 million gallons of fuel were transferred in flight by KC-135 tankers.

In addition to the B-47 and B-52 bombers, fighter bombers at U.S. bases in England, France, Italy, Turkey, Germany, South Korea, Japan, and the Philippines were also placed on alert and armed with ordnance, including nuclear, for striking targets in the Soviet Union or Eastern Europe.

There were three ICBM systems in the SAC inventory at the time: the Atlas, the Titan I, and the Titan II. A fourth, the solid-fuel Minuteman, would enter the inventory during the late days of the crisis. The Atlas missiles were deployed in so-called coffin configurations. The missile lay in its huge concrete coffin, topped by a four hundred-ton concrete-and-steel door. When the launch order is given, the door is drawn back, the missile is lifted, fueled, and readied for firing. Atlas missiles were deployed in ten complexes extending from New York to California. The Titan I system was deployed in silos but had to be elevated to the surface for firing. The Titans were deployed in five scattered complexes in Colorado, South Dakota, Idaho, Washington, and California. The Titan II system was fueled and stored in deep underground silos and could be fired from within the silos. There were three Titan II complexes, one each in Kansas, Arkansas, and Arizona.

McNamara received word from General LeMay late that evening that ninety-one Atlas and forty-one Titan missiles were being readied for firing.

Several U.S. Polaris missile-firing submarines left their base at Holy Loch, Scotland, and took up stations with other Polaris submarines in the North Atlantic. The United States had submarines at sea loaded with sufficient nuclear missiles to wipe out all of Russia's principal cities.

Matador and Mace cruise missiles deployed in tactical missile wings brought to a combat-alert status in West Germany were capable of striking military targets throughout East European countries. Aircraft carriers in the Mediterranean and in the Pacific, under Defcon 1, were prepared to assume general quarters. With so much at the ready, it was mandatory that the president maintain a steady finger on the nuclear trigger throughout the crisis. He knew, of course, that airborne SAC bombers carrying nuclear weapons were dispatched to predetermined points to await instructions whether to proceed to the designated targets in the Soviet Union or be recalled. Once the order was given to launch the land-based liquid-fueled ICBMs, he would only have moments to decide whether to stop the countdown. Even more difficult was the case of submarine-launched Polaris missiles: Once the order was given, there could be no recall.*

U.S. Department of Defense officials urged effecting a NATO alert during the course of the crisis. Prime Minister Macmillan was violently opposed and so informed General Lauris Norstad, NATO's supreme Allied commander. Macmillan said that mobilization had, at times, caused war. He also stated that a NATO alert would mean the call-up of British and other nations' reservists and he was strongly opposed to such action.†

---

* President Kennedy had visited the Navy's CINCLANT headquarters on April 19, 1962, and Admiral Robert Lee Dennison made sure that the president understood this fact. According to Admiral Dennison, the president was briefed in depth on Polaris firing procedures. Dennison asked if the president had any questions. "He didn't say anything and there was an appreciable pause, which seemed like a long time which was maybe six or seven or eight seconds. Finally he said, 'Can those missiles be stopped?' I said, 'No, sir.' These submarines are reeling in their underwater antennas, the countdown has started and there's no way to stop them." Dennison added, "I don't know whether he liked it or not, but I've wondered often what he was thinking about, what could happen in a matter of a few seconds—not half an hour or fifteen minutes for him to think about countermanding an order to shoot."[17]

† French armed forces, on October 25, were put on number-two alert, the final stage before general mobilization. Foreign Minister Couve de Murville, however, did not believe there would be any Soviet reaction with respect to Berlin.

The U-2 Era

1. The Lockheed U-2, with an 80-foot wing span, flew at over 70,000 feet and gathered not only information on Soviet strategic capabilities, but also data required in crisis situations.

2. Interpretation of U-2 photos of Soviet long-range bomber fields—revealing details and numbers of bombers—proved that the bomber gap was a myth.

3. U-2 photographs of the Soviet missile launch facilities at Tyura Tam, along with coverage of rail and road networks, also revealed that the missile gap didn't exist.

4. Arthur C. Lundahl, the brilliant director of the National Photographic Interpretation Center (NPIC), whose foresight, insight, and direction provided policy makers with current and irrefutable information.

Soviet Weapons to Cuba

5

6

5. Throughout the summer of 1962, U.S. intelligence agencies maintained close surveillance over the heavy volume of Russian shipping exiting the Baltic and Bosporus bound for Cuba.

6. ''Cratology,'' the intelligence technique for identifying deck cargos, was applied to photography of Soviet shipping en route to Cuba. These crates contain KOMAR guided-missile patrol boats.

7. The emerging picture of the military buildup in Cuba particularly worried John A. McCone, director of the Central Intelligence Agency. He increased U-2 overflights, concerned that the Soviets might introduce offensive weapons into Cuba.

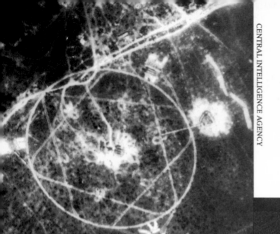

CENTRAL INTELLIGENCE AGENCY

Deployed Advanced Weapons

8

8. The first photographic proof of surface-to-air missile (SAM) deployment in Cuba was obtained on August 29, 1962. The SA-2 site's "signature" is its unique Star of David pattern.

9

CENTRAL INTELLIGENCE AGENCY

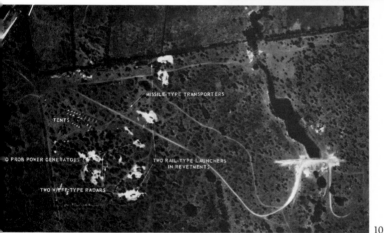

MISSILE-TYPE TRANSPORTERS

TENTS

O PROB POWER GENERATORS

TWO RAIL-TYPE LAUNCHERS IN REVETMENTS

TWO WIFFE-TYPE RADARS

10

U.S. AIR FORCE

9. That mission also confirmed seven KOMAR guided-missile patrol boats in the naval port of Mariel, twenty-seven miles west-southwest of Havana.

10. The combined efforts of intelligence analysts and NPIC photo interpreters finally identified a cruise-missile launch site near Banes in Oriente province, but not before incurring the president's displeasure.

11. From the missile site, a MiG-like cruise missile, similar to the Kennel air-to-air missile carried by Soviet bombers, could be launched against invading forces.

DEPARTMENT OF DEFENSE

11

Discovery of Offensive Missiles

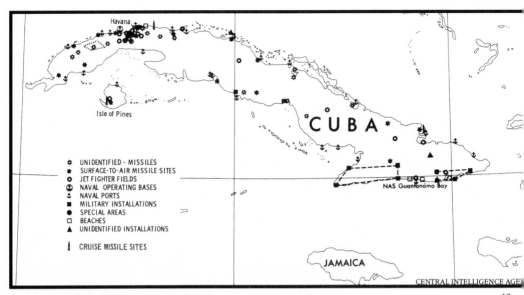

UNIDENTIFIED – MISSILES
SURFACE-TO-AIR MISSILE SITES
JET FIGHTER FIELDS
NAVAL OPERATING BASES
NAVAL PORTS
MILITARY INSTALLATIONS
SPECIAL AREAS
BEACHES
UNIDENTIFIED INSTALLATIONS

CRUISE MISSILE SITES

CENTRAL INTELLIGENCE AGE[NCY]

12

12. Intelligence objectives on October 5, 1962. Note the trapezoidal area in western Cuba identified by a CIA agent in Cuba as a possible area of missile-related activity and where the offensive missile sites were later discovered.

13

14

13. The first medium-range ballistic missile (MRBM) site found on the October 14 U-2 mission. A convoy is shown arriving at the site. Six MRBM transporters are present.

14. The second MRBM site, also found on that mission, was further along than the first, with erector/launchers in place and eight missile transporters nearby.

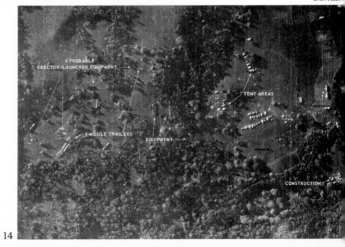

U.S. AIR

15. The SS-4 SANDAL MRBM on parade in Moscow. It could launch a three-megaton warhead to an estimated range of 1,020 nautical miles. 15

16. On Monday morning, October 15, a team of photo interpreters assigned to NPIC representing the Army, Navy, Air Force, and CIA made the crucial findings that would ultimately demand the attention of the world. Pictured are Lt. Richard Reninger, Joseph L. Sullivan, James P. Holmes, and Vincent N. DiRenzo. 16

17. When Bobby Kennedy first saw the photos of the missile sites, he asked humorously, "Will those damn things hit Oxford?" (a reference to the difficulties the Kennedys were having with the University of Mississippi). NPIC went along with the gag and placed Oxford in the same bold type as the principal southern cities on maps showing missile ranges.

18. The United States Intelligence Board (USIB) met daily to review the latest intelligence reports. They approved intelligence estimates and answered questions posed by the Executive Committee (EXCOM) of the National Security Council and the president.

19. The president learned of the offensive missiles on October 16. Two days later, Foreign Minister Gromyko (center) lied to Kennedy when he assured him that Soviet assistance was solely for the defense of Cuba. Note Kennedy's expression and an animated Gromyko. The president later referred to the foreign minister as "that lying bastard."

17

18

19

Discussions and Deliberations

20. The EXCOM received all source intelligence reports and recommended options for various courses of action to the president. Note an easel near the fireplace where the latest reconnaissance photography was displayed at each meeting.

20

21. A restless Bobby Kennedy at an EXCOM meeting. The president is at the right standing with Dean Rusk. Vice President Johnson is seated across from them.

21

Further Surprises

22

22. When the president demanded that Cuba be completely covered by U-2 photography, four additional MRBM sites were found, as well as three intermediate-range ballistic missile (IRBM) sites under construction. The IRBM sites are characterized by the slash-mark construction of the launch pads.

23. Also identified were four mobile combat groups geographically located to provide defense for construction. The precise positioning of the tents and the arrangement of the latest military equipment led interpreters to believe these were Soviet combat troops.

24. The Soviets later did not hide the fact that these were combat units. At one garrison, flagstones and flowers proudly displayed insignia symbols of Soviet units.

24

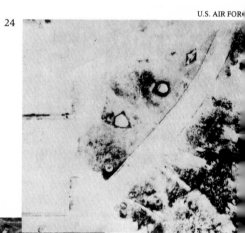

PROB MORTARS

AAA SITE

PROB. TANKS

AAA SITE

23

25

President Kennedy Returns to Washington

25. These new findings prompted the president to cancel his campaign trip to Chicago and head back to Washington. Reporters were told the president was suffering from a cold.

26. The Cuban missile crisis was made public by President Kennedy in a nationally televised address at 7 P.M. on Monday, October 22.

26

Low-Altitude Reconnaissance Begins

27

U.S. AIR FORCE

U.S. AIR FORCE

CHERRY PICKER

LAUNCH PAD WITH ERECTOR

LAUNCH PAD WITH ERECTOR

MISSILE READY BLDGS

OXIDIZER VEHICLES

FUELING VEHICLES

27. Low-altitude reconnaissance flights maintained close surveillance of Soviet activity on the island. The exposed film was rushed from the aircraft, processed, and then hurried to NPIC for analysis.

28. The low-altitude imagery added a new dimension to NPIC's reporting, allowing detailed and pinpoint analysis of military activity.

29. On October 23, in an unprecedented display of hemisphere solidarity, the Organization of American States (OAS) approved the U.S. quarantine. Only Uruguay abstained.

29

28

BOLIVIA

RASIL

COSTA R

30

33

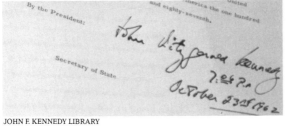

By the President:

Secretary of State

31

32

30. At 7:03 P.M. on October 23, the president signed the quarantine proclamation, "Interdiction of the Delivery of Offensive Weapons to Cuba."

31. He used his full name, John Fitzgerald Kennedy, rather than the usual John F. Kennedy.

32. The U.S. Navy's antisubmarine forces maintained a close vigil on four Soviet W-class submarines in the Atlantic.

33. On the deck of the *Poltava*, two uniquely configured trucks carrying IRBM launch rings were identified.

34. On Friday, October 26, the U.S. destroyers *Joseph P. Kennedy, Jr.*, and *John R. Pierce* stopped, boarded, and inspected the *Marcula*, a dry-cargo ship of neutral registry sailing under Soviet charter to Cuba.

34

35

The Crisis Heightens

35. On Thursday evening, October 25, in response to a challenge by Soviet Ambassador Zorin, Adlai Stevenson, the U.S. ambassador to the UN, presented to the Security Council the hard photographic evidence of Russian deployment of MRBMs and IRBMs in Cuba. Col. David S. Parker, deputy director of the NPIC, points out the photos while Stevenson describes them.

37

36. Two days later, at the height of the crisis, U.S. Air Force Major Rudolf Anderson, Jr., piloting a U-2, was brought down by a Soviet SA-2 surface-to-air missile.

37. That afternoon, low-altitude pilots reported that they were being fired on by Cuban anti-aircraft weapons. Soldiers can be seen running to their guns in a photo taken that day.

36

38

38. All of the MRBM sites were now considered capable of launching missiles at the U.S. within six to eight hours after command. At the San Cristobal MRBM Site No. 1, five MRBMs on transporters are apparent along with a missile ready tent. Fueling and checkout vehicles are positioned nearby.

UNCRATED FUSELAGE AND TAIL SECTION

BEAGLES BEING ASSEMBLED

39

39. The assembly of Il-28 Beagle light jet bombers was also continuing.

40. The climax of the crisis came after an ultimatum was given to the Soviets that the missiles had to be removed. The U.S. Air Force and U.S. Navy were prepared to strike Soviet bases in Cuba, and the U.S. Army and U.S. Marines were positioned to invade the island.

40

41

The Nuclear Warhead Base,
Bunkers, and Vans

41. The nuclear warhead processing base at the west end of the Mariel airfield. Warheads brought by ships in special containers were unpacked and checked at this facility, then transported to the missile sites in nuclear warhead storage vans.

42. Nuclear warhead bunkers were under construction at each of the MRBM and IRBM sites. Prefabricated concrete materials were brought from Russia.

42

PREFABRICATION MATERIALS

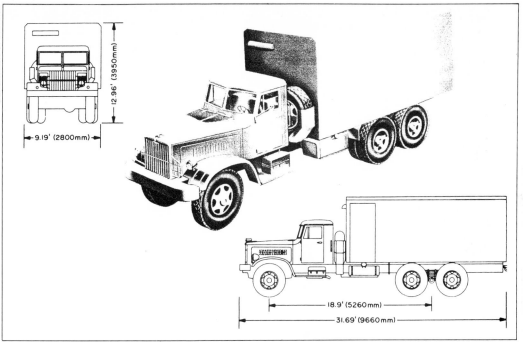

12.96' (3950 mm)

9.19' (2800 mm)

18.9' (5260 mm)

31.69' (9660 mm)

43. Details on the nuclear warhead storage vans, which were seen both at the Mariel facility and parked near the nuclear warhead storage bunkers.

43

44. Nuclear warhead storage vans at the port of Mariel awaiting loading and shipment back to Russia.

44

5 NOVEMBER 1962
MARIEL PORT

ERECTOR

3 MISSILE TRANSPORTERS

6 MISSILE TRANSPORTERS

OXIDIZER TRAILER

MISSILE TRANSPORTERS

PROB IRBM
PROPELLANT TRAILERS

OXIDIZER TRAILERS

PIC H-D148 (11/62)

6 MISSILE TRANSPORTERS

TRUCK

TRUCK CRANE

TRUCK

45

Missile Removal and Inspection at Sea

45. The MRBMs were hurriedly loaded as deck cargo. Six MRBMs can be seen aboard this Soviet freighter along with the loading of Soviet military personnel. (Note shadow of RF-101 reconnaissance jet taking the photograph.)

46. Inspections were also made at sea. Four missiles can be seen aboard the Soviet freighter *Volgoles,* bound for the Soviet Union.

46

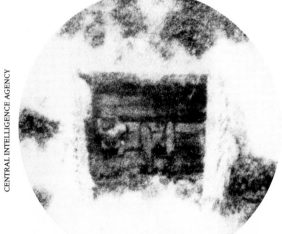

But There Were Moments of Humor

47. President Kennedy detested military jargon—particularly the reporting of MRBM launch positions as "occupied" (with launchers) and "unoccupied." A low-flying reconnaissance plane happened to photograph a soldier using an open three-hole latrine. When the photo was shown to the president as one "occupied," he laughed and asked why he didn't have this primer earlier.

47

· · ·

The U.S. Navy had been ordered to be prepared to conduct low-altitude aerial reconnaissance photo missions over Cuba and, on October 19, Light Photographic Squadron No. 62 had deployed sixteen Vaught Crusader aircraft to the Boca Chica Naval Air Station, outside Key West, Florida. But Washington planners still wanted firsthand verification of the Navy's ability to conduct the sustained low-level reconnaissance of Cuba that was required. Captain Edward Johnson, director of the Photographic Division in the Navy's Bureau of Weapons, along with Lieutenant Commander Whitney Wittrock, of the chief of naval operations Office of Photo and Reconnaissance, flew to Jacksonville to see Commander Robert A. Koch, executive officer of VFP-62, who was an expert on photo reconnaissance. Koch, nicknamed Daddy Photo, was a hard-nosed, driven individual who always demanded the best of his men and equipment. Captain Johnson asked if the squadron was prepared with men, machines, and materials to handle sustained high-speed low-level reconnaissance. He was concerned not only with conducting the reconnaissance but also with processing the photography at Jacksonville and rushing it to Washington. Koch informed the visitors of problems encountered in mounting the KA-45 and KA-46 cameras in the Crusader aircraft, and that he was also in dire need of some high-speed film-processing equipment—the Eastman-Kodak Versamats that he had requested so many times before. Koch assured the visitors, however, that VFP-62 had great aircraft, outstanding pilots and maintenance personnel, a fine technical team, and that the fleet photographic laboratory was a first-rate processing facility.

The chief of the photographic laboratory, Lieutenant Commander Gerry P. Pulley, was no stranger to photo processing. During the Truman administration, he was the official Navy photographer attached to the White House. Pulley supported Koch's demand for the high-speed processors, and by the middle of that week, two of them arrived from the NAVPIC in Washington.

Still anxious to make certain that the naval aviators cover the targets properly, the Joint Reconnaissance Center asked that a senior aviator be ordered to report to Washington immediately. Lieutenant

Commander Tad Riley flew to Andrews Air Force Base and was provided copies of U-2 photos of the various Cuban missile sites, along with special aeronautical and navigational charts showing the primary target areas.

On the evening of October 22, Captain Ted Dankworth of the Joint Reconnaissance Center met with Koch, Lieutenant Commander Tad Riley, and Lieutenant Junior Grade Kortge. Dankworth discussed the tactics that were to be employed, altitudes to be flown, and the results that were expected. That evening, orders also were received to prepare additional Crusader aircraft for possible deployment on carriers. Koch acknowledged that the barrel had been scraped for cameras, control systems, and crews. Not all of the Crusaders were equipped with the KA-45 and KA-46 cameras. They had been factory-equipped with Fairchild cameras, which had to be removed, and the KA-45's and KA-46's were literally shoe-horned into the camera bays. An all-out effort was made to equip as many Crusaders as possible with the newer cameras. The new camera mounts had to be custom-made and -fitted. There was no time to wait for the Bureau of Weapons to purchase the new mounts. The ingenuity of VFP-62 was exercised and camera mounts were custom-designed in Lieutenant Cecil Ogles's garage and fabricated by the VFP-62 camera repair shop.

The Navy had found through experience that high-speed low-level reconnaissance could be best performed with two aircraft working closely together. The lead aircraft would have a veteran pilot who was also an experienced navigator and pathfinder. The second aircraft, with a junior officer as pilot, would follow about 0.5 miles behind and about 0.25 miles to one side of the lead aircraft. The second aircraft would then maneuver as necessary to capture targets or objects that the lead pilot might have missed.

VFP-62 was prepared to launch six aircraft per mission, flying three separate flight tracks, two aircraft per track. Each aircraft had five cameras: a forward-firing KA-46, three tri-metrigon cameras providing horizon-to-horizon coverage, and a vertical KA-45. There was approximately 100 feet of film in each camera; some 3,000 feet would therefore be exposed by the six aircraft. The commanding officer of the squadron, Commander William B. Ecker, along with LCDR Tad T. Riley, LCDR James A. Kauflin, Lt. Gerald Coffee, Lt. Bruce Wilhelmy, and Lt. JG John Hewitt, were tapped to fly the first low-level mission over Cuba. They were briefed on their penetration and exit points, checkpoints, targets, and possible opposition. Communication and electronic procedures were also reviewed as well as escape and evasion.[18]

Fifteen minutes before the president's October 22 address, the nation's railroads were also put on the alert. The Pentagon asked the Association of American Railroads for 375 flatcars immediately to move air-defense and air-warning units to Florida. Later, the Pentagon would ask for 3,600 flatcars, 180 gondola cars, 40 boxcars, and 200 passenger coaches to move the 1st Armored Division from Texas to Georgia.[19] Television crews filmed the trains as they passed by cities along the routes. President Kennedy asked General Taylor if the move could be accomplished without attracting so much attention. It was almost impossible. Major General I. Sewell Morris, commander of the Defense Traffic Management Service, had told Taylor that the extraordinary demand for flat- and boxcars was close to bringing other Southwest rail traffic to a standstill. General Taylor said that the president was really not cognizant of what was required to move modern armies.

Admiral Ward informed Admiral Dennison that over 150 naval vessels were on station, forming an arc around Cuba to enforce the quarantine when it was announced. Forty-six of the 150 ships, along with 250 aircraft and some 30,000 men, were directly engaged in locating ships inbound or outbound from Cuba.

In Florida, 156 aircraft were ready to immediately strike targets in Cuba. If called upon, the Air Force and the Navy were prepared to conduct continuous air strikes until the missiles and the Cuban Air Force had been destroyed. It was estimated that a total of 1,190 sorties could be flown the first day.

On that evening of October 22, Colonel Oleg Penkovsky was in an isolated cell in Moscow, having been arrested by Soviet authorities. He was being interrogated by the KGB.[20] It was presumed that he was later executed. That evening, too, the U.S. Department of State in an "All Diplomatic and Consular Posts" cable warned: "It is very likely there will be a showdown on the quarantine inasmuch as we'll soon know whether the Soviets agree to respect it or not. We are going to stop all ships—Soviet and Allied—if they carry arms or munitions."[21]

In Berlin, the U.S. Army garrison, often referred to as the Berlin Brigade, consisted of some 4,000 officers and men. Duty with the brigade was considered a prestige assignment, and although the brigade was largely a "showpiece" unit participating in ceremonial affairs, the troops were fully combat trained. While combat against the onslaught of Soviet armor would have been futile, the U.S. troops were expected to employ delaying tactics. The Soviets knew, however, that an attack on Berlin would be an act of war that would bring swift retaliation from the United States. The garrison went on combat alert immediately after the president's address to the nation.

16

October 23–Quarantine: "Interdiction of the Delivery of Offensive Missiles to Cuba"

"We will at all times be ready to talk, if talk will help. But we must also be ready to resist with force, if force is used upon us. Either alone would fail. Together, they can serve the cause of freedom and peace."

—PRESIDENT KENNEDY

ABOUT 7 A.M., pilots from Light Photographic Squadron No. 62 manned their assigned aircraft at Boca Chica Naval Air Station. The pride of the squadron was evident in the condition of the aircraft and the efficiency of the ground crews. Each airplane had been checked out several times and the cameras had been loaded with film and prepared for activation. The pilots were strapped in their planes, ground checks accomplished, the chocks removed and Commander Ecker's aircraft moved out onto the taxiway. As each aircraft was launched, the ground crews began the apprehensive vigil that only ground-crew members experience. By the time coffee was brought to the flight ramp for the ground crews, the Crusaders were traveling at treetop level and at near sonic speeds, racing over cane-fields and ranchlands to the missile sites. The navigation was superb; all three flights had brought the reconnaissance aircraft over the target centers of the missile sites, and the cameras had functioned perfectly. On their way back, the pilots jotted notes on military activity observed at predesignated targets.

Admiral J. F. Carson, commander of Fleet Air Jacksonville, waited for the Crusaders to return from their first reconnaissance mission over Cuba. The first Crusader, No. 923, landed at the naval air station at Jacksonville and taxied to the flight line. When the aircraft stopped, there was an immediate flurry of activity as photographer mates unloaded the film magazines and rushed to the nearby Fleet Air Photo Laboratory. The activity inside the lab was just as intense as that on the flight line. The film was placed in the processors and within minutes the first negatives were finished. Koch, the principal photo officer of the squadron, carefully inspected the negatives: "They're beauties," he said. "Run the duplicate positives and let's get them to Washington."

Simultaneously, Admiral Carson and squadron intelligence officers busied themselves debriefing the pilots about their observations of targets and the mission. Of special concern were any defenses encountered. The pilots reported they had encountered no flak or small-arms fire.

As the flight crews were busy fueling and preparing the aircraft for another mission and photographer mates were reloading the cameras, a young enlisted man on the flight line decided that each mission should be recorded on the side of the aircraft. He made a stencil depicting a dead hanging chicken, the chicken an obvious reference to Castro's chicken episode at the UN and Washington. (Castro and his entourage cooked chicken in their hotel rooms, much to the consternation and disgust of hotel managers.) He began stenciling them on the side of each aircraft. It became a ritual for the pilot when he opened the canopy after each mission to call out, "Chalk up another chicken."

The Joint Chiefs of Staff wanted a firsthand report of the mission, and Commander Ecker was ordered to fly to Washington. He landed at Andrews Air Force Base and, still in his flying suit, was rushed to the Pentagon. He apologized for his appearance when he was ushered into the Joint Chiefs of Staff conference room. General LeMay said that he never would question anyone about his appearance when he is in a sweaty flying suit. The Joint Chiefs queried the commander about the mission and asked if any anti-aircraft fire had been seen. Ecker proudly reported that the mission was "a piece of cake."

The low-altitude photography added a new dimension to NPIC reporting. Each piece of equipment could be identified precisely, specific nomenclatures assigned, and its function in the missile system determined—launchers, transporters, generators, cranes, decontamination shower units, air compressors, shop trailers, oxidizer and fuel transporters. The briefing boards became more informative and annotations more detailed, and policymakers now could see clearly what was difficult to discern in the U-2 photos. There was no longer any doubt about the missiles or any other piece of military hardware that was being reported. Repetitive coverage also enabled interpreters to derive details of Soviet field operating procedures from the photography. All of the missions produced spectacular photography. When the interpreted photo enlargements were shown to the president by Lundahl, he could not believe that airplanes flying so low and so fast could accurately acquire such detailed images.

On the home front, Americans flocked to the department stores that morning of October 23 and bought up items they thought might be in short supply. Housewives headed for supermarkets and loaded up on food and drinks. There was panic buying of tires and automobiles. Refrigerators, television sets, and dishwashers were being purchased in huge quantities. Many filling stations reported runs on gasoline, some customers coming with 55-gallon drums to be filled. Prices on Wall Street—and on the stock exchanges in London and Canada—fell sharply. Firms that built atomic shelters were swamped with orders.

In *The New York Times* that day, James Reston, in a few concise words, captured the essence of the crisis: "It is now fairly obvious that Nikita Khrushchev, in planning Soviet policy on Cuba, misjudged the spirit of America and the character of President Kennedy. This is a common European habit, reaching from George III of Great Britain to Adolf Hitler, and in Khrushchev's case it is easy to explain. He never understood the president's policy on the invasion of the Bay of Pigs in Cuba in April 1961. As he has said in numerous private conversations, he would have understood a hands-off policy at that time or an effective strike that would have brought Castro down—as Moscow moved on Hungary or the Baltic states—but he could not understand how the United States could get involved in the exercise without seeing it through to a successful conclusion. Accordingly, he has been acting on the assumption ever since that President Kennedy is weak."

The president felt strongly that the handling of the crisis was in the hands of the executive. After the near-disastrous meeting with ranking members of Congress on the evening of October 22, the president did not openly further invite or seek the advice of ranking members of Congress. There would be no breakfasts, no meetings with either individual members, groups, or ranking committee heads. There was that expressed fear of criticism. Congressmen and senators in turn were skeptical and fearful of the president's actions. One senior senator would later explain, "I was afraid the president would get all bound up with that damn UN and not get anything done."

McCone received calls from powerful Senate and House leaders demanding to know what was happening. McCone understood and enjoyed the exercise of power. Between meetings of the EXCOM, McCone would call a powerful senator, congressman, or committee head to say that he had a few minutes to spare and was willing to brief on the latest information on the crisis. McCone would call Lundahl and they would hurry up to the Hill, and in a senator or congressman's private chambers, McCone would go over the latest information and Lundahl would brief the latest photography. During the week after the crisis became public, McCone and Lundahl visited at least ten ranking members of Congress and gained their respect and gratitude.

The first official Soviet reaction was a message received at the White House on October 23. It was obviously contrived, a rehash of previously issued statements on Cuba. Since the U.S. did not acquiesce in the placement of missiles in Cuba, the Russians resorted to their second fall-back position—force the United States to negotiate the issues. Khrushchev would ask, "If the U.S.A. is trying to secure lasting peace, as President Kennedy declared, it should accept the Soviet proposals to withdraw its troops and military equipment and close down its military bases on foreign territories in different parts of the world."

The Soviets also attempted to rally other nations to their cause. All governments and peoples were called upon "to raise their voices in protest against the aggressor actions of the United States with regard to Cuba and other states, resolutely to denounce these actions, and bar the way to the unleashing of thermonuclear war by the U.S. government."

The Soviets downplayed "evidence" provided by the aerial photos, referring to them as the "so-called indisputable evidence" and "so-called incontrovertible intelligence." In a round-table discussion broadcast to Soviet listeners, one of the participants referred to the photos as "some kind of faked photographs taken from spy planes." The missiles were justified because Cuba "had been subjected to continuous threats and provocations from the United States." The missiles were needed for Cuba's self-defense. The president's demand to remove the missiles was characterized by the Soviets as "a demand which no state that values its independence can meet."

Khrushchev, in his discussions with foreign diplomats, appeared to be signaling the U.S. that there had to be a change. In the Soviet mind, the road was clear—resolve the crisis through negotiation. The Soviets held that the U.S. was in a poor moral and negotiating position. Soviet statements also spoke of Soviet efforts to preserve the peace, feeling that nations fearing a nuclear war between the U.S. and the Soviet Union would support any negotiation effort. Soviet articles and editorials promoting negotiation were echoed by a strong supporting chorus from the Eastern European countries. The president had made it clear in his speech that the missiles had to be withdrawn. The president ordered the blockade and had overwhelming tactical superiority to enforce it. Khrushchev would later state that the threat "was not left to the Soviet imagination or its interpretation of American military buildup." As General Taylor, an avid tennis fan, would state after Kennedy's October 22 address to the nation, the ball was in Khrushchev's court.

To the U.S. military leaders, Khrushchev was an erratic leader—flamboyant and unpredictable. His mercurial nature was not compatible with careful planning. Rather, he seemed to be guided by improvisation and opportunity, and this made him even more dangerous. To the Joint Chiefs of Staff, especially General LeMay and Admiral Anderson, there was just one way to deal with Khrushchev—and that was to use tough and hard-nosed diplomacy. As Anderson would say, "unsheathing the cold blue steel of power." LeMay was even more brusque, "If there is to be war, there's no better time than the present. We are prepared and 'the bear' is not." Admiral Ward said later in several interviews that the Joint Chiefs of Staff also were extremely wary of President Kennedy. He reiterated that none of them were going to be "the Kimmel and Short of this generation" —an obvious reference to Admiral Husband Kimmel and Major General Walter Short, who were relieved of their commands after Pearl Harbor and who were subsequently objects of a long and tortuous investigation.

Soviet military strategists had written that heightened international tensions and steady deterioration of the political climate would precede an outbreak of hostilities. During this period, Soviet military preparations would be accelerated and Soviet forces brought to full combat readiness. A close watch was being maintained on Soviet naval, air, and ground forces by U.S. intelligence agencies. More attention was being paid by a variety of intelligence sources to Soviet forces in Berlin and East Germany. On October 23, the EXCOM would report to the president that the U.S. "had not detected any unusual activity or alerting of Soviet forces during the first few hours after the President's speech."[1]

The President knew that at some point he would have to seek the support of the Organization of American States for his Cuba policy, and it was decided that the OAS would be convened as soon as possible after the president's nationwide address. There was a problem, however. The secretary general of the OAS, Jose A. Mora, and the council chairman, Alberto Zuletta Angel, along with other delegates, were attending a conference of hemisphere economic ministers in Mexico City. Ironically, they were reviewing the gains of President Kennedy's Alliance for Progress economic programs. Calls were placed on the evening of October 22 summoning the delegates to a "most important" meeting in Washington at 9 A.M. on October 23. A number of delegates would arrive just in time for the meeting.

The president had some misgivings about approaching the OAS. If, as usual, the OAS members became embroiled in tangential discussions or hesitated inordinately while awaiting instructions from their governments, it would weaken and detract from the administration's position. If, on the other hand, the president gained the immediate backing and public support of the Latin American nations, it would enhance his position in dealing with the Soviets.

Few in the Kennedy administration had much faith in the OAS

since, historically, it had been unable to come to grips in a meaningful way with virtually any of the difficult problems it had considered. Its most glaring failure was an outright refusal to consider specific measures against the infusion of Communism into Cuba. Although the OAS Assembly was a forum for articulating the many problems of the hemisphere, it had a history of being unable to come up with many practical solutions. The outcome of most debates was a resolution recognizing the problem and empowering a committee to make more specific recommendations for later assembly considerations. It had, for the most part, taken the role of a spectator in the most vital issues confronting the hemisphere.

Strongly anti-Communist Latin American countries regarded Castro as a pariah. Other governments, though less hostile, were cool toward Castro and watched his every move with suspicion. Some member states, regardless of the problem being discussed, used the OAS as a forum for heaping invective on the U.S. Their usual complaint was that the United States exerted excessive influence over the inter-American system. Much of this was bombast, but there was real Latin American sensitivity about outside interference in matters of national policy.

U.S. ambassador Edwin M. Martin was well aware of this attitude. The principal issue to be resolved was the threat posed by the missiles and the unequivocal requirement that they had to be removed. He had convinced the Latin American ambassadors of the existence of the missiles by showing them the aerial photography on the evening of October 22. But to persuade the rest of the hemisphere that the U.S. was doing the decent and honorable thing would require a statesman who not only understood the nature of the Latin Americans but also their intense nationalism and materialism. It would, of course, also depend on the readiness of the OAS delegates to accept his explanation. Secretary of State Rusk said he would personally accept the challenge and prepared his presentation for the OAS. After a full day of negotiations, Rusk had obtained unanimous concurrence from the OAS in support of the quarantine. Some would later say that this was his "finest hour" as secretary of state.

At the UN that day, Adlai Stevenson, in a long speech, hit at the Soviet threat: "When the Soviet Union sends thousands of military technicians to its satellite in the Western Hemisphere, when it sends jet bombers capable of delivering nuclear weapons, when it installs in Cuba missiles capable of carrying atomic warheads and of obliterating the Panama Canal, Mexico City, and Washington, when it prepares sites for additional missiles with a range of 2,200 miles and a capacity to strike at targets from Peru to Hudson Bay—when it does these things under the cloak of secrecy and to the accomplishment of premeditated deception, when its actions are in flagrant violation of the policies of the Organization of American States and of the Charter of the United Nations, this clearly is a threat to this hemisphere. And when it thus upsets the precarious balance in the world, it is a threat to the whole world."[2] The Russians did not answer Stevenson's charges.

The United States would come under a barrage of criticism from the British press after the president's speech, and British leaders were surprised and disturbed by its ferocity. The president lashed out at British ambassador Ormsby-Gore with anger and some venom. He accused the British press of deliberately distorting the U.S. position and castigated the British government for maintaining a sideline attitude. The British were still rankled about the U.S. treatment of them during the Suez crisis of 1956, and the British press was also displaying considerable skepticism about the validity of the photographic evidence of the missiles being in Cuba, speaking of the "so-called missiles." There were implications that the missiles were only of the short-range variety. Macmillan later ordered that the photographs of the missile sites be interpreted by the best British photo interpreters at the Joint Air Reconnaissance Intelligence Center, at Brampton. Their evaluations not only substantiated the American interpretation but also established that the U.S. interpretation effort was far more comprehensive than the British could have accomplished within the same time frame.

British government officials openly expressed grave anxieties about the consequences of the president's actions regarding Cuba. One highly placed official stated that "a sugar and rum kingdom" was not worth a nuclear war. Macmillan and his ministers were also making it clear that Britain was not committed to aid the U.S. in the Caribbean with any naval or military support. When the news reached the White House, Bobby said sarcastically, "Those son of a bitches have a short memory." Angered by the continuing British criticism, the president stated, "I am not going to roll over and play dead like Chamberlain."

The British prime minister, the foreign minister, and the transport minister were being bombarded by British ship owners, whose freighters and tankers had been chartered by the Russians to carry nonmilitary cargo to Cuba. They appealed to Mr. Marples, the transport minister, to pressure the Americans to grant a special clearance for all British ships going to Cuba. British attacks on the Kennedy administration prompted several U.S. newspapers to criticize the Macmillan government. The anti-British Hearst newspaper chain assumed the offensive. *The New York Daily Mirror* brought the argument into focus: "It may be even smart for Great Britain to raise the issue of the freedom of the seas to help Russia to destroy us while we defend Great Britain with men and ships and NATO."

British ambassador Ormsby-Gore met with President Kennedy that afternoon and anxiously asked that the blockade line be moved closer around Cuba to allow Khrushchev more time to ponder his response to Kennedy's speech. The suggestion made Admiral Anderson livid. The arc five hundred miles out from Cuba had been set to keep U.S. intercepting ships out of the combat range of the MiG's in Cuba. Admiral Anderson said he would not move the blockade line nearer unless ordered to by the president.

It was obvious to the intelligence community that the Soviet diplomatic community around the world was not receiving instructions from Moscow and had not been made aware previously of the missiles being in Cuba. Those that were speaking out, however, were advocating a hard line. Dmitri Goryunov, director-general of the Soviet news agency, Tass, in Hiroshima claimed that Soviet ships would not stop on orders from the U.S. Navy and if the Soviet ships were attacked, it would surely bring on total war. A middle-ranking member of the Soviet UN delegation said that the Soviets would arm their ships to cope with the latest U.S. actions. Soviet military attachés at a reception at the Soviet embassy in Washington claimed that the Soviet ships steaming toward Cuba were under orders not to be stopped or searched.

President Kennedy had been in communication with General Eisenhower several times during the week, and at noon on October 23, Eisenhower made the following remarks at a rally of Adams

County, Pennsylvania, Republicans at Gettysburg College: "We meet in the aftermath of a grave message of the president of the United States. The decision he announced last night may seriously affect the lives of all Americans and the future of the republic. In the circumstances of this present time, as described by him, the decision had to be made. It has to be resolutely enunciated by one man who speaks for all of us in critical foreign affairs. As in all crises, America as a unit follows her constitutional leader. We must pledge him our help in whatever way we can be of help." When President Kennedy was shown a copy of the speech, he smiled and said, "That's what I expected from such a great man."

Castro's response to the president's address contained a variety of threats but none directed to the president personally. Castro assailed the quarantine as a total blockade that was "a violation against the sovereign rights of our people and all peoples." In his ninety-minute radio and television address, Castro gave the usual history of "Yankee aggression." There was an awkward denial of the presence of offensive weapons in Cuba. Castro declared that the weapons were for "defensive purposes." He elaborated, "We will acquire the arms we feel like acquiring and we don't have to give account to the imperialists. Cuba has the right to arm itself, and we had to do it." Castro employed an old axiom of the Communist revolutionaries. Answer a question with a question. "What have we done?" he said. "We have defended ourselves. That is all. Were the imperialists expecting that after their first hostile act, our people would surrender, that the revolution would raise the white flag?" Castro did not appear to be in a hurry to accommodate the U.S. on a settlement. In fact, Castro categorically refused to allow any inspection of Cuban territory. "If they attack us, we will resist. If they blockade us, we know how to resist it. Anyone who wants to inspect Cuba had better come prepared to fight their way in." But it was also obvious that the subdued tone of Castro's speech, together with the absence of any official comments on actions to be taken during the crisis, suggested that Castro was under constraint to let Moscow take the lead.

That evening, Secretary Rusk delivered the "quarantine" order to the president in the Oval Office for signing. The president closely read Proclamation No. 3504, "Interdiction of the Delivery of Offensive Weapons to Cuba." Mrs. Lincoln provided the customary wooden tray of pens for the signing ceremonies. President Kennedy dismissed the idea of using a number of pens as inappropriate and took only a single pen. He spread the four-page document in front of him. On the last page, he wrote firmly and boldly his full signature, John Fitzgerald Kennedy—one of the few documents he signed thus, normally using only his middle initial F. The president looked up and, sensing the magnitude of the moment in history, added the time, 7:06 P.M., and the date, October 23, 1962. As the photographers snapped additional pictures, he underlined the date for emphasis. He looked up again, smiled, and placed the pen his pocket, saying, "I am going to keep this one."

The president had barely signed the quarantine document when Press Secretary Salinger held a White House press conference at 7:15 P.M. on October 23. Salinger didn't have copies of the document to give reporters at the start of the conference, so he read his copy at a slow speed to the reporters. Abram Chayes, the State Department legal expert, was there to help answer questions, but the press conference was a disaster. The reporters wanted to know much more than either Salinger or Chayes could deal with.[3]

At 3 P.M. Moscow time on October 23—fourteen hours after President Kennedy's speech—Soviet defense minister Rodion Malinovsky, following an emergency meeting with Khrushchev and the Council of Ministers of the USSR, placed the Soviet armed forces on a war footing. All personnel due to be released from the Strategic Rocket Forces, the submarine fleets, and the defense forces (PVO Strany units) would be retained, and an immediate increase in the combat readiness and vigilance of all forces was ordered.

This announcement was followed by the news that Marshall Andrei Grechko, commander in chief of the Warsaw Treaty Forces, had summoned his commanders and given them orders to increase the combat readiness of their forces. These measures, Tass announced, were taken because of the "provocative action of the American government and the aggressive intentions of the American armed forces." It was significant, however, that there were no threatening moves by the Soviet Army in Berlin or by the Soviet naval forces in the Mediterranean. In Cuba, the Cuban Air Force, along with some of the naval and ground force units, were placed on a high state of alert but did not threaten U.S. reconnaissance aircraft.

On the evening of October 23, the Soviet embassy in Washington held its annual attaché reception and U.S. reporters swarmed about the military attaché, General Vladimir Dubovik. He stated defiantly that captains of Soviet ships headed for Cuba were under orders to defy the blockade. Apprised of Dubovik's statement, Bobby Kennedy contacted Dobrynin and demanded to know personally the Soviets' intentions regarding their ships bound for Cuba. Dobrynin, somewhat confused, said he did not know of any changes in instructions. That evening in Moscow, the Soviets broadcast a round-table discussion with a number of *Izvestiya* "observers." One of them remarked: "The Soviet Government publication today says: The Soviet Union is in favor of all foreign bases being withdrawn from foreign territory back to their national frontiers. If the United States really wants to strengthen friendly relations with states and wants to insure stable peace in the world, as President Kennedy said in his speech of 22 October, it ought to accept Soviet proposals, withdraw its troops and military equipment, and liquidate military bases on foreign territory in various parts of the world."[4]

On October 24, more than two of the six pages of *Pravda* were devoted to articles protesting President Kennedy's actions against Cuba and supporting various previous Soviet statements on Cuba. The editorial "Check the Criminal Plans of the Enemies of Peace" listed chronologically all the U.S. "criminal" and "aggressive" actions against Cuba. It threatened: "If the aggressors unleash a war, then the Soviets will deliver a very powerful retaliatory strike." The Soviet Union and the Socialist countries "have adequate means to place a straitjacket on the aggressor." There was a final warning, "The Soviet armed forces are equipped with the most modern combat equipment in the world."

The nerve center for implementing the quarantine was Navy Flag Plot, room 6D624 at the Pentagon. On a large wall chart of the Atlantic and the Caribbean, the estimated times of arrival of all foreign ships into the quarantine zone were carefully computed and their movements charted. The positions of U.S. warships along the quarantine line were also carefully plotted. The chart also depicted the principal shipping lanes used by all maritime nations engaged in trade with Cuba. Admiral Anderson frequently consulted the chart and assured himself that the Puerto Rico Trench, used by Russian ships to carry arms to Mariel and Havana, was being adequately monitored by U.S. warships. Soviet ships en route to Cuba's northern ports either used the Puerto Rico Trench, the Straits of Florida, or the Caicos Passage in the Bahama islands chain. Ships bound for Cuba's southern ports would normally navigate through the Mona Passage or the Windward Passage.

Admiral Anderson's office, just a corridor away from Flag Plot, was connected directly with the White House, the secretary of the navy, the secretary of defense, and CINCLANT. Through elaborate communication "patches," the destroyers on the picket line could also be brought into direct communication with Flag Plot.

From his Norfolk headquarters, Admiral Robert Lee Dennison, commander of the Atlantic fleet and NATO's supreme Allied commander, Atlantic, had ordered his forces into their assigned positions and paid particular attention to the blockading forces.

There were numerous merchant ships plying the seas and channels near Cuba. World shipping companies, fearing for the safety of their vessels, were asking for sailing instructions from the U.S. Navy. Foreign governments were calling in U.S. ambassadors and consuls asking what constituted safe passage in these waters for ships engaged in trade with nations other than Cuba. The U.S. State and Defense departments were deluged with calls they could not answer.

Lying in international waters off Morro Castle in Havana, the U.S. Navy ship *Oxford* observed the movements of Soviet ships into and out of Havana harbor. Although listed by the U.S. Navy as a technical research ship for experiments in communications and electromagnetic radiations, the *Oxford* was, in reality, loaded with very sophisticated electronic listening gear for intercepting Russian communications with Havana. Shortly after the crisis began, President Kennedy asked that the *Oxford* move further out to sea.

On September 27, four Soviet F-class long-range diesel attack submarines had slipped their mooring lines at their Northern Fleet base near Murmansk, transited the Barents Sea, and headed for the open Atlantic. It was an unusual move for these submarines, whose activities and patrols were in the past confined to waters in close proximity to their bases. The F-class submarine constituted the Soviets' first-line attack submarine and was assessed to be capable of firing a nuclear-tipped torpedo. During this same period, the Soviet auxiliary oiler *Terek* and a refrigerator ship also appeared in the open Atlantic. The *Terek* had been seen before in the Northern Fleet area, engaged in stern refueling of Soviet submarines at sea. The U.S. Navy correctly surmised that these two vessels might provide logistical support for the four submarines and began to follow them with surface vessels and air patrols. The Navy also maintained a close watch on the Soviet intelligence trawler *Skval*, convinced that it, too, was supporting the submarines.

Notified of this Soviet activity, Admiral Anderson ordered that the closest surveillance be maintained on the *Terek* and the refrigerator ship. Any movements of the submarines toward Cuba should be reported to him immediately. The Cubans had previously announced that the Russians intended to establish a "fishing port" in Cuba, and the U.S. Navy was justifiably suspicious that the port in reality would become a base for Soviet submarines. These submarines could be another Soviet ruse to test U.S. determination to resist further Soviet intrusions into Cuba. This was the first time that Soviet submarines had ventured so close to U.S. home waters. The movements of the submarines provided an ideal opportunity for the U.S. Navy to test its latest antisubmarine warfare equipment and personnel. Anderson had given the Navy wide latitude in this endeavor. After Kennedy's address to the nation on October 22 and the announcement of the quarantine on the next day, Admiral Anderson ordered U.S. destroyers, patrol aircraft, and helicopters to follow the Soviet submarines and ordered U.S. submarines to trail the oiler. Orders were also cut to sink the *Terek* and the submarines on direct command. At the time, the submarines were some six hundred miles from the quarantine line. Soviet Navy intelligence-collection trawlers kept close watch on U.S. naval movements, particularly aircraft-carrier task groups. These ships were undoubtedly providing the Soviet high command with a steady stream of naval intelligence of high value to decision makers. In the event of a conflict, the Navy had orders to immediately sink all such Soviet intelligence collectors.

Nuclear warheads for the MRBM missiles in Cuba had not been

found, and Admiral Anderson took particular note of USIB discussions on the possibility that the submarines could be transporting nuclear warheads for the missiles. Although Anderson's naval experts and the Office of Naval Intelligence doubted that Soviet submarines in the Atlantic would be used in such a role, Anderson nevertheless asked that the Navy stay alert to such a possibility. Although Soviet hydrographic ships had performed numerous surveys around Cuba, no Soviet submarine was ever known to have visited a Cuban port.

At 9:45 P.M. on October 23, Secretary McNamara was briefed in Flag Plot on the location of the Russian merchant ships and the location of U.S. blockading forces. He expressed particular interest in the location of the aircraft carriers *Enterprise* and *Independence* and their nine escort destroyers. When he asked why a number of ships on the chart were shown to be at or near Guantánamo, he was told that Amphibious Squadron 8 was involved in unloading the men of the 2nd Battalion of the 2nd Marines. Guantánamo was reinforced by three Marine battalions, with a fourth still afloat.

Some of the Soviet ships en route to Cuba and suspected of carrying missiles or missile equipment were the *Poltava, Ugrench, Kasimov, Dolmatovo, Krasnograd, Kimovsk,* and *Yuri Gagarin.* The *Poltava* and the *Krasnograd* were large-hatch ships capable of carrying eighty-foot-long missiles in their holds. The *Leninskiy Komsomol* was carrying as many as thirteen crated Il-28 Beagle bombers as deck cargo and the *Bolshevik Sukhanov* was carrying seven large crates on deck, presumed to contain aircraft.

At 10:10 P.M., the U.S. Navy and the State Department, in response to the concern of foreign nations for their ships in the Caribbean, sent to all stations Special Warning No. 30: "The President of the United States has proclaimed a quarantine of offensive military equipment under shipment to Cuba. Reactions may make the Windward Passage, Yucatán Channel and Florida Straits dangerous waters. Ships are advised to use Mona Passage. Ships transiting the Straits of Florida are advised to navigate in proximity to the Florida Keys. Ships passing through Yucatán Channel are advised to favor the coast of the Yucatán Peninsula."[5]

NPIC had searched aerial photography of Cuba thoroughly and had not found any SS-5 missiles but did find some ground-support equipment for the SS-5—a mobile service platform and a fuel transporter that were much larger than the SS-4 transporter. All of the equipment at the MRBM sites was carefully analyzed, and all of it, with the exception of the two pieces of SS-5 equipment listed above, was related to the SS-4 missiles. No missile-support equipment had been identified at the IRBM sites under construction. It was speculated that the large-hatch ships en route to Cuba were carrying SS-5 missiles and support equipment. All such vessels were photographed, but no missiles were seen on the decks of the ships. NPIC undertook a detailed analysis of the equipment carried as deck cargo. Two unique trucks were spotted on the deck of the *Poltava*. The trucks were identified as YAAZ-214's, but an odd offset in the truckbed drew particular attention. The bed was offset to accommodate a large metal ring. We measured the rings and quickly concluded that they were launch support rings for the SS-5. This was concrete evidence that the *Poltava* was carrying SS-5 missiles or SS-5 support equipment, and the *Poltava* therefore became a prime target for the U.S. Navy.

Soviet merchant ships were still proceeding toward Cuba, and at 10:45 P.M., Admiral Anderson met with McNamara to determine which Soviet merchant ship should be intercepted first. Since it was known that the *Poltava* had previously delivered missiles to Cuba, the *Newport-News* with her two destroyer escorts were assigned to stop her if ordered. The *Essex* and the cruiser *Canberra* were ordered to intercept the *Kimovsk*.

The U.S. Navy had also kept a close watch on the KOMAR guided-missile patrol boats the Soviets had given the Cubans in August 1962. The boats were stationed at two locations: eight at Mariel and four at Banes. Although the KOMAR guided-missile boats were only eighty-three feet long and weighed over seventy tons, they packed a lethal sting. Each had two missile-firing canisters twenty feet in length. The Styx missile fired from these tubes was radar-guided, with a range of about fifteen miles. The U.S. Navy's regard for the lethal effect of this missile had been underscored during the October 1956 Arab-Israeli War, when an Egyptian OSA boat had sunk the Israeli destroyer *Elath* with a single Styx missile. Reconnaissance photography and reporting from Navy patrol aircraft indicated consistently that the KOMAR remained at both ports unmanned and secured to their piers. Had the KOMAR ventured into international waters, both Navy fighter aircraft and destroyers were prepared to sink them upon the slightest indication of hostile activity.

At 7:30 P.M. on October 23, McNamara had called a press conference, ostensibly to announce particulars and status of the blockade initiated at 11 o'clock that morning. McNamara was surprised when asked by reporters for copies of the aerial photos they had seen on October 22. Unaware that the U-2 photos had been released to the British press, McNamara contended that security officers at the Pentagon felt that certain of the photographs should not be released because they might provide valuable "state-of-the-art" information on U.S. reconnaissance capabilities. When told that the British were featuring the aerial photos over the BBC television network, McNamara was stunned. This was not according to the White House plan as he understood it. He turned to Arthur Sylvester, assistant secretary of defense for public affairs, who shrugged his shoulders in disbelief. When pressed as to why the photos had not been released concurrently to the U.S. press, McNamara became irritated but promised that he would see to it personally that any photos released to the British would also be released in the United States.

After the press conference, McNamara, understandably furious at not having been told about the photos being released to the British, told John Hughes that "he felt like an ass out there" and demanded to know who had authorized the release of the photos. Hughes called Lundahl at the Center and asked the same question. Lundahl said he didn't know and that he was also getting calls that he could not answer. Neither McNamara, the CIA, nor the Center knew that, on October 23, the British ambassador to the United States, Sir David Ormsby-Gore, had again pressed President Kennedy to release the aerial photos in support of Macmillan's delicate position with respect to Parliament, the media, and British public opinion. Ormsby-Gore's endeavor was strongly supported by a cable from the U.S. ambassador to London, David K. E. Bruce. The president considered the British ambassador's request but did not release the photos.

Although it was never verified exactly how the release had come about, it was established that Macmillan had spoken to the president and forcefully made his position and views known subsequent to Gore's request. President Kennedy had stated that he would authorize the release of the photos but did not specify when. There was an apparent breakdown of communications because Macmillan assumed the release would be immediate and subsequently called Ambassador Bruce and informed him of his conversation with the president. Bruce, who had expressed his strong endorsement to Washington that the photos be released, did not question the prime minister. Bruce asked that Chet Cooper arrange for a briefing and release of the photos to the British press and media. Operational information on the briefing boards, classification, enlargement factors, and date of and number of mission were removed and at 5 P.M. on October 23, a background, nonattributable briefing was given by Sherman Kent to correspondents of the leading British newspapers, the BBC, and the Independent Television Network (ITV). The aerial photos were shown and the information on them was discussed in detail. In addition, Kent gave a description of the arms buildup that had occurred in Cuba throughout the summer and fall. Questions, according to Kent, were answered most frankly. British photographers took photos of the briefing boards. The briefing ended about 6:30 P.M. Within minutes, the BBC and ITV television were rushing the films to their studios for evening news programs.*

The president had planned to release the photos simultaneously at the UN, in Washington, and at various European capitals. It was resolved that a breakdown in communications between the president and Macmillan had caused their premature release. To ease things, the White House used the story that an "errant" U.S. embassy official in London had inadvertently distributed the pictures to the British press. The White House added that the administration had planned to release the photos later and that the London "mistake" only hastened the release by a few hours. Subsequently, the White House

---

* Another version frequently quoted is that Ormsby-Gore convinced President Kennedy to release the photos at a dinner party on the evening of October 23. That would not have been possible, since the chronology of events and the actual showing of the aerial photos on British TV on the evening of October 23 is not compatible. In any case, the British public thus were the first to see the U-2 photographs of the Cuban missile sites, along with an address by the foreign minister, who condemned the Russian actions and urged support for the U.S. position. The aerial photos did much to convince the British public of U.S. claims.

Press Office tasked NPIC to furnish twenty-five 8 × 10 sanitized copies of each photograph that had been shown in England as soon as possible. The copies were delivered to the Press Office at 1:30 A.M. on October 24. A short description of the detail depicted on each photograph was included. The White House sent the photos to the wire services for immediate release. Some of the prints made *The Washington Post* that morning, along with a number of other important morning newspapers around the country.*

As John McCone would later relate, "There was a lot of broken china in the White House Press Office that morning and it would require some diplomacy to pacify some of the White House correspondents, who felt they had been purposefully overlooked."

To placate newspapers that were unable to publish the photos released on the morning of October 24, the president authorized the release of twelve additional aerial photos, including some low-level photos, at 7:35 P.M. This seemed to pacify most of the reporters, who by now were totally engulfed writing about the crisis.

Late in the evening on October 23, word was flashed from the National Security Agency to the CIA Watch Office that its direction-finding efforts indicated that the Soviet missile-carrying ships bound for Cuba had not only changed course but were probably on their way back to Russia. The CIA Watch officer, Harry Eisenbiess, checked with the Office of Naval Intelligence. They were also in receipt of the NSA information but could not confirm the change of course. On-the-spot visual verification would have to wait until morning. The Navy felt that it might be a Soviet ploy. Eisenbiess was convinced of the validity of the NSA information and in the wee hours of the morning of October 24 went to McCone's home. McCone, aroused from a sound sleep, was told that at least five of the Soviet ships had

---

* Shortly after the photos were delivered, the Center received a call from the White House for an additional 150 copies of each print—50 of the copies to be delivered to either Carl Rowen or Donald Wilson of the United States Information Agency, and 100 copies would be released by Pierre Salinger on the morning of October 24. A total of over 2,000 prints had been printed and released by 1 P.M. on October 24. President Kennedy asked the USIA to send prints to every U.S. post throughout the world. The USIA asked for more copies, and by the next day over 5,400 prints of fourteen photos had been disseminated to 203 State Department posts in 107 countries and to press organizations all over the world.

changed course and were headed back to Russia but that the Navy could not verify the NSA information. McCone said he would convey the information to the White House immediately.[6]

At 5:40 P.M. on October 23, Castro gave the alarm for battle, *alarma de combate*, to his troops. The *alarma de combate* was the highest degree of alert for the Cuban armed forces. Later that evening, in a long interview, Castro ridiculed President Kennedy's October 22 speech paragraph by paragraph. In answer to a question as to why Cuba armed itself, Castro replied: "We armed ourselves against our own wishes, our desires, because we were forced to strengthen our military defenses on pain of endangering the sovereignty of our nation and the independence of our country."[7]

October 24 —
UN and Military Preparedness

"I hope you are in a position to prove beyond
a shadow of a doubt that the missiles
exist in Cuba."

—ADLAI E. STEVENSON

T HE NATIONS OF THE WORLD had to be convinced, and they would demand to see the evidence of the missiles in Cuba; the aerial photos were irrefutable. It was decided that the best forum for the confrontation was the United Nations Security Council and that, for maximum effect, the sooner the better. The president asked that the finest talent in the Washington area be dispatched to New York to "help" Ambassador Stevenson.

Adlai Stevenson and others at the U.S. mission to the UN were complaining that they were not being provided the same information as decision makers in Washington. While there was a constant flow of cable traffic between Washington and New York, few at the UN appreciated or understood the intricacies and procedures for reporting substantive intelligence derived from aerial reconnaissance.

Some of the responsibility for action and decision making regarding Cuba was beginning to devolve upon the U.S. mission and the UN, and the president directed that Adlai Stevenson, and later John McCloy, be shown the latest photography and kept informed on the latest diplomatic moves.

An incensed Stevenson called Mr. Lundahl on the evening of October 23 demanding that he come to New York at once and remain at the UN to advise him. Lundahl said he would contact McCone for guidance. As Lundahl expected, McCone, of course, would not let him go, but he did ask Lundahl to recommend who should be sent to New York for a one-day briefing. Lundahl responded quickly: his deputy, Colonel David S. Parker. Colonel Parker was an excellent choice. A graduate of West Point in 1940, he had performed a variety of important staff and line functions in his army career. Astute and articulate, Colonel Parker had served as an assistant professor in the Department of Military Topography and Graphics at the U.S. Military Academy. Commissioned in the Corps of Engineers, he was an expert in construction and construction equipment and had written a number of field and technical manuals on new equipment and field engineering and construction techniques that had been introduced into U.S. Army procedures during and since World War II. Colonel Parker also had a special ability to reduce highly technical subjects to layman terms and to communicate these subjects succinctly. Most pertinent of all, under Lundahl's tutelage, he became familiar with aerial photography and the photo interpretation being performed at the Center.

Colonel Parker and a number of other intelligence officers made preparations to be in New York the next morning. At the same time, Roger Hilsman and Leonard C. Meeker, the deputy legal counsel from the Department of State—the best-informed experts on the quarantine—would be arriving, along with Ray Cline, whom McCone had asked to go to New York to help Stevenson draft his speeches to the UN.

Lundahl, Parker, Gordon Duvall, Bob Boyd, and I reviewed all the aerial photography of the crisis processed by NPIC. Lundahl and Parker selected the briefing boards they thought provided the best evidence of the missile buildup in Cuba. Since the president had not yet approved declassification of some of the aerial photography, Dutch Scheufele, NPIC Operations and Classification Control Officer, was adamant that the security integrity of the briefing materials be maintained. TOP SECRET classification markings were to remain on the top and bottom of each board. I proposed, however, that Parker take an X-Acto knife with him, a bottle of india ink, and a brush, and if authority to declassify the boards was forthcoming, Parker could perform the function himself on the spot. Scheufele agreed.

Cline met Parker at National Airport, where, together, they

boarded a CIA aircraft. Once airborne, Cline asked to see the briefing materials. They were spread about the seats and aisles. As Parker spelled out details, Cline took copious notes. A flabbergasted courier watched. "I had visions," he later said, "of the aircraft blowing up and all that classified material floating down over the countryside." Landing at LaGuardia, Cline, Parker, and the courier were driven to Adlai Stevenson's office at the U.S. mission. Before Parker could open the large black satchel of briefing boards, Stevenson remarked, "I hope you are in a position to prove beyond a shadow of a doubt that the missiles exist in Cuba." Parker expressed surprise at Stevenson's attitude but assured him that the evidence was overwhelming. It was an accepted fact that Stevenson would be skeptical of any photographic information presented by the CIA. Stevenson's tenure at the United Nations was only a few months old when, as he later explained, he was "dropped on his head by the Washington establishment." During the Bay of Pigs episode, Stevenson had been put in the awful position of stoutly maintaining at the UN that a B-26 bomber that landed in Florida was piloted by a Cuban defector. As evidence of the defection, Stevenson had exhibited several photos of the pilot and the "Cuban" B-26. When he later learned that the Cuban "defector" was in reality a CIA-trained and -equipped pilot, he never forgave the State Department or Tracy Barnes of the CIA.[1]

Cline, McGeorge Bundy, and Arthur Schlesinger's association dated back to 1941, when they were junior fellows at Harvard. They always had gotten along and frequently consulted each other as their careers progressed. Schlesinger remembered clearly Stevenson's performance at the October 20 White House meeting, when he had incurred McCone and Bobby Kennedy's wrath by expressing doubts concerning the existence of missiles in Cuba. He was also aware that Stevenson's background knowledge of missiles was minimal, as was his knowledge of aerial reconnaissance and photo interpretation. Schlesinger also knew that it would be difficult for Stevenson to present the U.S. case successfully unless he was thoroughly convinced and provided continuing support.

Colonel Parker briefed Stevenson in depth on high-altitude photography and then on the specific differences in the IRBM and MRBM sites. Stevenson expressed particular skepticism about the estimated operational dates of the missile sites and the fact that one site at San

Cristóbal had been constructed in a little over twenty-four hours. Stevenson also asked a number of questions about the Il-28 bombers. Parker responded candidly and deftly. Parker found Stevenson "had a great deal of patience, intelligence, thoughtfulness, interest and picked up the material quickly."[2] Stevenson and Colonel Parker were compatible from the start, and a warm and cordial relationship was established, which endured years after the crisis. When the briefing was finished, Stevenson still appeared uneasy and remarked, "I've got a roomful of ambassadors waiting in the conference room. Are there any objections to showing them all of these materials?" Parker looked to Cline. Cline nodded assent.

Parker said that the TOP-SECRET code word classification markings should be removed from the briefing boards. The markings, however, were affixed with a stubborn adhesive and proved very difficult to take off. Everyone in the room, including Stevenson, had a hand in attempting to remove the tape. It was taking too long. Parker suggested pasting masking tape over the code words. When this also was taking too long, Cline said, "Let's take the boards on in."

As they entered the conference room, Hilsman had finished his briefing on the quarantine and the ambassadors were waiting. Stevenson had explained to Cline and Parker that most of the ambassadors were from West European and Latin American countries. Although Hilsman had hurried to New York to participate in the action as the State Department representative, his participation was characterized by others as "just getting in the way." Hilsman's principal task was to have been to brief representatives of third world nations who had initially declined the invitation by Stevenson to view the aerial photography.

Stevenson apologized to the ambassadors for having kept them waiting and proposed that the briefing boards be placed on the large conference table so that the ambassadors could inspect them closely rather than have Colonel Parker deal with individual boards. Cline, Parker, Hilsman, and Stevenson mingled among the ambassadors, pointing out details as well as answering their questions. The visual impact of the photography was substantial, even though a number of the ambassadors had served in the military and were familiar with such things.

The next briefing was to be with senior officials from the NATO countries. To lend an air of importance, McCloy had been designated by Stevenson to do this briefing. Before the briefing, Parker pointed out the salient details to McCloy, which he quickly grasped. McCloy complained, however, that he would like to have a large photo of the MRBM missile seen in the Moscow parades. Parker remembered that the Center had a number of photos of the SS-4 missile being towed on its transporter during the May and November parades, but he hadn't brought one with him. Comparisons would have been difficult anyway, Parker said. "I didn't think it was particularly useful because, at the time, we only had high-altitude U-2 photography and it was impossible really to make out what the missile looked like. To some extent, you had to take the briefing on faith."[3] According to Parker, McCloy made an admirable presentation considering the fact that he had little knowledge of photo interpretation.

After McCloy's briefing, Cline, Arthur Schlesinger, Ambassador Francis T. P. Plimpton, deputy U.S. representative to the UN, and Colonel Parker were sequestered in Stevenson's office to work on Stevenson's formal presentation to the Security Council if it became necessary to introduce the aerial photography as evidence. Since Cline was the best informed on all aspects of what had happened, he was the natural choice as the principal drafter. Parker worked on some sections dealing with the photography and provided Cline with some of the notes NPIC had prepared. As Cline finished each page of the draft, Plimpton would review it for State's input and Schlesinger added the Stevensonian touch to the final draft.

After the speech had been drafted, Parker and several of Stevenson's aides took the aerial photos back to the conference rooms. The informal briefings continued, this time to African, Asian, and Latin American delegates. Parker was surprised when he saw several Cuban delegates admiring the quality of the photographs and speaking about the "U-*dos*" photography. The Cuban delegates were amused to see a legend on the maps, used to key the sites of the photographs, which read: "These maps are for OFFICIAL USE ONLY and will not be reproduced or displayed or released without the approval of the Cuban government."

When the speech was drafted, Stevenson met with Cline, Schlesinger, and Parker. Some of the new photography sent to New York from Washington that afternoon was incorporated in the draft. Stevenson asked Parker if any of the missiles in Cuba could strike New York. When told that the MRBMs could reach points just north of Washington and that the IRBM sites under construction could easily launch missiles at New York, Stevenson insisted that his speech say so.

The consensus at the U.S. mission was that the Soviets would not deny the existence of the missiles in Cuba, so Cline headed back to Washington. Stevenson told Parker that he was also immediately free to return to Washington, but the colonel indicated that his air reservations were for that evening. Stevenson asked where he could be reached. Parker stalled for a moment and merely restated that he was returning to Washington that evening. Stevenson then changed his mind and asked Colonel Parker to remain in New York, volunteering to call Bob (Robert McNamara) if there were any problems. (Stevenson was unaware that Colonel Parker was attached to the CIA.) Parker, who had only a day's change of clothes, called Lundahl indicating Ambassador Stevenson's wishes and asked if Lundahl would contact Mrs. Parker and have her send some additional clothes up to New York. Parker expressed the feeling that he would probably be required to stay at the UN for the duration of the crisis.

On the morning of October 24, the president spotted one of the missile photos in *The Washington Post* and, not having been told that his miscommunication with Macmillan had caused its release, called Ray Cline asking if he had authorized Chester Cooper to release the photos on British TV and now in the *Post*. Cline later related that he "said no, which was true; the anger was over Stevenson's being scooped, although—as I pointed out—the TV image was bound to be pretty dim compared to our easel-size charts; later I discovered Chet simply had the photos shown [by Kent] with the concurrence of the U.S. Ambassador and felt he had no way to resist; it was a good thing anyway since it undoubtedly swayed British opinion in our favor."[4]

October 24 was also a day of tension and battle orders for the U.S. military. The Joint Chiefs of Staff issued Defcon 2, a maximum alert with the optimum posture to strike either Cuba or the USSR—or both.

Early on the morning of the twenty-fourth, a Soviet F-class submarine headed toward a rendezvous with a number of Soviet merchant vessels moving through the Atlantic Ocean toward Cuba. The U.S. Navy intensified its surveillance of the submarine. It was undetermined whether the submarine was sent to defend the Soviet merchant ships or to shoot its way through the blockade. Admiral Anderson dispatched two additional destroyers to the scene. The White House was informed of the movement of the submarine and a direct presidential order was imposed: "Trail, but take no offensive action against the submarine."

At 9 A.M., the secretary of defense received a briefing from the Navy on the status of the Soviet ships. Although the Navy had information that some of the ships had stopped or changed course, McNamara was not so informed. At a press conference that morning, McNamara said that about twenty-five Soviet ships were still on course for Cuba despite America's naval quarantine. McNamara said it was a "fair presumption" that some of the ships were carrying offensive weapons to Cuba. The defense secretary indicated that the first test of the blockade, a possible clash between American and Soviet ships, could come within twenty-four hours.

All morning long on October 24, the Navy Field Operational Intelligence Section at the National Security Agency, at Fort Meade, Maryland, bombarded the Office of Naval Intelligence and Flag Plot with telephone calls that their direction-finding efforts convinced them a number of Russian merchant ships had slowed, changed course, and that some might be on their way back to the Soviet Union. Later that day refined data was that sixteen of the eighteen ships, some with large hatches, were dead in the water or had turned back. Reports were also coming in from Navy reconnaissance, and surface units were confirming NSA's findings.

By 11:40 A.M., the Office of Naval Intelligence and Flag Plot were convinced that the NSA information was valid. The Office of Naval Intelligence notified Admiral Anderson, who personally called General Taylor. Taylor emphasized to Anderson that all necessary measures be taken to ensure that there should be no leak of this information until the president determined a course of action. Anderson also called the secretary of the navy and McNamara at the White House. Later that afternoon, when McNamara found that the information had been available since early morning and he had not been told, he was furious. He stormed into Flag Plot "like a madman," demanding to be briefed on the information at hand. According to one individual in the Flag Plot, "McNamara was chewing out one officer after another as they were attempting to explain their actions." The officer in charge called Admiral Anderson, who immediately came into Flag Plot and attempted to get McNamara aside. If McNamara had complaints, Anderson would be glad to listen to them. Anderson felt that McNamara's actions were unbecoming the secretary of defense. McNamara then turned on Anderson, complaining he was not pleased with the Navy's performance. Anderson said he would assume full responsibility for the Navy's actions. McNamara stormed from the room.

At 5:10 P.M. that evening in the White House Situation Room, Rostow, Ball, Nitze, Lovett, Bundy, Bobby Kennedy, and Admiral Claude Ricketts, vice-chief of Naval Operations, reviewed the evidence of the blockade that day. It appeared that the Russians did not want a missile-carrying ship seized and were trying to avoid a confrontation along the blockading line. Ball recommended that the U.S. not intercept any Soviet ship that might sail toward Cuba since it was now obvious that they would not contain contraband. Upon hearing this, the president said that it was a "good course of action." He asked that orders go out to all U.S. naval forces in the Caribbean not to board any Soviet vessel bound for Cuba. The directive to the commander of the Second Fleet was curt: "Do not board or stop. Keep under surveillance. Make continuous reports."

There had been a spate of rumors among the Washington media during the afternoon about the movement of Soviet ships. Both NBC and ABC reported in their evening news broadcasts that Russian ships were either dead in the water or had turned back. That evening, a Defense Department spokesman confirmed that "at least a dozen Soviet vessels have turned back, presumably because, to the best of our information, they might have been carrying offensive materials." Other vessels, however, were still proceeding toward Cuba. No intercept of a Soviet ship had yet been made necessary. At 7 P.M., Roswell Gilpatric asked that U.S. destroyers close in on the ships continuing to move toward Cuba.

Admiral Anderson said that he would pass all the information on to Admiral Dennison. He then warned Gilpatric, "From now on, I don't intend to interfere with Dennison or either of the admirals on the scene unless we get the additional intelligence information which were are hoping for." (He was referring to the removal of the missiles from Cuba.)

Late that evening, the president called McNamara. He wanted to confirm when our forces would be ready to invade Cuba. McNamara replied, "In seven days." When the president pressed whether all the forces would be well prepared, McNamara replied that they would be "ready in every respect in seven days."

The airborne-alert operations of the Strategic Air Command were particularly impressive. In normal times, 50 percent of SAC's bombers were in a ground-alert status, with their crews ready within minutes to launch their bombers. With Defcon 2, 1,436 bombers and 134 ICBMs were on constant alert; one eighth of the bombers were in the air at all times, and air crews were waiting near the rest of the bombers, prepared for takeoff on a moment's notice. The SAC missiles also were ready for launching.

General Thomas Power, the SAC commander, sent a message to all his commanders on October 24, stressing the seriousness and inherent dangers of the Cuban situation. Any questionable situation not covered in the various contingency plans must be forwarded to the highest levels for clarification—to himself if necessary. Nonessential operations were to give way to maintaining the alert. He called for strict security and, above all, the avoidance of any incident that could have deleterious results. The thorough discipline, rigid security, and regard for safety ingrained in SAC personnel by General LeMay during his tenure were brought into full play. General LeMay would be in constant touch with General Power throughout the crisis.

Admiral Anderson also reemphasized to his commanders the importance of maintaining a constant watch, since the submarines, in addition to being a threat, might also signal future Soviet intentions. He cautioned that the principal forces the Soviets could employ in the area were cruise missiles and torpedo-equipped submarines and bombers equipped with cruise missiles.

Senator Fulbright still insisted that the blockade would not work: It would bring on a confrontation with the Soviets rather than the

Cubans. "Put the pressure on the Cubans and maintain it," he again admonished.

Reports from the UN indicated that Western and Latin American nations were solidly behind the United States in the blockade, but there was concern regarding the uncommitted Afro-Asian countries. India was especially critical of the U.S. blockade actions.

In Havana, Castro spoke out, condemning the U.S. blockade, and said that anyone who tried to carry out inspection of Cuban armament or territory "had better come for combat." He reiterated the "legality of Cuban measures to ensure its security," and the "defense nature" of the weapons the Soviets had provided.

In Moscow, Ambassador Foy Kohler was called to the Foreign Ministry and handed a Soviet statement threatening that the blockade would "unleash a nuclear war." That declaration was broadcast every half hour for the remainder of the day on Radio Moscow.

In London, Macmillan and his cabinet were in turmoil over the turn of events and met for nearly three hours late on October 23. A statement expressing "deep concern at the provocative action of the Soviet Union in placing offensive weapons in Cuba" was later issued. Hugh Gaitskell, a personal friend of President Kennedy and the leader of the opposition Labour party, met with Macmillan late on October 23 and, along with some of Macmillan's cabinet members, urged Macmillan to go to Washington in an attempt to mitigate the U.S. provisions of the blockade. Kennedy was decidedly opposed to any such visit, which he felt would compromise his freedom of action to make further policy decisions. British ambassador Ormsby-Gore was so informed by the president the following day.

Not only was the British press critical, but Kennedy was particularly irked when Labour party spokesman Harold Wilson told a television audience that the U.S. should have taken the Cuban problem to the UN first rather than taking unilateral action of imposing the blockade. In debates in Parliament, Wilson went further—because the U.S. not only failed to notify the British but treated the British attitude with contempt, and risked total war with the Russians without consulting with its European allies, the "special relationship" that had existed with Britain over the years no longer applied. When word of Wilson's attack reached the White House,

Bobby contemptuously said, "Those sons a bitches do have a short memory!"

But the British leaders, regardless of their party affiliation, were determined that conversations between the Soviets and the United States should get under way as soon as possible and were eager to play a role in this endeavor. British ambassador Ormsby-Gore met with McGeorge Bundy on the afternoon of October 24 and summarized the position that Macmillan would take with the president that evening. "At some point there will clearly have to be a conference if there is not going to be war. Whose initiative would be helpful here—US? Secretary General or some other power, perhaps the UK."[5] Although not delineated as such, it was clear that the British were proposing a Cuba-for-Turkey missile exchange.[6]

The British had long espoused the "freedom of the seas" policy in international relations and could not understand why the U.S. could not revoke or retract provisions of its Cuba quarantine without insisting on the immediate removal of the missiles. The British couldn't appreciate U.S. concern that the photography acquired by the U-2 and low-level reconnaissance missions revealed that the Russians were working at a feverish rate and that Khrushchev had probably hoped for Allied disunity to provide the Soviets time to bring the missile sites to operational status.

On October 24, Khrushchev would make two informal public appeals to gain additional time to negotiate the crisis. He replied to a telegram sent by Lord Bertrand Russell on October 23: "The question of war and peace is so vital that we should consider useful a top-level meeting to discuss all the questions that have arisen, to do everything to remove the danger of unleashing a thermonuclear war."[7] On the evening of October 22, prior to the president's address to the American public, Lord Russell issued a press statement highly critical of President Kennedy. Russell's statement began, "It seems likely within a week you will all be dead to please an American madman."[8] He revealed that the American president had called members of his cabinet, congressional leaders, and ambassadors to meet in Washington on the twenty-second: "I appeal to my fellow countrymen to listen to this speech tonight. Should there be any suggestion of war or of an action calculated to provoke war, I urge every human being who loves life to come out in the streets of our country and demonstrate our demand to live and let live. There must be no WAR."[9] The British paid little heed to this latest statement by Lord Russell. His Ban the Bomb movement and the group demonstrations outside the American embassy had been a constant source of embarrassment to Macmillan and the government.

Lord Russell sent two telegrams on October 23. His message to President Kennedy was terse: "Your action desperate. Threat to human survival. No conceivable justification. Civilized men condemn it. We will not have mass murder. Ultimatums mean war. I do not speak for power but plead for civilized man. End this madness."[10]

To Premier Khrushchev: "I appeal to you not to be provoked by the unjustifiable action of the United States in Cuba. The world will support caution. Urge condemnation to be sought through United Nations. Precipitous action would mean annihilation for mankind."[11] Lord Russell also sent telegrams to Prime Minister Macmillan, Hugh Gaitskell, the leader of the Labour party, and to U Thant at the United Nations. He urged Macmillan to speak out to prevent nuclear war. He invited Gaitskell to join his protests against the Americans and he asked U Thant to condemn the American actions with regard to Cuba.

Khrushchev wrote, and released through Tass, a long letter to Lord Russell on October 24 expressing his willingness to negotiate the Cuban issue. Khrushchev portrayed the United States as threatening to unleash thermonuclear war. The Soviet Union, Khrushchev promised, "will not make any reckless decision." What is needed, he said, "is not only the efforts of the Socialist countries and Cuba—which has become, as it were, the focus of the world crisis—but also the efforts of all states, all peoples, and all sections of society to avert a military catastrophe." Playing on British fear and emotional reaction to the crisis, Khrushchev warned, "Clearly, if this catastrophe breaks out it will bring extremely grave consequences to mankind and will spare neither Right or Left, neither those who champion the cause of peace nor those who wish to remain aloof." Khrushchev had sensed that world public opinion was going against him and appealed for a summit meeting in an effort to recoup the propaganda initiative.

"The question of war and peace is so vital that we should consider useful a top level meeting in order to discuss the problems that have arisen."

Lord Russell hastily endorsed Khrushchev's appeal for negotiations, but his letter was greeted with understandable skepticism in the West. Lord Russell, for all his bravado and pomposity, did not realize that he had been used by Khrushchev. He sincerely believed that he was playing a leading role in resolving the crisis. He relished the attention he was receiving from television and world press coverage. That evening he sent the following telegram to Khrushchev: "Thank you for your heartening reply. I congratulate you for your courageous stand for sanity. I hope you will hold back ships in Cuban waters long enough to secure American agreement for your proposal. Whole world will bless you if you succeed in averting war. If there is anything I can possibly do please let me know."

To President Kennedy, he dispatched the following message: "I urge you most strongly to make a conciliatory reply to Khrushchev's vital overture and avoid clash with Russian ships long enough to make meeting and negotiations possible. After shots have been exchanged it will probably be too late. Appeal to you to meet Khrushchev. If there is anything I can do please let me know."[12]

President Kennedy was furious when shown Russell's endorsement of Khrushchev's negotiation proposal. Kennedy, referring to Russell's letter, was quoted, "He asked if he could do something for me. He can. He can go and soak his head. The last person in the world I want to talk to is that son of a bitch."

Although President Kennedy did not want to respond to Lord Russell's message, he was persuaded to do so by Bobby. On October 26, the president sent Lord Russell the following cable: "I am in receipt of your telegram. We are currently discussing the matter in the United Nations. While your messages are critical of the United States, they make no mention of your concern for the introduction of secret Soviet missiles into Cuba. I think your attention might well be directed to the burglars rather than to those who have caught the burglars."

William E. Knox, president of the Westinghouse International Company of New York, was in Moscow on a business trip on October 24. At 2 P.M., he was called at his hotel and told that Khrushchev would like to see him at 3 P.M. Shocked and flabbergasted, Knox was ushered into the premier's office at 3:30 P.M. The ensuing three-hour conversation ranged over a variety of topics before settling on Cuba. Khrushchev berated Kennedy for the blockade and desperately tried to convince Knox that the missiles were defensive. Knox would not agree. Khrushchev volunteered that the ballistic missiles in Cuba were equipped with conventional and nuclear warheads. This was the first Soviet admission of nuclear weapons being in Cuba. When Knox explained U.S. anxiety at having such complicated weapons in Castro's Cuba, Khrushchev quickly assured him that all of the sophisticated equipment was under the direct control of the Soviets and would not be fired except on his personal order. He avowed that he would never fire the missiles except in defense of Cuba or the Soviet Union. He also said that he would not be the first to fire a nuclear weapon. Knox diplomatically said that such reassurances would not appease Americans, since they were suspicious and apprehensive of him personally. According to Knox, Khrushchev appeared exhausted but, nevertheless, warned that if any Soviet ship was sunk, Soviet submarines would go into action.

Khrushchev then used an anecdote that he had told many distinguished visitors about the presence of nuclear bases surrounding Russia. A Russian peasant had come upon hard times and had to live in a stable with a goat. Although he learned to tolerate the goat's smell, try as he might, he could never learn to like the stench or living in the stable with the goat. Khrushchev said the Russians had been living with the American nuclear goat for some time. Rather flippantly, he said that although the U.S. didn't like it, they too would have to learn to live with unpleasant situations.[13]

Then Khrushchev finally came to the reason he had summoned Knox. He spoke of the necessity of averting a war and the need to meet personally with President Kennedy. He offered to meet Kennedy in Washington, Moscow, a neutral country, or at sea in his desire to put an end to the crisis on the basis of negotiation. Then he added, "If the United States insists on war, we'll all meet in hell."

Knox reported to Ambassador Kohler that Khrushchev looked tired but appeared cool and rational; Khrushchev had said he placed no restrictions on conversations with President Kennedy. Knox had assured the premier that he would not speak to anyone until he had notified the U.S. State Department. That was exactly what Khrushchev had hoped. Khrushchev's views were communicated to Washington, first in summary form and later in detail, by Ambassador Kohler.

Intelligence officers subsequently praised Mr. Knox for the quality of his reporting. Although not a trained intelligence officer, he had asked the right questions, elicited clear responses, and accurately committed Khrushchev's words to memory.

Although to a degree Lord Russell reflected the official British government view on the Cuban crisis, Macmillan was careful, and far too astute to be swayed by Khrushchev's negotiation scheme forwarded through Lord Russell. British students demonstrated against the U.S. in London, Liverpool, Leeds, and Manchester; British labor leaders were asking the prime minister to insist that President Kennedy call off the blockade. Macmillan regarded Khrushchev's move as a step to drive a wedge between the United States and Britain and thus fragment any prospect of European unity. The British position was further complicated by the overwhelming support accorded the United States by the OAS. Chancellor Adenauer had also pledged his full support to President Kennedy and had stated that Germany was ready to accept all risks associated with Cuba. General de Gaulle supported the president, and support also came from Norway, Tokyo, and Canberra. When Senator Russell was made aware of the British, German, and other international reaction to the crisis, he said, "Well now, that really tells you who your friends are, doesn't it?"

After carefully checked out cameras were placed into the reconnaissance aircraft and after all the electrical connections had been made and the camera settings checked, the cameras were activated by ground crews to check out the film transport mechanisms and shutter activations. Several frames of photography would be exposed. Shortly after a reconnaissance plane would be airborne, but when still over friendly territory, the pilot would again test the operation of all cameras. Several frames of photography again would be exposed.

When photography from the first low-altitude missions reached the Center, we noted that the test photos were clear and revealed details of nearby aircraft, ground support equipment and, frequently, personnel. The test photography taken in the air often revealed details of the air, naval, and ground force buildup at installations in Florida. On a particular mission, a Navy pilot, testing his cameras, unknowingly took a series of photos of the Key West area, showing a large number of fighters, fighter bombers, and helicopters at Boca Chica Naval Air Station. These photos were shown to Lundahl, who asked that we make enlargements of the air base. With those, he showed the USIB and the EXCOM the potential intelligence benefit to the enemy if the reconnaissance aircraft were shot down. Lundahl recommended that some sort of a screen be built to shield photographic acquisition during ground testing, and that airborne testing not be accomplished until the planes were over the sea. When the photos were shown to the president, he was overwhelmed with the number and type of aircraft that could be seen at Boca Chica and the fact that they were lined up wingtip to wingtip, easy targets for attack.*

There were three airfields in Cuba with air order of battle of concern to the United States. The MiG-15, MiG-17, and MiG-19 aircraft were parked in revetments or hangarettes at the San Antonio de los Baños airfield. The Beagle bombers were being assembled pell-mell at San Julián airfield and were scattered about the field. The only airfield in Cuba where the planes were parked in rows was Santa Clara airfield, where MiG-21's had been assembled and were parked along the taxiways.

Neither the U.S. Navy nor the Air Force took the precautionary measures of dispersing their aircraft as the president recommended because there simply was insufficient room at these airfields to dis-

---

* Bobby Kennedy's version differs substantially, stating that "when it was reported to him [the president] that our photography showed that the Russians and Cubans had inexplicably lined up their planes wingtip to wingtip on Cuban airfields, making them perfect targets, he requested General Taylor to have a U-2 fly a photographic mission over our fields in Florida. 'It would be interesting if we have done the same thing,' he remarked. We had. He examined the pictures the next day and ordered the Air Force to disperse our planes."[14]

perse the aircraft. There was also insufficient time to construct shields, so ground force personnel simply stood in front of the camera lenses during ground testing and pilots did delay airborne testing of their cameras until they were over the water.

The movement of ground combat units to Florida was under way. One of the most important units required for an invasion was the First Armored "Old Ironsides" Division. In February 1962, the division had been reactivated at Fort Hood, Texas. By August, with full complement of over fifteen thousand officers and men, it had been declared combat ready. When the missile sites were discovered, units from the division were engaged in the Joint Army-Air STRICOM maneuver exercise "Three Pairs." Early on October 22, the division was declared a new element of the combat-ready Strategic Army Corps (STRAC). Moments after the president's October 22 address, the division was ordered to move 1,100 miles to Fort Stewart, Georgia, forty miles from Savannah. Fort Stewart, the home of the U.S. Army Armor and Artillery Firing Center, was chosen because of its excellent firing facilities and because the terrain there resembled that of Cuba.

The Association of American Railroads had been notified that sufficient flatcars and passenger cars to move a division were required as soon as possible at Fort Hood. The railheads in the southern area of Fort Hood became a beehive of activity. Train after train arrived at the railyards. Tanks, armored personnel carriers, Honest John missiles, 105mm and 8-inch self-propelled howitzers, and weapons carriers were quickly loaded, chocked, blocked, and tied down. At night, activity continued under the glare of floodlights. In all, over 6,000 vehicles including trailers and thousands of tons of supplies were loaded. The move eventually required 38 trains, some up to 150 cars long, consisting of 2,418 flatcars and 299 equipment cars.

Personnel processing at Fort Hood continued around the clock. Medical records were checked; shots administered; clothing and equipment inspected. Five days of C rations were issued and troops started boarding the trains.

Although General Haines, commanding officer of the division, would have preferred that the trains be made up of integrated units—passenger cars along with flatcars, so as to keep the men and equipment together—it was obvious that air transport would be required to speed the movement. Ultimately, some 5,000 men would accompany the equipment while 10,000 would be airlifted by Air Force transports and 135 chartered commercial flights.

Later, some elements of the division would move to southern Florida. Mr. James Donn, Sr., owner of the Gulfstream Park Racing Course, at Hallandale, Florida, invited the U.S. Army to bivouac some of the troops of the Armored Division at the race course.[15] The Army accepted, and soon armed MPs were placed at all entrances; parking lots became motor pools and the infield was used for quartermaster purposes and messing stations. As the troops began to arrive in increasing numbers, cots were set up on the first and second floors of the grandstand building. Weapons and duffel bags were stacked outside the betting windows. Some soldiers whiled away the time sleeping in the grandstands; others picnicked or played touch football in the infield; the more devout attended church services in the photo-finish developing rooms. Although no racing program was under way at Gulfstream at the time—races were being held at Tropical Park, in Coral Gables—horses were in training at Gulfstream and the troops from the First Division enjoyed lining up along the rails to watch the thoroughbreds work out during the early-morning hours.*

The movement of such large numbers of troops to Florida was posing unprecedented logistical problems at military installations in that state. Although most troops were being moved with three-to-five days' combat rations, the feeding and care of these combat troops became the special concern of General Taylor. Headquarters of the 3rd Army at Fort Meade, Maryland, was responsible for feeding all the troops on the Florida peninsula. General Taylor directed the Army to complete activities of the Third Army Staging Area Command in Maryland and move to Florida as soon as possible.

Military hospitals, especially those along the East Coast, heretofore

---

* A bronze plaque on the wall of the Gulfstream Park Race Course Club House reads: "In grateful appreciation from the officers and men of the 1st Armored Division (Old Ironsides) who bivouacked here at the invitation of the owner, James Donn, Sr., during a period of national crisis in the fall of 1962."[16]

devoted primarily to treating service dependents, were being prepared to receive war casualties. Blood supplies were monitored and troops not involved in the movement to Florida were asked to give blood. There was also a call for an augmentation of chaplains. Two ambulance trains were activated for movement to Florida, along with an Air Ambulance detachment from Fort Benning, Georgia. One hospital unit was sent to Florida in chartered buses. Presuming that this movement was another exercise, the buses had stopped at several liquor stores along the way. When they arrived in Florida, according to one source, the unit itself was a casualty.

Cadres of expert communication specialists were being sent from the Pentagon to Florida to make all the necessary preparations to link the Florida military installations into an integrated communications net. Truck after truck left the Letterkenny Ordnance Depot in Chambersburg, Pennsylvania, and, loaded with ammunition, rolled to Florida. The war plans for Cuba called for the use of napalm, and hundreds of napalm drop tanks were arriving at the naval and tactical airfields, where they were stacked like "mountains of cordwood." Several ordnance plants were placed on three-shift, seven-day-a-week schedules to produce 20mm strafing ammunition required for the fighter aircraft deployed to Florida. The Navy also called for ordnance required for naval gunfire on Cuban installations to be moved to naval bases in Florida.

Boat units from Fort Eustis, Virginia, New Orleans, Louisiana, and Sunny Point, North Carolina, were directed to move to Fort Lauderdale and Port Everglades, Florida.[17] The Navy had promised a "dry foot" landing and had commenced practicing to ensure that promise.

The Army Intelligence Center at Fort Holabird was called upon to provide linguists, specialists in field-intelligence operations, and counterintelligence agents. Camp Jackson, South Carolina, was also queried for Russian and Spanish linguists. Crash courses on interrogation techniques for prisoners of war were being offered to the airborne divisions. Provost marshalls reviewed plans for holding prisoners of war and refugees and for the handling of Russian internees. Plans were progressing well until it was discovered that no rations had been programmed for the expected large numbers of prisoners of war. When the State Department was queried for funds, the reply came back that State had no such funds readily available and "none had been budgeted for."

The White House press secretary was being besieged by newsmen—as was the news desk at the Pentagon—demanding to know more about the reported buildup preparatory to an invasion of Cuba. The president, feeling that the Washington press would exercise control in reporting military information, was appalled by reports that local television reporters throughout the United States had stationed themselves near army camps and naval and air bases and were reporting military details unheard of during World War II and the Korean War. Reporters were also staked out along the arterial rail lines describing the number of passing military trains and their contents. The movement of the 1st Armored Division was being reported in detail.

The president decided that a nationwide reporting guideline had to be established and asked the Department of Defense to draft it. While assuring that he was not imposing censorship, the president did want "the public information media of all types to exercise caution and discretion."[18] Information on the employment of forces, degrees of alert, defenses, dispersal plans, vulnerabilities, command and control information, air- and sealift capabilities, and information relating to the offensive and defensive capabilities was considered "vital to our national security." Editors having doubt about release of such information were asked to contact the news desk at the Pentagon. The advice given would "be on an advisory basis and not considered finally binding on the editors."[19]

On the afternoon of October 24, Leo Szilard, the renowned scientist and nuclear weapons expert, was a registered guest at the Dupont Plaza Hotel in Washington, D.C. President Kennedy's public announcement of the Soviet missiles in Cuba and the U.S. quarantine of Cuba convinced him there would be a nuclear war between the United States and Russia. He telephoned his friends and bid them goodbye. Resplendent in his most prized possession, an Edwardian cape reminiscent of that worn by President Franklin Roosevelt, Szilard stood on the steps of the hotel and surveyed the city before departing for Switzerland. Spreading the cape to the full extent of his arms, as if in benediction, he mused that if he ever saw Washington again, it would be in ashes.

At 11:30 Moscow time on October 24, the Soviet Foreign Ministry delivered to the American embassy in Moscow a second letter from Khrushchev to the president.* In this message, Khrushchev protested that the quarantine was imposing "ultimate conditions" and added, in harsher language, that the president had no right to do this, saying, "You, Mr. President, have challenged us."[21] The Soviets, he said, could not agree to such a demand. "Try to put yourself in our situation and think how the U.S.A. would react to these conditions."[22]

Khrushchev also said that he could not instruct his vessels to comply with U.S. orders given by U.S. naval vessels and concluded that the Soviet Union would be compelled to take the necessary measure to protect its rights. (The necessary rights were interpreted by the U.S. military to be the Soviet F-class submarines in the Atlantic.) Although it appeared at the time to be a defiant statement, in hindsight, it was a plea.

"You, Mr. President, are not declaring quarantine but advancing an ultimatum and threatening that unless we subordinate ourselves to your demand, you will use force."

Khrushchev appeared to be saying that since Kennedy should know that Khrushchev had ordered his vessels carrying military cargo to stop (and later turn around), the president should allow general-cargo ships to proceed through the quarantine line. He was also telling Kennedy that he could not be totally humiliated and embarrassed.

Khrushchev's message created a great paradox for the U.S. military. At that very moment, two of the F-class submarines, trailed by the U.S. Navy antisubmarine warfare forces, began moving toward the Soviet cargo vessels dead-in-the-water while other Soviet vessels probably carrying offensive missiles had turned and headed back to Russia.

There appeared to be an implied threat in the second message

---

* Robert Kennedy misdates it as being October 23; Sorensen dates it correctly. It was received in Washington at 9:24 P.M. on October 24,[20] and was in reply to the president's October 23 letter, in which he asked Khrushchev to comply with the quarantine.

when, in closing the letter, Khrushchev stated that the Soviets would "be forced for our part to take the measures which we deem necessary and adequate to protect our rights. For this we have all that is necessary."[23]

To some U.S. military leaders it appeared that Khrushchev had disarmed himself in advance, by ordering his ships carrying missiles or missile-related equipment to turn around. To others, Khrushchev was implying that new threats were still to come. To the military, this meant Berlin and the U.S. military alert in Europe was increased.

The president asked that Khrushchev's October 24 letter be answered as soon as possible. He emphasized that he wanted "the monkey put squarely on Khrushchev's back" and all of Khrushchev's polemic questions answered with one strong statement. Bobby added that "we should rub their noses in it a little."

The Kennedy reply was communicated to the Soviet embassy in Washington at 1:45 A.M. Washington time on October 25 and began: "I have received your letter of October 24th, and I regret very much that you still do not appear to understand what it is that has moved us in this matter."[24] The Kennedy letter went on to review the president's warnings of September 4 and September 13. "After that time, this Government received the most explicit assurances from your Government and its representatives, both publicly and privately, that no offensive weapons were being sent to Cuba."[25] He asked Khrushchev to re-review the September 11 Tass statement where such assurances were given. The president said that he had relied on all these assurances and therefore had urged restraint upon those in the U.S. government who were urging action against Cuba. The president said that all of these Soviet public assurances were false and that "your military people had set out recently to establish a set of missile bases in Cuba."[26]

The implication was clear. Khrushchev had to either assume responsibility for the missiles in Cuba or deny that he was in control of the Soviet military. This was almost identical to the position that Khrushchev had tried to place Eisenhower in during the summit conference after the downing of Powers's U-2: to either apologize or admit that the flights were perpetrated without his knowledge.

The president then reminded Khrushchev to recognize that "it was not I who issued the first challenge in this case" and that the American responses were proper. President Kennedy stated that he could take no other course of action. He also knew that he was acting from a position of strength.

McNamara, who had been spending most of his time at the Pentagon, was tense and edgy and there would be still another confrontation with Admiral Anderson on the evening of October 24. A tired and bedraggled secretary of defense, accompanied by Roswell Gilpatric, entered Flag Plot. What ensued is open to question, depending on which version one accepts, including those of the people present. All agreed that a serious argument ensued between McNamara and Admiral Anderson.

McNamara, still smarting from his previous encounter with Anderson, was in a belligerent mood and began to question Anderson intensely about the Navy's operation of the blockade. When Anderson attempted to take McNamara aside to speak to him privately, the secretary's attitude became even more agitated.

They went back to the charts. McNamara noted that there were two U.S. destroyers several hundred miles from the quarantine line depicted on the chart as a semicircle around a dot. When McNamara asked why the destroyers were so far from the quarantine line, Anderson took him aside again to explain that U.S. forces were holding down a Soviet F-class submarine at that location.

McNamara demanded to know who had given those orders. Anderson explained it was just part of the overall naval strategy and that in such situations it was a common Navy practice to "trail" unidentified submarines.

"How sure are you that it is a Soviet submarine?" McNamara asked.

"Trust me," was Anderson's answer. Then he added that the reason these Soviet submarines were so far west in the Atlantic was undetermined and that he could not allow them to "pose any threat to my Navy."

"How does he know you are above him?" McNamara asked. Coming as it did from the secretary of defense, this appeared to be an ignorant question to anyone familiar with submarines.

"He can hear us," Anderson replied in a biting manner.

"How can he escape?" McNamara wanted to know.

Anderson replied with a certain amount of pride and sarcasm, "Just let him try."

"How long will you hold him down?"

"As long as he wants to stay down. The option is his."

"Isn't this dangerous?" McNamara asked.

"If he chooses to make it so. Otherwise, he can do as he has in the past few days—that is, come up for air and charge his batteries."

McNamara was dumbfounded that Russian submarines were being held down and was irritated by Anderson's casual attitude; and he was most concerned about provoking an incident or a direct confrontation with the Soviets that might get out of control. McNamara asked Anderson to issue an immediate order on his authority for a special submarine warning procedure. Anderson complied and on October 25, the Navy and the Department of State issued the following special warning: "The Secretary of Defense has today issued the following submarine surfacing and identification procedures when in contact with U.S. quarantine forces in the general vicinity of Cuba. U.S. forces coming in contact with unidentified submerged submarines will make the following signals to inform the submarine that he may surface in order to identify himself: Signals follow— quarantine forces will drop 4 or 5 harmless explosive sound signals which may be accompanied by the international code signal X 'IDKCA,' meaning 'rise to the surface.' The sonar signal is normally made on underwater communication equipment in the 8 KC frequency range. Procedures on receipt of signal: submerged submarines, on hearing of this signal, should surface on easterly course. Signals and procedures employed are harmless."[27]

The special order proved ineffective. The Russian submarines, when actually warned, failed to heed the order and continued to stay submerged until foul air and uncharged batteries forced them to surface.

Anderson perceived in McNamara an uncertainty, a confusion, and an emotional instability. When Anderson reassured the secretary that things concerning the blockade were going according to plan, McNamara asked, "What plan?" Anderson handed him a large black notebook containing the specific operational plan and said, "It's all there." McNamara disdainfully pushed the book aside.*

The Soviet tanker *Vinnitsa*, carrying 9,000 tons of fuel oil, was already within the quarantine zone when the quarantine was announced. The *Vinnitsa* was a Kazbeck-class tanker, built in the Soviet Union in 1957. This type of vessel was the backbone of the Soviet tanker fleet. The *Vinnitsa* was not stopped or searched and was allowed to proceed to Havana, where the crew was warmly received by Cuban officials. There was Cuban television coverage of the arrival, and still photography was provided to international wire services. Obviously, Havana wanted to convey the impression to the world that the United States was afraid to stop Soviet ships.

The Polish ship *Bialystok*, carrying general cargo, probably food-stuffs and machinery, was allowed to proceed through the blockade. The Poles had purchased the *Bialystok* in 1948. An old ship built in Bremerhaven in 1937, it had flown a number of flags before being purchased by the Poles. During the 1960s, the *Bialystok* had been very active on the "Cuban run" from Baltic ports, via the Kiel Canal.

Robert Kennedy had asked that a search be made to find a Cuban merchant ship that could be stopped in the Atlantic. This would have been an ideal situation for implementing the blockade. When no Cuban vessels were found on the open seas, he asked for a thorough search of aerial photography to find a Cuban ship the U.S. Navy could stop in Cuban coastal waters.

Most of the Cuban fleet was engaged in cabotage voyages between various Cuban ports. Cuba's export products were moved to foreign ports primarily in Russian bottoms. Cuban merchant ships consisted of American bottoms acquired during the Batista regime prior to 1959; a number were Liberty ships produced during World War II. Two ships, however, the *Comandante Camilio Cienfuegos* and the *Sierra Maestra*, had been recently purchased by Castro from Poland and

---

* After the crisis, Anderson remarked: "The presence of many Russian sub-marines in Caribbean and Atlantic waters provided perhaps the finest oppor-tunity since World War II for the U.S. Naval antisubmarine warfare forces to exercise their trade, to perfect their skills, and manifest their capability to detect and follow submarines of another nation."[28]

East Germany, respectively. Bobby felt these ships would be good ones to stop. Both ships were in port in Cuba; with vengeance in his voice, Bobby said, "If one of them comes out, try to take it in tow. If it resists, then sink it."

Admiral Anderson was also asked to designate a British ship that could be stopped and boarded the next day. The president (more probably, Bobby) thought it would be an ideal way to point out to the world that the United States was determined that no contraband would reach Cuba—that the United States was willing to stop friend and foe alike. The president requested that his views be checked out with the British ambassador. The British were furious, and Ormsby-Gore relayed to Rusk a plethora of reasons why a British ship should not be stopped. Subsequently, it was decided that a vessel of another nationality be selected for boarding. The Greek merchant ship *Sirius* appeared to be a good candidate and a destroyer was asked to close in on her.

Concurrently, a Soviet F-class submarine, which had been closely followed in the Atlantic throughout the night of October 23 and morning of October 24, surfaced and started its diesel engines, apparently to recharge its batteries. A U.S. destroyer eased alongside. Amidst a cloud of diesel smoke, several Soviet naval officers appeared on the bridge. In international Morse code, the destroyer flashed the message "Do you need help?" The Russians responded by frantically shaking their heads and attempting to wave off the destroyer. When Soviet naval officers whipped out cameras to take pictures of the destroyer, officers on the destroyer did the same. Before the crisis ended, all four Soviet submarines being tracked in the Atlantic would surface for battery recharging. In all cases, U.S. destroyers were alongside and, frequently, patrol planes were aloft. In the words of one destroyer skipper, "The antisubmarine activities during the crisis were textbook examples of what should be done in a crisis." In fact, the whole planning for implementing the quarantine had been meticulous. Dean Acheson in later years would go to the extreme of characterizing the Navy's performance during the crisis as "flawless." Although direction from the top commanders was clear, most line officers credited the superb seamanship of the experienced fleet officers for this success.

While the EXCOM continued to discuss stopping a ship as a test case, the president reiterated to Admiral Anderson that only the president would decide which ship or ships should be stopped and which ships should be boarded. All public announcements of such actions would come only from the White House. An elaborate command and control network was established that allowed the White House to speak directly with the captains of the intercepting destroyers.

The Soviet tanker *Bucharest* was steaming toward the quarantine line. The order had been given not to allow the *Bucharest* through the quarantine line, and destroyers had taken up positions to intercept her. Admiral Ward would record in his diary: "The *Bucharest* was tracked on and off for the next few days with orders coming from Washington to track her, then to trail her out of sight but within radar range, then to discontinue trailing, then to resume contact and resume trailing." Then the president reversed himself and ordered that the *Bucharest* not be intercepted and boarded, in view of Premier Khrushchev's apparent desire to avoid a direct U.S.-Russian confrontation and the fact that the *Bucharest* would not be carrying offensive weapons. At 11 A.M. on October 24, Admiral Claude V. Ricketts, vice-chief of naval operations, called the White House and asked to speak to either McNamara or Gilpatric to request clarifying instructions. Gilpatric came to the phone. His instructions were "Do not stop or harass the *Bucharest*, but continue to trail her."

At 0745 on October 25, the 21,000-ton 665-foot-long Soviet tanker flashed the message "My name is the *Bucharest*, bound for Cuba" to the U.S. destroyer *Larve*. The *Bucharest* slowed and the destroyer pulled alongside, photographed her, visually checked the tanker, but did not board. The *Bucharest* was allowed to proceed to Cuba. It was well known in the intelligence community that the *Bucharest* had made a number of trips to Havana carrying oil and oil products.

Later that day, the East German passenger ship *Volkerfreundschaft* was also approached by a U.S. destroyer and allowed to proceed to Havana. Built in Stockholm in 1949, the *Volkerfreundschaft* was the ex-Swedish-American liner *Stockholm*, which had been sold to the East Germans in 1959. The ship, pride of the East German passenger fleet, had become a cruise ship for East German officials and workers. It carried some six hundred passengers and its regular home port was Gdynia, Poland. It too had previously made a number of trips to Havana.

The *Maritsa*, a Greek merchant ship under Soviet time charter, also was considered for boarding, but allowed to proceed after declaring its cargo. Built in Canada during World War II, it had loaded general cargo in Leningrad. It was known Soviet policy never to permit free-world ships to carry Soviet military cargo.

At a JCS meeting early on October 24, CINCLANT, through Admiral Anderson, had asked for Air Force help in pinpointing the location of all Soviet shipping in the Atlantic search area. The Strategic Air Command was the only service equipped with long-range aircraft capable of searching such a large area. General LeMay, without consulting any of his senior staff officers, puffed on his cigar and confidently boasted that the U.S. Air Force would locate all the Soviet ships in the search area within four hours. It was a wild, impossible boast.* But LeMay was not aware, at the time, the Strategic Air Command had no reconnaissance units deployed that were knowledgeable to perform, or capable of performing, such reconnaissance. The only SAC forces that could be deployed immediately against this mission were tanker aircraft stationed in the Azores and Bermuda. LeMay ordered they take off immediately to search for Soviet vessels. Sixteen KC-97 tankers began flying search patterns over the Middle Atlantic. The Air Force tanker crews knew little about distinguishing specific merchant vessels or arms carriers and began reporting all ships seen as possible Russian vessels. A CINCLANT lieutenant commander remarked, "What in the hell does a SAC bomber crew know about ships at sea? Much less a SAC tanker crew." A number of ships reported to be Russian because they had a red star on their stacks turned out to be Texaco-owned and -operated. Other ships thought by SAC to be Russian were, in fact, American, British, or Greek freighters.

---

* LeMay may have been remembering a personal outstanding feat of navigation in 1938. Many doubted the usefulness of the Army Air Corps in naval warfare at the time and a test case was proposed—to find the Italian luxury liner *Rex* at sea. LeMay directed the successful intercept 776 miles at sea on May 12, 1938.

18

October 25— Confrontation at the UN

"Yes or no—don't wait for the translation—
yes or no."

—ADLAI E. STEVENSON

O N THURSDAY, OCTOBER 25, third-world nations at the UN, seeking
a solution to the crisis, began suggesting that the crisis could be
resolved without loss of face on either side if the United States
would remove its missiles from Turkey in exchange for Russia dismantling its missile sites in Cuba. The British, it was known, were
advocating such a proposal as one of three alternatives. Stevenson
had also suggested the same proposal to colleagues in Washington.
Two days before, Radio Moscow had first suggested the same exchange. Subsequently, Khrushchev had mentioned it to several foreign ambassadors in Moscow. Soviet diplomats in London and at
the UN were also promoting such an exchange.

That Thursday Walter Lippmann, too, found merit in the missile
exchange. Lippmann knew, of course, that the Joint Chiefs of Staff
were recommending a military strike and invasion of Cuba and that
the president had decided on a blockade, which could, in a few
months, ruin the Cuban economy. Lippmann also knew that the
Congress and the American public were demanding some sort of
positive action. Lippmann, drawing from his experience, wrote: "I
have lived through two World Wars, and in both of them, once we
were engaged, we made the same tragic mistakes. We suspended

diplomacy when the guns began to shoot. In both wars, as a result, we achieved a great victory but we could not make peace. There is a mood in the country today which could easily cause us to make the same mistake again. We must honor an attempt to avoid it."[1]

These words echoed the views of President Kennedy,* but Lippmann then added, "I hasten to say at once that I am not talking about and do not believe in a 'Cuba-Berlin' horse trade. Cuba and Berlin are whole different cases. Berlin is not an American missile base. It is not a base for any kind of offensive action as Cuba is by way of becoming. The only place that is truly compatible with Cuba is Turkey. This is the only place where there are strategic weapons right on the frontiers of the Soviet Union. There is another important similarity between Cuba and Turkey. The Soviet missile base in Cuba, like the U.S. NATO base in Turkey, is of little military value. The Soviet military base in Cuba is defenseless and the base in Turkey is all but obsolete. The two bases could be dismantled without altering the world balance of power."[2]

Soviet ambassador Dobrynin could only view the Turkey-for-Cuba missile exchange proposal Lippmann was advocating as a trial balloon floated by the White House. Lippmann was regarded by the Russians as an "insider" at the White House and one who had a host of friends at the policymaking level in the U.S. government.†

Early on the previous morning, Khrushchev had launched a new initiative. He let it be known to several foreign diplomats in Moscow that a meeting with Kennedy was not only desirable but a necessity. He again offered to meet privately with Kennedy in Moscow, Washington, a mutually agreeable neutral country, or at sea. Privately, Soviet representatives abroad were suggesting Vienna. Later that day, Khrushchev issued a public statement that he would consider a "top-level meeting useful." This suggestion was given prominence by Soviet newspapers and placed on Tass circuits for dissemination

---

* The president, on several occasions during the crisis, made reference to Barbara Tuchman's book *The Guns of August* about how miscalculations of German, British, French, and Russian diplomats allowed their nations to stumble into World War I.

† In retrospect, there is reason to believe that the president was aware on Wednesday that Lippmann was writing such a column but made no attempt to influence its substance or suppress it. In fact, some intelligence officers suspected that he discussed the idea with Lippmann.

abroad. Radio Moscow carried Khrushchev's message to North America throughout the day, to argue the need for summit talks.

The president, in his October 22 address, had implied that the United States would be receptive to proposals for high-level discussions with the Soviets. And in a letter to Soviet ambassador Zorin the same day, Ambassador Stevenson emphasized the need for a high-level meeting with the Soviets.[3] Powerful members in Congress, however, were against Kennedy meeting with Khrushchev. Senator Russell remarked, "The last time the president met with Khrushchev in Vienna, he lost his shirt. This time he'll lose his ass."

Two days later, acting UN secretary-general U Thant, at the request of more than fifty nonaligned nations, sent identical messages to President Kennedy and Chairman Khrushchev suggesting a two-to-three-week "voluntary suspension of quarantine measures involving the searching of ships to Cuba." This period, he suggested, would "greatly ease the situation and give time to the parties concerned to meet and discuss with a view of finding a peaceful solution to the problem." Then he offered to make himself available to all parties concerned.

U Thant's plea angered the president. He was reported to have said, "With friends like U Thant and Bertrand Russell, who needs enemies?" The president would in no way accede to negotiations involving the UN. The Congress and the Joint Chiefs of Staff had the same reaction. There was little respect for the UN, and besides, the aerial photography continued to provide evidence of the Soviets' perfidy.

Photography taken on October 24 and the morning of October 25 was shown to the president the same day by McCone and Lundahl. The pictures clearly showed that work on the missile sites was moving ahead rapidly, even faster than before. Lundahl pointed out that the nuclear warhead storage building at San Cristóbal site no. 1 had been completely assembled within two days—between October 20 and October 22. Photography taken early on October 25 confirmed that two Il-28 Beagle bombers had been assembled, three more were in the process, and crates for an additional twenty bombers were at San Julián airfield.

McCone also reported that as of six o'clock that morning, at least fourteen of the twenty-two Soviet ships that were known to be en route to Cuba had turned back. Five of the remaining eight were tankers. Two of the dry-cargo ships continuing on were probably not carrying military cargo. Those that had turned back had a history of carrying military cargo.[4]

Continuing reconnaissance of the missile sites was intense. Colonel Steakley had decided to try color photography on a low-level mission, though it had been shown that exploitation of color photography yielded little additional intelligence information, had drawbacks for mensuration purposes, and usually took longer to process. Yet the photo interpreters were anxious to look at the color mission. It did indeed fail to yield any additional intelligence information, but a color briefing board of the La Coloma SAM site clearly showed the SA-2 missiles and the guidance and control radars, and one could distinguish each swatch made by the bulldozers in the construction of the revetments. Copies of the photograph later became a highly sought after memento of the crisis. In fact, it was one of the photos selected by the president to hang in the Oval Office.

Even after the aerial photos of the missile sites had appeared in many newspapers on October 24, on the morning of October 25, the Soviet commentator Vavilov on Radio Moscow asked, "Can anyone say that he has seen these Soviet weapons of attack in Cuba? No," he said. "The USSR and the Cuban government have reiterated that there are no aggressive weapons in Cuba. Soviet aid to Cuba is of a purely defensive nature."

The president also heard an updated report from General Taylor on the contingent military movements under way in the United States, as well as concurrent Soviet military preparations. The president was pleased to note that the CIA had not seen any indications of Soviet "crash procedures in measures to increase the readiness of the Soviet armed forces" and that there was no indication of retaliatory action against the United States. On the other hand, the president was cognizant of Soviet defense minister Malinovsky's statement that the Soviet armed forces were in a state of "highest battle readiness." Malinovsky had also warned that at "the first signal all the might of our armed forces must be brought into immediate action against the enemy."

U.S. ambassador to the Soviet Union Foy Kohler had remained close to his Moscow telephone throughout the crisis. Now he was summoned to the Soviet Foreign Ministry. Expecting to receive a Soviet proposal or information for transmittal to Washington, he was surprised when he was ushered into the office of a lesser Foreign Ministry official, who immediately began to criticize the president's October 22 speech as "crude" and "full of anti-Soviet rhetoric." Because of its anti-Soviet tone, he said the speech would not be printed in the Soviet press or allowed on TV. He also maintained that the missiles in Cuba were strictly for defensive purposes. Kohler responded that his government thought otherwise. The Soviet official warned that the Soviet Union could not be treated like Belgium or Luxembourg. Then he reversed his argument and probably revealed the true reason for the meeting. The crisis could be worked out without war if the U.S. exhibited some desire to negotiate. He then pressed Kohler to determine whether the control of U.S. policy with regard to Cuba had shifted to the U.S. military. Kohler responded that the actions that the Russians took in the next few days would determine whether that fear would become a reality or not.

That evening, Khrushchev attempted to create an atmosphere of normalcy to convey the impression that he was in command and to forestall any speculation that he was in political trouble. At the same time, the Russians launched a broad diplomatic and public relations offensive, but the crisis was moving too fast and the results of diplomacy were uniformly negative, as the Soviets perhaps anticipated they would be.

At the UN Security Council meeting that afternoon, the Cuban representative, Dr. Mario Garcia-Inchaustegui, denied that the weapons the Cubans possessed constituted a threat to the Western Hemisphere. "The representative of the United States," he said, "presented no valid proof of the affirmations made by his president that Cuba constitutes a nuclear threat to the countries of the Western Hemisphere. The weapons that Cuba possesses are exclusively for defensive purposes." Sir Patrick Deane, the UK representative, facetiously remarked to his colleagues nearby, "By no stretch of the Cuban or Soviet imagination can a nuclear missile with a range of 2,000 miles be called defensive."

It was soon obvious to intelligence officers that Valerian Zorin, the Soviet ambassador to the UN, had no instructions from Moscow other than to continue the Soviet *maskirovka* line. It was also obvious that the Soviet UN delegation was in total disarray. Soviet diplomatic and press personnel were still denying the presence of missiles in Cuba and dismissing all such charges as falsehoods even though the aerial photos appeared in some morning newspapers. When Zorin spoke next, he took a different tack and chided Stevenson as to why the president had not confronted Gromyko with the "so-called" evidence when the president met with him on October 18. He added that the United States had not said "a word to the minister of foreign affairs of the Soviet Union with respect to these incontrovertible facts. Why? Because no such facts exist. The government of the United States has no such facts in hand except the falsified information of the United States Intelligence Agency, which are being displayed for review in the halls and which are sent to the press. Falsity is what the United States has in its hands—false evidence."

Zorin had perpetrated, perhaps, one of the most fatal blunders ever made in diplomacy. Had he not been informed of the missiles being in Cuba by his own government? Did the Soviets think that the U.S. would not display the photography because it might reveal the state of the art of U.S. photo technology? Or was Zorin simply caught out on a limb and forced to conform to the Soviet deception?

The president had watched the UN session on television that afternoon and had Bobby relay the message to the UN for Stevenson to "stick him," a reference to use the aerial photos on the floor of the Security Council.

At the Security Council meeting that evening, Zorin's remarks gave Stevenson a perfect opening. He asked angrily if Zorin still maintained that the missiles were defensive in nature or "if I heard you correctly say that they do not exist or that we haven't proved they exist, with another fine flood of rhetorical scorn." The usually elegant, courteous, brilliant Stevenson then departed from his script. With frustration and then fury, he launched a flamboyant challenge to Ambassador Zorin.

"All right, sir, let me ask you one simple question: Do you, Ambassador Zorin, deny that the USSR has placed and is placing medium- and intermediate-range missiles and sites in Cuba? Yes or no—don't wait for the translation—yes or no."[5]

The audience was transfixed by Stevenson's aggressive confrontation. (While his challenge was regarded as a brilliant move and immediately applauded by both the president and the American people, it would be viewed by him in later years as a most undiplomatic act.)

"I am not standing in the dock of an American court and I shall not answer at this stage" was Zorin's reply.

"You are in the courtroom of world opinion right now," Stevenson pressed him, "and you can answer yes or no. You have denied that they exist—and I want to know whether I have understood you correctly."[6]

Zorin asked that Stevenson continue with his statement and said he would have his answer in due course.

Stevenson shot back, "I am prepared to wait for my answer until hell freezes over, if that is your decision."[7]

The chamber roared with laughter and Zorin, taken aback, tried to smile. All eyes were on him. Zorin was desperate. Cornered, he sought an escape. As president of the Council and in an attempt to avoid further confrontation, Zorin recognized Daniel Schweitzer, the representative of Chile. The Council again roared with laughter when the Chilean representative refused to take the floor and urged Zorin to answer Stevenson's question.

Now Stevenson interjected that he had not finished his statement and called upon Colonel Parker, who was waiting in the corridor, to bring in the photographic exhibits. Colonel Parker remembered: "I was frantically moved into position where I could take the boards out in front of the Security Council at the magic signal from Ambassador Stevenson and was given the briefing script that he was going to read only a few seconds before I actually was called in. Somewhat to my horror, I discovered that his assistants, well-meaning no doubt, had rearranged the material that I had prepared. The words were there and the sentences were there, but they were in different order, so that my briefing boards were now in the wrong order and there would not be time for me to put them in order of the briefing script. . . . There was nothing I could do except take them all out when my time was called, put them on the floor in front of the briefing stand, and as Ambassador Stevenson went from one to another, I would have to take my cue from what he was saying and my knowledge of the photography to make sure that I got the right board up on the stand at the proper time."[8]

The easels had been erected as Stevenson began to read from the prepared script. The briefing boards were three-panel foldouts. The first showed the San Cristóbal area on August 29, 1962. Stevenson explained, "It was then, as you can see, only a peaceful countryside." The second photo, he explained, "shows the same area one day last week. A few tents and vehicles had come into the area, new spur roads had appeared, and the main road had been improved." The third photo "taken only twenty-four hours later, shows facilities for a medium-range missile battalion installed. There are tents for 400 or 500 men. At the end of the new spur road there are seven 1,000-mile missile trailers. There are four launcher-erector mechanisms for placing these missiles in erect firing position. This missile is a mobile weapon, which can be moved rapidly from one place to another. It is identical with the 1,000-mile missiles which have been displayed in Moscow parades." Then, to emphasize his point, Stevenson said, "All of this, I remind you, took place in twenty-four hours." Parker remembered that a hush fell over the chamber and delegates and representatives strained to see the details. It was the first time that aerial photography, with all its irrevocable authority and impact, had been used in any arena to resolve international disputes.

Stevenson then began to point out the metamorphosis of the Guanajay IRBM site. Again, it was a three-panel board. The first showed the area on August 29, the second when it was first identified on October 17, and the third the heavy construction activity involved in completing the site capable of firing a 2,000-mile missile. Finally, Stevenson showed photo documentation of Il-28 bombers being assembled at San Julián airfield. At the conclusion of the briefing, Stevenson announced that the photos would be placed in the Trusteeship Council Room following the meeting and that "one of my aides would gladly explain them to you in such detail as you may require."

Zorin made one more try to blunt Stevenson's attack by alluding to the B-26 photos that Stevenson had shown the Council before the Bay of Pigs invasion. Zorin said, "One who has lied once will not be believed a second time. Accordingly, Mr. Stevenson, we shall not look at your photographs."⁹ Zorin had only compounded his blunder. Stevenson, addressing Zorin, said that the authenticity of the pictures could easily be established if "the Soviet Union would ask their Cuban colleagues to permit a UN team to go to these sites. If so, Mr. Zorin, I can assure you that we can direct them to the proper places very quickly."[10] Stevenson then made a direct but embarrassing appeal to Zorin. "We know the facts, and so do you, sir, and we are ready to talk about them. Our job here is not to score debating points. Our job, Mr. Zorin, is to save the peace. And if you are ready to try, we are."[11]

Zorin's ability to argue persuasively had been crushed by Stevenson. It was now all too obvious that Zorin had little independent authority to negotiate further with Stevenson. The Soviet policy of secrecy had grave consequences on Soviet diplomacy. To many, it proved that the Soviets could no longer be trusted; they had proven to be brazen liars in one of the most visible debate chambers in the world.

The impact of bringing the aerial photos on to the Security Council floor was best described by DeWitt S. Copp: "No other proof could have been more irrefutable, and no other proof would have been acceptable to many among ourselves, our allies, and, of course, those unsympathetic to us. The UN could not debate away the iron reality of the aerial photographs, nor could the world."[12]

But the UN impasse on the Cuban problem crystallized when the Security Council debate failed. The debate between Stevenson and Zorin had produced no new initiatives, no hint of arbitration on the part of the Soviets. The question of inspection of the sites was lost in a mélange of accusations and bitter rhetoric. The Security Council adjourned at 7:25 P.M. It would not meet again during the crisis.

That night, Castro in a long harangue, condemned the U.S. blockade and the reconnaissance overflights: "The matter of Cuba's supervision—their supervision has been to violate our airspace daily—a violation of our airspace, our territorial waters, and they themselves admit it, because they talk of an alleged photograph their planes took. How could their planes take photographs if they did not violate Cuban airspace?"[13]

In Havana, Foreign Minister Roa stated once more there were no offensive weapons in Cuba. When President Kennedy was told of Roa's remark, he repeated one of his favorite phrases, "There's another son of a bitch that didn't get the word."

Castro continued to maintain a hard-line position. Although the intensity of his anti-U.S. oratory had been reduced, he refused to submit to Soviet overtures to negotiate the issues. Distrusting the Soviets, Castro attempted to buttress his case for a more prominent role by raising other U.S.-Cuban issues. He was disturbed over the possibility of unilateral U.S.-Soviet negotiations and openly critical of the Soviets for failing to support his demands. But Castro had few alternatives. Although he was alienating both the U.S. and the Soviets, he forged ahead, at least temporarily and tentatively.

That evening, an irate president called Ray Cline, who was attending a dinner party at the apartment of Mrs. Anna Chennault, widow of the late general. The president said that he had heard rumors that certain CIA officers were alleging that information on the missile bases had been available for several days before it was called to his attention. The president wanted to know who was responsible for the intelligence and how it had been brought to the attention of higher authorities. Cline told the president that he was responsible. Cline then reviewed with the president the reconnaissance mission flown on October 14, how it was processed and analyzed on October 15 and the information brought to the president's attention on the morning of October 16, in accordance with instructions from Mr. Bundy. The president seemed satisfied.

As the tension mounted and the days became longer and more difficult, the president sought surcease in an evening swim. He would call Dave Powers and, together, they headed for the White House pool. Powers liked to repeat that the president had once said while they were swimming, "You know, if it wasn't for the children, you could easily say the hell with it and push the button." Powers said he looked at the president in a quizzical manner, and the president added, "But I can't do that. Not for just Caroline and John, but for all the children all over the world—not only for those that are alive who will suffer and die, but all those who will have never lived." Then the president emerged from the pool, put on his terry-cloth robe, and returned to the family quarters. Powers did not follow, thinking there were moments that a man had to be left alone with his thoughts—and that this was such a moment. Later, passing through the living quarters, Powers heard the president reading Caroline a bedtime story. He listened attentively and wondered if this was the president's way of showing his love for his child and all the children of the world. Powers said that he never discussed the president's personal thoughts with him on that day or ever again.

19

October 26—
The Crisis Deepens

"It was a worried, preoccupied message—the
most tormented communiqué that
I have ever read."

—GENERAL MAXWELL TAYLOR

U THANT HAD APPEALED to Chairman Khrushchev not to challenge the quarantine imposed by the United States. Such a confrontation, U Thant said, "would destroy any possibility of the discussion I have suggested as a prelude to negotiations on a peaceful settlement. Khrushchev's reply, on October 26, was predictable. He promised to keep Soviet ships out of the quarantine area for "a limited time." He reaffirmed his desire to end the crisis and said he was still hoping to end the crisis "on the basis of negotiation." But fast-moving events on October 26 and 27 were to preclude any such hopes.

The CIA cautioned that "Khrushchev's prompt acceptance of U Thant's appeal was calculated to involve the U.S. in protracted negotiations. The Soviet leaders clearly believe that a temporary suspension of arms deliveries would be small price to pay for arrangements which, they hoped would effectively forestall further U.S. action against the military buildup in Cuba."[1]

Radio Moscow on the morning of October 26 was still protesting there were no offensive missiles in Cuba. *Pravda*, in an editorial, "Reason Must Triumph," urged the U.S. to exercise caution and realize that "the situation, aggravated to the extreme, can push the world into the abyss of war." *Red Star*, in an article entitled "Cuba Is Not Alone," trumpeted previous claims concerning the accuracy and destructiveness of Soviet rockets and that the peace-loving people have enough forces to curb a U.S. invasion of Cuba.

Moderate elements within the Politburo, however, joined with Khrushchev that morning to consider concessions to the United States. They knew that the United States had a clear superiority in both the quantity and quality of nuclear delivery systems and believed that any conflict between the U.S. and the Soviet Union could quickly escalate into a massive nuclear exchange. An uncompromising stand could jeopardize further Soviet negotiations. It was also too late for low-level demarches. Khrushchev shored up his position. War was to be averted at any cost.

Kennedy also didn't subscribe to the idea of an invasion or of a war over Cuba. His generals and admirals had strongly recommended it, rationalizing that this was the only sure way to eliminate the missiles. He was positive that the United States could easily accomplish the invasion, but it would be his last option. The president was also determined not to paint Khrushchev into a corner but to allow a "white alley," as he termed it, for him to withdraw the missiles. The president liked to quote Liddell Hart: "Never corner an opponent, and always assist him to save face. Put yourself in his shoes— so as to see things through his eyes. Avoid self-righteousness like the devil—nothing is so self-blinding." Kennedy would later tell Norman Cousins, "We never had any intentions of invading Cuba. Certainly there were those who advocated an invasion but I decided against for one simple reason: it would have killed too many Cubans."[2] Then, rejustifying his position during the Bay of Pigs: "That was why we didn't commit our forces in the Bay of Pigs episode."[3]

Nevertheless, U.S. planning for the invasion and war was in full swing. Military leaders openly predicted that an invasion of Cuba would be as bloody as Korea but were confident that they could land and sustain the invasion force and destroy the Cuban and Russian forces. Cuban forces would undoubtedly head for the hills, and the campaign would be a protracted one. Talk of organizing Cuban brigades in the United States was progressing, and the CIA was making preparations to air-drop agents and guerrilla forces behind Cuban lines. One U.S. general later remarked, "The most significant fact concerning intelligence during the Cuban crisis was that most intelligence planning had been completed before the crisis broke." That morning, on schedule, the Center packed hundreds of up-to-the-minute photos for dissemination to each of the Army divisions scheduled for operations against Cuba.

At the October 25 EXCOM meeting, after reviewing the status of shipping bound for Cuba, it was agreed that the *Marcula* was a good candidate to be stopped and boarded. The *Marcula*, a U.S.-built Liberty ship, Panamanian-owned, of Lebanese registry, was Greek-manned, under Soviet time charter, and had loaded cargo at the Soviet Baltic port of Riga. The president approved the recommendation, because the *Marcula* was not under Soviet or Eastern European registry, and he also knew it was not carrying contraband. The JCS were informed of the president's decision, and they, in turn, notified Admiral Dennison.

At first efforts to pinpoint the location of the *Marcula*, however, had been frustrated. Finally, at 9 P.M. on October 25, planes from the carrier *Essex* spotted the *Marcula* and radioed her position and course to Admiral Ward and CINCLANT. The orders from Washington were explicit. The *Marcula* would be boarded when found, day or night. Admiral Beakley suggested to Admiral Ward that it would be nice if the destroyer *Kennedy* was one of the first ships to board a ship suspected of carrying forbidden cargo. Not long after, Commander Nicholas Mikhalevsky, commander of the destroyer *Joseph P. Kennedy, Jr.* (DD 850), on station east of the Bahamas, received a message from Admiral Ward to proceed at once to join the destroyer *John R. Pierce* (DD 753) and be on-scene commander to intercept the *Marcula*.

The *Pierce* made initial contact with the *Marcula* at 10:30 P.M. and shortly after midnight was joined by the *Kennedy*. Admiral Ward, ignoring orders, had decided not to attempt a boarding at night. He later explained: "Since boarding under any conditions would be tricky, and inspections during darkness only partially effective, it was decided to postpone boarding until daylight."[4]

The two destroyers trailed the *Marcula* at a distance of about two miles throughout the night. Orders were then received from Ward to intercept and board the *Marcula* at first clear light. The destroyers had established and maintained radio contact with the *Marcula* throughout the night and the *Marcula*'s skipper had been notified of the intent to stop and board his ship. The skipper expressed a willingness to cooperate.

At 6:50 A.M. on October 26, the *Kennedy* hailed the *Marcula* with flashing light signals and ran up the international flag hoist OSCAR NOVEMBER—"You should heave to; stop at once!" The *Marcula* complied. The *Kennedy* radioed the *Marcula*'s location: 26 degrees 30 minutes north, 74 degrees 30 minutes west.

Admiral Anderson was in Flag Plot to follow the boarding. At 7:29 A.M., a longboat was lowered over the *Kennedy*'s side. In the boarding party were Lieutenant Commander Dwight G. Osborne, executive officer of the *Pierce*, and Lieutenant Commander Kenneth G. Reynolds, the *Kennedy*'s executive officer, along with Ensign Edward A. Mass, Ensign P. W. Sangaer, and Signalman Second Class J. P. Ruppenthal, all from the *Kennedy*. The men were in dress whites and unarmed.[5]

The *Marcula* lowered a Jacob's ladder for the boarding party. The Americans were greeted by Captain Condorrigas, the *Marcula*'s skipper, his chief mate, and his radio operator. They all spoke fluent English. Captain Condorrigas led the party to his cabin.

Lieutenant Commander Reynolds, in charge of the boarding party, announced the purpose of his visit and asked to see the ship's manifests. Captain Condorrigas complied and stated that he was aware of President Kennedy's quarantine order. After a review of the ship's manifests and records, the boarding officers proceeded with the search, accompanied by the master of the *Marcula*, the chief mate, and the radio operator. On deck, they examined twelve trucks. Belowdecks, they were shown rolls of paper, truck parts, machine parts, and sulphur cargo. The U.S. officer asked that one crate labeled PRECISION INSTRUMENTS be opened. The skipper complied. Captain Condorrigas told the U.S. officers this would be his first visit to Cuba.

After nearly three hours of inspection, at 10:20 A.M. the boarding party left the *Marcula* and returned to their respective destroyers. A cable was dispatched to Admiral Ward stating that the boarding operation had proceeded without incident and that no prohibited cargo had been found. The *Marcula* was allowed to proceed toward Cuba.

Admiral Ward responded to the *Pierce* and the *Kennedy* with a

"Well done" and ordered the destroyers to resume their stations.

The president had followed the boarding and had made his point to Khrushchev and the world. It was only the first move; plans for stopping a Soviet ship were still in force.

That afternoon, however, the Swedish freighter *Coalangatta* would again test the quarantine and communications system. Intercepted by a U.S. destroyer, she refused to respond or stop. An urgent message for instructions was sent to Admiral Ward, who consulted Washington. The *Coalangatta* was under charter to the USSR and had departed Leningrad on October 9 with general cargo. The Swedish Shipowners' Association had recommended that all Swedish ships submit to American search under protest, reserving the right to claim damages. From Washington word came back, "Allow her to proceed."

In Cuba, Radio Havana reported that morning that Raul Castro, the vice-premier and the minister of the armed forces, had gone to Oriente province, his usual post during previous military alerts, to "coordinate military activity." Che Guevara reportedly had established a military command post at the town of Corral de la Palma, in Pinar del Río province. Fidel remained in Havana.[6]

A highly polarized military situation was further aggravated by a number of Soviet submarine contacts that day. At 8:25 A.M., U.S. Navy patrol planes of the Atlantic Fleet reported an F-class submarine on the surface, probably recharging its batteries.

Meanwhile, at the Center, analysis of both the U-2 and low-level photography had clearly shown that the Soviets were working hard to achieve full operational capability for all the missile sites in the shortest possible time.

Construction activity in the Remedios area strongly suggested that a second IRBM site was in the making. Bulldozers and construction equipment were present, along with large amounts of prefabricated concrete forms and construction materials. Construction was also continuing at the Guanajay IRBM sites.

Detailed analysis of the MRBM sites clearly showed that an additional MRBM site—San Cristóbal no. 2—was now considered operational, making a total of twenty MRBM positions, and that Sagua la Grande no. 1 would probably be operational within hours. Launch stands and erectors had been or were being placed on the prepared MRBM launch positions. Cabling led from a number of the launch stands to camouflaged control centers in wooded areas nearby. Theodolite stations, containing the optical gear for precise alignment of the missile on the pad, and one of the last items needed for a missile site to be considered operational, had appeared at each of the launch sites.

Activity near the missile checkout tents appeared to be at a high level. Vans with large ducts extending into the tents were visible, suggesting that the tents were being heated, air-conditioned, or dehumidified. Cabling from the tents led to control areas or to generators, indicating that missiles were being checked out or held in a state of readiness. Fuel and oxidizer trailers were nearby.

Missile support equipment—such as generators, vans, propellent transporters, and pumps, used in preparing the missile for firing—had been moved into the close proximity of many of the MRBM launch stands.

What was even more disturbing to the interpreters and to Lundahl was that the Russians had begun to employ concealment measures at the missile sites. In addition to using trees, shrubbery, and bushes to conceal missile equipment, various forms of camouflaging was also being used. Garnished netting had been erected over some of the missile support equipment. Plastic camouflaged sheathing appeared over a number of the launchers and erectors. The canvas covers of some of the missiles and missile transporters had been painted with disruptive patterns.

Lundahl was shown something even more ominous. Heavy track activity in the wet soil, not present on late-afternoon coverage of October 24, appeared on early photographic coverage of October 25, suggesting that the missile systems had been checked out or exercised during the previous evening or night.

Lundahl realized the impact that all of this information would have on the policymakers. He knew that it had to be clearly conveyed, neither overstated nor underplayed, and in any event, he must not "create a fear or stampede." As Lundahl related it: "I had mulled over in my mind what I was going to say. It was to be stated succinctly—very, very conclusive, without any dramatics, so that the decision makers would be convinced, just as the photo interpreters were, that the crisis was entering a new phase."

Lundahl said he had experienced the dilemma of the messenger carrying the bad news to the king. Lundahl's clear and articulate presentation to the USIB, the EXCOM and, later, to the president himself successfully expelled any dilemma.

The president reacted to the information by shaking his head in disbelief. He felt that the Russians were testing him and his room for maneuver was being constricted. He then thought for a few moments and asked that a public statement, based on the information Lundahl presented, be prepared.

That afternoon, the following statement was released by the White House: "The development of ballistic missile sites in Cuba continues at a rapid pace. Through the process of continued surveillance directed by the President, additional evidence has been acquired which clearly reflects that as of Thursday, October 25, definite buildup in these offensive missile sites continued to be made. The activity at these sites apparently is directed at achieving a full operational capability as soon as possible.

"There is evidence that as of yesterday, October 25, considerable construction activity was being engaged in at the Intermediate Range Ballistic Missile sites. Bulldozers and cranes were observed as late as Thursday actively clearing new areas within the sites and improving the approach roads to the launch pads.

"Since Tuesday, October 23, missile related activities have continued at the Medium Range Ballistic Missile sites resulting in progressive refinements at these facilities. For example, missiles were observed parked in the open on October 23. Surveillance on October 25 revealed that some of these same missiles have now been moved from their original parked positions. Cabling can be seen running from the missile-ready tents to power generators nearby.

"In summary, there is no evidence to date indicating that there is any intention to dismantle or discontinue work on these missile sites. On the contrary, the Soviets are rapidly continuing their construction of missile support and launch facilities, and serious attempts are under way to camouflage their efforts."[7]

At the USIB meeting that morning, concern was expressed about the Soviet "surging" the construction of the sites. A lengthy discussion developed regarding photographing the missile sites during the night. Colonel Ralph D. Steakley, a reconnaissance expert, was asked to comment on the possibility of using night flash photography. He said the Strategic Air Command had special flares for this purpose. These flares, dropped by parachute, provided light of noontime intensity for a substantial period of time. One aircraft, a pathfinder, would drop the flares while a second would do the photographing.*

The Air Force had RB-47E and RB-66 aircraft equipped with the proper cameras and dispensers to perform this task. The mission for optimum results would be flown at 7,000 to 10,000 feet. Steakley had copies of aerial photos taken during night exercises, and the USIB was impressed with the results that could be obtained from such reconnaissance.

When a decision was about to be reached recommending to the EXCOM that night photography be attempted, Sherman Kent asked, "When these bombs go off, they make a noise like a French 75, don't they?"

Steakley said, "Oh, much larger than that."

"And the light?" Kent asked.

"Oh, the whole countryside will be lit up."

Lundahl had made Kent aware of the night photographic experiments that Goddard had conducted over U.S. cities, including New York in the 1930s, and how the telephones of authorities rang for hours with calls from the scared populace when Goddard lit up the skies. The experiments generated such concern that Goddard was forbidden to conduct any further experiments over populated areas.

---

* The use of night pyrotechnics to obtain night photography had been experimented with by the Army as far back as the 1920s. During World War II, a need was established, especially in the Pacific, to learn more about Japanese resupply activities. Primarily through the dedicated efforts of Major (later General) George Goddard, of the Wright Patterson Photography Laboratory, powerful flash bombs were developed.[8] Lighting a relatively small and poorly illuminated area was one thing, but illuminated scores of square miles of an area was another. After the war, the Wright Patterson Laboratory continued its work on pyrotechnics. The geometry of taking proper night pictures, along with the proper heights and exposures, was computed and tested. Ejectors in the bomb bay of the reconnaissance aircraft could dispense either bombs or cartridges with the proper fusing or ignitors to have the device explode at the proper optimum point in its downward trajectory. The pyrotechnics source was either finely powdered magnesium or aluminum along with an oxydizer that would produce 50 to 100 million candle seconds. The camera shutters were synchronized to expose film with the peaking time of the flash. Bright flashes would be strung across the night sky by exploding bombs or photo flash cartridges. In 1959, night photography had been made part of the Royal Flush reconnaissance competition among the NATO countries.

The discussion then centered on the effect of such reconnaissance on the Cubans. Kent said there was no doubt in his mind that it would scare the hell out of the Cubans and the Russians, and the detonation of the flash cartridges would also considerably increase the chance of a hostile response by the Russian and Cuban air defense units, which would believe they were under attack. Kent asked about the possible danger to the flash-dispensing aircraft. Steakley admitted that both the flare-dropping aircraft and the photographing aircraft would be illuminated for some time, making them distinct targets for anti-aircraft forces.

After a long discussion stimulated by Kent's lucid arguments, the USIB decided that it would not be a good idea to use night reconnaissance, and General Carter reported to McCone that the discussion resulted in a firm recommendation against the night photography. McCone thanked Carter, commenting that he was happy that the pros and cons had been discussed and that he would report such to the EXCOM. Lundahl later assured McCone that with repeated low-altitude photography over the missile sites throughout the day, we could accurately measure the amount of construction accomplished each night, precluding the need for night photography.

The president now knew he had to seize the diplomatic initiative and strive to keep the pressure on the Soviets and Cubans. He had decided not to agree to UN negotiations and to focus instead on the missile sites in Cuba, insisting that the only solution to the crisis lay in their removal. There was a lingering fear in the president's mind that Castro might not have been told by the Russians, or did not fully realize, the magnitude of the threat to Cuba posed by the presence of the Russian missiles. The president decided that a message should be dispatched to Castro succinctly explaining the inherent dangers and a proposal advocating the removal of the missiles. He asked U. Alexis Johnson to draft such a message.

The president also hoped that a representative of a Latin American country friendly to both the U.S. and Castro could meet with Castro personally and make certain he understood the U.S. position. The logical man was the Brazilian ambassador in Havana, Luis Batian Pinto. A cable would be sent to Rio for transmission to Batian Pinto in Havana. Late on October 26, U. Alexis Johnson's draft of the cable was sent to McGeorge Bundy. The draft message to Castro stated that the Soviets were concerned only with their own interests, their ships had turned around, and they had put out numerous feelers to allied governments "for exchanges of their positions in Cuba for concessions by NATO countries in other parts of the world. Thus you are not only being used for purposes of no interest to any Cuban, but deserted and threatened by betrayal."[9]

Castro also would be told that the United States was closely watching the frantic work pace to make the missile installations operational and to complete assembly of the Il-28 bombers. Time was growing short, and the United States could not sit still while "the threat against them is being increased in this fashion. Further steps will have to be taken against Cuba and very soon." The cable proposed that if the missiles were removed, there would be no need for the United States or the OAS to invade Cuba.

A number of EXCOM members were opposed to the message. General Taylor, especially, felt that it would be regarded by Castro as a mark of weakness, and it was not sent.

When the U.S. Air Force learned that the Navy had been tasked to fly the low-level missions, it asked that it also be allowed to fly low-level missions. The Air Force, however, was not prepared to assume such responsibilities. It had assigned its low-altitude-reconnaissance responsibilities to the Tactical Air Command (TAC), and its reconnaissance efforts were in disarray. In contrast to the Navy, TAC had no integrated reconnaissance system. It had been experimenting with a multipurpose camera, in-flight processing, and a variety of aircraft, none of which had been developed into an effective low-altitude-reconnaissance system.

TAC had selected the McDonnell RF-101C, Voodoo, as its reconnaissance vehicle.* The Tactical Reconnaissance Center was located at Shaw Air Force Base, in Sumter, South Carolina, and was responsible for field modifications to all tactical camera systems. Tactical reconnaissance was performed by the 363rd Tactical Recon-

---

* The Voodoo had been originally developed as a tactical fighter, but because of its poor performance in that role, the aircraft was subsequently used for reconnaissance. The Voodoo was factory-equipped with the KA-1 and KA-2 cameras. They were of variable focal lengths of 12, 24, and 36 inches. The film load was 9½ inches wide and more than 400 feet long. The aircraft and cameras, however, were designed for medium- and high-altitude reconnaissance.

naissance Wing, also stationed at Shaw. The 363rd consisted of two squadrons of the RF-101's and one squadron of RB-66 photo reconnaissance and EB-66 elint aircraft. On Sunday, October 21, the entire wing had been deployed to MacDill Air Force Base, outside Tampa, Florida, ostensibly to fly reconnaissance over Cuba. The B-52's stationed at MacDill were given a two-hour notice to depart and were flown to Warner-Robbins Air Force Base, near Macon, Georgia.

In Florida, the Air Force flew several practice low-level missions with the KA-1 and KA-2 cameras. The camera systems failed to perform properly at low altitudes. The camera cycling rates were too slow, causing misframing, and the image motion compensation was inadequate, causing blurring. The Air Force quickly realized that the cameras were not suited for the low-altitude, high-speed missions and frantically cabled Air Force headquarters for help. Colonel Frank Grossman, of TAC headquarters, called Chicago Aerial Industries, manufacturer of the KA-45 cameras, asking if the company had any spares. The company had two and flew them to MacDill field, where they were quickly installed in an RF-101. The camera was tested in the aircraft for one day and the Air Force's first successful low-level reconnaissance mission over Cuba was accomplished early on the morning of October 26.

Brigadier General Horace Aynesworth of TAC contacted Chicago Aerial Industries to inquire if any more KA-45's were available. He was informed that twenty-two KA-45 cameras were ready for shipment to the Navy. General Aynesworth attempted to procure some of the cameras from the Navy but was refused. Aynesworth called General Sweeney, commander of the Tactical Air Command, who pleaded with General Curtis LeMay to approach Admiral Anderson. LeMay emphasized to the admiral that as commander of SAC, he had frequently been generous to the Navy; Admiral Anderson agreed to split the shipment.

The story of the Navy bailout of the Air Force low-altitude reconnaissance predicament became a muted classic of the Cuban missile crisis. In a round-the-clock effort, the Chicago Aerial Industries cameras were installed in the RF-101's. Colonel A. A. McCartan, the commander of the 363rd, his deputy, Colonel Earl Butts, and Colonel Robert L. Ramsey, deputy commander for matériel, worked closely with their reconnaissance specialists until six additional RF-101's were ready to fly low-altitude missions over Cuba.

The Tactical Air Command not only had failed to develop a low-altitude reconnaissance capability but also had not properly trained its photo interpreters to interpret strategic targets. Furthermore, its photo-interpretation units were seriously understaffed. The command was aware of these deficiencies and immediate action was taken to rectify them. Brigadier General Robert N. Smith, director of intelligence at SAC, was asked to provide photo-interpretation assistance to support TAC's reconnaissance evaluation effort. He agreed, but not before informing General LeMay at the Pentagon, who fumed, "Don't they do anything right in that damn command?"

Early on the morning of October 21, eighteen SAC photo interpreters received orders to proceed immediately to MacDill AFB. Six interpreters came from the 2nd Reconnaissance Technical Squadron, at Barksdale AFB, Louisiana, while others came from the 8th Reconnaissance Technical Squadron, at Westover AFB, Massachusetts, and the 15th Reconnaissance Technical Squadron, at March AFB, California.

Arriving at MacDill, the SAC photo interpreters were briefed by a TAC major who was himself poorly informed on the TAC mission at MacDill. The photo interpreters had been given specific assignments—i.e., accomplish a preliminary examination of various targets to determine the quality of coverage and provide feedback to the mission planners. The eighteen TDY (temporary duty) SAC interpreters would be integrated with seven officers and twenty-two enlisted men of the 363rd Tactical Reconnaissance Wing. The Air Force photo interpreters, after being divided into three eight-hour shifts, started collecting source materials, plotting targets, and trying to assemble a data base from which to work. Serious communication gaps developed between operations personnel and the photo interpreters. No one seemed to know when the film would arrive from the processing site or what areas in Cuba had been covered. Reconnaissance pilots often came to the photo interpreters and made their flight charts available inasmuch as the majority of the interpreters were unfamiliar with Cuban terrain. When photography from an Air Force low-level mission was totally unusable, SAC photo interpreters tried to help the pilots to make sure that their velocity/altitude settings on the cameras were correct. A number of pilots admitted that they were flying at 200 to 250 feet with a camera setting of 500 feet.

The shift-work arrangements fell into shambles, with shifts and personnel constantly being changed. As a result, some men were off duty for the first four to five days, while others were working straight through for twenty-four to thirty-six hours. It was somewhat unreasonable to have a shift from midnight to 8 A.M. because no missions were being flown at night.

A contingent of Army photo interpreters also was sent to bolster the TAC effort, but on reporting, they were told by 363rd personnel they were not needed. The SAC and TAC photo interpreters were instructed not to talk to Army personnel or to tell them what was being seen or done.

When, at last, interpretable imagery was received, General Sweeney, the TAC commander, hurried over to see it. He asked the TAC major in charge to point out the missiles on the film. Reyes Ponce, an expert SAC interpreter, was flabbergasted. Finally, he could resist no longer. "Sir, what the major is showing you is a fallen palm tree." Needless to say, the major was quickly replaced.

Aleksandr Semenovich Fomin was officially listed as counselor of the Soviet embassy in Washington. He was in reality the KGB *rezident*, the chief Soviet intelligence officer in the United States, the equivalent of a CIA chief of station. He was a capable and impressive officer, one of the few in the Russian embassy who thoroughly understood the American government. It was rumored he had been personally selected by Khrushchev for the position. Fomin had first served in the United States during World War II and had returned on successive tours, each time with a promotion. He had numerous contacts with American journalists and frequently at prearranged luncheons solicited their opinions on U.S.-Soviet relations or U.S. reactions to Soviet pronouncements or policies.

One of those he lunched with was John Scali, State Department correspondent for ABC. At 1:30 Friday afternoon, Scali received an urgent call from Fomin asking for an immediate meeting. Scali, aware of Fomin's real position and function, felt that something major was up and arranged to meet Fomin at the Occidental Restaurant, on

Pennsylvania Avenue. Fomin had suggested that since Scali had highly placed friends at the State Department, they might be interested in a compromise position that might prove to be the solution to the crisis. The proposal he advanced was for Soviet withdrawal of the missiles, UN supervision and verification of the withdrawal, and a Soviet pledge not to reintroduce such weapons, in exchange for the lifting of the blockade and a public American pledge not to invade Cuba. Fomin further intimated that if Adlai Stevenson were to pursue this compromise proposal with Soviet deputy foreign minister Valerian A. Zorin, the chairman of the UN Security Council, he would find "a fertile ground for his ideas."[10] Then Fomin did something unusual for a KGB operative: He gave Scali his home telephone number and stressed the fact that Scali could call him at any hour since this was an urgent situation.

Scali hurried to Roger Hilsman's office and laid out the Russian's proposals. Hilsman asked Scali to dictate the proposals. Hilsman immediately sent copies to the EXCOM members and to the White House.

At the Agency, Sherman Kent regarded the Fomin proposal as probably genuine and surmised that Fomin was obviously acting on instructions from the Kremlin. There was some debate among Agency Russian experts that the proposal might prove to be false, or misleading as the Bolshakov messages had been. Others argued that it was a stalling or delaying tactic until all the missile sites became fully operational. Although McCone advised caution, he was convinced that no Soviet official of that rank could make such a suggestion without the expressed approval of Premier Khrushchev.

Rusk scribbled instructions for Scali and asked him to contact Fomin. Fomin had said he could meet Scali that afternoon at the Statler Hotel Coffee Shop. Rusk had authorized Scali to inform Fomin that the United States was interested in the proposal, but there was a deadline for an agreement. Testimony differs as to whether Scali was instructed to specify "forty-eight hours" or "two days" or simply to say "time was of the essence." At 7:45 P.M., Scali told Fomin of the American interest in the proposition and that the authorization "came from the highest level." Scali read the message to Fomin but did not reveal it had been handwritten by Rusk: "I have reason to believe that the USG [United States government] sees real possibilities and supposed that the representatives of the two governments in New York could work this matter out with U Thant and with each other. My impression is, however, that the time is very urgent." (Scali still retains the note and displayed it to reporters on August 4, 1964.) Fomin was further encouraged by Scali to place the Russian initiative into diplomatic channels.

Fomin, however, suddenly reversed his condescending attitude. He proposed that if Cuba was to be inspected by the UN, then why shouldn't the United States forces in Florida also be inspected? This clearly was an intelligence officer's desperate attempt to make the best of an uncertain situation. Scali dismissed these conditions to the proposal, stating that he was not authorized to speak for the State Department and went on to belittle it in view of the urgency of the situation. Scali reemphasized to Fomin the importance of a quick response. Fomin and Scali parted shortly after 8 P.M.

The Agency knew that Fomin's KGB position gave him a separate secure channel of communications with Moscow KGB head-quarters, independent of Ambassador Dobrynin and Foreign Minister Gromyko.

The president had demanded all week long that the Soviets had to withdraw the missiles, stating that this issue was nonnegotiable. He was still beleaguered, however, feeling that he had lost prestige and credibility both at home and abroad in his previous dealing with the Russians. This time he would have to be totally affirmative. Consternation among powerful members of Congress continued to grow that Khrushchev might interpret Kennedy's action as symp-tomatic of America's lack of nerve to wage nuclear war. There were calls, however, from others complimenting the president's stand.[11]

Even in a crisis, politics prevailed. Douglas Dillon remarked during an early-morning meeting of the EXCOM that there was the very real possibility that if the United States did not get the missiles re-moved promptly from Cuba, the next House of Representatives was likely to have a Republican majority and that this would completely paralyze the U.S. ability to react sensibly and coherently to further Soviet advances.

There was no doubt among the Democratic leadership in Congress that if the missiles were still in Cuba by the time of the November elections, it would be disastrous for both Kennedy and the Democratic party. There might even be calls for the president's resignation or impeachment. The administration would not be able to accommodate a Soviet fait accompli. At the height of the crisis, President Kennedy and Bobby had discussed the presidential decisions. Bobby said, "I just don't think there was any choice—and not only that, if you hadn't acted, you might have been impeached." According to Bobby, "The president thought for a moment and said, 'That's what I think—I would have been impeached.' "

At about 6 P.M. that Friday, October 26, the White House began to receive transmission of yet another letter from Khrushchev. This one was a long, rambling message—troubled but conciliatory, rather than belligerent. It had been delivered to the U.S. embassy in Moscow early on Friday morning. Llewellyn Thompson was convinced that it had been written by Khrushchev personally, and because of its length and complexity, it was thought it had been written before any Soviet-U.S. naval confrontation—certainly Thursday and possibly even Wednesday. Could it be that Khrushchev was making decisions personally and speaking for the Central Committee? General Taylor would later tell me: "It was a worried, preoccupied message—the most tormented communiqué I have ever read." He said that the question of a possible revolt in the Kremlin could not be overlooked. When Llewellyn Thompson was questioned about the letter, he said the tone of the letter could indicate a change in command, but he didn't think a revolt was likely.

Khrushchev put on record once again that the missiles were for defensive purposes—that he had put the missiles in Cuba because of the Bay of Pigs invasion. He questioned the legality of the quarantine and dwelt at length on U.S. designs on Cuba. He related his experiences in World War II, how he had lost a son and how much Russia had suffered. He declared he was a peaceful man. The letter was full of polemics: "Mr. President, you and I should not pull on the ends of the rope in which you have tied a knot of war, because the harder you and I pull, the tighter this knot will become. . . . Therefore, if there is no intention of tightening this knot, thereby dooming the world to the catastrophe of thermonuclear war, let us not only relax the forces straining at the ends of the rope, let us take measures for untying this knot. We are agreeable to this." The letter was ambiguous enough to suggest that any dramatic changes in the

Soviet position would be unlikely in spite of the pressure the U.S. was applying.

The October 26 letter remained unpublished for thirteen years. There were several interpretations of the letter by those who saw it at the time. General Taylor saw it as a stalling tactic; Khrushchev was still holding out for negotiations. It was completely rebuffed by the Joint Chiefs of Staff. LeMay said it was "a lot of bullshit" that the missiles were put into Cuba for defensive purposes. He said that Khrushchev must think "we are a bunch of dumb shits, if we swallow that syrup." Sorensen referred to it as "long, meandering, full of polemics but in essence appearing to contain the 'germ' of reasonable settlement; inasmuch as his missiles were there only to defend Cuba against invasion, he would withdraw the missiles under UN inspection if the U.S. agreed not to invade."[12] Bobby saw the key passage as being "If assurances were given that the President of the United States would not participate in an attack on Cuba and the blockade lifted, then the question of the removal or the destruction of the missile sites in Cuba would then be an entirely different question."[13] Bobby interpreted the letter in this way: "This is my proposal he said. No more weapons to Cuba and those within Cuba withdrawn or destroyed, and you reciprocate by withdrawing your blockade and also agree not to invade Cuba."[14]

Reconnaissance missions were flown until dusk on October 26. While the Soviets were mounting a diplomatic offensive, it was also obvious from our interpretation of the imagery from these missions that the Soviets were working overtime to bring all their missiles in Cuba to an operational status. That night we reported that five of the six MRBM sites were now fully operational; the sixth would be operational within hours.

Khrushchev's overall behavior in the week of the crisis appeared unsure and erratic. He continued to lie about the missiles, even after their presence had been established beyond doubt. His soldiers at the Cuban bases were working frantically while he attempted to pacify the United States. He threatened to run the blockade using submarines after ordering his ships to turn around. He threatened to fire missiles but had taken no overt offensive action that might cause the United States to further increase its alert status. Much concern was expressed as to whether Khrushchev's erratic behavior was indicative of the possibility of irrational acts.*

General Taylor said that Khrushchev's peasant vernacular and colloquialisms in drawing analogies were extremely difficult to translate and even more difficult to understand for those untrained in Russian history. The president's problem, as General Taylor would relate, was which voice meant what it said and which did not. But Khrushchev's days of decision were numbered. Quite apart from the confusion that his vacillation had created, the United States could not condone the continued feverish construction of the IRBM sites and the operational status of the MRBM sites.

General Taylor expressed a particular concern about the Soviet command and control system in such an emergency. The system relied on an echelon-to-echelon communication system involving human processing networks that become quickly overloaded in times of stress. Because of the bureaucratic maze through which Soviet directives had to pass, the command system was also frequently inflexible and slow in reacting to new situations. The system, essentially monolithic, had individual commanders often responding to new situations by buck-passing or indecisively seeking guidance at a higher level. There was a great need in the Soviet armed forces for automatic command networks using complicated computer supported systems. But in 1962, most of the Soviet commanders had received their command training in World War II and either were afraid of or had an aversion to automatic communication systems. The poor responsiveness of Soviet commanders at all levels contrasted sharply with that in the U.S. The Soviet system simply did not permit latitude to commanders at all levels in responding to crisis situations. Aggravating the rigid Soviet command system was the

* Medical intelligence reports on Khrushchev's health revealed that he suffered from hypertension, exhibited periods of irritability, lack of memory of recent events, and stubbornness. These were all signs of cerebral arterial sclerosis. The fact that he was known to be diabetic could account for some of his erratic behavior. Some reports indicated that he had suffered a coronary. Khrushchev also had become subject to fits of deep depression, occasional outbursts of violent temper, and an obsession to hit back. Most of all, Khrushchev was naturally impulsive and reckless, and he had the ability to be ruthless when desperate. It was also known that Mrs. Khrushchev was a major softening influence on Khrushchev's stern and unyielding personality.

fact that in Cuba, the commanders were even further removed from the ultimate decision makers, increasing already existing delays.

As the crisis deepened, one day blurred into the next and fatigue among the policymakers was beginning to show. Some were sleeping on couches in their offices after working sixteen-hour days, meals were taken on the run, and the fatigue was particularly evident in USIB and EXCOM discussions. "It was getting to sound like a broken record," Kent would remark. "You had heard it all before." Another participant remembered, "The faces grew longer, the tension increased and the sweaty concern on many faces was now becoming apparent. A certain irritability was showing up." Kent remarked: "Everybody was holding himself down in his chair and spoke in a low voice with consideration of the frayed nerves of everybody else in the room." Kent also observed, "The days of the long drawn out estimates were over. It was the day of the fire-bucket brigade. Policymakers were demanding a simple answer to complicated problems. The photo-collection programs were forcing analysts and policymakers to react to that information."

There was the fear that the unrelenting drain of emotional energy might make it impossible for them to fully utilize their intellectual capacities. One member stated later that McNamara was sleeping on his couch in the Pentagon and was "unraveling," and Rusk, much to the consternation of the Kennedys, especially Bobby, was leaving details of the crisis handling to George Ball. The president had to be spared this drain. Although curtailed, some visitor activities were maintained by the president; he kept his normal working hours. He slept regular hours, ate hearty meals, went swimming regularly with Dave Powers, and took hot baths. When he met with the EXCOM or took regular morning briefings from McCone and Lundahl, his thinking, judgment, and decision-making process remained clear and decisive. He was never testy or angry with his subordinates. In fact, he went out of his way to be pleasant.

McGeorge Bundy also was well aware of the strain on the policymakers and became very solicitous in his relations with them. He would ask if they had had a good lunch or dinner and if they were getting enough sleep. His concern was not restricted to the policymakers; he was especially concerned about the photo interpreters. Bundy recognized they were the key to this crisis and that if they missed some crucial information or made faulty judgments, the overall effect could be damaging at the highest levels. The EXCOM was now accepting the photo interpreters' judgments with a high degree of confidence, with no questioning. Bundy was aware that the interpreters, too, must be feeling the pressure and experiencing the fatigue. He kept asking Lundahl about the continued efficiency of the photo interpreters. He was much relieved to learn that the photo-interpretation efforts were being conducted on a shift basis.

Long after the crisis, when Bundy would see people who he knew had contributed considerable effort to the crisis, his opening gambit would be something like, "Caught up on your sleep yet?" or, "Ready for another crisis?"

On the afternoon of October 26, the FBI reported that the Soviets were burning their archives not only at the Washington embassy but also at the Soviet UN enclave at Glen Cove, Long Island. The burning of sensitive files is normally the last diplomatic act in preparation for war. When asked by the Hungarian chargé if there were any plans to evacuate the dependents of the Soviet personnel, Dobrynin replied in the negative.

If nuclear war became a distinct possibility, the Office of Emergency Preparedness had formulated plans for the evacuation of the president from Washington. The coordinator within the White House staff for preparing such a move was General Chester V. "Ted" Clifton, the president's military adviser. However, there appeared to be some conflict of responsibilities, because Secret Service chief Jim Rowley also was checking out details of his own plan for the evacuation of the president. The prepared evacuation shelter, located beneath a mountain, contained all the necessary records and facilities for the government to function. One principal drawback was that if it became public that the president had moved the U.S. government from Washington to an emergency location, the deleterious impact on the nation would most certainly cause widespread panic, especially in Washington and other large cities. The impression would be created that the president had abandoned the people, as well as the capital city, to nuclear attack. President Kennedy was not willing to execute this evacuation scheme unless there was all-out war, but he did dispatch his own family to their new home at Glen Ora, in the Virginia countryside.

20

October 27–All the MRBM Sites Are Operational

"A smell of burning hung in the air."
—NIKITA KHRUSHCHEV

LUNDAHL ARRIVED at the Steuart Building early on the morning of October 27. There was much work to be done. At the usual morning staff briefing he was shocked when told that all twenty-four MRBM sites in Cuba were now considered fully operational. The Soviets were capable of salvoing twenty-four MRBM missiles against U.S. targets six to eight hours after a decision to launch was made. The Soviet state of readiness also postulated a refire capability four to six hours after the initial salvo. An assumption was made that there were two MRBM missiles for each launch pad in Cuba. This could mean there could be forty-eight MRBM missiles in Cuba.

Lundahl also was told that Guanajay IRBM site no. 1 would probably be fully operational by December 1 and Guanajay IRBM site no. 2 and Remedios IRBM site no. 1 would probably become operational on or about December 15. He pondered all the boards and notes. He asked for a count of the missile-ready tents and MRBM transporters seen on photography and was told that thirty-three MRBM transporters and thirty-three missile-ready tents had been identified. As Lundahl studied the photography, he was apprised that additional fresh mud tracks indicated more missiles had probably been moved into the missile-ready tents and checked out during the night. It was our opinion that the entire MRBM missile force in Cuba had been checked out. Later, the formal intelligence report to USIB indicated that the MRBM force in Cuba was in an "integrated operational readiness posture."

Construction of the nuclear storage bunkers at the missile sites was continuing. The bunker at Guanajay appeared to be externally complete on October 26 photography. A white-water sealant was being applied to its roof. There were, however, no indications on photography that nuclear warheads had been placed within the bunker.

Photo-interpreter specialists in electronics called Lundahl's attention to the construction of new microwave towers being positioned near the MRBM sites and oriented toward a high-frequency communications site the Soviets had constructed near the town of Bauta. The photo interpreters pointed out that these were the same type of microwave towers that had been constructed by the RCA Corporation during the Batista regime. But these towers appeared new and were probably Soviet. This was another indication that the MRBM sites were being tied into an integrated command and control operational net.

Another disturbing new development: Automatic weapons and anti-aircraft artillery sites were being installed around the MRBM sites, and zigzag personnel trenches had been dug at a number of the sites to defend against air attacks. Camouflaging activity seen at the MRBM sites on the previous day was continuing. Clearly, the Russians were preparing to defend the MRBM sites against air attack.

In times of international crisis, little time or effort is usually expended at the federal level to keep state governments informed of the details of fast-breaking international situations. There are no formal mechanics for informing state governors of highly sensitive intelligence details or for coordinating policies affecting national decisions. In truth, the federal government would prefer not to be bothered by another body of opinion. The usual solution is to call the governors to Washington for a series of briefings and then seek their support. The Cuban missile crisis was no exception. The governors found out about the missiles being in Cuba at the same time their constituents did—when the president addressed the nation on October 22. The Civil Defense Committee of the Governors' Conference was invited to meet in Washington on October 27. The following governors or their representatives on the committee attended: Nelson Rockefeller, New York; Edmund Brown, California; Elmer L. Anderson, Minnesota; George D. Clyde, Utah; Albert D. Rosellini, Washington; John A. Volpe, Massachusetts; Ferris Bryant, Florida; William W. Barron, West Virginia; and Ernest Vandiver, Georgia. General Frances A. Woofley, civil defense director, represented Governor Jimmie H. Davis of Louisiana and General John McGreedy, civil defense director, represented Governor John H. Notte, Jr., of Rhode Island.

As the governors were assembling at the Pentagon on the morning of October 27, Lundahl spent a few minutes with us before he went into his office and rehearsed in his mind what photography he was going to show them and what he was going to say. This would be the first time that most of these distinguished men would be exposed to aerial reconnaissance, and Lundahl felt the briefing should be a "tutorial." McCone called for Lundahl at the Center in his personal car. On the way to the Pentagon, McCone informed Lundahl that he would personally conduct the briefing. He wanted to impress the governors with both his and the president's credibility. Lundahl appreciated that McCone had a lot at stake politically and wanted to look good. Arriving at the Pentagon, McCone quickly sought out Nelson Rockefeller, chairman of the committee, and chatted amicably with him. The tables were arranged in a U shape and the easel to hold the aerial photos was placed in the center of the U.

At 8:40 A.M., McCone began his briefing, using some of the latest aerial photography. Lundahl pointed out details on the photography as McCone painted a rather bleak picture—that while the Russians were proposing to negotiate the crisis, the photographic evidence clearly indicated that they had embarked on a "crash program" to make all the missile sites operational. The aerial photos had a tremendous impact on the governors. The evidence could not be denied. Governor Anderson recalled that he was shocked to see "the missiles in place, pointed toward the United States."[1] McCone emphasized that at least thirty missiles could now be fired at the U.S. In response to a question, "What will we do if they do not remove the missiles?" McCone replied, "Then we'll have to go in and dig them out."

Following McCone's presentation, Roswell Gilpatric briefed the governors on the state of U.S. military preparedness. Gilpatric stressed that while a number of U.S. troops were still in transit to Florida, others were poised to strike or invade Cuba if called upon by the president. Governor Rockefeller asked Gilpatric if an invasion date had been set. When Gilpatric responded that troops could well be moving against Cuba by Tuesday, Rockefeller grimaced. Governor Pat Brown was so disturbed that he demanded a joint meeting of the governors and the EXCOM. There was speculation among the governors that the prestige factor would not permit the Soviets to bow easily to defeat. Governor Anderson pondered the fact "that the U.S. was so close to attacking Cuba." Brown asked, "Just what does a governor do, if we are attacked?"[2] It brought a ripple of laughter, but the governors were not sure the crisis could be resolved peacefully. Anderson remarked that Brown "was clearly very upset at the possibility that we could be facing attack."[3] Others, like Governor Rosellini, placed full faith and confidence in the president.[4]

Gilpatric was followed by Steuart I. Pittman, assistant secretary of defense for civil defense, who briefed on a new proposed federal civil defense program.[5] Under the program, the marking of civil-defense shelters would be given priority and shelter stocking accelerated. Congress would be called upon to provide additional funds for new shelters as soon as possible.[6] The governors were appalled at how unprepared some states were. Governor Volpe would later comment: "As far as my feeling about the state of our Civil Defense Program at that time, I can only say I didn't feel we were as well prepared as we should have been, although some states were ahead of others. In our State, we did have a contingency plan but it was not a complete plan."[7] Governor Bryant expressed fear that Florida would be a likely target for attack because of the military buildup there. Governor Rosellini was concerned as to what could be done in such a short period of time, but when Khrushchev later announced that he would remove the missiles, Rosellini said, "It was a feeling of relief, and I felt a real sense of accomplishment on behalf of President Kennedy and our country."[8]

Following the Pentagon briefings, the governors were driven to the White House to meet with the president. Arriving at the White House at 11:56 A.M., they were greeted warmly by the president, who asked each of them if they had received all of the information they deemed essential. The governors nodded agreement. Governors Volpe, Rosellini, and Brown, who had met the president at political and social gatherings before, thought the president was unusually somber and harried. There was a consensus among the governors that the president might not have been forceful enough with Khrushchev.

Governor Brown asked, "Mr. President, many people wonder why you changed your mind about the Bay of Pigs and aborted the attack. Will you change your mind again?"[9] Some of the governors were surprised and uncomfortable at such a question. The president paused and was extremely serious as he responded, "I chose the quarantine because I wondered if our people are ready for the bomb." Governor Volpe agreed, but related, "I felt that the Russians, as they so often do, will push you to the wall, and if you do not react strongly, they just push a little further."[10] The president reiterated that the missiles had to be removed from Cuba. He then urged governors to implement accelerated civil-defense programs in their states. Governor Rockefeller, as chairman, reaffirmed full support for presidential firmness in this period of national emergency and advised the president to stick to his guns. He subsequently stressed the need for Congress "to make nuclear fallout shelters a reality for all Americans." Volpe later commented: "The President was very gracious in his appreciation to the governors for their support and indicated that he would not retreat from the position he had taken and hoped that Khrushchev would understand that he was not saying words just for the sake of saying them, but rather he meant business."[11]

Politics, it seems, remains paramount even in such a critical time. It was the last week of Pat Brown's reelection campaign against Richard Nixon for governor of California. As Brown walked out of the meeting with the president, he sought out Rockefeller and said, "You take care of this crisis and I will take care of Nixon, so he won't be a threat to you for the presidency." According to Brown, "Rockefeller looked at me with a puzzled expression, and I smilingly walked away."[12] The governors departed the White House at 12:19 P.M., but not before one of them, commenting on the inadequacy of the U.S. civil-defense program, complained, "It was all empty, so empty." That afternoon the president reviewed National Security

Action Memorandum No. 200, accelerating the civil defense program. He signed it on October 28.

On the morning of October 27, Khrushchev still obviously felt that he had time to maneuver and negotiate, but already, SAC B-52 bombers loaded with nuclear weapons were flying patterns to pre-designated points in the Arctic and at an H-Hour Control Line (HHCL) waited for the message from SAC headquarters that would either send them on to Soviet targets or return them to their home bases. Throughout the previous day and night, bomber after bomber had made its rendezvous over the Arctic. These flights were monitored by the Soviet air defense network and reported to Moscow, where they were particularly unnerving to the Soviet military. That day, the first Minuteman ICBM was placed on alert. By October 30, nine Minuteman missiles were ready for firing and Polaris missile-firing submarines were on station prepared to launch their missiles.

That afternoon, Mr. Pittman met with representatives of the U.S. Conference of Mayors, the American Municipal Association, and the National Association of County Officials. To each, he presented a statement of the status of civil defense applicable to cities and counties.

John Scali, on the morning of October 27, was called to the State Department to be briefed in depth by Roger Hilsman on the Soviet proposal to swap Turkish for Cuban missiles. Scali was also shown some of the latest photography of the operational missile sites in Cuba. Carefully rehearsed in approaching Fomin again, Scali played his role to the hilt. He telephoned Fomin and demanded a meeting; Fomin agreed to meet him that afternoon at the Statler Hotel. Fomin was waiting when Scali arrived. Scali immediately accused Fomin of perpetrating a "stinking double cross." Scali claimed it was all a Soviet ruse—the Soviets were engaged in a huge stalling maneuver until the Cuban missile sites became operational. When the Russian protested innocence, Scali fumed that he wasn't anyone's stooge, least of all a Russian's. When Fomin raised the Turkish-for-Cuban missile swap to Scali, Scali feigned anger and said it was not acceptable. Fomin then began to offer excuses and, at one point, attempted to blame the crisis on Castro. Scali flew into a rage. Did Fomin really think he was that big a fool? Then Scali emphasized that the Russians were frittering away valuable time and reminded Fomin that soon it would be too late. American troops were already making preparations to invade Cuba. At that point, Fomin repeated that his original proposal was sincere and genuine. Perhaps, he explained, there had been a delay in communications from Moscow. Fomin promised Scali he would try to get in direct touch with Moscow. Scali reported back to Hilsman and, together, they went to the White House, where the EXCOM waited to hear the results of his talks with Fomin. Scali affirmed that he thought Fomin was sincere and was convinced that Fomin was acting on instructions from a higher authority, probably Khrushchev himself.

(There are two footnotes of historical interest to the Scali-Fomin talks. After the crisis, Fomin again lunched with Scali and told him that Khrushchev himself had instructed Fomin to tell Scali that his "explosion on Saturday"[13] when Scali had charged "a stinking double cross" had helped Khrushchev make up his mind very quickly. The president was so pleased with Scali's performance that he had planned to give Scali public recognition for his efforts shortly after Fomin had completed his tour. Unfortunately, the president was assassinated before he was able to honor Scali properly.)

Lundahl and McCone had hurried from the governors' meeting to the EXCOM, which met, as usual, at 10 A.M. After hearing that all twenty-four MRBM sites were considered operational and that the construction of the IRBM sites was progressing at a rapid rate, Lundahl recalled that everyone seemed to be holding his breath. Lundahl also had informed them that additional Il-28 bombers had been assembled. After listening to Lundahl's ominous briefing, the EXCOM began to discuss the draft of a reply to Khrushchev's October 26 letter. Moments later, the Foreign Broadcast Information Service flashed a message to the White House that a new Khrushchev message was being broadcast by Radio Moscow. The immediate reaction of the EXCOM was that it might be a public broadcast of the October 26 letter. It was soon determined, however, that an entirely new letter was being broadcast.

This letter was also lengthy. While it applauded President Kennedy's action in trying to avoid a military confrontation and not introducing the "laws of war," it also contained a proposal that the Soviets would withdraw their missiles from Cuba in exchange for the U.S. withdrawal of missiles from Turkey. Khrushchev stated: "We agree to remove these weapons from Cuba which you regard as offensive weapons. We agree to do this and to state this commitment in the United Nations. Your representatives will make a statement to the effect that the United States, on its part, bearing in mind the anxiety and concern of the Soviet state, will evacuate its analogous weapons from Turkey. Let us reach an understanding on what time you and we need to put this into effect."[14] There would be UN supervision of the withdrawals. The Soviets also proposed that the U.S. and the Soviet Union support mutual "no invasion" pledges.

Although the message appeared to be boilerplate Khrushchev, it raised questions in the mind of the EXCOM members as to whether Khrushchev's October 26 proposal had been overruled by the Politburo or whether this letter had been drafted earlier than the October 26 letter. This was puzzling, since the October 26 offer was, of course, more attractive to U.S. leaders. The situation was further complicated because specific information was lacking as to what was happening politically in Moscow. Khrushchev had not been seen in public since October 25. There had been no recent direct Western contact with Khrushchev, and a careful review of all information, published and unpublished, did not portray any particular member of the Politburo in either a favorable or unfavorable light to indicate a possible change in leadership. The October 27 letter was an anomaly explainable either by bureaucratic bungling or a last desperate attempt by Khrushchev to get a more favorable deal than unilateral withdrawal. Some intelligence officers later felt that Soviet intelligence had gained information on discussions being held in the White House from Soviet spies in the British intelligence system, since this was the position being espoused by British leaders. If the Cuba-for-Turkey swap could be made, Khrushchev would save face both with the Politburo and the Communist nations.

Khrushchev, it was known, had been under increasing pressure from his critics since the outset of the crisis. General Taylor read and reread the second letter and reached the ominous conclusion that Khrushchev was in trouble. In a JCS meeting, Taylor stated, "the Russians are wavering. We will soon have peace or war." The JCS viewed Khrushchev as a master of the unexpected, and this heightened tension and uncertainty among the staff as to what action the Russians would take. The consensus was that the next Soviet move might well be in Berlin. General Taylor also was disturbed by Khrushchev's reference to "the arms that you describe as offensive." General Taylor characterized it as another indication of Soviet maintenance of their position. He still believed, however, that Khrushchev had backed himself into a corner. "He was faced with either inglorious withdrawal or the use of nuclear weapons—either one a helluva choice." While there was still room for negotiations under the circumstances, the JCS believed that the U.S. armed forces should be brought to a higher state of alert. The JCS concern was communicated to Admiral Dennison at Norfolk.

There was widespread feeling in Washington that the Soviet political and military tactics were being fully coordinated with Castro. This later proved to be untrue. Although letters and messages were being exchanged, the Soviets did not want to put themselves in a position where they could be attacked by the U.S. When Castro learned of the Turkish-for-Cuban missile proposal, he was furious. Castro later related to Senator George S. McGovern: "I would have taken a harder line than Khrushchev. I was furious when he compromised. But Khrushchev was older and wiser. I realize in retrospect that he had reached the proper settlement with Kennedy. If my position had prevailed, there might have been a terrible war. I was wrong."[15]

Premier Castro, angry with the Russians, threatened on the morning of October 27 to open fire on any U.S. aircraft that violated Cuban airspace. Concern was expressed at USIB for the low-level reconnaissance missions inasmuch as aerial photography had revealed that bunkered automatic weapons and anti-aircraft positions were being installed near the MRBM sites.

That morning, the Cuban air-defense network underwent a major reorganization. It became obvious that the Russians had taken complete control of the command network. Broadcast channels and the loose communications linkage with the SA-2 sites were now tightly integrated. Russian control of the defense system was also apparent in the introduction of Russian call signs, codes, and procedures now being heard by U.S. monitoring centers. The tracking of all U.S. reconnaissance aircraft was more intense and persistent. An October

26 *Red Star* editorial had reflected the Russian concern: "It is no secret in the USA that the ill-famed reconnaissance plane—the U-2—in violation of all the norms of international law, has penetrated Cuban airspace to photograph its defenses and other objectives." Castro, meanwhile, was demanding an assurance from Moscow that if the U.S. invaded Cuba, the Soviets would launch the missiles against the U.S.

The leadership of Strategic Air Command, responsible for conducting U-2 overflights, was still extremely sensitive and possessive of its authority. Although Agency U-2 pilots and flight personnel had been sent to McCoy Air Force Base to assist in flight operations, they were seldom called upon. The number of U-2 flights had been increased after the missiles were found in Cuba, and concern was expressed in Washington about the possible fatigue factor imposed upon the only two SAC pilots, majors Anderson and Heyser, who were each flying as many as two missions a day. Washington was demanding more and more photo-reconnaissance coverage, but it was not known how long the need for such sustained reconnaissance would continue. General LeMay had suggested, however, to the undersecretary of the Air Force, Joseph V. Charyk, that Agency pilots were not needed and Charyk had agreed. The CIA had always been careful in preparations of its U-2 missions over Cuba, ensuring that adequate safety measures were employed. Major Anderson's October 27 flight, however, was not supported with radar, sigint, or optical tracking coverage. There were no support aircraft with elaborate sigint or elint monitoring equipment flying the periphery of Cuba while Anderson's U-2 was over the island. The CINCLANT land-based radars were not capable of reaching the eastern end of Cuba, and SAC had not requested naval vessels with sufficient radar capacity to act in a "fill-in" mode in monitoring Anderson's U-2. Because of the number of missions being flown by Anderson and Heyser, SAC could not provide a second U-2 to fly the periphery of Cuba with the capability of visually observing and conversing with the photo-taking U-2.

The ill-fated U-2 mission of Major Rudolf Anderson on October 27 was designed to cover the eastern section of Cuba. He left McCoy Air Force Base, at Orlando, Florida, at 8:10 A.M. for an estimated 3.5-hour flight. He made landfall on the northern coast of Cuba at

9:15 A.M., flew southward to Santiago de Cuba, over Guantánamo, and then northward to Banes. Suddenly, at about 10 A.M., and without any warning or any voice transmission, his mission apparently ended near Cuba's northern coast. It was not immediately apparent whether Anderson's flight had terminated because of hypoxia—i.e., a failure in the oxygen system—or if he had been downed by an SA-2 missile. At first, military experts favored the first hypothesis because Major Anderson had equipment in his plane to detect an SA-2 fired at him and would have reported it. Representatives of the JCS hurried to the Steuart Building, and after tracking the flight plan and times against photography, it became obvious that the culprit had been the Los Angeles SA-2 site near Banes. It took NSA several hours to sort their data and conclude that Anderson's U-2 had been downed by an SA-2 missile.

(There have been a number of reports that Castro gave the command to down the U-2 or that there had been a firefight between the Russians and Cubans and that the Cubans had taken over the SA-2 site. Another version was that Castro had visited an SA-2 site and, knowing that the site was tracking a U-2, pressed the fire button, much to the consternation of the Soviet commander. The intelligence community would believe none of this.)

The CIA reported that the SA-2 system was under the total and complete control of the Soviets: "The SA-2 surface-to-air missile sites have been assembled and are being manned exclusively by Soviet personnel; the speed with which the SAM sites have become operational precludes any significant participation of Cuban personnel in the firing batteries, fire control elements or support elements."[16] The Agency reported further there was no evidence that a special cadre of Cubans had been sent to Russia for training to man an SA-2 site. Neither was there any evidence that there was a SAM training facility or program in Cuba. There was evidence that "the sole function of Cuban nationals is to provide security personnel and some support facilities."[17] (Kuznetsov would later lie, telling McCloy that all anti-aircraft weapons, including the SAM sites, were in Cuban hands. He never gave any details, however, on who downed the U-2. It wasn't until 1989 that the former Soviet ambassador to Cuba, Alekseyev, would admit that the downing of Anderson's U-2 was the result of a "trigger-happy Soviet air defense commander." Sergei

Mikoyan, however, would identify General Igor D. Statsenko, commander of Soviet forces in Cuba, as the person who had authorized the shoot-down.)

The Joint Chiefs of Staff Operations Plan No. 312 specifically directed CINCLANT to be prepared to strike a single SA-2 site, or all Cuban SA-2 sites, within two hours of a U-2 shoot-down. The established policy, agreed to by the president, was that if an SA-2 site fired at a U-2, that site was to be immediately neutralized. Sixteen armed F-100 fighters stood by at Homestead Air Force Base on thirty-minute alert to attack that site.

The Soviet military establishment was regarded as a large and complex organization with rigid standards and operating procedures. Soviet doctrine and practice reflected a do-it-by-the-book attitude. The Soviet air defense, especially, operated by established guidelines. The intelligence community could come up with no rational reason why the Soviets, who had been tracking the U-2 flights, would select this time to down a U-2. Most feared that the Soviets were escalating the crisis.

When word of termination of the Anderson flight reached General LeMay, he ordered the F-100's readied to strike. The most modern weapons for the destruction of the SAM sites had been issued to Air Force and Navy strike aircraft. Zuni 5-inch high-velocity unguided air-to-surface rockets had been rushed to Florida. The Zuni had proved especially effective against pillboxes, gun positions, trains, convoys, small ships, and ammunition and fuel depots. As many as forty-eight Zunis could be carried on the Air Force F-100 Super Sabre or the Navy's A-4 Skyhawk. The Zunis would be used to knock out the extremely vulnerable guidance and control radars. Other aircraft armed with the latest in fragmentation munitions—clustered bomb units (CBU) that had been designed for antipersonnel and antimaterial purposes—were rushed to Florida. The CBU were later used in Vietnam, with devastating results. The combination of the two weapons would be more than enough to destroy any SA-2 site.

The White House, realizing that there was a standing order for the immediate destruction of a firing SAM site, frantically contacted General LeMay and asked if the strike aircraft had been launched. LeMay replied that they were being briefed and prepared for launch. LeMay was admonished not to launch the aircraft until he received direct orders from the president. Angered, LeMay hung up. "He chickened out again. How in the hell do you get men to risk their lives when the SAMs are not attacked?"

When an aide said he would wait at the phone for the president's order, LeMay disgustedly said, "It will never come!"

At 2 P.M. on October 27, the EXCOM met with the president to discuss the loss of Anderson's U-2 and the fact that pilots of low-level reconnaissance missions were beginning to report their airplanes were being fired on by small arms and light anti-aircraft weapons. The U-2 shoot-down had escalated the crisis, and General Taylor was concerned that some kind of retaliatory action had to be taken. As he would later relate, in the military when you are shot at, you must let your men shoot back. If not, you shouldn't commit them to a mission in the first place. There were a variety of recommendations. McCone felt that President Kennedy should send a strongly worded letter to Khrushchev protesting the shoot-down. He added, "If there's any continuation of this, we just take those SAM sites out of there."[18] McCone's idea of a strong letter to Khrushchev, however, was not seriously considered.

There was general agreement that aerial surveillance of Cuba had to continue and that the SAM site that downed the U-2 should be destroyed, but no time for its destruction was agreed to. Downing of the U-2 had also raised the prospect that continued high-altitude reconnaissance of Cuba was now out of the question. Reconnaissance experts began to review options. One possibility was to use the new SR-71 aircraft. Although it had been test-flown, it had not achieved operational status. Use of the 240-inch camera also was reviewed, along with employing the Firebee reconnaissance drone. The EXCOM agreed that U-2 reconnaissance would be suspended temporarily, but low-altitude reconnaissance would be continued and expanded, with the reconnaissance aircraft escorted by armed fighters.

The Joint Chiefs of Staff were concerned that the longer the EXCOM deliberations took, the more advanced the Soviets' preparations and defenses became. In addition to all of the MRBM sites being operational, so too were all of the SA-2 sites, making it more difficult and more costly to destroy them.

The EXCOM then returned to the two Khrushchev letters. General

Taylor's opinion was that the Soviets were vacillating and he saw in this vacillation a reluctance to conciliation, with the attendant loss of face. The general also felt that the letter could reflect a genuine shift in Soviet policy. Taylor pointed out, however, that Moscow's military posture did not suggest any impending action against Berlin. Taylor thought it was extremely unlikely that the USSR would choose to go to war on "a worst-case basis." The Russians, traditionally, had always taken the time needed to ensure full military preparedness, but in this particular instance, Soviet military behavior seemed to suggest uncertainty and indecision. McNamara raised the possibility of an escalation to nuclear war in the event that a deal could not be worked out with Khrushchev and if events kept going in the same direction. Yet, as Taylor would later relate, "I never heard any expression of fear of nuclear escalation on the part of any of my colleagues. If at any time we were sitting on the edge of Armageddon, as nonparticipants have sometimes alleged, we were too unobservant to notice it."[19]

A very fragile and volatile situation existed that could explode into a major conflict with little or no warning. It could be only hours away. Secretary Rusk decided it was imperative to warn NATO members of the increasingly dangerous situation. U. Alexis Johnson composed a long cable that Rusk sent to all U.S. ambassadors to NATO countries. After discussing the downing of the U-2 and the missile sites' achieving operational status, Rusk instructed the U.S. ambassadors: "You can report that message from Khrushchev to President received night October 26, while full of polemics, seemed to offer real hope solution could be found within framework supervised withdrawal offensive weapons from Cuba in exchanges for commitment by United States not invade Cuba. U Thant's conversations in New York and broad hints in Cuban speeches at UN also seemed offer hope settlement along these lines could promptly be reached. Khrushchev's message to U Thant agreeing keep vessels temporarily outside quarantine area also seemed favorable sign. These hopes have been diminished by subsequent public letter from Khrushchev to the President linking Cuban settlement to withdrawal of NATO Jupiters from Turkey, but we continue to press for solution in Cuban framework alone."[20] After stating that the missile sites were operational and that some Soviet vessels were continuing to proceed toward the quarantine area, in direct violation of Khrushchev's assurances, Rusk warned: "In these circumstances the United States may find it necessary within a very short time in its own interest and that of its fellow nations in the Western Hemisphere to take whatever military action may be necessary to remove this growing threat to the Hemisphere."[21] Rusk then warned that: "US action in Cuba may result in some Soviet moves against NATO."[22]

On the diplomatic front, Cuban representatives were saying that Havana would be receptive to UN mediation, but there was a prerequisite—that the U.S. would not invade Cuba. Soviet spokesmen around the world continued to play down the possibility that the Cuban crisis could lead to general war. One important Soviet diplomat stated that "Cuba is not important enough to go to war." The Soviets were also floating trial balloons regarding an immediate Kennedy-Khrushchev meeting. Austrian foreign minister Bruno Kreisky was approached by the Soviets to offer Vienna as the site for such a summit. Kreisky suggested to U.S. representatives that Premier Khrushchev had enjoyed himself so during the 1961 Kennedy-Khrushchev meeting that Vienna would be the ideal location. It was unlikely that President Kennedy would be amenable to Vienna, considering the outcome of the 1961 meeting. Kreisky had an ulterior motive, of course, in that it would increase his prestige and boost his chance in the forthcoming Austrian elections.

Some EXCOM members considered the Cuba-for-Turkey missile swap an ideal exchange at this time. The principal argument advanced in favor of that arrangement was that the Jupiter missiles were obsolete and that Polaris missile-firing submarines would soon be deployed in the Mediterranean. When the missile-swap proposal was first raised by the Soviets, the president was furious. "I thought I had issued orders that those missiles were to be removed over a year ago."

At that moment, according to one source, Rusk gazed out the window into the Rose Garden. It was due to Rusk's inaction that the U.S. missiles were still operational in Turkey. Kennedy had raised the issue of missile removal at a National Security Council meeting nearly a year earlier and Rusk had been specifically assigned the task of making the appropriate overtures to the Turkish foreign minister. He did so during the NATO meetings held in Oslo in May 1962. In defense of Rusk, it should be noted that he had met resistance from both the U.S. ambassador to NATO, Thomas K. Finletter, and Selin Samper, the Turkish foreign minister. The matter was subsequently dropped. Then, too, it was U.S. policy that the Jupiters were not to be removed until Polaris submarines were deployed to the Mediterranean and the Turks provided with F-104 fighter aircraft. (Polaris submarines would not be deployed to the Mediterranean until April 1, 1963.) Again, on August 23, 1962, the president, in National Security Action Memorandum No. 183, directed George Ball to raise the issue of missile removal, this time with the Turkish ambassador to the United States. Turkish resistance remained, and Ball, in State Department parlance, "shelved the negotiations."

The United States at the time had fifteen Jupiter missiles in Turkey and thirty in Italy, under the control of the U.S. Air Force.[23] The missile had a range of 1,500 nautical miles, bringing most of European Russia, including Moscow, within range. Nuclear warheads for the Jupiter were under control of the U.S. Air Force. There were sixty U.S. Thor IRBM missiles deployed in Britain, each with a range of 1,600 nautical miles. They were operated and maintained by the RAF Bomber Command, but the nuclear warheads were under control of the U.S. Air Force. On August 1, 1962, it had been announced that the Thor missile force in England would be dismantled in 1963 and the missiles returned to the United States. Some of the returned missiles subsequently were used as space boosters for U.S. satellite reconnaissance.

On October 27, *Red Star* reiterated "arms-swapping" as potential bargaining of the crisis: "The U.S. demands the removal from Cuba of Soviet equipment provided by her exclusively for defensive purposes. Why then not remove American military equipment and troops from the hundreds of military bases ringing the Soviet Union."

W. Averell Harriman, assistant secretary of state for Far Eastern affairs, had sent a memo to the president stating that Khrushchev had been under pressure "from his military and from the more aggressive group"[24] in the Kremlin to do something about the U.S. ring of nuclear bases about their borders. Harriman did not define who constituted "the more aggressive group," but he stated that Khrushchev had been compelled to act in sending the missiles to Cuba "to offset the humiliation to which they consider they had been subjected by U.S. nuclear bases close to their borders."[25] Harriman went on to state that U.S. placement of missiles in Turkey and Italy, in his opinion, had been a mistake and had been "counterproductive, both in our relations with the Soviet Union and domestically, particularly in Italy."[26] Harriman deduced that there was a conflict in the Kremlin and that "Khrushchev had been induced to take this dangerous action in Cuba by the tougher group." Again, he did not identify the "tougher group." Harriman's unstated recommendation was that the U.S. should remove the missiles from Turkey "in such a way as to make it possible for Khrushchev to save his own face, to blame this tough group and to swing in a more cooperative direction."[27] It was the same position that Adlai Stevenson had advocated. In fact, to some of the EXCOM participants, it was obvious that Stevenson had spoken to Harriman and prompted him to write the letter.

The U.S. military, especially General Lyman L. Lemnitzer and NATO commander Lauris Norstad, opposed unilateral withdrawal of the Jupiter missiles from Turkey and Italy for two reasons. They felt strongly that withdrawal of the missiles should be used in negotiations with the Soviets aimed at having the Soviets eliminate some of their SS-4 MRBM and SS-5 IRBM missile sites in Russia targeted against NATO countries. Secondly, the Jupiters should not be removed under any circumstances before U.S. deployment of Polaris submarines to the Mediterranean.

Military leaders argued forcefully that the withdrawal of the missiles without accompanying defensive measures would pose acute problems and dangers for the NATO alliance. They went so far as to say that unilateral withdrawal of the missiles from Turkey would have serious repercussions and could lead to the downfall of the Turkish government. In a rare instance, the State Department supported the U.S. military position: "Neither Italy or Turkey can be expected to accept being made the bone of appeasement thrown to the UN or the Russians."[28] It was also argued that de Gaulle and Adenauer would be alert to any sign of U.S. withdrawal from the European continent and would regard such a unilateral move as another sign of weakness in foreign affairs by the Kennedy administration. The military remained adamant that the Jupiter missiles should not be removed. They argued that since Khrushchev had created the issue, the missiles should not be removed on principal. Every time Khrushchev made a move and we displayed a readiness to negotiate away our strengths and assets, he would be encouraged to conduct forays all over the world. The military felt that the time for a facedown was now, and Khrushchev could not have chosen a worse place than Cuba.

Questions about the accuracy and reliability of the Jupiter missiles were also raised. Although the Air Force would vouch that the Jupiter's reliability and accuracy had been proven in numerous flight tests, President Kennedy, in the course of discussions, would note in an aside, "In the course of discussing missiles in Turkey and Italy—Douglas Dillon stated that the reasons Jupiters were sent was they were flops—they couldn't have been fired if they had to."[29]

The events that day were making the JCS extremely uneasy. One of the more forceful criticisms that General LeMay would make during this period was that the president simply couldn't make up his mind. The military were determined not to let anything "happen on their watch." They remembered the Bay of Pigs review. Most felt that blame had unfairly been placed on the JCS and the CIA, while some spoke openly that Kennedy had lost his nerve at the crucial moment. Would he lose it again? they questioned. Dogmaticly and firmly, LeMay would summarize his feelings in this manner: "The Russian bear has always been eager to stick his paw in Latin American waters. Now, we've got him in a trap, let's take his leg off right up to his testicles. On second thought, let's take off his testicles, too."

EXCOM concern about the downing of Anderson's U-2 and the Turkish-Cuban missile swap were discussed deep into the afternoon of October 27. McCone was impressed with McNamara's concern about nuclear war and proposed, "I think that we ought to take this case to—send directly to Khrushchev by fast wire the most violent protest, and demand that he stop this business and stop it right away, or we're going to take those SAM sites out immediately."[30] The CIA director, much to the surprise of General Taylor, was now advocating to trade the Jupiter missiles in Turkey to defuse the crisis. He cautioned that the president should be firm with Khrushchev: "I wouldn't try to negotiate a deal. I would send him a threatening letter. I'd say, you've made public an offer. We'll accept that offer."[31] McCone then presented to the EXCOM a letter he had drafted to

Khrushchev, incorporating the points discussed in the meeting. Bobby Kennedy and Llewellyn Thompson maintained that the president should respond only to Khrushchev's first letter. According to Taylor, this left a hollow feeling, since nothing had been agreed to concerning the downing of the U-2.

Shortly after the Soviet Cuba-for-Turkey missile proposal was received at the White House, Vice-President Johnson called General Lemnitzer to the White House. Johnson stated he thought the Khrushchev proposal was a reasonable one and should be accepted by the U.S. Lemnitzer later wrote: "I had great difficulty in convincing Vice-President Johnson that our Jupiter missiles in Italy and Turkey were there by NATO's approval and were an important part of NATO's deterrent posture. Accordingly, they were not there as U.S. weapons."[32] The vice-president adopted a rather belligerent attitude, stating that "since we damn well gave them to the Turks, we can damn well take them back." Then Johnson, in his inimitable manner, said, "We can make it up to the Turks."

At 3:35 P.M., the Pentagon announced that a U.S. reconnaissance plane was missing on a flight over Cuba and presumed lost. A large air and sea search for Major Anderson continued throughout the afternoon and evening.

At 4:36 P.M., two low-level-reconnaissance pilots returning from a mission over Cuba reported that they had been fired on, apparently by 20mm or 37mm anti-aircraft guns, as they flew near the San Cristóbal and Sagua la Grande missile sites. Photography acquired by the reconnaissance aircraft showed anti-aircraft personnel running to man three 57mm and two 37mm anti-aircraft guns at a site immediately east of San Cristóbal MRBM site no.1; none, however, could be identified actually firing at the reconnaissance aircraft.

At 4:34 P.M., the White House issued a press release on the missile crisis, acknowledging that "several inconsistent and conflicting proposals had been made by the Soviet government. The statement confirmed that "work on the offensive missiles is still proceeding at a rapid pace." The president emphasized that it was imperative that before any Soviet proposal could be considered, work on the Cuban bases had to cease and the missiles rendered inoperable; that further arms shipments must cease; and that all of this activity be placed under effective international control.

That evening at 5 P.M., General Lyman Lemnitzer met with the president. The president explained Khrushchev's Turkey-for-Cuba swap. Lemnitzer later recalled, "In discussing this matter, I pointed out to the president that the missiles in Italy and Turkey had been provided by the U.S., they were now in fact a NATO—not a U.S.— matter. He said he had called a meeting (held after our conference) to discuss the reply he would make to Khrushchev."[33] The president nodded that he was aware of the NATO objection. General Lemnitzer was scheduled to leave for Europe the next morning, to replace General Lauris Norstad as NATO's supreme Allied commander, and accordingly, the president reviewed the European situation with him. He told General Lemnitzer to strive to achieve support for the U.S. position with the NATO allies. The president was certain that problems would arise with the European leaders, especially with General de Gaulle. He told General Lemnitzer about de Gaulle's remarks to Dean Acheson and de Gaulle's fear that the U.S. might take some military action without consulting him and other European allies. The president said he was thinking of sending Dean Acheson to brief the NATO Council. He also expressed concern about Berlin. According to Lemnitzer, "The President was particularly concerned about the possibilities of incidents in Berlin or along the ground and air corridors to Berlin."[34] He asked General Lemnitzer to warn NATO commanders of his concern. They both agreed, however, that there was no justification for the U.S. or other Berlin forces (British and French) to stay in their barracks. Lemnitzer said that if conditions worsened, "We also discussed possible measures to be taken to alert the NATO forces and the Berlin garrison after I assumed my new commands which were scheduled to take place on 1 November."[35] Lemnitzer reassured President Kennedy that the Soviets had made a foolish move in challenging the U.S. in an area where it had overwhelming superior air and sea power. The U.S. was in a position to strike first against Cuba and inflict intolerable damage on the Soviet Union as well.

One of the president's favorite words when talking to his advisers during the crisis was *prudent*. To make a point, he would often single out an individual's oblique statement and state rather categorically that the individual should be careful in making such statements lest they be misunderstood. In order to ensure that no inadvertent action be taken in regard to the Jupiter missiles in Italy and Turkey, he ordered that all the Jupiter missiles be taken off their pads and the nuclear warheads removed. Later, General Lemnitzer and other military observers would say it was a most stupid move—that in the event of war, it would have deprived the U.S. and NATO of a strategic strike force.

Each day during the crisis, McCone was still able to report that the Soviet Union and Bloc Eastern European nations were not taking steps to achieve a heightened level of readiness.[36] The forward Soviet forces in East Germany were in a defensive readiness posture, but Allied officers roaming the roads reported no-large scale movement and there were no suggestions that any move would be made on Berlin. That afternoon, however, tension was heightened when a U.S. T-29 aircraft outbound from Berlin in the central corridor to Berlin was intercepted by two Soviet fighters. The Soviet fighters made three passes but did not fire at the trainer. U.S. European Command (USEUCOM) braced for harassment by the Soviets in the air and ground corridors and promptly informed Washington of the incident.

The president was fully aware that U.S. forces were on a heightened state of alert and that orders had been sent to Admiral Dennison to be especially watchful of any change in Soviet naval moves. The president had been concerned throughout the crisis that the JCS or U.S. Navy commanders might inadvertently bypass him and issue orders to individual ships on the picket line, provoking an incident that would escalate to general war. On October 26, the Soviet tanker *Groznyy* was spotted steaming toward the quarantine line. The *Groznyy*, a Kazbeck-class tanker built in the Nikolayev Yard in Russia in 1954, had been converted in 1960 to carry liquid ammonia to Cuba. The *Groznyy* on this trip carried 566 tons of ammonia in deck tanks. The ammonia was normally discharged at Nicaro and was used in the nearby nickel refinery. The *Groznyy* had previously made a number of trips to Cuba, so its mission and cargo were well known to the intelligence community. It was not known, however, whether the *Groznyy* had been chosen to test the quarantine and could thus signal a change in Soviet intentions.

The U.S. Navy had lost track of the *Groznyy* and had frantically called on the Strategic Air Command to locate, track, and photograph the tanker. RB-47K's from the 55th Reconnaissance Wing based at Forbes Air Force Base, Kansas, flew to the Kindley Naval Air Station, in Bermuda. The crews were briefed on the approximate location of the *Groznyy* and searched until dark on October 26. Early on the morning of October 27, four RB-47K's took off from Kindley and began the search once again. One of the RB-47K's, heavy-laden with fuel, crashed on takeoff and the crew of four was lost. At 8:07 A.M. local time, Captain William F. Haynes, a navigator of the 338th Strategic Reconnaissance Squadron, spotted the tanker in the Puerto Rico Trench steaming toward Cuba. Captain Joseph Carney, the pilot, flew low and parallel to the *Groznyy* in order to make a positive identification. The crew was able to read the name *Groznyy* on both the fantail and bridge wings.

CINCLANT was immediately informed and, in turn, asked the RB-47K to remain on station until a destroyer could be dispatched to trail the tanker. The RB-47K took a series of aerial photos of the tanker. For more than two hours, Captain Carney circled his target, made repeated simulated bombing runs, and periodically reported the location and heading of the *Groznyy*. He then spotted a U.S. destroyer steaming toward the tanker. When the destroyer reported that she had taken the *Groznyy* under surveillance, the SAC crew proceeded back to Bermuda. Upon hearing of the success of the mission, General John D. Ryan, commander of the 2nd Air Force, recommended that the four crew members be awarded the Air Medal.

As the *Groznyy* entered the quarantine line, the U.S. destroyer pulled alongside but the *Groznyy* appeared to ignore the destroyer. The destroyer commander asked CINCLANT for instructions. CINCLANT, in turn, called for instructions from Washington. It has never been determined why the Russians permitted the tanker to proceed through the quarantine line. The *Groznyy* may not have received proper orders from Moscow, although this is doubtful. More likely, since it was a tanker and since the tankers *Vinnitsa* and *Bucharest* had already been allowed through the quarantine line, the *Groznyy* skipper may have thought he had permission to proceed without further instruction.

When CINCLANT asked the Pentagon for orders, it brought on still another confrontation between Admiral Anderson and Robert

McNamara in Flag Plot. McNamara asked what would happen if the *Groznyy* did not stop. Anderson said the instructions were clear: If after agreed-to warnings the *Groznyy* did not stop, a shot would be fired at its rudder. McNamara, in the words of several that were in the room, "blew his cork." He said that there was to be no firing on any Soviet ship without his express permission and he would not give such permission until he received the president's approval.

Anderson, who had had his fill of McNamara, stated, "The Navy has been handling quarantines and blockades since John Paul Jones, and if you people will let us handle it, we'll handle it right." McNamara replied, "I don't give a damn about John Paul Jones, but there will be no firing on Soviet ships." Then, with an antagonistic attitude, he stated, "Is that understood?" and stormed out.

After the *Groznyy* failed to heed the warning by the U.S. destroyer, several other destroyers that had also begun trailing the tanker loaded their guns on orders from CINCLANT. The entire incident could have easily precipitated events that might have led to the sinking of the tanker. With the tanker violating the quarantine and with the destroyers' guns loaded, the destroyer commanders awaited further orders. The only order received from CINCLANT was to clear their guns by firing the shells at sea. The clearing of the guns was heard and reported by observers to Guantánamo and elsewhere as firings on the tanker. According to Paul Nitze, the destroyers fired star shells close enough to the *Groznyy* to "show that we meant business." The skipper of the *Groznyy* panicked and frantically called Moscow for instructions. It quickly reversed its course, proceeded beyond the quarantine line, and lay dead in the water for several days. The *Groznyy* was permitted to proceed without having been boarded.

Totally incensed with McNamara's performance that day, Admiral Anderson flew to Norfolk that afternoon to attend the Navy-Pitt football game. Although his box had been rigged to receive special communications from the Pentagon and his special plane stood ready at the Norfolk Naval Air Station to rush him back to Washington, he would be criticized for being away from his command post at this critical period. He would not arrive back at his post in the Pentagon until late that evening.

There were additional difficulties along the quarantine picket line. Once the quarantine was imposed, the U.S. Navy, at regular intervals, broadcast special warnings to all ships approaching the quarantine zone. These warnings advised that reactions to the quarantine might make the Windward Passage, the Yucatán Channel, and the Florida Straits "dangerous waters—i.e., places where there could be confrontations between the U.S. and the Soviets."

But it was also obvious to high U.S. administration officials that provisions had to be made to allow cargo bound for areas other than Cuba through the quarantine zone. As early as October 24, these same officials admitted that consideration was being given to a clearance certification system. Although it was to be an integral part of the quarantine plan, the clearance certification was specifically designed to minimize interference with non-Cuba trade and also to placate Latin American and Western European nations.

At 4:06 P.M. on October 26, the Joint Chiefs of Staff approved the clearance certification (Clearcert) plan proposed by the U.S. Navy. It had been coordinated with State, Treasury, and appropriate Defense agencies. Early on October 27, the Department of State announced the institution of "a system of clearances to assist vessels which transit waters in the vicinity of Cuba and vessels destined for Cuba with cargoes containing no offensive weapons or associated materials."[37] The U.S. Navy, along with custom authorities, through advisories and periodic broadcasts, announced the details of the plan. The U.S. Treasury, through customs, would issue certificates for any vessel departing a U.S. port, while any vessel departing from a foreign port would obtain a clearance from any American consulate.

That evening, Defense Press Secretary Arthur Sylvester issued additional information on the downed U-2: "The Defense Department stated tonight that a military reconnaissance aircraft conducting surveillance over Cuba is missing and presumed lost. Surveillance missions will be continued and appropriate measures will be taken to insure that such missions are effective and protected."[38]

At 9:15 P.M. the White House notified the U.S. UN mission that: "An unarmed aircraft on a high altitude mission over eastern Cuba was probably attacked and shot down between 10:15 and 11:00 A.M. EST. Two unarmed aircraft were attacked while on low-altitude reconnaissance missions near San Cristóbal and Sagua la Grande at about 4 P.M. EDT. These aircraft were fired upon by small arms as well as by light anti-aircraft weapons but escaped undamaged."[39]

The Cubans—watching the U.S. buildup at Guantánamo, seeing the U.S. naval task forces off their shores, and undoubtedly receiving reports from their agents in Florida on the U.S. buildup in Florida and fearful that an attack was imminent—transmitted their fears to Khrushchev. Time was short, and Khrushchev was to place heavy emphasis on the extreme urgency of the moment. Khrushchev would relate: "On the morning of October 27 we received information from our Cuban comrades and from other sources which directly stated that this attack would be carried out within the next two or three days. We regarded the telegrams received as a signal of the utmost alarm, and this alarm was justified. Immediate actions were required in order to prevent an attack against Cuba and to preserve peace. A message was sent to the U.S. President which suggested mutually acceptable solutions."[40]

When McNamara returned to the Pentagon from the EXCOM in the early evening hours of October 27, he was thoroughly briefed on the firing at the low-altitude reconnaissance planes. He subsequently had the following statement issued: "Today U.S. unarmed reconnaissance aircraft, conducting surveillance of the buildup of the offensive weapons secretly introduced into Cuba by the Soviet Union, were fired upon. Such surveillance operations were in accordance with the resolution adopted on October 23, 1962, by the Organ of Consultation of the Inter-American System under the provisions of the Rio Treaty of 1947. To ensure that the nations of the Western Hemisphere continue to be informed on the status of the threat of their security, it is essential that such reconnaissance flights continue. The possibility of further attack on our aircraft and the continued buildup of the offensive weapons system in Cuba require that we be prepared for any eventuality. Therefore, tonight, acting under the authority granted me by Executive Order 11058, dated October 23, 1962, I have instructed the Secretary of the Air Force to order to active duty 24 troop carrier squadrons of the Air Force Reserve with their associated support units."[41] Over 14,000 Air Force reservists were recalled to man twenty-one C-119 and three C-123 troop carrier squadrons. These squadrons would be engaged in dropping paratroopers and delivering supplies to the ground units to be placed ashore in an invasion of Cuba.

That evening, too, Radio Havana boasted that Cuban anti-aircraft batteries had driven off unidentified planes. That night, soldiers were seen unloading medicine and surgical equipment in the basements of all the large buildings in Havana. The anti-aircraft guns around Havana were all manned. Shortly after midnight, hundreds of women reported to nursing stations. Havana, it appeared, was fully alerted for an attack. At midnight, Radio Havana would wearily announce that "This ends one of the longest nights of these times in Cuba."

With no U-2's flying, low-altitude missions were directed to fly near the Los Angeles SAM site in an attempt to locate Anderson's downed U-2. The U.S. Navy was directed to also search the sea, since the Los Angeles SAM site was near the coast. The secretary of defense declared Major Anderson missing in action after all rescue and search efforts failed. The Cubans would later admit that Major Anderson was "downed by our anti-aircraft weapons." (In the November 5 edition of *Revolution*, two photographs of Major Anderson's plane were published. It had fallen on land and, from the look of the wreckage, had fallen hard.) That night, President Kennedy wrote to Mrs. Anderson and her two sons, offering his personal condolences. He also authorized the awarding of the Distinguished Service Medal posthumously to Major Anderson, the highest honor that can be bestowed in peacetime. McCone had suggested that Major Anderson be awarded the Congressional Medal of Honor since the crisis was in a near wartime environment, but he was overruled by McNamara.

The downing of Anderson at the eastern end of the island led to speculation that there were additional undiscovered offensive missile bases there or some military activity so significant that the Russians would risk downing a U-2 to protect it. The premise that nuclear warheads were stored somewhere in this area was also raised. Photographic searches of all target areas of Major Anderson's flight track were ordered by the Defense Department, but nothing of significance was found.

The timing of the U-2 shoot-down was particularly unfortunate because the U.S. military was now strongly advocating that the only solution to the crisis was an immediate air strike and invasion of Cuba, since it was now obvious that the Russians and Cubans were preparing for war. The president was in the precarious position of losing control of the crisis. A military solution seemed to be the only solution.

October 27 was extremely busy at NPIC, and the Center prepared up-to-the-minute briefings of the day's happenings. That evening, Lundahl and McCone went to see the president. The downing of the U-2, the firing on the low-altitude aircraft, and the operational capability of all of the MRBM sites were most disturbing to the president. One of the newly apparent phenomena at the missile sites was the Soviet attempts to camouflage them. The effort was all in vain because, with the excellent quality of the low-altitude photography, we could easily discern all the military activity. The continued digging of thousands of defensive trenches, not only at the military installations but also near the principal Cuban cities, was covered in the presidential briefing, as was the dispersal of personnel and equipment. The president, his manner grave, was more absorbed than usual. He listened intently and then thanked Lundahl and McCone.

The president was confronted with a fateful choice if the Russians did not remove the missiles—the aerial bombing and invasion of Cuba. That evening (the best time estimates are about 10 P.M. rather than 7:45 P.M., as Bobby states in his book), at the urging of the president and Secretary Rusk but with some evidence that it was instigated by Bobby himself, Bobby met with Ambassador Dobrynin and made explicit the ultimatum that was implied in the president's October 26 letter to Khrushchev.

There have been numerous versions of what happened that evening. Khrushchev, in *Khrushchev Remembers*, reported that Bobby Kennedy had gone to see Dobrynin on an unofficial basis and that Bobby stated that "the President was in a grave situation and that he was under strong pressure from the military to use force against Cuba. If the situation continues much longer, the President is not sure that the military will not overthrow him and seize power."[42] In a speech in 1963, Bobby stated that he had informed Dobrynin that "strong and overwhelming retaliation" would be taken unless the president received immediate notice that the missiles would be withdrawn. Roger Hilsman, in his book, relates that Bobby's message was that "the United States could wait no longer but would have to proceed toward an agreement and peace if the missiles were withdrawn or toward strong and overwhelming retaliatory action."[43] Sorensen, in his book, relates that in addition to delivering a verbal message to Dobrynin, Bobby gave him a copy of the president's October 26 message to Khrushchev. According to Sorensen, Bobby told Dobrynin that "the point of escalation was at hand; the United States could proceed toward peace and disarmament; as the Attorney General later described it, we could take "strong and overwhelming retaliatory action unless the President received immediate notice that the missiles would be withdrawn."[44] President Kennedy's letter and Dobrynin's account of the meeting reached Khrushchev in Moscow in the early morning hours of October 28.

In several off-the-record discussions to an intelligence officer writing a history of the crisis, Bobby later stated that the ultimatum was direct and final. The United States was prepared to act militarily within forty-eight hours of Sunday morning. In his book, however, Bobby states that he told Dobrynin that "We had to have a commitment by tomorrow that those bases would be removed. I was not giving them an ultimatum but a statement of fact. He would understand that if they did not remove the bases, we would remove them."[45]

Dobrynin raised the question of U.S. removal of the Jupiter missiles from Turkey in what appeared to be the last desperate hope of the Soviets retrieving something from the crisis. Bobby said that the missiles could not be bartered. Although Bobby said there could be no quid pro quo, he did state that "President Kennedy had been anxious to remove the missiles from Turkey and Italy for a long period of time. He had ordered their removal some time ago, and it was our judgment that, within a short time after the Crisis was over, those missiles would be gone."[46] There can be little question that Bobby Kennedy promised Dobrynin that the Turkish missiles would be withdrawn—but after the crisis. This unpublished deal was above and beyond the "no invasion of Cuba" pledge.

Dobrynin agreed to pass Bobby's message to Khrushchev, who had an overriding concern that the prospect of nuclear escalation and a threat to USSR's very existence were inherent in the Cuban crisis. Bobby later stated to the intelligence officer that he had made clear to Dobrynin that the war could go nuclear, with unpredictable consequences, including a massive nuclear strike against the Soviet

Union. Khrushchev also knew that if the Soviet Union gave any appearance of going on a war footing, the U.S. might deliberately choose war on a first-strike basis.

British diplomats in Washington, aware of the sudden gravity of events, were beside themselves. There were urgent messages from British officials in Washington to Prime Minister Macmillan asking him to try to mediate the crisis. There was a fear that the U.S. would take the ultimate step and the UK could only stand idly on the sidelines and watch its possible destruction.

The U.S. Strategic Air Command went on full alert.* Adlai Stevenson began telling UN representatives of Western nations on the evening of October 27 that the U.S. was preparing to bomb the Cuban missile sites if the Soviets didn't dismantle them and soon.

The Russians probably knew that the Strategic Air Command had targeted the seventy principal Russian cities for immediate destruction with nuclear weapons. The Soviet military was undoubtedly interpreting the heightened SAC status and the alerting of the troop carrier squadrons as a move toward war and probably informed Khrushchev that the crisis was at a critical stage.

The president had invited Dave Powers to go swimming with him in the White House pool while Bobby had gone off to see Dobrynin. After emerging from the pool, the president, wearing a terry-cloth robe, decided to have something to eat and went with Powers to the White House kitchen. Both were eating chicken salad sandwiches and drinking milk when Bobby returned.

Bobby reported that the news was glum and then proceeded to recount in detail his conversation with Dobrynin. Bobby said he tried desperately to persuade Dobrynin that it was mandatory that the Russians remove the missiles or war between the U.S. and the Soviets could occur. Dobrynin, according to Bobby, was not encouraging but did say he would report Bobby's views to Moscow.

Powers tells the story that while the president had ceased eating, he continued to eat with gusto.

---

* President Kennedy later alluded to the fine performance of SAC during the Cuban crisis. "The record of SAC in mobilizing the forces of the United States was unprecedented in the long history of SAC. The amount of flights made during that period of time, the amount of men that were involved, was a record unparalleled by any country in the history of air power."

Bobby looked at Powers and said kiddingly, "Good God, Dave, you are eating as though it was your last supper."

Powers responded dryly, "The way you fellows are talking, it well may be."

Early the next morning, Castro sent a message to U Thant that while Cuba was ready to discuss its differences with the United States, it "equally rejects outright the attempt by the United States to determine the acts that we have a right to undertake in our country, the type of weapons it considers proper for our defense, our relations with the USSR, and the steps of international policy which, within the norms and the laws that regulate relations between the countries of the world and the principles that regulate the United Nations, we have a right to take steps to guarantee our security and sovereignty."[47]

That night, interpreting aerial photography taken of the Guanajay IRBM complex on October 27, interpreters spotted fuel transporters, vans, and other equipment at the site. Although it was known that many of the pieces of ground-support equipment were interchanged between the MRBM and IRBM missile systems, two pieces of equipment were identified that, because of their size, were definitely associated only with the IRBM system: the SS-5 fuel transporter, 69.5 feet long (versus the MRBM fuel transporter, which was 30 feet long) and the SS-5 service platform, which also is much larger than that for the SS-4. Although an exhaustive search was conducted for SS-5 missiles in Cuba, none were found.

By the morning of October 28, Khrushchev was fully aware that he had only a maximum of forty-eight hours and a minimum of twenty-four hours to decide. After receiving Bobby's ultimatum via Dobrynin, Khrushchev stated, "We could see that we had to orient our position swiftly. Comrades, I said, we have to look for a dignified way out of this conflict."[48] This was an indirect criticism of the Turkish-Cuban missile deal, a proposal probably arrived at by the Presidium.

Prior to the crisis, McNamara and Rusk had advocated a thoughtful doctrine of controlled response, up to and including nuclear war. Their subordinates had listed a carefully orchestrated step-by-step process of escalation that could lead to war, but what was happening in Cuba was not in the scenario. "A full retaliatory response to the

Soviet Union" could result in the stopping of a Soviet ship, the downing of another reconnaissance plane, the Cuban firing on Guantánamo or the torpedoing of a U.S. destroyer. Events that day were near the point of moving out of the control of either Khrushchev or the president. In testimony before a congressional subcommittee in February 1963, Robert McNamara said, "Khrushchev knew without any question whatsoever that he faced the full military power of the United States, including its nuclear weapons. We faced that night [October 27] the possibility of launching nuclear weapons and Khrushchev knew it, and that is the reason, the only reason, why he withdrew those weapons."

My deputy, Burt Betters, liked to post signs up on his office wall reflective of events, the mood, or the times. That afternoon, he put up the following sign: "A search for sanity in the face of insanity, a search for reason and the impossible in a world of distrust."

Like many privy to details of the burgeoning crisis, I succumbed to the general mood of apocalypse that evening. Seeing no earthly way out of this conflict except war and complete destruction, I told my wife that on call, she should take our two children, get in the car, and head for my parents' home in Jefferson City, Missouri.

In subsequent days, October 27 would be referred to as black Saturday by both the president and EXCOM members. Khrushchev remarked that "a smell of burning hung in the air."

21

October 28–
The Soviets Capitulate

"We were eyeball to eyeball, and I think the
other fellow blinked."

—DEAN RUSK

THAT MORNING when Lundahl was briefed on the previous day's
photography, he was still concerned about all the MRBM sites
being operational and that the camouflaging of the missile sites
was continuing. What worried him most, however, was that activity
at the IRBM sites was proceeding at an unusually high rate. The
number of vehicles noted at Guanajay site no. 1 increased from
around forty-four on October 26 to sixty-one on October 27. Additional missile support equipment had also been moved to this site.
At Guanajay site no. 2, a significant amount of construction had been
completed just the day before. At the Remedios IRBM site, construction was also continuing at a frantic pace. Lundahl asked if the
December 1 date for the Guanajay site no. 1 becoming operational
was still valid. After studying the aerial photography of the site himself, he concluded: "The way they are going, it looks as though it
may be operational before that date."

The stand-down of U-2 flights over Cuba continued, pending an
investigation of Major Anderson's shoot-down. Early on the morning
of October 28, U.S. Air Force RF-101's and U.S. Navy F-8U low-
altitude reconnaissance planes were again over the missile sites. This
time, however, they were escorted by fighter aircraft armed to the

teeth—both alongside and prowling offshore. There were also fighters flying cover. There was no attempt to disguise the mission of the escort aircraft, which were prepared, on orders, to strike any anti-aircraft gun or surface-to-air missile site that fired on the unarmed reconnaissance aircraft. General LeMay was eager to avenge Major Anderson's death. He was also prepared to go to war. There were not only a substantial portion of his bombers in the air, but SAC and TAC crews were on alert status in ready rooms, their aircraft fueled and loaded with appropriate ordnance, including nuclear weapons. External power supplies were connected to the aircraft. That morning 1,576 U.S. Air Force bombers and 283 missiles stood poised to strike the Soviet Union.

That morning, too, the Lake City Ordnance Plant, outside Ogden, Utah, was placed on a three-shift, seven-day-a-week basis to produce ammunition for fighter aircraft. At Andrews Air Force Base, outside Washington, D.C., Military Air Transport Service (MATS) crews were preparing a number of transport aircraft to evacuate casualties resulting from a Cuban invasion. Selected military hospitals along the East Coast were told to be prepared to receive the wounded. Navy picket ships were on offshore patrol around the entire island of Cuba. Aircraft carriers stood poised to launch their aircraft to strike the missile sites. On the beaches, the Cubans were nervously bracing for an attack.

There were reports that the Soviet leadership was bickering, debating, and divided in its determinations regarding actions that Khrushchev would take that day. There were other reports that the Soviets were prepared to go to war rather than submit to the humiliation of removing the missiles. If indeed they were planning war, there was again no evidence of increased readiness on the part of Soviet military forces. No general alert was issued, nor was there any movement of forces. On the contrary, throughout the crisis, the Soviets were at great pains to assure the U.S. that they would not engage in a first strike. Ambassador Zorin told a group of neutral African and Asian UN delegates on October 27 that "the Americans are thoroughly mistaken if they think we shall fall into their trap. We shall undertake nothing in Berlin, for action against Berlin is just what the Americans would wish."[1]

In Cuba, over 35,000 men had been mobilized and deployed since

October 22. The digging of defensive trenches continued and was clearly apparent on aerial photography. Yet the Cuban Air Force maintained a stand-down posture and the Cuban Navy remained in port.

Although the Russians had not gone on alert, they were firmly convinced that President Kennedy was now ready to employ the hemispheric superiority he possessed and, if necessary, the U.S. strategic superiority against Russia. Khrushchev later admitted that his decision was a simple one—a Soviet-controlled Cuba without missiles was of more advantage to the Soviet Union than a U.S.-occupied Cuba. Afterward, Khrushchev told U.S. ambassador Kohler that he made the decision to withdraw the missiles with little declared opposition, just as it had been he who made the decision to send the missiles to Cuba. The Soviet party organ, *Kommunist*, in December 1962, probably stated it best when it said the party "had soberly weighed the balance of power" and made the decision to remove the missiles.

It was early Sunday afternoon, Moscow time, on October 28 when the Soviets sent a communiqué to the U.S. embassy that a formal diplomatic letter would be forthcoming. President Kennedy had planned to attend ten o'clock mass at St. Stephen's Church, while McCone, as was his custom, went to one at nine o'clock. On his way to church, McCone heard on his car radio from a Washington radio station that the Russians would make an important announcement within the hour. McCone would later relate that it was the longest mass he ever attended.

The Soviets, obviously concerned about the time it would take for a diplomatic message to be encoded, transmitted, decoded, and translated, and knowing that U.S. invasion planning was proceeding at a rapid rate, did something unique in diplomatic history. They had Radio Moscow broadcast the message in the clear at 9:04 EST.

At 9:09 A.M., the Foreign Broadcast Information Service flashed by Teletype the following bulletin to the White House and the intelligence community.

"Moscow Domestic Service in Russian at 1404GMT on 28 October, Broadcast a message from Khrushchev to President Kennedy stating that the USSR had decided to dismantle Soviet missiles in Cuba and return them to the Soviet Union 28 October 908a-FRR/HM."

The initial bulletin was followed at 9:11 A.M. by a more substantive alert from the service:

"Moscow Domestic Service in Russian at 1404 GMT on 28 October broadcast a Khrushchev message to Kennedy. He declares: I received your message 27 October and I am grateful for your appreciation of the responsibility you bear for world peace and security.

"The Soviet Government has ordered the dismantling of bases and the dispatch of equipment to the USSR. A few days ago, Havana was shelled, allegedly by Cuban émigrés. Yet someone must have armed them for this purpose. Even a British cargo ship was shelled. Cuba wants to be mother of their country. The thought of invasion has upset the Cuban people. I wish to again state that the Soviet Government has offered Cuba only defensive weapons. I appreciate your assurance that the United States will not invade Cuba. Hence, we have ordered our officers to stop building bases, dismantle the equipment and send it back home. This can be done under U.N. supervision.

"We must not allow the situation to deteriorate [but] eliminate hotheads of tension, and we must see to it that no other conflicts occur which lead to a World Nuclear War.

"We are ready to continue to exchange views on relations between NATO and the Warsaw Bloc, disarmament, and other issues of peace and war."[2]

By 9:40 A.M., an extensive paraphrase of the entire message had cleared the wires; this was followed in the next hour by the complete text, as translated from the Russian. Subsequently, the official text, as transmitted by the Soviet news agency Tass, was also carried.

The president was given copies of the messages almost paragraph by paragraph as they were received by the monitoring service's Teletype station at the White House's Situation Room.

Immediately after mass, McCone called the CIA headquarters and was informed of the details of the Russian messages. He asked if they had been relayed to the White House and was told that they had. McCone then went directly to the White House, where he encountered an air of jubilation among the White House staff.

The president, probably reflecting on the October 18 White House meeting, when Gromyko had lied to him, still had doubts regarding real Russian intentions. He knew that all the MRBM sites were operational, and there was some fear that Khrushchev's announcement might be a subterfuge. Showing some evidence of impatience and scorn, he said rather sharply to McCone, "Get some planes in the air and check on the missile sites." McCone immediately called the CIA operations center to relay the order. He was told that low-altitude-reconnaissance missions were already over the sites.

Dobrynin called Bobby Kennedy at his Justice office stating he was coming over with an important message for the president. What he received was substantially the same as the Radio Moscow broadcast. Bobby hurried to the White House only to find that the president had already received the broadcast message through the Foreign Broadcast Information Service. On learning of this, Bobby commented, "That's a hell of a way to run a railroad."

Over thirty minutes after the Moscow radio broadcast, the official text in Russian was given to Ambassador Foy Kohler in Moscow. When the president was told that it would take several hours for that transcript to arrive in Washington via diplomatic channels, he asked that a response to the broadcast message be drafted. He also wanted the EXCOM meeting postponed until 11 A.M.

At 9:54 A.M., President Kennedy, Dave Powers, and K. LeMoyne Billings, who was on the staff of the National Cultural Center and a personal friend of the president, went to mass at St. Stephen's Church. As they entered, the president turned to Dave Powers and said, "Dave, this morning we have an extra reason to pray."

The rapid and changing pace of events, and the flow of photographic-intelligence information, had far outstripped the available communications technology during the crisis. The delays caused by encoding, transmitting, decoding, translating, and retransmitting messages to the intended recipients were far too time-consuming. The flow of intelligence required for decision-making purposes was of such volume, and arriving at such speed, that it was often necessary to make policy decisions while additional vital information was still being transmitted.

The need for a surer, quicker, more direct method of communication between Moscow and Washington became all too apparent. This was not a new idea. It had been discussed and proposed many times but was always blocked by the State Department. The Cuban missile crisis stimulated renewed interest in improving direct communications between the U.S. and the Soviets—but this time at the presidential level.

A wave of euphoria swept over the White House. When the president returned from mass, he was in a calm and reflective mood. McCone, however, was thinking ahead. He was subsequently described "as the only realist in a family of romantics." Although there might be cause for jubilation, McCone knew the crisis was far from over. There was the problem of missile inspection, and other problems—such as the disposition of the Il-28 bombers and the MiG-21 fighters, and to see there was no possibility that Castro would be left in a position to continue to promote insurgency throughout Latin America.

Ambassador Stevenson wanted a statement made by the president "in order to prevent the Soviets from capturing the peace offensive." He suggested: "The United States never had any territorial designs against Cuba, but, of course, we cannot tolerate Soviet-Cuban aggression against us or our sister Republics. So the Soviet offer to withdraw all weapons from Cuba is welcome. There is no obstacle to further assurances of our peaceful intentions toward Cuba. But in the meantime it is imperative that further development of the Soviet bases stop while discussions proceed with the Secretary General of the United Nations in New York."[3]

At the EXCOM meeting at 11 A.M., the following message to Khrushchev was finally drafted: "I am replying at once to your broadcast message of October twenty-eight, even though the official text has not reached me, because of the great importance I attach to moving forward promptly to the settlement of the Cuban Crisis. I think that you and I, with our heavy responsibilities for the maintenance of peace, were aware that developments were approaching a point where events could have become unmanageable. So I welcome this message and consider it an important contribution to peace."[4] The president said he considered his letter of October 27 and Khrushchev's reply as "firm undertakings on the part of both our governments which should be promptly carried out. I hope that the necessary measures can at once be taken through the United Nations, as your message says, so that the United States, in turn, will be able to remove the quarantine measures now in effect. I have already made arrangements to report all these matters to the Organization of American States, whose members share a deep interest in genuine peace in the Caribbean area."[5]

The president also explained that the U.S. violation on the Chukotsk Peninsula had been a navigational error made by a nuclear sampling aircraft. He appealed that "both of our countries have great unfinished tasks and I know that your people as well as those of the United States can ask for nothing better than to pursue them free from the fear of war. Modern science and technology have given us the possibility of making labor fruitful beyond anything that could have been dreamed a few decades ago.[6] Finally, the president expressed the hope that "now, as we step back from danger, we can together make real progress in this vital field. I think we should give priority to questions relating to the proliferation of nuclear weapons, on earth and in outer space, and to the great effort for a nuclear test ban. But we should also work hard to see if wider measures of disarmament can be agreed and put into operation at an early date. The United States Government will be prepared to discuss these questions urgently, and in a constructive spirit, at Geneva or elsewhere."[7]

The first nuclear confrontation had ended. Armageddon had been postponed. The president had averted war and had secured the peace, and in his view this was the ultimate attainment. There were two casualties directly related to the crisis: Major Rudolf Anderson and Colonel Oleg Penkovsky had given their lives for freedom, and they were both engaged in intelligence.

The mood at the White House on October 28 was described by one participant as "a miasma of self-congratulation." In this moment of extreme jubilation, the president warned the celebrants not to overdo it because there was still a rocky road ahead. He was, however, in a confident, happy, and relaxed mood but had no intention of responding immediately to the flood of media inquiries generated by Khrushchev's message and his response. Rather than lunching at the White House, the president ordered his helicopter immediately to the White House lawn. Before departing, he requested that a formal message be drafted to Khrushchev once the final text of his message was received. At 1:39 P.M., the president, along with his naval aide, Captain Tazewell T. Shepard, and K. LeMoyne Billings, left for the president's home at Glen Ora, near Middleburg, Virginia, where his wife and family waited.

At 4:30 P.M., President Kennedy's formal response to Khrushchev was dispatched: "I welcome Chairman Khrushchev's statesmanlike decision to stop building bases in Cuba, dismantling offensive weapons and returning them to the Soviet Union under United Nations verification. This is an important and constructive contribution to peace.

"We shall be in touch with the Secretary General of the United Nations with respect to reciprocal measures to assure peace in the Caribbean area.

"It is my earnest hope that the governments of the world can, with a solution of the Cuban Crisis, turn their urgent attention to the compelling necessity for ending the arms race and reducing world tensions. This applies to the military confrontation between the Warsaw Pact and NATO countries as well as to other situations in other parts of the world where tensions lead to the wasteful diversion of resources to weapons of war."[8]

The Cuban missile crisis was over, but the "Cuban problem" remained. That afternoon, the FBIS Teletypes would chatter again. This time, there was a bulletin from the Havana desk of the service. Fidel Castro had released the following communiqué: "In statements made today, the U.S. Government intends to invest itself with the official prerogative of invading our airspace. Cuba does not accept the vandalist and piratical privilege on the part of any war planes to violate its airspace because such actions would essentially affect its security and would facilitate conditions for a surprise attack on our territory. This legitimate right of defense cannot be surrendered and, therefore, any combat plane that invades Cuban airspace will only do so at the risk of encountering defensive fire. Fatherland or death: We will win."[9] Castro, in a pique, had issued his own conditions for ending the crisis—an end to economic sanctions against Cuba, cessation of all subversive activities against Cuba, cessation of pirate attacks, cessation of violations of Cuban space by U.S. ships and planes, and U.S. withdrawal from Guantánamo.

Continuing concern about the safety of low-altitude reconnaissance aircraft flying over Cuba prompted Arthur Sylvester to issue the following statement: "Surveillance flights over Cuba were made today. All aircraft returned safely. The readouts will not be completed until tomorrow."[10]

The fear of rash actions by Castro to deliberately involve the U.S. and the Soviets loomed as a danger that both the U.S. and Soviets would have to face. Khrushchev's admonition to Kennedy that violation of Cuban airspace by U.S. aircraft could have "dangerous consequences" was viewed as a warning that he could no longer deter Castro's forces from firing on the unarmed reconnaissance aircraft. A quick check of low-altitude reconnaissance units, however, indicated that none of their aircraft flying over Cuba that day had been fired on. Intercepted Cuban radio broadcasts and messages to their field units directed that there would be no firing on U.S. aircraft except in case of attack.

That afternoon and evening, the Center reviewed all of the photography acquired by reconnaissance aircraft on October 28, but there was no evidence whatsoever that the Russians were preparing to dismantle the missile sites in Cuba. In fact, when the imagery was compared with that of the previous day, construction at some of the sites was still proceeding.

At 6:40 P.M., the president, Caroline Kennedy, LeMoyne Billings, Miss Shaw, Captain Shepard, and Maria Shriver departed Glen Ora and flew by helicopter, arriving at the White House at 7 P.M.

When Kennedy left his office that night, the memorandum pad on his desk had only five words—"Berlin, Berlin, Berlin, Berlin, Berlin."

October 29–
The Beginning of Negotiations

"We have to match a hard ass with
a hard ass."

—BOBBY KENNEDY

T
HE DAY FOLLOWING the Soviet capitulation was characterized by
one highly placed U.S. official as "ego day high and low." There
was a flood of congratulatory cables and letters to the president
from around the world. Prime Minister Macmillan praised Kennedy,
saying the way was now open for East-West negotiations. Adenauer
remained steadfast in his support of the president and regarded the
Russian missiles in Cuba as the strongest challenge ever addressed
to the Western world. He would later address the National Press
Club: "In order to understand what was going on in the mind of
Khrushchev when he was placing the missiles in Cuba, I would like
to quote to you a remark Khrushchev made to a Western diplomat.
He told this Western diplomat that he did not understand why I,
Chancellor Adenauer, was so much interested in this particular question, because all of these missiles would now be shipped to Russia
and they were just the right range for being deployed against Germany. So that, in other words, gentlemen, was what he had in mind
for the United States of America."[1] Adenauer went on: "This attempt,
as I said, was not only directed against the United States, but was
directed against the whole Free World, and that is the reason why
all countries of the Free World must do their utmost to establish the

strength and unity which is required to serve the cause of peace and freedom and liberty and to put all resistance against Communist aggression."[2] Bonn's All-German Affairs Minister Lemmer found the settlement "wonderful, astounding," while Mayor Willy Brandt, of Berlin, expressed the hope that his city "would feel something of the change which is going around the world."

General de Gaulle, always the military man, had accepted the fact that the United States might have to strike Cuba and the Russians might retaliate somewhere in Europe. Although he was displeased that Kennedy had not consulted him earlier in the crisis, de Gaulle watched the buildup of U.S. forces with considerable satisfaction.* He understood military power and expected Kennedy to use it to the maximum and knew that Khrushchev understood that the U.S. was prepared to go to war.

Canadian Liberal leader Lester Pearson remarked that Cuba being turned into an offensive base was a shock not only to U.S. citizens but to Canadians and to citizens in every free country. Pearson stated that if the settlement could lead to disarmament, then "we can be even more grateful to President Kennedy for his firm stance."[3] Jean Monnet of France was immensely impressed by the president's determination and moderation. When asked about the lack of consultation with many nations, he said, "Goddamn consultation. It's action that counts."[4] Norwegian prime minister Gerhardson said, "This is an almost unbelievably happy outcome of a situation that could have had the most disastrous consequences." A Japanese government statement called the Kennedy-Khrushchev exchanges "a matter for much rejoicing."

There was both surprise and elation at the White House at the Soviet capitulation. In the April 1963 issue of *Foreign Affairs*, McGeorge Bundy concluded that the missile crisis "came out better than President Kennedy or any of his assistants expected."

While Western European countries greeted the news of the dismantling of the missile bases with surprise, joy, and relief, there were also some notes of caution. A British Foreign Office spokesman said

---

* De Gaulle pondered the events of the Cuban missile crisis for some time. Concerned that unilateral actions by the U.S. could drag NATO and France into war, he seriously considered and later pulled France out of NATO and began developing France's own nuclear air, missile, and submarine strike forces.

that while his government was pleased by the news of Khrushchev's agreement to accept UN inspection and dismantling, difficult problems remained. The conservative *Daily Telegraph* stated that since the USSR had accepted the "verification principle" in Cuba, "a long barred door may have been set ajar." Copenhagen radio was more sober and realistic, expressing the opinion that the reason for the Khrushchev capitulation was to be found in two events that occurred the previous evening. First, it was alleged that Ambassador Stevenson had warned Allied ambassadors that the U.S. would strike the missile and bomber bases within twenty-four hours if work was not stopped; secondly, the mobilization of the U.S. transport aircraft meant that the U.S. was serious in its announced intent to invade Cuba.

For the U.S. military leaders, the end of the crisis was greeted with a great sigh of relief. Admiral Ward would later write me "about the trying days of the real Crisis when it seemed to waver back and forth as to whether or not we were destined to have a holocaust such as the world has never seen. Fortunately, Mr. Khrushchev and President Kennedy took the side of statesmanship."[5]

Other military leaders would later write that it was the strategic strength of the U.S. that forced Khrushchev to remove the missiles, thereby justifying all that had been spent on U.S. strategic weapons.

Admiral Anderson would remark: "The entire operation has been a magnificent testimonial not only to the senior leaders of our Government, but also to those commanders and commanding officers at lower levels who were so quickly able to move their troops—large numbers of troops—many ships—and their aircraft of many types in position to carry out lengthy, tedious, and often very sensitive operations with a high degree of leadership, professional competence, courage, and diplomatic skill."[6]

The volume of Soviet propaganda on the crisis sharply declined on October 29 for the first time since early October. President Kennedy's reply to the Khrushchev broadcast, however, was repeated throughout the day on Radio Moscow. Khrushchev displayed unusual sensitivity to assertions by Western commentators that the Soviet Union had capitulated and had suffered a setback. Radio Moscow continued to emphasize Khrushchev's calm determination throughout the crisis. Soviet commentators played heavily on the theme that by extracting disclaimers of U.S. military action against

Cuba, they had achieved a major victory for world peace. *Pravda* claimed, "a situation had taken shape in which it is impossible to implement the initial Pentagon plans for a military invasion of the island of freedom, and the military blockade has been renounced. The Pentagon had to beat a retreat."

The Communist Bloc press was effusive in its praise for Moscow's stand—that unilateral action by the U.S. had been averted by Khrushchev's moves, his action in averting thermonuclear war thereby opening the way for solving other questions by peaceful means.

That day, in addition to receiving plaudits from foreign sources, President Kennedy took a number of calls from congressional leaders expressing their firm support for his stand. There was a flood of positive mail to the White House from civic organizations, veterans organizations, and private citizens.

President Kennedy was back on top now, firmly in control—the darkest days behind him. He decided he wanted to thank the pilots personally who had flown the reconnaissance missions that had contributed so much to resolving the crisis. At 11:15 A.M., October 29, the president met with Lieutenant Colonel Joe M. O'Brady, a low-level-reconnaissance pilot; Major Richard S. Heyser, the U-2 pilot who had flown the October 14 mission on which the missiles had been found; Colonel Ralph D. Steakley, the photo-reconnaissance chief for the Joint Chiefs of Staff; Brigadier General Godfrey McHugh, Air Force aide to the president; and General Curtis LeMay, chief of staff of the USAF. For about twenty minutes, the president told the officers how much he appreciated their efforts during the crisis and how he marveled at the quality and quantity of photography they had taken. He said he hoped he could speak personally to a few of the other reconnaissance pilots and wanted to thank all of the units that had participated in the crisis.

This was the first crisis in which the analysis of aerial photography was often precursing analytical thinking. The pace of events during the crisis had moved so fast that policy papers prepared by the Policy Planning Council of the Department of State were just being delivered. On October 29, McGeorge Bundy received three papers from Walt Rostow suggesting ways of achieving a peaceful resolution of the crisis, and the diplomatic moves necessary for removing the Jupiter missiles from Turkey and Italy and how to placate those governments. Bundy frequently displayed the papers as an example of poor planning on the part of a governmental agency.[7]

Fidel Castro, of course, had been confronted with a profound setback to his prestige and vented his anger on the Russians. The confidence that permeated the Castro government—that the United States would take no offensive action against Cuba without an implied threat of nuclear retaliation from the Soviets—had evaporated. Castro, instead, attempted to pressure the Soviets to support his demands for major U.S. concessions prior to the removal of the missiles. Raul Castro, the defense minister, ridiculed the idea that the U.S. could be trusted to abide by any "nonaggression guarantee," saying that, "Whatever happens, whatever President Kennedy says, Cuba will remain mobilized until its commander in chief orders the contrary." Orders were again issued by Raul that day cautioning military units not to open fire unless attacked. Such orders apparently had been in effect since October 23, but Premier Castro's warning on October 27 that foreign aircraft flying over Cuban territory might be attacked, and the downing of Major Anderson's U-2 on October 27, had created some confusion among Cuban defense units as to whether the order of October 23 had been rescinded.

In a desperate move, on October 28, Castro had invited U Thant to visit Cuba "with a view to direct discussion on the present crisis prompted by our common purpose of freeing mankind from the dangers of war." Thant had been assured by Mario Garcia-Inchaustegui, Cuba's permanent representative to the UN, that he would be warmly welcomed in Cuba. Castro even offered a Cuban plane to transport the secretary-general and his aides to Cuba. Thant replied that he preferred to charter his own plane, and there are indications that this infuriated the hypersensitive Castro. Thant had informed representatives of a number of nations that before sending UN inspectors to Cuba, he would formally request Castro's permission. This action was based on precedent established by his predecessor, Dag Hammarskjold, who asked for and received from President Nasser of Egypt agreements to arrange stationing UN forces in Egypt following the Suez crisis of 1956. The Security Council suspended all debate on the Cuban crisis, and Mohmoud Riad of the

UAR, soon to assume presidency of the Council, said he would not convene another Council meeting until Thant returned from Cuba.

The Soviet ambassador to the UN, Zorin, had been rendered totally ineffective by Adlai Stevenson's attack and the presentation of the "hard" photographic evidence on October 25, which established the presumption that he had lied on the question of the presence of Soviet missiles in Cuba. In his October 28 letter to President Kennedy, Khrushchev announced that he had dispatched First Deputy Foreign Minister Vasily Vasilyevich Kuznetsov to New York "to help Mr. Thant in his noble efforts aimed at eliminating the present danger."

Kuznetsov was no stranger to the UN, having been a delegate to the founding conference in San Francisco in 1945. Neither was he a stranger to the U.S., having earned his master's degree in engineering in 1933 from Carnegie Tech as an exchange student. In connection with his engineering studies, he had worked in the Open Hearth Division of the Ford Motor Car Company in Detroit. He admired U.S. technology in private conversation, but he couldn't be characterized as easy to deal with. Cold and formal in manner, collected in speech, careful in action, he was still a Stalin-era diplomat—aggressive, hard-nosed, knowledgeable of the U.S. and the concessions he could make and, in turn, those he could demand and expect to gain. He was well known to U.S. diplomats, having been involved with such problems as the release of two crewmen of a U.S. Air Force RB-47 that was shot down near the Soviet coast* in the early days of the Kennedy administration, the Congo debates, the Geneva Indo-China Conference in 1954, and the Geneva Conference on Surprise Attack in 1958.

Kuznetsov arrived in New York on October 28 and wasted no time establishing who was now in charge of Russian negotiations. He proceeded on the premise that there had been no previous negotiations by Zorin. A personal friend of Khrushchev, Kuznetsov obviously had been given wide latitude in conducting negotiations at the UN.

The day after his arrival, Kuznetsov met with U Thant and assured him that the missiles were being dismantled and prepared for re-

* The RB-47 was shot down near the Kola Peninsula on July 1, 1960, and two crew members were freed by Premier Khrushchev on January 25, 1961, and returned to the United States on January 27, 1961.

shipment to the Soviet Union. Kuznetsov also said that he would be leaving soon for Cuba. When all of the missiles had been removed, he promised to inform the Security Council. No inspection team would be required until this announcement. U Thant later met with Stevenson, McCloy, and Yost and relayed Kuznetsov's insistence that inspection and verification would not be permitted until the dismantling had been completed. Kuznetsov was also adamant that the Soviets would not allow Soviet ships returning equipment and missiles to be inspected by UN personnel. He said further that the Soviets would only approve inspection of their ships en route to Cuba by representatives of the International Committee of the Red Cross from neutral nations. He purposely left any further details ambiguous. Thant was doubtful that the Red Cross would undertake such a responsibility.

The secretary-general was also concerned whether a provision in President Kennedy's October 27 letter to Khrushchev—"to insure the carrying out and continuation of these commitments"—meant the U.S. expected the UN to continue the inspection of Cuba for an indefinite period. This might provoke Castro to make counter-demands for inspection of so-called "CIA training camps for exiles in the U.S. and in certain Caribbean countries." McCloy reiterated the U.S. position that inspection was an absolute and that unilateral aerial inspection was going to be maintained. Furthermore, there would be no lifting of the quarantine until verification was established.[8]

Given Kuznetsov's outspoken and direct nature, the Kennedy White House became concerned that he might intimidate Adlai Stevenson. Bobby was the most blunt: "We have to match a hard ass with a hard ass." Stevenson was shunted aside, and John McCloy became the principal U.S. negotiator with Kuznetsov. If Kuznetsov was a tough negotiator, he was to meet his match in the person of John J. McCloy. McCloy had turned down a cabinet position in the Kennedy administration but had agreed to perform a number of special tasks for the president—most notably, presidential adviser on disarmament in negotiations with the Russians. On October 29, the president named George Ball, Roswell Gilpatric, and John J. McCloy to the Special Coordinating Committee on the Cuban crisis, with McCloy as chairman.[9]

Although the Special Coordinating Committee was a complex arrangement for negotiations, one member calling it a "troika within a troika," it was staffed with people in whom the president had explicit trust. All were experienced diplomats, and McCloy in particular was regarded by the president as a "hard-nosed" negotiator. When questioned by reporters as to who would be principally dealing with Kuznetsov—Stevenson or McCloy—Salinger replied the Special Coordinating Committee, meaning McCloy. It was essentially another move by the Kennedy administration to frustrate Stevenson. When Stevenson was asked to pose with the group for a picture-taking session, he refused.

Stevenson understandably took the appointment of the committee as a slap in the face and moped about the UN following the announcement. Although the Special Committee members would act under the supervision of the three cabinet members concerned—Secretary Rusk, Secretary McNamara, and Ambassador Stevenson—they also reported directly to the president. They were instructed by the president "to give full time and attention to the matters involved in the conclusion of the Cuban crisis."[10] Pierre Salinger amplified the president's position: The three officers would stay at the UN until the UN verified "the fulfillment of Premier Khrushchev's promise to dismantle Soviet offensive weapons and ship them back to the Soviet Union."

Lundahl asked that I meet with John Hughes and Roswell Gilpatric to coordinate preparation of a "negotiating book" for the committee. Gilpatric requested that an 8- × -10-inch photo of each missile site, airfield, cruise missile, and SAM site, along with a map of Cuba showing their locations, be placed in a notebook to be used as a quick reference by the negotiators. He also wanted updated photos sent to him each day at the UN.

On the afternoon of October 29, U Thant met with Stevenson, McCloy, and Ambassador Charles W. Yost, deputy U.S. representative to the Security Council, to review his discussions with Kuznetsov that morning. U Thant praised Soviet compliance with the secretary-general's appeal to suspend arms shipments to Cuba and avoid confrontations at sea and noted that there had been no U.S. response to his request. At that point, Stevenson handed Thant President Kennedy's response; Thant didn't bother to open the envelope.

Thant emphasized to the U.S. representatives that he would like to have the blockade lifted when verification procedures were established. He stated that Kuznetsov had said the Soviets would also allow UN personnel to verify the missile removal by Soviet ships. Kuznetsov added that "the USSR was prepared to agree to the proposal that Red Cross representatives inspect Soviet ships going to Cuba in order to ascertain that they carry no weapons as the U.S. is worried about offensive weapons to Cuba." Kuznetsov told Thant that the Red Cross personnel would be allowed to board Soviet ships at sea from either neutral or Soviet ships. When U Thant mentioned inspection of incoming Soviet ships in Cuban ports, Kuznetsov said that would depend on Cuba. The secretary-general appealed to McCloy for some U.S. concessions, stating that if the Soviets were willing to submit to inspection by the Red Cross, it was obvious they were no longer shipping arms to Cuba.

Kuznetsov had reassured Thant that the missile sites were being dismantled and would be shipped out soon. Stevenson said it was imperative that the U.S. have reassurances that dismantling was in progress. At Kuznetsov's insistence, Thant requested that the quarantine be lifted and that aerial reconnaissance be suspended. The quarantine could not be lifted, McCloy responded, until it had been certified that the missiles had been removed; low-level reconnaissance would continue. He said the president was adamant on these points. Thant argued that he could not go to Cuba and hold negotiations with Castro while U.S. spy planes boomed over Havana, but McCloy insisted on continued aerial inspection. Stevenson was anxious that U Thant dissuade Castro from introducing any negative or extraneous elements into the discussions, such as his five-point declaration, which could only complicate and perhaps even jeopardize any settlement reached between the United States and the Soviet Union.

President Kennedy finally agreed that for the period the secretary-general was in Cuba, the U.S. would, at the secretary-general's request, temporarily suspend the quarantine and all aerial reconnaissance.

U Thant's ego was bolstered by the agreement between the U.S. and the Soviets on inspection of the missile sites. He had reached the pinnacle of his career. The UN, he would later state, had come of age during this crisis, and he was vain enough to believe that it was through his actions that nuclear war had been averted. Thant announced on October 29 that he would be leaving for Havana the next day.

The intelligence community, informed of the proposed inspection of Soviet ships by Red Cross representatives, initiated frantic biographic searches to identify International Red Cross personnel who had served in their country's armed forces and might be knowledgeable of military equipment. When General LeMay heard about the Red Cross inspectors, he said disgustedly, "Jesus Christ, what in the hell do a bunch of gray ladies know about missiles?" That, of course, was the Soviet ploy. They knew that military officers from nations friendly to the United States, properly briefed as to what to look for, could gain considerable information on Soviet military equipment unobtainable from aerial photography alone. This would be especially true of military and factory markings on the equipment. Kuznetsov also knew that this plan would give the Soviets additional time to remove the missiles without any inspection at all.

Worldwide press and diplomatic reporting began carrying reports of the "Thant plan," but U Thant, in reality, had no plan or plan of action. Confused and disoriented when pressed for details, Thant avoided specifics, saying that his military adviser, Indian brigadier Indar Jit Rikhye, would supply all the details. William Tidwell, a CIA expert in aerial reconnaissance and a military reserve officer, was sent to New York to seek clarification from Brigadier Rikhye. But if U Thant was confused, Rikhye was completely out of touch with reality. A short, stocky Punjabi with a deceptive smile, Rikhye's first service with the UN was as a colonel commanding an Indian unit in the Gaza Strip during the Middle East cease-fire in 1957. He had helped organize the UN force sent to the Congo in 1960–1961 and, in 1962, had worked to supervise the peacekeeping force in Netherlands New Guinea. During World War II, as a major, he commanded an armored unit of the famed Bengal Lancers in General Mark Clark's 5th Army.

Tidwell soon determined Rikhye knew British and American military equipment but knew absolutely nothing about Soviet MRBM and IRBM sites. He had no plans for site inspection or UN-sponsored aerial reconnaissance overflights of the missile sites. He said that in accordance with U Thant's instructions, he would select inspectors from neutral nations, including the UAR, Brazil, Mexico, Switzerland, Ethiopia, Sweden, Yugoslavia, Ghana, and Nigeria. A survey of the qualifications of those nations revealed that none had military officers familiar with Soviet missiles or with high-altitude or combat-type photo reconnaissance. Neither did they possess state-of-the-art photo-interpretation capabilities.

Neither U Thant nor Brigadier Rikhye had the slightest idea of where the missile sites were located or even what actually constituted a missile site. McCone was vehemently opposed to giving U Thant photographs of the missile sites unless an American was assigned to accompany the UN delegation to Cuba. Since Thant would not hear of anyone except neutrals in his inspection party, it was decided at the U.S. UN mission that Brigadier Rikhye should be briefed on the location and composition of the missile sites and Colonel Parker was again selected to go to the UN. A three-ring binder containing forty-two aerial photos and maps was compiled, with a duplicate copy for the U.S. UN mission. Parker briefed Brigadier Rikhye, using the photos, on the various components of both an MRBM and IRBM site. Parker also showed photos of the larger pieces of missile equipment such as the transporters, launch-erectors, and fuel and oxidizer transporters should Brigadier Rikhye be allowed to visit Cuban ports. McCone directed, however, that Brigadier Rikhye was not to take the photographs to Cuba. Brigadier Rikhye clipped aerial photos of the missile sites from *The New York Times* and other newspapers and placed them in a portfolio, which he took to Cuba. We suspected that he also took the binder with him but never had an opportunity to use it.

In Washington, another rhubarb was developing. Newsmen were protesting retention of the administration-imposed "security guidelines" of October 24 and October 27. Pierre Salinger assured them that the government's request for "caution and discretion" in the handling of news on the crisis would be removed "as soon as feasible." At a Pentagon press conference, however, Arthur Sylvester, assistant secretary of defense for public affairs, announced that the regulations would "of course continue just as firmly as they have in the past." When angry newsmen claimed that they were being misled and denied information, Sylvester asked for specific examples. They were quick in coming: The president hadn't come back from Chicago because of a cold; the movement of troops across the United States had not been a "normal exercise"; naval movements in the Caribbean had not been called off because of hurricane Ella; and the administration had known that the missiles in Cuba were offensive weapons while stating publicly that they were defensive. The press conference became increasingly heated as reporters hurled questions.

Sylvester reminded the press that the release of military information during a crisis was "part of the arsenal of weaponry" available to the administration. He said, "In a kind of world we live in, the generation of news by actions taken by the government becomes one weapon in a strained situation; the results in my opinion justify the methods we used." What about the half truths issued during the crisis? "It would seem to be basic, all through history, that a government's right and in government I mean a people . . . that it's inherent in the government's right, if necessary, to lie to save itself when it's going up into a nuclear war. This seems to be basic." It wasn't "basic" to the news reporters, editorial writers, and television and radio reporters who quoted Sylvester's remarks widely the following day that lying to the public would be a normal practice during a crisis.

For the president the crisis was not over, and he still wanted restrictions on information; he so informed the secretaries of State and Defense. As late as November 1, Arthur Sylvester issued a memorandum requiring all Defense Department officials to report the substance of their remarks to newsmen to the Press Office. In the case of interviews, a press officer must be present. At the Department of State, the substance of all information given to newsmen had to be reported to Robert J. Manning, assistant secretary of state for Information.

Low-altitude reconnaissance missions continued to range far and wide over Cuba, covering most of the missile sites, until dusk. The processed film was rushed to the Center for analysis. The launch stands at all the missile sites in Cuba were still in place. There was no evidence that cable connections between the various components had been removed. A number of missile erectors had been moved back from the launch stands, but this did not detract from the missile launch capabilities. Several erectors were seen hidden under nearby trees. Camouflage and concealment activities continued at a number of the sites. Some missile-ready tents, however, had been struck. Comparison of the morning and evening photography made it obvious that construction was continuing at the San Cristóbal MRBM sites and at the nuclear storage bunker nearby.

That evening, Lundahl reviewed the substance of the day's photo analysis with all the Center photo interpreters and intelligence analysts. The NPIC SITSUM that night indicated that the Soviets had not dismantled any site. On the contrary, all MRBM sites were still considered fully operational.

That evening, too, NPIC implemented a revised worksheet reporting missile, military, air, and naval activity in Cuba: 1) no significant change noted; 2) general construction continuing; 3) major change: a) missiles or missile launchers no longer observed, b) other evidence of evacuation, c) evidence of AW (automatic weapons) being emplaced vicinity site, d) other significant construction noted, e) aircraft count change (Il-28/MiG-21), f) KOMAR PT boat change, and g) changes in vicinity of nuclear storage facilities.

23

October 30 –
U Thant Goes to Cuba

"Analysis of aerial pictures entails a meticulous
review of material disclosed and a painstaking
comparison of that material with our previously
obtained material in order to obtain
accurate findings."

—ARTHUR SYLVESTER

T HE U.S. NEWS MEDIA was demanding that the Kennedy administration release details relative to the dismantling of the missile
sites in Cuba. Arthur Sylvester, who knew there was no evidence
of missile dismantling, waffled and issued an official Department of
Defense statement on the morning of October 30: "I have talked this
morning with the top officials responsible for the evaluation of the
results of our aerial surveillance of Cuba. As a consequence, I can
report the following: "Analysis of aerial pictures entails a meticulous
review of the material disclosed and a painstaking comparison of
that material with our previously obtained material in order to obtain
accurate findings. One has to be careful about making conclusions
because there are certain evaluation procedures to be observed in
order to insure accuracy of the results obtained. All of this takes time,
despite reports to the contrary. In addition, the time since Chairman
Khrushchev's message of Sunday morning is too short to allow us
to expect conclusive evidence."[1]

That morning, U Thant and a staff of eighteen advisers, including
Brigadier Rikhye; Omar Loutfi of the UAR, the UN undersecretary
for Special Political Affairs; and Hernane Tavares de Sa of Brazil, the
ranking Latin American of the Secretariat and undersecretary for

political information, landed at José Martí airfield, outside Havana. The UN negotiating party was hurried to a meeting with Premier Castro, President Osvaldo Dorticos, and Foreign Minister Raul Roa.

Thant found Castro in an angry and intractable mood; one participant said Castro was "like a gored wild bull bleeding all over the place and attacking everything and everybody." Speaking softly, U Thant said that he had come to Castro as a friend, to bring peace to the area. Castro reacted angrily, saying he too wanted to bring peace to Cuba and if his five points were accepted, it would produce that peace. U Thant had been told by the Russians, both in New York and in Havana, that the UN could inspect all the missile sites and the incoming ships. When U Thant explained that his mission was to work out arrangements for UN supervision of the dismantling and removal of the Soviet missiles, Castro pounded the palm of his hand with his fist and told U Thant unequivocally there would be "no inspection of any kind on Cuban soil, before, during, or after the missile removal. Those coming to inspect Cuba had better come armed." When Thant spoke of what the Russians had promised, Castro became furious, stating he didn't care what the Russians had said or promised, that he, Castro, was the leader of the Cubans. Pointing to the secretary-general, Castro accused him of being a lackey to the two major powers, pulling first one and then another of their chestnuts out of the fire. "Can't you see what they are doing to the little nations like yours and mine?" U Thant responded by agreeing with Castro and conveying that he was only performing another of his distasteful duties as secretary-general.

As for the Russians, Castro was quoted as saying, "I gave them my heart, but now I wouldn't give them the cockles off my ass." Cuban-Soviet relations, he said, could be characterized only one way—extremely bad. Castro asked the secretary-general, "What do you think of a country that you allow to install missiles in your country but who wouldn't allow Cuban military men to visit the sites?" Shaking his head as though he had made a big mistake, he said, "No foreign country will be allowed to speak in Cuba's name again."

Castro appeared unwilling to make any concessions. He threatened to boycott any discussions and, if necessary, to fight alone. He saw the removal of the missiles and a U.S. military withdrawal from

Guantánamo as bargaining chips. He was not simply content to survive the crisis, he was attempting to recover the position he had held among emergent nations before the crisis. U Thant tried halfheartedly to bring Castro around, but the Cuban premier remained adamant. Thant, mindful of McCloy's admonition that any armed action against U.S. aircraft would invite prompt and serious reprisals, warned Castro. "This airspace is mine and we aim to defend it," Castro boasted.

The discussions between U Thant and Castro ended acrimoniously. Although the collapse in negotiations was thought to be temporary, it resulted in a new polarization of positions. The Cuban communiqué issued after the meeting reflected the lack of any agreement. "The meeting lasted two hours and fifteen minutes and during that time Cuba clearly outlined its position and its points of view without reaching any agreement." In retrospect, Thant's trip only complicated the work of Kuznetsov, Stevenson, and McCloy. The overeager Thant caused Castro to toughen his position, and the question of inspection was lost in a mêlée of accusations and bitter rhetoric.

In a meeting with Ambassador Stevenson and McCloy in New York on October 30, Kuznetsov again assured them that the missiles were being dismantled and that verification could be accomplished "by any means the United States desired." Kuznetsov, however, cautioned McCloy that all of the anti-aircraft weapons were in the hands of the Cubans and that the Soviets could no longer vouch for what Castro might do. McCloy knew this was an outright lie—that the SA-2 sites in Cuba were still in firm control of the Soviets. He looked Kuznetsov straight in the eye and warned him that U.S. flights would be resumed on November 1 and that "a most dangerous situation would arise if U.S. reconnaissance were fired upon or downed."

Meanwhile, during the stand-down, Western diplomats were asked to check on any movement of Soviet missiles to Cuban ports. Friendly attachés in automobile trips from Havana to Mariel saw no signs of any such activity.

President Kennedy, concerned about protecting any American elements that might be sent to Cuba as inspectors, had the Army come up with contingency plans. On October 31, the president met with General Earle Wheeler, U.S. Army chief of staff, along with Lieutenant General Theodore W. Parker, deputy chief of staff for Military Operations, and Lieutenant General Hamilton W. Howse, commanding general of the XVIII Airborne Corps. General Wheeler brought with him a large book containing detailed plans for a number of contingencies. The president seemed pleased that the Army was more than ready if called upon.

The next day, Thant and Brigadier Rikhye met in Havana with Soviet ambassador Alekseyev and Major General Igor D. Statsenko, who identified himself as commander of all the Soviet military forces in Cuba. Statsenko informed U Thant that Khrushchev's order to begin dismantling the bases had been received between 1 and 3 P.M. on Sunday, October 28, and that the dismantling began at 5 P.M. Statsenko further said that all major pieces of equipment would be removed in two days and the remaining "bits and pieces" would be destroyed and bulldozed. The crating of the equipment and the movement to the ports would take additional time. Statsenko expected to depart Cuba with the missiles.[2]

Statsenko showed little concern about the resumption of U.S. reconnaissance of the missile sites. There appeared to be some doubt in Brigadier Rikhye's mind as to which anti-aircraft weapons were in Cuban hands and which were controlled by the Soviets, and he expressed some concern that those in Cuban hands might go into action against U.S. overflights.

General Statsenko told Brigadier Rikhye that U.S. information he possessed on Soviet missile installations was "about correct." Although none of the IRBMs were operational, "six or eight" of the MRBMs were. Statsenko said there were about five thousand Soviet military personnel and three to five thousand Soviet civilian construction workers in Cuba. He implied that all of the military and civilian personnel would be evacuated along with the missiles. U Thant had been told by the Soviet delegation at the UN that he could visit any Russian missile site in Cuba, but the secretary-general felt that such an act would irritate the sensitive Castro. U Thant thereupon prepared to leave Cuba.

In addition to the standard signs and placards in Havana proclaiming the glory of the Cuban revolution, two new slogans had begun to appear in September and October 1962. One portrayed Russian troops on the march and bore the caption "Cuba Is Not Alone";

another displayed a Cuban soldier holding up his hand in the manner of a traffic policeman, proclaiming, "Stop, Mr. Kennedy! Cuba Is Not Alone." Still another proclaimed, "Our Friendship with the Soviet Union Is Unbreakable." As U Thant and his party moved through Havana on their way to the airport, they noticed that a number of these signs already had been, or were being, painted over. At José Martí airfield, U Thant expressed his thanks to the government of Cuba and departed for New York. At Idlewild airfield, he reported that although he and Castro had held a "fruitful negotiation," he had not obtained any agreement in his attempt to get Cuba to allow UN observers to verify the removal of the missiles. He said that Soviet representatives had informed him that dismantling of the missiles and launching systems was under way and that the work would be completed by Friday, November 2. Arrangements were also being made for the "shipment and return" of all the missiles and their supporting equipment to Russia.

Although the quarantine had been lifted for U Thant's visit, Soviet submarines in the Atlantic were still being tracked and harassed by U.S. Carrier Division No. 18. On the morning of October 31, a Soviet F-class submarine, Pendant No. 945, surfaced about 420 miles north of the Leeward Islands. Destroyer *Lloyd Thomas* watched the surfacing. As naval patrol planes swooped low to photograph the submarine, a harried Soviet skipper appeared on the bridge. When the *Thomas* flashed a conciliatory, "Do you need help?" the Soviet captain replied with a brisk, "Nyet." It was a known Soviet deceptive practice to paint out original pendant numbers on the sails of submarines on patrol and substitute new ones. This was normally done while the submarine surfaced in the early morning hours. During the crisis, a submarine was spotted on the surface with different numbers on either side of its sail.

The mechanics of implementing UN verification of the removal of the missiles from Cuba posed a number of problems. The UN had no photo-reconnaissance aircraft or photo-interpretation capability. While a number of nations participating in the proposed verification procedures had pilots and photo interpreters trained to work with low- or medium-altitude photography, with the exception of the

United Kingdom none had the capability to interpret the high-altitude photography acquired by the U-2. McCone had a low opinion of U Thant and the UN and argued vehemently that neither the U-2 nor U-2 photography should be made available to the UN. He proposed instead that older or obsolete Air Force reconnaissance aircraft and aerial cameras be assigned to the UN.

General Taylor was taking a lot of heat from the JCS that the military were losing complete control of the situation. General LeMay reminded Taylor, "I told you that yellow banty-legged bastard would fuck up the works." LeMay now pressed for the U.S. to position a large naval task force off Havana and a fleet of his SAC bombers overhead. Then he would demand that Castro allow U.S. forces to inspect the sites. If this demand was rejected, bombing of the Cuban military command center in Havana would begin immediately. LeMay's simplistic attitude was that both the Russians and the Cubans only recognize force. General Taylor characterized it later as another of General LeMay's "half-assed" recommendations during the crisis.

The JCS reluctantly accepted McCone's suggestion that older U.S. reconnaissance aircraft be offered to the UN and ordered that RB-66 airplanes of the 363rd Tactical Reconnaissance Wing be readied for transfer to UN authority. The aircraft were made ready, the cameras checked, and film stocks allocated. The RB-66's were flown from Shaw Air Force Base, South Carolina, to MacDill Air Force Base, in Florida. U.S. insignias were painted out and replaced with the white-and-blue insignia of the UN. However, while the aircraft were at MacDill, the UN insignias were kept covered by tarpaulins.

At White House meetings, both Bobby Kennedy and John McCone felt that U Thant's actions were eroding the U.S. position. The idea of using Red Cross inspectors was chaffing both of them. McCone pressed to resume low-altitude reconnaissance missions as soon as possible. On the afternoon of October 31, the president decided to resume the quarantine and the reconnaissance flights. Word was relayed to the Russians in New York that reconnaissance over Cuba would resume early on the morning of November 1. Later that day, the president ruled against the use of nuclear weapons in Cuba and the JCS ordered that nuclear weapons at the Tactical Air Force bases and in the ships of the U.S. Navy be returned to storage. SAC bombers, however, continued their airborne alert armed with nuclear weapons.

At the UN, Adlai Stevenson felt totally left out. McCloy was now carrying on most of the direct negotiating with Kuznetsov. His role had been diminished and he was convinced that his position was becoming purely perfunctory. He felt abandoned and went to visit his dear friend Eleanor Roosevelt, who was succumbing to a succession of terminal ailments.

November 1 – The Missiles
Are Removed from Cuba

*"You let a good milk cow bellow for a while
before you milk her."*

—ANASTAS MIKOYAN

AT DAWN ON NOVEMBER 1, U.S. Navy, Marine, and Air Force low-altitude reconnaissance planes were on their way to the Cuban missile sites. The missions were described as "milk runs"—the reconnaissance airplanes were not challenged or fired on by either the Soviets or the Cubans.

That afternoon, Lundahl was at the White House when word was flashed to him that based on the readout of the most recent photography, MRBM sites in Cuba had been or were being dismantled. Low-level reconnaissance showed that the missile erectors had been moved off the pads at nine of the eighteen launch positions observed. Missiles had already been removed from a number of the sites, the launch stands were being crated, the missile-ready tents struck, the theodolite stations dismantled, and some of the launch pads were being destroyed by bulldozers. Some of the missile transporters and launch erectors were being prepared for movement from the sites to the ports; oxidizer trailers and fuel transporters were observed grouped for movement, some with prime movers attached. Camouflage netting and polyvinyl sheathing had been removed from the sites. Convoys of trucks and equipment were being formed at several of the sites. Construction had ceased at most of the nuclear warhead storage sites, and scaffolding was being removed. Construction continued, however, at two of the nuclear storage areas, though construction had ceased at the IRBM sites and bulldozing of the launch stand foundations had begun. Cable troughs and other concrete structures were being destroyed; bulldozers, graders, and other equipment sat idle in some construction yards. The exact location of some of the missiles and support equipment could not be determined from the photography; most likely the missiles were on their way to designated Cuban ports. The assembly of the I1-28 bombers was continuing at San Julián airfield.

The limited filmloads in the cameras of the low-altitude reconnaissance planes were insufficient to photograph the missile sites along with the roads and port facilities in a single mission. McCone made a strong recommendation on November 2 to reinstitute U-2 overflights of Cuba but was refused by McNamara.

The mood at the White House when the news of the dismantling was received was described by an observer as "one eager, unrestrained display of emotion." The president asked that the aerial photos of the dismantling be shown to him first thing on the morning of November 2. Lundahl and McCone complied with Kennedy's request at the White House early the next morning. The president, turning to Lundahl, said, "These are mighty fine photographs—both in quality and in content." Smiling, he added, "Keep bringing that type of information and you'll always be welcome."

The president selected photo prints of the San Cristóbal and Sagua la Grande MRBM sites and asked that they be prepared for release to the press and media. He said that he planned to report to the nation on TV that evening and requested a summary of the information presented by McCone and Lundahl. Lundahl left a copy of his notes for the president. The president then pretended to swing a golf club, a habit that those in the White House got to know when the president was in a good and happy mood.

Since the president was going to address the nation that evening, he wondered about the strengths and weaknesses of U.S. broadcasting capabilities to Cuba. He wanted his message to be heard by the Cubans. It was estimated that there were about 1.3 million radio sets in Cuba, and Donald Wilson, the acting director of the United States Information Agency, was asked to give a rundown of the various radio stations in the U.S. that were broadcasting to Cuba and their effectiveness.[1]

That evening, on national television, Kennedy began his address: "My fellow citizens: I want to take this opportunity to report on the conclusions which this Government has reached on the basis of yesterday's aerial photographs which will be made available tomorrow, as well as other indications, namely that the Soviet missile bases in Cuba are being dismantled, their missiles and related equipment are being crated, and the fixed installations at these sites are being destroyed. The United States intends to follow closely the completion of this work through a variety of means, including aerial surveillance, until such time as an equally satisfactory international means of verification is effected."[2] The president also announced during his address that the U.S. would accept Red Cross inspection of Soviet vessels bound for Cuba.

Since SAC was going to continue to conduct all future U-2 reconnaissance over Cuba with its own U-2's, questions were raised whether these aircraft should not be upgraded with Agency electronic countermeasures (ECM) equipment. General Taylor called McCone and told McCone that nothing should be done about retracting the Agency U-2's until General Power, the SAC commander, completed a study on the "implications of installing this [ECM] equipment in these aircraft."

In Havana, Castro felt betrayed and neglected by the Soviets. On television, he appeared nervous and hesitant, belching frequently throughout his speech. Much of the rhetoric from Havana emphasized Castro's irritation with the trend of U.S.-Soviet negotiations and he reiterated his five points for settling the crisis.

Castro refused to see or speak to Soviet ambassador Alekseyev,[3] and Alekseyev warned Moscow that he could no longer control Castro: He might, by some irrational act, provoke a renewed Soviet-American confrontation.

As in many previous instances when a seasoned negotiator was needed, the Soviets turned to First Deputy Premier Anastas I. Mikoyan. Mikoyan arrived in New York on November 1 and, meeting newsmen at the Soviet UN mission, confidently predicted that "if every side will adhere to their documents [on the missile removal] the problem will be solved."

Castro, in a radio-TV address, on November 1 again specifically rejected UN on-site inspection of missile dismantling and removal, UN inspection of Soviet ships bound for Cuba, and International Red Cross inspection of Soviet ships in Cuban ports. He said, "We have not violated any law and have not carried any aggression against anyone whatsoever. Therefore, the inspection is another attempt to humiliate our country. Therefore, we will not accept it." He went on to warn Mikoyan: "We will sit down with the Soviet Union as equals and discuss in the light of reason and principle on a government-to-government basis."

When Mikoyan arrived in Havana, he quickly realized that the warm atmosphere of his first visit to Havana in 1960 had been totally dissipated. He was received formally but coldly by Castro at José Martí airfield. In his first meeting with Castro, Mikoyan was kept waiting for nearly two hours. When Castro finally emerged, Mikoyan was prepared to listen. Despite the tension and Castro's raving and tantrums, Mikoyan sought from time to time to keep the state-to-state relations on a relatively even keel. But Castro kept extolling military preparations for war, threatening to down U.S. reconnaissance planes, calling for additional Soviet concessions, and admonishing the United States for not accepting his five-point proposal. Castro was desperate to drive a wedge between the United States and the Soviet Union. Above all, he was worried about the direction the Soviets would now take. It now appeared to him that the Soviet attitude toward Cuba was ambivalent.

Mikoyan succeeded in taking some chill out of Soviet-Cuban relations by endorsing Castro's five points, but resolving the basic differences between the two countries would require further meetings. Mikoyan later remarked, "You let a good milk cow bellow for a while before you milk her."

Publicly, Mikoyan proclaimed: "We entertain feelings of sincere friendship and deep respect for the Cuban people and their government," but in private, he labeled Castro a psychopath. The Cubans, he would later remark, were never known for their logic. In subsequent meetings, Mikoyan attempted to put relations on a better footing by reassuring Castro that with the removal of the missiles, the Soviets would press the United States that there would no longer be a need for inspecting Cuba. He also promised Castro that there would be additional shipments of military equipment and economic aid in the future. He invited Castro to be Khrushchev's personal guest in Moscow at a later date. He also informed him that he was being considered for the Lenin Prize, the highest Soviet award.

Mikoyan appealed to Kuznetsov in New York to ask the United States to stop the low-level reconnaissance missions. Kuznetsov, in an obvious move to placate Castro, proposed to Ambassador Stevenson that the Soviets could give the United States all the necessary photographic proof of the dismantling of the missile sites. If this were done, he insisted, there would no longer be the need for intensive U.S. reconnaissance of the island. Washington quickly and categorically denied the request. Kuznetsov was warned again that any armed action against a U.S. low-altitude plane would invite ''prompt and serious reprisals.''

On November 3, in an interview with the Havana newspaper *Hoy*, Mikoyan declared that ''These are difficult days for the Cuban people, but the Soviet people are with Cuba body and soul.'' That same day, the Mikoyan-Castro talks nearly collapsed when Mikoyan approached Castro about allowing UN inspection of the missile sites. Castro stormed out of the meeting. Mikoyan was taken on tours of beaches and farms outside Havana, but no further meeting with Castro had been arranged. Adding to his diplomatic difficulties, Mikoyan was notified that afternoon that his wife, Ashken Lazaryevna, had died.

Mikoyan was under considerable pressure from Moscow, as well as from Kuznetsov at the UN, to prevent a complete breakdown of the talks with Castro. Sensing that he had perhaps made some progress with Castro, Mikoyan decided not to return to Moscow for his wife's funeral. Instead, he dispatched his son, Sergei, on November 4 to return to Moscow and arrange for his mother's burial. In later years, several Soviets would remark that Mikoyan never forgave Castro for forcing him to miss his wife's funeral.

With the talks in Havana stalled, it was obvious that Moscow had to initiate other alternatives to urge Castro to show some flexibility. Mikoyan warned Antonio Núñez Jiménez, director of the National Agrarian Reform Institute and one of Castro's closest associates, that he might go back to Moscow and let someone else of lesser rank talk to Castro, since it appeared they were getting nowhere. Mikoyan was continuing his "sightseeing" tours in the Cuban countryside when Castro called him back to Havana.

This time, Mikoyan pursued an entirely different approach. He listened patiently, but when Castro again reiterated that the Cubans were prepared to fight as they had at the Bay of Pigs, Mikoyan drew Castro up short. He said: "You won't have a ragtag brigade against you this time. You have the full might of the U.S. armed forces. If you want to fight, you can fight—but alone." When Castro declared that he was prepared to fight to the death, Mikoyan remarked, "That's exactly what the Kennedy brothers are prepared to give you. Nothing would please them more than to see you hanging from the highest light pole in Havana." Mikoyan tightened the screws. He threatened to return immediately to Moscow and to cut off all Soviet economic aid to Cuba. Castro countered that he would seek support from China. Mikoyan remained persistent. The discussion continued and the differences between Castro and Mikoyan narrowed. Mikoyan promised that all other disagreements could be settled later, when Castro visited Moscow. Castro, however, remained suspicious of the Soviets; the promise of aid had become self-serving and face-saving. It would not be until November 30 that Mikoyan would leave Cuba for the United States.

Washington's hopes for progress toward a final resolution of the crisis had suffered a setback by the bungling of U Thant in Cuba. The Kennedy administration still felt confident that it could pressure the Russians who, in turn, could force Castro to submit to inspection. In a meeting with McCloy and Stevenson in New York on the afternoon of October 31, Kuznetsov had shifted his position: Verification of missile removal had to be worked out between the UN and Castro. McCloy strongly objected, but Kuznetsov assured him that the USSR, in any event, would "fulfill its obligation." A number of U.S. military chiefs were not satisfied with the Cuban outcome. General LeMay continued to harry General Taylor with an I-told-you-so attitude. General Thomas White would refer to this period as "our national orgy of self-congratulations." He parodied Rusk's statement with, "When we were eyeball to eyeball, the other fellow winked."

In that meeting with Stevenson and McCloy, Kuznetsov had acknowledged that there were forty-two Soviet medium-range missiles in Cuba and that these missiles would be removed in such a manner that the removal could be verified. He also had said that once the missiles had been loaded and the ships had put to sea, U.S. naval units could pull alongside and view the missiles. Then, indicating Soviet good faith, the wily Kuznetsov began to press the U.S. to remove a base that threatens the USSR—an obvious reference to Turkey.

Anticipating that the NPIC ultimately would be called upon to verify removal of the MRBMs from Cuba, Lundahl directed the Center to review and restudy its analysis of the total number of MRBMs seen on the photography. In an elaborate review of all aerial photography, we again reaffirmed that the largest number of MRBMs seen on aerial photography was thirty-three. The Joint Chiefs of Staff sent representatives to the Center to verify that count. The JCS had postulated that based on the number of known launch positions and sites in Cuba, the Soviets could have as many as forty-eight MRBMs and either twenty-four or thirty-two IRBMs in Cuba. We pointed out that no SS-5 IRBM missiles had ever been seen on aerial photography. The JCS did not believe Kuznetsov's figure of forty-two MRBMs and thought that we should attempt to verify forty-eight missiles as they were loaded aboard Soviet ships.

Roswell Gilpatric, later appearing on the ABC-TV program *Issues and Answers*, stated he "could not be sure that forty-two was the maximum number that the Soviets brought to Cuba" until on-site inspection had been carried out.

Communist China now supported Cuban demands that the U.S. withdraw from Cuba and lent vigorous support to Castro's five points. The Chinese also urged Castro privately to resist Soviet pressure for an early settlement. At a meeting of the Presidium of the World Peace Council in Stockholm, the Chinese characterized Soviet behavior in the Cuban crisis as "cowardly." In the meantime, the Soviet press shifted its tone, emphasizing that U.S. pledges to respect the integrity of Cuban territory had to be honored. U.S. acceptance of Castro's five points would contribute to "normalizing" the situation in the Caribbean.

McCone and General Taylor realized that in shifting the diplomatic action to the UN, the United States would leave the Russians and

U Thant in control of events and the U.S. would never be likely to regain the diplomatic initiative. Kuznetsov would plead one delay after another. Kuznetsov also was a fresh player in the game, while those in the White House were becoming tired, impatient, and weary. Everything had slowed down. There was confusion, even a seeming paralysis, on the part of the Kennedy administration. Bobby was disappointed that there were no new initiatives emanating from the State Department.

At his first meeting with McNamara following his return from Glen Ora, the president demanded, "Let's make damn sure we get plenty of pictures of the missiles leaving Cuba. Allow the press to witness as much of it as possible." He added prophetically, "The Republicans will surely accuse us that the Russians allowed a few missiles to remain in Cuba."

With the continuing U-2 stand-down, NPIC recommended that more low-altitude missions would be required to adequately perform the job of verifying removal of missiles. The task confronting reconnaissance planners and the Center was formidable. Close coordination was required to ensure that the number of missiles leaving Cuba could be accounted for and confirmed without a shadow of a doubt. Commencing on November 1, from dawn until dusk, U.S. low-altitude reconnaissance planes bore in on the missile sites and overflew Cuban ports and the roads leading to them. An elaborate photographic record was compiled of the dismantling of the sites, the loading of the equipment, the movement of the equipment along the roads, and its arrival at the ports. All the components of the missile systems were counted and checked as they left the sites, and recounted and rechecked as they reached the ports and loaded aboard Soviet ships.

The EXCOM was concerned with the number of ships required to remove the missiles and how long the entire operation would take. CIA estimated that it would take six to eight ships to transport the missiles and an additional four to carry the missile-support equipment back to the Soviet Union. It was believed that the missiles would be removed in large-hatch ships similar to those that had brought the missiles to Cuba.[4] But when Khrushchev made his decision to remove the missiles on October 28, there were no large-hatch ships available to the Soviets in Cuban waters. The Soviets chose to remove the missiles as soon as possible, using whatever ships were available; consequently, the missiles would be returned to the Soviet Union as deck cargo. This was to be an obvious advantage to the United States in observing the removal of the missiles.

NPIC produced a number of briefing boards derived from the intensified low-level reconnaissance missions. The boards chronicled the dismantling of the missile sites and the movement of equipment toward the ports in great detail. Some of the missiles and equipment had arrived at Mariel and were parked in the dock area; at Punta Gerardo, a convoy of six oxidizer trucks had arrived. McCone and Lundahl briefed the president, and again he asked that some of the photos be made available to the press as soon as possible. Aerial photos released showed that missiles and missile equipment from the Sagua la Grande MRBM sites were being evacuated through the ports of La Isabela in the north and Casilda in the south. Missiles and equipment from the Guanajay and San Cristóbal MRBM sites were removed through the port of Mariel. The Soviet merchant ships *Dvinogorsk, Metallurg Anasov,* and *Bratsk* had been berthed at the Mariel pier since October 27.

By November 3, the ports were jammed with both missiles and support equipment. In all, twenty-eight MRBMs would be evacuated from Mariel: Four missiles were loaded aboard the *Dvinogorsk,* eight aboard the *Metallurg Anasov,* and two aboard the *Bratsk.* As soon as these three ships pulled away from the pier, the Soviet freighters *Ivan Polzunov, Labinsk,* and *Volgoles* arrived. Five missiles were loaded aboard the *Ivan Polzunov,* two aboard the *Labinsk,* and seven aboard the *Volgoles.* At the port of Casilda, on November 6, the Soviet merchant ship *Fizik Kurchatov* arrived and later took on six missiles. On November 7, the *Kurchatov* left the pier and the *Leninsky Komsomol* arrived and took aboard eight missiles. The *Bratsk* and *Dvinogorsk* put to sea on November 5, the *Metallurg Anasov,* the *Fizik Kurchatov,* and the *Labinsk* on November 7, the *Volgoles* on November 8, and the *Leninsky Komsomol* and the *Ivan Polzunov* on November 9.

The Soviet delegation to the United Nations had provided the U.S. Department of State with the names of the nine Soviet ships that would carry the missiles out of Cuba. Also provided was the number of missiles that each ship would carry. The secretary of state, in turn, provided the Soviets with the locations at sea where U.S. naval ships would rendezvous with the Soviet ships and inspect their cargo. The names, call signs, and numbers of U.S. naval combatants doing the inspecting were also given to the Soviets.

Adlai Stevenson, concerned about Eleanor Roosevelt's deteriorating health, was notified on November 7 that she had died of anemia and a lung infection.

Also on November 7, the Department of Defense announced: "The Soviet Union has reported that ships are leaving Cuba with missiles aboard. Arrangements are being made with Soviet representatives for contact with these ships by U.S. naval vessels and for counting the missiles being shipped out."[5]

"Close-alongside" scrutiny and photography of departing Soviet merchant ships was initiated, with Soviet cooperation. The Soviet ships, however, did not depart on the days specified, and the first ship to leave port, the *Bratsk*, made no effort to pass through the designated "alongside" inspection areas. Neither did the Soviets give the speed, course, or routes that the ships would take. Based on information provided by NPIC reporting, however, U.S. destroyers took up positions outside the ports where the missiles were observed being loaded.

As the Soviet ships put to sea, low-flying reconnaissance planes and helicopters photographed their deck cargoes and movement. Destroyers of the U.S. task forces moved close alongside once the Soviet ships entered international waters. The agreement between Kuznetsov and McCloy required that the Soviets remove the outer tarpaulins covering the missiles when asked to do so. The inner covers, made of clear plastic, need not be removed. Most of the Soviet ships cooperated fully, but the captain of the *Volgoles* refused to acknowledge signals and steamed past the waiting U.S. destroyers *Perry* and *Vesole*. The *Perry* twice flashed the message "uncover missiles," with negative results. The *Perry* repeated the message a third time and, after a pause, added the word *"Please."* When the *Volgoles* again refused, the *Perry* and *Vesole* began to trail her. The *Perry* transmitted the message of refusal to CINCLANT, which relayed it immediately to Admiral Anderson. Anderson contacted Roswell Gilpatric, who informed Rusk. John McCloy was contacted at the UN and asked to lodge an immediate protest with Kuznetsov. McCloy suggested strongly to Kuznetsov that the *Volgoles* return to its rendezvous point and uncover its missiles. Kuznetsov asked that he be granted a brief period, and then the U.S. destroyers could contact the *Volgoles* again. Gilpatric asked Admiral Anderson to order the *Perry* to proceed abreast the *Volgoles* and signal the following message: "Your government has agreed to uncover missiles. Please do so." This time, the *Volgoles* complied.

Kuznetsov protested to Stevenson that force had been used against the *Aleksandrovsk, Dvinogorsk,* and *Volgoles,* that these ships had been told by U.S. commanders they must open their cargo hatches under threat of force if they did not comply. This was a gross misunderstanding of the U.S.-Soviet agreement, according to Kuznetsov. He was especially vehement about the *Aleksandrovsk,* since it had no missiles aboard.

The U.S. destroyer *Biddle* came alarmingly close to the *Leninsky Komsomol* to get the necessary verification pictures. The captain of the *Leninsky Komsomol* sounded the danger signal with several short blasts of his horn. The destroyer remained alongside, however, until all the necessary photos had been taken. The captain of the *Leninsky Komsomol* complained by loudspeaker in poor but understandable English. An officer aboard the *Biddle* replied in poor but understandable Russian. The captain of the *Leninsky Komsomol* spoke again, this time in Russian and the U.S. naval officer again responded in Russian. The ships were so close that both parties could see each other, and both began smiling. In an effort to surmount the language difficulties, Captain Roth, skipper of the destroyer, invited the Soviet captain to come aboard for lunch. There was a long silence and the Soviet captain responded that he was sorry but he had a previous commitment.

The U.S. heavy cruiser *Newport News* intercepted the *Ivan Polzunov*. Using signal flags and international code, good morning messages were exchanged. Pulling alongside, voice communication was established in English. The captain of the *Polzunov* expressed his sympathy on the death of Eleanor Roosevelt. When asked to uncover the missiles, the master replied that he had been intercepted the previous day and had been cleared. Without delay, however, he had the tarpaulins pulled back again, exposing the missiles. In departing, the *Newport News* sent the message "Wish you good sailing on your trip home. Goodbye and good luck." The *Polzunov* replied, "Thanks to you. Goodbye."

The aircraft carrier *Wasp* intercepted another of the missile-carrying ships. A helicopter with a Russian-speaking officer was sent from the *Wasp* to hover above the Soviet ship to get the necessary pictures. The crew of the Soviet ship were very cooperative, removing the tarpaulins from the missiles. It was obvious to the helicopter crew that a number of missile technicians were aboard the ship. They were distinguishable because they were not wearing traditional navy-blue uniforms, and most were shirtless—apparently trying to get a suntan. They were smiling and waved greetings. Captain Middleton, chief of staff to Admiral Paul B. Buie, was in the helicopter. He took off his Navy tie clasp and lowered it on a line to the Russians below. As the helicopter began to lift, the Russians motioned for it to return. Asking that the line be lowered again, the Russians attached a bottle of vodka. Now the smiles came from the helicopter.

The U.S. Navy followed the Soviet missile-carrying ships into the Mediterranean and the Baltic Sea. Admiral Anderson had ordered, "I want to report to the boss when they are all back in Russia."

Throughout the crisis, Lundahl had alerted his staff to post him of any evidence of comic relief observed on the photography. President Eisenhower had appreciated a number of humorous briefing boards prepared during critical situations. Lundahl felt that President Kennedy would also welcome a little humor in this situation. President Kennedy, himself adept at clear, concise usage of the English language, particularly disliked anything smacking of military jargon. On several occasions during the crisis, he had shown a certain displeasure with daily intelligence reports referring to the number of missile launch positions "occupied" and "unoccupied." He felt that, somehow, there must be a better way to describe how many of the four launch positions at each of the missile sites had missile launchers on them. McCone had struggled unsuccessfully to find appropriate terms of clarification throughout the crisis, until the stage had been reached when the missiles were on their way out. At that point, a U.S. reconnaissance plane flying very low over a military camp happened to photograph a soldier using an open "three-hole" latrine. We produced a briefing board from the photography, and Lundahl showed it to McCone and included it in the White House briefing package. Lundahl finished his routine briefing of the president and McCone asked if the president would like to see a new three-position military site discovered in Cuba, with one position occupied. The president's face froze momentarily, since he was aware that each of the missile sites in Cuba had four positions rather than three. As the president studied the photo, there came first a smile and then a booming laugh. When he finally stopped, he asked, "Why didn't I have this earlier? Now I understand the occupied/unoccupied problem perfectly."

The president was grateful and generous with his thanks and praise to those in his administration and throughout the federal service who had supported him so loyally and contributed so much to the successful management of the crisis. For a select group of his closest advisers, he personally designed a unique commemorative calendar to be executed in silver by Tiffany Jewelers of New York. The silver calendar leaf displaying the month of October 1962, with the critical dates of the sixteenth through the twenty-eighth more heavily embossed, was mounted on a walnut base. The initials JFK and those of the recipient were engraved, respectively, in the upper left and upper right corners. No public announcement of the gifts was made, and they were presented to the thirty-four recipients privately. The calendar recipients included Secretaries Rusk and McNamara, Adlai Stevenson, each of the Joint Chiefs of Staff, CIA director McCone, members of the National Security Council, presidential aides Pierre Salinger and Ted Sorensen, and Arthur C. Lundahl. Two of the calendars were presented to women: one to his wife, Jacqueline, and the other to his personal secretary, Mrs. Evelyn Lincoln.

McCone was the first to recognize the work of the National Photographic Interpretation Center with a formal memo of commendation on November 2, 1962: "As Director of Central Intelligence and on behalf of the entire intelligence community as well as the United States Government, I wish to commend you and the personnel under your command for the outstanding work you have been performing, especially during the past four months of the Cuban buildup."[6]

On November 8, 1962, the president sent the following letter to Lundahl:

"While I would like to make public the truly outstanding accomplishments of the National Photographic Interpretation Center, I realize that the anonymity of an organization of your high professional competence in the intelligence field must be maintained.

"I do want you and your people to know of my very deep appreciation for the tremendous task you are performing under most trying circumstances. The analysis and interpretation of the Cuban photography and the reporting of your findings promptly and succinctly to me and to my principal policy advisers, most particularly the Secretary of State and the Secretary of Defense, has been exemplary.

"You have my thanks and the thanks of your government for a very remarkable performance of duty and my personal commendation goes to all of you."

John F. Kennedy

The Center continued to monitor the missile sites and the removal of missile equipment and also was closely watching San Julián and Holguín airfields in Cuba, where a number of Il-28 Beagle bomber crates remained. At San Julián, thirty-three unassembled bombers had been delivered in crates during early October. Thirteen of the sixty-foot-long fuselage crates had been opened and the fuselages removed. Assembly of the Il-28's at San Julián had continued throughout the crisis. At the height of the crisis, the Soviets used canvas, tarpaulins, and nets to conceal their assembly activities. Thirty of the remaining crates were dispersed throughout the airfield and concealed with camouflage netting.

On November 1, an Il-28 was seen taxiing on the San Julián runway; an additional five Il-28's were observed assembled on hardstands. The EXCOM was briefed by Lundahl on November 3 that the uncrating and assembly of Il-28's was continuing. McCone felt strongly that the assembly of the bombers had to be stopped, by bombing if necessary.

The presence of the bombers made it even more imperative that there be a system for inspection and verification of the removal of all offensive weapons, and a system of aerial inspection and on-site verification to prevent the reintroduction of offensive weapons in Cuba. After it appeared that Mikoyan had failed to persuade Castro to accept on-site inspection and UN observers, McCone argued, and the EXCOM agreed, that the best means of acquiring data and monitoring Cuba was the use of high-altitude aerial reconnaissance. He proposed full U-2 coverage of the island every seven days. Because of the frivolous nature of Cuban weather, this meant that on clear days, two U-2 missions might have to be flown.

McCone added that not only the Il-28's but the MiG-21 fighters as well had to be removed. As one member stated, "It was another of McCone's clay pigeons that was shot out of the air." The EXCOM and the president agreed, however, that the Il-28's had to be removed, but not the MiG-21's.

McCloy had asked McCone for intelligence support on the Il-28 problem; McCone appointed Huntington B. Sheldon to keep McCloy informed on CIA monitoring of the Il-28's. We provided Sheldon with information derived from analysis of aerial and ground photography, along with all collateral information available at the CIA. Sheldon departed Washington and shortly after met with both Stevenson and McCloy in New York.

On November 4, Stevenson and McCloy met with Kuznetsov and took up the question of the removal of the Il-28's. McCloy said that the U.S. took a "most serious" view of the bombers' presence. Kuznetsov maintained that the Il-28's were not included in the "offensive weapons" category. But McCloy pressed the point that the bombers were capable of striking the United States and therefore could certainly not be considered defensive weapons. McCloy then raised the ante. He said that as long as the bombers were in Cuba, the United States could not lift the blockade but might even have to intensify it. McCloy added that the United States refused to guarantee not to invade Cuba unless the bombers were removed. He stated there was pressure within the Kennedy administration and in the Congress to bomb the aircraft if they were not removed. Kuznetsov ended the meeting abruptly, saying that the problem could be discussed again at a later date. It was obvious to McCloy that Kuznetsov had no specific instructions regarding the Il-28's and that the Soviets hoped that Mikoyan could resolve the issue in his negotiations in Havana. The Havana negotiations with Castro, of course, were on dead center.

On Sunday, November 5, McCloy, with additional support from Sheldon, met with Kuznetsov again. McCloy emphasized again that some U.S. administration experts, frustrated with Castro, were still strongly advocating the bombing of the two airfields where the bombers were located. Castro remained firm, claiming that the bombers had been purchased from Russia and belonged to Cuba. President Kennedy remained just as adamant that the Il-28's had to be removed from Cuba. Premier Khrushchev, in several notes to Kennedy, had made proposals regarding the Il-28's, all of which were labeled unacceptable by the White House. The president had implied politely but firmly that Khrushchev should not delay removing the "offensive" bombers as he had promised to do with the missiles.

At 4:15 P.M. on November 5, Cuban authorities, in keeping with a promise to U Thant, surrendered the body of Major Rudolf Anderson to the Swiss ambassador in Havana. Brigadier Indar Jit Rikhye flew from Miami to Havana and brought Anderson's body back to the United States. An autopsy revealed that fragments from the SA-2 had penetrated the pilot's pressurized suit and that instant decompression had occurred. There were small flesh wounds on the body where fragments had been taken from it. The suturing of the wounds was that of a mortician rather than of a surgeon. Major Anderson was buried with full military honors at Woodlawn Memorial Park in Greenville, South Carolina.

Eleanor Roosevelt would be buried beside her husband in the rose garden at Hyde Park, New York. President Kennedy, Vice-President Johnson, and ex-Presidents Truman and Eisenhower attended the funeral. Others attending were Adlai Stevenson, Chief Justice Earl Warren, Justice Arthur Goldberg, Governor Nelson Rockefeller, ex-Governor Herbert H. Lehman, and cabinet members of Franklin Roosevelt's administration. President Kennedy, although recognizing Stevenson, paid more attention to Presidents Truman and Eisenhower before hurrying back to Washington. More than ever, Stevenson felt that the Washington establishment had forgotten him. He instead turned to his friends. A week later, Stevenson would be the principal speaker at a memorial service for Mrs. Roosevelt at the Cathedral of St. John the Divine in New York City.

The U.S. midterm elections on November 6 resulted in a Democratic victory, with the Democrats winning twenty-five of the thirty-nine contested Senate seats, a net gain of four seats, and losing only four seats in the House. The clear majority won by the Democrats was a personal victory for President Kennedy, and newspapers regarded the election as evidence of national support for Kennedy's Cuba policies. The president was in a buoyant mood. When Lundahl routinely went to the White House to brief him the next day, the president was swinging at imaginary golf balls in the Oval Office.

Meanwhile, at the Center, we continued to carefully note what was happening at the two Cuban Il-28 airfields. On both November 4 and 5 coverages, there were at least nine Il-28 fuselage crates at Holguín but no apparent effort to assemble the bombers. However, the assembly of bombers continued at San Julián.

McCloy, alternately threatening and cajoling, was determined to sustain Kennedy's insistence that the bombers be removed, and he doggedly pursued the issue with Kuznetsov at UN headquarters and at the Soviet UN mission at Glen Cove, Long Island. Kuznetsov maintained that the bombers had been given to the Cubans. If this were the case, McCloy maintained that the Cubans could simply return them. Kuznetsov then charged that a demand to remove the Il-28's, together with the removal of the missiles, would make it virtually impossible for the Soviets to control Castro. In Havana, there were signs of concern that Washington was pressing the Russians too hard. Castro had attempted without success to get involved in negotiations at the UN. He also continued to demand unsuccessfully that the U.S. abide by his five points.

On November 8, Kuznetsov met with Stevenson and U Thant at the UN and reversed himself; implementation of the on-site verification procedures depended on Cuban agreement, which was not forthcoming. He stated rather forcibly that all of the missiles and warheads, as the U.S. knew, had been removed from Cuba. Kuznetsov also argued that since the Soviets had removed the missiles, there would be no need for International Red Cross inspection at sea. He said he had discussed the matter with U Thant and that U Thant was cancelling all plans to send inspectors to the missile sites in Cuba. Then, in a rather oblique manner, Kuznetsov added that Castro was complaining about Moscow's policy toward Cuba, but he didn't elaborate.

Stevenson became increasingly concerned with the stalemate and drafted a message to the president: "Unless there is some break from Moscow or Havana, I think the situation is deadlocked, and I suggest trying to conclude the transaction with the Russians to enable us to get into contact with Cuba through the OAS or directly. Realizing that the Soviets may not be able to control Cuba, I suggest consideration as a contingency a formula for terminating the present transaction." Stevenson then proposed several solutions through Security Council arrangements. Stevenson's fallback on the inspection issue was to use aerial reconnaissance ("I assume our reconnaissance will also verify without any agreement by the Soviets or Cubans").[7]

On November 11, Gilpatric publicly announced, with the president's approval, that the United States would no longer condone the presence of the Il-28 bombers in Cuba. He said that since the Soviets had given the bombers to Cuba, "we regard the removal of these bombers as within the capacity of the Soviets."

McCloy had sensed that there was a certain mounting frustration within the Soviet UN delegation, and felt that it was an opportune time to press Kuznetsov further. He also felt, however, that he could not accomplish his objective in the UN atmosphere. He therefore invited Kuznetsov to the more conducive atmosphere of his farm in Stamford, Connecticut, for discussions. They walked about the farm alone for some time and then paused at a rail fence. McCloy had carefully rehearsed what he was going to say. He told Kuznetsov that the two nations were allowing a petty matter to destroy their present and future relations; that the longer the Soviets allowed the bombers to remain in Cuba, the more difficult they would make Kennedy's position in his relations with Congress, which would demand that Kennedy take an even harder line against the Soviets. McCloy reiterated that there were some in the Kennedy administration and in the Congress who advocated bombing of the Il-28's. McCloy then told Kuznetsov that a foolish act by Castro could bring the two nations into direct confrontation again. He reassured Kuznetsov that a new era in U.S.-Soviet relations could arise from the ashes of the crisis if the bombers were removed. Kuznetsov hesitated momentarily and then agreed with McCloy that the Il-28 bombers should be removed. He turned and said to McCloy, "This time, but never again." McCloy reported to Rusk and the president that the Russians would regain ownership of the Il-28's but advised the president that pressure would have to be maintained until the aircraft were actually removed.

The EXCOM met on November 13, and Rusk proposed that the U.S. tie in the removal of the Il-28's with the lifting of the quarantine. The president agreed, and the Center was asked to closely monitor the two Il-28 airfields and aid in planning the reconnaissance required to verify their removal.

The CIA chairman of interdepartmental COMOR, James Reber, called a meeting for November 14 to consider long-range planning for reconnaissance of Cuba. Reber, noting the deactivation of the IRBM and MRBM launch sites, coupled with evidence of missile-associated equipment aboard ships on their way to Russia, asked if daily low-altitude coverage of the missile sites was necessary any longer. Reber proposed that coverage of the ports or any other interior target considered significant would continue to be accomplished by low-level missions. He indicated that USIB had recommended, and the president had approved, that the entire island also be covered once a week by U-2 photography.

On November 16, the president met with the Joint Chiefs of Staff to discuss removal of the Il-28 bombers. While the president stated that he was pleased with the progress of the McCloy-Kuznetsov negotiations, he asked individual JCS members for contingency recommendations if the Soviets, because of Castro's intransigence, failed to remove the Il-28's in consideration of the president's no-invasion pledge. The recommendatins were unanimous—bomb them, or go into Cuba and remove them forcibly.

Castro was, reportedly, livid when told that the Soviets were going to remove the bombers. It had become apparent to McCloy in his conversations with Kuznetsov that Mikoyan was making little progress in bridging the differences between the USSR and Cuba. Mikoyan avoided acrimonious exchanges with Premier Castro that could lead to a further deterioration of relations, but on the issue of removal of the Il-28's, they remained far apart. Castro steadfastly maintained that the bombers were his and therefore not negotiable.

On November 16, in a letter to U Thant, Premier Castro again warned that Cuba would shoot down U.S. planes if aerial reconnaissance was not terminated. President Kennedy forcefully stated the reconnaissance flights would continue until an "equally satisfactory international means of verification is effected."

Castro continued that "violations have increased in number every day, the incursions of war planes over our territory have become more alarming. Military aircraft harass our air bases, make low-level flights over our military defenses, and photograph not only the dismantled strategic missile installations but in fact our entire territory, foot by foot and inch by inch." He stated that a captured CIA agent* "had shown us how the photographs taken by the spying planes serve for guidance in sabotage and also revealed, among other things, a design to cause chaos by provoking the deaths of 400 workers in one of our industries."

McCloy also continued to insist aerial reconnaissance be continued. "We can't think of giving up overflights, which everybody in the Hemisphere now knows have played such an important role in maintaining the security of the hemisphere."[8]

There was agreement among the members of EXCOM that the low-altitude aircraft were probably very disconcerting to the Cubans, but there also was a desire to restrict the missions since there was no longer an intelligence-collection need. Then, too, a number of these aircraft, because of the heavy flight activity since October 23, were scheduled for maintenance. McCone insisted that U-2 flights be resumed as the low-altitude flights were scaled down. The EXCOM agreed and the last low-altitude mission over Cuba's interior was flown on November 15. From time to time, however, low-altitude missions continued to be flown over Cuban ports to check on Russian ships. Between October 22 and December 6, a total of eighty-two U-2 missions were flown. On January 3, 1963, Castro would take credit for the discontinuance of the low-level missions: "And they showed [up] with their planes; in the days of the crisis, during the truce, they started to fly over and buzz our bases and over our artillerymen until they received orders to fire; then the

* For sabotage operations, Cuban CIA agents were frequently provided aerial photographs.

Americans went as high as they could, and they quit flying low."[9]

President Kennedy, in a December 17 news conference, credited the eventual removal of the Il-28's to aerial reconnaissance: "One of the reasons, I think, that the Soviet Union withdrew the Il-28's was because we were carrying on very intensive low-level photography. No one would have guessed, probably, that that would have been such a harassment. Mr. Castro could not permit us to indefinitely continue widespread flights over his island at two hundred feet every day. And he—and yet he knew if he shot down one of our planes that then it would bring back a much more serious reprisal on him."

McCloy, a staunch Republican, had consulted General Eisenhower to solicit his opinions on concluding the crisis. Eisenhower shared McCloy's view "that we have a victory in hand and should now wind the matter up promptly." General Eisenhower also agreed that U.S. reconnaissance overflights and the intelligence derived were much better means of verification than some undefined UN inspection personnel, and he expressed the view that "we might get tied on too hard to this kind of thing."[10]

On Sunday, November 18, McCloy met with Kuznetsov and Zorin in New York. Kuznetsov stated that he felt that the U.S. was stalling further negotiations and had done little to effect a rapid solution to remaining problems regarding Cuba. It was obvious that the Soviets wanted a rapid solution, and after a long, frank, and detailed review, McCloy told Kuznetsov that although U.S. low-altitude missions over the island interior had been canceled, "he wanted to have it clear that we were not in any way contemplating stopping overflights in Cuba unless and until we were sure that there was not going to be any reintroduction of these weapons. We were doing the utmost to keep overflights to a minimum, but in the absence of any adequate verification, this was the only thing we could do and he repeated that overflights had probably saved us from war and they might do so again." McCloy made it clear to Kuznetsov and Zorin that "we would return fire if our planes were shot at; that we were going to do as we had been doing in the past, i.e., keep overflights to a minimum necessary to protect ourselves and hemisphere."[11] McCloy further alerted Kuznetsov that the reconnaissance of Cuba would henceforth be accomplished by U-2's.

Stevenson was still concerned about ending the crisis quickly and, in a memo to the White House, again reviewed the situation, stating that negotiations appeared to be deadlocked. He proposed that if the Soviets removed the Il-28's, other problems could be resolved through Security Council arrangements. Verification could be effected through ex post facto relations between Cuba and selected Latin American nations. The Soviets and Cuba would provide public assurance in the Security Council that such weapons would not be reintroduced into Cuba. If this were done, the U.S. would end the quarantine and give Cuba formal guarantees against invasion and ask other Latin American countries to do the same.[12]

U Thant on November 18 received a surprise letter from Castro stating he was willing to accede to the Soviet decision to remove the Il-28's, claiming that the bombers were too obsolete to be of any value to Cuba. On November 20, Khrushchev agreed to disassemble the bombers and remove them from Cuba. The same day at 6 P.M., President Kennedy announced that the quarantine would be lifted and as many of the blockading vessels as possible would return to port. Admiral Anderson reported that 183 ships had participated in the quarantine at its height. With justifiable pride, Anderson said, "Again, the U.S. had turned to seapower to wield the iron fist in a velvet glove and again the Navy and ships of the Atlantic fleet had shown this confidence was not misplaced." The president, a former Navy man himself, was in total agreement.

Based on the understanding between President Kennedy and Khrushchev, the Soviet premier instructed Marshall Malinovsky to abrogate the measures established on October 23 for increased combat readiness of Soviet troops and fleets. At the same time, President Kennedy authorized the secretaries of the Navy and Air Force to terminate the extension of tours of duty and release those reservists called to active duty in connection with the Cuban crisis.[13] The Department of Defense also authorized payment of lump-sum emergency relocation expenses to dependents of military personnel evacuated from Guantánamo.[14] The Navy later assumed responsibility for packing the household goods and personal belongings of those evacuated from Guantánamo for shipment to the United States.[15]

The question as to whether the United States had the right to continue aerial surveillance of Cuba under the Khrushchev-Kennedy agreement prompted a debate between Stevenson and the White House and intelligence community. On November 22, Ambassador Stevenson sent a memo to the president regarding Cuban refusal of inspection proposals and the possibility of the president retracting his noninvasion pledge: "If the real objective is not to give the invasion pledge at this time, I think it would be best to break off the negotiations over an agreement on interpretation of the contract, rather than by insisting on the right to continue over-flights which were not contemplated by the contract. I think we can make a strong case for insisting, in accordance with your letter of October 27, on safeguards in the form of UN observers at the ports, airfields, and so forth in Cuba. I submitted exact language on this several days ago, but I don't have it at hand. To break off over their refusal to give us what we are reasonably entitled to under the agreement would be better than breaking off over their refusal to tolerate over-flights, which were not contemplated by the agreement."[16]

NPIC, looking at the bulldozed missile sites on aerial photography, was acutely aware of Castro's foolishness, even stupidity, in not allowing UN inspectors to view the dismantled sites. These inspectors, in general, would have been limited to reporting back only that the sites had been dismantled, but the continued aerial photography was providing intelligence bonuses on a wide spectrum of Cuban military and economic life. By tacitly allowing periodic U-2 reconnaissance of the entire island, the Cubans provided the United States an opportunity to glean a wealth of intelligence information, not only on Cuba itself but also on its efforts in "exporting the revolution" to foreign areas.*

The advantages to the U.S. of periodic aerial reconnaissance missions versus on-site UN observer teams were clear to anyone familiar with intelligence operations, and McCone had strong support among

---

* Periodic U-2 reconnaissance of Cuba continued until the Jimmy Carter administration, when he directed it be cancelled. It was reintroduced, however, during the MiG-23 controversy and whenever U.S. national security interests dictated a look-see at what military equipment and supplies the Cubans might be receiving from the Russians. The aegis of continuing U-2 reconnaissance was a U.S. need to assure itself that no offensive-weapons capability was being reintroduced into Cuba. At no time did Castro interfere with U-2 or subsequent SR-71 aerial reconnaissance missions.

EXCOM members who pressed his case with the president and Bundy that aerial reconnaissance had to be continued. McCone stated bluntly that he could not support Stevenson's proposal in that we could not rely on words from the Soviets and Cubans alone or from UN observer groups. He reiterated forcefully that the Soviets had lied on numerous occasions and would probably do so again if it was in their interest or to their advantage. He insisted, and the president agreed, that aerial reconnaissance be continued.

A draft by Bundy of the president's instructions to Stevenson specified: "The United States has never wanted to be forced to invade Cuba. The sudden and secret actions of others in September and October created a danger which might have compelled an invasion. On the evidence and assurances now presented, the threat of offensive weapons is receding, and in this situation invasion of Cuba is neither required or justified. On the understanding, therefore, that offensive weapons are removed and kept out of Cuba in the future, the United States is able to give assurances against invasion."[17] To assure that aerial reconnaissance would be continued, the memo emphasized: "In the absence of the verification and safeguards contemplated by the President's letter of October 27, these assurances can be sustained only if there is no interference with other means of obtaining satisfactory information on the absence of offensive weapons systems."[18]

A "Guideline for the Planning of Cuban Overflights" was approved by National Security Action Memorandum No. 208 and signed by the president on December 4, 1962. It allowed continued U-2 reconnaissance of Cuba.

While the president was pleased with the Soviet promise to remove the bombers, in another set of instructions to McCloy he requested that the Soviets be made to understand that it is "our desire that this be wound up very promptly, a desire Chairman Khrushchev evidently shares."[19] The president emphasized that "there is, in fact, no present danger of invasion of Cuba, but we cannot be put in a position of giving blanket guarantees to a man who has refused to cooperate with the UN to fulfill the understanding of October 27 and 28."[20] The president instructed that if Kuznetsov raised any inspection scheme of the U.S., the U.S. would insist that inspections be also performed in the Soviet Union. Both countries, however, seemed content to wind down the crisis—and seemed to agree that any other side issues could be discussed later in Geneva, where future negotiations on safeguards against surprise attack were to be conducted.

Both Stevenson and McCloy had reported that in their negotiations with Kuznetsov, they had observed repeated indications that the Soviets were anxious for broader détente with the U.S. The president was deeply interested and would exploit this interest later in speeches at American University and the Irish Parliament in 1963. The president's purpose was not to intensify the Cold War but to create conditions moving toward better relations with the Soviet Union.

Although intensified military and intelligence operations attendant to the crisis were winding down, NPIC was again called upon to monitor the removal of the Il-28 bombers. U-2 missions continued to cover San Julián and Holguín airfields. Surprisingly, assembly of the bombers at San Julián was continuing. It wasn't until November 25 that disassembly was first observed there. The twenty open aircraft-shipping crates that had been seen dispersed throughout the airfield during the crisis were seen collected along a central taxiway and aircraft component parts had been placed inside them. The crates were reported as ready for transfer to the ports. At Holguín airfield, the aircraft-shipping crates were seen ready for transfer on November 25, and on photo coverage of November 27 they were no longer present. On December 4, the Center reported that all of the bombers had been removed from San Julián airfield.

The Soviets did not specify to U.S. representatives at the UN where or when the Il-28's would be removed. The Center kept a close watch on Cuban ports for the loading of the Il-28's. The Soviet merchant ship *Okhotsk* arrived in the port of Mariel, where it picked up three Il-28 fuselages transferred from San Julián. It moved along the coast to the port of Neuvitas, where it picked up nine Il-28 fuselage crates transferred from Holguín airfield. The Soviet merchant ship *Kasimov*, which had brought some of the Il-28's to Cuba originally, moved into the port of Mariel, and on December 15 eleven Il-28 fuselages in shipping crates and four canvas-covered fuselages were loaded as deck cargo. Fifteen additional fuselage crates were observed parked at Mariel port. The Soviet merchant ship *Krasnograd*, a large-hatch ship, docked at Mariel and loaded the fifteen fuselage crates and departed Cuba on December 15. All the ships were closely followed at sea and photographed by the U.S. Navy. The Soviets partially removed the tops of the Il-28 shipping crates so that the fuselages could be seen inside. The Center verified that all forty-two Il-28's seen in Cuba during the crisis were on their way back to the Soviet Union.

McCloy later characterized his meetings with Kuznetsov at the UN and on Long Island as a "sparring match that never seemed to end." Kuznetsov continually had raised many extraneous issues. He had claimed that provisions of the Rio Pact under which the U.S. was operating were not in accord with Article 51 of the UN Charter. He also criticized the Rio Pact as authorizing the use of force without the approval of the Security Council under Article 53. McCloy said that they were "swatting the hell out of gnats and letting the elephants go by."

Cuba made it apparent that it was not going to accept terms of the agreement inherent in the Khrushchev-Kennedy exchange of October 27. The State Department took the position that there were two major options for concluding the negotiations: "1) continued efforts to get parallel declarations put before the Security Council where minimum stated position of each side is tolerable to the other; 2) wind up the problem by issuing unilateral government statements delineating respective positions."[21] The State Department favored the latter option, and the crisis ended with many issues unresolved. This was acceptable to the president. The missiles and Il-28 bombers were out of Cuba, and Kennedy seemed satisfied.

Once the missiles and bombers had been removed, little concern was expressed about the Russian troops remaining in Cuba. Notes taken at a November 29 EXCOM meeting reflect a diminished level of concern: "There was a discussion of Soviet personnel, whether they would stay in Cuba and why. The conclusion was unclear. It was not thought they would stay as assurance. The conclusion, which seems to have been Bundy's, was that the personnel were planted as a presence."[22]

Nuclear Warhead
Postmortem

"My views of the intelligence taken from the
U-2 was the view I would have of
a holy miracle."

—Sherman Kent

WHEN LUNDAHL had first briefed the president and his advisers on the discovery of MRBM missiles in Cuba on October 16, McNamara asked if nuclear warheads for the missiles had been found. Lundahl replied in the negative: There was no evidence of a nuclear warhead storage facility, but it was assumed that there were nuclear warheads in Cuba, probably near the missile sites. NPIC interpreters had developed a number of photographic "signatures" for identifying Soviet practices for storing nuclear weapons. These signatures comprised specially constructed bunkers surrounded by elaborate security measures—security fences and walls, guard towers, control and check points—lightning arrestors and fire prevention zones. Tent camps for a Soviet guard force would also be evident.

The president had ordered Cuba completely covered by aerial reconnaissance on October 17 and 18. Late on Wednesday evening, October 17, a photo interpreter, after finding an IRBM site, spotted a nuclear warhead storage bunker under construction, similar to those seen in Russia. A security fence was being erected around the bunker. Prefabricated construction materials (concrete arches, beams, fenceposts, etc.) were scattered about the area. When Lundahl viewed the bunker, he asked the Center's nuclear-weapons specialists, Chris Dole, Joe Seng, and Wilbur Dodd, numerous questions about its construction and whether any indications of weapons storage had been seen. He was sure McNamara would ask the same questions of him. The photo interpreters replied in the negative. Lundahl was acutely aware that these bunkers would become a prime target, not only for bombing but also for any special-operations military mission that might be sent to the area.

A number of other nuclear warhead storage bunkers were found under construction near other missile sites in Cuba, and all were carefully studied. It was established that none of the bunkers were present on aerial photography of August 29 or September 5. Refugee reporting had indicated that materials for the construction of one of the storage sites arrived about September 29.[1] There were two basic types of bunkers: the Guanajay type measured 112 feet in length; while the San Cristóbal type measured 71 feet in length. Four lightning arrestors were identified at the Guanajay bunker. San Cristóbal-type nuclear warhead storage bunkers eventually were identified under construction at all the MRBM sites, except San Cristóbal MRBM sites 2 and 4. There was, however, some ground scarring at those sites and scattered construction materials, indicating construction of a bunker was planned. Only one bunker was identified at the Guanajay IRBM launch area, which consisted of two IRBM launch sites. A San Cristóbal-type bunker was also identified under construction at the Remedios IRBM launch site.

Construction at each bunker site began with leveling an area and digging a rectangular ditch for footings. After the footings were poured, the floor of the bunker was leveled and a layer of gravel applied. Precast concrete arches brought from the Soviet Union were then erected. Each arch, spanning 18.5 feet of ground space, was 18.5 feet high and 1 meter wide. Cranes and dollies were employed to hold the arch semisections in position while they were placed on the footings and joined at the center. This operation was repeated, with consecutive arches emplaced to form the roof. A concrete floor was poured after the roof sections had been erected. The end walls were constructed of masonry blocks two feet thick to serve as retaining walls for the earth mounding. A buttress reinforced each end wall. The joints between the arches were caulked and waterproofed. Drainage ditches were dug parallel to the bunkers, and drainpipes were laid in the ditches and covered with earth. A layer of gravel was placed on the roof before bulldozers and dump trucks were employed to cover the bunker with about a yard of earth. Entrance doors, 12 feet wide and 13 feet high, were installed. A lightning arrestor was emplaced near each corner of the bunker. A hardstand was poured adjacent to the entrance. A crane was probably installed inside the bunker for handling the warheads.

A number of vans usually seen in and around the missile sites were postulated as equipped to fuel, check out, erect, and maintain the missiles in the field. Identical vans, subsequently labeled U/I (unidentified) vans, were observed near the bunkers. While it was noted that construction of the bunkers required special scaffolding and equipment, there never appeared to be activity around these vans. There were usually four to eight of these vans at each bunker. The van chassis was a KRAZ/YAAZ-219; the van body had a flat roof, with slightly beveled edges. Spare tires were mounted on each side of the cab, between the cab and the van body. A protrusion on the van body above the cab of the truck was thought to be either an air conditioner or a ventilator. There were double rear doors, vertically hinged, as well as a small access door at the right front of the van body. Two parallel rail-like extensions, a cranelike mechanism allowing for the transfer of objects from the van to a dolly or truck, sometimes projected from the rear of the van. The entire van body apparently could be removed from the truck chassis for shipment or storage. These vans were always seen in the open, parked separate from other vehicles and equipment. No special fencing, security devices, or guard forces were observed about the vans. No activity was ever seen that might have made them suspect.

Three distinct elements of missile technical support were required to deploy missiles in the field: the missile airframes, the propellents, and the warheads. Warheads and airframes for Soviet missiles were handled by separate support elements, probably a combination of organizations then under the aegis of former marshall Nedelin's Chief Artillery Directorate. Propellents, along with other fuels, were handled by the Armed Forces Rear Services' Fuel Supply Directorate. The warheads were thought to be under the overall control of the KGB. The three supply lines converged at a Strategic Rocket Forces rocket-technical base (*raketno-tekhnicheskaya baza*), which was deployed to support combat missile operations.

The U.S. intelligence community was in agreement that the KGB was responsible for guarding the nuclear warhead storage depots in the Soviet Union, involving elaborate security measures to prevent unauthorized or accidental use of nuclear weapons. One of the features of nuclear installations in the Soviet Union seen on overhead photography was a series of heavily guarded internal security fences. It was believed that KGB officers would exercise even more caution and physical security when such weapons were deployed outside the Soviet Union. It was also postulated that extensive security would be employed in Cuba, since there would be fear that the United States could mount a special-operations mission to capture the warheads or that they would have to be in a secure area in the event of U.S. invasion. It was also believed that the Soviets did not have the equivalent sophisticated Permissive Action Links (PAL) system, electronic or mechanical locks that prevent unauthorized use of the weapons, and that there would be a Soviet command organization near the weapons. It was therefore believed that there would be a communication center near any nuclear weapons storage area.

Very little information was available on Soviet practices in the transport and storage of strategic nuclear weapons. Even less was known on tactical or field deployment of nuclear weapons. While Oleg Penkovsky had provided information and documents on field deployment of Soviet weapons, he had not provided any information on the deployment of nuclear warheads. It was generally agreed that nuclear warheads for the SS-4 missiles would be guarded and handled by a separate unit not subordinate to the missile regiment. The warheads would be mated to the missiles only when a combat-readiness alert was given. Since it was assumed that the warheads were under control of the KGB, it also was assumed that the warheads would be stored in separately controlled and secured areas near the missile sites. There was no doubt, however, that if the Soviet missile units in Cuba moved into an operational posture, the warhead and support equipment elements would be observed at the launch pads on aerial photography.

Photography acquired by the U-2 missions over Cuba subsequent to October 17 was searched intensively at the Center for newly secured facilities or old facilities that could have been used or converted for the storage of nuclear weapons. Munitions storage areas were scrutinized, particularly, for any newly constructed or modified bunkers or any areas that displayed more than the usual security measures or for any area that had newly installed lightning arrestors. None was found. It was postulated that if existing storage bunkers at airfields or ammunition areas were being used to store nuclear warheads, a Soviet presence would be evident in the form of additional security, structures, tents, or equipment.

Punta Gerardo, a small molasses and sugar port in the bay of Bahía Honda, forty-seven nautical miles west-southwest of Havana, caught the eye of a photo interpreter. He noted that the port area had been double-fenced, in typical Soviet fashion, with guard tents along the outer perimeter of the fences. A number of Soviet pitched tents were also inside the enclosure. An excavation some three hundred feet in diameter, a number of warehouses, and a cylindrical storage tank also were under construction within the enclosure. Because of its remote location, the security measures, and the construction activities observed, this port became the principal candidate for search and identification of a nuclear weapons storage facility in Cuba. On subsequent aerial photographic missions, however, the positive identification of oxidizer trailers and oxidizer storage tanks, along with pipeline connections to the port, resulted in the identification of the facility as a missile-fuel transfer and storage area.

The possibility that there was a temporary nuclear storage facility, i.e.—holding the warheads aboard a Soviet freighter in a Cuban port—was also considered. Again, it was surmised that such a ship would undoubtedly be closely guarded and berthed in an isolated port or harbor. A review of all Cuban ports failed to reveal any such ship.

Concern was expressed that the nuclear warheads might be delivered aboard Russian missile-firing submarines. It was reasoned that the missile-firing tubes of existing Soviet submarines could be modified to carry the warheads. At the time, the Soviets had seven types of submarines capable of firing either ballistic or cruise missiles.* None of these submarines, however, had been detected patrolling in the Atlantic during the crisis. Even assuming that they had sailed recently from bases near Murmansk, it would have taken twenty to thirty days to reach Cuba. Based on an estimate that at least thirty to forty nuclear warheads would be required to arm the missiles in Cuba, it was doubtful if the Russians would attempt to transport the warheads with a flotilla of such submarines. It also would have been extremely difficult for the Russians to get such a flotilla to Cuba without being detected.

There still remained some concern that the four F (Foxtrot)-class submarines known to be in the Atlantic could deliver the warheads. Detailed analysis of the U.S. Navy photographs of these submarines surfaced charging their batteries revealed that they had the standard 1-meter hatches, which made it impossible for them to load the 5-foot-4-inch missile warheads.

(At a conference of Soviet and American leaders held in Moscow in January 1989, Soviet General Dmitri Volkogonov said that during the crisis, twenty nuclear warheads arrived in Cuba and twenty more were aboard the Soviet merchant ship *Poltava*, which turned back when the blockade was announced. At the same conference, Sergei N. Khrushchev, son of Nikita Khrushchev, said that the twenty nuclear warheads in Cuba were never mated to the missiles but easily could have been.)

When the low-altitude aerial reconnaissance missions were initiated on October 23, it was believed that they would acquire detailed information on the missile sites and some idea of where the warheads were stored. The president constantly questioned Lundahl and McCone as to whether the warheads had been located; their location became an obsession with McNamara. All agreed, however, that it had to be assumed that the warheads would be present when the missile sites achieved operational status.[2]

---

* The nuclear-powered H-1 (Hotel)-class submarine carried three ballistic missiles. The G-1 (Golf)-class was diesel-powered and carried three ballistic missiles. The Modified Z (Zulu)-class was diesel-powered and carried two ballistic missiles. The E-1 (Echo)-class was a nuclear-powered submarine with six cruise missiles. The W (Whiskey)-class Long Bin was a diesel-powered submarine with four cruise missiles. The W (Whiskey)-class Twin Cylinder carried two cruise missiles and the W (Whiskey)-class Single Cylinder carried a single cruise missile.

McNamara had been asked about the presence of nuclear warheads when the press was first briefed on October 22. He answered, "I believe the question was, are there nuclear warheads in Cuba. We don't know. Nuclear warheads are of such a size that it is extremely unlikely we would ever be able to observe them by the intelligence means open to us. I think it is almost inconceivable, however, that there would be missiles, as I have indicated, without the accompanying warheads."[3]

Those who felt most strongly that nuclear warheads had been delivered to Cuba were convinced that they were transported by the large Soviet Tu-114 Cleat cargo aircraft in flights via Dakar, Senegal, and Conakry, Guinea, on the west coast of Africa. It was estimated that the Cleat could carry at least fifteen nuclear warheads. The Cleat had first flown nonstop from Moscow to New York City on June 28, 1959. On September 26, 1959, a Cleat carried Khrushchev on his first visit to the United States, landing at Andrews Air Force Base, outside Washington, D.C. Hundreds of photographs of the aircraft had been taken, and measurements derived from these photos had clearly shown that the door of the Tu-114 was much too small to accommodate the SS-4 warhead. Some intelligence analysts postulated that the warheads might be shipped disassembled in the Tu-114 and later assembled in Cuba. This was ruled highly unlikely, but a detailed search of all known Russian facilities in Cuba was instituted for any special facilities or buildings or areas that exhibited more than unusual security for such a mission. None was found.

On October 24, William Knox, president of Westinghouse Electric International, was in Moscow on business when he had been summoned to a meeting with Khrushchev. The premier admitted that the missiles in Cuba were equipped with both conventional and nuclear warheads. Since the Russians had obviously carefully prepared for the Cuban venture, there could also have been a *maskirovka* scheme with regard to the nuclear warheads.

The intelligence priorities, however, were still the individual launch sites, and low-altitude reconnaissance aircraft were directed to fly directly over the launch pads. The prime concern of the photo interpreters was to maintain careful counts and the whereabouts of the missiles, the missile launchers, and the missile-ready tents. The nuclear warhead storage bunkers, when they were seen, were usually imaged by the oblique cameras, and since they were all still under construction, no particular attention was paid to the vans that were always parked nearby. There was still no activity or special security or fencing near them.

The movements of the Soviet merchant ship *Aleksandrovsk* during the crisis are worthy of mention.* It was known that the *Aleksandrovsk* had been active in the Russian arms trade to third-world nations emanating from such Baltic ports as Leningrad and Tallinn. Later, the *Aleksandrovsk* was engaged in regular sailings from Murmansk.

There was nothing unusual about the ship or its previous voyages. In October 1962, the *Aleksandrovsk*, sailing from Murmansk, arrived in the port of La Isabela, Cuba, and remained there until October 28. It had slipped through U.S. air surveillance and its cargo therefore had not been photographed. After Khrushchev agreed to remove the missiles, the *Aleksandrovsk*, on October 29, mysteriously weighed anchor at La Isabela and hurried to the port of Mariel.

The first objects to arrive at the port of Mariel from the dismantled launch sites were not the missiles but rather the "unidentified" vans. The vans had been separated from their truck chassis, and a number were loaded aboard the *Aleksandrovsk* the same evening they arrived. The ship departed Mariel immediately. This was during the period of the stand-down on U.S. reconnaissance missions while U Thant was visiting Havana, and no photos were obtained of the *Aleksandrovsk* while it was in the port of Mariel. On November 10, the *Aleksandrovsk* was photographed in the North Atlantic with ten of the vans on deck. The hatches of the *Aleksandrovsk* were partially open, suggesting that a large number of personnel were on board. The rapid movement and transshipment of the vans in the port revealed their real purpose: They were nuclear warhead storage vans.

Further postmortem reviews of all previous photography over Cuba revealed that, indeed, the nuclear warheads were stored in the "unidentified" vans. The secret of the Russian handling of nuclear warheads for the missiles in Cuba was uncovered at the Mariel naval air station. The short runway had fallen into disuse and disrepair

---

* It was one of ten ships of the Dolinsk class and had been built at the Abo yard in Nystad, Finland, between August 1957–61. This class of ship was typical of Scandinavian state of the art and represented the type known as the split superstructure, popular with world shippers following World War II.

during the Castro regime and the facility had been used primarily for temporary storage of Soviet arms shipments, particularly equipment for the KOMAR guided-missile patrol boats stationed nearby. On aerial photography of August 29, 1962, however, when SAMs were first discovered in Cuba, no equipment or weapons were on the runway at Mariel.

Photo coverage of October 14 revealed that a nuclear warhead processing facility had been sited at the western end of the runway. A barricade had been placed across the runway, and within a fenced area, there were four steel-frame buildings measuring 28 by 26 feet, two general-purpose tents, and four squad tents measuring 32 feet by 20 feet. The steel-framed structures were probably the warhead check-out buildings, as indicated by several lightning arrestors installed nearby. It was postulated that the warheads arrived at the port of Mariel and were carried to the runway facility in coffin-shaped nose-cone containers. The Soviets attempted to conceal the nose-cone containers from low-altitude photo reconnaissance missions with netting, and although it was difficult to see the end points of the containers under the netting, they were measured with sophisticated mensuration equipment to be approximately 14+ feet long and 5+ feet wide. Comparative analysis of Moscow parade photography of Soviet SS-4 missiles showed that its nose cone was approximately 13.2 feet long and had a base diameter, at its widest, of 5.3 feet.

Also present at Mariel were a number of uniquely configured dollies for handling the nuclear warhead, each measuring about six feet by four feet. It was postulated that the warheads were removed from their coffin-shaped containers, placed on the dolly, and trundled into the steel-framed building for check out. On low-altitude photography of October 25, the Mariel nuclear warhead handling facility was a beehive of activity. There were at least twenty-three net-covered coffin-shaped warhead containers aligned in two separate rows, so that at least twenty-three warheads were present in Cuba. Twelve warhead vans were parked nearby. One of the coffin-shaped warhead containers was open. After the warheads were checked out at Mariel, they were loaded onto the warhead vans and dispatched to the various MRBM sites. On one of the aerial photographs of the Mariel facility, a warhead van was observed with its rear doors open and the rail extending from the roof of the van for loading the warhead. The vans, arriving at the missile sites, would probably transfer the warhead to the dolly for mating with the missile. At the San Cristóbal MRBM launch site no. 3, on October 23, there were six warhead vans. One of the vans had its rails extended and appeared to be transferring a warhead to a truck that had parallel rails in its bed.

None of the nose-cone coffin-shaped containers remained at Mariel facility after the *Aleksandrovsk* left. The Soviets had expedited the vans from the missile sites back to the Mariel facility, where the nose cones were transferred from the vans, repacked in the coffin-shaped containers, and prepared for shipment back to the USSR. It was now clear that the *Aleksandrovsk* had been diverted quickly to Mariel to receive the warheads. The Soviets obviously didn't have sufficient time to repack all the warheads in their coffin-shaped containers before U.S. reconnaissance would resume, and in some cases, the van body with a probable nuclear warhead was removed from the truck chassis and loaded as deck cargo. A number of vans, probably empty, were seen on the loading dock after the *Aleksandrovsk* had left.

During a filmed special Cuban wrap-up briefing by Secretary of Defense McNamara and John Hughes on February 6, 1963, a reporter asked: "Were any atomic weapons ever identified or distributed in Cuba, and if they were, what happened to them?" McNamara answered, "The movement of nuclear weapons into Cuba, I believe, occurred. I believe we observed it in certain vehicles and we observed the movement of those vehicles out of Cuba, and we traced the shipment of those vehicles on ships back into the home waters of the Soviet Union."

The postcrisis review of past photography made it obvious that the Soviets had fueled and mated the warheads and had practiced moving the missiles to the erectors. On the October 23 photography of the Sagua la Grande MRBM launch site no. 1, the missile fueling, check-out, generator, and water vans are positioned and connected to a missile inside the missile-ready tents. It has to be presumed that the warhead was also mated to the missile.

We know from photographic observation that the Soviets practiced moving fueled and checked out missiles from the missile-ready tents to the erectors on the launch pads during the night. The month of October was very rainy in Cuba, and tracks that could only have been made by missile transporters could be seen in the mud, on a number of instances, leading from missile-ready buildings to erector launchers.

Subsequent to the crisis, the same type vans were seen not only at nuclear weapons storage areas within the Soviet Union but also at Soviet nuclear weapons storage areas in East European countries. The vans were also seen in field-deployment exercises of MRBMs and IRBMs in the Soviet Union and in Soviet field exercises with tactical missiles in East German training areas.

Statements by responsible U.S. officials during that period, and articles written subsequent to the crisis, maintaining that nuclear weapons were never seen in Cuba simply weren't true. The fact was they weren't discovered until the postcrisis review of aerial reconnaissance photography taken during the crisis period. Khrushchev and other Soviets have testified that Soviet warheads were in Cuba, but the Soviets have never revealed where the weapons were stored and how they were moved to the missile sites. Maybe now they will.

(It was not known to the U.S. military planners that when the 101st Airborne Division would be dropped on the Mariel airfield, they would land atop the main Soviet nuclear weapons base in Cuba. Although many of the nuclear warheads were in vans at the missile bases, some undoubtedly would have remained at the Mariel base. The landing of the 101st could have resulted in a myriad of complexities—from the capture of the warheads to an unintentional explosion leading to a nuclear disaster.)

Postlude

"The Center served as the focal point for the
receipt and immediate analysis of intelligence
photography and was instrumental in identifying the nature and magnitude of the threat
to world peace."

—NPIC COMMENDATION

RELATIONS BETWEEN Moscow and Washington entered a period
of relative calm as the strain of the crisis eased. Premier Khrushchev, along with other Soviet officials, expressed a desire for
improved relations.

Lundahl and McCone continued to brief President Kennedy on
Cuban developments. The president, now fully aware of the capabilities of aerial photography, engaged in a long discussion with Mr.
Lundahl on one occasion—inquiring about the capabilities of aerial
reconnaissance to monitor a disarmament agreement with the Soviets. In commenting on the problems of monitoring adherence to
an arms agreement, Kennedy expressed the opinion that the camera
would probably turn out to be our best inspector. The president said
he was serious about the idea of conducting discussions with the
Soviets on disarmament. Lundahl replied that the quality of the
U-2 photography would allow such monitoring but doubted that the
Soviets would allow a U-2 to fly over Russia again. Lundahl explained the tremendous advances being made in satellite photography and advised that in the future, satellite reconnaissance would
be applicable to monitoring disarmament agreements. The president
asked a number of other questions pertaining to the qualifications

and training of the photo-interpretation personnel necessary to adequately monitor such agreements.

The president frequently expressed his admiration for the accomplishments achieved during the crisis using aerial photography. Cline asked both the president and Bundy, "if they would tell me how much that single evaluated piece of photographic evidence [the missile sites] was worth, and they each said it fully justified all that CIA had cost the country in all its preceding years."[1]

General Taylor, before the troops assembled in the southeastern United States were disbanded, wanted the president to see firsthand the military machine and personnel involved with the projected invasion of Cuba. He considered it would also be an excellent way of educating the president on military matters. General Taylor realized he would be showing the president only a small portion of the force that had been alerted and also felt this would be a good time for the president to honor the Army, Navy, Air Force, and Marine units that had been most directly involved in the crisis. On November 26, 1962, the president, accompanied by the Joint Chiefs of Staff and the chairman of the House Armed Services Committee, arrived at Fort Stewart, Georgia, and reviewed one of the three brigades of the First Armored Division. The president, in his open limousine, passed in review of all of the men and equipment. The president alighted from his car five times to inspect or speak directly to men of the First Armored. The inspection completed, the president addressed the division, praising them and expressing the nation's appreciation for "your past service, and most especially your present actions during the difficult period of the last four or five weeks." He then recited a poem supposedly found on a British sentry box at Gibraltar:

> God and the soldier; all men adore,
> In time of danger and not before
> When the danger is passed
> And all things righted,
> God is forgotten and the old
> soldier slighted.

The president added, "The United States forgets neither God nor the soldier upon which we now depend."

The president flew on to Homestead Air Force Base. Escorted by General Walter C. Sweeney, Jr., commander of the Tactical Air Command, the president presented the Presidential Unit Citation to the 4080th Strategic Wing and the 363rd Tactical Reconnaissance Wing, in recognition of the contribution in acquiring the photography on which so many vital decisions had been based. The president praised the skill of the low-level pilots of the 363rd and the speed and precision with which their film had been developed. President Kennedy strolled over to the U-2 flyers. Colonel John A. Des Portes, commander of the 4080th, stood at attention while the president affixed a streamer and presented the Presidential Unit Citation. The president addressed the group: "I may say, gentlemen, that you take excellent pictures and I have seen a good many of them, beginning with the photographs which were taken on the weekend in the middle of October which first gave the conclusive proof of the buildup of offensive weapons in Cuba." Later, he remarked: "The 4080th contributed as much to the security of the United States as any unit in our history and any group of men in our history." After the presentation, the president made small talk with several of the U-2 pilots, saying that someday he would like to fly in a U-2 and see what the world is like from 70,000 feet. One of the pilots offered to take the president up in the two-seater trainer version of the U-2. At Homestead, the president also reviewed paratroopers from the 101st and 82nd airborne divisions. He also witnessed a flyby of more than seventy F-100's, F-102's, F-104's, F-105's, F-84's, and RF-101's.

At Boca Chica Naval Air Station, the president presented the Presidential Unit Citation to the U.S. Navy Light Photographic Squadron No. 62 and the U.S. Marine Corps Light Photographic Squadron VMC-12. The citation for the Light Photographic Squadron read, "For extraordinary achievement in the planning and execution of aerial reconnaissance during 1962 on missions of support of operations of the utmost importance to the security of the U.S. The successful completion of these flights in the face of adverse circumstances was in keeping with the highest traditions of the United States Naval Service."

The president concluded this day of honor on a pier at the U.S. naval base in Key West, Florida, with the men and ships that had effectively patrolled the seas while he was charting the nation's course of action.

Arriving back in Washington, the president sent the following message to Admiral Robert L. Dennison, commander in chief of U.S. Forces, Atlantic: "Please accept my thanks and congratulations for the wonderful day afforded me by my visit to your command. It would be an inspiration to every citizen to see the high state of readiness of the soldiers, sailors, airmen and marines whom I visited. A sincere well done to all ranks."

The president made sure that all those involved in the crisis would be recognized and sent a number of personal letters during January 1963. On January 7, he sent the following letter to Adlai Stevenson: "Dear Adlai: As the negotiations to wind up the Cuban Missile Crisis come to an end, I want to send my thanks and congratulations to you personally, and through you, to all those who have worked so hard in support of you and Mr. McCloy. This negotiation has been conducted with great skill and it has been marked, all the way through, by prompt reporting, skilled drafting, and responsible execution of instructions. I know that this has meant hard work, late hours, and high professional performance under pressure for many members of your mission. You know better than I which particular officers deserve particular commendation, but I do want all of the United States Mission to the United Nations to have my hearty thanks and warm appreciation."[2]

The continued exemplary performance of the National Photographic Interpretation Center—first in finding the missiles and the Il-28 bombers and then monitoring their withdrawal—impressed the president greatly, and he decided to present a presidential commendation to the center. It read:

> The President of the United States takes pleasure in commending the NATIONAL PHOTOGRAPHIC INTERPRETATION CENTER for outstanding achievement and service to the security of the United States and the Free World during a time of grave international crisis.

CITATION:

The National Photographic Interpretation Center distinguished itself by exceptionally meritorious service during the period from 1 May 1962 through 31 December 1962. During the period of international crisis, the Center served as the focal point for the receipt and immediate analysis of intelligence photography and was instrumental in identifying the nature and magnitude of the threat to world peace. Although working under great stress, personnel of the Center were able to carefully analyze and process a massive volume of critical intelligence material thereby enabling the United States to respond immediately and effectively to the developing threat. The outstanding achievement of the members of the National Photographic Interpretation Center is in keeping with the finest traditions of service to the United States.

THE WHITE HOUSE
9 January 1963

On January 9, the president also sent the following letter to Mr. McCone, chairman of the United States Intelligence Board: "I wish to express to you, the members of the United States Intelligence Board, and to the individual members of the intelligence agencies my deep and sincere appreciation for your outstanding service to our nation—and the Free World—during the recent international crisis.

"In the course of the past few months I have had occasion to again observe the extraordinary accomplishments of our intelligence community, and I have been singularly impressed with the overall professional excellence, selfless devotion to duty, resourcefulness and initiative manifested in the work of this group. The fact that we had timely and accurate information, skillfully analyzed and clearly presented, to guide us in our judgments during the crisis is, I believe, the greatest tribute to the effectiveness of these individuals and agencies. The magnitude of their contribution can be measured, in part, by the fact that the peace was sustained during a most critical time.

"It is, of course, a great source of strength to me to know that we have such dedicated and skilled men and women in the service of our Nation in these times of peril. Although I cannot personally commend each member of the intelligence community for their individual effort, I would like for you to convey to them, through the members of the United States Intelligence Board, my personal word of commendation, my deep admiration for their achievements, and the appreciation of a grateful Nation."[3]

On January 26, 1963, the president sent the following letter to Commander William B. Ecker of Light Photographic Squadron no. 62:

"My Naval Aide has delivered to me the excellent photographs taken by your squadron on the first low-level reconnaissance flight over Cuba last October. I appreciate your thoughtfulness in presenting it to me, and ask that you convey my gratitude to your officers and men. You will be interested to know that it is now hanging in my outer office.

"I would also like to take this opportunity to reaffirm my thanks to your hard work during those weeks. As I said at our meeting in Boca Chica, the reconnaissance flights which enabled us to determine with precision the offensive build-up in Cuba contributed directly to the security of the United States in the most important and significant way."

After a lengthy Senate investigation of the crisis, the report concluded that "the CIA and military intelligence, by use of their highly developed photographic capability, were able to give a unique performance in intelligence operations. They ultimately placed in the hands of the president and his advisers and U.S. diplomatic representatives incontrovertible proof of the presence of Soviet strategic missiles in Cuba in direct contravention of Soviet government assurances. This visual proof unquestionably played a major part in the united actions of the Organization of American States and world acceptance of the correctness of our position."

The military recognized those that performed their duties in an exemplary manner. The following U-2 pilots were awarded the Distinguished Flying Cross by General Thomas S. Power, commander of the Strategic Air Command: Majors Emerling, Brown, Heyser, Qualls, McIlmoyle, and Primrose, along with Captains Herman, Bull, and Kern.

The president, on January 5, sent the following letter to Lieutenant Colonel William J. Gregory, USAF WRSP-4, at Edwards Air Force Base, California:

It has been my pleasure to visit a number of military units in the Southeast which took part in a very direct way in support of our Government's position in the Cuban crisis in October of this year. I thus had the welcome opportunity to personally congratulate their officers and men on the very real contribution they had made at a critical time in this Nation's history, and to express to them their Government's gratitude for a job well done.

Circumstances did not permit me to acknowledge openly your Detachment's significant and extended contribution to what was accomplished in the days and months prior to the climax of the Cuban situation. In spite of this, I want you, your fellow officers and men, your skilled civilian pilots, staff employees and supporting technical representatives, to know of my real and abiding appreciation for a fine job you have done so quietly for so long, not only in Cuba but in other areas of the world where vital intelligence must continue to be obtained in order to guarantee the cause of freedom. The dangers are no less real, the hardships no less difficult and your achievement no less important to your country than those experienced by the men whom we can honor publicly.

Please accept assurances of my gratitude for your efforts, and extend to your entire command my sincerest thanks for their sustained superior performance.

With esteem and personal regards, John F. Kennedy.[4]

Later, the secretary of the Navy commended Marine Composite Reconnaissance Squadron 2 for its service during the missile crisis. The citation read: "For exceptionally meritorious service during the period 1 September 1960 to 1 December 1962 in connection with the planning and executing of aerial reconnaissance missions in support of operations of the utmost importance to the security of the United States. The consistent and outstanding high record of accomplishment attained by Marine Composite Reconnaissance Squadron Two attests to the professional competence, diligence, and resourcefulness of its officers and men. Their inspiring and zealous devotion to duty in the face of adverse circumstances reflects great credit upon themselves and the United States Naval Service. All personnel attached to and serving with Marine Composite Reconnaissance

Squadron Two during the above period, or any part thereof, are hereby authorized to wear the Navy Unit Commendation Ribbon. Signed Paul H. Nitze, Secretary of the Navy."[5]

The Russian press and radio commentators continued to portray Khrushchev's performance during the crisis not as a failure but as a victory for a sane approach to solving an international crisis and a successful peace initiative. Defense Minister Malinovsky would later relate that the "Soviet Union demonstrated maximum self-restraint and discretion" and that "the Soviet government and its head, Comrade N. S. Khrushchev, by their sage proposals showed the way to a reasonable compromise."[6] Khrushchev displayed unusual sensitivity to the Western view that he had backed down and later, at a meeting with Ambassador Foy Kohler, he defended the necessity of flexibility in foreign policy. He said it was futile to indicate who had won or lost. He smacked Kohler on the back and said, "We are both alive, aren't we?" Still later, speaking to newsmen, Khrushchev said, "A week ago we were on the edge of a precipice of nuclear war and we were both ready for it."

At a meeting of the Moscow Soviet on November 6, 1962, A. N. Kosygin continued to blame the U.S. for the crisis: "The Soviet Union gave Cuba the necessary aid in strengthening its defense. We were forced to do so, for the United States was openly promoting some kind of 'special rights' to interference in Cuban affairs. . . . Who yielded to whom in those circumstances? We believe that this was a concession on the part of both sides, a concession to reason and peace. Who is to be blamed for this conflict? Militarism and the aggressive imperialism of the United States. It created this conflict which could have cost mankind huge casualties."[7]

After the crisis, Soviet Foreign Ministry personnel confirmed Soviet frustration with their inability to develop a strategy to settle the crisis in a manner that would save face in the eyes of the Chinese and the Communist world without creating a nuclear confrontation with the United States. The Chinese referred to the Soviet agreement to remove the missiles as a Soviet Munich. The Cuban failure became Khrushchev's failure. It provided the Chinese with additional arguments that Khrushchev's deployment was "adventurist" and his withdrawal of them was "appeasement." Khrushchev criticized the Chinese for their continued acceptance of "colonial outhouses" in Hong Kong and Macao. The Chinese responded that in the 1860s, over 1 million square miles of Chinese territory in Soviet Siberia had been annexed, which was also a colonial enclave tolerated by the Chinese.

The announcement of the missile withdrawal from Cuba was very popular among the nonaligned nations and momentarily strengthened Khrushchev's hand internationally. Third world nations, while relieved that there had been no nuclear confrontation between the superpowers, later criticized the Soviets for having yielded so quickly to American pressure and began to regard with suspicion any future promises or military commitments extended by the Kremlin. At the same time, the credit Moscow won abroad for showing good sense and military restraint was beneficial to its European relations. Moscow sensed the international mood and began to play its levelheaded role in both domestic and foreign policies. The Cuban misadventure, coming on top of the embarrassing Powers U-2 incident, was one of the most serious liabilities of Khrushchev and his domestic political allies.

The Soviet withdrawal from Cuba also had an adverse impact on the Soviet military. It revealed fundamental flaws in Soviet strategic planning, military policy assessment, and in command and control authority and procedures. It was also a blow to Soviet military pride and prestige. The Soviet leadership had extended themselves much further, in terms of military risks taken, than they could hope to gain in international power and prestige. There was evidence that the hard-liners in the Soviet military had opposed the withdrawal, or at least favored a much harder bargaining position on the removal of the missiles. They would be reminded by Marshall V. I. Chuikov, in a November 17, 1962, article in *Red Star*, that some military leaders were displeased about the political leadership blemishing the Soviet military record. But Chuikov strongly reminded that the military was subordinate to the Party and that they must abide by the decisions of the political leadership.

Khrushchev himself acknowledged that his Cuban venture had been criticized. On December 12, he stated: "Some say that the United States forced us to retreat. If this is their attitude, then these same people must also admit that the United States was forced to make concessions."[8] One military casualty was Marshall M. V. Zakharov, chief of the general staff, who was removed and replaced by Khrushchev's crony Marshall Biryuzov.

Western European reaction was perhaps best expressed by Chancellor Adenauer: "The case of Cuba, the adventure in Cuba, has, I believe, shown that the power of the Soviets also has limitations, and the Soviets have probably also learned from this course of adventure."

Khrushchev had become increasingly arbitrary and more of a recluse; he rarely listened to dissenting views or considered the advice of his colleagues. It was evident to CIA Russian intelligence analysts that wide cracks had begun to appear in the solid front that Moscow wanted to portray to the world. It was no longer a question of whether Khrushchev would fall but when. In October 1964, Khrushchev was abruptly removed and replaced by a triumvirate headed by L. I. Brezhnev, N. V. Podgorny, and A. N. Kosygin. Although some of Khrushchev's marshalls remained, a number resigned and retired. Those who had opposed Khrushchev's capricious decisions regarding the military soon began to speak out. Probably the most vindictive was Marshall Zakharov, who was reinstated as chief of the general staff. In a lengthy article in the Soviet press in 1965, he condemned Khrushchev's "hare-brained" schemes. He also made references to Khrushchev's "subjectivism and military dilettantism" and derided Khrushchev's claim of "strategic farsightedness." He insisted that Khrushchev had only a "rudimentary knowledge of military strategy."

The Soviet military, reacting to the Cuban crisis, would press to rectify the strategic disparity with the United States by expanding its ICBM force toward a goal of strategic superiority with the development of large megatonnage and throw weight intercontinental missiles. The Soviets also began development of a nuclear-powered submarine fleet. The Soviet surface navy would change from a coastal defense and inland sea role to a bluewater offensive mission. The Soviet Air Force would be augmented with new supersonic bombers carrying air-to-surface missiles; their strategic airlift capability would be expanded. The Soviets also began upgrading their defensive systems to protect against U.S. retaliatory strike capabilities, and continued development of an antiballistic-missile defense system.

As Cuba prepared to celebrate the fourth anniversary of the Castro revolution, on January 2, 1963, the American intelligence community was particularly interested in any Soviet military equipment that might be paraded and, therefore, remaining under Castro's control. In a long speech, Castro blasted both the United States and the Soviet Union. Vowing that Cuba would act independently regardless of U.S.-Soviet agreements on the missile removal, he said: "The Soviet government has reached certain accords with the American government. But this does not mean that we have renounced the right to have the weapons we deem convenient and to take steps in international policy we deem convenient as a sovereign country."[9] Castro hinted that Cuba was inclined toward China in the Moscow-Peiping ideological split.

It was time for Khrushchev to make amends to Castro, and he was invited to visit the Soviet Union as his personal guest. Castro arrived in the Soviet Union on April 27, 1963, for a month-long visit. Greeted in Murmansk by Mikoyan, he was flown to Moscow, where he was met by Khrushchev and other Communist dignitaries. Moscow provided an unusually warm welcome, and Soviet officialdom went out of its way to demonstrate a friendly attitude toward Cuba. Khrushchev took Castro to his dacha and treated him as a member of his family. At Khrushchev's personal direction, Castro was accorded the highest protocol honors. Castro's visit was regarded by the U.S. as a hand-holding session designed to reassure the volatile Castro that the Russians would not sacrifice his interests during further discussions with the United States. As the ultimate honor, Castro was awarded the Order of Lenin.

Prior to the crisis, the unpredictable Castro had devoted much time and attention to cultivating support for his revolution among the Latin American countries in the hope that his renunciation of the U.S. would receive broad backing. The effort had met with some success. But now, he had been isolated and his harsh ideological stands and complete dependence on the Soviet Union had nullified all his previous successes. To demonstrate that the revolutionary movement had continued viability, he engaged in a desperate attempt to carry the revolution to Latin America, which climaxed with his sending Che Guevara to Bolivia. He had hoped for some dramatic action, some means of capturing international attention, of promoting Latin American support for his insurgent capabilities. It ended with Che dead on a wooden table and the Latins laughing at the stupidity of the Cuban revolutionaries.

The Russians, in the absence of any pressure to remove the troops, left behind a 2,800-man combat brigade, which would go undetected until the Carter administration. In addition, the Soviets would leave behind another 2,800 military advisers, along with about 2,100 technicians, at the Lourdes electronic intelligence collection facility, which was regarded as "the most sophisticated Soviet collection facility outside the Soviet Union itself."[10] This listening post enabled the Soviets to monitor sensitive U.S. maritime, military, and space communications, as well as telephone conversations in the United States.

On November 4, 1962, Senator Keating charged that Soviet missiles and launching equipment had been stored in caves and tunnels in Matanzas province. Senator Keating admitted that his source was not an official one. That same day, the Anti-Castro Student Revolutionary Directorate in Miami also reported that some of its operatives had reported missiles being hidden in Cuban caves. Reports persisted that missiles were being concealed in caves and that the number of Soviet troops remaining in Cuba was far in excess of that reported by the intelligence community. Speleological studies conducted prior to the Castro regime had established that there were literally hundreds of caves and underground caverns in Cuba, and it was known that a number were large enough to accommodate the storing of missiles. There was no photographic evidence, however, to sustain any of the "missile cave" claims.

President Kennedy was disturbed by the continuing reports of additional missiles in Cuba. A November 29, 1962, memorandum states: "The President showed great concern over refugee reports and the CBS report of 88 missiles. There is also a Mirror story which gives details and a map of remaining missiles based on refugee reports. The Secretary indicated that the press could not be controlled, and that the policy should be to follow up quickly and stamp out such stories. It might be possible to have an understanding with the press to check such stories in advance. The agreement was that Helms would work out some scheme with Manning and Salingerts.[11]

The president called Cline one evening, stating that he had just read an article in a Washington newspaper indicating that many missiles had been hidden in Cuban caves. Cline remembered: "Since he had got the press before I did, he read the whole crazy story to me over the phone and wanted to know what I could tell him. The president said he wanted me to check everything and help him shoot down the cave story. Naturally I said I would check it overnight and report to him in the White House the next morning. I found some of my Cuba task force members still on duty and asked them about the caves. Amazingly one of the analysts was an amateur speleologist and had a 5-by-7 card in a file box on every sizable cave in Cuba. It was a bonanza for me and someone brought the file up to me. Even better, there was photography of the entrances to the caves. Many of them were used to store ammunition and several had narrow-gauge rail lines into the entrances of the caves. The speleologist said that the rail lines into the only big caves curved through rock formations obstructing access to the caves. It was evident that none of these rails could handle a flatbed as long as an SS-4 without being derailed. The next morning I went to the White House, met with President Kennedy in the Cabinet Room, told him my story and plunked down the actual card file. The story of intelligence is that you have facts, it is taken for granted, and you do not get much credit. Kennedy thanked me rather casually and turned to other questions."

A *U.S. News and World Report* story of February 4, 1963, particularly disturbed the president: "Forty-six medium range missiles still on the island. Authoritative sources who just left Cuba reported this: My people counted 88 medium range Soviet missiles in Cuba, of which only 42 were taken out by Russian count. That leaves 46 missiles still on the island. There are 10,000 Russian troops and 12,000 non-Russian Communists in international brigades." Another report listed seven Soviet "subterranean installations" in which the missiles were stored.

The disturbing effect of these reports on the president prompted

NPIC to check out each report against photography. The Center's finding, forwarded to McCone, reemphasized repeatedly that an MRBM complex comprised a number of components* and that not only were no missiles seen on photography, but there was also no other missile-related equipment. Testifying before the Senate Preparedness Investigating Subcommittee, McCone would report: "Many rumors and reports of the continued presence of the offensive weapons in Cuba have been received. For instance, there have been a number of reports that offensive weapons have been concealed in caves. Some of these reports evidently derive from the known Cuban practice of using caves for storage of small-arms, ammunition and other items of military hardware. All statements alleging the presence of offensive weapons are meticulously checked. So far the findings have been negative. Absolute assurance on these matters, however, could come from continuing, penetrating on site inspection."[12]

McCone attempted to show that "Refugees themselves are not always the best observers. They come out in a distraught frame of mind, many of them agitated and disturbed. Over a period of two or three years, we have had countless reports from refugees of missiles here, there, and the other place. You have had them, as have I. We have gone back with photography and with other sources of intelligence to find if they were wrong. Another unfortunate part of refugee reporting is that many of them are lobbyists. They would like to agitate us into some kind of action. They would like to direct our policies with respect to Cuba. Therefore, they are inclined to overexaggerate the situation, and all too often their statements are taken by the press or by others as facts."[13]

Charges persisted in the press and media that the Soviets had not removed all their missiles from Cuba but had concealed them in caves and that Russian submarines had been seen in Cuban ports. President Kennedy decided that the American people should be briefed on the photographic evidence that the Russians had indeed removed the missiles and bombers. The president preferred that Lundahl handle the report to the nation, but McCone was reluctant to surface Lundahl and the National Photographic Interpretation Cen-

---

* the missile, the transporter, its launching platform, the fuel and oxidizer generators, guidance control elements, and all other required pieces of equipment

ter. Lundahl recommended that John Hughes, who had been outstanding in his service at the National Photographic Interpretation Center as an Army lieutenant and became special assistant to General Joseph Carroll, director of the Defense Intelligence Agency, conduct the public briefing. NPIC supported Hughes in preparing the briefing, and at 5 p.m., February 6, 1963, in the State Department Auditorium, Hughes and Secretary of Defense McNamara presented a comprehensive photographic review of the introduction of Soviet missiles, military personnel, aircraft, and equipment into Cuba—and the removal of the missiles and the bombers—on nationwide TV. The presentation did much to allay the fears of the American public, but some intelligence specialists questioned whether too much had been revealed about photo-interpretation methods and the quality and quantity of intelligence information that the U.S. was deriving from photographic sources.

James Jesus Angleton, CIA chief of counterintelligence, intrigued by conspiratorial aspects of the crisis, was convinced that the Russians were being tipped off on U.S. moves. Angleton was further convinced of high-level penetration of British intelligence by the KGB. He was especially suspicious of MI5 and the British equivalent of the U.S. National Security Agency, Government Communications Headquarters (GCHQ), based in Cheltenham, England. Specifically, Angleton suspected that the Soviets currently had a mole in the British intelligence system, operating in the same manner as the Kim Philby team. He also had been concerned with the Profumo affair, in which Christine Keeler, in addition to having an affair with Defense Minister Profumo, was involved with a Russian operative, Evgeny Ivanov. Angleton was regarded by most at the Agency as an eccentric, a paranoid, or as the "superspook." He was admittedly difficult to plumb. Everywhere, he was consumed by the pervading Soviet deceit and deception. Angleton asked for all documents prepared by NPIC during the crisis. Supposedly, Angleton had undertaken a study of the Cuban crisis and Soviet penetration of the British intelligence system. The results of neither study was ever published.

After years of mutual distrust and harsh propaganda diatribes on both sides, there remained in both the United States and the Soviet

Union a basic skepticism about the extent to which relations could be reestablished. Both sides, however, had an interest in seeing that former relationships were not totally destroyed. President Kennedy saw denouement of the Cuban crisis as an opportunity for bettering the relationships between the two countries. Many had predicted that there would be a heightening of East-West tensions, but a mood of détente prevailed that was recognized by both the Soviets and President Kennedy. In July 1963, the president announced that the United States and the Soviet Union had agreed on a treaty banning nuclear tests in the atmosphere. The president called it "an important first step," while Khrushchev announced that it was a beginning toward liquidating the Cold War. NPIC was assigned the task of verifying Soviet compliance with the agreement.

Probably the most important lesson learned in the Cuban missile crisis was to keep all lines of communication—political, military, and diplomatic—open at all times. Whether direct or indirect, maintaining communications was indispensable to resolving the crisis. It became dangerously apparent that there had to be a better method of communicating between governments than the antiquated Department of State and Foreign Ministry methods of encoding, transmitting, and translating diplomatic messages. A month after the crisis, in an interview with a CBS television correspondent, Secretary Rusk, responding to a question about the urgency of communications in crisis-management situations, said: "I think that there was a question of speed of communications through normal channels. The sheer physical problem of transmitting messages to people who use another language, requiring decoding and translation, with differences in office hours in their respective capitals, did remind us all over again that immediate communications is important; and I think these public communications turned out to be the fast communications, so that this was, I think, the importance of the broadcast message on October 28. It was a fast response to the president's message of the day before and perhaps could not have been handled through the elaborate channels of code and translation and normal diplomatic patterns."

But the most significant statement on the need for rapid communications was made at a presidential press conference on December 12, 1962. A reporter asked: "Mr. President, the administration proposed in Geneva today some sort of direct communications between the White House and the Kremlin, either telephone or Teletype. Could you tell us what was in your mind in proposing this and how it is related to the Cuban affair and the fact of the delay?"

The president replied: "There was a delay, as you know, in the communications back and forth, in the Cuban affair. In some degree I think on one or two occasions it was necessary to rely on open broadcasts of messages rather than sending them through the coding procedure, which took a number of hours. What was happening was that when we finally concluded our day and sent the messages to the Soviets, they were just waking up, and when they finished their day and prepared their messages for us, we were just waking up, so that it was taking time. The coding procedures were slow.

"In a nuclear age, speed is very desirable. So we are hoping that out of this present conversation we can get instantaneous communication, or at least relatively instantaneous communications."

(Former Soviet ambassador Dobrynin, in an address at Georgetown University in November 1989, lamented that the Soviets in the Washington embassy did not have a fast direct telephone or radio communications line to Moscow in 1962. He had entrusted urgent encoded messages to Western Union messengers, who may have stopped for lunch or to chat with friends, completely oblivious to the world-shaking messages they were carrying.)

Discussions between U.S. and Soviet representatives to establish a sure and quick communications link between Moscow and Washington began in Geneva in April 1963 and a formal agreement was signed on June 20, 1963. The "hot line," perhaps the most tangible result of the crisis, ironically was not placed in the Department of State, much to Secretary Rusk's chagrin, but rather in the National Military Command Center at the Pentagon.

The Cuban crisis had ended without a formal agreement between the U.S. and the Soviet Union. In the unpublished understanding reached between Khrushchev and President Kennedy, the Soviets had agreed to remove the offensive missiles and the Il-28 bombers —and not to reintroduce them into Cuba. Neither had the Russians and Cubans reached any formal agreement regarding on-site inspection to verify removal of the missiles, and President Kennedy had made the pledge not to invade Cuba conditional to on-site inspection. Secretary Rusk, in an interview after the crisis, stated: "President Kennedy has made it utterly clear that we would not accept a reintroduction into Cuba of weapons which could strike at its neighbors, including the United States."[14] While there were comments in the U.S. press and media that the Soviets and Cubans had signed an economic agreement to end the crisis, the Cubans were emphatic in denying "the speculations of American news agencies regarding the alleged signing of a new agreement on economic assistance between the Soviet Union and Cuba."[15] Later, the Cubans would add: "During the course of the present crisis, Cuba has not entered into any agreement with the government of the Soviet Union."[16]

The successful application of U-2 photographic intelligence during the crisis was to have a number of important consequences for the Central Intelligence Agency. Perhaps William Colby put it best: "One of the most important consequences of the missile crisis was on the morale of the Agency: it soared. The CIA had done just the sort of thing it was supposed to do in the defense of the nation, and done it well. And that splendid performance did much to repair the damage done to its reputation by the Bay of Pigs debacle. Beyond that, the photographs and the like demonstrated the value to intelligence of the most sophisticated advances in science and technology, and they spurred McCone to push for new work in this area, including spy-in-the-sky satellites and ultrasophisticated electronic equipment. Increasingly, as a result, the customers of intelligence began demanding 'hard' evidence of this sort on all information and in just such indisputable technical and measurable forms, instead of generalized academic conclusions, and Kennedy's pleasure at seeing the raw photographs themselves produced an appetite for the same sort of raw reports, direct from the source in field reporting as well."[17]

Epilogue

"Art Lundahl has done as much to protect the
security of this nation as any man I know."

—ALLEN DULLES

THE GENUINE mutual friendliness between Presidents Eisenhower
and Kennedy continued following the Cuban missile crisis, as
did Eisenhower's interest in the various U.S. reconnaissance
programs. President Kennedy solicited General Eisenhower's counsel
on international matters a number of times and saw to it that the
general was kept informed on current intelligence problems, as well
as updates on the new performance of photographic systems, through
periodic briefings conducted by McCone and Lundahl. Normally,
these briefings were accomplished at the former president's guest
home in Palm Springs, California. Each fall, General and Mrs. Eisenhower departed Gettysburg for Palm Springs to enjoy the weather
and golf outings in the California desert; McCone also had a home
there. McCone would telephone the general from Washington to say
that he had "another chapter of the story," and General Eisenhower
would respond, "Come out, the golfing and weather is fine."
McCone, Lundahl, and his courier, Frank Beck, would depart
Washington for California. General Eisenhower usually arrived at
McCone's home in golf togs, driving a golf cart. After an exchange
of pleasantries, the briefing would begin. The briefing package included annotated photography and notes detailing highlights of aer-

ial and spatial reconnaissance intelligence data acquired since the last time the general had been briefed. Eisenhower was always an attentive listener, contributing his own observations and comments on both the progress of the various photographic-collection systems and the intelligence content of the briefing materials. According to Lundahl: "He was always gracious. He would thank McCone and me for taking the time and interest to brief him."

General Eisenhower's intense personal and professional interest in the importance of reconnaissance to the national security continued throughout his life. After rallying from his fourth heart attack at Walter Reed Hospital, with time heavy on his hands, he requested that President Nixon furnish an update on the status of various U.S. reconnaissance programs. The president forwarded the request to Richard Helms, director of the CIA. Helms in turn tasked Lundahl to prepare a briefing for presentation to the general at an appropriate time.

Mr. Lundahl asked me to coordinate production of the briefing, making special note of the improvements and ongoing research and development in photographic-collection and -exploitation systems since the first U-2 mission in 1956. Almost every analyst in the Center participated in the research and selection of materials, which came to be known as the Eisenhower Package.

Helms, Lundahl, and Tom Logan, Lundahl's special assistant for briefings, delivered the package to Walter Reed Hospital on February 13, 1969. Lundahl recalls the visit: "Eisenhower looked better there than the last time I had seen him, at the White House. He was more loquacious; there was no stumbling of words. His ideas were crisp; his gaze was clear, and he was lying propped up in his bed. He shook hands with us and recalled all the times we had briefed him under many different conditions.

"Mr. Helms sat to the left of the bed; I stood on the right, and with Tom Logan standing at the foot of the bed holding up the briefing boards, I went through the 'how it was and how it is.'

"The general was just absolutely flabbergasted about the improvements achieved in the systems. He was apparently writing a book. He had a manuscript—long yellow sheets of paper—and was writing things down. Every once in a while he asked me to stop, saying he wanted to make some notes about something I had just said. He asked about ABMs [antiballistic missiles] and about our ability to detect them. He also wanted to know about the ABMs around Moscow. He talked about the precision of our photographic effort and its possible usefulness if arms control or disarmament were initiated. We got into many things like that. Everything he wanted to know, we had in spades, before and after. It was a very pleasant and very, very energetic exchange. He could not have been nicer. When we finished, he shook hands with us, saying that it had been very exhilarating and most enjoyable. I really felt as we left the hospital that here was a man who was going to recover. He had all the vitality signs showing, and I would have bet anyone ten to one that he was going to get out of there."

President Eisenhower died at Walter Reed Hospital six weeks later, on March 28, 1969.

President Kennedy and Bobby started to concentrate on the presidential campaign of 1964, but not before authorizing the release of heretofore classified national security information about administration successes during the crisis to favored columnists and authors. Bobby, commenting on the crisis, remarked at a symposium: "We let the spear carriers and the horse holders from the various agencies take up the load. In fact, we were happy to have it lifted from our shoulders."

One information release caused particular consternation in Washington. In a December 8, 1962, *Saturday Evening Post* article titled "In Times of Crisis," Adlai Stevenson was accused of "wanting a Munich" during the crisis. Although the president denied having anything to do with the article, it didn't go unnoticed in Washington that it was written by two close friends, Stewart Alsop and Charles Bartlett. In an article published in the December 14 issue of *Life* magazine, John Steele, the chief of the Time-Life Washington bureau, defended Stevenson, but the damage had been done. Although McGeorge Bundy tried to reassure him, Stevenson would write Bundy: "I hope this 'foolish business'—to use your apt words—is over. But I hear that minutes of these meetings are kept, and if there is any misrepresentation of my position, I hope soon to find the time to deposit at the appropriate place a clear exposition of my views during that memorable week." To my knowledge, that was never done. Stevenson resisted pressure from his admirers to resign because of the shabby treatment by the Kennedys. He died of a heart attack in London on July 14, 1965.

The president would be dead before the 1964 election and Bobby before that of 1968. Bobby was writing a book about the crisis. Shortly after Bobby's death, the Agency was sent a galley of the book, with a request for comments. I was asked to review it and I listed a number of errors or inaccuracies. From what I was to understand, others who read the galley did the same. When these were shown to the publisher, it was decided not to correct the errors but to allow the book to stand as written.

McCone found Lyndon Johnson colorless and crude in intelligence matters and, as president, clumsy and heavy-handed in international affairs. Instead of personally carefully considering prepared intelligence memorandums on intelligence matters, he preferred to be briefed by trusted advisers. Increasingly, the president sought intelligence information almost exclusively from Secretary McNamara and the Defense Department. McCone's advice simply was no longer actively sought by the president. His role diminished, his influence faded, and the ready access he had enjoyed during the Kennedy administration became very limited. Perhaps, too, since McCone was close to both the Kennedy brothers, he mourned the president's loss, and as an aide would remark, "It was never the same with the boss." McCone's restlessness became pronounced. Finally, he asked to be relieved and decided to return to his beloved California.

There can be little doubt that the Cuban missile crisis hastened Khrushchev's ouster. After his fall, his role in World War II would be minimized by Soviet historians. The Stalingrad group of marshalls and generals would be shoved aside or forced to retire and would only be seen on historic occasions. Foreign Minister Gromyko lasted through a succession of premiers, until Gorbachev. Although he had witnessed the great diplomatic events in the past half century firsthand and was knowledgeable of the events surrounding the sending of missiles to Cuba, Gromyko's memoirs were full of boilerplate Communist ideology and contained little of historical interest. Gromyko died on July 3, 1989, after refusing several opportunities to explain his role in the crisis at a meeting of American and Soviet crisis experts in Moscow in January 1989.

President Johnson replaced McCone with a fellow Texan, retired U.S. Navy vice-admiral William F. Raborn, Jr. The admiral had played an important role in development of the Polaris missile system but had no experience in intelligence, which soon became apparent to CIA veterans. To counterbalance this inexperience, Richard Helms, an extremely able CIA veteran, was selected to replace General Marshall Carter as deputy director of the Agency. Raborn's tenure as director was rated by senior Agency officials as one of the least effective; the congressional briefings, which he insisted on delivering himself, were characterized by Senator Symington as "one disaster after another." Helms succeeded Raborn as DCI in July 1966 and, until retiring to become U.S. ambassador to Iran in 1973, kept the Agency in the forefront of the development of technological intelligence resources.

Members of the Joint Chiefs of Staff, EXCOM, and others prominent in the crisis for the most part saw their careers decline afterward. General Maxwell Taylor, the melder of theory and practice, became a proponent of the flawed U.S. strategy in Vietnam. General LeMay, during the Vietnam War, recommended bombing the Vietnamese "back into the Stone Age." He emerged from retirement in 1968 as the vice-presidential running mate of George Wallace in his ill-fated bid for the presidency. Where once his speeches at SAC had been listened to with respect by military audiences, his political campaign speeches, especially his remarks on his feelings about the use of nuclear weapons, were ridiculed by the press and the media. Following his defeat in the 1968 election, LeMay adopted an antagonistic attitude toward the press and media that continued to his death. He became a partial recluse, refusing to grant interviews and rejecting invitations to attend ceremonies celebrating milestones in aviation. He would only meet with fellow SAC cronies who still praised and idolized him.

General Shoup left the Marine Corps and began writing poetry. In later years, a Marine critic would say that in searching Shoup's four-year tenure as commandant of the Marine Corps, he could find only two significant contributions—Shoup had designated the traditional swagger stick carried by officers "optional"; another order ended the practice of drummers playing the death march while court-martialed Marines were marched off post. Although President Kennedy had hailed his accomplishments in a news conference on May 9, 1963, Admiral Anderson was relieved of command as CNO and was appointed ambassador to Portugal on May 22, 1963. General Wheeler became Chairman of the Joint Chiefs and was embroiled in the Vietnam conflict. He endured the wrath of Congress for concealing the fact that U.S. bombing raids had been conducted in Cambodia.

Llewellyn Thompson, the brilliant chain-smoking diplomat, would die of cancer in February 1972, at the age of sixty-seven. Theodore Sorensen, who left the White House on February 29, 1964, to write a book on the Kennedy administration, was nominated by President Jimmy Carter in 1977 to head the CIA, but because of growing opposition in Congress, his nomination was withdrawn. Relations between President Johnson and Pierre Salinger soured and Salinger abruptly resigned as press secretary in the spring of 1964. After writing a book on Kennedy, Salinger became an ABC correspondent in Paris. Douglas Dillon left government to return to the New York financial world. McGeorge Bundy would remain in Washington for a time, but his influence lessened with President Johnson and he resigned in 1966 to become president of the Ford Foundation.

The Kennedys had frequently considered replacing Secretary Rusk and infusing new ideas into the "fudge factory." Yet Rusk remained not only throughout the Kennedy administration but the Johnson administration as well. Rusk held the position for the second longest period in history; he compared his tenure as being second only to Cordell Hull's, and a State Department official once remarked, "That's about the only comparison that could be made."

As the U.S. became more and more embroiled in Vietnam, Secretary McNamara, who had presidential ambitions himself, became more and more assertive, and feuding erupted between the CIA and the DIA on many intelligence estimates regarding Vietnam. The "tell it as it is" derived from photo intelligence that existed in the Kennedy administration was changed, with McNamara insisting that the Department of Defense, through the Defense Intelligence Agency, assume prime responsibility for intelligence reporting in support of military forces in the field. And therefore, McNamara argued, the DIA must have a larger role in the briefing of President Johnson. Admiral Raborn played a role in McNamara's effort.

In contrast to the Cuba missile situation, Lundahl was never permitted to brief Johnson directly on the situation in Vietnam. During this period, thousands of briefing boards produced by NPIC depicted both the favorable and unfavorable aspects of the conflict. Much to NPIC's chagrin, McNamara was using Center-produced briefing boards showing only favorable progress of U.S. forces, replacing the NPIC logo and control numbers with those of the DIA. McNamara and the Joint Chiefs began to control tightly the flow of information to the president. It was later established that unfavorable military-intelligence information was cast aside and seldom shown to the president. One DIA briefer stated that the president "got very depressed and hard to handle when shown bad news."

Aerial reconnaissance of the Ho Chi Min Trail is a case in point. Observation of the heavily bombed and cratered roads on high-altitude photography created the impression of a successful military operation, but on low-level photography, large numbers of Vietnamese soldiers could be seen pushing bicycles laden with supplies, weaving their way through the heavily cratered areas. NPIC briefing boards showing the Vietnamese resupplying their forces—not only by bicycle, but by river boats and pack animals, through a variety of trails from Cambodia—were never shown to the president, we were told. Although Secretary Rusk was aware of the unfavorable intelligence, Rusk was reluctant to challenge the aggressive McNamara, fearing a State-Defense split. McNamara and the Joint Chiefs of Staff were allowed to set U.S. Vietnam policy unchallenged by unfavorable intelligence.

Colonel David Parker, deputy director of NPIC during the Cuban missile crisis, became lieutenant governor, and later governor, of the Panama Canal Zone. He also served in Vietnam, retiring as a major general.

The untimely death of President Kennedy was emotionally wrenching for Mr. Lundahl. He continued as director of NPIC, participating in the ongoing development and application of increasingly sophisticated photo-intelligence technology. A severe arthritic condition forced him into early retirement in June 1973. Since his retirement, his interest has been in the application of multisensor technology and photo interpretation and photogrammetry to resolving the many economic and environmental problems besetting our planet. Over the span of his distinguished career, he received numerous important honors, including President Kennedy's silver calendar memento of the crisis; the National Security Medal, awarded by President Nixon in 1973; the National Civil Service League Award in 1963; and the CIA Distinguished Intelligence Medal, upon his retirement. The CIA citation read that Mr. Lundahl was "a superb technician in the science of photographic interpretation and photogrammetry with few, if any, peers. His skills during times of crisis and periods of comparative calm have brought him high praise from world leaders and senior government officials at home and abroad." Lundahl was also awarded the Defense Intelligence Agency's Director's Exceptional Civilian Service Award. On December 17, 1974, Her Majesty Queen Elizabeth II conferred on Mr. Lundahl the Most Excellent Order of the British Empire in the rank of Honorary Knight Commander (KBE), in recognition of his outstanding scientific and technical services to the Crown. The KBE is rarely awarded outside the United Kingdom. In 1985, Lundahl was awarded the Pioneer in Space Medal by the U.S. government for his role in the development of satellite reconnaissance.

Of all the awards and honors Lundahl achieved, one he seldom displays reflects most appropriately his contributions to this nation. It is an autographed photograph of Allen Dulles and himself, which reads: "Art Lundahl has done as much to protect the security of this nation as any man I know. Allen W. Dulles."

Notes

1. Eisenhower and Reconnaissance

1. Also quoted in Brigadier General George W. Goddard, *Overview, a Lifelong Adventure in Aerial Photography* (New York: Doubleday, 1969), p. 381.

2. Dino A. Brugioni, "Photo Interpretation and Photogrammetry in World War II," *Photogrammetric Engineering and Remote Sensing*, Vol. L, No. 9 (September 1986): 1313–1318.

3. Allen Dulles, *The Craft of Intelligence* (New York: New American Library, 1963), p. 139.

4. James R. Killian, *Sputnik, Scientists, and Eisenhower: A Memoir of the First Assistant to the President for Science and Technology* (Cambridge, Mass.: MIT Press, 1967), p. 68.

5. Dino A. Brugioni and Robert F. McCort, "Personality: Arthur C. Lundahl," *The Art of Aerial Photography, Photogrammetry and Remote Sensing*, Vol. LIV, No. 2 (February 1988): 270–272.

6. Ibid.

7. James R. Killian, op. cit, p. 82

8. Dino A. Brugioni and Robert F. McCort, op. cit., pp. 270–272.

9. Letter from Lawrence R. Houston to author, 25 January 1988.

10. Memorandum, dated April 23, 1975, from Charles A. Cravotta, Jr., to author, "Description of 'Life Support' Equipment Used with the Agency U-2 Aircraft During the Cuban Missile Crisis."

2. Eisenhower Uses the U-2 to Provide Vital Strategic and Tactical Information

1. Dwight D. Eisenhower, *Waging Peace* (New York: Doubleday, 1965), p. 545.

2. Embassy of the Union of Socialist Republics, Note No. 23, dated July 10, 1956, John F. Kennedy Library.

3. Department of State, Press Release No. 398, dated July 1956, John F. Kennedy Library.

4. Dwight D. Eisenhower, op. cit., p. 677.

5. Ibid. p. 390.

6. George B. Kistiakowsky, *A Scientist in the White House* (Cambridge, Mass.: Harvard University Press, 1976), p. 313.

7. Averell Harriman, "My Alarming Interview with Khrushchev," *Life*, 13 July 1959, p. 33.

8. Ibid. p. 34.

9. Foreign Broadcast Information Service, FBIS in Retrospect, Washington, D.C., June 1971, p. 28.

10. Foreign Broadcast Information Service, Daily Report Supplement No. 1, "Khrushchev Speech at Supreme Soviet," January 14, 1960, p. 18.

11. Letter from John M. Clarke to author, dated 20 March 1989.

12. Dwight D. Eisenhower, op. cit., pp. 552–553.

13. *The New York Times*, 24 May 1962.

14. "President Eisenhower Reports to the Nation," Department of State Bulletin 1093, 6 June 1960, p. 899.

15. Ibid. p. 900.

16. Dwight D. Eisenhower, op. cit., p. 559.

17. Ibid.

18. Frances Gary Powers, *Operation Overflight* (New York: Holt Rinehart and Winston, 1970), pp. 357–358; Edward J. Epstein, Legend: *The Secret World of Lee Harvey Oswald* (New York: McGraw-Hill, 1970), p. 103.

19. Report of the Warren Commission on the Assassination of President Kennedy, *The New York Times* edition, McGraw-Hill, October 1964.

20. "Khrushchev Speech to All-Russian Teachers' Congress," *The Current Digest of Soviet Press*, Vol. XII, No. 28 (August 10, 1960): 5.

21. General Electric Company, Summary, U.S. Air Force Discoverer Satellite Recovery Vehicle Program, I thru XIV, Philadelphia, no date, p. 7.

3. President Kennedy and "the Cuba Problem"

1. See Professor Lyman B. Kirkpatrick, Jr., "Paramilitary Case Study, The Bay of Pigs," *Naval War College Review*, Vol. XXV, No. 2 (November-December 1972).

2. See memorandum for the president from Maxwell D. Taylor, dated June 13, 1961, declassified May 8, 1977.

3. Charles J. V. Murphy, "Cuba: The Record Set Straight," *Fortune*, September 1961, 92–97.

4. When the president read Murphy's article, according to Murphy, the president "went ballistic." He sent Maxwell Taylor to New York to meet with Henry Luce and to demand an apology from Murphy. Murphy and Taylor met with Mr. Luce in his office and Luce demanded to know where Murphy's article was erroneous. After a very acrimonious discussion, there was only one error found in Murphy's article, relating to the name of an aircraft carrier. At that point, Luce demanded an apology from Taylor. Taylor replied, "It is not within my instructions to apologize," and walked out. Murphy would later reveal to Time-Life correspondents that this was "his finest hour in journalism."

5. Address by President Kennedy, 20 April 1961, "The Lesson of Cuba," Department of State Publication No. 7185.

6. Knoche would later serve as deputy director, from July 7, 1976, to August 1, 1977, and acting director of the agency, from January 20 to March 9, 1977.

7. Interview of Congressman Whitten by author, October 1972.

8. Interview of Senator Stuart Symington by author, October 1972.

9. U.S. Senate, Senate Select Committee to Study Governmental Operations, *Alleged Assassination Plots Involving Foreign Leaders with Respect to Intelligence Activities*, 94th Congress, 1st session, 20 November 1975, Report No. 94–465.

10. See also Taylor Branch and George Crile II, "The Kennedy Vendetta," *Harpers*, August 1975, 49–63.

11. "Senator J. W. Fulbright Calls for a New Approach to the Latin American Policy of the United States, May 9, 1961," *Congressional Record*, 87th Congress, 1st session, 1961, Vol. 107, No. 77, pp. 717–19.

12. Senator J. W. Fulbright, "Some Reflections Upon Recent Events and Continuing Problems," *Congressional Record*. 87th Congress, 1st session, Senate, 29 June 1961, p. 11704.

13. Roswell L. Gilpatric, "Present Defense Policies and Program, United States Does Not Seek to Resolve Disputes by Violence," delivered

before the Business Council at the Homestead, Hot Springs, Virginia, 21 October 1961.

14. Ibid.

15. Foreign Broadcast Intercept Service, "Text of Malinovsky Congress Speech," Russia, 24 October 1962, p. 25.

16. Ibid. pp. 19–20.

17. Stewart Alsop, "Kennedy's Grand Strategy," *The Saturday Evening Post*, 31 March 1962.

18. R. A. Malinovsky, "Vigilantly Stand Guard Over the Peace," U.S. Department of Commerce, Office of Technical Service, Joint Publications Research Service, 19, 127, p. 12.

19. Robert S. McNamara, "Defense Arrangements of the North Atlantic Community," 16 June 1962, Department of State Bulletin, 9 July 1962, p. 67.

20. "Conversations with Fidel," *Oui*, January 1975, p. 158.

21. Address to the American Newspaper Editors, Washington, D.C., by the Honorable Richard Helms, Director of Central Intelligence, 14 April 1971, p. 9.

22. Excerpts from the Speech Delivered by N. S. Khrushchev at the World Congress for General Disarmament and Peace, USSR, *Soviet Life Today*, September 1962, pp. 22–23.

23. Ibid.

24. Ibid.

25. Ibid.

26. Foreign Broadcast Information Service, Cuba, 4 July 1962, pp. HHHH 1–17.

27. *The New York Times*, 3 July 1962.

28. Department of State, Incoming Telegram from Mexico to Secretary of State, No. 3515, 5 June 1962, John F. Kennedy Library.

29. Ibid.

30. John A. McCone Interview, 19 August 1970, John F. Kennedy Library, Oral History Collection.

31. National Security Action Memorandum No. 181, 23 August 1962, John F. Kennedy Library.

32. Central Intelligence Agency, Current Intelligence Memorandum, 22 August 1962, John F. Kennedy Library.

33. Public Papers of the President, "The President's News Conference of August 29, 1962," pp. 352–353.

34. Ibid.

35. Ibid.

36. Ibid.

37. Department of State Airgram No. A-297, from AmEmbassy Mexico, "Cuban Exiles Report Soviet Troops in Cuba," 31 August 1962, John F. Kennedy Library.

38. Arthur M. Schlesinger, Jr., *A Thousand Days* (Boston: Houghton, Mifflin, 1965), p. 665.

39. Central Intelligence Agency, "Recent Soviet Military in Cuba," August 1962, John F. Kennedy Library.

40. Department of State, Outgoing Telegram No. 104, to American Embassy, Bern from Rusk, 31 August 1962, John F. Kennedy Library.

41. Department of State Airgram No. A298, "Subject Cuban Complaint and Denial of Attack on U.S. Vessel, Department of State from USUN Stevenson, 10 September 1962, John F. Kennedy Library.

42. "Capehart Charges Kennedy is Lax on Cuban Build-Up," *Indianapolis News*, 28 August 1962.

43. "GOP Blast Kennedy Concessions and Retreats," *New York Herald Tribune*, 31 August 1962, cited in U.S. Senate, *Congressional Record*, 31 August 1962, p. 18359.

44. U.S. Senate *Congressional Record*, 31 August 1962, p. 18360.

45. Ibid.

46. *Soviet Union*, 152 (1962).

47. Department of State, Bulletin, No. 1213, 24 September 1962, p. 450.

48. Robert Kennedy, *Thirteen Days* (New York: W. W. Norton, 1969), pp. 25–26.

49. "Goldwater Urges U-2 Flights," *The New York Times*, 6 September 1962.

50. "Khrushchev's Collected Works on Agriculture," U.S. Department of Commerce, JPRS 20,000, September 1963.

51. Theodore Sorensen, *Kennedy* (New York: Harper and Row, 1965), p. 667.

52. Ibid.

53. Ibid.

4. The Soviet Buildup in Cuba

1. Roger Hilsman, *To Move a Nation* (New York: Doubleday, 1967), p. 171.

2. Memorandum for James R. Killian, Jr., Chairman, President's Foreign Intelligence Advisory Board, from McGeorge Bundy, 9 January 1963, John F. Kennedy Library.

3. Ibid.

4. For details on the development of the SR-71, see Clarence L. John-son, "Development of the Lockheed SR-71 Blackbird," *Lockheed Horizons*, Winter 1981/1982.

5. The U-2 is a fragile aircraft. Kelly Johnson, the U-2 designer, once compared the U-2 to an eggshell. He said it was designed only for level flight. If SAMs or fighter aircraft could reach it, the U-2 was extremely vulnerable. We were all impressed with this fact, and most remembered an incident in the early days of U-2 operations staged out of Wiesbaden, West Germany. A U-2 was climbing to gain altitude and a Canadian jet fighter pilot, seeing this odd aircraft, cut in front of it to take a closer look. The turbulence caused by his aircraft caused the U-2 wing to break off and we lost an aircraft and a pilot. After that incident, the surrounding skies would be cleared when a U-2 took off.

6. Abram Chayes, *The Cuban Missile Crisis* (New York: Oxford University Press, 1974), p. 19.

7. Tass statement, "Put an End to the Policy of Provocations," *The Current Digest of Soviet Press*, Vol. XIV, No. 37 (October 10, 1962): 14–15.

8. Department of State, Lima, to Secretary of State, No. 373, 19 September 1962, John F. Kennedy Library.

9. Department of State, Bulletin, Vol. XLVII, No. 1214, 1 October 1962, pp. 481–482.

10. Ibid.

11. Adlai Stevenson's remarks at the UN, dictated over phone to Mr. Waller State, 21 September 1962, John F. Kennedy Library.

12. See Sherman Kent, "Estimates and Influence," *Foreign Service Journal*, Vol. 66, No. 5 (April 1969): 6–18.

13. The attitude of the intelligence community was summed up best by General Robert A. Breitweiser, assistant chief of staff, intelligence, USAF, testifying before the Senate Preparedness Investigation Subcommittee of the Committee on Armed Services after the crisis was over: "The establishment on Cuban soil of Soviet nuclear striking forces which could be used against the U.S. would be incompatible with Soviet policy as we presently estimate it. It would indicate a far greater willingness to increase the level or risk in U.S.-Soviet relations than the USSR has displayed thus far, and this would have important implications in other areas. However, Soviet military have almost certainly considered the contribution which Cuban bases might make to the Soviet strategic posture and, in that connection, the feasibility and utility of deploying nuclear delivery systems to Cuba. Therefore, this contingency must be

examined carefully, even though it would run counter to current Soviet policy. Soviet planners might see utility in deploying MRBMs or IRBMs to Cuba in order to supplement the limited number of ICBMs now believed to be operational in the USSR and to reach targets beyond the range of submarine launched missiles. The establishment on Cuban soil of a significant strike capability with such weapons has so far not been installed even in satellite territory. Serious problems in command and control would arise. There would also have to be a conspicuously larger number of Soviet personnel in Cuba, which, at least initially, would be a political liability in Latin America. The Soviets might think that the political effect of defying the U.S. by stationing Soviet nuclear striking power in so menacing a position would be worth a good deal if they could get away with it. However, they would certainly estimate that this could not be done without provoking a dangerous U.S. reaction."

14. Central Intelligence Agency, "The Military Buildup in Cuba," 19 September 1962, SNIE 85-3-62, John F. Kennedy Library.

15. John A. McCone interview, 19 August 1970, Oral History Collection, John F. Kennedy Library.

16. For details on CIA estimative process, see Chester L. Cooper, "The CIA and Decision-Making," *Foreign Affairs*, Vol. 50, No. 2 (January 1972): 223–236.

17. Sherman Kent, op. cit., p. 16.

18. Letter from Samuel Halpern to author, dated 20 May 1990.

19. For details, tonnage, draught, dimensions, etc., on both the *Omsk* and *Poltava*, see Ministry of Merchant Marine Chartering Corporation, Sovfracht, Soviet Merchant Sea-Going Dry Cargo Ships and Oil Tankers Reference Books, Moscow, 1969.

20. Ibid.

21. Roger Hilsman, op. cit., pp. 186–187.

22. See B. N. Zakharov, Historical Development of Lumber Carriers in the USSR, U.S. Department of Commerce, JPRS, 45,019, 11 April 1968.

23. U.S. Congress, *Congressional Record*, 87th Congress, 2nd session, Vol. 108, No. 170, 20 September 1962, pp. 18892–18951.

24. *Pravda*, 23 September 1962.

25. Ibid.

26. Adlai Stevenson's Remarks at the UN, 21 September 1962, John F. Kennedy Library.

27. U.S. Congress, *Congressional Record*, 87th Congress, 2nd session, Vol. 108, No. 174, 26 September 1962, pp. 19702–19753.

28. Khrushchev's Collective Works on Agriculture, U.S. Department of Commerce, JPRS 20,000, September 1963.

29. Department of State, Bulletin, XLVII, No. 1217, 22 October 1962. Also, Secretary Discusses Cuban Situation on "News and Comment" Program, Bulletin, No. 595, 22 October 1962.

30. Ibid.

31. Ibid.

32. The Reminiscences of Admiral G. Ward, U.S. Navy (Retired) U.S. Naval Institute, Annapolis, MD, 1972, pp. 7–168.

33. George W. Ball, "Trading Relations between the Free World and Cuba," made before the House Committee on Export Control, Press Release No. 595, State Department Bulletin, 22 October 1962, p. 594.

34. Hearings Before the Select Committee on Export Control, H. R. 87th Congress, 2nd session, Pursuant to House Resolution 403, part 3, pp. 810–811.

35. Hearings Before a Subcommittee on Appropriations, House of Representatives, Department of Defense Appropriations for 1964, part 2, 14 February 1963, p. 35.

36. Ibid. p. 364.

37. U.S. Senate Preparedness Investigation Subcommittee on Armed Services, "Interim Report on Cuban Military Buildup," dated 9 May 1963.

38. Letter from Samuel Halpern to author, dated 14 June 1989.

39. United Nations General Assembly, 1145B Plenary Meeting, 8 October 1962, "Address by Osvaldo Dorticos, President of the Republic of Cuba," p. 375.

40. Ibid.

41. Ibid. p. 373.

42. Foreign Broadcast Information Service, Cuba, "Raul Castro Opens University Games," 9 October 1962, p. HHHH-9.

43. Foreign Broadcast Information Service, Cuba, "Lyndon Johnson's 'Encouraging,' " 10 October 1962, p. HHHH-10.

44. Ibid.

45. Walter Lippmann, "On the War over Cuba," Washington Post, 9 October 1962.

46. For more details, see Sen. Kenneth Keating, "My Advance View of the Cuban Crisis," Look, 3 November 1964.

47. Roger Hilsman, "The Cuban Crisis: How Close We Were to War," Look, 25 August 1964, p. 18.

48. Betty Beale, "Clare Booth Luce Weaves a Fascinating Tale," Washington Star, 16 November 1975.

49. Foreign Broadcast Information Service, Cuba, "Castro Welcomes President Dorticos," 10 October 1962, p. HHHH-5.

50. Ibid.

51. Foreign Broadcast Information Service, Cuba, "Castro Visits Law Students, Professors," 15 October 1962, p. HHHH-7.

52. Chester Bowles, *Promises to Keep* (New York: Harper and Row, 1971), p. 418.

53. Foreign Broadcast Information Service, Daily Report No. 123, USSR International Service, "Kennedy Sees Soviet Journalists," 27 June 1961.

54. Robert Kennedy, op. cit, p. 27.

55. In his book, *With Kennedy*, Pierre Salinger discusses a meeting with Bolshakov in Moscow in 1965. According to Salinger, Bolshakov was the head of a radio-TV department of Novosty, a Soviet news agency.

56. Public Papers of the Presidents, John F. Kennedy, Government Printing Office, Washington, D.C., 1962, p. 772.

57. Ibid.

5. October 14—The U-2 Reconnaissance Mission

1. Roger Hilsman, *To Move a Nation* (New York: Doubleday, 1967), p. 168.

6. October 15—Discovery of Offensive Missiles in Cuba

1. See Dino A. Brugioni, "Genetrix—The Intelligence Balloon," *Military Intelligence* (January-March 1989): 26–27.

2. *No Return for U-2*, Foreign Language Publishing House, Moscow, 1960.

3. *The Trail of the U-2*, Translation World Publishers, Chicago, 1960, pp. 84–87.

4. Ibid. p. 86.

5. See also Amron Katz, "The Soviets and the U-2 Photos—A Heuristic Argument," Rand Corporation, Memorandum RM-3584-PR, March 1963.

6. Stanislav Kondrashov, "Once More About the Caribbean Crisis," *Izvestiya*, 28 February 1989.

7. Theodore Sorensen, *Kennedy* (New York: Harper & Row, 1965), p. 673.

7. October 16—The President Is Informed

1. The Ballad of the Conference on Intelligence Methods, 15–20 October 1962.

> Ten little analysts, sittin' round a table,
> Were running the Conference as well as they were able.
> But the work load piled on Round Ray Cline,
> We looked round—and then we were nine.
> Who would next be caught up by Fate?
> Who would be the next departer?
> The answer came soon, we were down to eight,
> Oh, who had called General Carter?
> Some pictures came in, as if sent from heaven;
> Art Lundahl left, and we were seven.
> Loud screams were heard; the atmosphere rent,
> This obviously called for Sherman Kent.
> And then there were only six.
> How were we to keep the Conference alive
> Without pulling an awful blooper?
> But a few minutes passed and we became five.
> For we just lost Chester Cooper.
> The analysts huddled together and bore
> A look like a monolith,
> But alas, there were only four,
> As out went R. Jack Smith.
> The breeze was blowing; there must be a flap
> The Conference was up a tree.
> Someone woke poor Tidwell up from his nap,
> Leaving Analysts now only three.
> Then Sir Kenneth nudged Bowen and Bowen nudged King
> And they wondered just what they could do.
> Then one of them asked, "My God, where is Ting?"
> For analysts they saw only two.
> No Scoville, no Wheelon, no Helms, and no Kirk,
> And the Conference was hardly begun.
> They all somehow had got caught up by their work,

And of analysts there was now only one.
And that was Pforzheimer, And he don't rhyme with nuthin'

2. Tom Wicker, "Eisenhower Calls President Weak on Foreign Policy," *The New York Times*, 16 October 1962.

3. Robert F. Kennedy, *Thirteen Days* (New York: W. W. Norton, 1969), p. 7.

4. Letter from Douglas Dillon to author dated 1 March 1978.

5. Elie Abel, *The Cuban Missile Crisis* (New York: Lippincott, 1966), p. 43.

6. Charles E. Bohlen, *Witness to History* (New York: Norton, 1973), p. 488.

7. Ibid. p. 489.

8. Robert Kennedy, op. cit., pp. 23–24.

9. Maxwell D. Taylor, "Reflections of a Grim October," *Washington Post*, 15 October 1982, p. A–19.

10. Letter from Sampson Field to author, dated February 25, 1978.

11. Letter from O. D. Johnson, of the Chicago Aerial Industries, Inc., to author dated, January 11, 1973, along with brochures of the KA-45A and KA-46A cameras.

12. U.S. Navy, Squadron History—Light Photographic Squadron Sixty-Two, no date given.

13. The instructions were:

A. Six aircraft flying three separate tracks (2 aircraft per track)
B. Each aircraft has five cameras as follows:
I1. 1st camera—forward firing KA-46. Film format 4½" × 4½." Focal length 6 inches
I2. 2nd, 3rd and 4th cameras—horizon to horizon tri-met. 70mm film. Focal length 1½"
I3. 5th camera—vertical KA-45, 4½" × 4½" format. Focal length 6 inches
C. 100 ft. of film per camera. Total footage expected–3,000 feet.

14. Bobby's style can be best illustrated by a story that William J. Crockett, who was appointed early in the Kennedy administration to be assistant secretary of state for administration, loved to tell. Bobby told Crockett that he was selected to reorganize and get some new ideas into the State Department and that he would be given specific instructions at a later date. Crockett waited and waited, and when none still was forthcoming, he called Bobby. Bobby asked him to come to his office, and Crockett expected a detailed and specific list of recommen-

dations. When none was still forthcoming, he pointedly asked Bobby what was expected with regard to State's reorganization. Bobby replied, "Go and kick asses so hard at the top that teeth will rattle throughout the department." With that, Crockett went back to reorganize the State Department.

15. The White House, Washington, National Security Action Memorandum, signed by John F. Kennedy, 22 October 1962.

16. Countner, Sorensen to JFK memo, 17 October 1962, John F. Kennedy Library.

17. Charles E. Bohlen, op. cit., p. 491–492.

8. October 17—Options and Courses of Action

1. Letter from Martin J. Hillenbrand to author, dated 19 April 1978.

2. Letter from William A. Tyler to author, dated 29 March 1978.

3. Countner, Sorensen to JFK memo, 17 October 1962, John F. Kennedy Library.

4. Ibid.

5. Ibid.

6. Ibid.

7. Arthur M. Schlesinger, *A Thousand Days* (Boston: Houghton Mifflin, 1963), p. 760.

8. Countner, Sorensen to JFK memo, op. cit.

9. Ibid.

9. The Joint Chiefs of Staff

1. See SIOP-62 Briefing, *International Security*, Vol. 12, No. 1 (Summer 1987): 50–51.

2. Letter from General L. L. Lemnitzer to author, dated 17 March 1978.

3. "General Shoup Critical of Article by Kennedy on '62 Crisis," *The New York Times*, 25 October 1968.

4. Robert Kennedy, "Thirteen Days," *McCall's*, November 1968, p. 9.

5. *Time*, 26 October 1962, pp. 23–24.

6. The Reminiscences of Admiral Alfred G. Ward, U. S. Navy (Retired), U. S. Naval Institute, Annapolis, Maryland, 1972.

7. Letter from Admiral Alfred G. Ward to author, dated 6 August 1976.

10. October 18—More Surprises

1. Ward would later tell me that most around the table knew very little about how a blockade would be conducted. They left the details to the Navy but indicated that they would be concerned when intercepts of Soviet vessels would be made. Ward and Dennison flew back to Norfolk that evening arriving at midnight and arranged to meet the next day to work out all the details of getting all the blockading ships at sea.

2. Letter from Michael V. Forrestal to author, dated 27 February 1978.

3. The memo, which was declassified in 1978, read: "Dear Mr. Chairman: For the first time since the Korean War, the United States is confronted with a hostile development to which we have an inescapable commitment to respond with military action. Consequently, the purpose of this note is to inform you that, shortly after the close of your conference with my emissary, I have no choice but to initiate appropriate military action against the island of Cuba. Should those in your government who fail to grasp the meaning of total war urge upon you any countermeasures or threats which affect other vital interests of this nation, I ask you to remember that the United States possesses both the will and the weapons to take whatever action is needed in the defense of those interests." Theodore C. Sorensen, draft letter for the president, 18 October 1962, John F. Kennedy Library.

4. Chalmers M. Roberts, "A Diplomat with a Rare Intuitive Touch," *Washington Post*, 8 February 1972.

5. During a conference between Americans and Russians in Moscow in January 1989, Dobrynin still insisted that he had been kept in the dark about the missiles. Confronted by reporters, Gromyko joked that he thought he had told Dobrynin shortly before he had left to return to the Soviet Union in October 1962.

11. Military Preparations

1. Department of Defense, Office of Public Affairs, News Release No. 1698–62, 18 October 1962.

12. October 19—Return to Washington

1. Lawrence F. O'Brien, *No Final Victories* (New York: Doubleday, 1974), p. 142.

2. Letter from Michael V. DiSalle to author, dated 24 February 1978.

3. Letter from Frank J. Lausche to author, dated 5 March 1978.

4. Upon his arrival in Cleveland, the president strode over to Brother Siegel, director of the Saint Edward High School Band, and after a warm and vigorous handshake said, "I think your band played 'Hail to the Chief' exceptionally well, Brother. Very fine." The president was invited to visit the school. He said he would if time permitted. In addition to the spiritual bouquet, Robert Cutter, the student body president, presented the president with a football inscribed: "To the Kennedy Touch Football Team from the Faculty and Students of St. Edward, Lakewood." The president engaged in an impromptu touch football game aboard *Air Force One* en route to Springfield with the football. In the main corridor of the high school, there is a plaque commemorating the president's visit with the inscription: "You may be sure my visit to St. Edward High School was a memorable occasion for me and I greatly appreciate the warm hospitality extended to me there." Letter from J. E. Nieberling, St. Edward High School, to author, dated 10 February 1977, and letter from Brother George Klawitter, Brothers of Holy Cross, to author, dated 2 October 1976.

5. Letter from Sidney R. Yates to author, dated 6 March 1978.

6. Central Intelligence Agency, "The President's Intelligence Checklist," 19 October 1962, John F. Kennedy Library.

7. The models were subsequently given by the CIA to the Air and Space Museum of the Smithsonian Institution.

8. Central Intelligence Agency, "Major Consequences of Certain Courses of Action on Cuba," SNIE 11-19-62, 20 October 1962, John F. Kennedy Library.

9. Ibid.

10. Ibid.

11. Central Intelligence Agency, "Soviet Reactions to Certain US Courses of Action on Cuba," SNIE 11-18-62, 19 October 1962, John F. Kennedy Library.

13. October 20—Setting the Course of Action

1. Letter from Adlai E. Stevenson to Arthur M. Schlesinger, Jr. (no date), p. 2, John F. Kennedy Library.

2. Ibid.

3. Ibid.

4. Foreign Broadcast Information Service, USSR International Affairs,

Moscow Domestic Service in Russian, 1930 GMT, 23 October 1962, p. BB18.

5. Letter from John J. McCloy to author, dated 9 March 1978.

6. Department of Defense, "Fallout Protection. What to Know About Nuclear Attack," Publication H-6, December 1961.

14. October 21—Notifying the Allies

1. Kenneth Harris, "Pungent Memories from Mr. Acheson," *Life*, 23 July 1971; and C. L. Sulzberger, *The Last of the Giants* (New York: Macmillan, 1970), p. 931.

2. Letter from William Tidwell to author, dated 9 June 1989.

3. Ibid.

4. Ibid.

5. Admiral George W. Anderson, Jr., "The Cuban Crisis," Proceedings Naval History Symposium, U.S. Naval Academy, Annapolis, Maryland, p. 8.

6. The Reminiscences of Admiral Ward, U.S. Navy (Retired), U.S. Naval Institute, Annapolis, Maryland, 1972, pp. 9–237.

7. See also "You Have 15 Minutes to Pack, All Hands," Bureau of Naval Personnel Information Bulletin, December 1962, pp. 6–10.

8. Department of Defense, News Release, Office of Public Affairs, No. 1731–62, 24 October 1962.

9. Ibid.

10. "Soviet Military Participant Views Cuban Missile Crisis," *Latinskaya Amerika*, (November-December 1977): 110.

15. October 22—Address to the Nation

1. Letter from Martin J. Hillenbrand to author, dated 19 April 1978.

2. Department of State, Outgoing Telegram, All Diplomatic and Consular Posts, 22 October 1962, John F. Kennedy Library.

3. Note File, John F. Kennedy Library.

4. Letter from G. Mennen Williams to author, dated 20 February 1978.

5. Letter from Orville L. Freeman to author, dated 4 January 1978.

6. Letter from Walter W. Heller to author, dated 16 February 1978.

7. Letter from John W. McCormick to author, dated 8 March 1978.

8. Ibid.

9. Letter from Dr. Thomas E. Morgan to author, dated 10 March 1978.

10. Ibid.

11. Letter from Leverett Saltonstall to author, dated 23 March 1978.

12. Letter from George A. Smathers to author, dated 3 March 1978.

13. *Newsweek*, 5 November 1962.

14. Letter from Edmund C. Hutchinson to author, dated 14 February 1978.

15. Note to the president from McGeorge Bundy, dated 22 October 1962, John F. Kennedy Library.

16. Background Briefing on Cuban Situation, the Pentagon, 22 October 1962, 8 P.M. E.S.T., pp. 17–18.

17. "The Reminiscences of Admiral Robert Lee Dennison, U.S. Navy (Retired), U.S. Naval Institute, Annapolis, Maryland, August 1975.

18. Letter from Robert Koch to author, dated 5 May 1975.

19. Letter from Diane S. Liebman, Information and Editorial Specialist, Association of American Railroads, to author, dated 3 April 1975. Also, Association of American Railroads, News, P6305, 137164, dated 9 January 1963.

20. See V. Kutuzov, *Penkovsky, Facts and Fancy*, (Moscow: Movosti Press Agency Publishing House, no date).

21. Department of State, Outgoing Telegram. No. 725 dated October 22, 1962, John F. Kennedy Library.

16. October 23—Quarantine: "Interdiction of the Delivery of Offensive Missiles to Cuba"

1. Executive Committee, National Security Council, Untitled Memorandum Summarizing Intelligence on Cuba, John F. Kennedy Library.

2. "U.S. Charges of Soviet Military Buildup in Cuba," Statements by Adlai E. Stevenson, U.S. Representative in the Security Council, 23 October 1962, Department of State Publication 7458, Released November 1962.

3. News Conference No. 795, White House, Pierre Salinger, 23 October 1962, 7:15 P.M.

4. Foreign Broadcast Information Service, USSR International Affairs, USSR Roundtable Discussion, 24 October 1962, pp. BB–24.

5. U.S. Navy, NAVOCEANO, Washington, D.C., DTG 240007Z, October, Control 17456, 23 October 1962, 10:10 P.M., John F. Kennedy Library.

6. Central Intelligence Agency, Memorandum: The Crisis USSR/ Cuba, October 25, 1962, John F. Kennedy Library.

7. Foreign Broadcast Information Service, Cuba, "Fidel Castro's 23 October Interview," 24 October 1962, p. HHHH-15.

17. October 24—UN and Military Preparedness

1. Letter from Ray Cline to author, dated 3 April 1978.

2. Letter from Major General David S. Parker to author, dated 1 September 1979.

3. Ibid.

4. Letter from Ray Cline to author, dated 3 April 1978.

5. McGeorge Bundy, Memorandum for the president, 24 October 1962, John F. Kennedy Library.

6. See Harold Macmillan, *At the End of the Day 1961–1963* (New York: Harper & Row, 1973), p. 187.

7. Foreign Broadcast Information Service, USSR International Affairs, 25 October 1962, p. BB-8.

8. Bertrand Russell, *Unarmed Victory* (New York: Simon & Schuster, 1963), p. 34.

9. Ibid. p. 35.

10. Ibid. p.36.

11. Ibid. p. 37.

12. Ibid. p. 46.

13. For further details, see W. E. Knox, "Close-up of Khrushchev During a Crisis," *The New York Times*, Part VI, 18 November 1962.

14. Robert Kennedy, *Thirteen Days* (New York: Norton, 1969), pp. 59–60.

15. Letter from George F. Gilbody, assistant information director, Gulfstream Park Racing Assn., to author, dated 28 April 1975.

16. Ibid.

17. For details on orders given to units to proceed to Florida and Georgia, see Department of the Army, DA Washington Situation Report No. 2-62 as of 240500 October 62.

18. Office of the White House Press Secretary, Memorandum to Editors and Radio and Television News Directors, 24 October 1962, John F. Kennedy Library.

19. Ibid.

20. This letter was released on November 19, 1973.

21. Department of State, Bulletin, Vol. LXIV, No. 1795, 19 November 1973.

22. Ibid.

23. Ibid.

24. Ibid.

25. Ibid.

26. Ibid.

27. U.S. Navy, NAVOCEANO to Secretary of State, Control 18428. Received 25 October 1962.

28. *Washington Post*, 10 November 1962.

18. October 25—Confrontation at the UN

1. Walter Lippmann, "Blockade Proclaimed," *Washington Post*, 25 October 1962.

2. Ibid.

3. Department of State, Outgoing Telegram, Circular Priority 725, 22 October 1962, John F. Kennedy Library.

4. Central Intelligence Agency Memorandum, The Crisis USSR/Cuba, 25 October 1962, John F. Kennedy Library.

5. Department of State, "U.S. Charges of Soviet Military Buildup in Cuba," Statement by Adlai E. Stevenson, U.S. Representative in the Security Council, Bulletin No. 0-666502.

6. Ibid.

7. Ibid.

8. Letter from Major General David S. Parker to author, dated 1 September 1979.

9. Department of State, Bulletin, Volume SLVII, No. 1220, 12 November 1962.

10. Ibid.

11. Ibid.

12. George W. Goddard with DeWitt S. Copp, *Overview* (New York: Doubleday, 1969), p. xi.

13. Foreign Broadcast Information Service, Cuba, 24 October 1962, p. HHHH–8.

19. October 26—The Crisis Deepens

1. Central Intelligence Agency Memorandum, The Crisis, USSR/ Cuba, 26 July 1962, John F. Kennedy Library.

2. Norman Cousins, *The Improbable Triumvirate* (New York: Norton, 1972), p. 24.

3. Ibid.

4. Address by Vice-Admiral Alfred G. Ward, USN, Committee of One Hundred of Miami Beach, at the Surf Club, 16 February 1963.

5. For further details, see Jerry McDonnell, USN, "Incident in History—Intercept of MARCULA," *All Hands*, December 1962.

6. Central Intelligence Agency Memorandum, The Crisis, USSR/ Cuba, 26 October 1962, John F. Kennedy Library.

7. Public Papers of the President, John F. Kennedy, 1962, No. 489, 26 October 1962.

8. Fairchild Camera and Instrument Corporation, *Focusing on Victory: The Story of Aerial Photography at War* (New York, 1944).

9. Department of State, Deputy Undersecretary of State, Memorandum for the Honorable McGeorge Bundy, Proposed Message to Castro, 26 October 1962, John F. Kennedy Library.

10. Marguerite Higgins, "Emissary in Missile Crisis," *Washington Star*, 4 August 1944.

11. The White House, Senator Olin Johnson Call, 26 October 1962, John F. Kennedy Library.

12. Theodore C. Sorensen, *Kennedy* (New York: Harper & Row, 1965), p. 803.

13. Robert F. Kennedy, *Thirteen Days* (New York: W. W. Norton, 1969), pp. 88–89.

14. Ibid.

20. October 27—All the MRBM Sites Are Operational

1. Letter from Governor Elmer L. Anderson to author, dated 23 March 1978.

2. Ibid.

3. Ibid.

4. Letter from Governor Albert D. Rosellini to author, dated 8 March 1978.

5. Department of Defense, Office of Public Affairs, Press Release, 27 October 1962.

6. A Report on National Civil Defense Readiness by Steuart L. Pittman, Assistant Secretary of Defense for Civil Defense, to the Committee on Civil Defense and Post Attack Recovery of the National Governors' Conference, 27 October 1962, John F. Kennedy Library.

7. Letter from Governor John A. Volpe to author, dated 14 March 1978.

8. Letter from Governor Albert D. Rosellini to author, dated 8 March 1978.

9. Letter from Governor Anderson, op. cit.

10. Letter from Governor Volpe, op. cit.

11. Ibid.

12. Letter from Governor Edmund G. Brown to author, dated 28 April 1978.

13. Marguerite Higgins, "Emissary in Missile Crisis," *Washington Star*, 4 August 1964.

14. Foreign Broadcast Information Service, USSR International, 29 October 1962, p. BB-2.

15. U.S. Senate, Committee on Foreign Relations, "Cuban Realities: May 1975," a Report by Senator George S. McGovern to the Committee on Foreign Relations, August 1975, p. 14.

16. Central Intelligence Agency Memorandum, The Crisis USSR/Cuba, November 1, 1962, Annex, John F. Kennedy Library.

17. Ibid.

18. EXCOM Meeting, 27 October 1962, Presidential Recording Transcripts, 27 October 1962, John F. Kennedy Library.

19. Maxwell D. Taylor, "Reflections of a Grim November," *Washington Post*, 5 October 1982.

20. Department of State, Outgoing Telegram from Rusk to all NATO Ambassadors, Eyes Only Ambassadors, No. 578, 26 October 1962, John F. Kennedy Library.

21. Ibid.

22. Ibid.

23. The Jupiter missiles were developed by the Army Ballistic Missile Agency under Dr. Werner von Braun and produced by Chrysler. The same agency had fielded the successful Redstone missile. The Jupiter was 58 feet long and 105 inches in diameter. The smooth cylinder body had no wings or fins. The motor was gimbaled to correct changes in course. Tested by the Army, the Jupiter was fielded by the Air Force because a 1956 decision had limited the Army responsibility to missiles with ranges under 200 miles. As a compromise, the development of the

missile continued by the Army but it was field-deployed by the Air Force. The First Strategic Missile Squadron completed its training at Redstone Arsenal and the missiles were first deployed in Europe in 1959 in semihard configurations.

24. W. Averell Harriman, Memorandum on Kremlin Reactions, 22 October 1962, EXCOM files, John F. Kennedy Library.

25. Ibid.

26. Ibid.

27. Ibid.

28. Department of State, Policy Planning Council, Scenario, 26 October 1962, John F. Kennedy Library.

29. Kennedy Doodles, John F. Kennedy Library.

30. EXCOM meeting, 27 October 1962, Presidential Recording Transcripts, John F. Kennedy Library.

31. Ibid.

32. Letter from General L. L. Lemnitzer to author, dated 17 March 1978.

33. Ibid.

34. Ibid.

35. Ibid.

36. Central Intelligence Agency Memorandum, The Crisis USSR/Cuba, 27 October 1962, John F. Kennedy Library.

37. Department of State, Press Release No. 644, 27 October 1962.

38. Department of Defense, Office of Public Affairs, News Release, 27 October 1962.

39. USUN Mission, Incidents Involving Attacks on US Forces Over Cuba Today, dictated to USUN in New York at 9:15 P.M., John F. Kennedy Library.

40. *Pravda*, 13 December 1962.

41. Department of Defense, Office of Public Affairs, statement by Secretary McNamara, 27 October 1962.

42. *Khrushchev Remembers* (Boston: Little, Brown, 1970), p. 497.

43. Roger Hilsman, *To Move a Nation* (New York: Doubleday, 1967), p. 224.

44. Theodore C. Sorenson, *Kennedy* (New York: Harper & Row, 1965), p. 806.

45. Robert F. Kennedy, *Thirteen Days* (New York: W. W. Norton, 1969), pp. 108–109.

46. Ibid.

47. Foreign Broadcast Information Service, "Text of Fidel Castro's

Messsage to U Thant," *Havana Prensa Latina* in Spanish to Latin America, 2130 GMT 27 October 1962, Cuba, 29 October 1962, pp. HHH 16–17.

48. *Khrushchev Remembers*, p. 498.

21. October 28—The Soviets Capitulate

1. Central Intelligence Agency Memorandum. The Crisis, USSR/Cuba, 27 October 1962, p. III-3, John F. Kennedy Library.

2. Foreign Broadcast Information Service, FBIS in Retrospect, 30th Anniversary Issue, 1941–1971, Washington, D.C., 1971, p. 28.

3. Memorandum for the president from MVFW, 27 October 1962, John F. Kennedy Library.

4. Message Reply to a Broadcast by Chairman Khrushchev on the Cuban Crisis, 28 October 1962, Public Papers of the President, John F. Kennedy, Government Printing Office, Washington, 1963, pp. 814–815.

5. Ibid.

6. Ibid.

7. Ibid.

8. Statement by the President Following the Soviet Decision to Withdraw Missiles from Cuba, Public Papers of the President, John F. Kennedy, Government Printing Office, Washington, 1963, p. 815.

9. Foreign Broadcast Information Service, Daily, Latin America, 29 October 1962, p. HHHH-5.

10. Department of Defense, Office of Public Affairs, No. 1760–62, 29 October 1962.

22. October 29—The Beginning of Negotiations

1. National Press Club, Washington, D.C., Press Conference of His Excellency Konrad Adenauer, Chancellor, Federal Republic of Germany, 5 November 1962.

2. Ibid.

3. Department of State, Telegram from Ottawa to secretary of state, No. 521, dated 29 October 1962, John F. Kennedy Library.

4. Memorandum for McGeorge Bundy from J. Robert Schaetzel, deputy assistant secretary for Atlantic Affairs, Department of State, 8 November 1962, John F. Kennedy Library.

5. Letter from Admiral Alfred G. Ward to author, dated 24 August 1977.

6. Statement by Admiral Anderson sent to author by Admiral Ward, 24 August 1977.

7. Department of State, Policy Planning Council, Memo to McGeorge Bundy from Harry Owen, 29 October 1962, John F. Kennedy Library.

8. Department of State, Incoming Telegram, from New York to secretary of state, No. 1535, 29 October 1962.

9. White House News Conference No. 805, with Pierre Salinger, 29 October 1962, 11:20 A.M. E.S.T.

10. Ibid.

23. October 30—U Thant Goes to Cuba

1. Department of Defense, Office of Public Affairs, News Release No. 1765, Statement by Assistant Secretary of Defense, Arthur Sylvester, 30 October 1962.

2. Central Intelligence Agency Memorandum, The Crisis, USSR/ Cuba, 1 November 1962, p. 1, John F. Kennedy Library.

24. November 1—The Missiles Are Removed from Cuba

1. Memorandum for the president from Donald M. Wilson, acting director, United States Information Agency, 2 November 1962, John F. Kennedy Library.

2. Statement of the president, Office of the White House Press Secretary, 2 November 1962.

3. Michael Dobbs, "Soviet and Cubans to Give Their Versions of '62 Missile Crisis," *Washington Post*, 9 January 1989.

4. Central Intelligence Agency, "Number of Ships Required to Remove Soviet Weapons System from Cuba," no date, John F. Kennedy Library.

5. Department of Defense, Office of Public Affairs, Statement by Secretary Sylvester; News Release, 5:50 P.M., 7 November 1962.

6. Central Intelligence Agency, Office of the Director, Memorandum for Director, National Photographic Interpretation Center, Subject: Commendation, 2 November 1962.

7. Memorandum of Governor Stevenson Proposing Solution Through Security Council Arrangements, no date, John F. Kennedy Library.

8. Department of State, Executive Secretary, Memorandum for

McGeorge Bundy from William H. Brubeck, "Conversation with Mr. McCloy on Cuba," 28 November 1962, John F. Kennedy Library.

9. Foreign Broadcast Information Service, Cuba, "Castro's Fourth Anniversary Speech," 3 January 1963, p. HHHH-12.

10. Memorandum for the president, Proposed Declaration on Cuba, signed by McGeorge Bundy, 24 November 1962, John F. Kennedy Library.

11. Department of State, Incoming Telegram to secretary of state from Stevenson, Subject: Meeting Between McCloy and Kuznetsov, November 18, 1962, No. 1856, 19 November 1962, p. 8, John F. Kennedy Library.

12. Memorandum of Governor Stevenson Proposing Solution Through Security Council Arrangements, no date, John F. Kennedy Library.

13. Department of Defense, Office of Public Affairs, News Release No. 1896–62, 21 November 1962.

14. Department of Defense, Office of Public Affairs, News Release No. 1891–62, 21 November 1962.

15. Department of Defense, Office of Public Affairs, News Release No. 1847–62, 14 November 1962.

16. Memorandum from Adlai E. Stevenson to President Kennedy, 22 November 1962, John F. Kennedy Library.

17. Letter to General McHugh for the president from Bundy, 22 November 1962, John F. Kennedy Library.

18. Ibid.

19. Instructions to McCloy, 23 November 1962, John F. Kennedy Library.

20. Ibid.

21. Department of State, Letter for Stevenson and McCloy: New York Negotiations, 11 December 1962.

22. Memorandum to Mr. Hilsman from Allan Evans, November 29, 1962, Subject: Debriefing re Executive Committee Meeting, 29 November 1962, John F. Kennedy Library.

25. Nuclear Warhead Postmortem

1. Central Intelligence Agency Memorandum, The Crisis, USSR/Cuba, 25 October 1962, John F. Kennedy Library.

2. Central Intelligence Agency Memorandum, The Crisis, USSR/Cuba, 24 October 1962, John F. Kennedy Library.

3. Background Briefing on Cuban Situation, 22 October 1962, 8 P.M., EST, p. 9.

26. Postlude

1. Ray Cline, *Secrets, Spies and Scholars* (Washington, D.C.: Acropolis Books Ltd., 1978), p. 197.

2. Letter to the Honorable Adlai E. Stevenson from President John F. Kennedy, 7 January 1963, John F. Kennedy Library.

3. Letter to the Honorable John A. McCone, chairman, United States Intelligence Board from President John F. Kennedy, 9 January 1963, Central Intelligence Agency.

4. Letter to Lieutenant Colonel William J. Gregory, USAF, WRSP-4, Edwards Air Force Base, California, from President John F. Kennedy, 5 January 1963.

5. Secretary of the Navy, Washington, Commendation of Marine Composite Squadron Two, no date.

6. Marshall Rodion Yakovolich Malinovsky, Vigilantly Stand Guard Over the Peace, U.S. Department of Commerce, Office of Technical Services, Joint Publications Research Service, JPRS 19, 127, 9 May 1963.

7. *Izvestiya*, 6 November 1962.

8. *Pravda*, 13 December 1962.

9. Foreign Broadcast Information Service, Cuba, "Castro's Fourth Anniversary Speech," 3 January 1963, p. HHHH-11.

10. Department of State and Department of Defense, "The Soviet-Cuban Connection in Central America and the Caribbean," Washington, March 1983, p. 3.

11. Memorandum for Mr. Hilsman from Allan Evans, "Subject Debriefing re Executive Committee Meeting," 29 November 1962, John F. Kennedy Library.

12. John A. McCone, Statement on Cuba to the Preparedness Investigating Subcommittee of the Senate Committee on Armed Services, 6 February 1963, John F. Kennedy Library.

13. Ibid.

14. Interview of Secretary Rusk by representatives of the General Federation of Women's Clubs, Department of State Bulletin, May 6, 1963.

15. *Hoy*, 22 November 1962.

16. *Revolución*, 26 November 1962.

17. William Colby, *Honorable Men, My Life in the CIA*, (New York: Simon and Schuster, 1978), p. 189.

Index

About the Author

DINO A. BRUGIONI is a native of Missouri and attended schools in Bevier and Jefferson City. During World War II, he flew in sixty-six bombardment and a number of reconnaissance missions over Europe. After the war, he received BA and MA degrees in foreign affairs from George Washington University. He joined the Central Intelligence Agency in 1948 and became an expert on Soviet industrial installations. In 1955, he was selected as a member of the cadre of founding officers of the National Photographic Interpretation Center. As a senior officer at the Center, he was involved in the exploitation of U-2, SR-71, and satellite imagery in strategic and crisis situations. He also discovered and analyzed World War II aerial photography of the Auschwitz-Birkenau death camp. Mr. Brugioni has received a number of awards for his work including a citation from President Kennedy for his performance in the Cuban missile crisis. Since his retirement from the CIA in 1982, he has written extensively on the application of aerial and spatial imagery to intelligence and environmental problems. Mr. Brugioni is also a Civil War buff and has written a number of articles and a book dealing with the war in the West.